PACIFIC SYMPOSIUM ON
BIOCOMPUTING '97

PACIFIC SYMPOSIUM ON BIOCOMPUTING '97

Maui, Hawaii, USA
6–9 January 1997

Editors

Russ B. Altman
Section on Medical Informatics
Stanford University

A. Keith Dunker
Department of Biochemistry/ Biophysics
Washington State University

Lawrence Hunter
National Library of Medicine
National Institutes of Health

Teri E. Klein
Department of Pharmaceutical Chemistry
University of California, San Francisco

World Scientific
Singapore • New Jersey • London • Hong Kong

Published by

World Scientific Publishing Co Pte Ltd
5 Toh Tuck Link, Singapore 596224
USA office: 27 Warren Street, Suite 401-402, Hackensack, NJ 07601
UK office: 57 Shelton Street, Covent Garden, London WC2H 9HE

British Library Cataloguing-in-Publication Data
A catalogue record for this book is available from the British Library.

BIOCOMPUTING
Proceedings of the 1997 Pacific Symposium

ISBN-13 978-981-02-3005-0
ISBN-10 981-02-3005-2

Pacific Symposium on Biocomputing 1997

The second Pacific Symposium on Biocomputing (PSB-97) has once again brought together key researchers from the international biocomputing community. The importance of biocomputing is now widely recognized, and a set of critical meetings has emerged providing access to peer-reviewed reports of exciting new techniques and results. The PSB has been designed to be maximally responsive to the need for critical mass in subdisciplines within biocomputing. For that reason, it is the only meeting whose tracks are defined dynamically (in response to specific proposals) each year, organized by leaders in the emerging subdisciplines, and targeted to provide a forum for publication and discussion of research in biocomputing's "hot areas." In this way, PSB provides an early forum for serious examination of emerging methods and approaches.

As usual, the cultures of biology and computer science clash in the organization of a biocomputing meeting. The desire to have the latest ideas, the biggest names, and the most diverse attendance (typical of biology conferences) causes some to question the utility of providing rigorous peer review of the manuscripts (typical of computer science conferences). The organizers believe that the value of the proceedings to posterity rests on the quality of the review process. This year, every manuscript was examined by at least two anonymous reviewers (as well as the track organizers and meeting chairs), and some manuscripts were examined by as many as five reviewers when significant differences arose. We trust, therefore, that the proceedings will have significant scientific and academic legitimacy.

The session chairs performed admirably in soliciting high quality submissions, and moderating the review process. This year there were sessions in several critical areas within biocomputing, including:

Molecular Visualization (Chris Henn, Conrad Huang, Arthur Olson & Michael Teschner)

Computational Simulation and Hybrid QM/MM models (Toshiko Ichiye, Charles Brooks III, Mark Thompson & Kenneth Merz)

Protein Structure Prediction (Fischer, Adam Godzik, Su Chung, Subbiah Subramanian & Richard Lathrop)

Structure evolution (Richard Goldstein & Erich Bornberg-Bauer)

Distributed and Intelligent Databases (Pat Argos, H. Werner Mewes & Dmitrij Frishman)

Extracting Biological Knowledge From Sequences (Francisco De La Vega, Julio Collado-Vides & Denis Thieffry)

Metabolic Pathways (Peter Karp & Monica Riley)

Computing with Biomolecules (Tom Head & Takashi Yokomori)

In addition, there were workshops and discussion groups organized on the following topics:

Molecular Modeling (Teri Klein & Jurgen Bajorath)

Taxonomic Information Systems (Gary Waggoner)

Biocomputing Education (Susan Johns & Steven Thompson)

Information and Complexity (Greg Dewey & H. Eugene Stanley)

Stochastic Models and Grammars (Kiyoshi Asai & Hidetoshi Tanaka)

The organizers wish to thank the invited plenary speaker, Dr. I. D. Kunz, as well as the speakers invited by track organizers for particular track sessions. We would also like to thank Sharon Surles, Kevin Lauderdale, the Stanford Section on Medical Informatics, and the UCSF Computer Graphics Lab for excellent administrative and technical assistance.

The meeting was supported by grants from the National Science Foundation, the Department of Energy and the National Institutes of Health. In addition, corporate sponsors included Molecular Applications Group, Pharmacia & Upjohn. The PSB has now firmly established a tradition of success and excellence, and we look forward to future versions as biocomputing comes to maturity.

Russ B. Altman,
Section on Medical Informatics, Stanford University

Keith Dunker,
Department of Biochemistry/Biophysics, Washington State University

Lawrence Hunter,
National Library of Medicine, National Institutes of Health

Teri E. Klein,
Department of Pharmaceutical Chemistry, University of California, San Francisco

Pacific Symposium on Biocomputing, 1997 Co-Chairs

CONTENTS

Session Introductions

SESSION TITLE: Distributed and Intelligent Databases

P. ARGOS
European Molecular Biology Laboratory,
Mayerhofstr. 1, 69012 Heidelberg, Germany

H.-W. MEWES, D. FRISHMAN
Martinsried Institute for Protein Sequences,
Max-Plank-Institute for Biochemistry
Am Klopferspitz 18a, 82152 Martinsried, Germany

Presently molecular biological databases are rapidly increasing both in number and information content; however, their interpretation is rapidly becoming a bottleneck in molecular biology. An outstanding example is afforded by amino acid sequence collections and their doubling every few years with entries now exceeding 100 000; and yet there is no comprehensive database multiply aligning them as families with conserved motifs. The information in the banks has not been integrated since the originators (often scientists in a given field) have focused on their specific specialty such as tertiary protein structures or only immunoglobulin sequences. Mere collection was sufficient when the information content was relatively small, the opposite of the present status given the dominance of genome sequencing projects and commercial pharmaceutical biotechnology. Large databases need classification, interpretation, and analysis. Furthermore, they need synthesis for optimal use of information necessary for new discoveries of peviously unknown relationships. The integration required is extensive and should span across genetic mapping and sequence data, evolutionary development, protein structure and function, and cellular processes and organization.
The session will focus on recent advances in delivering high quality information to the biological community. New approaches include interconnecting existing databases distributed over many computer sites for simultaneous information retrieval through Internet tools, knowledge-based expert systems, interface languages, and multiserver management as well as methods that make the primary databases more intelligent and yield newly synthesized and interpreted databases, exemplified by careful clustering of the available data, incorporation of experimental data, functional and structural characterization of whole genomes using novel techniques such as structure prediction, threading, and pattern recognition. It is clear that major discoveries in molecular biology will be severely inhibited without automatic access and association of available information.

MODERN CONCEPTS IN MOLECULAR MODELING

Jurgen Bajorath
Bristol-Myers Squibb Research in Institute
3005 First Avenue, Seattle, WA 98121

Department of Biological Structure
University of Washington, Seattle, WA 98195

Teri E. Klein
Department of Pharmaceutical Chemistry
University of California, San Francisco, CA 94143

Computational methods to predict and analyze the structural and energetic properties of small or macromolecules and their interactions play an increasingly important role in chemistry and biology. The wealth of available sequences, structures, and mutagenesis data provide an enormous database for computational efforts to predict structures, simulate molecular interactions, and understand them in quantitative energetic terms.

The field of molecular modeling is very diverse and difficult to define. Primary goals of the workshop, **Modern Concepts in Molecular Modeling,** were to highlight major directions of computer modeling efforts and to reflect the diversity of current research. How are molecular structures and properties analyzed? How are biomolecules and their interactions modeled and energetically characterized? What are the successes, caveats, and limitations?

The majority of contributions to the session have focused on the development and application of various energy functions to study the structure, energetics, and dynamics of proteins and their interactions with ligands. These include molecular dynamics, free energy calculations and empirical free energy functions, quantum mechananics, and molecular field analysis.

Other contributions have targeted structure comparison, prediction, and assessment.

In aggregate, these studies provide an exciting view of current developments in computer-aided molecular modeling and theoretical analysis or biological molecules. The research presented in this session certainly contributes to the wide spectrum of methods and applications in the biocomputing arena.

Participants in this workshop included: **B. Hess**, University of Groningen, *Model for the Long Term Dynamics of Proteins;* **P. A. Kollman**, University of California, San Francisco, *Molecular Dynamics and Free Energy Calculations;* **T. P. Lybrand**, University of Washington, *Evaluation of Three-Dimensional Models for Proteins and Protein-Ligand Complexes;* **G. M. Maggiora**, Pharmacia & Upjohn, *MIMIC: A Field-Based Approach to Molecular Similarity with Applications to Small Molecules and Proteins;* **T. Mirzadegan**, Roche Bioscience, *Homology Modeling of Immunoglobulins;* **J. Novotny**, Bristol-Myers Squibb Research Institute, *Empirical Free Energy Calculations on Mutants of the HyHEL-10-Lysozyme Complex;* **R. E. Stenkamp**, University of Washington, *Protein Superfamilies as Targets for Computer Modeling: The Carbohydrate Recognition Domain of a Macrophage Lectin;* and, **A. Tempzcyk**, Agouron Pharmaceuticals, Inc., *Combined Quantum and Molecular Mechanics: Catalytic Mechanism of the Protein Serine/Threonine Phosphatase Family.*

Acknowledgments

We would like to acknowledge the financial support of the Computer Aided Drug Discovery, Pharmacia & Upjohn for this workshop.

EXTRACTING BIOLOGICAL KNOWLEDGE FROM DNA SEQUENCES

F. M. DE LA VEGA[1], D. THIEFFRY[2,3], and J. COLLADO-VIDES[3]

[1]*Departamento de Genética y Biología Molecular, CINVESTAV-IPN. A.P. 14-740, México D.F. 07000, México*

[2]*Département de Biologie Moléculaire, Université Libre de Bruxelles. Rue des Chevaux, 67, B-1640 Rhode-Saint-Genèse, Belgium*

[3]*Centro de Investigación sobre Fijación de Nitrógeno. Universidad Nacional Autónoma de México. Cuernavaca A.P. 565-A, Morelos 62100, México*

We are experiencing the time when sequencing genome projects of various organisms are already being completed. No doubt the understanding or deciphering of these large amounts of DNA sequences represents, at least conceptually, one of the major challenges for those working in computational biology.

This track focuses on the different theoretical and computational approaches aimed to extract biological information from DNA sequences. The approaches utilize among others, methods from statistics, information theory, artificial intelligence, linguistics, as well as combinations of these. The variety of approaches exemplified by the different contributions to this track illustrates how computational biology is quickly progressing.

The purpose is to identify functional units in sequences, looking for characteristic patterns and regularities found in a set of examples. Some of the identified units also maintain complex relationships among themselves, allowing to explain regulatory phenomena, or evolutionary relationships. As some complete genomic sequences become available, questions involving properties of the whole cell can be addressed, as well as comparisons of complete genomes across species. A new type of sequence analysis focusing on higher order sequence patterns is emerging.

It is important to note that ultimately what all these methods do is to make use of biological knowledge that has been in one way or the other obtained experimentally, and to transform this knowledge into a predictive tool. Therefore the importance of organized databases and biological knowledge as a resource to decipher genomes and sequences.

In this sense, it is interesting to think about the conclusions that anthropologists have drawn from their lessons in deciphering ancient human languages. Some of "the fundamental pillars" summarized by Michael Coe on which successful deciphering enterprises have rested are the following: i) the database must be large enough; ii) there should be a bilingual inscription, such as the rosette stone; and iii) the language must be known [1]. Etruscan is an example where condition three is not fulfilled, therefore, it can be read but not understood.

In the case of molecular biology, the first condition is being fulfilled by the genome sequencing projects; the second one by the organized biological knowledge in databases where sequences and functions can be matched; the third one is quite an astonishing condition. We leave it as food for thought to the reader.

The organizers of this track acknowledge all anonymous referees who helped in selecting and improving the papers submitted.

References

[1] Coe M. *Breaking the Maya Code* (Thames and Hudson, New York, N.Y., 1992).

UNDERSTANDING AND PREDICTING PROTEIN STRUCTURE

Daniel Fischer
Molecular Biology Institute, University of California, Los Angeles, CA 90095, USA

Adam Godzik
Dept. of Molecular Biology, Scripps Research Institute, La Jolla, CA 92037, USA

Su Chung
Uniformed Services University of the Health Sciences, Bethesda, MD 20814, USA

S. Subbiah
The Wistar Institute, 3601 Spruce Street, Philadelphia, PA 19104, USA

Richard Lathrop
Information and Computer Science, University of California, Irvine, CA, USA

Protein structure prediction from sequence remains a premiere computational problem for modern molecular biology. Just as protein structure prediction may be divided into sub-problems of main-chain and side-chain placement, so the protein structure prediction track this year has been divided into sub-tracks of protein threading (organized by Daniel Fischer and Adam Godzik) and side-chain packing (organized by Su Chung and S. Subbiah). The result is an unusually rich tour through different levels of protein structure prediction, from coarse-grained prediction of the tertiary fold to the fine-grained atomic detail of individual side-chains.

1 Protein Threading

Organized by Daniel Fischer and Adam Godzik.

All threading and folding algorithms depend crucially on the quality of the energy parameter set. For many years such sets were built by analyzing interaction regularities in known protein structures. Despite a long history of such derivations, fundamental problems with the theoretical background persist till today, with many existing derivations containg important omissions or even errors. Reva et al. tackle this problem by providing a very formal derivation protocol. While the practical difference their derivation makes can only be demonstrated by empirical tests in a predictive setting, their derivation provides a well thought out standard that other derivations can compare to.

In a second paper, Zheng et al. extend their original work presented last year in this conference. In their work they explore a new picture of a protein structure, described as a space filling aggregate of irregular tetrahedra with vertices at C-alpha atoms. This model puts an emphasis on the spatial arrangement of residues, rather than on their position along the chain. In a natural way it also allows to develop a four body interaction potential. Although it still remains to be tested on actual threading, it is an interesting generalization of most other existing empirical interaction potentials used in threading and folding algorithms.

Delarue and Koehl return to the roots of the inverse folding problem, which addresses the question of finding a sequence compatible with a given protein structures. Using a mean field theory they develop a generalized sequence profile compatible with a given C-alpha atom trace. The sequence matrix, as it is called in the paper, is derived purely from the structural information, but can be used in the framework of standard sequence alignment programs.

Two papers in the threading session attempt to combine several prediction methods to create hybrid approaches addressing two different stages in protein structure prediction. Ortiz et al. analyze multiple aligned protein sequences to derive possible constraints on the final structure in terms in secondary structure elements and contacts between them. By combining state of the art secondary structure prediction, analysis of correlated mutations, and inverse folding, they derive a small number of distance constraints. These in turn are used to guide a lattice folding algorithm to arrive at a low resolution protein model. On three examples they show that, given a sufficient number of homologous protein sequences, it is possible to obtain final models with correct topology and 4-4.5 Angstrom root mean square deviation from the native structure.

Pawlowski et al. combine a semi-automatic comparative modelling and threading to build full atom models of proteins close to the limits of recognizable sequence similarity. For very distantly homologous proteins sequence alignments become unstable, changing dramatically with small changes in gap penalties and mutation matrices; recognition of a structurally correct alignment is impossible on the sequence level. At the same time, differences between alignments become more pronounced when full atoms models are built on their basis. Structurally correct alignments lead to higher quality models, as measured by the threading algorithm. This promising method is shown to work on two examples of notoriously difficult sequence alignments, and is also used to suggest a possible model for a currenlty unknown structure of S100A1 dimer. This paper also suggests an interesting approach to verifying the results of threading.

Mamitsuka and Abe use a stochastic tree grammar method to predict location and structure of beta sheet regions in proteins. Using a formalism developed to study natural languages, they are able to discover amino acid patterns defining localization of beta strands which go beyond simple sequence similarity. This method stands half way between secondary and tertiary structure prediction method; it concentrates on predictions of secondary structure elements, but predicts their mutual structural organization within the beta sheet as well as their location along the sequence. On a set of several beta proteins this method is able to predict the correct position of most beta strands, and in two cases correctly suggests the entire protein topology.

2 Side-chain Packing, or "The Importance of Being Well-Packed"

Organized by Su Chung and S. Subbiah

Starting in the mid-70's and through the mid-80's there was much well-publicized literature by many groups that claimed to have solved the homology modeling problem to a significant degree. The general lay-biologist was led to think that, save for some long loops and solvent-exposed residues, the modeling of side-chains onto a template backbone from a homologue protein was in the main a solved problem. The combination of "sex appeal" from the advent of exciting color computer graphics and the "above-reproach" mathematically sophisticated, computationally complex energy calculations was a potent mix that could not be subjected to honest and critical assessment of (1) what was really being predicted as opposed to being merely copied and (2) what the prediction accuracy relative to random was.

In a typical modeling exercise, a protein sharing 50% sequence identity with a known homologue protein structure was modeled based on the homologue's main-chain providing the template scaffold on which the new side-chains were added. Since, roughly speaking, half the atoms in an average protein belong to either the main-chain or the C-beta side-chain location (which is in practice totally defined by the coordinates of the main chain atoms), at best only half the atoms — those in the post-C-beta side-chain positions — actually were predicted. Further, it is well-known that side-chains that are identical between homologous proteins very frequently assume the same or very similar conformation. It is also well-known that the backbone atoms between 2 proteins sharing 50% sequence identity typically differ by only about 1 Angstrom root mean square deviation (r.m.s). This is not a lot when compared with studies suggesting that when the same exact protein is solved in two different X-ray crystallography labs using different software, etc., the backbone atoms differ by as much as 0.5 Angstroms r.m.s. Thus for our typical modeling exercise where there is 50% sequence identity between target and template, simply accepting the template as a starting point for further modeling guarantees the "prediction" of half the atoms in the final completed model to about 1 Angstroms r.m.s. Moreover, the fact that 50% of the side-chain conformations can be simply adopted as is, "predicts" another one quarter of the atoms in the complete final model at significantly better than 1 Angstrom r.m.s. — possibly even 0.5 Angstrom r.m.s. Thus, barring the loops and highly solvent-exposed residues where modelers (then and now) a priori concede defeat, there was at best one quarter of all atoms that truly remained to be predicted. One could expect that even a random method might get some of these right by chance. Thus, no matter how badly this quarter of atoms were predicted, one could always count on the final complete predicted model being judged relatively accurate when compared to the known experimental answer. It also helped that there were no established numbers — in r.m.s. Angstroms, or equivalently chi angle degrees — on what constituted a totally random prediction. Any seemingly low r.m.s. error to report, accompanied by detail-obscuring superpositions of predicted model vs. known experimental truth that emphasized the general backbone similarity and ignored the details of the side-chain conformational similarity, could be trumpeted as success. The dictum — "Don't get it right; just get it in color" — was often an apt description of the state of affairs.

By 1989 some investigators began to point at the true difficulty of the problem [1,2]. Despite this dawn of pessimism, a little earlier in 1986 Ponder and Richards [3] pointed out that the exhaustive enumeration of the so-called side-chain rotamers could in principle allow side-chains to be predicted with great accuracy, using the perfect native backbone as a rigid constraint. However, in practice, this task of enumerating all the possibilities was well beyond the computing power of modern day computers. Assuming just 5 rotamer choices on average per side-chain, the typical 200 residue protein would require enumerating 5^{200} conformations. For an ab initio chi angle enumeration at 10 degree intervals the number would be even more astronomical at more than 10^{600}.

In 1991, 3 groups working independently of each other — one using an ab initio approach and two using rotamer-based ones — proved that the foresight of Ponder and Richards was indeed correct [4,6]. When a protein is stripped of all its side-chains and the perfect native backbone is used as a constraint to re-pack all the side-chain atoms, these varied methods could depend on achieving 1.25, 1.5 and 1.6 Angstroms r.m.s. accuracy on the 30-40% of the least solvent-exposed residues. Using only extremely simple and crude van der Waals packing-oriented energy functions without electrostatics or solvent considerations, these methods circumvented the astronomical combinatorics of exhaustive enumeration. At this time the r.m.s. deviation averaged over all side-chain types that could be expected for a random prediction was established to be about 3.1 to 3.3 Angstroms, which has since been confirmed [4,7]. Since then there has been a flood of different methods and improvements of earlier ones — mostly using rotamers or database-derived information — that have confirmed our ability to crack this seemingly large combinatorial problem at even higher accuracies of 1 and sub-1 Angstrom r.m.s. for the buried side-chain residues. It is worth noting that when two X-ray labs solve the structure of the same protein, side-chain r.m.s. deviations, albeit over all side-chains and not just buried ones, can differ by as much as 1 to 1.5 Angstroms r.m.s.

Despite the success at breaking the back of the basic side-chain packing combinatorial problem, many workers, as illustrated by the contributions from Koehl and Delarue and from Desmet et al. in the following pages, are busy trying to refine the methodologies further. More recently, other workers have extended these methods to the practically more important real-life homology modeling situation; again using a rigid-backbone, but one that is a less accurate template from the homologue protein. While these studies show that even imperfect backbones can be used to produce side-chain information that is better than random, it is increasingly clear that the backbone needs to be simultaneously adjusted. While this problem has been solved recently in a very specialized instance[8], a general solution still is lacking. This problem, the problem of handling side-chain packing at loops, and the problem of allowing for solvent and electrostatic effects, all are beginning to take center-stage in theoretical side-chain packing.

In parallel with the success at defeating the combinatorics of the packing problem, methods relying on this success have been proposed to predict the packing energies and relative stabilities of mutants. In the following pages both Kono and co-workers and Lee and Levitt compare their predictions with experiments. Related algorithms that allow side-chain flexibility during protein-ligand docking are also under study.

It is clear, that in the last few years we have convincingly shown that the combinatorial problem of side-chain packing is reliably solved. This theoretical success, viewed in the context of supporting experimental evidence, suggests that to first order good side-chain packing is an important, if not the dominant, factor in the architecture of proteins. Many hurdles remain to turn this discovery into truly practical tools to aid the experimental biologist. Nevertheless this appears an opportune moment to take stock of our theoretical successes and chart the way forward that will allow predictive success to migrate from the computer to the test-tube. Recalcitrant backbone shifts, wayward loops, slippery energy potentials, troublesome electrostatic effects and even the mystical medium of water - Let's get it all right and in living color.

Acknowledgments

The session co-chairs gratefully thank the session referees, whose careful reviews of the submitted papers and insightful, judicious suggestions for improvement are materially reflected in the high quality of the presented papers: N. Alexandrov, M. Bass, G. Crippen, S. Doniach, R. Dunbrack, A. Elofson, J. Fetrow, L. Gregoret, M. Grisbkov, J. Hirst, A. Kolinski, S. LeGrand, K. Olszewski, B. Park, M. Pellegrini, F. Pettit, D. Rice, D. Ripoll, E. Shakhnovich, J. Skolnick, A. Tempczyk, M. Vasquez, M. Wilmanns, T-M. Yi, R. Zimmer. Special thanks to all crystallographers who deposited their coordinates in the international scientific databases.

This work was supported in part by a grant to S.S. from the Department of Energy, DE-FG03-95ER62135. We also acknowledge financial and other support for the session from the Bioinformatics Center at the National University of Singapore, The Program in Mathematical Biology at University of California, Berkeley, Molecular Applications Group of Palo Alto and Digital Equipment Corporation.

References

1. L. Reid and J. Thornton, Proteins 5, 170 1989.
2. N. L. Summers and M. Karplus, J. Mol. Biol. 210, 785 (1989).
3. J. W. Ponder and F. M. Richards J. Mol. Biol. 193, 775 (1987).
4. C. Lee and S. Subbiah, J. Mol. Biol. 217, 373 (1991).
5. P. Tuffery et. al., J. Biomol. Struct. Dynam. 8, 1267 (1991).
6. L. Holm and C. Sander, J. Mol. Biol. 218, 183 (1991).
7. R. Tanimura, A. Kidera and H. Nakamura, Prot. Sci. 3, 2358 (1994)..
8. P. Harbury, B. Tidor and P. Kim, Proc. Natl. Acad. Sci USA 92, 8408 (1995).

BIOPOLYMER STRUCTURES: WHERE DO THEY COME FROM? WHERE ARE THEY GOING? EVOLUTIONARY PERSPECTIVES ON BIOPOLYMER STRUCTURE AND FUNCTION

RICHARD A. GOLDSTEIN
Chemistry Department, Biophysics Research Division, University of Michigan
Ann Arbor, Michigan, USA - 48109 - 1055
richardg@umich.edu

ERICH BORNBERG-BAUER
Abt. Theoretische Bioinformatik, Deutsches Krebsforschungszentrum
Im Neuenheimer Feld 280, D - 69 120 Heidelberg
and
Institut für Mathematik, Universität Wien, A - 1090 Wien
Bornberg@dkfz-heidelberg.de

Biological polymers such as DNA, RNA, and proteins are the result of eons of evolution. In order to understand these macromolecules, it is necessary to understand the evolutionary pressures that determined their form and function. Conversely, the properties of these macromolecules encode this heritage, and can provide insight into the process of evolution.

The effort to understand, reconstruct, and simulate the evolution of biopolymers, including their structure and function, has become a key task involving such diverse fields as evolutionary biology, molecular biology, structural biology, and biophysical chemistry. The rapid growth of sequence and structure databases, combined with the continuing geometric increases in computer speed, has made this field fertile ground for biocomputing and bioinformatics. In this session a number of diverse contributions to this effort are presented.

There has been much interest in using simple models to investigate basic principles that govern the relationship between biopolymer sequence and structure. In their paper, Abkevich, Gutin, and Shakhnovich develop a model where proteins are confined to cubic lattices. They apply optimization procedures to find evolved sequences that fold faster than initial random sequences, and show that the ability of proteins to fold may actually have arisen as a side-effect of other physiochemical factors.

In their contribution, Renner and Bornberg-Bauer use the popular "HP-type" lattice model to explore the fitness landscapes of lattice proteins. By generating large ensembles of random structures, they can characterize the relationship of sequence to structure using statistical methods. They find structure landscapes to be rugged, and this ruggedness to be sensitive to alphabet and shape space size. This suggests that simple HP-models may be too crude for realistic analyses of evolutionary issues.

Many applications, such as identifying and aligning homologous proteins, require the use of some sort of "similarity matrix" which measures how much different amino acid types resemble each other. In their paper, Wei, Altman, and Chang develop a novel approach to the generation of these matrices, looking at similarities in the *environments* in which different amino acids are more likely to be found. In addition to enabling homology searches with a sensitivity comparable to that obtained using matrices based on relative substitution rates, this approach helps us to understand the relationship between amino acid property and local environment.

The exceedingly growing abundance of sequence data poses the need for new and efficient methods to scan data bases quickly and efficiently. Matsuda, Taniguchi, and Hashimoto introduce a method to tackle the notorious sequence-to-structure alignment problem. They present a simple algorithm to represent structures by mapping dihedral angles to an alphabet of 20 letters. Using Smith-Waterman local alignment algorithms and appropriate scoring matrices, their method appears to be more sensitive than standard procedures for performing motif searches.

The evolutionary process may leave intriguing residual clues that can be uncovered by increasingly sophisticated statistical methods. Korotkov and Phoenix present a method based on information theory to look for latent periodicities in the DNA sequences, and suggest that such periodicities may be quite widespread. In addition to suggesting duplication events during evolution, these features may also have certain physiologically-important roles.

Acknowledgments:

We are thankful to all researchers who submitted work to this track. We are indebted to the reviewers who found the time to provide useful comments and criticisms.

Introduction to the session: COMPUTING WITH BIOMOLECULES

Tom Head
Department of Mathematics, Binghamton University, Binghamton, New York 13902-6000 USA
tom@math.binghamton.edu

Takashi Yokomori
Department of Computer Science and Information Mathematics, University of Electro-Communications, 1-5-1 Chofugaoka, Chofu, Tokyo 182, Japan
yokomori@cs.uec.ac.jp

As one of the sessions in PSB'97, this session is unique in that it was set up to provide an opportunity to present works that deal with the use, as computational units, of molecules that either occur naturally in living systems or that are manufactured in imitation of molecules that occur in living systems. In other words, the work presented in this session deals with what might be described as applications of biology and biochemistry to computing and to the broader understanding of the nature of computation. Thus this session intends to deal with applications in the direction opposite to that of the other sessions in PSB series.

More specifically, this session consists of three presentations. They concern biomolecular behaviors that may be incorporated into computations, used as computations, or viewed as computations.

The first paper concerns an incorporation of the protein bacteriorhodopsin into an artificially constructed light sensitive receptor which provides visual input to computational processes. This work links naturally occurring biomolecular behavior with conventional silicon hardware.

The second paper provides a new conceptual approach to the use of DNA molecules and enzymes to implement algorithmic computations. The naturally occurring actions of restriction enzymes and ligases on DNA molecules are shown to provide a basis for universal test tube 'wet' computing.

Using newly created formal models, the third paper reports the computational generative capabilities of three mobile behaviors exhibited by subsegments of DNA molecules. This work, which was inspired by considerations of genome evolution, establishes relationships in generative power among the operations of inversion, transposition, and duplication.

(Presentation #1:)
Towards a BacterioRhodopsin-Silicon Neuromorphic Photosensor
by C.H. Martin, Z.P. Chen, and R.R. Birge
W.M. Keck Center for Molecular Electronics and the Department of Chemistry, Syracuse University, Syracuse, New York 13244, USA

(Presentation #2:)
Test Tube Systems with Cutting/Recombination Operations
by Rudolf Freund (`rudi@logic.tuwien.ac.at`)
Institut fur Computersprachen, Technische Universitat Wien, Resselgasse 3, 1040 Wein, Austria
Erzsebet Csuhaj-Varju (`CSUHAJ@luna.aszi.sztaki.hu`)
Computer and Automation Institute, Hungarian Academy of Sciences, Kende u. 13-17, 1111 Budapest, Hungry
Franz Watchler (`franz.wachtler@univie.ac.at`)
Institut fur Histologie und Embryologie, Universitat Wein, Schwartzspanierstr. 17, 1090 Wein, Austria

(Presentation #3:)
On Some Operations Suggested by Genome Evolution
by Jurgen Dassow (`dassow@irb.cs.uni-magdeburg.de`)
Faculty of Computer Science, University of Magdeburg, P.O.Box 4120, D-39016, Magdeburg, Germany
Victor Mitrana (`mitrana@math.math.unibuc.ro`)
Faculty of Mathematics, Department of Computer Science, University of Bucharest, Str. Academiei 14, 70109 Bucharest, Romania

* * * * * * * * * * * * * * * * * * *

Finally, we would like to thank all of those who contributed to making this session possible by submitting their work or reviewing submissions.

Session on Computation in Biological Pathways

P.D. Karp
AI Center, SRI International, EJ229
Menlo Park, CA 94025, pkarp@ai.sri.com

M. Riley
Marine Biological Laboratory
Woods Hole, MA 02543, mriley@mbl.edu

The computational management and analysis of biological pathways is at the intersection of a surprisingly diverse set of disciplines, including biochemistry, chemical engineering, genomics, developmental biology, artificial intelligence, simulation, and control theory. These disciplines encompass both a range of biological pathway types, and a range of analysis techniques. A PSB session on this topic is timely for two reasons: Several new information sources on biological pathways have appeared on the WWW in the last year, resulting in a surprisingly large number of pathway-database projects.[a] Communication among the developers of these databases will allow them to build on each others efforts in the areas of schema design, and user-interface design, and may reduce duplicate data entry, and encourage data validation. Communication among database developers and users will inform developers of user needs, and inform users of database capabilities. In addition, the recent completion of several genomic sequencing projects, along with the imminent completion of several others, provides a driving force for the prediction of pathways from sequence data.

The papers in this session indeed encompass both pathway databases and computational tools for pathway analysis. Goto et al discuss a database of metabolic pathways for several organisms whose genomes have recently been sequenced. Okamoto et al present a toolkit for use by chemical engineers in modeling, optimizing, and visualizing pathways. Bergeron et al describe techniques for studying regulatory pathways such as those involved in transcription, translation, and signaling. Papers by Mittenthal, and by Sellers and Wagg, explore the problems of enumerating the possible pathways present in a set of reactions, in the areas of transport and protein–protein interactions.

[a]For an overview of these resources, see `http://www.ai.sri.com/~pkarp/pathways.html`.

Invited Reviews

New Challenges in Computational Biochemistry

B. HONIG
Department of Biochemistry and Molecular Biophysics
Columbia University
630 West 168 St.
New York, NY 10032

The application of physical chemical methods to the simulation of biological macromolecules has become an important area of scientific research (which I will term computational biochemistry). Molecular dynamics simulation methods, continuum electrostatics and a variety of empirical solvation models have become widely used tools in physical biochemistry and structural biology. Algorithms and computer programs that have been developed for the purposes of simulation have become an integral part of the methodological repertoire of experimental scientists in these fields. In biologically oriented research, the adaptation of theoretical methods and concepts by experimentalist is often taken as a sign of success and by this criterion, theory has indeed had significant impact. The existence of software companies that market the wares of computational biochemists provides further evidence of the acceptance of simulation methodologies. This is a non-trivial accomplishment given the fact that as recently as ten to fifteen years ago, the results of simulations on proteins, membranes and nucleic acids were not taken very seriously by the experimental community.

The successes of computational biochemistry have resulted from a number of factors. First and foremost in my view was the willingness of many investigators to defy the conventional wisdom which posited that large molecules could not be gainfully studied until simpler systems could be better understood. From a practical standpoint, essential accomplishments included the development of potential functions that could effectively mimic physical reality and the parallel development of simulation methods that could relate these potential functions to physical observables. Improved representations of the aqueous phase, ranging from atomic level descriptions to continuum approximations, have played a crucial role in this process. Another factor has been the ability of workers in the field to relate their results to experimental questions that were under concurrent investigation in the larger biochemical and biophysical communities. In this way, the results of simulations have been extensively tested and refined. The many successful correlations between theory and experiment that have been reported in the literature testify to the effectiveness of this approach as does the integration of many theoretical concepts into the every day language of biochemistry and structural biology.

Despite the enormous progress that has been made, a number of challenges have been elusive. Perhaps the most glaring of these is the inability of existing methods to consistently predict the relative binding free energies of different substrates to the same protein. A number of impressive successes have been reported but, in a general sense, the problem remains unsolved. The same can be said about the prediction of the relative free energies of different protein or nucleic acid conformations. For example, the prediction of the conformation of loops which connect two fixed secondary structure elements is an extremely important problem for which anecdotal successes have been reported but for which no general solution is available. It is useful to consider possible sources of the difficulties inherent in these problems but before doing so, it is of interest to consider challenges of a very different nature to the field of computational biochemistry. These come from computational biology at the one extreme, and combinatorial chemistry at the other.

Combinatorial chemistry poses a "threat" of sorts to the entire field of structure based drug design. As has been widely discussed, the ability to simultaneously test a large number of different compounds for binding affinities reduces the need for the precise design of a compounds that binds tightly to a specific target. With regard to computational methods, one might inquire as to the point of carrying out a complicated calculation of a binding free energy when, at least in principle, it is straightforward to test thousands or even millions of potential substrates. Clearly the "binding problem" will remain one of great theoretical interest but is it of practical interest as well?

The challenge of computational biology arises from an entirely different source. The vast quantity information now accumulating in biological databases provides an approach to the prediction of biological structure and function that in many ways bypasses approaches based on physics and physical chemistry. A clear example is provided by the protein folding problem. Despite the range of methods that have been applied to understanding the physical and chemical principles upon which protein folding is based, the fact remains most of the successes to date in actual fold prediction have resulted from database mining of one type or another. It is somewhat sobering for example that despite the extraordinary progress that has been made in understanding the physical basis of secondary structure formation, the most successful secondary structure prediction methods are based solely on database analysis, for example using neural networks. The same can be said about tertiary structure prediction based on "threading" and 3-D profile fold recognition methods.

One response to these comments is to point out that not all science need be immediately practical. Database mining does not necessarily lead to the type of deep understanding that is satisfying to physical chemists while the existence of combinatorial chemistry does not really detract from the interest and importance in elucidating the principles of molecular recognition. On the other hand, there are many practical elements to academic science of which we are all aware; such as the difficult in obtaining funding, or in finding jobs. I find it difficult to ignore the enormous disparity in job availability for individuals trained to carry out comparative analysis of amino acid sequences and individuals trained in simulation methods. Both fields involve computational research but the former has become so "hot" that the absence of trained researchers has become a frequent subject of commentary in Science and other journals.

How can computational biochemistry respond to these theoretical and practical challenges. The difficulties in calculating accurate binding and conformational free energies may arise from a number of sources. First, it is possible that available potential functions are simply not good enough. There is some evidence to this effect; for example it has been shown recently in a number of studies that the relative solvation free energies associated with a number of functional groups cannot be explained with existing force fields. The problem seems to result from non-electrostatic contributions to hydrogen bonding which are difficult to reproduce with the reliance of all widely used force fields on atomic partial charges. Moreover, it is essential to find a way to properly account for electronic polarizability. There has been much effort in this direction for some time but a new generation of "polarizable force fields" has not yet emerged.

A second major problem concerns conformational sampling. There is a need to develop methods that effectively sample conformational space based on a physically meaningful energy function. The integration of continuum solvent representations and molecular mechanics methods may prove useful in this regard and has indeed been attempted on a number of occasions. However here again, much work remains to be done. Of course, there may be problems that are simply intractable. If for example, the difficulties in calculating relative binding free energies are due in large part to different entropy changes distributed over an entire protein associated with the binding of different substrates, the prospects for a general solution to the binding problem are dim.

It is likely that much theoretical effort will be devoted to these problems in the coming years and it is likely that the effort will be worthwhile. However, even in the absence of methodological progress, there are clearly many ways to exploit existing techniques in computational biochemistry in the study of biological macromolecules; for example in the analysis of the structure and function of the large numbers of proteins and nucleic acids whose three dimensional structures have been determined. Enzyme mechanisms, the nature of ligand induced conformational changes, the effects of mutations on protein stability and protein folding pathways are examples of problems of great current interest that will not soon disappear. On the other hand, computational biochemistry may also have answers to the two practical challenges mentioned above.

Regarding the challenge of combinatorial chemistry, a more optimistic view is that this technology effectively relieves the pressure to calculate binding free energies at better than kcal/mole accuracy. Rather, developing approximate methods to screen combinatorial libraries based on their ability to bind to a specific target or to possess properties similar to a known pharmacaphore has become an important goal. This in turn requires an accurate description and understanding of the properties of isolated molecules in aqueous solution and existing methods are already quite successful in this regard.

An optimistic view of the challenge of biological database mining suggests even greater opportunities for computational biochemistry. Specifically, in the absence of a well-defined physical model, statistical methods used in the analysis of databases, though extremely powerful, are ultimately limited in their ability to extract meaningful information. Their effectiveness can be enormously enhanced if they are combined with the tools and insights of computational biochemistry. As an example, it seems clear that threading methods could be significantly improved if the scoring functions they use to distinguish correct from incorrect protein folds were based on meaningful physical rather than statistical potentials.

The integration of computational biochemistry and computational biology offers many exciting opportunities. One can envision the day where the process of multiple sequence analysis, structural prediction, the design of combinatorial libraries and binding free energy calculations will be carried out in a single group by researchers who understand the intricacies of each of these problems. For this to occur will require new training modes for graduate students and postdoctoral fellows and, perhaps, new modes of thinking for their more senior colleagues.

Papers

COMPUTER SIMULATIONS OF PREBIOTIC EVOLUTION

V.I. ABKEVICH, A.M. GUTIN, and E.I. SHAKHNOVICH
Harvard University, Department of Chemistry
12 Oxford Street, Cambridge MA 02138

This paper is a review of our previous work on the field of possible ways of prebiotic evolution[1,2]. We propose an algorithm providing sequences of model proteins with rapid folding into a given native conformation. Thermodynamical analysis shows that the increase in speed is matched by an increase in stability: the evolved sequences are much more stable in their native conformation than the initial random sequence. We discuss a possible origin of the first biopolymers, having stable unique structure. We suggest that at the prebiotic stage of evolution, long organic polymers had to be compact in order to avoid hydrolysis and had to be soluble and thus must not be exceedingly hydrophobic. We present an algorithm that generates such sequences of model proteins. The evolved sequences turn out to have a stable unique structure, into which they quickly fold. This result illustrates the idea that the unique three-dimensional native structure of first biopolymers could have evolved as a side effect of a nonspecific physico-chemical factors acting at the prebiotic stage of evolution.

The problem of how first biopolymers could have evolved prebiotically is one of the most fundamental in modern science. The first macromolecules which served as enzymes must satisfy two conditions: (i) the structure must be thermodynamically stable and (ii) it must be kinetically reachable in a biologically reasonable time. The important question, from the evolutionary point of view, is how likely that such sequences, having unique 3-dimensional structure have appeared in the primordial soup. Assuming that initial polymerization of organic molecules at the prebiological stage resulted in the set of random sequences, it can be be formulated as what fraction of all sequences can fold to and be stable in a unique structure? This question concerns the very essence of the concept of prebiological evolution. Indeed, if the fraction of foldable sequences among all random sequences is large, then there may be no need in prebiotic selection, and protein-like sequences could have been selected randomly out of multitude of randomly synthesized biopolymers. Alternatively, if the set of foldable sequences constitutes vanishing fraction of all sequences, then some selection was likely to had been acting even at the prebiotic stage. In this paper we show that this is in fact the case. However, the main problem here is that at the prebiotic stage such property as unique structure (and ability to perform catalytic functions) was not likely to be a factor in selection (that is why this stage is *prebiotic*). Therefore in this case some other factors could have been guiding synthesis of prebiological polymers, and sequences with unique structure could have evolved as a byproduct of other physico-chemical processes. In this paper we suggest a principle possibility of a scenario of this type.

It was shown analytically[3,4] and numerically[4-7] for different models of proteins that the condition of the thermodynamic stability of the native state is not restrictive. It was conjectured[3,4] that there exists a critical temperature T_c such that a significant fraction of random sequences have a stable unique structure at $T < T_c$. It was also pointed out[1] that the probability for a random sequence to have a stable unique structure at $T < T_c$ does not depend on its length N (this result was confirmed in a more recent numerical study[7]). However, at low temperatures folding rate decreases and the native conformation becomes kinetically less accessible. The implication is that random sequences mostly are not able to fold into a unique structure[8].

The principal way out is to find special sequences which have their native structure stable at temperatures when the folding is fast, resolving therefore the contradiction between the thermodynamic and kinetic requirements characteristic for random sequences[9]. The requirement that a sequence has a native structure stable at higher temperatures imposes the necessary condition that it is a pronounced energy minimum separated by a large energy gap from the set of non-native conformations[8-10].

The probability of finding such sequence by simply pulling it out at random from the "soup" of all possible sequences is very small for chains of realistic length. However, this difficulty may be overcome by a simple sequence design algorithm suggested[10,11]. This algorithm generates sequences which have sufficiently low energy in a chosen target conformation. The energy gap in designed sequences was indeed large enough to enable them to fold fast to the stable native conformation[12] which coincided with the target conformation used at the design stage. The design algorithm is based on the idea of Monte Carlo (MC) search in sequence space. It proceeds by making mutations in a sequence, biasing them to ones which decrease the relative energy of the native state at given amino acid composition, or relative energy. The algorithm made it possible to find sequences having relative energies sufficient for folding in spite of the fact that the fraction of such sequences among all possible ones is small.

The results of refs. 10 and 12 demonstrate that sequence design aimed at generating thermodynamically stable sequences makes this conformation accessible - i.e., that thermodynamic stability is a sufficient condition for fast folding. We may ask now, is it also a necessary condition for fast folding? This question is exceptionally important for our understanding of prebiotic evolution of any biopolymers with a unique native state. If thermodynamic stability is a sufficient condition for fast folding then two conditions to which enzymes must satisfy (see above) are equivalent to each other and one could easier imagine prebiotic process in which the first enzymes evolved.

To address this question, we use a simple algorithm of sequence selection based on the principles similar to biological evolution, i.e. random substitutions and selection pressure. The requirement of rapid folding into one specific conformation modeled the selection pressure via acceptance of substitutions which result in faster folding and rejection of substitutions which slow down the folding rate.

Due to the fact that the mean first passage (to the native conformation) time (MFPT) is determined only approximately we developed the following 3-step algorithm for evaluation of the kinetic consequence of a point mutation. In step 1, we perform 2 folding runs and estimate very roughly the new MFPT. If it is longer than the original one, then the mutation is rejected; if the new MFPT is shorter, then we estimate the new MFPT more precisely in step 2. The purpose of the step 1 is to reject outright obviously poor mutations, which constitute the majority of all mutations. In step 2 we perform 10 folding simulations and therefore get much more precise estimate for the MFPT. If it is less than the original MFPT by 20%, then the mutation is accepted; otherwise it is rejected. If the mutation is accepted, then an additional 100 folding runs are performed (step 3) to get a reasonably good estimate for the new MFPT. This estimate is used as a current MFPT for comparisons with the MFPT of the next mutations.

Due to computer time limitations we restricted our study to chains of 27 monomers on a cubic lattice. The energy of a conformation of the chain is the sum of energies of pairwise contacts:

$$E = \sum_{1 \leq i < j \leq N} (B_0 + B(\xi_i, \xi_j))\Delta_{ij} \tag{1}$$

where $\Delta_{ij} = 1$ if monomers i and j are lattice neighbors and $\Delta_{ij} = 0$ otherwise. ξ_i defines the type of amino acid residue in position i. $B(\xi, \eta)$ is a magnitude of contact interaction between amino acids of types ξ and η. We expect that the choice of the specific set of parameters for our study is not very essential (for more detailed discussion of this problem, see ref. 13). We used parameter set published[14]. This set of parameters was derived from statistics of contacts in proteins. B_0 is an energetic parameter having the meaning of overall attraction, it was introduced to bias conformations toward more compact ones making the native state belong to the set of maximally compact conformations. The motion of the chain is modeled by the standard cubic lattice MC algorithm[15,16]. Simulations were performed at temperature $T = 0.32$ and with $B_0 = -T = -0.32$.

We started our selection algorithm with random sequence which folded in its native conformation at temperature $T = 0.32$ in about $5 \cdot 10^6$ MC steps. The result of selection is presented in Fig.1. which shows the MFPT as a function of the number of accepted mutations. It can be seen that for about 100 accepted mutations the MFPT decreased almost two orders of magnitude.

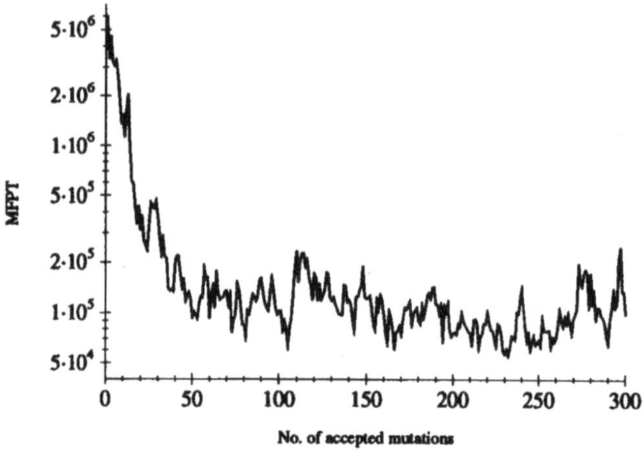

FIG. 1. Evolution of the MFPT (in MC steps) under the requirement of fast folding. This figure is taken from the ref. 1.

As we mentioned before, one way to make a chain fold rapidly is to make the energy E_{nat} of its native conformation as low as possible. The absolute value of the energy itself is not directly related to stability; what is important is the relative value of energy, or Z-score introduced by Eisenberg and coauthors[17]:

$$Z = \frac{E_{nat} - E_{av}}{\sigma} \tag{2}$$

where E_{av} is the average energy of compact non-native conformations. It could be estimated as $E_{av} = K \cdot e_{av}$, where $K = 28$ is the number of contacts in a maximally compact conformation and e_{av} is an average energy of all possible contacts with a corresponding dispersion σ.

The evolution of the relative energy of the native conformation Z is shown on Fig.2. It is seen that for the first 50 accepted mutations, when the MFPT decreases, Z decreases noticeably too, though because of strong fluctuations of Z the effect is not so pronounced. To get a clear impression of the properties of the ensemble of selected fast-folding sequences, we calculated the distribution of Z over 250 sequences starting from 50th accepted mutation. The corresponding histogram is shown on Fig.3. For comparison we also plotted a similar histogram for 250 random sequences with the same amino acid composition. It is clearly seen that the distribution of the parameter Z for fast-folding

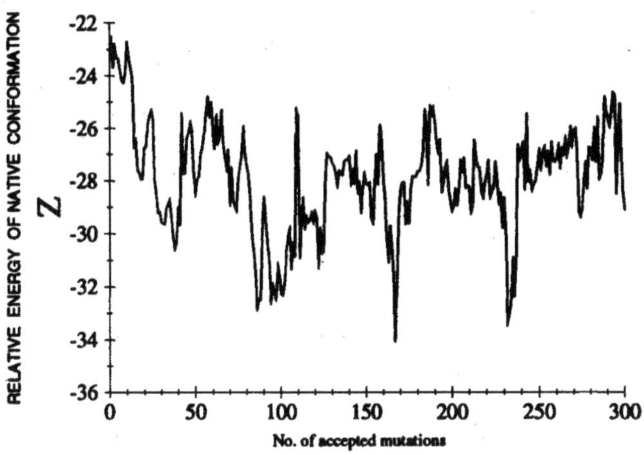

FIG. 2. Evolution of the relative energy of the native conformation Z under the requirement of fast folding. This figure is taken from the ref. 1.

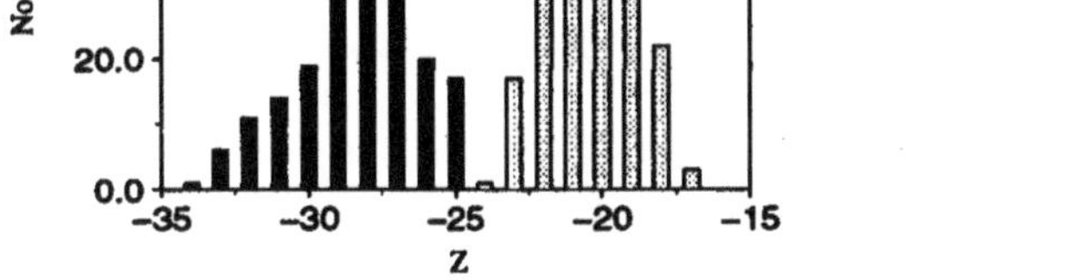

FIG. 3. Distribution of the relative energy of the native conformation Z for random sequences (white bars) and for the fast-folding sequences generated by the selection algorithm under the requirement of fast folding (filled bars). This figure is taken from the ref. 1.

sequences generated by the selection algorithm is clearly shifted to smaller values as compared to random sequences. The most probable value of Z for fast-folding sequences is about -27.5; at the same time for random sequences this number is close to -20. The distribution of Z for random sequences can be fit very well by a Gaussian. It is possible to determine from such a fit the probability to have a random sequence with $Z = -27.5$ corresponding to the median of the Z distribution for selected sequences. The elementary estimate gives $P(Z = -27.5) \approx 10^{-6}$. Therefore one out of million random sequences for 27-mer will behave like average fast-folding sequence from the pool of "evolutionary selected" ones. Even though thermodynamical stability is matched with increase in speed it is not the only factor which determines a folding rate. Two equally stable sequences might have very different folding time. We have compared folding time of evolved sequences and equally stable sequences obtained by a simple sequence design algorithm[10,11]. We found that evolutionary designed sequences fold in average ten times faster. However we were not yet able to find what makes evolutionary designed sequences so exceptionally fast-folding.

It was shown in a number of previous calculations that thermodynamic stabilization results in rapid folding. In this work, we have shown that the opposite is true as well: optimization of folding rate results in a pronounced thermodynamic stabilization of the native state. This result show that both key conditions for polypeptide sequences to be protein-like (i.e., thermodynamic stability and fast folding), can be achieved when one parameter, the relative energy *or* folding time, is minimized under the evolutionary pressure. This is due to the fact that one parameter, the relative energy, governs, to a large extend, both quantities.

Such schemes may model some aspects of protein evolution only at the biological stage where sequences, which reliably fold into their native conformations, have already evolved, and the evolutionary process presses for their improvement as more stable and fast-folding proteins. This fact manifests in both algorithms where the concept of unique native structure is introduced from the beginning, at the stage of formulation of selection rules.

This implies that such evolutionary improvement schemes must be "seeded" in the sense that first protein-like sequences, which are able to fold into their unique native conformations must have evolved at the stage of prebiological evolution.

It is quite clear that at the prebiological stage of evolution the notion of unique structure could hardly exist, and instead of "selection pressure", at which specific biological advantages were memorized and inherited, there could be only relatively nonspecific physico-chemical factors which governed synthesis and hydrolysis of the first organic polymers. Then question arises, how such nonspecific physico-chemical factors could have selected first protein-like sequences?

In this paper we give a possible example of such "pre-biological" selection. While being unlikely to reproduce the actual process of prebiological evolution, it may illustrate an important idea of how biopolymers might have evolved as a result of nonspecific physico-chemical factors.

We consider a model where "physico-chemical" pressure consists of two factors: possibility of aggregation and hydrolysis[18]. The latter could be catalyzed by other existing low- and high molecular weight compounds. It is clear that a simple way to protect polypeptide from hydrolysis would be to make chains compact. This biases equilibrium distribution over sequences towards more hydrophobic ones, with prevailing attraction between residues. However, hydrophobic sequences tend to aggregate.

The real prebiotic selection of biopolymers precursors was likely to involve synthesis of large number of sequences over long period of time ($\sim 10^9$ years). The polymers which are less compact had higher probability to get hydrolyzed. This factor gradually shifts the sequence distribution towards more compact and, as will be shown in this work, more stable sequences with unique structure.

In this work we propose a simple algorithm which is similar in spirit to the one we described above and biases sequence sampling towards compact and water-soluble sequences. While being unlikely to reproduce the details of the actual process of pre-biological evolution, it generates in a computationally reasonable time the ensemble of sequences which meet these two criteria of compactness and solubility. Compactness can be measured directly in the simulation through the number of intramolecular contacts which chain forms: the greater this number, the more compact the chain is. As regards to solubility, it is computationally very costly to faithfully reproduce interactions of macromolecules with solvent while making the search in sequence space. The unrestricted condition of compactization would generate mainly hydrophobic sequences with tendency to aggregate. To prevent this we will impose the simple condition of solubility as a requirement that sequence search proceeds over sequences with constant amino acid composition. To model the requirement of solubility further, we introduced slight overall repulsion between molecules by taking $B_0 = 0.05$. Simulations were performed at temperature $T = 0.15$.

Now the main idea of the algorithm can be formulated: beginning with random sequences, we make substitutions preserving the overall composition of amino acids. If the chain becomes more compact, or gets compact faster, the substitution is accepted, otherwise it is discarded. After a number of cycles the procedure will generate sequences which will be compact and still not exceedingly hydrophobic. The ensemble of such sequences can be then studied to see whether their properties deviate from such of random sequences.

We changed the selection procedure in the following a way. Instead of optimization of the folding time, we optimized the average compactness over a half of million MC steps starting with a random coil conformation. In other words, the requirement now is not only to reach a compact state rapidly, but also to keep the compactness over the course of simulation. This is a more faithful representation of the idea that compactness should protect the chains from hydrolysis. This combines two requirements: that compactization will be fast and that it will lead to persistent compact conformations.

Our selection mechanism is close to the described above. In step 1, 50 folding runs were performed to get a reasonably good estimate of average compactness during the first $5 \cdot 10^5$ MC steps. In step 2, an attempt of pairwise substitution is made. This corresponds to picking randomly two sites and "swapping" amino acids between them. This is the natural way of changing sequence without changing amino acid composition. If the new average compactness (number of intrachain contacts) during the first $5 \cdot 10^5$ MC steps is smaller, then the substitution is rejected. If it is larger, then we perform ten folding simulations and get a more precise estimate of the new average compactness during the first $5 \cdot 10^5$ MC steps in step 3. If it is at least 1 % higher than the original compactness, then the substitution is accepted; otherwise, the substitution is rejected.

Thirty two substitutions were accepted. For all of the generated sequences, we determined conformations (not necessarily maximally compact) with the lowest energy. This was done by means of extensive MC simulations. These conformations were identified as the native ones. Some of them are shown on Fig.4. After analyzing native conformations, we found that most of them differ one from another. Although for the first 7 substitutions, native conformations changed dramatically, for the next substitutions, the number of common contacts between native conformations for different sequences became large ($> 80\%$) so that sequences which evolved at the later stage of the procedure had structurally similar native conformations.The evolution of average compactness of the native conformations, with substitutions is shown on Fig.5. It is clear that the compactness of the native conformations grows rapidly and reaches its plateau value corresponding to conformations having 25 contacts.

Most importantly, the relative energy of the native conformation (Z) decreases with substitutions (Fig.5b). It implies that as a result of selection aimed at large average compactness the procedure, after some substitutions, decreases the relative energy of the native conformation to as low value as -33. One might see on Fig.3 that probability to choose such sequence randomly is vanishingly small. In other words, the requirement of a rapid compactization can lead to a result different from the compactization itself, that is, to the stable native conformation with very low energy. This conclusion is supported by the next plot on the Fig.5c which shows evolution of the thermodynamic probability of the native conformation. One can see that the native conformation of the starting randomly chosen sequence is extremely unstable: its

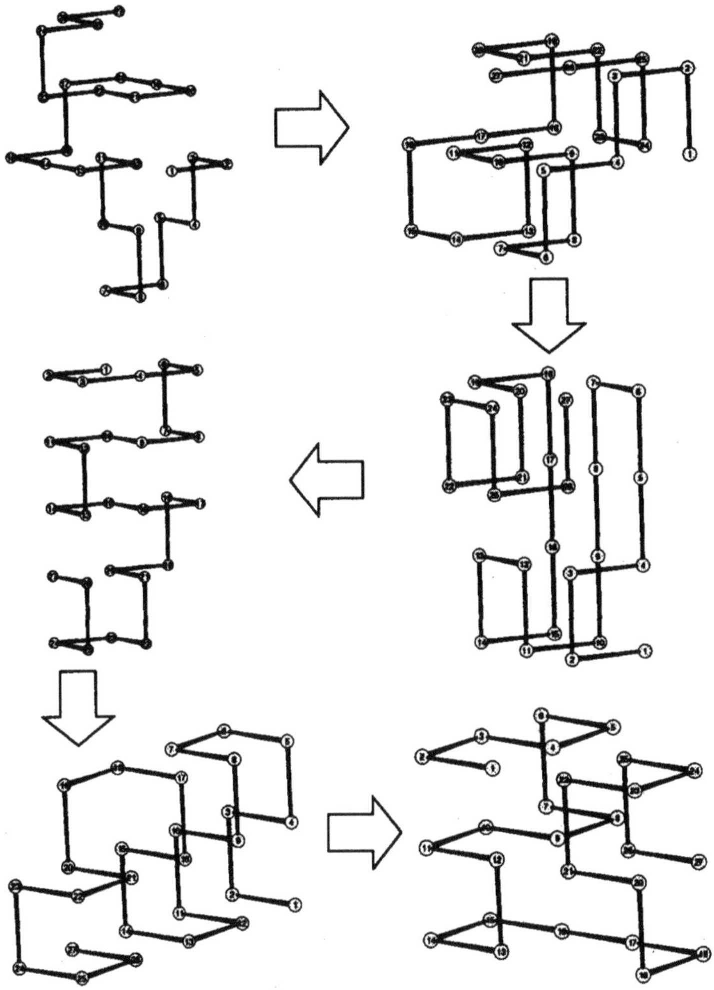

FIG. 4. Selection of sequences under the requirement of large average compactness over a half of million MC steps starting with a random coil conformation. Evolution of the native structure is shown. On this figure shown the native conformations of the original random sequence, sequence after the 5th substitution, sequence after the 10th substitution, sequence after the 20th substitution, sequence after the 25th substitution and sequence after the 32nd (last) substitution. This figure is taken from the ref. 2.

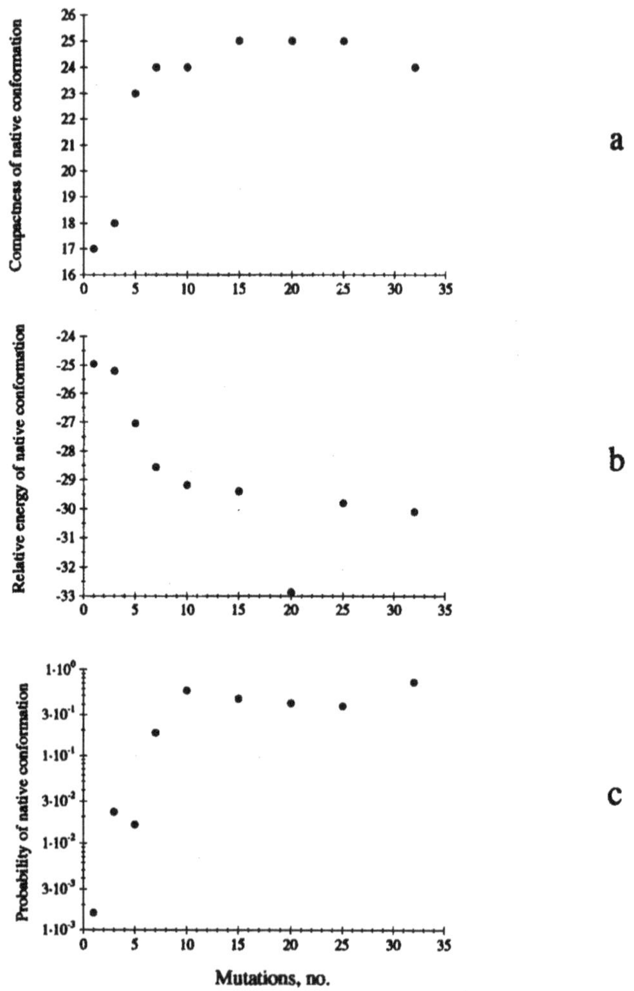

FIG. 5. Selection of sequences with 27 residues under the requirement of large average compactness over a half of million MC steps starting with a random coil conformation. (a) Evolution of compactness (the number of contacts in the native structure). (b) Evolution of the relative energy of the native conformation. (c) Evolution of the stability of the native conformation. This figure is taken from the ref. 2.

Boltzmann probability is only about 0.1%. At the same time for the selected sequences the Boltzmann probability of the native conformation is close to 50% after about 10 substitutions.

This suggests an idea of how proteins with stable native structures might have evolved. The main point here is that such stable structures could be a side effect of a different requirement, for example, the requirement on compactization. In the primordial "soup" different species with different sequences were in equilibrium. Some fractions aggregated; some were soluble but noncompact and were hydrolized. Our results suggest that a small fraction of all sequences were able to satisfy mutually conflicting non-specific requirements, and these sequences could have had a unique structure.

It is commonly believed that in the earliest cells, both the genetic and enzymatic components were RNA molecules[19–21]. If this hypothesis is correct, proteins evolved during biological evolution. However, the question remains as how ribozymes with unique native structure have evolved? The model described above can be used to understand better the driving forces of prebiological creation of any biopolymers with stable native structure.

The selection algorithm that we used herein may resemble rather biological selection than prebiological one since some favorable substitutions were accepted and passed by to further "generations" of sequences. This resemblance is superficial. The possible feedback in prebiological evolutionary scenario could be that more compact polypeptides were more likely to avoid hydrolysis. In the situation when polypeptides got synthesized randomly, this factor gradually shifted the sequence distribution to increase probability of polypeptides with stable native state. The possible physical mechanism of it is very simple: in spite of the fact that probability to randomly synthesize polypeptides with stable native state is very small, these sequences were not hydrolyzed and accumulated over many cycles of hydrolysis and synthesis; whereas other sequences underwent many turns of recycling.

Synthesis of random sequences represents a random walk in sequence space. Within the framework of this analogy, the stability of folded structures, which makes sequences nonhydrolyzable, is equivalent to absorbing walls; it is clear that the concentration of species at or near adsorbing boundaries is increased. This gives an equivalent explanation of the observed phenomenon and suggests the way how to construct analytical model of prebiological evolution.

Another striking result of this study is that, though the fraction of sequences with a stable unique structure is very small, the algorithm generated them after a small number of mutations. This is the common feature of evolution-like algorithms: selection pressure generates a directed drift in sequence space that makes generation of desirable (in our case compact) chains much more feasible than if such sequences were searched for randomly.

Our model does not consider such important properties of proteins as chirality and enzymatic activity. But we found that the requirement of compactness without aggregation can cause a stable three-dimensional native conformation, without which enzymatic activity is unlikely to be possible. The model presented in this work, while being unlikely to reproduce the details of prebiotic evolution, illustrates a general idea that a stable native structure could have evolved as a side effect of equilibrium conditions that selected sequences satisfying simple physicochemical requirements.

Acknowledgments

This work was supported by a Packard Fellowship.

References

1. A.M. Gutin, V.I. Abkevich, and E.I. Shakhnovich, *Proc. Natl. Acad. Sci. USA* **92**, 1282 (1995).
2. V.I. Abkevich, A.M. Gutin, and E.I. Shakhnovich, *Proc. Natl. Acad. Sci. USA* **93**, 839 (1996).
3. E.I. Shakhnovich and A.M. Gutin, *Nature* **346**, 773 (1990).
4. A.M. Gutin and E.I. Shakhnovich, *J. Chem. Phys.* **98**, 8174 (1993).
5. E.I. Shakhnovich and A.M. Gutin, *J. Chem. Phys.* **93**, 5967 (1990).
6. H.S. Chan and K.A. Dill, *J. Chem. Phys.* **95**, 3775 (1991).
7. C. Camacho and D. Thirumalai, *Phys. Rev. Lett.* **71**, 2505 (1993).
8. A. Sali, E.I. Shakhnovich, and M. Karplus, *J. Mol. Biol.* **235**, 1614 (1994).
9. R. Goldstein, Z.A. Luthey-Schulten, and P. Wolynes, *Proc. Natl. Acad. Sci. USA* **89**, 9029 (1992).
10. E.I. Shakhnovich and A.M. Gutin, *Proc. Natl. Acad. Sci. USA* **90**, 7195 (1993).
11. E.I. Shakhnovich and A.M. Gutin, *Protein Engineering* **6**, 793 (1993).
12. E.I. Shakhnovich, *Phys. Rev. Lett.* **72**, 3907 (1994).
13. V.I. Abkevich, A.M. Gutin, and E.I. Shakhnovich, *Protein Science* **4**, 1167 (1995).
14. S. Myazawa and R. Jernigan, *Macromolecules* **18**, 534 (1985).
15. P.H. Verdier, *J. Chem. Phys.* **59**, 6119 (1973).
16. H.J. Hilhorst and J.M. Deutch, *J. Chem. Phys.* **63**, 5153 (1975).
17. J.U. Bowie, R. Luthy, and D. Eisenberg, *Science* **253**, 164 (1991).
18. A. Grosberg and A. Khohlov, *Unsolved Problems in Physiccs of Polymers*, preprint NCBI, Puschino (in Russian) (1981).
19. G.F. Joyce, *Nature* **338**, 217 (1989).
20. S.A. Benner, A.D. Ellington, and A. Tauer, *Proc. Natl. Acad. Sci. USA* **86**, 7054 (1989).
21. C. Wilson and J.W. Szostak, *Nature* **374**, 777 (1995).

Ubiquitous Distributed Objects with CORBA

Frédéric Achard, Emmanuel Barillot
Gis Infobiogen
7 rue Guy Môquet, BP 8
94801 Villejuif Cedex, FRANCE

Database interoperation is becoming a bottleneck for the research community in biology. In this paper, we first discuss the question of interoperability and give a brief overview of CORBA. Then, an example is explained in some detail: a simple but realistic data bank of STSs is implemented. The Object Request Broker is the media for communication between an object server (the data bank) and a client (possibly a genome center). Since CORBA enables easy development of networked applications, we meant this paper to provide an incentive for the bioinformatics community to develop distributed objects.

1 Introduction

1.1 Why interconnect?

The process of discovery in science greatly relies on the ability of researchers to link previously unrelated data or knowledge. This is true at all levels of research, from the daily task of information gathering to the merging of two theories into one new dogma based on the accumulation of knowledge involving links between different fields [a]. In biology, the problem of linking data is becoming more and more crucial: since the discovery of the genetic code, genetics unifies the biological sciences by offering a common basis for various disciplines such as biochemistry, embryology, taxonomy, cytology and evolution. The 'physics of particles' plays a similar role with regard to 'hard sciences'. However, biology has the advantage that the scale-up between the basic science and the others is much more manageable than in physics. Thus, the community would greatly benefit from an interconnection of the data generated by biologists. This has been particularly true since the explosion of molecular biology: there is a dramatic need to relate mapping data to sequence data and functional data, as well as to relate the genetic data of different species (e.g. model organisms or mammalian comparative mapping).

This need advocates for the interconnection of biological databases. Nevertheless, the biological data is dispersed in a large number of different databases. These databases are often not interconnected in a satisfactory way either for

[a] A good example is the discovery of the double helix [1].

programmers or for users; at the most, they offer reliable hypertext links toward some other databases but very rarely permit one to program easily distributed data gathering. Moreover, biological databases are managed by heterogeneous systems, which may not necessarily follow international standards. Examples of such systems include Relational DBMS, Object-Oriented DBMS, flat files and home-made systems.

The interconnection can be described at several levels:

- *physical interconnection:* the databases should be accessible through the Internet. Unfortunately, there are some highly specialized databases, with interesting and sometimes unique expertise, that can not be accessed via the Internet. This problem is out of the scope of this paper.

- *syntaxic interconnection:* databases are managed by a variety of heterogeneous system that are not interconnected. They use different data models and data manipulation languages. A common language is required.

- *semantic interconnection:* for both data and meta-data levels. At the data level, it can be difficult to reveal a semantic link between related data wich come from distinct databases (or even from one single database). This problem is discussed elsewhere[2]. At the meta-data level, terms are understood by scientists with regard to their experience and culture. For example, molecular biologists, geneticists and epidemiologists have not the same understanding of the term *gene*. This leads to a semantic barrier and prevents the scientists from going outside their specialty.

- *operational interconnection:* having an operational way to manipulate data to and from diverse databases is the purpose of the interconnection. In addition to the types of interconnection described above, adequate user interfaces are required. Such developments would clearly benefit from the use of an architecture-independent language, such as Java™ .

1.2 Which interconnection?

Interconnection is a generic term that can be applied to simple references as well as any arbitrary complex system linking distinct databases. Therefore its meaning should be further explained. Basically, the goal is to *interoperate* data from various sources, typically to provide a single end user interface. Therefore, what is needed is more than simple accession number references or hypertext links, which can be considered as the minimum level of interconnection. A productive *interoperation* between databases is required. For example, biologists expect to be able to query all the databases of interest in one row and to process the data using a tool box of methods such as sequence alignment and EST mapping. In that respect, an interconnection system must:

- provide a unified view of heterogeneous databases,
- ensure the portability of the existing databases and the adaptation of softwares,
- facilitate the evolution of the components of the system,
- be applicable both for large databases as well as for small specialized databases and
- be accessible from heterogeneous architectures.

It follows that one must:

- use an architecture, DBMS and language independent metalanguage to describe the structure of each data to be shared,
- provide a structured description of the data for computation (hypertext is not powerful enough) and
- have an excellent scalability. Data are accumulated at an exponential rate, and the number of areas of knowledge to be connected are increasing too.

The success of projects involving a large number of heterogeneous components is generally achieved through standardization. SQL is a good example of such a success. This standardization can arise de facto as when a product is progressively proved better and adopted by the community, or after a formal consensus as when needs are well specified and the product designed after a general agreement.

Besides, a realistic solution must leave a large degree of autonomy to each database. It is unrealistic to impose a common DBMS or a common metaschema. A relational structure can be perfectly suited to describe a laboratory notebook for some precisely standardized biological manipulation, while the complexity of a genome mapping schema clearly requires an object-oriented approach. This means that an upper layer should be used on top of the existing databases to provide a syntaxic interconnection. The problem of semantic interconnection has to be solved separately.

Some pioneering attempts to address the problem of interconnection have been proposed, such as the Object Protocol Model [3] and the Integrated Genomic Database[4]. Those approaches have been enriching the debate, but they are not yet universal standards. One can classify those approaches in two categories:

- data warehouse: data is centralized in an integrated database.
- data interoperation: the queries are distributed over the different databases, and results are grouped back.

Data warehouse is seldom practical because it is costly to curate, maintain and keep large databases evolving. Data interoperation increases the network traffic, but smooths it among the interconnected sites. Each data manager keeps control on his data and is responsible for its quality.

We will now briefly describe a standard that could be used for interconnection, the Common Object Request Broker Architecture, and a first application we have developed on top of it.

2 An overview of CORBA

CORBA [5,6], Common Object Request Broker Architecture, is the result of the work done by major actors of the hardware and software industry to set up a communication framework. The goal is to facilitate the development of distributed applications over a heterogeneous network. In a distributed environment, clients are talking to objects. The services that can be delivered to a client by an object are described in an interface. The means of communication are handled by an Object Request Broker (ORB). The idea behind CORBA is to provide an intermediary layer that handles access requests on data. It frees the developer from most of the portability issues. It enables the development of "distributed objects": objects that are somewhere on a network, some place that will not always remain the same.

CORBA defines a two-fold set of specifications. To be CORBA compliant, a vendor must implement at least the CORBA core: the CORBA Object Model, the CORBA architecture, the Interface Definition Language (IDL) syntax and semantics, an ORB (which supports the Dynamic Invocation Interface, Dynamic Skeleton Interface, the Interface Repository) and one language mapping. In addition, the vendor is free to implement a number of services. Those services, if implemented, are granted a separate compliance point. The main CORBA services are Lifecycle, Events, Naming, Persistent Object Service and Relationships. The points of interest for our work will be further discussed in sections 2 to 4.

CORBA is already a *de facto* industry standard. We strongly believe that it will become a standard in the bioinformatics community. The long term goal is to allow a true and productive interoperation between distributed programs and databases.

CORBA developments can be featured as follows:

- Object Oriented technologies gives the best model to capture the richness of data in biology.
- The data and methods to operate an object are described by means of the Interface Definition Language (IDL), a strongly typed language.
- The IDL compiler generates a stub for the client side and a skeleton for the object implementation side. The ORB must store the IDL definition of each object in the Interface Repository. It means that a client can possibly access a CORBA object with no prior knowledge of its implementation scheme. It is the foundation for interoperability.
- CORBA provides a set of services that prevents one from reinventing the wheel. The Object Management Group, the large industry consortium which accredits CORBA products, guaranties the benefits from an Industry Standards: scalability, robustness, support, long-term future. It is commonly admitted that Bioinformatics developments suffered from a lack of consistent standards.

3 An illustrated view of CORBA

We have sketched out a working example to illustrate how the objects are defined and how to access them. This code was written and compiled on a Sun workstation using the ORBeline™ environment. The scenario models a distributed environment and demonstrates CORBA interoperability. Although we meant it to be quite close to real life issues, we deliberately kept the example simple. Data descriptions are minimal. For this example, we write a simplified "STS bank object".

We chose this example because "Sequence Tag Sites" are essential objects in genome study. They are the skeleton of physical maps, the basis of genetic maps and a keystone in positional cloning. Typically there are pieces of information that need to be shared via a computer media since the biological object can be generated from an electronic description. Moreover, STSs are of interest for any group working in a genomic region.

The object's goal is a management system for STSs. It accepts deposit, deletion and query by name. We first write the IDL interface and then write a client implementation that accesses this object. Purposely, the object implementation details are not given. We only describe how to register the object. Although we developed the facilities[b] to manage the STSs, the technical implementation is out of the scope of this paper. Our point is to demonstrate a client implementation to an object for which the IDL interface is known. The C++ language is used for this example.

3.1 Interface Definition

First we define the structure of an STS as it will be stored within the object:

```
// Specification of an STS
struct STS {
    string Name;
    string Species;
    string CA_primer;
    string GT_primer
    long Length;
    float Heterozygosity; // in percentage
};
```

Then we define the services that we are going to offer, related to STS objects. The `interface bank` describes a new CORBA object type. The object can be manipulated by means of the three methods defined within it: `add_sts`, `del_sts`, `get_sts`.

```
// hold the STSs interface bank {

  boolean add_sts ( in STS sts_info);

  boolean del_sts ( in string name);

  boolean get_sts ( in string name ,
                    out STS sts_info);
};
```

Then the Orbeline™ IDL-to-C++ interpreter generates a stub, used to implement the client side, and a skeleton, used to implement the object side. The key points of the client implementation are further explained in the next section.

[b]the object source program is available on request

3.2 Client implementation

First the program makes a connection to the ORB, then asks whether the ORB knows an object called **bank** (which refers to the `interface` **bank** of the IDL). In case of success, the ORB provides the client with a proxy object. Here the binding is straightforward because the ORB knows where objects are located within a local network. However client may specify the use of an instance of the object that resides on a specific host.

```
// connection to the ORB
CORBA::ORB_var orb = CORBA::ORB_init(argc, argv);

// bind to the object
bank_var sts_object;
sts_object = bank::_bind();
```

Once the binding is done, methods can be applied to the object.

- Adding an STS to the bank is done by calling the method `add_sts` on the `sts_object`. The method takes an STS description as argument and returns `true` on success.

```
CORBA::Boolean success;
STS a_sts;

a_sts.Name = "AFM115xf2";
a_sts.Specie = "human";
a_sts.CA_primer = "ttcaaaggtggagacccttc";
a_sts.GT_primer = "ttttggtcagaatggagtgg";
a_sts.Length = 107;
a_sts.Heterozygosity = 77;

success = sts_object->add_sts( a_sts);
if( !success) cout << "'add_sts' failed" << endl;
```

- Deleting an STS from the bank is done by calling the method `del_sts` on the `sts_object`. It takes a name as argument (a string in IDL terminology, which maps to a C++ `const char *`) and returns `true` on success.

```
CORBA::Boolean success;

success = sts_object->del_sts( "AFM115xf2");
if( !success) cout << "'del_sts' failed" << endl;
```

- Fetching an STS from the bank is done by calling the method **get_sts** on the sts_object. It takes a name as **in** argument (a string in IDL terminology, which maps to a C++ const char *), an STS as **out** argument (a pointer to STS, passes as a reference) and returns true on success.

```
CORBA::Boolean success; STS *& to_sts = new STS;

success = sts_object->get_sts( "AFM115xf2", to_sts);
if( !success) cout << "'get_sts'" failed << endl;
```

CORBA provides facilities for error checking via the C++ exception mechanism. Each time a method is applied to a CORBA object, we encapsulate it with a try which allows to catch errors such as network failure or wrong argument calls. For example, the **add_sts** method is called as follows:

```
try {
    status = sts_object->add_sts( a_sts);
}
catch( const CORBA::Exception& excep) {
    cout << "Error add_sts " << endl << excep ;
    exit( 2);
}
```

3.3 Object implementation and running the example

The object side implements the facilities described within the IDL interface. The object is registered to the ORB with the following code (note that methods of implementation are not reproduced):

```
int main(int argc, char **argv) {
    // Initialize ORB and the Basic Object Adaptator
    CORBA::ORB_ptr orb = CORBA::ORB_init(argc, argv);
    CORBA::BOA_ptr boa = orb->BOA_init(argc, argv);

    Bank bank_server;
    boa->obj_is_ready( &bank_server);

    // get ready to receive requests
    boa->impl_is_ready();

    return(1);
}
```

We then compile and link our C++ code with the IDL compiler-generated stubs for the client side and the skeleton for the object side. The ORB is started with **osagent**™ (Orbeline smart agent). The object is registered to the ORB by running its code. Then clients can access it via the ORB for each type of method, as described earlier.

By this example we attempt to demonstrate that developing a CORBA client is surprisingly easy and effective. Note that issues such as identification and security should be addressed for a real life program. In addition, a very powerful aspect of CORBA is the use of the Dynamic Invocation Interface which allows one to discover the methods associated to an object at run time. This feature is not demonstrated in this paper.

4 A prospective view on CORBA

The ORB by itself only provides basic mechanisms for brokering object requests. All other services are provided by objects with IDL interfaces that reside on the top of the ORB (see 2). Unfortunately, we were restricted to discussing these services in the "prospective" section because only few of them are currently implemented. Some of these services represent the cutting edge of distributed objects and client/server technologies. However, we believe that most of the basic services will soon be available from ORB vendors. Software developers in the biological community will benefit from some of these services in ways that are briefly discussed in the following sections.

4.1 Persistence Object Service

We expect, from the client side, that an instance of the object is always running and always preserves its state. This requirement represents an obligation on the object side and some coding to do so is necessary. The "Persistent Object Service" (POS) provides the means to standardize this process. In other words, vendors are expected to provide means for easy storage, either by developing their own scheme or supporting bridges to other database systems such as relational ones.

4.2 Object Query Service

This service will allow one to find objects whose attributes meet the search criteria one specifies using a query. Three query languages will be supported: OQL (ODMG-93's Object Query Language), SQL with object extensions or a subset of the two previous ones.

4.3 Collections and Relationships

This service will let you create relationship between objects. It is a dynamic process; one can relate objects without modifying the object. Object itself is not aware that it is part of a relationship. This service, associated with the Object Query Service, will allow queries that are arbitrarily complex.

4.4 Authentification and Authorization

In our example (see 3), the addition and the deletion of an STS are accessible to any client. A real life object server should enforce security of its data. Therefore, when a client connects to an object, the object should be able to check

- if the client is really what it claims to be
- what resources the client can access

Facilities to do so are provided with the Authentification and Authorization Services.

5 Conclusion

A loose system of interoperation that lends autonomy to data managers is mandatory to be widely accepted. In particular, it is not necessary to give an access to the database as a whole, because some data may be redundant or irrelevant. Another important point is to use a recognized standard; it is clear that too many standards exist in biology. CORBA can play this role, though it is not the answer to every question about interconnection. In particular, it does not address the issue of semantic interconnection. Nevertheless, we think that it will provide the basis for sharing objects in an unified way and that semantic questions will be solved on top of CORBA.

The implementations of CORBA are not very complete at the present time. However as CORBA-compliant ORBs will provide more and more of the services, programming will become easier, both on the object and the client side, and at the same time, distributed objects will become much more dependable. Still, it is difficult to forecast the availability of all the CORBA services. And the network performance is an issue that needs to be addressed.

On the other hand, a very appealing aspect of CORBA lies in the vertical facilities. This term denotes the services that are industry specific. Currently, OMG has established working groups in various domains such as health care or financial services. We believe that the creation of such a group will benefit to the biology community. We hope that such a group will be initiated soon because we believe that the proliferation of biological objects, in the CORBA sense, over the network will be the foundation for a productive interoperation of biological data.

Our middle term project is to offer a CORBA interface to HuGeMap, our local database for human genome data. As a test case, the objects defined will be accessed by the EBI to complement the data of the RHdb database. In that respect, an Object Database Adapter will be developed for the OODBMS we use [c]. The interoperation of this mapping data should facilitate the development of tools to help the cloning of new genes.

Acknowledgments

This paper greatly benefited from Tom Flores and Patricia Rodriguez-Tomé of the EBI for first suggesting the use of CORBA to address the interoperability problems and for profitable discussions [7].

We are thankful to Guy Vaysseix for valuable discussion, Claude Scarpelli and Philippe Gesnouin for providing excellent informatics support.

We also wish to thank Jennifer Fitzpatrick for smart critical reading of the manuscript.

We would like to acknowledge contribution of Visigenic and PostModern Computing for providing their Orbeline^{TM} ORB.

[c] IDB_system by Eric.Viara@infobiogen.fr

This work was supported by the European Community under grant BIO4-CT95-0037 for the BIOTECH Research and Technological Development Program.

References

1. J.D. Watson. *The double helix.* Laffont, 1968.
2. Frédéric Achard. Proposal scheme for storing links among genomic databases. In *Hugo's Human Genome Meeting*, Heidelberg, March 1996.
3. I-Min A. Chen and Victor M. Markowitz. An overview of the object-protocol model (OPM) and OPM data management tools. *Information Systems*, 20(5), 1995.
4. Otto Ritter, P. Kocab, M. Senger, D. Wolf, and S. Suhai. Prototype implementation of the integrated genomic database. *Computers and Biomedical Research*, 27:97–115, 1994.
5. Robert Orfali, Dan Harkey, and Jery Edwards. *The Essential Distributed Objects Survival Guide.* Wiley Computer Publishing Group, 1996.
6. Jon Siegel. *CORBA, Fundamentals and Programming.* Wiley Computer Publishing Group, 1996.
7. European Bioinformatics Institute. *Linking Biological Databases workshop*, Hinxton Hall, November 1995.

Towards a density functional treatment of chemical reactions in complex media

D. R. Berard, D. Wei
Centre de Recherche en Calcul Appliqué, 5160 Boulevard Décarie, Bureau 400, Montréal, Québec, Canada H3X 2H9

D. R. Salahub
Département de Chimie, Université de Montréal, C.P. 6128, Succursale Centre-ville, Montréal, Québec, Canada H3C 3J7 and Centre de Recherche en Calcul Appliqué, 5160 Boulevard Décarie, Bureau 400, Montréal, Québec, Canada H3X 2H9

We discuss two techniques involving density functional theory (i.e., *ab initio* molecular dynamics simulations and frozen density functional theory) which show promise for applications directed towards understanding reactions in complex media. Preliminary results for the simulation of the conformational dynamics of an isolated analogue of alanine dipeptide and for the interaction between F^- and H_2O are included. These results represent the first steps towards a combined theoretical approach of reactions in complex media.

1 Introduction

Theoretical studies play an important role in the understanding of chemical processes. In complex environments, such as in solution or enzymes, and at metal-liquid interfaces, traditional quantum mechanical methods must be supplemented with approximate techniques and model potentials in order to reduce the demands of these problem to computationally feasible dimensions. While a number of approaches have been developed in this regard, the accurate description of chemical processes in complex environments still presents a major challenge. An ideal theoretical approach should provide an accurate description of the chemically interesting region (for example, the solute, reacting system or adsorbate). This must be provided by a quantum mechanical approach and clearly the accuracy will depend on the method chosen. Here we will consider methods based on density functional theory. One difficulty in studying complex systems is providing an accurate (yet theoretically simple) description of the environment at the electronic level. This is particularly important in systems which interact strongly with the environment such as charged solutes in aqueous solution or enzyme active sites interacting with the rest of the protein. Another important challenge in treating complex systems is to include the reaction dynamics in real-time. In this case, an effective potential approach is not adequate since a detailed time-dependent description of the electron density is necessary to describe bond breaking and making during a reaction. An *ab initio* molecular dynamics (AIMD) [1] approach has been developed [2] to study the dynamic motion of atoms in the chemically interesting region. The target of the current research is to develop theoretical methods and computing software to study reaction dynamics in complex media which combines the AIMD method with an accurate description of the solvent environment.

The standard QM-MM technique [3,4] of modeling the environment using force fields (i.e., a point charge and Lennard-Jones representation) can often lead to an inaccurate description of the potential fields at the electronic level. The culprit in these cases is the environment immediately neighboring the quantum mechanically interesting region such as the first solvation layer. In order to ameliorate this problem, a number of techniques have been attempted to better represent the field due to neighboring particles. One technique that looks promising is the frozen density approximation in density functional theory [5,6,7]. In this method, particles in the immediate vicinity of the quantum center are represented by their nuclei and frozen electron density.

The AIMD simulation method was pioneered by Car and Parrinello (CP)[8]. The CP-AIMD simulation involves the solution of coupled dynamical equations of motion for the nuclear coordinates and molecular orbital expansion coefficients. Our AIMD simulation is carried out at the Born-Oppenheimer (BO) level[2,9,10]. In this approach, it is assumed that the motion of the nuclei is much slower than that of electrons and is always in equilibrium with the electronic structure. Therefore, the classical dynamical equations of motion can be used to give complete trajectories if the potential surface is known. At each time step in the molecular dynamics simulation, the forces on the nuclei are given by the energy gradients and the molecular orbitals are updated by solving a Schrödinger-type equation within the BO approximation. It has been found recently [11], that trajectories obtained using the BO-AIMD approach can be both more accurate and less costly than their Car-Parrinello counterparts [8].

In this paper, we present a sketch of some recent results of an AIMD simulation of an isolated alanine dipeptide analogue and for a frozen density calculation of a fluoride ion (with a fixed electron density) interacting with a (free-electron) water molecule. We consider these results as early steps towards a unified theoretical approach to chemical processes in solution.

2 Theory

2.1 QM-MM DFT theory

In the Kohn-Sham density function theory (DFT) [12,13,14,15], the ground state energy is a functional of the electron density $\rho(\mathbf{r})$ and external fields. For a system consisting of $2N_e$ electrons and M nuclei, the ground state energy is given by

$$E_q[\rho(\mathbf{r})] = -\frac{1}{m}\int\sum_i^{N_e}\psi_i^*(\mathbf{r})\nabla^2\psi_i(\mathbf{r})d\mathbf{r} + \int v_e(\mathbf{r})\rho(\mathbf{r})d\mathbf{r} + E_{xc}[\rho(\mathbf{r})] + E_{nn} \,, \quad (1)$$

where ψ_i denotes a molecular orbital wavefunction, E_{xc} is a functional describing the energy contribution from exchange and electron correlation and ρ is the electron density calculated from

$$\rho(\mathbf{r}) = 2\sum_i^{N_e}\psi_i^*(\mathbf{r})\psi_i(\mathbf{r}) \,. \quad (2)$$

In Eq. (1), E_{nn} is the interaction energy between nuclei and v_e represents the electrostatic potential due to the nuclei and the average electron density. This potential is given by

$$v_e(\mathbf{r}) = \sum_{i=1}^{M}\frac{Z_i}{|\mathbf{r}-\mathbf{r}_i|} + \int\frac{\rho(\mathbf{s})}{|\mathbf{r}-\mathbf{s}|}d\mathbf{s} \,, \quad (3)$$

where Z_i denotes the nuclear charge of an atom located at $\mathbf{r}_i$. In the Kohn-Sham procedure, the electron density is obtained from the self-consistent solution of the Schrödinger equation

$$\left(-\frac{\hbar^2}{2m}\nabla^2 + v_{\text{eff}}(\mathbf{r})\right)\psi_i(\mathbf{r}) = \varepsilon_i\psi_i(\mathbf{r}) \quad (4)$$

$$v_{\text{eff}}(\mathbf{r}) = v_e(\mathbf{r}) + \frac{\delta E_{xc}[\rho(\mathbf{r})]}{\delta\rho(\mathbf{r})} \,. \quad (5)$$

Density functional theory is an appealing method since accurate quantum mechanical results can be obtained with relatively short computation times compared to other equally accurate methods. However, the computational demands of large complex systems has led to the development of approximate methods of incorporating environmental effects such as the QM-MM approach. In this method, the solvent or environment is treated with classical molecular models. Using a simple point charge and Lennard-Jones model to represent the solvent, the effective potential in the quantum Hamiltonian is modified to include these model point charges. With environmental point charges included, the electrostatic potential of Eq. (3) in the QM-MM approach is now given by

$$v_e(\mathbf{r}) = \sum_{i=1}^{M} \frac{Z_i}{|\mathbf{r}-\mathbf{r}_i|} + \int \frac{\rho(\mathbf{s})}{|\mathbf{r}-\mathbf{s}|} ds + \sum_i \frac{q_i}{|\mathbf{r}-\mathbf{r}_i|} , \tag{6}$$

where q_i denotes the charge of a model site located at $\mathbf{r}_i$ and the sum is over all model sites. The total energy of the QM-MM system is given by

$$\begin{aligned} E_{q,s} = E_q &+ \sum_{i<j} \frac{Z_i q_j}{r_{ij}} + \sum_{Mi} u_{LJ}(r_{Mi}) \\ &+ \sum_{i<j} \frac{q_i q_j}{r_{ij}} + \sum_{i<j} u_{LJ}(r_{ij}) , \end{aligned} \tag{7}$$

where E_q is evaluated from the electron density calculated from Eqs. (4) and (5) using the electrostatic potential of Eq. (6). Here, $r_{ij} = |\mathbf{r}_j - \mathbf{r}_i|$ and the Lennard-Jones potential is given by

$$u_{LJ}(r_{ij}) = 4\epsilon_{ij}\left[\left(\frac{\sigma_{ij}}{r_{ij}}\right)^{12} - \left(\frac{\sigma_{ij}}{r_{ij}}\right)^{6}\right] . \tag{8}$$

The QM-MM method provides an adequate representation of the environment at the quantum level when the QM and MM parts are weakly interacting or far apart. The local environment of, for example, an ion or quantum water molecule in aqueous solution is not adequately represented by a point charge model of the solvent. In these cases, a better representation of the neighboring solvent is needed.

2.2 Frozen-DFT Theory

In density functional theory, the total electron density is the basic variable from which all ground state properties are determined and is an additive quantity. In the frozen density approximation (frozen-DFT) this property is exploited by fixing the electron density of the solvent while solving the electron density of the quantum region. This frozen solvent-density region needs to only extend a small distance from the quantum center—for example, the first solvation shell.

Solvent molecules further away can be represented using a traditional force-field approach in the QM-MM method. Denoting the electron density of the quantum domain and environment as $\rho_q(\mathbf{r})$ and $\rho'(\mathbf{r})$, respectively, the total electron density is given by

$$\rho(\mathbf{r}) = \rho_q(\mathbf{r}) + \rho'(\mathbf{r}) \, . \tag{9}$$

Using this partition, the electrostatic potential can also be divided into regional contributions,

$$v_e(\mathbf{r}) = v_{e_q}(\mathbf{r}) + v_{e'}(\mathbf{r}) \, , \tag{10}$$

where the subscript q denotes contributions from the quantum domain and the prime denotes contributions from the frozen-solvent domain. The frozen-DFT method seeks to determine the electron density ρ_q using the 1-electron wavefunctions of the quantum region,

$$\rho_q(\mathbf{r}) = 2 \sum_i \psi_i^*(\mathbf{r})\psi_i(\mathbf{r}) \, , \tag{11}$$

while keeping the environment frozen. In a full quantum calculation including the solvent, the wavefunctions are required to be orthogonal over the whole system. In the frozen-DFT method of Wesolowski and Warshel [5], the orthogonality of the wavefunctions between the two domains is relaxed. However, Wesolowski and Warshel add a kinetic energy functional to the effective potential which corrects for the nonorthogonality between domains. In this way, the wavefunctions and electron density of the quantum region can be solved using the DFT method with the following effective potential

$$v_{\text{eff}}(\mathbf{r}) = v_e(\mathbf{r}) + \frac{\delta}{\delta \rho_q} \left(E_{xc}[\rho_q + \rho'] + \Delta T[\rho_q, \rho'] \right) \, , \tag{12}$$

where ΔT represents the nonadditive kinetic energy functional that corrects for the nonorthogonality of the wavefunctions between the quantum and environmental domains and is defined as

$$\Delta T[\rho_q, \rho'] = T[\rho] - T[\rho_q] + T[\rho'] \, . \tag{13}$$

In this work, we use the Thomas-Fermi approximation for the kinetic energy functional which is given by

$$T[\rho; \mathbf{r}] = C_{\text{TF}} \int \rho(\mathbf{r})^{5/3} d\mathbf{r} \, , \tag{14}$$

where $C_{TF} = \pi^{4/3}3^{5/3}/10$. The total energy of the system is now

$$\begin{aligned} E[\rho_q, \rho'] &= T_q + T' + \Delta T[\rho_q, \rho'] \\ &+ \int v_e(\mathbf{r})\rho(\mathbf{r})d\mathbf{r} \\ &+ E_{xc}[\rho_q + \rho'] + E_{nn} , \end{aligned} \tag{15}$$

where Eqs. (9) and (10) are used and E_{nn} includes interactions among all nuclei in the quantum region and environment. The term T_q is calculated using the one-electron wavefunctions evaluated for the quantum region,

$$T_q = -\frac{1}{m}\int \sum_i \psi_i^*(\mathbf{r})\nabla^2\psi_i(\mathbf{r})d\mathbf{r} . \tag{16}$$

The quantity T' is evaluated similarly using the frozen wavefunctions localized in the environment.

3 Computational details

3.1 Frozen density calculations

The frozen-DFT calculations were carried out for F^--H_2O. In this work, a full density functional calculation is performed for H_2O in the presence of the ion with frozen electron density distribution. The frozen electron density used to represent F^- was obtained from a full DFT calculation of the isolated ion. Results from these calculations were compared with DFT results for the complete four-atom cluster. All free-electron calculations were done at the all-electron level using the TZVP+ orbital basis set [16] (which is of triple-zeta quality and includes field-induced polarization functions) and both local and generalized gradient approximations (GGA) for the exchange and correlation energy. In the local-density (LDA) calculations, the Vosko-Wilk-Nusair (VWN) correlation functional [17] is employed. In the GGA calculations, the exchange and correlation functionals of Becke [18] and Perdew [19] (BP), respectively, were used. The geometry of the water molecule was fixed in all calculations using the experimental structure [20] ($R_{\mathrm{OH}} = 0.957$Å and $\angle$(H-O-H) $= 104.5°$).

3.2 Alanine dipeptide analogue

Traditionally, alanine dipeptide has been used as a model system for simulations of peptides. To reduce the computational demand, we use an analogue of the dipeptide [21] which is formed by replacing the terminal methyl groups

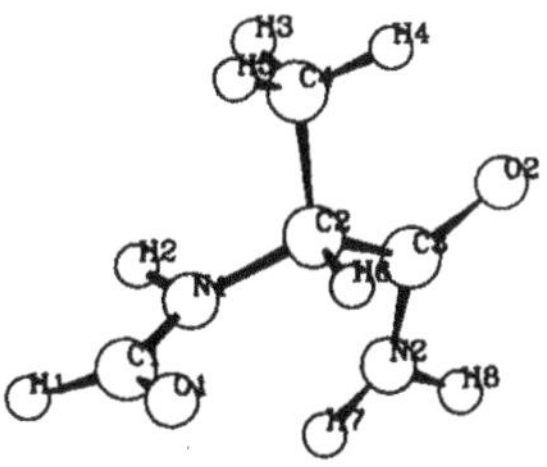

Figure 1: Schematic diagram of alanine dipeptide analogue.

by hydrogen atoms. A schematic diagram of the alanine dipeptide analogue (ADA) is shown in Fig. 1. It is found that[21] the terminal methyl groups play an insignificant role in the structure and energetics of alanine dipeptide. One important question that needs to be answered concerns the time scales and forces activating and stablizing secondary structure formation (i.e., formation of α- and β-sheet). A first-principles molecular dynamics simulation should be able to answer these questions. Here we consider an isolated ADA molecule and start the simulation with the β-like structure. The velocity is distributed in such a way that there is no overall translational and rotational motion in any direction, and the initial velocity norm is given so that the kinetic temperature is about 298K. The Verlet integrator[22] was used to propagate the equations of motion for the nuclei. The time step is taken to be 50 a.u. (i.e., 1.21 fs) and the simulation is run for about 7000 time steps. The quantum DFT calculations were carried out using the DZVP basis set, which is of double-zeta quality and includes field-induced polarization functions. Also in these calculations, the BP approximation was used for the exchange and correlation functional. The calculations were performed on an SGI-R8000 processor over a period of about two months.

4 Results and Discussion

4.1 Alanine dipeptide

The conformation space of the alanine dipeptide is conveniently described by the backbone dihedral angles ϕ [$\angle$(C1-N1-C2-C3)] and ψ [$\angle$(N1-C2-C3-N2)]. High-level *ab initio* studies[21] have shown that the internally hydrogen bonded conformations, the cyclic hydrogen-bonded $C7_{eq}$ structure [O1$\cdots$H7] and the extended C5 [O2$\cdots$H2] structure, are of lowest energy. The $C7_{eq}$ and C5 structures have (ϕ,ψ) angles of (-86°, 79°) and (-157°, 160°), respectively. Those

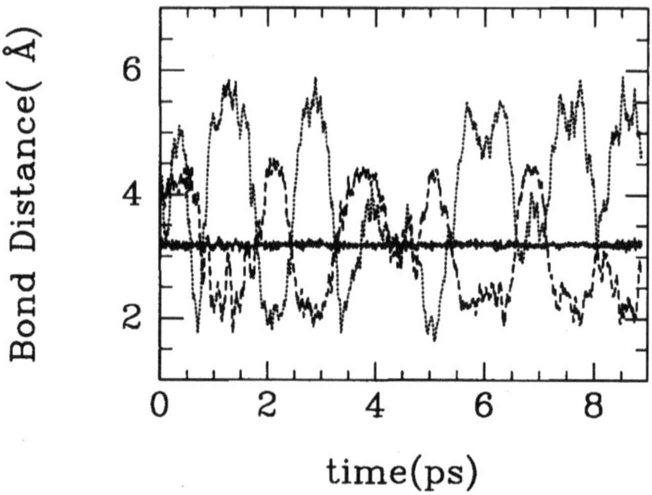

Figure 2: Time evolution of the H-bond lengths. The solid, dotted and dashed lines are for the O_1-H_2, O_1-H_7 and O_2-H_2, respectively.

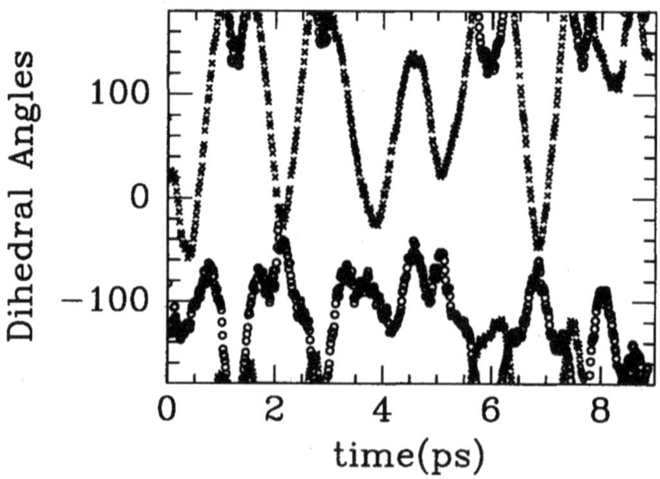

Figure 3: Time evolution of the dihedral angles. The open circles and crosses are for the ϕ and ψ angles, respectively.

structures analogous to α and β helical conformation are of higher energy. In Fig. 2, we plot the bond lengths as a function of time. The dotted and dashed lines correspond to the O-H bond lengths for the two internally hydrogen bonded conformers $C7_{eq}$ and C5, respectively. If the O-H bond length is about 2.0Å or less we define a hydrogen bond to be formed. By monitoring the forming and breaking of the two types of hydrogen bonds we can observe the conformational dynamics in the simulation. We clearly see the conversion from the $C7_{eq}$ to the C5 conformation. The frequency of transition occurs in a few picoseconds. This time scale is much shorter than the result obtained by Smith, Pettitt and Karplus[23]. However, they have employed Langevin dynamics in a fully classical molecular dynamics simulation. The O-H bond length for the $C7_{eq}$ conformation (also shown in Fig. 2) reaches a lower value than the C5 conformation. The C5 hydrogen bond tends to have a longer duration. In Fig. 3, we show a plot of the dihedral angles ϕ and ψ as a function of time. Again we see the interchange of $C7_{eq}$ and C5. In addition, we see a significant population of the β-conformation (-57°,134°). The α-conformation (-60°, -40°) is populated less frequently.

4.2 Frozen density calculations

Figure 4 shows results for the interaction energy between a water molecule and a fluoride ion as a function of the water-ion separation and for two angles of approach (along the principle axis and along the OH bond vector). In the frozen-DFT approximation, the fluoride ion is represented by its unpolarized electron density in the gas phase. Compared to the full calculations (solid and dotted curves), the result shows the correct shape for the interaction potentials. However, the potential well is too shallow and occurs at a larger separation. Within the current theoretical model, our results for H_2O–F^- agree well with those of Stefanovich and Truong at the same level of approximation[7]. Stefanovich and Truong have shown that the frozen density approximation can lead to an inaccurate description of the electron density in the core region of F^- when the species are close. Upon use of a model core potential for F^-, they obtain significantly improved results for the pair potential[7]. Two additional factors are expected to contribute to the discrepancy between the full and frozen-DFT results. These include the neglect of ion polarization in the frozen density approximation and the Thomas-Fermi approximation used for the nonadditive kinetic energy functional. In both cases, a better representation of the frozen density in the presence of the water molecule is expected to further improve the results.

In the full DFT calculation, the BP results yields a more accurate estimate

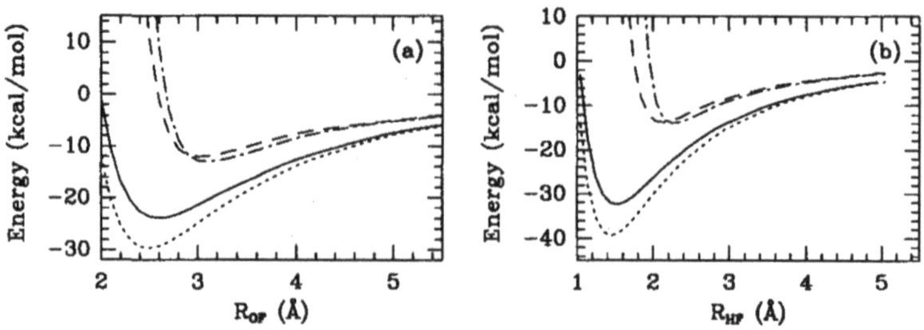

Figure 4: Interaction energy curves for H_2O–F^- with F^- positioned on the H-side of water and (a) along the principle axis of symmetry; (b) along the OH bond vector. Results are included for a full 4-atom DFT calculation using the LDA (····) and BP (——) approximations, and for a frozen F^- calculation using the LDA (–·–·) and BP (– – –) approximations.

of the interaction potentials. In the frozen-DFT calculation, a comparison of the local and BP approximations shows that the potential well is similar for both approximations. However, the potential well in the BP calculation is located approximately 0.2Å closer to the full results.

5 Conclusions

The results reported here should be taken as part of a progress report on two techniques involving density functional theory that shows promise for applications aimed at understanding reactions in complex media. Both AIMD method and the frozen density approach to solvation (and their eventual combination) are undergoing extensive testing and development that will be reported in due course.

Acknowledgments

The financial support of the Natural Sciences and Engineering Research Council of Canada is gratefully acknowledged. We are grateful to Dr. Hong Guo for stimulating discussions.

1. M. E. Tuckerman, P. J. Ungar, T. von Rosenvinge and M. L. Klein, *J. Phys. Chem.* **100**, 12878 (1996) and references therein.
2. D. Q. Wei and D. R. Salahub, *J. Chem. Phys.* (submitted).
3. M. J. Field, P. A. Bash and M. Karplus, *J. Comput. Chem.* **11**, 700 (1990).
4. D. Q. Wei and D. R. Salahub, *Chem. Phys. Lett.* **224**, 291 (1994).

5. T. A. Wesolowski and A. Warshel, *J. Phys. Chem.* **97**, 8050 (1993).
6. T. A. Wesolowski and J. Weber, *Chem. Phys. Lett.* **248**, 71 (1996).
7. E. V. Stefanovich and T. N. Truong, *J. Chem. Phys.* **104**, 2946 (1996).
8. R. Car and M. Parrinello, *Phys. Rev. Lett.* **50**, 55 (1985).
9. R. Barnett and U. Landman, *Phys. Rev.* B **48**, 2081 (1993).
10. X. Jing, N. Troullier, D. Dean, N. Binggeli, J. R. Chelikowsky, K. Wu and Y. Saad, *Phys. Rev.* B **50**, 122234 (1994).
11. D. Gibson, I. Ionova and E. Carter, *Chem. Phys. Lett.* **240**, 261 (1995).
12. W. Kohn and L. J. Sham, *Phys. Rev.* **140A**, 1133 (1965).
13. P. Hohenberg and W. Kohn, *Phys. Rev.* **136B**, 864 (1964).
14. R. G. Parr and W. Yang, *Density functional theory of atoms and molecules* (Oxford University, Oxford, 1989).
15. D. R. Salahub, R. Fournier, P. Mlynarski, I. Papai, A. St-Amant and J. Ushio in *Density functional methods in chemistry*, ed. J. Labanowski and J. Andzelm (Springer, Berlin, 1991).
16. J. Guan, P. Duffy, J. T. Carter, D. P. Chong, K. C. Casida, M. E. Casida and M. Wrinn, *J. Chem. Phys.* **98**, 4753 (1993).
17. S. H. Vosko, L. Wilk and M. Nusair, *Can. J. Phys.* **58**, 1200 (1980).
18. A. D. Becke, *Phys. Rev.* A **38**, 3098 (1988).
19. J. P. Perdew, *Phys. Rev.* B **33**, 8822 (1986).
20. W. S. Benedict, N. Gailar and E. K. Plyler, *J. Chem. Phys.* **24**, 1139 (1956).
21. T. Head-Gordon, M. Head-Gordon, M. J. Frisch, C. L. Brooks III and John A. Pople, *J. Am. Chem. Soc.* **113**, 5989 (1991).
22. L. Verlet, *Phys. Rev.* **159**, 98 (1967).
23. P. E. Smith, B. M. Pettitt and M. Karplus, *J. Phys. Chem.* **97**, 6907 (1993).

COMBINATORIAL TOOLS FOR THE ANALYSIS OF TRANSCRIPTIONAL REGULATION

A. BERGERON, E. GAUL
LACIM, Université du Québec à Montréal
C.P.8888 Centre-Ville, Montréal, Canada, H3C 3P8
{anne, gaul}@lacim.uqam.ca

D. BERGERON
Département de microbiologie et immunologie, Université de Montréal
C.P. 6128 Centre-Ville, Montréal, Canada, H3C 3J7
bergerdo@ere.umontreal.ca

In this paper, we discuss virtual experiments for the study of major regulatory processes such as translation, signalization or transcription pathways. An essential part of these processes is the formation of protein clusters held together by a small number of binding domains that can be shared by many different proteins. Analysis of these clusters is complicated by the vast number of different arrangements of proteins that can trigger a specific reaction. We propose combinatorial tools that can help predict the effects on the rate of transcription of either changes in transcriptional factors concentration, or due to the introduction of chimeras combining domains not usually present on a protein.

1 Introduction

Most regulatory proteins consist of a combination of discrete modules or *domains* which have been shuffled during evolution[1,2]. Many of these domains are involved in protein-protein interactions modulating various processes within the cell, including gene expression. A domain is a specific region of the protein surface, created by the folds of an amino acid chain. An interaction consists essentially in the transient apposition of two complementary domains. Structural data show that the number of different domains is relatively small, but the great diversity of protein function is partly due to the vast number of arrangements generated by these basic domains.

Along the multiple folds of their polypeptide, a protein harbors several distinct interaction domains. Theoretically, a protein could thus be involved in the formation of clusters composed of several interaction partners. A large number of regulatory proteins, such as transcriptional factors, do not have intrinsic enzymatic activity, but modulate cellular processes by their involvement in the formation of intermolecular clusters central to specific enzymatic activity. The function of these proteins could thus be explained by their ability to drive cluster formation.

In this paper, we present a combinatorial and probabilistic study of the various clusters that can be formed through protein-protein or protein-DNA interactions. We discuss computational experiments based on this model that attempt to replicate experimental findings on human Ewing's tumors. In this case, the accidental exchange of two DNA strands results in the expression of a chimeric protein that combines domains not normally present in a transcriptional factor. In vitro, this protein has been shown to activate transcription at a rate 30 times fold the rate observed in natural conditions, leading to tumoral growth [3].

The proposed computational tools can be helpful in rapidly conducting virtual experiments with new or suspected regulatory proteins. The program can readily adapt to the introduction of new proteins, even when their structure is only partially known. However, the predicting value of the model will depend on networking with databases and other analytical software [4,5] which will provide growing information on the nature of protein domains, their location, and their binding properties.

2 Biological Background

2.1 Signaling Pathways

In response to external stimulus, like growth hormones or cell contacts, biochemical cascades are initiated in the cell, ultimately resulting in changes in gene expression. These signal pathways involve several steps in which specific proteins - the *targets* - are chemically altered, due to the action of kinases or phosphates, for example. The study of molecular mechanisms involved in signaling pathways has shown that each step of the pathway is characterized by the formation of transient protein clusters, necessary to bring the appropriate presented substrat near the proper enzymatic activity, by the intermediate of molecular glue [6]. The phosphorylation state of the target protein in turn determines its capacity of forming subsequent clusters [7] (see Figure 1).

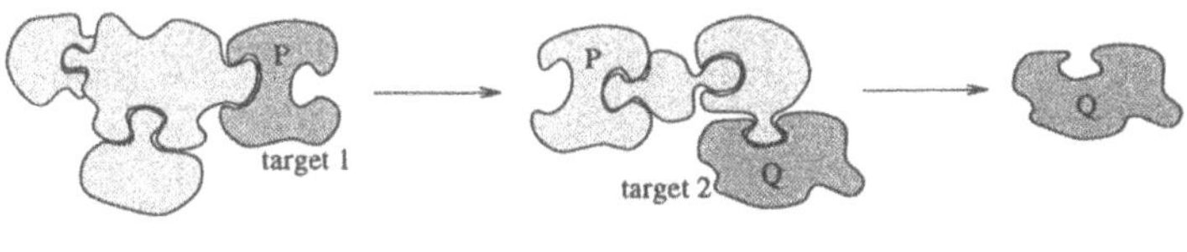

Figure 1: Signaling Pathway

The final step of a signaling pathway is generally connected with the phosphorylation of a transcriptional factor [8], thus modulating gene expression.

2.2 Transcriptional Regulation

A gene, coded by a strand of DNA, contains the necessary information for the synthesis of a protein. The actual synthesis, *gene expression,* is initiated by a process called *transcription* in which gene information is transferred to mRNA. One particular enzyme (DNA-dependent RNA polymerase II, denoted as Pol II) is responsible of the transfer, and must be correctly positioned along the gene in order to initiate transcription. Transcriptional regulation refers to the various mechanisms used by the cell to control the rate at which transcription occurs.

The recruitment and positioning of Pol II is done by clusters of proteins - called *transcriptional factors* - that are formed on a promoter-enhancer section of DNA preceding the actual gene (Figure 2). Each protein in a cluster has a set of *binding domains* on its surface. A particular domain will bind the corresponding domain of another protein or of DNA, allowing the cluster to grow in a Lego-like fashion, and occasionally recruiting Pol II. If Pol II is readily recruited, gene expression is activated [9].

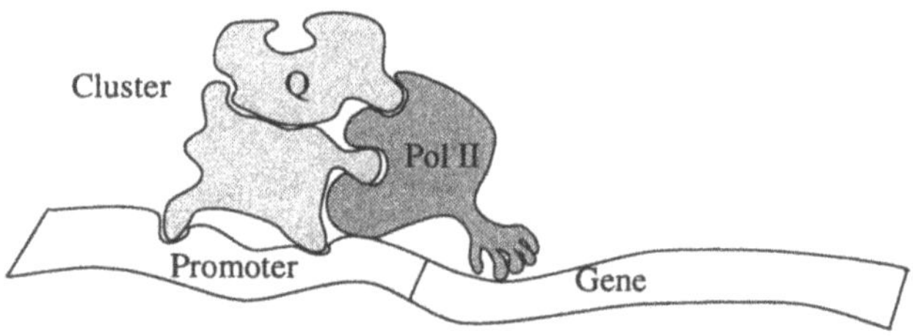

Figure 2: Promoter, Cluster and Gene

In this model, and as observed in molecular processes of signaling pathways, the majority of transcriptional regulators act simply as linkers in the cluster. A given binding domain is not specific to a transcriptional factor. In fact, the number of different domain families is relatively small - see Table 1-, and domains with similar binding properties can be present on several different proteins [1,2,9]. Binding domains can thus be viewed as connectors that can build many different clusters. This combinatorial aspect of cluster formation complicates the prediction of protein function in transcription.

The composition and size of a cluster able to recruit Pol II are predicted to affect the level of gene expression: a higher complexity is expected to correlate with a reduction of expression. Activation will also depend on both the structure of the promoter, and the nature and concentration of the proteins available in the environment - called here a *medium.*

2.3 Molecular Cluster Formation

Clusters are formed by the aggregation of proteins through *interaction* or *binding domains*[9,10]. These are amino acid residue portions - often, but not necessarily a consecutive sequence - that configures into a unique three dimensional shape displaying specific charged and/or hydrophobic groups[11]. Two domains with the same binding properties, but not necessarily the same composition, are considered of the same *type*.

A basic condition for formation of a cluster is that each type of domain t (ex. a basic domain) has one - or more - complementary type t' (ex. an acidic domain) such that there is a non-covalent attraction between t and t' (ex. basic:acidic) encouraging the formation of clusters. A similar kind of binding occurs between protein domains that recognize small specific sequences of DNA,like the TATA-binding factor[9]. By analogy, we will also call binding domains the specific regions of a promoter that are involved in these interactions.

3 The Combinatorial Model

The formal definition of molecular clusters will suppose that some properties of actual clusters are abstracted. In this first attempt, we model the interconnections of the different proteins involved in a cluster. Our goal is to give a precise meaning to *"the ability of a medium to form clusters that will recruit a given protein P"*. This notion will be cast as the mathematical expectation of a random variable defined on a population of clusters.

3.1 Basic Definitions

Let T be a finite set of *types of domains*. The *binding relation* $\mathcal{B}$ is a symmetric relation on $T \times T$. This relation stores the information on which pairs of types are complementary. A *protein* is a pair $P = (Ident, Domains)$, where $Ident$ is the name of the protein, and $Domains$ is the multi-set of its domains, consisting of elements of T with their multiplicities. Figure 3 shows an example of a protein with three domains.

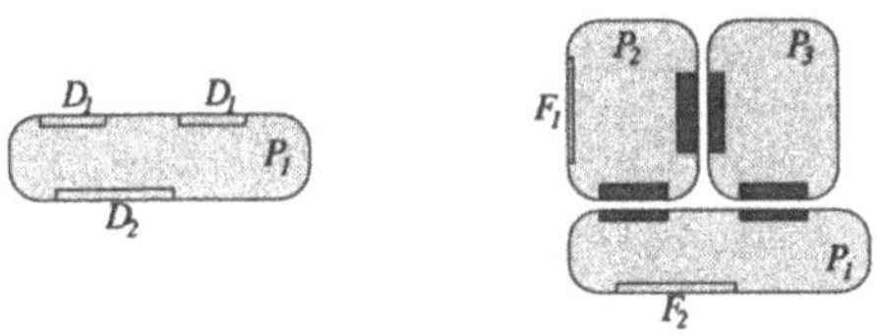

Figure 3: The Protein $P_1 = (Ident, \{2 \times D_1, D_2\})$ and the Cluster $(\{F_1, F_2\}, \{P_1, P_2, P_3\})$

A *cluster* is given by a pair $C = (Free, Members)$, where $Free$ is the multi-set of its free domains, and $Members$ is the multi-set of proteins that are members of the cluster (Figure 3). Note that a protein can be present in several copies in a cluster. A cluster with free domains, but no member, is a *promoter*.

3.2 Recruitment

A *link* is a pair of domains (D, E) such that the types of D and E are complementary, ie. the pair (D, E) belongs to $\mathcal{B}$. The *first projection* of the link (D, E) is D, and its *second projection* is E. Given a cluster C and a protein P, we will say that C *recruits* P *with links* $L_1, \ldots, L_k$ *yielding* C', noted

$$C \xrightarrow[L_1,\ldots,L_k]{P} C'$$

to describe the process of forming a new cluster with C and P. Figure 4 gives a simple example of the recruiting operation.

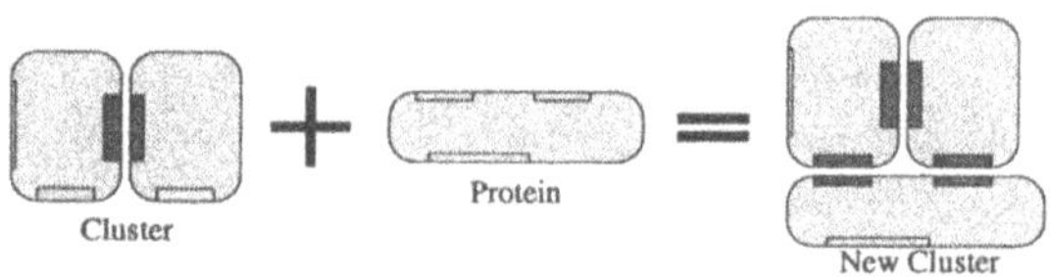

Figure 4: Recruitment

The recruitment of P by C with links $L_1, \ldots, L_k$ is *possible* if: 1) The multi-set of the first projections of $L_1, \ldots, L_k$ is included in the free domains of C, and 2) The multi-set of the second projections of $L_1, \ldots, L_k$ is included in the domains of P.

If C recruits P with links $L_1, \ldots, L_k$, the new cluster C' is obtained from C by erasing the domains of C that participate in the binding, adding those of P that do not participate in the binding, and by adding P to the members of C. Note that there is an element of non-determinism in choosing which domains of P will be bound. If additional information is available on the structures of the proteins involved, it can eventually be used to reduce the number of possible clusters.

A *medium* is a multi-set of proteins. These are the proteins available for recruitment by a cluster. Given an initial medium and a promoter I, a recruitment *chain* is an unbounded sequence: $I \longrightarrow C_1 \longrightarrow C_2 \longrightarrow C_3 \longrightarrow \cdots$ such that, at each step, either a protein is recruited by cluster C_i - and removed from the medium - or no further recruitment is possible and the chain becomes constant (ie. $C_i + 1 = C_i$).

The set Pop_n of clusters after n recruitments is the set of nth clusters from all possible recruitment chains of length n. A cluster in Pop_n contains at most n proteins, and clusters that contain less than n proteins are ***stable*** - they cannot grow anymore. (Note that we model *growth* of clusters, we do not, yet, account for the fact that a cluster could release a protein.)

Example 3.1 Consider the following situation. A promoter has two DNA-binding sites, named X and Y, and the medium is composed of five proteins: one copy of protein P with binding domain $\{X'\}$; one copy of protein Q with domains $\{X', A\}$; and three copies of protein R with domains $\{Y', A'\}$. Assuming that the binding relation is given by all pairs of the form (D, D'), one recruitment chain is:

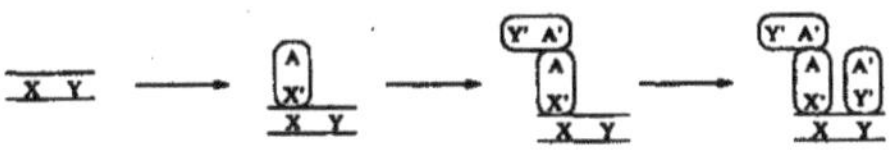

Note that in the middle step, the new protein could have been recruited in two other different ways, with link (Y, Y'), or both (A, A') and (Y, Y'). ∎

3.3 Probability distribution on Pop_n

We next define a probability distribution on a population of clusters. This distribution will depend essentially on the probability of recruiting events, given a medium M:

$$p\left(C \xrightarrow[L_1,\ldots,L_k]{P} C', M\right).$$

The probability of such an event depends on many variables such as the concentration of the molecule P in the medium, the number of other binding partners in M that can compete with P, the stability of the clusters, affinities between domains, the physical realizability of links $L_1, \ldots, L_k$, etc. The simplest model, and for which probabilities can be readily computed, is based on the following:

Given a medium M, and assuming recruitment is possible, the probability that a cluster C recruits a protein $P \in M$ with links $L_1, \ldots, L_k$, is given by the quantity $n/(cN)$, where n is the total number of domains of P proteins that can bind to a free domain of C, N is the total number of domains in the medium M that can bind free domains of C, and c is the number of different ways that C can recruit P - that is, the number of different configuration of used and unused links between C and P.

Given a sequence of recruitments $s = I \longrightarrow C_1 \longrightarrow \cdots \longrightarrow C_n$, the probability $p(s)$ of the sequence is given by the product of the probabilities of each recruiting event in the sequence, with the convention that the probability of an event $C \longrightarrow C$ is equal to 1. Fixing the initial medium I, we have:

Definition 3.1 *The probability of a cluster in Pop_n*
Let $C \in Pop_n$, then the probability $p(C) = \sum_{\substack{s \text{ is a sequence of} \\ \text{length } n \text{ from } I \text{ to } C}} p(s)$. ■

Proposition 3.2 Definition 3.1 yields a probability distribution on Pop_n. ■

3.4 Random variables

It is now possible to define and compute the value of random variables defined on clusters. The most interesting are the number $N(C)$ of a specific protein P in a cluster. The mathematical expectation of these quantities in Pop_n is given by:

$$E_n(N) = \sum_{C \in Pop_n} N(C)p(C).$$

An interesting property of these quantities is expressed in the following proposition. It gives a recursive formula for the computation of $E_n(N)$. With this formula, the value of the expectation can 'accumulate' as soon as clusters are formed by an algorithm. Since a population of clusters can be very large, it might be wise to monitor the increasing approximations of $E_n(N)$ during the computation.

Proposition 3.3 $E_n(N) = E_{n-1}(N) + \sum_{\substack{s \text{ has recruitment} \\ \text{of } P \text{ as last event}}} p(s)$. ■

Example 3.2 Consider the problem described in Example 3.1, where the medium is composed of $1 \times \{X'\}, 1 \times \{X', A\}$ and $3 \times \{Y', A'\}$. The different clusters of Pop_1, Pop_2 and Pop_3 can be constructed in a tree-like fashion, with the promoter at the top (see Figure 5).

The elements of Pop_3 are found on either the third level - downward - of the tree, or at the end of branches that did not grow. The probability of the different clusters for a population can be obtained by labelling the branches of the tree with the different probabilities of recruitment.

For example, in labeling the top right arrow illustrating the recruitment of R from the initial promoter, there are $n = 3$ domains of R proteins that can bind to the promoter, $N = 5$ domains in the medium that can bind to the promoter, and $c = 1$ way that the promoter can bind an R protein, yielding a probability of $3/5$ for this particular event.

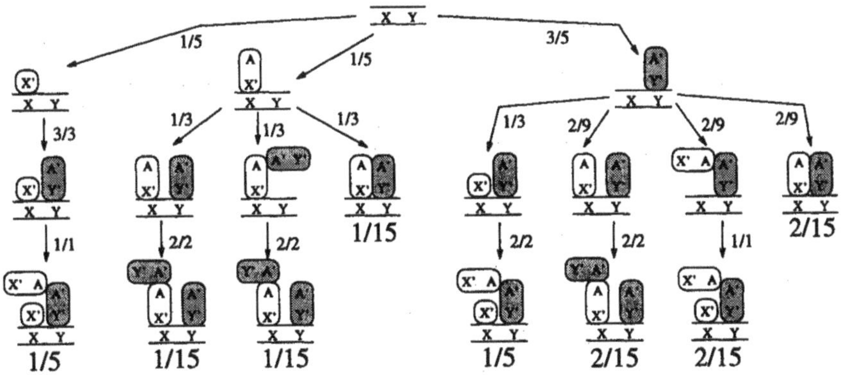

Figure 5: Construction of Pop_1, Pop_2 and Pop_3

The probability of a particular sequence of recruitment is then obtained by multiplying all the numbers along the sequence. The number under each Pop_3 cluster corresponds to the probability of obtaining this particular cluster with this particular sequence of recruitments. In the tree, we have highlighted all occurrences of protein R. The successive values of $E_n(N_R)$ are: $0, 3/5, 3/5+2/5$ and $3/5 + 2/5 + 2/15 + 2/15$, yielding an expectation of about 1.27 for the number of R proteins.

4 Virtual Experiments

4.1 *The problem*

Aberrant expression and structural alteration of transcription factors are frequent, primary molecular mechanisms in oncogenesis. Our target is the 11:22 chromosomal translocation found in human Ewing's tumors that results in the expression of a chimeric protein. This fusion protein combines the DNA-binding domain of the known transcriptional factor Fli-1, with domains - QSY repeats - derived from the EWS (for Ewing's) gene [12]. In vitro, the EWS-Fli-1 fusion protein has been shown to activate transcription at a rate 30 times fold the rate observed with the normal Fli-1 product [3]. Our goal is to perform experiments combining transcriptional factors with, or without, this protein.

4.2 *The Virtual Laboratory*

Setting up the virtual laboratory proved harder in practice than in theory. Many simplifying decision were taken with respect to biological reality in order to track down the combinatorial complexity of the problem. The first task was to list, with the help of databases, known transcriptional factors, including two of the basal transcriptional machinery and RNA Pol II, which could be present in human hematopoietic cells [13,14](see Appendix). For each of the 32 chosen proteins, we identified known domains[5] presumably involved in protein-protein or protein-DNA interactions. These interactions are listed in Table 1.

Table 1 cannot be used immediately as a formal table of interaction: structural information on the DNA-binding sites of the chosen promoter reveals that NF-kB and Ets-1 sites are overlapping: they also must be considered of the same type, implying equality of types of both NF-kB and Ets-1 binding sites. Finally, in some cases pairs of proteins are experimentally known to interact, without the explicit knowledge of the domains through which these interactions occur. In order to take this fact into account, we added pairs of domains D? and D?', adding these to the set of domains of participants in known interactions.

As a target promoter in our virtual laboratory, we artificially introduce in blood cells a gene under the control of the Human Immunodeficiency Virus-1 (HIV-1) promoter sequence [15] - which has a complex set of protein binding sites - retaining the following multi-set of domains: { 2× AP-1, 1× TBP, 1× Myb, 1× TCF, 2× NF-kB (including 2× Ets-1), 1× USF, 3× Sp1, 1× YY1 }.

A *virtual experiment* consists in choosing the relative concentration n_P of each of the protein P in the medium, where n_P is a non-negative integer. This choice can reflect either a coarse estimate of relative concentration, or a measure of the relative affinities of different proteins for the same target. For proteins that are not currently under study, we set $n_P = 0$.

4.3 Examples of virtual experiments

In the first experiment, we want to compare the effect of binding EWS-Fli-1 or Fli-1 on the Ets Site of the promoter. The medium consists here of Pol II and the set $\{1, 6, 10, 13, 14, 15, 16\}$ where the numbers refers to proteins in Appendix. A QSY' domain was assigned to 10, 13 and 15. Results on the expected number of Pol II are shown in Table 2. These results show that the expected number of Pol II is increased at least three-fold for nearly every size of clusters, suggesting that the presence of EWS-Fli-1 could increase transcription as observed *in vitro*[3].

Experiment 2 was designed to measure the inhibitory effect of transcriptional factor. The medium consists here of Pol II, the multi-set $\{4, 5, 18, 2\times 19, 24\}$, and graded concentrations of SCL. The factor SCL was chosen for the sake of its Basic domain, theoretically competing with the RNA Pol II repeats domain of Pol II for acidic domains. Results on the expected number of Pol II are shown in Table 3. An inhibitory dose-dependant effect is observed.

5 Conclusions

Our biological model is based on the assumption that the function of several regulatory proteins could be defined by their ability to form transient multi-molecular clusters. The formation of clusters occurs through non-covalent interactions which are dependent on the protein 3D structure. In this paper we described computational tools, based on combinatorial analysis of cluster formation, that can provide guidelines to experiments on the function of regulatory proteins in biological processes.

Although presently limited by our software knowledge on domains, we believe that this approach could be useful in the design of laboratory experiments that could tap into the tons of biological data accumulating on computing networks.

We are also aware of the elementary aspect of defining probabilities of reruitment on purely combinatorial grounds. Further implementations will incorporate more sophisticated knowledge on cluster formation, which could take into account the equilibrium constant of each two-by-two relation.

Table 1: The binding relation

Name of protein domain	Name of target interaction domain - Protein or DNA -
A. Protein-protein interactions	
1. Basic domain	Acidic domain
2. RNA Pol II repeats	Acidic domain
3. Gln-Ser-Tyr domain (QSY)	QSY'
4. Glutamine rich domain (Q-rich)	Q-rich
5. Helix-loop-helix (HLH)	HLH
6. Hydrophobic domain	Hydrophobic domain
7. Leucine zipper (Leu zip)	Leu zip
8. Proline rich domain (Pro-rich)	Pro-rich
9. Rb pocket	Rb pocket interaction
10. D1 - D6	D1' - D6' (experimental results)
B. Protein-DNA interactions	
1. AP-1 BD	AP-1 Site
2. Ets-1 BD	Ets-1 Site
3. USF BD	USF Site
4. NF-kB BD	NF-kB Site
5. Sp1 BD	Sp1 Site
6. YY1 BD	YY1 Site
7. A-T hooks (HMG)	TCF Site
8. WWW motif	Myb Site
9. TBP BD	TBP Site

Table 2: Experiment 1

n	With EWS-Fli-1		With Fli-1	
	Number of clusters	Expected number of Pol II	Number of clusters	Expected number of Pol II
3	26	0.99	9	0.00
4	92	1.33	26	0.33
5	211	1.71	41	0.48
6	335	2.30	45	0.62
7	352	2.65	38	0.77
8	257	2.98	28	0.93
9	157	3.11	22	1.05
10	118	3.19	21	1.08

Table 3: Experiment 2

n	Control		1× SCL		2× SCL		5× SCL	
	Number of clusters	Expect. number of Pol II	Number of clusters	Expect. number of Pol II	Number of clusters	Expect. number of Pol II	Number of clusters	Expect. number of Pol II
3	72	0.60	87	0.53	89	0.48	89	0.38
4	134	0.90	181	0.80	211	0.71	211	0.52
5	165	1.32	280	1.16	415	1.01	420	0.71
6	126	1.61	232	1.39	514	1.20	566	0.83
7	98	2.20	196	1.90	545	1.58	743	1.03
8	48	2.39	96	2.05	323	1.71	634	1.13
9	34	3.07	68	2.58	199	2.04	528	1.31
10	30	3.12	60	2.62	141	2.14	298	1.38

Appendix: Transcriptional Regulatory Proteins

A- Transcript. regulatory prot. which do not bind to the target DNA promoter

	SWISS-PROT NUMBER	NAME	DOMAINS
1.	P49715	C/EBP-a	Basic, Pro-rich, Leu zip
2.	Q01658	DR1	Q-rich
3.	P15923	E2A/E47	HLH
4.	?	E2f	Leu zip, Rb pocket interaction, acidic
5.	P01100	Fos	Basic, Leu zip
6.	P12980	Lyl1	HLH
7.	Q00987	MDM2	Acidic
8.	P01106	Myc	Basic, Leu zip, HLH, Q-rich, D2'
9.	P43354	NOT	Q-rich, 2× Pro-rich
10.	P04637	P53	Basic, Acidic, Pro-rich, Hydrophobic
11.	Q01094	RABP	Rb pocket interaction
12.	P06400	Rb	Rb pocket, D2, D3, Pro-rich
13.	P11831	SRF	2× Acidic
14.	P17542	SCL	Basic, HLH
15.	P21675	TAFII 250	Acidic, Pro-rich, D1'
16.	P19484	TFEB	Q-rich, HLH, Leu zip, Pro-rich
17.	P19532	TFE3	Basic, HLH, Leu zip, Pro-rich
18.	P24928	RNA Pol II	52× RNA Pol II repeats, (Catalytic domain for RNA synth.)

B- Transcript. regulatory prot. which can bind to the target DNA promoter

	SWISS-PROT NUMBER	NAME	DOMAINS
19.	P05412	AP-1	AP-1 BD, Leu zip, Q-rich
20.	P43268	E1A-F	Ets-1 BD, Q-rich, Acidic
21.	P32519	Elf-1	Ets-1 BD, Rb pocket interaction, Acidic
22.	P14921	Ets-1	Ets-1 BD, HLH, D4
23.	Q01844	Ews	31× QSY
24.	Q01543	Fli-1	Ets-1 BD, HLH
25.	P01242	Myb	WWW motif, Leu zip, Acidic
26.	P19838	NF-kB	NF-kB BD, D5'
27.	P17947	Pu.1	Ets-1 BD, HLH, 3× Acidic, Q-rich, D3', D4
28.	P08047	SP1	Sp1 BD, Q-rich, D5, D6'
29.	P20226	TBP	TBP BD, Q-rich, Basic, D1, D4'
30.	P36402	TCF-1	HMG, Pro-rich
31.	P22415	USF	USF BD, HLH, Leu zip
32.	P25490	YY1	YY1 BD, Acidic, D6
33.	-	Ews-Fli-1	Ets-1 BD, 31× QSY

References

1. Baron M., Norman D.G., Campbell L.D., Trends Biochem. Sci. **16**, 13-17 (1991).
2. Patthy L., Current Opinion in Structural Biology **1**, 351-361 (1991).
3. May W.A., Lessnick S.L., Braun B.S., Klemsz M., Lewis B.C., Lunsford L.B., Hramas R., Denny C.T., Molecular and Cellular Biology **13**, 7393-7398 (1993).
4. Fischman, J., Science **273**, 591-593 (1996).
5. Bairoch A., Bucher, P., Hofman, K., Nucleic Acids Res. **24**, 189-196 (1996).
6. Faux, M.C., Scott, J.D., Cell **85**, 9-12 (1996).
7. Alberts B., Bray D., Lewis J., Raff M., Roberts K., Watson J.D., Molecular Biology of the Cell, (3rd Ed.), Garland Pub. Inc., NY, (1994).
8. Boulikas, T., Critical Reviews in Eukaryotic Gene Expression **5**, 1-77 (1995).
9. Tijian R., Maniatis T., Cell **77**, 5-8 (1994).
10. Cohen G.B., Ren R., Baltimore D., Cell **80**, 237-248 (1994).
11. Branden C., Tooze J., Introduction to Protein Structure, Garland Pub. Inc., NY, (1991).
12. Rabbits T.H., Nature **372**, 143-149 (1994).
13. Faisst S., Meyer S., Nucleic Acids Res. **20**, 3-26 (1991).
14. Wingender, E., Dietze, P., Karas, H., Knuppel, R., Nucleic Acids Res. **24**, 238-241 (1996).
15. Gaynor R., AIDS **6**, 347-363 (1992).

THE GENERALIZATION METHOD OF RELATIONSHIPS AMONG NUCLEOTIDE SEQUENCES REVEALS AN ORDER IN ASSIMILATION OF AMINO ACID CODONS DURING THE ISOACCEPTOR tRNAs EVOLUTION.

M.B. CHALEY, E.V. KOROTKOV
117312 Russia, Moscow, Prospect 60-letiya Oktyabrya, 7/1,
Center "Bioengineering" Russian Academy of Sciences

ABSTRACT

A new method, generalization of relationships among the nucleotide sequences has been used to analyze divergency both within and across the families of isoaccepting tRNAs. Dendrogram, dipicting relations between tRNA sets with different amino acid specificities, presents the results of analysis. The method allowed to interpret dendrogram, as a reflection of final stage of the evolution of ambiguous molecules-adaptors to highly specific tRNAs. We have proposed a model of amino acid codons assimilation at this stage. According to the model, the final formation of specific adaptors was followed by assimilation of codon clusters (four codons, differing in the third position), the first dinucleotides of which were connected by transitions. Alternate steps along double-stranded coding DNA accompanied the establishment of tRNA sets with strict specificities. Complementary codons, to which specific adaptors were assigned at step the last, were involved into the process afterwards.

INTRODUCTION

Sequences of transfer RNAs (tRNAs) have always been popular objects for comparative analysis. First phylogenetic trees of isoaccepting tRNAs have shown the divergency of tRNA's sequences among different species [1]. The phylogenetic tree for two superfamilies of tRNAs, VAL and GLY, has shown that the divergency of tRNAs was followed by divergency of anticodons and later - the divergency of species [2]. The evolution of transfer RNAs was considered in detail by Cedergren et al. [3]. Other authors [4] revealed conservative cloverleaf structural elements in each isoacceptor tRNA family and archetypical features in all families, by comparing the known tRNAs and their genes. Because of important function of tRNAs as adaptors to the genetic code they have been chosen to check up a hypothesis of ambiguity reduction in the origin of the genetic code [5]. Eigen et al. [6] acknowledged that in spite of structural conservatism tRNAs contain enough informational sites (52 of total length 76) for comparative analysis. New method of statistical geometry in sequence space has suggested that at the moment of archaebacteria and eubacteria division the divergency level between the sequences was already equal to one third of the current RNAs divergency [6]. Transfer RNAs as witnesses of the genetic code structuring to its current state have been put into the focus [7,8,9] for discussions on: whether the main reasons in establishing of the universal genetic code were biosynthetical relations among amino acids [10,11] or physical and chemical properties [12,13,14]. The method of statistical geometry in sequence space has been offered as more reliable for revealing of hidden kinship of nucleotide sequences, although the methods of comparative analysis of nucleotide sequences were developed and widely used by the moment [15]. As already mentioned, this method was successfully used for tRNAs [6]. The goal of our paper is to describe a method of generalization of nucleotide sequence relationships and to show how informative its application may be with respect to analysing the evolutionary divergency of tRNA families and their relation with the genetic code.

MATERIALS AND METHODS

The sequences were taken from the compilation of tRNA sequences and tRNA genes in EMBL database [16] and aligned according to the standard cloverleaf structure. Modified RNA bases were substituted the original ones. The tRNAs sequences, whose anticodons suggested a linkage with known exceptions from the universal genetic coding [17], were excluded from comparative analysis. These exceptions, according to the mechanisms of "codon reassignment" [18] and "codon swapping" [19], are due to the later evolution of genomes rather than the originally established correspondence between codons (anticodons) and amino acids. tRNAs of cellular organelles were also excluded from analysis, basing on the symbiotic theory of the origin of cellular organelles [20]. There are grounds to believ that cellular tRNAs were evolving independendently and, therefore, deserve a separate study. Some facts support this suggestion, e.g., frequent unstandard secondary structures of mitochondrial tRNAs [21] and deviations from the universal coding [17].

Isoacceptor tRNAs and their genes were put into the distinct sets according to different amino acid specificities. Elongator and initiator methionine tRNAs were also divided into separate sets. Totally 756 tRNAs and their genes for twenty amino acids were divided into separate sets according to their specificities: 46 ALA, 40 ARG, 28 ASN, 26 ASP, 10 CYS, 25 GLN, 34 GLU, 46 GLY, 23 HIS, 30 ILE, 61 LEU, 42 LYS, 25 MET, 46 MET_f, 39 PHE, 42 PRO, 62 SER, 34 THR, 20 TRP, 35 TYR, 42 VAL. Anticodons of isoacceptor tRNAs spaned the whole table of amino acid

Table 1. The number of representatives in all Kingdoms of living organisms for each set of isoaccepting tRNAs and their genes. Sets are given in order from left to right as shown on the dendrogram (Fig.1).

	HIS	GLN	LEU	PRO	SER	GLY	GLU	ASP	CYS	TRP	ARG	VAL	ALA
VIRUSES	1	2	2	4	3	2	-	1	-	1	1	1	2
ARCHAEBACT.	4	3	11	6	7	8	5	4	2	3	5	7	15
EUBACTERIA	8	8	28	16	17	21	10	8	5	7	15	12	17
PROTISTA	5	6	6	3	14	1	6	4	1	3	10	7	5
PLANTS	1	-	1	3	9	4	3	1	-	3	1	2	1
ANIMALS	4	6	13	10	12	10	10	8	2	3	8	13	6

	METf	TYR	ILE	MET	THR	PHE	ASN	LYS
VIRUSES	1	-	2	2	2	-	1	1
ARCHAEBACT.	7	3	4	4	7	3	5	5
EUBACTERIA	13	9	17	10	16	11	10	11
PROTISTA	8	6	4	2	5	6	5	8
PLANTS	5	10	1	3	-	6	2	1
ANIMALS	12	7	2	4	4	13	5	16

codons. Table 1 shows distribution of the sequences by Kingdoms of protista (separately for viruses, archaebacteria and eubacteria), plants and animals. In most cases there were representatives from all Kingdoms in each set.

The method of generalization of relationships among nucleotide sequences

It can be described as follows:

1) The nucleotide sequences of tRNAs and tRNA genes were compared in pairs within each set of different amino acid specificities and across all sets. The measure of similarity in pairwise comparing was a doubled value of mutual information 2I:

$$2I = 2\left(\sum_{i=1}^{4}\sum_{j=1}^{4} m_{ij}\ln m_{ij} - \sum_{i=1}^{4} m_{i.}\ln m_{i.} - \sum_{j=1}^{4} m_{.j}\ln m_{.j} + L\ln L\right) \qquad (1)$$

$$L = \sum_{i=1}^{4} m_{i.} = \sum_{j=1}^{4} m_{.j} \qquad (2)$$

$$m_{i.} = \sum_{j=1}^{4} m_{ij}\ , \quad m_{.j} = \sum_{i=1}^{4} m_{ij} \qquad (3)$$

Here, m_{ij} are elements of the 4*4-dimensionary matrice M of base coincidences. The matrice M contained numerical values of all kinds of coincidences among A, G, U, C bases, when two tRNAs were compared. It was shown 2I value distributed as χ^2 statistic with degrees of freedom equal to (n-1)*(n-1) [22], in our case n=4. Basing on chi-square value, we determined the consistency of the statistical significance of similarity. For each pair of the sets, X and Z, matrice R_{XZ} of tRNA pairs similarity were constructed. The elements of R_{XZ} matrice were the values of 2I statistic for each pair, respectively.

2) The sets, having different amino acid specifics, contained unequal numbers of the sequences. As we had a different numbers of the sequences within sets, matrices R_{XZ} of pairwise comparing of the sets had different dimensions. Due to this we have tried to establish the similarities between tRNA sets integrally, i.e., independently from R_{XZ} matrices dimensions. We have done a statistical analysis of matrice elements to reach the goal. The distribution of 2I value was considered over the following twelve intervals:

$$[0,20),\quad [20,25),\quad \ldots,\quad [60,65),\quad [65,70),\quad [70,+\infty) \qquad (4)$$

Experimental frequencies of 2I value distribution over the intervals have been denoted as f_n, n=1,...,12. Theoretical probabilities e_n for 2I value to belong to each interval have been calculated by integration of probability's density of χ^2 distribution with nine degrees of freedom. The measure of interrelationship between two sets of tRNAs, i.e., the measure of deviation of comparison matrice R_{XZ} from any accidental matrice was as follows:

$$F_{XZ} = K_{XZ}\left(\sum_{n=1}^{r} f_n \ln f_n - \sum_{n=1}^{r} f_n \ln e_n\right) \qquad (5)$$

Here, K_{XZ} is a dimension of comparison matrice R_{XZ} for any pair of tRNA sets: X and Z. r - the number of discrete intervals of 2I value, r=12.

3) It was earlier shown $2F_{XZ}$ value is distributed as χ^2 with (r-1) degrees of freedom [22]. Therefore we can introduce G_{XZ} value as the measure of interrelationship between tRNA sets, which is independent from the dimension of comparison matrice R_{XZ}:

$$G_{XZ} = \frac{2F_{XZ}}{K_{XZ}} K_0 \tag{6}$$

Here K_0 - is a certain average dimension of the comparison matrice for all pairs of tRNA sets. In further calculations, $K_0 = 1296$.

4) For a more adequate description relationships between the sets of isoacceptor tRNAs we shifted from χ^2 distribution with eleven degrees of freedom to the standard normal distribution using the formula [23]:

$$N_{XZ} = \sqrt{2G_{XZ}} - \sqrt{2r-1} \tag{7}$$

5) Finally, strength of an interrelationship between a set pair was expressed as an argument of standard normal distribution, basing on wich N(x,z) - a similarity matrice for twenty and one sets of isoacceptor tRNAs was constituted. A dendrogram based on N(x,z) similarity matrice was constructed, using the well-known algorithm of cluster analysis, the "nearest neighbor" [24]. When constructing a dendrogram, the arguments of normal distribution were expressed in round numbers. Each set was reflected by a separate branch, whose gorisontal end value corresponded to the strength of a generalized interrelationship of sequences within the set (Fig.1).

RESULTS AND DISCUSSION

Fig. 1 shows dendrogram of interrelationships among the tRNA sets, with different amino acid specificities. The values of interrelationship are given as arguments of standard normal distribution ranging from 185 to 335. For this case a difference between values even in one unit leads to difference in accidental probabilities in more than one order of magnitude. One can see that lysine tRNAs have the most closely related sequences. Analysis of tRNA sequences suggests two factors might have influenced interrelation levels of isoacceptor tRNA sets. First, some time passed before, when a group of molecules-adaptors had been finally formed as a set of high specificity to concrete amino acid. Second, the evolution of species. The influence of the second factor - the evolution of species - can be reduced to minimum by constructing common ancestral sequence [5,9]. But such methods are very labor-intensive. Besides, the statistical testing of phylogenetic hypotheses presents a difficult problem [25,26].

Table 1 shows the number of representatives of each Kingdom: viruses, archaebacteria, eubacteria, protista (except two last groups), plants and animals, for twenty and one sets of tRNAs. The tRNA sets in Table 1 go from left to right, as in Fig. 1. It should be noted that no clear correlation between the number of kingdom representatives in each set and the placing of the sets on the dendrogram seems to exist. Therefore, we can suppose the order of tRNA sets on the dendrogram mainly reflects the evolutionary process, during which tRNAs of precise amino acid specificities were formed. Also, Fig. 1 reveals a clear trend: the smaller a strength of internal relationship is, the less isoacceptor tRNA family is related with other tRNA sets. Naturally, the more ancient the sequences of isoacceptor tRNAs are, the more divergent they are between themselves. Their relations with different isoacceptor tRNAs, which have been formed later, are weaker as well. The results strongly

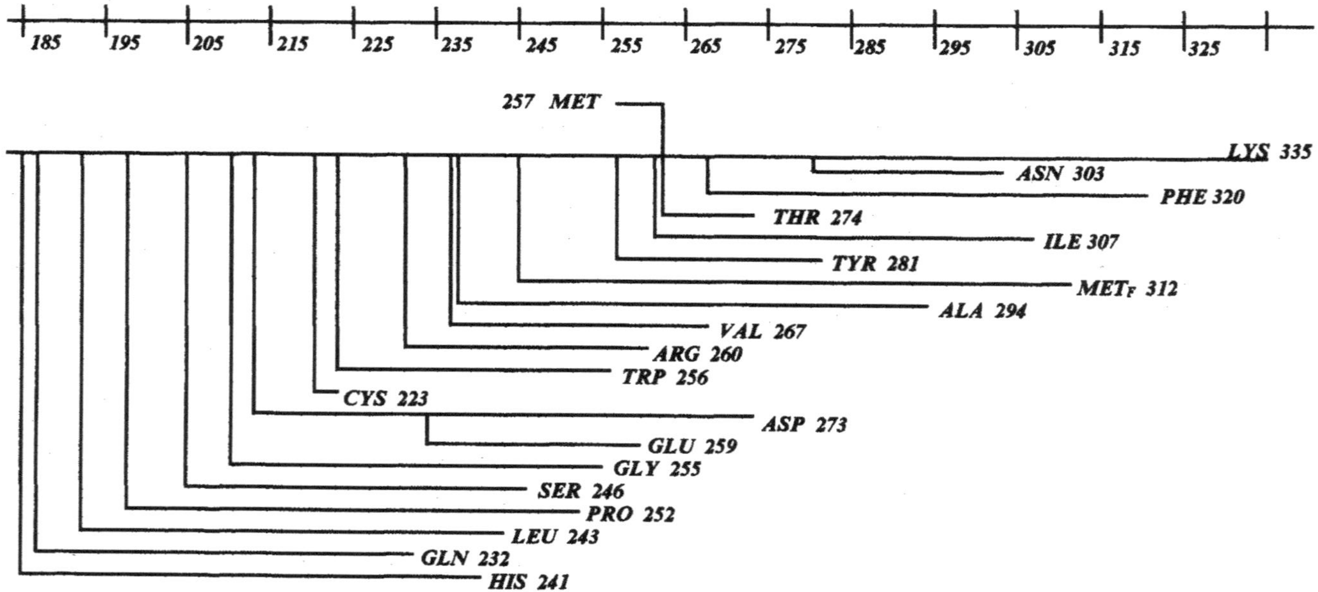

Figure 1.
Dendrogram constructed on N(x,z) matrice of generalized interrelationships between the isoacceptor tRNA sets. The method of clustering is nearest neighbor (single-link). Values of internal and external relationships are the arguments of standard normal distribution. The horizontal growth of each branch ends on the level of generalized interrelationship value within isoacceptor tRNA set. See text for further explanation.

suggest that the dendrogram in Fig. 1 correctly reflects the evolutionary process, settling highly specific adaptors between the genetic code and amino acids.

Arrangement of methionine tRNA sets on dendrogram is unexpected. Methionine tRNAs providing only elongation of amino acid chain arise simultaneously with threonine tRNAs, the first being more related with $tRNA^{THR}$ set than among themselves. Besides, the interrelationship of the methionine elongator tRNA set has the same value as that of $tRNA^{TYR}$ set with the rest of tRNAs, when it is separating into a set with high specificity. The explanation of the unexpected behavior of methionine tRNAs will be given below, in discussion of the proposed model for settling tRNA sets of high specificity. This process occurred according to assimilation of the amino acid codon clusters (the four codons differred in the third position).

The model of high specific tRNAs settlement

The following assumptions are used here to model the process during which tRNA sets with precisely determined specificities are settled (see Fig. 1):

1) When the first set of precisely specific tRNAs appeared, the genetic code in its current state had been already formed. That is, due to physicochemical [13,27,28] or stereochemical [29] correspondences between amino acids and their codons (anticodons), or biosynthetical relations among amino acids [10,11], or by any accidental reasons [30] all codons have been assigned to amino acids and vice versa.

2) tRNAs are already well-developed molecules-adaptors. Nevertheless, they do not reproduce precise amino acid sequences from nucleotide templates. The completing period of separate sets of tRNAs with highly determined specificities formation is going on. Factors, active in this period, are not in the focus of present study.

3) Both DNA strands are considered as coding. This implies, that translation of protein sequences occurs either from both strands or from their RNA transcripts. This assumption is based on a recent proof of neutral adaptation of the genetic code to double-stranded coding [31,32]. The process of double-stranded coding, if it did take place in the past, could significantly accelerate the evolution of biomolecules.

As was discussed above, the dendrogram in Fig. 1 reflects the order of establishment of precisely specific adaptors between amino acids and their codons. We would like to point out that forming of tRNAs, having high adaptor specificities, occurred discretely, step by step. It corresponds to assimilation of amino acid codon clusters (four codons, differing in the third position). Frequently, several clusters were assimilated at one step. These are clusters, in wich the first codon dinucleotides are connected with each other by transitions. The codons complementary to already assimilated codon clusters have determined what clusters will be assimilated at the next step of specific tRNAs formation.

Let us consider in detail how the process of highly specific tRNA sets establishment is reflected in the ordering of amino acid codons. As far as both DNA strands are coding in our model, let us refer to the scheme of double stranded DNA in Figure 2. In this study, the lower strand will be reffered to as "sense", the upper - as "antisense". In reality, amino acid codons, for which highly specific tRNAs are forming at given moment, may be scattered along both strands. Nevertheless, on the scheme in Fig.2 they are drawn on only one of the two DNA strands. Amino acid codons shown by bold Roman letters are placed from left to right in the same order as isoacceptor tRNA sets are from left to right in Fig.1. The alternate clusters are shadowed. Vertical arrowheads between DNA strands are marking the transfer from one strand to another. Hence, the scheme is divided into separate steps or stages corresponding to the "sense" or "antisense" DNA strands. Amino acid codons,

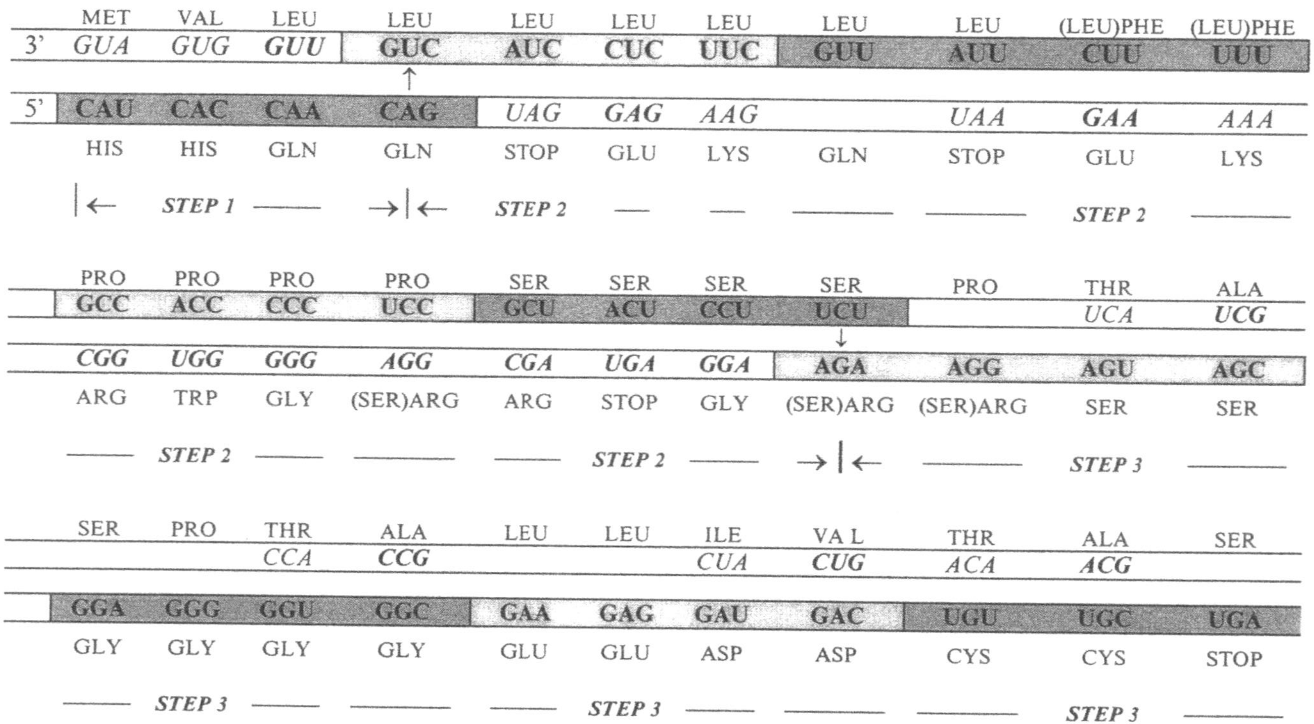

Figure 2. Seven steps model for assimilation of amino acid codons, in settling highly specific tRNAs. Both DNA strands are considered as coding. Amino acid codons, shown by bold Roman letters, are placed from left to right in the same order as isoacceptor tRNA sets are from left to right in Fig.1. Shadowed bars distinguish the alternate codon clusters. Vertical arrowheads between DNA strands are marking the transfer from one DNA strand to another. Codons, which will be assimilated at the next step, are shown by bold Italics. The codons, which already have strict moleculs adaptors, are omit. See text for further details and explanation.

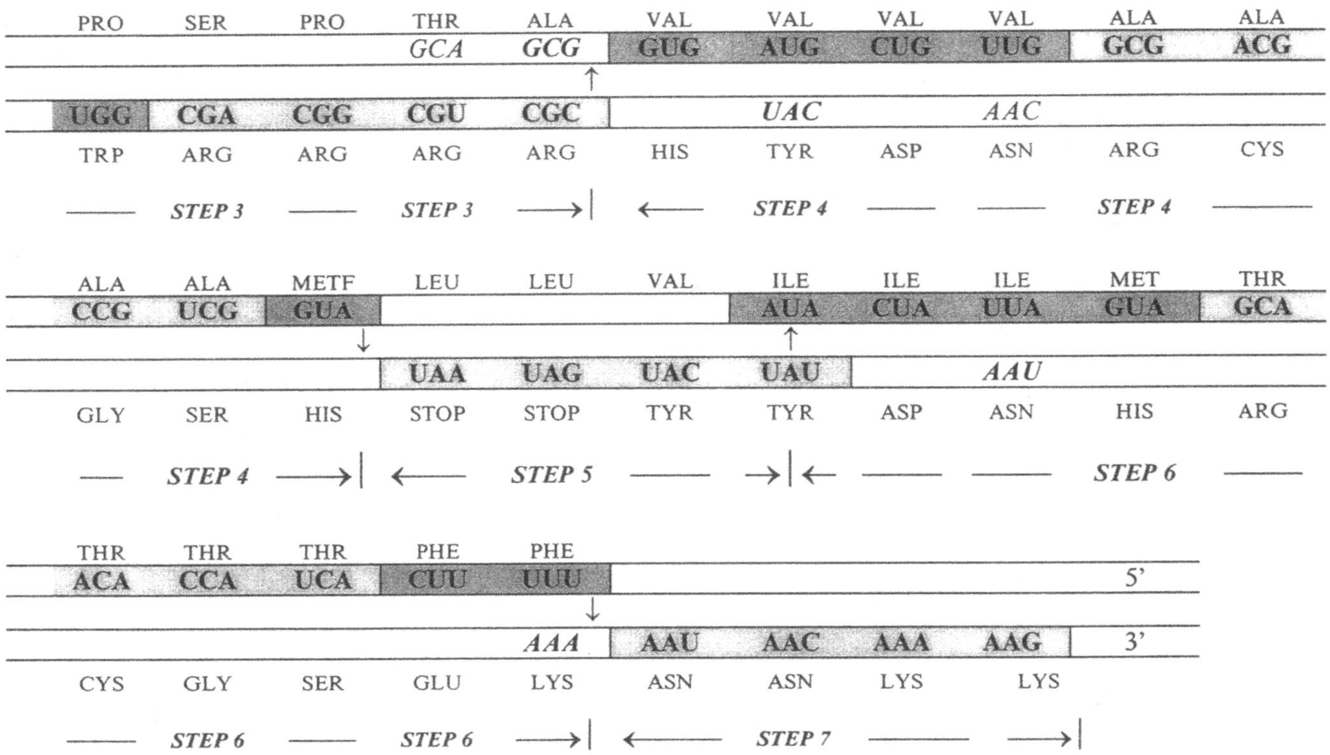

Figure 2 (continued)

involved into the process of strictly specific tRNAs formation at the next step, are shown by bold Italics. The codons, which already have strict molecules-adaptors, are omit. Now, let us consider the scheme in Fig.2 step by step.

Step 1. The first precisely specific tRNA sets, according to Fig.1, were acylated by histidine and glutamine. Codons for these amino acids constitute cluster CA*. One can notice that glutamine codons at the sense strand, CAA and CAG, are complementary to two of the six leucine codons: UUG and CUG. This initiates the transfer of the process of determined tRNA's formation from sense strand to antisense strand.

Step 2. The next sets of tRNAs in Fig.1 are $tRNAs^{LEU}$, $tRNAs^{PRO}$ and $tRNAs^{SER}$. Let us consider the codon's succession of amino acids LEU, PRO and SER. One can see, that with phenylalanine codons UUU and UUC, they constitute a chain of clusters CU*→UU*→ CC*→ UC*. This means that, precisely specific sets of tRNAs accepting amino acids, whose codons are related between each other by transitions, are created. Therefore, it can be supposed that, leucine tRNAs have also recognized phenylalanine codons UUU and UUC. We have put the name LEU in round brackets in Figure 2. While tRNAs of amino acids LEU, PRO, and SER were settled on the antisense strand, codons of amino acids without strictly specific tRNAs have been accumulated at the sense strand, and the process of establishing of specific tRNAs returns to the sense strand.

Step3. Cluster AG* was first to be assimilated after the transfer to the sense strand. As far as serine codons: AGU and AGC are part of the cluster, it is logical to suggest that primarily, AGA and AGG codons were also recognized by $tRNAs^{SER}$. Because of this, we have put the name SER in round brackets. Mistakes in the reading of codons stopped to occur much later. The process of forming tRNAs specific to amino acids SER, GLY, GLU, ASP and CYS, TRP, ARG passed through the codon clusters: AG*→GG*→GA* → UG*→CG*. Except for two stop-codons and two lysine codons, these clusters include sense strand codons, which are complementary to antisense strand codons, whose specific tRNAs were formed at the second step (see Fig.2). It should be noted again that codon clusters AG*→GG*→GA* and UG*→CG* are interrelated between themselves by transitions. When passing the sense strand at the third step, the antisense strand accumulated amino acid codons, which had not get strictly specific tRNAs yet. That induces transfer to the antisense strand.

Step 4. Clusters GU* and GC* are assimilated. Methionine codon AUG joins them at the fourth step.

Step 5. Recurrence to the sense strand, where unassimilated UAC tyrosine codon has emerged. One of the tyrosine codons - UAU is complementary to isoleucine AUA codon at the antisense strand. This initiates the continuation of the process along the antisense strand.

Step 6. Further, assimilation of codon clusters AU* and AC* is taking place at the antisense strand. After that, there are no codons unassimilated by tRNAs at the antisense strand. So, transfer to the sense strand follows.

Step 7 (final). Establishment of precisely specific adaptors for ASN and LYS amino acids is going on at the sense strand. Assimilation of codon cluster AA*.

A closer look at the scheme in Fig.2, might lead to a question about possible deviations from the proposed order in the establishment of precise adaptors between amino acids and codons. First, why assimilation of the clusters, containing methionine codon AUG and valine codon GUG, did not occur at the second step? Why did it take place only at the fourth step? We believe that such facts can be explained by the character of clusters assimilation at the second step. The cluster chain CU*→UU*→CC*→UC* contains all variants of pyrimidine dinucleotides. Specific tRNAs for these codons can be established more easily, even if anticodon changes have been passing also through transitions. Second, why the fourth step was interrupted with methionine codon AUG, and assimilation of AU* cluster was not finished? According to Fig.1, the next set settled after alanine tRNAs, was the set of methionine-initiator tRNAs. Consequently, during initiator tRNAs formation, additional requirements to binding with initiating factor and small ribosomal subunit were set. So, one may suppose, that the period of methionine-initiator tRNAs formation was significantly longer than for the rest tRNAs. Due to a prolonged pause in the assimilation of the codon cluster, it became possible to take tyrosine codon, which appeared at the fourth step on the sense strand and had not got specific tRNAs yet. Further, a return to the antisense strand occurred, where AU* cluster was totally assimilated. However, methionine AUG codon here corresponded only to elongating tRNAs. Threonine codon cluster was assimilated after that. The fourth and the sixth steps could be considered as a single step, in spite of brief pause.

Now, it seems possible to explain why methionine tRNAs are more weakly related within themselves than with tyrosine tRNAs. The strength of relationship within $tRNA^{MET}$ set has the same value as $tRNA^{TYR}$ set has with the other tRNA sets (see Fig.1). It might have occured, because specific methionine-elongator tRNAs originated from tRNAs, which preferably accepted methionine, were unfit to provide initiating function. So, only some time later, when codon cluster AU* was assimilated, they united into a separate isoaccepting set.

The weaker interrelationship within $tRNA^{MET}$ set (if compared with its relationship with $tRNA^{THR}$ set) may reflect a possibility of the biosynthetic transformation of THR to MET [10] as well. A final forming of $tRNA^{PHE}$ set occurs at the antisense strand in the end of the sixth step, and codons UUU and UUC are unambiguously reassimilated by phenylalanine tRNAs. This initiates the assimilation of codon cluster AA* at the sense strand and the establishment of strictly specific sets of $tRNA^{ASN}$ and $tRNA^{LYS}$. However, the problem arises: why AA* cluster was not assimilated earlier, at the third or at the fifth step? A reasonable explanation is the specific role of poly(A) sequences in RNAs functioning. For instance, poly(A) sequence at 3'-end of plant mRNA stabilizes transcripts and influences the expression level [33]. Because poly(A) is frequently used sequence, and "wobble" rule [34] is effective in mRNA and tRNA binding, $tRNA^{ASN}$ and $tRNA^{LYS}$ must discriminate the third codon position with a special accuracy.

Figures 1 and 2 reflect biosynthetical relationships of some amino acids in accordance with the coevolution hypothesis [10]. Such relations are precursor-product convertions: GLN→HIS, SER→GLY, ASP→GLU, (SER→TRP, SER→CYS), (THR→ILE, THR→MET). Comparing amino acid polarities ([13], Table 1), one can see that amino acids of the nearest neighboring tRNA sets in Fig.1: (GLN, HIS), (SER, GLY), (ASP, GLU), (ILE, MET), have the nearest polarity values.

The proposed model of amino acid codon clusters assimilation during the forming of precisely specific molecules-adaptors agrees with the hypothesis of ambiguity reduction in the genetic code origin, which has been also tested on transfer RNAs [5]. This hypothesis assumes that the genetic code has been influenced by the development of adaptors' selectivity initially to purines and pyrimidines at the first codon dinucleotides and later to the purine-pyrimidine type. Fig.2 shows that, when the formation of precisely specific tRNAs started, adaptors could already discriminat purines and pyrimidines at the second codon's position. Both DNA strands were involved simultaneously into the process. Codons with purines in the central position are located along one strand, whereas those with pyrimidines in the central position occupy the complementary strand. Further, the process tends to be discriminatory against specific types of purine or pyrimidine at the second codon position, as well as against purines and pyrimidines at the first position.

In this study, we avoided discussing which gives a more adequate explanation of the genetic code structuring. Recent reports [7,8] have given some additional evidence in favour of coevolution hypothesis. This paper shows, that evolution of specific tRNAs has been continued after the genetic code establishment. Also it reveals the possible order in the assimilation of codons, during the formation of precisely specific adaptors. Formation of highly specific adaptors occurred according to the assimilation of successions of codon clusters, differing from each other only by nucleotide transitions. Their complementary codons were involved into formation of precise adaptors at the next step.

REFERENCES

1. B. LaRue et al, J. Mol. Evol. 14, 287 (1979)
2. R.J. Cedergren et al, Proc. Natl. Acad. Sci. USA 77, 2791 (1980)
3. R.J. Cedergren et al, CRC Crit. Rev. Biochem. 11, 35 (1981)
4. K. Nicoghosian et al, J. Mol. Evol. 26, 341 (1987)
5. W.M. Fitch and K. Upper, Cold Spring Harbor Symp. Quant. Biol. 52, 759 (1987)
6. M. Eigen et al, Science 244, 673 (1989)
7. E. Szathmary and E. Zintzaras, J. Mol. Evol. 35, 185 (1992)
8. M. Di Giulio, Origins Life 24, 425 (1994)
9. M. Di Giulio, Origins Life 4, 1 (1995)
10. J. T.-F. Wong, Proc. Natl. Acad. Sci. USA 72, 1909 (1975)
11. F.J.R. Taylor and D. Coates, BioSystems 22, 177 (1989)
12. T.M. Sonneborn in: Evolving genes and proteins, Eds. V. Bryson and H..J. Vogel (Academic Press, New York, USA, 1965)
13. C.R. Woese et al, Proc. Natl. Acad. Sci. USA 55, 966 (1966)
14. C.R. Woese et al, Cold Spring Harbor Symp. Quant. Biol. 31, 720 (1966)
15. M. Eigen et al, Proc. Natl. Acad. Sci. USA 85, 5913 (1988)
16. S. Steinberg et al, Nucl. Acids Res. 21, 3011 (1993)
17. S. Osawa et al, Microbiol. Rev. 56, 229 (1992)
18. S. Osawa and T.H. Jukes , J. Mol. Evol. 28, 271 (1989)
19. E. Szathmary, J. Mol. Evol. 32, 178 (1991)
20. B. Alberts et al, Molecular biology of the cell, 3d Ed. (Garland Publishing Inc, New York, USA, 1995).
21. R.J. Cedergren ,Canad. J. Biochem. 60, 475 (1982)
22. S. Kullback, Information theory and statistics (John Wiley and Sons, Inc., New York, 1958)
23. V.S. Koroljuk et al, The handbook of the theory of probability and mathematical statistics (Nauka, Moscow, 1985)
24. R.O. Duda, P.E. Hart, Pattern classification and scene analysis (John Wiley & Sons, New York, London, Sydney, Toronto, 1973).
25. J. Felsenstein, Ann. Rev. Genet. 22, 521 (1988)
26. L. Jin and M. Nei, Mol. Biol. Evol. 7, 82 (1990)
27. J.R. Jungck , J. Mol. Evol. 11, 211 (1978)
28. J.C. Jr. Lacey and D. W. Jr. Mullins, Origins Life 13, 3 (1983)
29. L.B. Hendry et al, Origins Life 11, 203 (1981)
30. F.H.C. Crick , J. Mol. Biol. 38, 376 ((1968)
31. J. Konecny et al, J. Mol. Evol. 36, 407 (1993)
32. T. Yomo and I. Urabe, J. Mol. Evol. 38, 113 (1994)
33. D.R. Gallie et al, translation" Plant Cell 1, 301 (1989)
34. F.H.C. Crick, J. Mol. Biol. 19, 548 (1966)

Using Tcl for Molecular Visualization and Analysis

Andrew Dalke and Klaus Schulten
Beckman Institute, 405 N. Mathews,
Urbana, IL 61801, USA

Reading and manipulating molecular structure data is a standard task in every molecular visualization and analysis program, but is rarely available in a form readily accessible to the user. Instead, the development of new methods for analysis, display, and interaction is often achieved by writing a new program, rather than building on pre-existing software. We present the Tcl-based script language used in our molecular modeling program, VMD, and show how it can access information about the molecular structure, perform analysis, and graphically display and animate the results. The commands are available to the user and make VMD a useful environment for studying biomolecules.

Introduction

There are many programs for molecular visualization (RasMol [1], Quanta [2], GRASP [3], SETOR [4]) and analysis (Naomi [5], Modeller [6], MD Toolchest [7], STRIDE [8]). They all perform many of the same basic tasks: they read in molecular structure data, perform some analysis, and display the results. Visualization programs usually analyze the data to display some aspects of it, while programs for analysis often return their results as detailed textual information.

As visualization and analysis tasks become more complex and the expectations for programs continues to rise, it becomes harder to build new software from scratch. Fortunately reusable code libraries like PDBlib++ [9] and the MMDB-API [10] have simplified program development. However, such libraries do not provide much assistance to the user, who often wants a high degree of interactivity and the ability to implement new features or combine existing features in new and novel ways without altering the underlying program code.

To address this problem, many programs implement script languages which allow the user to execute various commands and analysis routines. Some of the best known script languages are found in X-PLOR [11] , NAOMI [5] and SETOR [4] . Because the languages were developed *ad hoc*, they are rather incomplete, and do not handle some common programming abstractions. An alternate method is to extend one of the many embeddable scripting languages, such as Tcl [12] , Python [13] or Perl [14] . Over the last few years as scripting languages have matured and people have become more experienced in using them, a new generation of modeling tools have been developed based on them, e.g. Molviewer-ogl [15] , gOpenMol [16] and Chimera [17] .

We have developed several ways to use one such language, Tcl, in our molecular graphics and analysis program, VMD [18] . Originally written to display molecular dynamics trajectories and support interactive molecular dynamics, VMD now includes Tcl language extensions for controlling the graphics display, accessing the internal database of molecular information, analyzing atom selections, displaying user-defined 3D graphics, and acting on specified events. Combined with the base scripting language, these extensions provide a powerful environment for molecular modeling and suggest interesting directions for future developments.

Tcl

Tcl [12] is one of the most popular scripting languages. It is freely available and contains many of the standard language features such as variables, control loops, and procedures as well as more advanced utilities, including file I/O, process spawning, and exception handling. The most interesting aspect of its design, at least from the aspect of software development, is its use as an embeddable and extensible controller.

Embedding Tcl in another program is done through a C library interface. The library contains the interpreter and the core set of Tcl commands. Text commands are passed to the library, which evaluates the string and calls the appropriate functions. The language is extended by adding new functions, either through a Tcl procedure definition or by adding a call-back to a C function. Figure 1 shows how the components are arranged. Because of its popularity and ease of extensibility, many extensions have been built for Tcl (Tk, expect, Dp, Extend). The only thing that connects the different pieces together is the interpreter, which is why Tcl is often called a "glue" language.

VMD Extensions to Tcl

The VMD scripting language uses Tcl along with two of the common extensions, Tcl-Extend (which adds many generally useful functions) and Tcl-Dp (for network communications), and adds many molecular modeling specific extensions. Since the rest of this paper describes the various extensions, it is helpful here to elaborate more on extensions and some of the issues concerning them.

One of the simplest Tcl extensions in VMD is a set of commands for manipulating vectors and 4x4 matrices. Structural analysis often involves vector

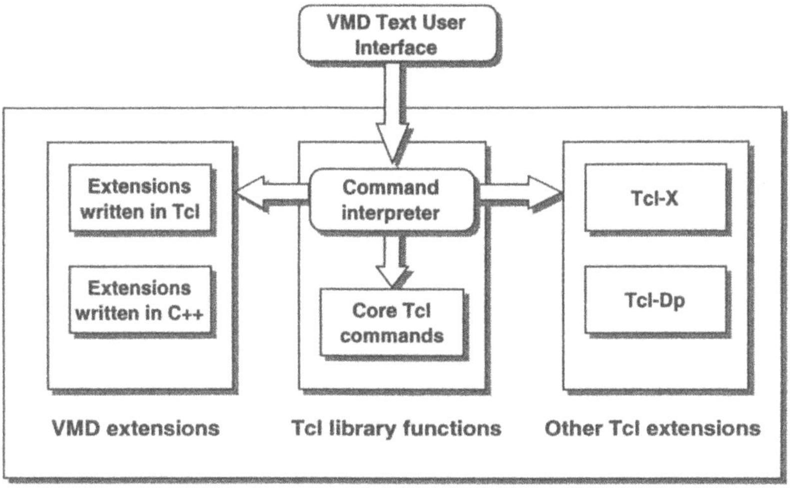

Figure 1: Organization of the Tcl interpreter, basic command library and extensions

algebra, but Tcl is a string-based language with limited provision for mathematical operations and no commands for manipulating vectors and matrices. Thus, the new commands include methods for vector addition and subtraction, dot and cross product evaluation, matrix multiplication, and various methods to construct specific types of matrix transformations.

The commands were originally developed as a set of procedures implemented in Tcl, but the constant interpretation and conversion from Tcl strings to numbers and back to strings made many of the more commonly used commands quite slow. This is especially noticeable in routines like `vecadd` which are likely to be in inner loops. As Tcl can use functions written in C or C++ just as easily as ones in Tcl, several of the most heavily used functions were converted into C, resulting in performance increases ranging from 5- to 40-fold.

Atom Selections

All of the molecular analysis routines in VMD depend on an atom selection, which is both a reference to the atoms which match a given selection text and a way to access the data associated with those atoms. A selection contains a selection text, the molecule from which the selection derives, and a list of atoms meeting the selection criteria. Since a molecule may have multiple animation

Selection Text	Selected Atoms
name N CA C O	backbone atoms in proteins
hydrophobic protein backbone	
x > 0 and y > 0 and z > 0	atoms in the first octant
segname == "PRO1"	same as "segname PRO1"
same residue as name "S.*"	all residues containing an atom name starting with S
resid 5 to 10	residues with index between 5 and 10
sqr(x-1)+sqr(y+2.3)+sqr(z) < sqr(6)	atoms within 6 Å of (1, -2.3, 0)
helix within 5 of resname HEME	atoms on an alpha helix within 5 Å of the heme

Table 1: Examples of atom selection text

frames, the selection also contains a reference to the specific frame to use.

The text used to make a selection consists of four main types of primitives. These can be combined with boolean operators to form more complex selections (see Table 1 for examples). The simplest primitive is of the form "keyword," as in "`backbone`." An atom is selected if it has the given attribute. The next simplest is of the form "keyword *value1 value2* ...." If the value of the attribute for an atom matching any of the values in the list, it is selected. Comparison expressions are allowed, so the nonsense selection "`mass * cos(x) / 5.0 < sqrt(abs(charge))`" is acceptable. The operators are the same as those used in the Perl scripting language so the somewhat more useful "`name =~ 'H.*'`" is also acceptable; in this case it finds atoms whose name matches the regular expression which says the first character must be an "H," e.g., hydrogen and mercury atoms. The fourth set of selection primitives include specialized forms for distance searches and set relations.

The selection text parsing is done at the C++ level and uses a keyword symbol table and a lex/yacc grammar. The constructed parse tree is evaluated to produce a boolean array of flags indicating which atoms were selected. The most interesting of these is the symbol table which contains a list of the various keyword terms recognized in a selection. Each element of the table consists of a display string, a regular expression, and accessor function pointers to "get" and "set" the keyword attribute values. The table is used in every stage of the selection evaluation; the graphical browser uses the display string, the lexer uses the regular expression to identify keywords in the selection text, and the evaluation step calls the gettor function to check attribute information. New keywords can be readily added because the symbol table is dynamically built

(a)

```
set dna_sel [atomselect $molecule_id {segname DNA} ]
set total_mass 0.0
foreach mass [$dna_sel get mass] {
  set total_mass [expr $total_mass + $mass]
}
puts "The total mass is: $mass"
```

(b)

```
proc total_mass_proc {selection} {
  eval "vecadd [$selection get mass]"
}
puts "The total mass is: [total_mass_proc [atomselect 0 \
  {segname DNA}]]"
```

Figure 2: (a) Script to compute the molecular weight of a segment; (b) rewritten as a function

from function pointers added when the program is run.

The different parts of the evaluation are encapsulated in the VMD script language by the `atomselect` command, which takes as arguments the molecule number, selection text, and optional animation frame number, calls the C++ functions, and creates a new Tcl function. Using one function to construct another one dynamically is one way in Tcl to implement object-oriented programming. The newly created function is specific to the selection and can be called with various parameters to get information about it, such as the original selection text, a list of selected atom indices, and the current frame. More important for analysis, the atom selection object can call the accessor functions from the keyword symbol table to get and set information about the selected atoms, making all the data attributes available to a script.

Analysis of Atom Selections

A major benefit of the VMD script language is that the details of reading the structure data and evaluating its contents are left to the program and the results are made available to the user in a form amenable to analysis. With the atom selections and the standard Tcl commands, a wide range of routines can easily be implemented. As a simple example, Figure 2 (a) computes the molecular weight of the segment named DNA by adding all the mass terms returned by the atom selection. The evaluation of the mass can be written as a function for general use, as shown in Figure 2 (b), though in this case the function was simplified by means of the **vecadd** command.

Several of the more common analysis routines are already built into VMD, such as finding the center of mass of a selection or the RMS deviation between two selections. We plan to include other routines for analysis more specific to molecular modeling, such as finding hydrogen bonds and computing surface and volume terms. Since many specialized analysis programs are developed and made available by other groups, we have found it often easier to use Tcl to communicate with an external process than to rewrite the program. The secondary structure determination used in VMD, for example, is actually performed by calling the program STRIDE [8] . In the future, with the run-time loading feature of Tcl, it will even be possible to add new, compiled routines without recompiling VMD.

User-defined Graphics

The analysis commands described in the previous section use the standard Tcl commands to create text output. Another possibility in VMD is to take advantage of the 3D graphics commands to position various simple geometric primitives such as lines, spheres, cylinders, and triangles in the same display as the visualized molecules. This option was originally included for adding arrows and text to a scene for making images for publication, and as such has been used to draw the unit cell, highlight hinge motions, and display specific bonding patterns. Because of the dynamic versatility of Tcl, the graphics commands have also been used to display the output of other programs including the results of MDToolchest analysis and the surface generated from MS [19] .

When combined with atom selections and the analysis routines, the graphics commands add an exceptionally useful means to test and visualize molecular data in ways not directly implemented in VMD. One proposed visualization method, prototyped using the code in Figure 3 , draws a sphere for each residue with the sphere centered at the residue's center of mass with radius equal to the residue's radius of gyration. The sphere is colored with the color assigned to the residue name.

The combination of routines described have even been used to draw 2D plots. Figure 4 shows the protein bacteriorhodopsin above a C_α-C_α distance plot. The solid protein structure, computations and plot were done in VMD.

Event Call-Backs

Saying that VMD uses a script language is somewhat of a misnomer. Scripts are usually thought of as a sequence of commands which are executed one after another, but Tcl can be used to call functions based on asynchronous events, such as using the mouse to pick an atom. There are two ways to implement these actions in Tcl; we chose to use the `trace` command, which associates a function call-back with specified Tcl variable being read, modified, or deleted. For example, every time an animation frame changes for a molecule the Tcl variable "vmd_frame($molecule_id)" is set to the new frame number, where the molecule identifier is denoted by $molecule_id. The interpreter looks up the functions to be called when that array element changes, and executes each of them.

This type of call-back is used in viewing trajectories where the user-defined graphics may change during the course of the playback. A notable example computes and draws the best-fit line through each of two protein helices that move during a molecular dynamics simulation. A new call-back function was set up so that when the animation frame changed, the best-fit lines were updated, and the angle between the two printed. In that way, the researcher could see that the calculations were correct, visualize the motions of the helices, and get an analytical value for each time step.

Another trace variable, and the only event directly related to the graphical user interface, occurs when an atom is selected with the mouse. Two variables are set, which define the atom index and molecule identifier of the selected atom. The associated user function can act on the event, for instance, by printing extra information about the selected atom, computing some property of the molecule, or modifying the secondary structure of the residue. It has even be used to develop hyperlinks in a molecule: a group of atoms can be associated with a URL, and when one of the atoms is selected, a web browser will be updated accordingly.

Program Availability

The complete, documented source code for VMD and a precompiled binary for IRIX 5.x is available via anonymous ftp from ftp.ks.uiuc.edu. A detailed User's Guide is also available as is a Programmer's Guide for those interested in modifying the code. Please see the VMD home page at http://www.ks.uiuc.edu/Research/vmd/ for more information.

Conclusion

Molecular modeling software can require the use of many different types of features. Since it is impossible to predict all the combinations of options a user may want, the dynamic nature of an embedded scripting language like Tcl is a useful way to increase the utility and interactivity of a program. Complex code and functions that demand intensive calculations can be written in C or C++ and organized by Tcl so components which are orthogonal in design, such as making atom selections and adding graphical primitives, are tied together to form a synergistic combination.

More importantly, the flexible nature of Tcl along with the modeling extensions added by VMD has provided a way for users to implement new features that were not considered when VMD was developed. With commands to access the internal structure database, new analysis routines are easier to write, especially since the details of reading and determining the inital structure are automatically performed. The results can be presented as text, or displayed as 3D graphics; allowing a wide range of new display methods to be constructed and even animated.

The next stage in VMD development will add more analysis routines, provide support for viewing kinemage files and electron density maps, and develop methods for user interactions. One of the most popular Tcl extensions is the Tk library for writing graphical menus, and adding Tk to VMD will allow others to design menus to handle new tasks, such as graphically modifying the secondary structure definitions. The mouse controls will be expanded to allow for selecting user-defined objects in the graphics display. A major goal of VMD is to develop methods for interactive molecular dynamics, where VMD is used to visualize and alter a system undergoing simulation. The basic interface exists, but there are very few definite ideas on how it should be expanded so the highly extensible and configurable nature of VMD will play a key role in testing the various possibilities.

Acknowledgments

We thank Bill Humphrey for his original design and development of VMD, and everyone else in the Theoretical Biophysics group for offering suggestions and testing out new features. This work is supported by the National Institutes of Health (grant number PHS 5 P41 RR05969-04), and the National Science Foundation (grant number BIR-9318159).

References

1. Roger A. Sayle and E. J. Milner-White. *RasMol: Biomolecular graphics for all*, TIBS 20(Sept):374-376 (1995). http://www.umass.edu/microbio/rasmol/
2. Quanta, Polygen Corporation. Waltham, MA. http://www.msi.com/marketing/life/ls_software.html#Quanta

3. A. Nicholls, K. A. Sharp and B. Honig. *Protein Folding and Association: Insights From the Interfacial and Thermodynamic Properties of Hydrocarbons*, Proteins: Structure, Function and Genetics 11:282-290 (1991). http://tincan.bioc.columbia.edu/grasp/
4. Stephen Evans. *SETOR: Hardware-lighted three-dimensional solid model representations of macromolecules*, J. Mol. Graph. 11:134-138(1993).
5. Simon M. Brocklehurst and Richard N. Perham. Protein Science 2:626-639 (1993). http://www.ocms.ox.ac.uk/~smb/Software/N_details/naomi.html
6. A. Sali and T. L. Blundell. *Comparative protein modelling by satisfaction of spatial restraints*, J. Mol. Biol. 234:779-815 (1993). http://guitar.rockefeller.edu/modeller/modeller.html
7. G. Ravishankar and David L. Beveridge. Molecular Dynamics Analysis Toolchest, Department of Chemistry, Wesleyan University.
8. Dmitri Frishman and Patrick Argos. *Knowledge-based secondary structure assignment*, Proteins: structure, function and genetics, 23:566-579 (1995). http://www.embl-heidelberg.de/stride/stride_info.html
9. W. Chang, I. N. Shindyalov, C. Pu, and P. E. Bourne. *Design and Application of PDBlib, a C++ Macromolecular Class Library*, CABIOS 10(6):575-586 (1994). http://www.sdsc.edu/CompSci/pb/pdblib/pdblib.html
10. Christopher W. V. Hogue, Hitomi Ohkawa, and Stephen H. Bryant. *A dynamic look at structures: WWW-Entrez and the Molecular Modeling Database*, TIBS 21: 226-229 (1996). See ftp://ncbi.nlm.nih.gov/pub/mmdb/README for API information.
11. Axel Brünger. **X-PLOR, Version 3.1, A System for X-ray Crystallography and NMR**, Yale University (1992). http://xplor.csb.yale.edu/xplor-info/xplor-info.html
12. John Ousterhout. **Tcl and the Tk Toolkit**, Addison-Wesley (1994). http://www.sunlabs.com/research/tcl/
13. The Python home page is at http://www.python.org/
14. The Perl home page is at http://www.perl.org/perl/
15. Molviewer-ogl is described at http://www.yorvic.york.ac.uk/~mjh/molviewer-ogl/about-molviewer-ogl.html
16. gOpenMol is described at http://laaksonen.csc.fi/gopenmol/gopenmol.htmls
17. Chimera is described at http://www.cgl.ucsf.edu/home/chimera/introduction/
18. W. F. Humphrey, A. Dalke and K. Schulten. *VMD – Visual Molecular Dynamics*, J. Molec. Graphics 14(1):33-38 (1996).

http://www.ks.uiuc.edu/Research/vmd/
19. M. L. Connolly. *Analytical Molecular Surface Calculation*, J. Appl. Crystal. 16:548-558 (1983).

```
proc find_rgyr {sel} {
  # get the center of mass
  set com [measure center $sel weight mass]
  # compute the numerator
  set I 0 ; set M 0
  foreach m [$sel get mass] pos [$sel get {x y z}] {
    set I [expr $I + $m * [veclength2 [vecsub $pos $com]]]
    set M [expr $M +  $m]
  }
  # compute and return the radius of gyration
  return [expr sqrt($I/$M)]
}

### find the sphere parameters for every residue except waters
set sel [atomselect top "not water"]
set molid [$sel molindex]
foreach residue [luniq [$sel get residue]] {
  set ressel [atomselect $molid "residue $residue"]
  ## find the center of mass and radius of gyration
  set com [measure center $ressel weight mass]
  set radius [find_rgyr $ressel]
  ### draw the sphere with the correct color assigned to the residue
  lassign [$ressel get resname] resname
  draw color [colorinfo category Resname $resname]
  draw sphere $com radius $radius
}
```

Figure 3: VMD script to compute the radius of gyration for a given atom selection. $R_{gyr} = (\sum_{all\ atoms} mass(i) \cdot \|\vec{r}(i) - \vec{r}_{com}\|^2)/total\ mass)$

Figure 4: C_α-C_α distance plot of the bacteriorhodopsin protein. The protein visualization, distance calculations, and 2D plot were made in VMD

ON SOME OPERATIONS SUGGESTED BY GENOME EVOLUTION

J. DASSOW
Faculty of Computer Science, University of Magdeburg
P.O.Box 4120, D-39016, Magdeburg, Germany

V. MITRANA[a]
Faculty of Mathematics, University of Bucharest
Str. Academiei 14, 70109 Bucharest, Romania

Three operations involved in the genome evolution namely, inversion, transposition and duplication, are considered as operations on strings and languages. We show that, for any pair of these operations, there is a language family which is closed under one of the operations and not closed under the second one, however, under some mild conditions the closure of a language family under one of the operations implies that it also closed with respect to another one.

1 Introduction and definitions

The genomes of complex organisms are organized into chromosomes which contain genes arranged in linear order. Much of the current data for genomes is in the form of maps which are now becoming available and permits the study of the evolution of such organisms at the scale of genome for the first time [3].

It is rather commonly asserted that DNA is a language for specifying the structures and processes of life. Despite this opinion biological sequences has not been investigated very vivid so far by methodes developed in the field of formal language theory. A pioneer's work has been reported in [1] where very simple genes were described by means of regular grammars. Since then most investigations on the topic have used grammar formalism [4, 2, 15].

In the course of its evolution, the genome of an organism mutates by different processes. At the level of individual genes the evolution proceeds by local operations (point mutations) which substitute, insert and delete nucleotides of the DNA sequence. Evolutionary and functional relationships between genes can be captured by taking into considerations only local mutations [14]. These operations viewed as operations on strings and languages have been considered from different points of view [15] and the references thereof.

However, the analysis of the genomes of some viruses (Epstein-Barr and Herpes simplex viruses, see for instance [6, 9]) have revealed that the evolution

[a] Research supported by the Alexander von Humboldt Foundation

of these viruses involved a number of large-scale rearrangements in one evolutionary event. This non-local rearrangements include: ***inversion, transposition, duplication*** and ***splicing.***

- Inversion replaces a segment of a chromosome with its reverse DNA sequence.
- Transposition moves a segment to a new location in the genome.
- Duplication copies a segment to a new location.
- Splicing results in recombination of genes in a pair of homologous chromosomes by exchanging segments between parental chromatides. Splicing can be modelled as a process that exchanges segments at the end of two chromosomes.

The splicing operation was introduced as a language theoretic operation in [7] and then vividly investigated in a series of papers e.g. [11, 12, 5, 10]. A survey can be found in [8].

The other aforementioned operations appear very attractive to us, too. Consequently, in the present paper we shall investigate the other operations from the formal language theory point of view.

It is worth mentioning here that these operations on languages have been considerated in [15] as well. The operations investigated in the present paper are generalizations of the operations studied in [15]. Furthermore, the iterated versions of operations in debate are also considered.

We now recall some notation from formal language theory and formalize the operations mentioned above.

We denote by V^* the free monoid generated by V under catenation, by λ the empty string and by V^+ the free semigroup generated by V, i.e. $V^+ = V^* \setminus \{\lambda\}$. The length of the string x is denoted by $|x|$ whilst the number of occurrences of the letter $a \in V$ in x is denoted by $|x|_a$.

Further we define the *mirror image* $mi(x)$ of a word $x = a_1a_2\ldots a_n$, $a_i \in V$ for $1 \leq i \leq n$, by

$$mi(a_1a_2\ldots a_n) = a_na_{n-1}\ldots a_1$$

and, for a word $x \in V^*$, let

$$Perm(x) = \{y \mid |y|_a = |x|_a \text{ for } a \in V\},$$

be the set of all words over V which are permutations of x.

Moreover, we recall that a family $\mathcal{F}$ of languages is called a *trio*, if $\mathcal{F}$ is closed under (λ-free) homomorphisms, inverse homomorphisms and intersections with regular sets. It is well-known that any trio is closed under restricted homomorphisms, too [13].

For further details in formal language theory we refer to [13].

Definition 1 *An inversion scheme is a pair $I = (V, I')$, where V is an alphabet and I' is a finite subset of V^*.*

For a given inversion scheme $I = (V, I')$ and a string $x \in V^*$, we define

$$Inv_I(x) = \{x_1 mi(x_2)x_3 \mid x = x_1x_2x_3,\ x_2 \in I'\}$$

Definition 2 *A transposition scheme is a pair $T = (V, T')$, where V is an alphabet and T' is a finite subset of $(V^*)^3$.*

For a given transposition scheme $T = (V, T')$ and a string $x \in V^*$ we define

$$Tr_T(x) = \begin{cases} x_1x_3x_4x_2x_5x_6 & \text{for } x = x_1x_2x_3x_4x_5x_6,\ (x_2, x_4, x_5) \in T' \\ x_1x_2x_5x_3x_4x_6 & \text{for } x = x_1x_2x_3x_4x_5x_6,\ (x_5, x_2, x_3) \in T' \end{cases}.$$

Obviously, if $(u, \lambda, \lambda) \in T'$, then u can be shifted to every place in the given word x.

Definition 3 *A duplication scheme is a pair $D = (V, D')$, where V is an alphabet and D' is a finite subset of $(V^*)^3$.*

For a given duplication scheme $D = (V, D')$ and a string $x \in V^*$ we define

$$Dupl_D(x) = \begin{cases} x_1x_2x_3x_4x_2x_5x_6 & \text{for } x = x_1x_2x_3x_4x_5x_6,\ (x_2, x_4, x_5) \in D' \\ x_1x_2x_5x_3x_4x_5x_6 & \text{for } x = x_1x_2x_3x_4x_5x_6,\ (x_5, x_2, x_3) \in D' \end{cases}.$$

If the applied scheme is obvious from the context, we write Inv, Tr and $Dupl$ instead of Inv_I, Tr_T and $Dupl_D$, respectively.

For all $S \in \{mi, Perm, Inv, Transp, Dupl\}$, the operation can naturally be extended to languages by

$$S(L) = \bigcup_{x \in L} S(x).$$

The iterated versions of the above operations are naturally defined as follows. For $S \in \{Inv, Transp, Dupl\}$ we set

$$\begin{aligned} S^0(L) &= L, \\ S^{i+1}(L) &= S(S^i(L)), \\ S^*(L) &= \bigcup_{i \geq 0} S^i(L). \end{aligned}$$

2 Relations between the operations

The inversion operation looks similar to the mirror image operation *mi*. It consists in the application of *mi* to a subword. However, the two operations are quite different as shown in the following proposition.

Proposition 1 *There are families of languages closed under mi but not closed under inversions and vice versa.*

Proof. It is known that the family of D0L languages is closed under *mi*. Consider the D0L language $L = \{a^{2^n} b^{2^n} \mid n \geq 0\}$ and the inversion scheme $I = (\{a, b\}, \{ab\})$. The language

$$Inv_I(L) = \{a^{2^n-1} bab^{2^n-1} \mid n \geq 0\}$$

cannot be generated by a D0L system. Indeed, let us suppose that there exists a D0L system $G = (\{a, b\}, w, h)$ such that $L(G) = Inv_I(L)$. Since $h(a^{2^n-1} bab^{2^n-1}) \in Inv_I(L)$, for some $n \geq 2$, it follows that $|h(a)|_b = |h(b)|_a = 0$. Therefore, $h(a) = a^k$ and $h(b) = b^p$ for some $k, p \geq 1$.

If $k = p = 1$, then $L(G)$ is finite, which contradicts the infinity of $Inv_I(L) = L(G)$.

If $k > 1$ or $p > 1$, then $h(a^{2^n-1} bab^{2^n-1})$ contains a substring of the form $b^p a^k$, which contradicts the form of the words in $Inv_I(L) = L(G)$.

Now, we shall provide a family of languages closed under inversions but not closed under the mirror image. To this end, take the language $L_0 = \{a^n b^n \mid n \geq 1\}$ and construct recursively the following sequence of language classes:

$$\begin{aligned} \mathcal{F}_0 &= \{L_0\}, \\ \mathcal{F}_{k+1} &= \{Inv_I(L) \mid L \in F_k, I \text{ is an inversion scheme}\}. \end{aligned}$$

The family

$$\mathcal{F} = \bigcup_{k \geq 0} \mathcal{F}_k$$

is obviously closed under inversions.

The following fact is essential in our proof.

Fact. *For every language $L \in \mathcal{F}$ and any $n \geq 1$ there exists a finite set $A(L, n) \subseteq L$ such that every string x in $L \setminus A(L, n)$ can be expressed as $x = a^p y b^q$ with $p, q \geq n$ and $y \in \{a, b\}^*$.*

If $L = L_0 \in F_0$, then the assertion is trivially true.

Assume that the assertion is true for any language $L' \in F_k$ and take $L \in F_{k+1}$. Then there exists an inversion scheme $Inv = (\{a, b\}, I)$ such that $L = Inv_I(L')$. Let $n \geq 1$ be a given integer and $m = max\{|x| \mid x \in I\}$. By the induction hypothesis it follows that $L' = A(L', n+m) \cup \bar{L}$, where $A(L', n+m)$ is a finite set and every string x in $\bar{L}$ can be written as $x = a^p y b^q$, $p, q \geq n+m$. Consequently,

$$L = Inv_I(L') = Inv_I(A(L', n+m)) \cup Inv_I(\bar{L}).$$

Note that $Inv_I(A(L', n+m))$ is a finite set and any string w in $Inv_I(\bar{L})$ can be decomposed as $w = a^r z b^s$ with $r, s \geq n$ and $z \in \{a, b\}^*$, which completes the proof of the fact.

Now it is clear that the mirror image of any language in $\mathcal{F}$ cannot be in $\mathcal{F}$ because it does not satisfy the requirements of the aforementioned fact. □

We now prove that the three operations introduced above also differ in that sense that the closure under one operation do not imply the closure with respect to another one.

Theorem 2 *For any pair (X, Y) with $x, y \in \{Inv, Tr, Dupl\}$, $x \neq Y$, there is a language family $\mathcal{L}$ such that $\mathcal{L}$ is closed under X and is not closed under Y.*

Proof. First we consider the family $\mathcal{F}$ defined in the second part of the proof of Proposition 1. By construction $\mathcal{F}$ is closed under inversion. On the other hand, if we apply the transposition scheme

$$T = (\{a, b\}, \{(aa, b, b)\})$$

to the language $L_0 \in F$ we obtain a language, which contains the set of all words $a^{n-2}b^{n-1}aab$ with $n \leq 2$. This contradicts the fact shown in the proof of Proposition 1. Therefore $\mathcal{F}$ is not closed under transposition.

Moreover, if we consider T as a duplication scheme we can prove by analogous arguments that F is not closed under duplication.

Let V be an alphabet. Then we consider the family $\mathcal{L}$ consisting of all languages L such that there is an integer $n \geq 1$ with $L \subseteq V^n$. Obviously, $\mathcal{L}$ is closed under inversion and transposition since these operations do not change the length of a word.

On the other hand, applying the duplication scheme

$$(V, \{(a, \lambda, \lambda), (aa, \lambda, \lambda)\}),$$

where $a \in V$, to the language $\{a^2\} \in \mathcal{L}$ yields the language $\{a^3, a^4\}$ which is not in $\mathcal{L}$.

Let $V = \{a, b\}$. Then let $\mathcal{L}'$ be the family of all languages L over V such that each word in L can be expressed as $x_1 a x_2 b x_3$, i.e. any word of L contains ab as a scattered subword. Obviously, $\mathcal{L}'$ is closed under duplication, since duplication adds additional subwords and does not destroy scattered subwords.

On the other hand, the application of the inversion scheme (V, ab) and the transposition scheme $(V, \{a, b, \lambda)\})$ to the language $\{ab\} \in \mathcal{L}'$ yields $\{ba\} \notin \mathcal{L}'$, which proves the nonclosure of $\mathcal{L}'$ under inversion and transposition. □

However, the situation changes if we restrict the families of languages under consideration.

Theorem 3 *Let $\mathcal{L}$ be a family of languages which is closed under homomorphisms and inverse homomorphisms. Then the following statements hold.*

i) $\mathcal{L}$ is closed under transpositions iff $\mathcal{L}$ is closed under duplications.

ii) The closure of $\mathcal{L}$ under transpositions (or duplications, respectively) implies the closure of $\mathcal{L}$ under inversions.

iii) If $\mathcal{L}$ is closed under union and inversions, then $\mathcal{L}$ is closed under transpositions and duplications.

Proof. i) First, we shall prove that the closure under transposition implies the closure under duplication. Let $D = (V, \{(x_i, y_i, z_i) \mid 1 \leq i \leq n\})$ be a duplication scheme. We consider the homomorphisms

$$h_1 : (V \cup \bigcup_{i=1}^{n} \{c_i, d_i\})^* \longrightarrow V^*,$$

$$h_1(a) = a \text{ for } a \in V, \quad h_1(c_i) = x_i, \ h_1(d_i) = y_i z_i \text{ for } 1 \leq i \leq n$$

$$h_2 : (V \cup \bigcup_{i=1}^{n} \{c_i, d_i\})^* \longrightarrow (V \cup \bigcup_{i=1}^{n} \{c_i, d_i, c_i', d_i'\})^*,$$

$$h_2(a) = a \text{ for } a \in V, \quad h_2(c_i) = c_i c_i', \ h_2(d_i) = d_i d_i' \text{ for } 1 \leq i \leq n,$$

$$h_3 : (V \cup \bigcup_{i=1}^{n} \{c_i, q_i, q_i', p_i\})^* \longrightarrow (V \cup \bigcup_{i=1}^{n} \{c_i, d_i, c_i', d_i'\})^*,$$

$$h_3(a) = a \text{ for } a \in V,$$

$$h_3(q_i') = d_i c_i' d_i', \ h_3(q_i) = c_i c_i', \ h_3(c_i) = c_i, \ h_3(p_i) = d_i d_i' \text{ for } 1 \leq i \leq n,$$

$$g : (V \cup \bigcup_{i=1}^{n} \{p_i, q_i', q_i, c_i \mid 1 \leq i \leq n\})^* \longrightarrow V^*,$$

$$g(a) = a \text{ for } a \in V,$$

$$g(q_i') = y_i x_i z_i, \ g(q_i) = g(c_i) = x_i, \ g(p_i) = y_i z_i \text{ for } 1 \leq i \leq n$$

and the transposition scheme

$$T = (V \cup \bigcup_{i=1}^{n} \{c_i, c_i', d_i, d_i'\}, \{(c_i', d_i, d_i') \mid 1 \leq i \leq n\}).$$

Every string in the language $Tr_T(h_2(h_1^{-1}(L)))$ is either of the form

$$xc_iyd_ic_i'd_i'z \quad \text{or} \quad xd_ic_i'd_i'yc_iz$$

with

$$x, y, z \in (V \cup \bigcup_{i=1}^{n} \{c_ic_i', d_id_i'\})^*.$$

Now, it is easy to see that

$$Dupl_D(L) = g(h_3^{-1}(Tr_T(h_2(h_1^{-1}(L)))))$$

Conversely, for the transposition scheme

$$T = (V, \{(x_i, y_i, z_i) \mid 1 \le i \le n\})$$

we construct the homomorphisms h_1 and h_2 as above and consider the homomorphisms

$$h_3' : (V \cup \bigcup_{i=1}^{n} \{p_i, p_i', q_i, q_i'\})^* \longrightarrow (V \cup \bigcup_{i=1}^{n} \{c_i, d_i, c_i', d_i'\})^*,$$

$h_3'(a) = a$ for $a \in V$,

$h_3'(q_i') = d_id_i'$, $h_3'(q_i) = c_ic_i'$, $h_3'(p_i) = c_id_ic_i'$,

$h_3'(p_i') = d_id_ic_i'd_i'$ for $1 \le i \le n$,

$$g' : (V \cup \bigcup_{i=1}^{n} \{p_i, p_i', q_i, q_i'\})^* \longrightarrow V^*,$$

$g'(a) = a$ for $a \in V$,

$g'(q_i') = y_ix_iz_i$, $g'(q_i) = x_i$, $g'(p_i') = y_iz_i$, $g'(p_i) = \lambda$ for $1 \le i \le n$

and the duplication schemes

$$\begin{aligned} D_1 &= (V'', \{(d_i, c_i, c_i') \mid 1 \le i \le n\}), \\ D_2 &= (V'', \{(d_ic_i', d_i, d_i') \mid 1 \le i \le n\}) \end{aligned}$$

with

$$V'' = V \cup \bigcup_{i=1}^{n} \{c_i, c_i', d_i, d_i'\}.$$

Then we obtain

$$Tr_T(L) = g'((h_3')^{-1}(Dupl_{D_2}(Dupl_{D_1}(h_2(h_1^{-1}(L)))))).$$

ii) By i) it is sufficient to give a proof for transpositions. Let

$$I = (V, \{x_1, x_2, \ldots, x_n\})$$

be an inversion scheme. Then we construct the homomorphisms h_2 and h_3 and the transposition scheme T as in the proof of i) and modify h_1 and g to

$$\begin{aligned}
&h_1' : (V \cup \bigcup_{i=1}^{n} \{c_i, d_i\})^* \longrightarrow V^*,\\
&h_1'(x) = x \text{ for } x \in V \cup \{c_i \mid 1 \le i \le n\}, \quad h_1'(d_i) = \lambda \text{ for } 1 \le i \le n,\\
&g'' : (V \cup \bigcup_{i=1}^{n} \{p_i, q_i', q_i, c_i \mid 1 \le i \le n\})^* \longrightarrow V^*,\\
&g''(a) = a \text{ for } a \in V,\\
&g''(q_i') = \lambda,\ g''(q_i) = x_i,\ g''(c_i) = mi(x_i),\ g''(p_i) = \lambda \text{ for } 1 \le i \le n.
\end{aligned}$$

Then we obtain

$$Inv_I(L) = g''(h_3^{-1}(Tr_T(h_2((h_1')^{-1}(L))))).$$

iii) Again, by i) it is sufficient to give a proof for transpositions. Obvously, if $T = (V, \{t_1, t_2, \ldots, t_n\})$ is a transposition scheme and $T_i = (V, \{t_i\})$ for $1 \le i \le n$, then

$$Tr_T(L) = Tr_{T_1}(L) \cup Tr_{T_2}(L) \cup \cdots \cup Tr_{T_n}(L).$$

By supposition, $\mathcal{L}$ is closed under union, and thus it is sufficient to show that $\mathcal{L}$ is closed under applications of transpositions schemes of the form $\bar{T} = (V, \{(x, y, z)\})$. We consider the homomorphisms

$$\begin{aligned}
&f_1 : (V \cup \{c, d\})^* \longrightarrow V^*,\\
&f_1(a) = a \text{ for } a \in V, \quad f_1(c) = x, \quad f_1(d) = yz,\\
&f_2 : (V \cup \{c, d\})^* \longrightarrow (V \cup \{c, d, c', d'\})^*,\\
&f_2(a) = a \text{ for } a \in V, \quad f_2(c) = cc', \quad f_2(d) = dd',\\
&f_3 : (V \cup \{q, q', p, p'\})^* \longrightarrow (V \cup \{c, d, c', d'\})^*,\\
&f_3(a) = a \text{ for } a \in V,\ f_3(q) = cc',\ f_3(q') = dd',\ f_3(p) = c'c,\ f_3(p') = d'd,\\
&f : (V \cup \{p, p'q, q'\})^* \longrightarrow V^*,\\
&f(a) = a \text{ for } a \in V, \quad f(q') = yz, \quad f(q) = x, \quad f(p) = \lambda, f(p') = yxz
\end{aligned}$$

and the inversion schemes

$$I_1 = (V \cup \{c, d, c', d'\}, \{cc'\}) \quad \text{and} \quad I_2 = (V \cup \{c, d, c', d'\}, \{dd'\})$$

and obtain

$$Tr_{\mathcal{T}}(L) = f(f_3^{-1}(Inv_{I_1}(Inv_{I_2}(f_2(f_1^{-1}(L)))))).$$

□

3 Closure properties of some families

We first study the closure under (non-iterated) inversion, duplication, and transposition.

Theorem 4 *Any trio is closed under duplications, transpositions and inversions.*

Proof. Let $\mathcal{F}$ be a trio and $L \subseteq V^*$ be a language in $\mathcal{F}$. Further let $D = (V, \{(x_i, y_i, z_i) \mid 1 \leq i \leq n\}$ be a duplication scheme. We define the homomorphisms

$$h_1 : (V \cup \bigcup_{i=1}^{n} \{c_i, d_i\})^* \longrightarrow V^*, \quad \begin{array}{l} h_1(a) = a \text{ for } a \in V, \\ h_1(c_i) = x_i \text{ for } 1 \leq i \leq n, \\ h_1(d_i) = y_i z_i \text{ for } 1 \leq i \leq n, \end{array}$$

$$h_2 : (V \cup \bigcup_{i=1}^{n} \{c_i, d_i\})^* \longrightarrow V^*, \quad \begin{array}{l} h_2(a) = a \text{ for } a \in V, \\ h_2(c_i) = x_i \text{ for } 1 \leq i \leq n, \\ h_2(d_i) = y_i x_i z_i \text{ for } 1 \leq i \leq n \end{array}$$

and the regular set

$$R = \bigcup_{i=1}^{n} (V^*\{c_i\}V^*\{d_i\}V^* \cup V^*\{d_i\}V^*\{c_i\}V^*).$$

It is easy to see that

$$Dupl_D(L) = h_2(h_1^{-1}(L) \cap R)$$

which proves the closure of $\mathcal{F}$ under duplications.

Since the erasing homomorphisms used in the proof of Theorem 3 i) are 1-restricted and trios are closed under restricted homomorphisms (see [13]), the statement follows for transpositions, too.

Now let $I = (V, \{x_1, x_2, \ldots, x_n\})$ be an inversion scheme. We consider the homomorphisms

$$h_1 : (V \cup \{c_i \mid 1 \leq i \leq n\})^* \longrightarrow V^*, \quad \begin{array}{l} h_1(a) = a \text{ for } a \in V, \\ h_1(c_i) = x_i \text{ for } 1 \leq i \leq n, \end{array}$$

$$h_2 : (V \cup \{c_i \mid 1 \leq i \leq n\})^* \longrightarrow V^*, \quad \begin{array}{l} h_2(a) = a \text{ for } a \in V, \\ h_2(c_i) = mi(x_i) \text{ for } 1 \leq i \leq n \end{array}$$

and the regular set

$$R = \bigcup_{i=1}^{n} V^*\{c_i\}V^*$$

and obtain

$$Inv_I(L) = h_2(h_1^{-1}(L) \cap R)$$

which proves the closure of $\mathcal{F}$ under inversion. □

Corollary 5 *All families in the Chomsky hierarchy are closed under duplications, transpositions and inversions.*

We now start the study of closure under iterated versions. The following lemma is a helpful tool.

Lemma 6 *Every family of languages closed under iterated inversions or iterated transpositions is closed under permutations.*

Proof. For any language $L \in V^*$ let us construct the inversion scheme $I = (V, \{ab \mid a, b \in V, a \neq b\})$ and the transposition scheme $T = (V, \{(a, \lambda, b), (a, b, \lambda) \mid a, b \in V\})$. The relations

$$Inv_I^*(L) = Tr_T^*(L) = Perm(L)$$

follow immediate. □

Theorem 7 *The family of regular languages is not closed under iterated inversions, iterated transpositions and iterated duplications.*

Proof. Since the family of regular languages is not closed under permutations, the nonclosure with respect to iterated inversions and iterated transpositions follows by Lemma 6.

In order to prove the non-closure under iterated duplications we consider the regular language L consisting of the only word $abab$ and the duplication scheme $D = (\{a, b\}, \{(ab, a, b)\})$. It is easy to see that

$$Dupl_D^*(L) = \{a^n b^n a^m b^m \mid n \geq 1, m \geq 1\}$$

which is not a regular language. □

Theorem 8 *The family of context-free languages is closed neither under iterated inversions nor under iterated transpositions.*

Proof. Because the family of context-free languages is also not closed under permutations, the statement follows by Lemma 6, again. □

It remains as an *open problem* whether or not the family of context-free languages is closed under iterated duplications.

Theorem 9 *The families of context-sensitive and recursively enumerable languages are closed under iterated inversions, iterated transpositions and iterated duplications.*

Proof. Let L be a context-sensitive language generated by the context-sensitive grammar $G = (N, T, S, P)$ and let (V, I) be an inversion scheme. We construct the context-sensitive grammar $G' = (N', T, S, P')$, where

$$\begin{aligned} N' &= N \cup \{X_a \mid a \in T\}, \\ P' &= \{X_{a_1}X_{a_2}\dots X_{a_k} \longrightarrow X_{a_k}\dots X_{a_2}X_{a_1} \mid a_1a_2\dots a_k \in I\} \\ &\quad \cup \{X_a \longrightarrow a \mid a \in T\} \\ &\quad \cup \{h(\alpha) \longrightarrow h(\beta) \mid \alpha \longrightarrow \beta \in P,\} \end{aligned}$$

and $h : (N \cup T)^* \longrightarrow N'^*$ is the homomorphism given by

$$h(A) = A \text{ for } A \in N \quad \text{and} \quad h(a) = X_a \text{ for } a \in T.$$

The equality $L(G') = Inv^*(L)$ can be easily checked.

We are going to prove that $Tr^*(L)$ is a context-sensitive language for any transposition scheme $(T, \{(x_i, y_i, z_i) \mid 1 \leq i \leq n\})$, $n \geq 1$. To this end, we construct a phrase-structure grammar $\bar{G}$ working in the following way. A string of the form X_iw, with $w \in L$ and $1 \leq i \leq n$ is firstly generated. The symbols X_i scan the string w from left to right in order to perform a transposition rule (x_i, y_i, z_i). During this process two situations may occur. In the first one, the substring x_i is identified in w, it is erased, and the substring y_iz_i is looked for further. If this substring is identified, then x_i is inserted between y_i and z_i and the current scanning symbol becomes Y.

The second situation assumes that the substring y_iz_i is firstly identified and then the substring x_i. Now the process may be iterated arbitrarily many times, afterwards the scanning symbols are erased. With the above explanations we infer that $L(\bar{G}) = Tr^*(L)$. Since the grammar $\bar{G}$ has a linear bounded working space, it follows that $Tr^*(L)$ is a context-sensitive language (see[13]).

The closure of the recursively enumerable languages class follows immediately. By a similar proof one can show the closure under iterated duplications. □

Finally we remark that in this paper the three operations inversion, transposition and duplication have been studied isolated from each other as this was done in the papers on splicing. However, if we want to model the evolution it is necessary to consider schemes which contain rules for inversion as well as for transposition, duplication, splicing and deletion. It remains to investigate operations based on such schemes. A grammatical approach in this direction is presented in[4] as well as[15].

References

1. V. Brendel, H. G. Busse, Genome Structure Described by Formal Languages, *Nucleic Acids Res.*, **12**, 2561(1984).
2. J. Collado-Vides, The Search for Grammatical Theory of Gene Regulations is Formally Justified by Showing the Inadequacy of Context-free Grammars, *CABIOS*, **7**, 321(1991).
3. N. G. Copeland et al. A Genetic Linkage Map of the Mouse: Current Applications and Future Prospects. *Science*, **262**, 57(1993).
4. J. Dassow, V. Mitrana. A Grammatical Model for Genome Evolution: Evolutionary Grammars. *Proc. GCB'96*, 1996.
5. J. Dassow, V. Mitrana. Self Cross-over Systems. Submitted, 1995.
6. D. J. McGeoch. Molecular Evolution of Large DNA Viruses of Eukaryotes. *Seminars in Virology*, **3**, 399(1992).
7. T. Head, Formal Language Theory and DNA: An Analisys of the Generative Capacity of Specific Recombinant Behaviours, *Bull. Math. Biology*, **49**, 737(1987).
8. T. Head, Gh. Păun, D. Pixton, Language Theory and Molecular Genetics, a chapter in the forthcoming *Handbook of Formal Languages* (G. Rozenberg, A. Salomaa, eds.).
9. S. Karlin, E. S. Mocarski, G. A. Schachtel. Molecular Evolution of Herpesviruses: Genomic and Protein Comparisons. *J. of Virology*, **68**, 1886(1994).
10. V. Mitrana, Crossover Systems: A Language-theoretic Approach to DNA Recombination. Submitted, 1995.
11. Gh. Păun, The Splicing as an Operation on Formal Languages, *Proc. of INBS-IEEE Conference*, Washington, 176(1995).
12. D. Pixton, Regularity of Splicing Languages, *Discrete Appl. Math.*, in press.
13. A. Salomaa, *Formal Languages*, Academic Press, New York, 1973.
14. D. Sankoff et al. Gene Order Comparisons for Phylogenetic Inference: Evolution of the Mitochondrial Genome. *Proc. Natl. Acad. Sci. USA*, **89**, 6575(1992).
15. D. B. Searls, The Computational Linguistics of Biological Sequences. In *Artificial Intelligence and Molecular Biology* (L. Hunter ed.), AAAI Press, The MIT Press, 47(1993).

THE INVERSE PROTEIN FOLDING PROBLEM: SELF CONSISTENT MEAN FIELD OPTIMISATION OF A STRUCTURE SPECIFIC MUTATION MATRIX.

M. DELARUE
Laboratoire d'Immunologie Structurale, Institut Pasteur, 25 rue du Docteur Roux, 75015 Paris, France.

P. KOEHL
UPR 9003 du CNRS, Boulevard Sebastien Brant, 67400 Illkirch Graffenstaden, France.

The goal of the inverse folding problem is to supply a list of sequences compatible with a known protein structure. If two-body interactions are taken into account in energy calculations, an exhaustive exploration of the energy landscape in sequence space cannot be achieved because of the huge number of possible combinations. To circumvent this problem, we propose a method in which multiple copies corresponding to every possible side-chain type are attached to each Cα position in the protein. The weights of each copy (stored in the sequence matrix SM) are refined using mean field theory : each side-chain copy interacts with the mean field generated by all possible side-chain copies at neighbouring positions, weighted by their respective probabilities. The potential energy is simply taken to be amino acid pair potentials of mean force. The method converges in a few cycles to a self-consistent solution. The refined matrix does not depend on the starting point; therefore the method succeeds in removing memory effects. Starting solely from the backbone of the known structure, and without information from the initial sequence, the final sequence matrix **SM** is shown to be able to retrieve significant sequence information, as observed through a series of structure-recognizes-sequence(s) computer experiments. The issue of specificity is discussed in detail.

1. Introduction

The Protein Data Bank[1] which gathers most known protein structures to date, contains a number of structures exceeding several times the number of distinct folds[2]. This has led to the hypothesis that the total number of different folds is finite, and roughly of the order of one thousand[3, 4]. Should examples of every fold be known, protein structure prediction would reduce to the inverse protein folding problem, which consists in identifying which sequences are compatible with a given fold[5]. Elaboration of this alternative view is not only theoretically interesting but is also important for protein design and engineering, as well as structure prediction.

Ponder and Richards[6] provided the first step towards this goal. They systematically tested combinations of sidechains fitting in the core of small proteins, based on steric overlaps, hydrogen bonding and packing density criteria. The number of residues included in the combinatorial search is however limited for practical computing reasons. In fact, as soon as energy calculations contain two-body interaction terms, which are indeed ubiquitous in the classical treatment of proteins then a huge combinatorial problem arises. To alleviate this problem, current methods either refine a single sequence, or limit the search to available sequence databanks (for review, see [7]). Two major approaches have been derived.

In the first one, each known protein structure is represented as a contact map containing position dependent residue-residue contact preferences; aligning a sequence using these contact maps requires a double dynamic programming algorithm[8]. This approach has been successfully applied by Jones et al[9], and is now referred to as the "threading" algorithm. Its drawback however is that it is computationally slow.

Alternatively, the protein structure information can be reduced into one dimension, yielding the so-called 3D-1D profile[10]. In this approach, a position and structure dependent scoring table is built, which contains as many rows as residues in the structure, and a column for each of the twenty amino acids. Aligning a sequence on such profiles resorts to dynamic programming methods developed for pairwise sequence comparisons[11]. In previous applications, scores were usually calculated from the residue environment in the known protein structure (the so-called frozen approximation). One possible caveat is that this is based on the hypothesis that residue environments are conserved within proteins adopting similar folds. This hypothesis has recently been questioned by Russell and Barton[12].

In this paper, we present a new strategy for profile construction based on a self consistent mean field (SCMF) optimisation protocol (for review, see [13]), which does not resort to the frozen approximation. The basic idea of our method is to attach to each Cα of the known structure multiple copies of the side-chain, corresponding to all twenty common amino acids. Each type of side-chain is given a probability, or weight, stored in a sequence matrix, **SM**. This matrix is initialised such that each amino acid type has the same probability, for all residues in the protein (i.e. the system has no memory of the native sequence). Each residue is then considered in turn : the matrix row corresponding to the residue is updated, based on the mean field generated by the multiple side-chains at neighbouring residues, and the procedure is repeated till convergence (i.e. self consistency) is reached.

One of the main results of the paper is to show that the sequence matrix **SM** refined through this procedure, based only on the coordinates of the backbone of the protein, recovers significant sequence information. The discriminatory power of **SM** this matrix is evaluated both in the sequence-recognises-structure protocol[14], in which a given sequence is threaded through an ensemble of profiles derived from known protein folds, as well as in the structure-recognises-sequence assay, in which a large number of sequences is threaded through a given profile.

2. Materials and Methods

A complete description of the self consistent mean field (SCMF) approach is described in our previous works[13, 15]. Specific problems related to optimisation in sequence space are discussed below.

2.1. *The chimeric molecule: the multiple copy representation.*

The mainchain atoms (N, Cα, C, O) of the known protein structure are fixed in all subsequent calculations. All twenty amino acids are attached to each Cα .

Let us denote as N the total number of residues in the protein. The chimeric molecule described above will be characterised by the sequence matrix **SM** of dimension Nx20, such that SM(i,j) is the probability that residue i is an amino acid of type j. **SM** is initialised such that each residue type is given the same probabiliy.

2.2. *Mean Field Theory : a tool for efficient energy minimisation.*

2.2.1. The effective energy of the chimeric molecule The multiple copies of side-chains on a given Cα do not interact with each other; they do interact however with the mean field exerted by all multiple copies of interacting neighbouring positions in the protein. The energy function that we seek to minimize is taken to be:

$$E_{eff} = \sum_{i=1}^{N} \sum_{j=1}^{20} SM(i,j) f[E(i,j)] \tag{1}$$

where:

$$E(i,j) = \sum_{\substack{k=1 \\ k \neq i}}^{N} \sum_{l=1}^{20} SM(k,l) W(\mathbf{x}_{ij}, \mathbf{x}_{kl}) \tag{2}$$

here $\mathbf{x}_{ij}$ are the coordinates of sidechain type j at position i in the sequence, W the pair potential energy function, and

$$f[E(i,j)] = E(i,j) \tag{3}$$

corresponding to the classical formulation of the effective energy function[13]; subsequent applications of equation (3) will be referred to as Method A.

We also studied an alternative form for f, which will be denoted Method B :

$$f[E(i,j)] = \frac{1}{2}\left[\frac{E(i,j) - U_{av}(j)}{U_{sig}(j)}\right]^2 \tag{4}$$

where $U_{av}(j)$ is the average energy for an amino acid of type j as observed in native proteins, and $U_{sig}(j)$ the width of the distribution of U(j) over these states. It should be noted that replacing equation (4) in equation (1) leads to an E_{eff} which does not correspond anymore to a term having the dimension of a true energy.

2.2.2. The potential energy function W. W is taken to be the amino acid pair potentials of mean force defined by Sippl[16], which are of the form:

$$W(\mathbf{x}_{ij}, \mathbf{x}_{kl}) = -RT \ln\left(\frac{f_t^{jl}(r_{ik})}{f_t(r_{ik})}\right) \tag{5}$$

where j and l correspond to the two amino acids at position i and k in the protein, respectively, t=j-i is the separation of these residues along the sequence, and r_{ik} is the spatial distance between the C_α atoms of i and k. The pair interactions are represented by several variants of potentials, depending on the separation t along the sequence. In the short range, t = 1,2,3,4,5, and 6 individual potentials are compiled for each value of t. For medium, $7 \leq t \leq 9$, and large separations, $10 \leq t$, the pair potentials are condensed to a single type of potential. A cutoff at r=20Å was imposed[17]. Potentials described by Equation (5) were shown to be adequate both for protein folding and inverse protein folding problems[18].

The required density distributions f (corrected for the problem of small dataset, as described by Sippl[16]) were compiled from a database of 83 structurally unrelated proteins (see [19] for a list), excluding all $(\beta/\alpha)_8$ folds and globin folds since triosephosphate isomerase and myoglobin will be used as the main test molecules.

U_{av} and U_{sig}, defined in equation (4) were calculated from the same database, with the restriction that in all protein energy calculations, the respective protein is substracted from the database and the potentials are recompiled (i.e. the jack-knife procedure).

2.2.3. Self-consistent mean field optimisation. Mean field theory consists in finding the minimum of the free energy with respect to all variables[20]. This leads to[13, 21]:

$$SM(i,j) = \exp\left[-\frac{V(i,j)}{RT}\right] \Big/ \sum_{k=1}^{20} \exp\left[-\frac{V(i,k)}{RT}\right] \qquad (6)$$

where

$$V(i,j) = \frac{\partial E_{eff}}{\partial SM(i,j)} \qquad (7)$$

V(i,j) can be seen as the local mean field experienced by amino acid type j at position i in the protein.

Given the initial uniform matrice **SM** and the backbone of the protein, a series of steps is taken to define new probabilities for all amino acids at all positions in the protein. First, all effective potentials are calculated based on Equations (1) and (7). The effective potentials are converted into probabilities using equation (6) and the procedure is iterated as many times as required to reach convergence (i.e. no further modification of **SM**), yielding the final self consistent sequence matrix. To avoid convergence problems such as oscillations, a "memory" was set to the system [15,22].

2.3. Evaluation of Sequence-structure fitness.

The dynamic programming algorithm provides an efficient means of determining the best arrangement of a particular sequence in a particular structure, represented by its sequence matrix. We used a straightforward adaptation of the Smith and

Waterman alignment algorithm[11]. The dynamic algorithm requires additivity and independence. Independence is inherent to the use of the mean field approximation. In order to fulfill the additivity requirement, the sequence matrix is transformed into a profile matrix **PM**:

$$PM(i,j) = \log\left[\frac{SM(i,j)}{Prand}\right] \qquad (8)$$

where Prand is the probability to observe residue type j at position i by chance (Prand is set to 0.05). If SM(i,j) is zero, SM(i,j) is reset arbitrarily to 0.01. The profile matrix was further linearly modified so that its larger and smaller elements are respectively set to 1 and -0.5. This is similar to what is done in recent works[23,24]. For the results reported here, all alignments were performed with a gap opening penalty and a gap elongation penalty of 4.5 and 0.1, respectively, in regions involved in secondary structure, and 0.45 and 0.01 otherwise (typically, a gap can be compensated by 4 or more optimal residue fits in a secondary structure). Secondary structures were defined using the program DSSP[25].

If gaps are not allowed, the score of a particular sequence on a given profile matrix **PM** of the same length is obtained directly as the sum over all positions of the scores of the amino acid type in the sequence, as read in the corresponding row of **PM**.

2.4. The database of test proteins.

108 well refined proteins were included in the database. The corresponding entries in the PDB[1] are : 451c, 156b, 8abp, 8adh, 3adk, a8atc, b8atc, a2aza, 3blm, 1bp2, 2ca2, 1cc5, 1ccr, a2ccy, 3cd4, 2cdv, 3cla, 3cna, a4cpa, 5cpa, 2cpp, 1cpv, 1crn, 2cro, e1cse, i1cse, 1ctf, 2cy3, 2cyp, 8dfr, a4dfr, a1dhf, e2er7, 12fb4, 1fd2, 1fx1, 3fxc, 4fxn, a3gap, 2gbp, 1gcr, o1gd1, 1hip, a2hla, b2hla, 1hoe, 1i1b, 3icb, 7icd, 1l01, 2lbp, 6ldh, 31lrd, a2ltn,1lz1, a4mdh, 2mhr, 2mlt, 2ovo, a2pab, 9pap, 2paz, 1pcy, a1pfk, 3pgk, 3pgm, 1phh, 5pti, 4ptp, 1rhd, 2rhe, 2rnt, 7rsa, 5rxn, 2sga, 3sgb, 1sn3, 2sns, o2sod, 2ssi, 2stv, i1tgs, 6tmn, 4tnc, a1tnf, 1ubq, 1utg, a9wga, r2wrp, b1wsy, 5 globins : 1eca, a1hhb, 1lh1, 5mba, 1mbd and 13 $(\beta/\alpha)_8$ barrels : 2aaa, 4enl, 1fba, a1fcb, 1gox, a5rub, 2mnr, a1pii, b1pii, 1tim, a1wsy, a4xia, and a2ypi.

3. Results

3.1. The sequence matrix recovers information on the native sequence of the protein.

In previous works, self consistent mean field optimisations based on Method A (i.e. equations (1) and (3)) were used for side-chain conformation prediction[15] as well as for homology modelling[26], with reasonable success. Both applications concerned optimisation in the conformational space : the sequence is known, and the conformation is changed untill a minimum is found. Direct extension of this approach to the problem of optimisation in sequence space leads however to poor results, as illustrated on figure 1 in the case of chicken triosephosphate isomerase (PDB code 1TIM; 245 residues). Calculation of the sequence matrix was carried out over 120 cycles and convergence is achieved in more than 15 cycles (figure 1A).

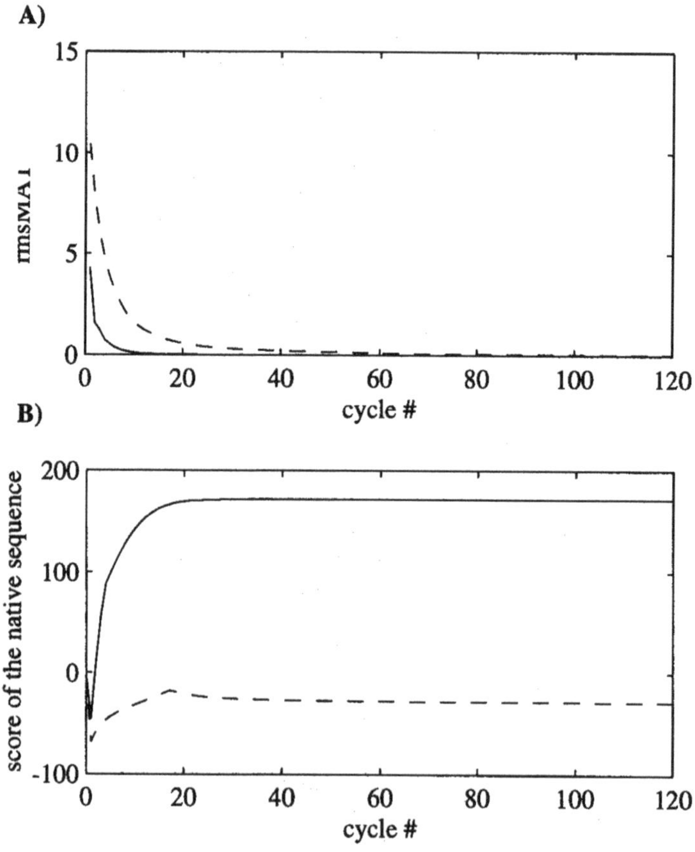

Figure 1 : Illustration of the convergence of the SCMF approach in sequence space in the case of TIM (245 residues) for method A (solid lines) and method B (dashed lines): (A) Starting with a uniform matrix, **SM** is computed iteratively using equations 1, 6 and 7; the r.m.s. difference (rmsMAT) between the successive sequence matrices **SM** are given versus the iteration or cycle number (B) At each cycle of the SCMF refinement, a profile matrix is computed from **SM** using equation (8); the score of the native sequence threaded without gap on this profile matrix is shown versus the cycle number.

The final **SM** shows no specificity towards the native sequence of TIM (figure 1B). In fact, **SM** ends up strongly biased towards sequences of unrealistic amino acid composition. In searching for a minimum of E_{eff}, the procedure selects residue types which provide the lowest contact energies; this happens to be observed for cysteine-cysteine contacts (cysteine has a probability higher than 0.9 in 62 out of the 245 rows of the converged sequence matrix), hence a drift in sequence space. This phenomenon is similar to the design of 'superstable' HP sequences for a given fold just by making all buried residues non polar and surface residues polar[27]. Preliminary experiments (unpublished results) showed that, even at constant amino acid composition, a simple Monte Carlo minimisation in sequence space is able to decrease the total potential energy proteins of known structure to a value lower than the native sequence (for details on the Monte Carlo procedure, see [27]). This means that native structures are not even local minima for the potential energy function we have used; therefore, this energy should not be minimized *per se*, but, rather, should be constrained to take values that are commonly observed for native proteins. We have consequently chosen a new form of total effective energy, based on equation (4) to take this into account. This new formulation, i.e. method B, bears similarity with a procedure adopted in applications of spin glass theory to protein folding[28], as well as in the modified Monte Carlo method of Shakhnovich et al[29, 30].

An example of the convergence of the SCMF approach based on Method B is also given in Fig. 1 in the case of TIM. Calculation were carried out over 120 cycles, but convergence is achieved in less than 20 cycles. The matrix obtained is independent of the starting point. If the initial matrix is set to reflect the initial sequence (probability of 1. for the wild type amino acid type and zero for all others), the refined matrix is identical to the one obtained with an initial random matrix (data not shown). As expected, the total energy of the system (Eq. 1) is minimised during the optimisation. An interesting feature of the specific function given in Eq. 4 is that it succeeds in gradually retrieving information concerning the native sequence (Fig. 1B). In all subsequent calculations only method B is used.

To test if the sequence information achieved through this procedure is significant, a computer experiment was performed. 10,000 random sequences obtained by shuffling the native sequence of TIM are threaded either directly (i.e. without gaps) or by dynamic programming (allowing gaps) on the profile matrix derived from the refined sequence matrix. In both cases, it is seen that the native sequence is well discriminated, with significant z-scores (calculated as (Snat-Sav)/σ, where Snat is the score of the native sequence, Sav the average score over all sequences and σ the corresponding standard deviation) of 4.66 when no gaps are considered, and 4.11 when gaps are allowed. Both values can be seen as measures of the fitness of the native sequence on the native structure. Fig. 2 summarises the z-scores (allowing gaps) obtained on the database of 108 protein structures, representing a wide range of tertiary folds (α, β, $\alpha\beta$ and $\alpha+\beta$) whose sizes vary from

26 (melittin, 2mlt) to 476 residues (α-amylase, 2aaa). The lowest z-scores are found for small proteins in which only few non local contacts are present.

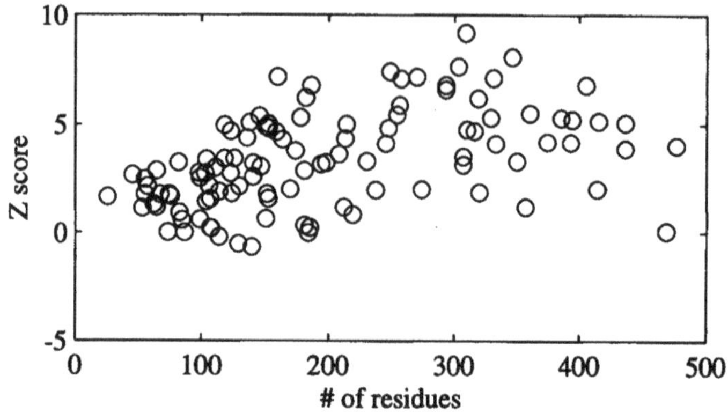

Figure 2 : Sequence profile fitness (expressed as z-scores) as a function of protein size. All z-scores are calculated with respect to an alignment allowing gaps of 5,000 shuffled sequences. Results are shown for the 108 protein structures in our database (see Materials and Methods).

3.2. Sequence-recognises-structure.

In this test, a given protein sequence is aligned to the database of 108 protein structures, one at a time, presented as SCMF profile matrices. The fitness of each sequence-structure alignment is evaluated by means of a z-score calculated from an ensemble of 1000 shuffled sequences. The native sequence scored highest for 63 out of the 87 sequences containing more than 100 residues (smaller sequences were not considered since their fitness values on their native profiles were found to be small; see Fig. 2). Of course, the ultimate practical aim of this kind of experiment is the prediction of the 3D structure of a protein, given its sequence. It is expected to work at least for homologous structures. This was observed for the globin fold, using the SCMF profile matrix (Fig. 3A). The same procedure was applied on TIM, in which case structurally related β/α barrels other than TIM sequences were not detected to a significant level (figure 3B); for a successful application of 3D-1D profile in this difficult test case, see Wilmanns and Eisenberg[31]. In order to improve our method it might be advisable not to give the same weight to all positions in the profile; the question then arises of how to identify those positions that are to be considered with a large weight.

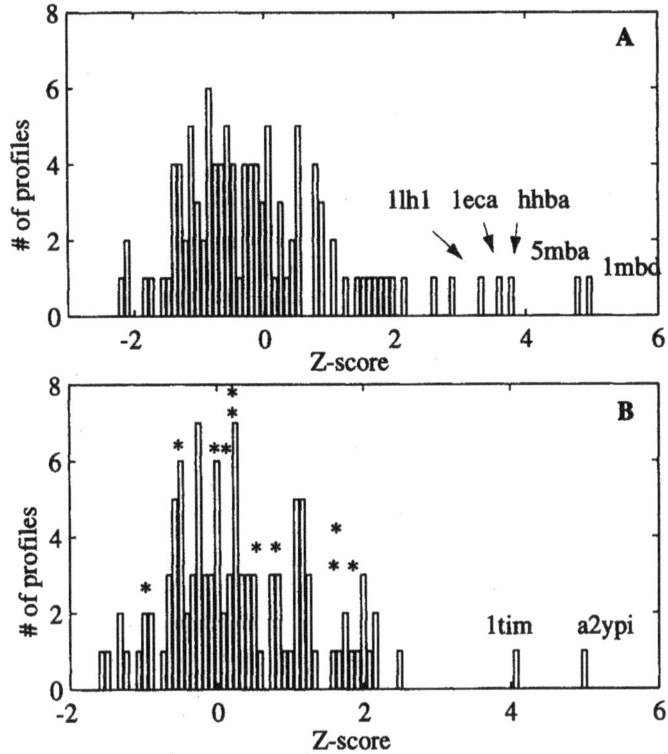

Figure 3 : A) threading histogram of the sperm whale myoglobin sequence (PDB code 1mbd, referred to as MBD) on the SCMF matrices derived from the 108 proteins in our database. All proteins with a globin fold score first. The sequence identity between MBD and A1HHB, 5MBA, 1LH1, 1ECA is 29%, 24%, 17% and 18%, respectively.
B) threading histogram for TIM on the same database of SCMF matrices. The profile matrix derived from the native structure for TIM, i.e. 1tim, scores second after 2ypia, which corresponds to a triosephosphate isomerase from yeast (the 2 proteins have 53% sequence identity). Other related α/β fold are shown as *.

4. Discussion

When searching for all sequences, or just the optimal sequence, that fit to a given protein fold, minimisation of the free energy will usually yield sequences that do not fold into unique conformations. This was observed in the HP model, in which case superstable sequences were designed with all H inside and all P at the surface of the protein[27]; these sequences are not specific in that they can fold into many native conformations; this was demonstrated for 2D lattice simulations[32, 33]. Successful sequence design requires then additional constraints. A sequence is optimal for a given fold if, in addition, it is incompatible with all other possible folds. Yue and Dill[33] have designed a series of rules to 'design out' incorrect conformations, for HP models on 2D lattice. Dill and coworkers[34] have recently proposed another promising approach for HP model. It is based on a modified energy function containing two terms, the first being designed to favour hydrophobic-hydrophobic contacts, while the second tends to avoid contacts between the solvent (not included explicitly) and hydrophobic monomers. The sequence generated by this method on a given protein structure agree reasonably well with the native sequence, and is shown to fold uniquely on a lattice model. Applications of these strategies [33, 34] to real proteins (i.e. including the 20 amino acids) have not yet been developed; this would be important because there are indications that 2 letter code proteins do not adequately describe real polypeptides[35]. The amino acid composition of a protein is known to be highly dependent on its folding class[36]; this can be imposed as one *global* constraint (see for example [37, 38]). However, even if this condition is necessary, it is certainly not sufficient[38] Another approach consists in maximising the so-called 'energy gap', defined as the difference in energy between the native state and either the best non native conformation[39], or the mean energy of all non native states[40-42]. The energy gap condition was found to be necessary and sufficient for a 27 mer model fitted on a 3x3 lattice[43]. It should be mentioned that a sequence design experiment based on this criteria was shown to fail for larger HP sequences[44], but was found successful for long lattice chains designed in 20-letter code[45-47].

We confine ourselves to the profile formalism. The major novelty of our approach is to provide a rigourous treatment of two-body interactions without having to resort to the frozen approximation. A sequence matrix **SM** is calculated from the backbone only of the protein of interest using a self consistent mean field minimisation of the difference in energy of each residue with average energies found in native structures. The sequence matrix designed here recovers sequence information, yielding a significant sequence-structure fitness value (Fig. 2). It was also found to recognize structurally related proteins with low sequence identity, in cases in which the fold is well preserved, such as the globin fold (Fig. 3A). This success however was not found to be general (Fig. 3B). Limitations of **SM** may be related to the constraint of using a too precise structural template and/or to insufficently discriminative potentials. The profile formalism itself may be questioned: it is based on the independence of each position in the protein, which are then given the same weights. Positions however are not truly equivalent, depending on the presence of secondary structure elements.

The procedure described here is based on pair potentials of mean force derived from known protein structures[16]. Similar potentials have already successfully been used for protein sequence design[37], with a different cutoff. Words of caution are however in order here. Statistical residue-residue pair potentials derived from preferences observed in the Protein Data Base (potentials of mean force) are by no means equal to the true two body interaction potentials; therefore, their use should always be considered with caution[48]. Improvements including different potential energies as well as optimisation of these potentials are currently being investigated.

5. Acknowledgements

We are grateful to H. Orland, T. Garel, B. Reva, A. Finkelstein and A. Godzik for fruitful discussions. Also, thanks are due to A. Godzik for communicating manuscripts prior to publication. We also acknowledge encouragement and support of D. Moras and J.F. Lefèvre, in whose laboratories part of this work was done.

6. References

1. Bernstein, FC, Koetzle, TF, Williams, G, Meyer, DJ, Brice, MD, Rodgers, JR, Kennard, O, Shimanouchi, T & Tasumi, M (1977). J. Mol. Biol. 112:535-542.
2. Orengo, CA, Flores, TP, Jones, DT, Taylor, WR & Thornton, JM (1993). Current Biology 3:131-139.
3. Orengo, CA, Jones, DT & Thornton, JM (1994). Nature (London) 372:631-634.
4. Chothia, C (1992). Nature (London) 357:543.
5. Drexler, KE (1981). Proc. Natl. Acad. Sci. (USA) 78:5275-5278.
6. Ponder, JW & Richards, FM (1987). J. Mol. Biol. 193:775-791.
7. Bowie, JU & Eisenberg, D (1993). Curr. Opin. Struct. Biol. 3:437-444.
8. Taylor, WR & Orengo, CA (1989). J. Mol. Biol. 208:1-22.
9. Jones, DT, Taylor, WR & Thornton, JM (1992). Nature (London) 358:86-89.
10. Bowie, JU; Lüthy, R & Eisenberg, D (1991). Science 253:164-170.
11. Smith, TF & Waterman, MS (1981). J. Mol. Biol. 147:195-197.
12. Russel, RB & Barton, GJ (1994). J. Mol. Biol. 244:332-350.
13. Koehl, P & Delarue, M (1996). Curr. Opinion Struct. Biol. 6:222-226.
14. Hendlich, M, Lackner, P, Weitckus, S, Floeckner, H, Froschauer, R, Gottsbacher, K, Casari, G & Sippl, MJ (1990). J. Mol. Biol. 216:167-180.
15. Koehl, P & Delarue, M (1994). J. Mol. Biol. 239:249-275.
16. Sippl, MJ (1990). J. Mol. Biol. 1990:859-883.
17. Sippl, MJ & Jaritz, M (1994). In *Predictive power of mean force pair potentials*. Edited by H. Bohr and S. Brunak. IOS Press, Amsterdam. 113-134.
18. Rooman, MJ & Wodak, SJ (1995). Prot. Eng. 8:849-858.
19. Koehl, P & Delarue, M (1994). Proteins: Struct. Funct. Genet. 20:264-278.
20. Kubo, R (1965). *Statistical Physics*. North Holland Publishing Co, Amsterdam.
21. Rabow, AA & Scheraga, HA (1993). J. Mol. Biol. 232:1157-1168.
22. Finkelstein, AV & Reva, BA (1991). Nature (London) 351:497-499.

23. Ouzounis, C, Sander, C, Sharf, M & Schneider, R (1993). J. Mol. Biol. 232:805-825.
24. Abagyan, R, Frishman, D & Argos, P (1994). Proteins: Struct. Funct. Genet. 19:132-140.
25. Kabsch, W & Sander, C (1983). Biopolymers 22:2577-2637.
26. Koehl, P & Delarue, M (1995). Nature Struct. Biol. 2:163-170.
27. Shakhnovich, EI & Gutin, AM (1993). Protein Eng. 6:793-800.
28. Goldstein, RA, Luthey-Schulten, ZA & Wolynes, PG (1992). Proc. Natl. Acad. Sci. (USA) 89:4918-4922.
29. Abkevich, V, Gutin, A & Shakhnovich, EI (1995). J. Mol. Biol. 252:460-471.
30. Mirny, L, Abkevich, V & Shakhnovich, EI (1996). Folding & Design 1:103-116.
31. Wilmanns, M & Eisenberg, D (1993). Proc. Natl. Acad. Sci. (USA) 90:1379-1383.
32. Chan, HS & Dill, KA (1991). J. Chem. Phys. 95:3775-3787.
33. Yue, K & Dill, KA (1992). Proc. Natl. Acad. Sci. (USA) 89:4163-4167.
34. Sun, S, Brem, R, Chan, HS & Dill, KA (1995). Prot. Eng. 8:1205-1213.
35. Onuchic, JN, Wolynes, PG, Luthey-Schulten, Z & Socci, ND (1995). Proc. Natl. Acad. Sci. (USA) 92:3626-3630.
36. Nakashima, H, Nishikawa, K & Ooi, T (1986). J. Biochem. 99:153-162.
37. Jones, DT (1994). Prot. Sci. 3:567-574.
38. Hinds, DA & Levitt, M (1996). J. Mol. Biol. 258:201-209.
39. Shakhnovich, EI & Gutin, AM (1990). Nature (London) 346:773-775.
40. Finkelstein, AV & Reva, BA (1992). Prot. Eng. 7:617-624.
41. Godzik, A (1995). Prot. Eng. 8:409-416.
42. Deutsch, JM & Kurosky, T (1996). Phys. Rev. Lett. 76:323-326.
43. Sali, A, Shakhnovich, EI & Karplus, M (1994). J. Mol. Biol. 235:1614-1636.
44. Yue, K, Fiebig, KM, Thomas, PD, Chan, HS & Shakhnovich, EI (1995). Proc. Natl. Acad. Sci. (USA) 92:325-329.
45. Shakhnovich, EI (1994). Phys. Rev. Lett. 72:3907-3910.
46. Abkevich, V, Gutin, AM & Shakhnovich, EI (1995). Prot. Sci. 4:1167-1177.
47. Shakhnovich, EI, Abkevich, V & Ptitsyn, O (1996). Nature (London) 379:96-98.
48. Thomas, PD & Dill, KA (1996). J. Mol. Biol. 257:457-469.

7. Appendix

7.1 Method A : the total effective energy of the chimeric molecule is given by :

$$E_{eff} = \sum_{i=1}^{N} \sum_{j=1}^{20} SM(i,j)E(i,j) \qquad \text{(A.1)}$$

where E(i,j) is defined by equation (2).

The local mean field exerted on amino acid type b for residue a is (see equation 7) :

$$V(a,b) = \frac{\partial E_{eff}}{\partial SM(a,b)} = 2E(a,b) \qquad \text{(A.2)}$$

7.2 Method B : the effective energy of the chimeric molecule is defined as :

$$E_{eff} = \sum_{i=1}^{N} \sum_{j=1}^{20} SM(i,j) \left(\frac{E(i,j) - U_{av}(j)}{U_{sig}(j)} \right)^2 \qquad \text{(A.3)}$$

in which case :

$$V(a,b) = \left(\frac{E(a,b) - U_{av}(b)}{U_{sig}(b)} \right)^2 + 2 \sum_{\substack{i=1 \\ i \neq a}}^{N} \sum_{j=1}^{20} SM(i,j) \frac{W(x_{ab}, x_{ij})}{U_{sig}(j)} \frac{E(i,j) - U_{av}(j)}{U_{sig}(j)} \qquad \text{(A.4)}$$

THEORETICAL AND ALGORITHMICAL OPTIMIZATION OF THE DEAD-END ELIMINATION THEOREM

J. DESMET
Interdisciplinary Research Center, K.U.Leuven Campus Kortrijk, B-8500 Kortrijk, Belgium

M. DE MAEYER, I. LASTERS
Center for Transgene Technology and Gene Therapy, Flanders Interuniversity Institute for Biotechnology, K.U.Leuven Campus Gasthuisberg O&N, B-3000 Leuven, Belgium

The dead-end elimination theorem has proved to be a powerful method to reduce the theoretically accessible conformational space when modeling protein side chains by using a rotameric representation of possible conformations. In this work, theoretical details about variants to the original criterion are discussed. We also provide information on how the equations can be algorithmically implemented in such a way that both computational performance and structural accuracy are optimized. In addition, we discuss the theoretical and practical aspects of three new methods called the "bottom line theorem", dead-end elimination assisted by local modeling and a combinatorial search combined with conventional dead-end elimination. It is shown that the algorithm in its current form enables the determination of the global minimum energy side chain conformation of large proteins on a time scale of hours while for small proteins of up to 30 residues the calculations are done on a time scale of seconds. The latter opens a way to combine a main chain sampling algorithm with the dead-end elimination method to locally model entire fragments of a protein chain.

1. Introduction

Today many useful methods for side chain modeling have been published (reviewed in ref. 1). The remarkable interest in this sub-domain of protein folding arises from the fact that in many cases a fairly accurate three-dimensional structure for a protein main chain is available for the protein of interest. To a first approximation, the backbone structure can then be kept fixed when it comes to finding the optimal conformation of one or more side chains. Examples of this kind of applications range from the simple design of point mutations to the simultaneous positioning of large sets of side chains as in the case of homology modeling.

As a simple rule of thumb one can state that the root-mean-square (r.m.s.) deviation for the main chain coordinates is usually less than 1 Å if two proteins are more than 50% identical in sequence[2]. In such cases fairly accurate predictions are possible and various studies have reported scores ranging from 60 to 90% correctly predicted side chain conformations[3-7]. We believe that these scores can be further improved in different ways. While the modeling of solvent exposed side chains would certainly benefit from a more accurate solvent representation, buried side chains apparently require more scrupulous search techniques which can at the same time avoid very strong repulsive forces and identify the optimal pattern of very weak interactions. Because of the dense packing and the entanglement of core residues side chain modeling is fundamentally a combinatorial problem. In addition, and for the same reason, a very detailed representation of the conformational freedom of the individual side chains is necessary. While these two aspects make the side chain problem far from trivial, it is also true that the local main chain fold is an important (but not the only) determinant for the side chain conformations[8].

With respect to these considerations the dead-end elimination (DEE) method[9-12] provides a suitable solution to the side chain modeling problem. It operates by systematically eliminating side chain rotamers which are incompatible with the global minimum energy conformation (GMEC). Rotamer elimination occurs on basis of energetic criteria which balance rotamers against each other by comparing their main chain interactions and a lower or higher limit for their interactions with other side chains. In this work we describe three previously unpublished modifications to the original algorithm[9] which facilitate the final determination of the GMEC. We discuss both the theoretical and practical aspects of the various criteria and illustrate their effectiveness and performance by three proteins of very different size.

2. Theoretical considerations

2.1 Preliminary Remarks

In general, side chain modeling is a problem of global optimization. The premise is that by minimizing a given cost function (usually but not necessarily a potential energy function) one will arrive at the most probable side chain arrangement. Here we will not further discuss the validity of the previous assumption, nor do we want to discuss the various possible cost functions. In stead we will assume that the premise is correct and focus on the computational *feasibility* of the minimization problem by a specific approach called the dead-end elimination (DEE) method.

Prior to going into some mathematical aspects we want to emphasize that the DEE-method can be very helpful in reducing the complexity of the minimization problem but *does not guarantee* that, in a practical situation, the global minimum energy conformation (GMEC) can be determined. Since the DEE-method works by systematically eliminating side chain conformations which satisfy a given mathematical expression (the DEE-criterion), convergence to the GMEC is achieved only if, for all residues considered, all but one conformations can be eliminated. Alternatively, if the DEE-method fails to reach a unique structure by itself, an additional step is required like, for instance, a brute force combinatorial search or a clustering approach on the remaining conformations[9]. We have found that the original theorem in combination with different variants and a final DEE-assisted combinatorial search procedure does allow GMEC-determination for all globular proteins studied until now. The different DEE-criteria are hereafter discussed.

2.2 The Original Dead-end Elimination Theorem

The necessary and sufficient conditions for the DEE-theorem to be applicable to a given problem are the following.

1) The quality of a solution to the problem must be assessable by a particular cost function C which is a function of a set of different, independent variables x_1, x_2, ..., x_i, ..., x_N, where N is the total number of variables defining the system. The minimum of the cost function must provide the optimal solution.

2) It must be possible to write the cost function as a sum of terms c which are themselves function of maximally two variables.

In its most general form, the original DEE-theorem states that *a particular value for the ith variable x_i cannot be consistent with the globally optimal solution if another value for the same variable, x_i', can be found so that*

$$c(x_i)+\sum_{j=1}^{N}\min c(x_i,x_j) > c(x'_i)+\sum_{j=1}^{N}\max c(x'_i,x_j)\,;\, j\neq i \tag{1}$$

This theorem can be proved by analogy to the proof given earlier for the DEE-theorem applied to protein side chains[9]. For a system of protein side chains, attached to a fixed template structure (i.e. all atoms which do not move by rotating around the side chain dihedrals), the above-mentioned conditions are indeed fulfilled. The total potential energy, E_{total}, can be written as a sum of (i) a constant term, $E_{template}$, which is the template self-energy, (ii) terms which are a function of only one variable, $E(r_i)$, being the self-energy of the ith side chain in conformation r_i plus its interaction with the template – this sum is also called the *inherent* energy of a rotamer – and (iii) the terms indicating the non-bonded interaction between two side chains i and j in their respective conformations r_i and r_j, $E(r_i,r_j)$:

$$E_{total} = E_{template} + \sum_{i=1}^{N} E(r_i) + \sum_{i=1}^{N-1}\sum_{j=i+1}^{N} E(r_i,r_j) \tag{2}$$

N is the number of rotatable side chains. Side chains which are kept fixed can simply be included in the template so that modeling can potentially be performed on part of the protein. The side chain conformations, symbolized by the variables r_i, denote a particular combination of dihedral angles for side chain i. The side chain conformations can either be continuous or discrete. In the latter case the variables r_i are indices on a list of theoretically possible conformations as stored in a rotamer library.

Using the same notations as in Eq. 2, the DEE-criterion can be written as

$$E(r_i)+\sum_{j=1}^{N}\min E(r_i,r_j) > E(r'_i)+\sum_{j=1}^{N}\max E(r'_i,r_j)\,;\, j\neq i \tag{3}$$

The min and max functions, which operate on the pairwise non-bonded interaction energies, yield, for each residue j, the conformation which interacts in the most favorable way with r_i (or in the most unfavorable way with r_i'). The left hand side of Eq. 3 can therefore be simply interpreted as "the inherent energy of side chain conformation r_i plus the best possible interaction with the other side chains". The right hand side represents "the inherent plus the worst possible interaction energy for any other conformation r_i' of the same side chain i".

According to the DEE-theorem, any side chain conformation r_i which satisfies Eq. 3 cannot be part of the global minimum. Although the DEE-criterion is valid for continuous modeling, from a practical point of view it is much more convenient to work with discrete rotamers. Then, in a search for the GMEC, rotamers satisfying Eq. 3 can safely be discarded from further consideration thereby reducing the accessible conformational space. This, in turn, may lead to gradually higher values for the left hand side or, especially in a densely packed protein system, to lower values for the right hand side when Eq. 3 is iteratively applied to all remaining rotamers. For all systems tested so far we have observed that the ***logarithm*** of the conformational space decreases in a pseudo-exponential fashion as a function of the number of iteration cycles until it settles at a value which is usually below one half of the starting value (see also ref. 9, 12).

2.3 The DEE-criterion for Rotamer Pairs

Since the original DEE-criterion alone is usually not powerful enough to determine the GMEC, the help of additional elimination criteria is required. Fortunately, the conditions in paragraph 2.1 leave room for some creativity in formulating alternative versions of the original DEE-criterion. For instance, it is possible to group multiple side chains into so-called "super-rotamers" the conformations of which are simply all possible combinations of the individual side chains rotamers. The inherent energy of a super-rotamer R_I covering a collection of n individual rotamers $\{r_1, r_2, .., r_n\}$, $\mathcal{E}(R_I)$, can be expressed as

$$\mathcal{E}(R_I) = \sum_{i=1}^{n} E(r_i) + \sum_{i=1}^{n-1} \sum_{j=i+1}^{n} E(r_i, r_j) \tag{4}$$

while the interaction of R_I with other single rotamers, $\mathcal{E}(R_I, r_j)$ equals

$$\mathcal{E}(R_I, r_j) = \sum_{i=1}^{n} E(r_i, r_j)\,;\; i \neq j \tag{5}$$

Conversion of the DEE-criterion for single rotamers to super-rotamers is readily achieved by substituting the terms $E(r_i)$ and $E(r_i, r_j)$ in Eq. 3 for their super-rotamer counterparts:

$$\mathcal{E}(R_I) + \sum_{j=1}^{N} \min \mathcal{E}(R_I, r_j) > \mathcal{E}(R'_I) + \sum_{j=1}^{N} \max \mathcal{E}(R'_I, r_j)\,;\; j \notin I \tag{6}$$

In view of the combinatorial nature of super-rotamers, working with super-rotamers consisting of more than two single rotamers is practically prohibited in the early stages of dead-end elimination and therefore Eq. 6 is applied only to pairs. Also, a dead-ending pair means that the *combination* of two rotamers is incompatible with the GMEC while it is very well possible that one of both is a GMEC-rotamer. Therefore, great care must be taken when using this information in trying to identify additional dead-ending rotamers by Eq. 3. We have proved earlier[10] that ignoring dead-ending pairs is only permitted for the left hand side of Eq. 3.

2.4 The Goldstein Criteria.

Recently, Goldstein[11] has discovered an elimination criterion which is much more effective than Eq. 3. This criterion guarantees that r_i is dead-ending if

$$E(r_i) - E(r'_i) + \sum_{j=1}^{N} \min\left[E(r_i, r_j) - E(r'_i, r_j)\right] > 0 ; j \neq i \tag{7}$$

The main difference between Eq. 3 and 7 is that the latter considers the *same* conformation for the *j*-residues when balancing rotamer r_i against r'_i while our criterion (3) allows independent minimization and maximization of the interactions with r_i and r'_i, respectively. As a consequence, our method is "overly restrictive" and therefore less effective. On the other hand, criterion 7 is computationally slower than criterion 3 and this may cancel out its greater effectiveness when applying it to rotamer pairs (see ref. 12 and section 3.3).

Another more effective (but computationally slower) elimination criterion has been put forward by Goldstein[11] and proved and optimized later[12], where all T available rotamers for the *i*-residue, $r_i^1, r_i^2, ..., r_i^t, ..., r_i^T$ are given normalized weight coefficients C_t

$$E(r_i) - \sum_{t=1}^{T} C_t E(r_i^t) + \sum_{j=1}^{N} \min\left[E(r_i, r_j) - \sum_{t=1}^{T} C_t E(r_i^t, r_j)\right] > 0 ; j \neq i \tag{8}$$

This criterion essentially means that, when evaluating r_i, the inherent and the interaction energies of all possible rotamers r'_i may be allowed to contribute for only a fraction of their total value. Therefore, the determination of an optimal set of coefficients C_t is required for each rotamer r_i, which can be done by linear programming[12]. In other words, while criterion 7 involves a search for just one rotamer r'_i satisfying the inequality, it is also permitted to consider all r'_i together, each of them to a certain extent.

The most surprising aspect of criterion 8 is that the bottom line in searching for dead-ending rotamers was not yet reached by Eq. 7. Given the validity of criterion 8 and its greater effectiveness compared to Eq. 7, one may wonder whether even more effective criteria can be formulated. For this purpose, we have to go back to the fundamental background of dead-end elimination.

2.5 The "Bottom Line" Criterion

On basis of simple logic grounds a given rotamer r_i cannot be part of the optimal solution (the GMEC) *if, for whatever conformation of the non-i residues, another rotamer r_i' exists such that switching from r_i to r_i' always results in a better solution.* Indeed, such rotamers always face a possible downhill movement while for GMEC-rotamers there is at least one conformation for the non-*i* residues for which a downhill switch is impossible, namely the GMEC itself. This is illustrated in Fig. 1 displaying hypothetical inherent-plus-interaction energy profiles of the rotamer under study r_i and two alternatives r_i' and r_i'' as a function of the conformational space of non-*i* residues. This (N-1)-dimensional hyper-space can be conveniently notated as $\{R_J\}$, the set of possible rotamers for the super-residue *J* not comprising *i*. In view of its combinatorial nature, $\{R_J\}$ can be extremely large (>10^{100} individual super-rotamers). The bottom line DEE-criterion therefore faces a serious practical problem: while for the previous criteria it was possible to minimize the interactions with the *j*-residues on a one per one basis, the bottom line criterion requires minimization *over all possible values of R_J*. Until now, no optimal solution to this problem has been found although a partial solution is presented in section 3.4.

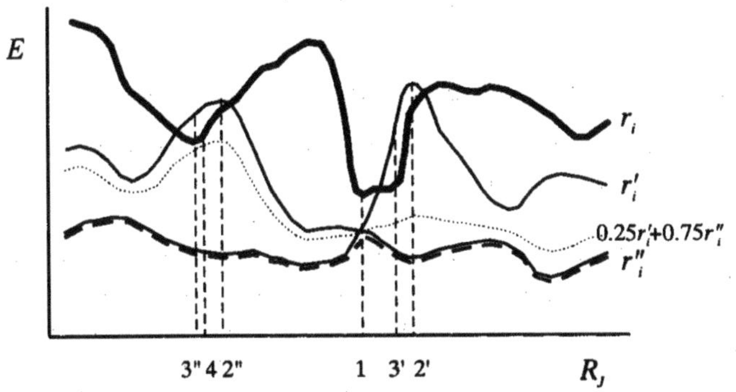

Figure 1: Illustration of dead-end elimination by the different DEE-criteria. The residue under study has three rotamers, r_i, r_i' and r_i''. Their inherent-plus-interaction energy with the rest of the protein (*E*) is expressed as a function of the conformational space of the system. The latter is described using the "super-rotamer terminology", where all non-*i* residues are combined into one super-residue *J* possessing a set of super-rotamers R_J. According to the original DEE-criterion (Eq. 3) r_i cannot be declared dead-ending on basis of r_i' since the minimum of the r_i profile (point 1) is *not* higher than the maximum of the r_i' curve (point 2'). The same is true for r_i relative to r_i''(compare 1 and 2"). The Goldstein criterion (Eq. 7) also fails to identify r_i as dead-ending because the minimal difference between the curves for r_i and another rotamer is *negative*, both for r_i' and r_i''(points 3' and 3", respectively). The generalized Goldstein criterion (Eq. 8) does allow to identify r_i as dead-ending since a linear combination of curves exists (dotted line) which falls below the entire r_i curve: the minimal difference (point 4) is *positive*. However, if the dotted curve were slightly higher, elimination by Eq. 8 would also be impossible. Yet, the conditions of the bottom line DEE-theorem would be fulfilled: for each point on the r_i curve a lower point on another curve exists. The bottom line curve (dashed line) represents the rotamer to which residue *i* would spontaneously switch if the surrounding side chains would adopt a particular conformation R_J. Since for the entire R_J space a favorable switch is possible, r_i can be identified as dead-ending.

3. Algorithmical implementation and results[a]

3.1 Initializations

The DEE-algorithm has been incorporated in the BRUGEL modeling package[13]. Our potential energy function is based on the CHARMM force field parameters[14]. Other groups have also successfully applied the DEE-method using three other force fields[11,15,16]. Usually, all atoms are included in the energy calculations but a united-atom representation is optional.

The program starts by reading in the starting structure of a protein (usually a PDB-structure[17]), the rotamer library and the list of rotatable residues. In this work, all rotatable side chains, including solvent exposed ones, have been modeled. Next, the side chains are given standard bond angles and lengths. Then, each side chain is assigned a number of rotamers according to its residue type and its description in the rotamer library. Our library currently contains 859 elements describing the theoretically possible conformations of the 17 non-Gly/Ala/Pro residue types (De Maeyer *et al.*, submitted). Finally, for all rotatable side chains all possible conformations are generated and their coordinates are stored to avoid the repeated application of rotation matrices when calculating the interaction energies.

3.2 Elimination of Template and Side-chain incompatible Rotamers

Two types of energies are required, being the inherent energy, $E(r_i)$, which is itself the sum of a rotamer self-energy and its interaction with the template, and the pairwise interaction energy between two rotamers, $E(r_i,r_j)$. After having calculated the values for $E(r_i)$ all rotamers for which $E(r_i)$ > 30 kcal mol^{-1} are removed. We have recently found that a relative cutoff of only 12 kcal mol^{-1} is also safe when using our detailed library (rotamers for which $E(r_i)$–$E(\text{lowest}_i)$ > 12 kcal mol^{-1} are also removed). By these eliminations, the original number of rotamers can be reduced by about 50-70% on average (De Maeyer *et al.*, submitted). For the remaining set of rotamers the pairwise energies, $E(r_i,r_j)$, are then calculated and stored. Rotamers which are incompatible with all side chain rotamers of an adjacent residue (min $E(r_i,r_j)$ > 30 kcal mol^{-1} for a particular *j*-residue) are eliminated as well.

3.3 Dead-end Elimination Routines

In the theoretical section we have discussed a number of possible DEE-criteria which varied from "computationally fast but moderately effective" to "computationally slow but very effective". At different stages of dead-end elimination the

---

[a] The routines described in sections 3.1-3.6 are performed consecutively so that this chapter actually describes the complete DEE-algorithm in its current state.

effectiveness and speed of the various criteria have different offsets. For instance, applying the most effective but very slow criterion 8 at the beginning of the DEE-calculations may well cause a huge number of eliminations but at a terribly high computational cost. Conversely, applying Eq. 3 after Eq. 7 is almost instantaneous but never leads to further elimination. Certainly the testing of rotamer pairs has to be done with great care since the number of possible pairs changes quadratically with the number or residues. More important however, is the need to search for each pair $[r_i,r_{i'}]$ the optimal "switch-pair" $[r'_i,r'_{i'}]$ over all rotamer combinations of side chains i and i'. When using the Goldstein criterion for pairs (Eq. 7, where $E(r_i)$ is substituted by $\mathcal{E}([r_i,r_{i'}])$ and $E(r_i,r_j)$ by $\mathcal{E}([r_i,r_{i'}],r_j)$), this requires eight nested search loops: two for all possible residue pairs $[i,i']$, two for their rotamers $[r_i,r_{i'}]$, two to find the best switch-pair $[r'_i,r'_{i'}]$, one over all j-residues and one over their rotamers r_j.[12]

The fine tuning of the program flow has been subject of extensive testing, the results of which have been published earlier[12]. In summary, first the Goldstein criterion (Eq. 7) is applied iteratively to single rotamers until no dead-ending rotamers can be found. Then the Goldstein criterion with optimized coefficients (Eq. 8) is used in the same way. Next, dead-ending rotamer pairs are exhaustively searched using the original DEE-criterion for pairs (Eq. 6). This is followed by cycling back to the previous two stages. Only when no more dead-ending pairs can be identified using Eq. 6, the much slower Goldstein criterion for pairs is used. All previous steps are applied until exhaustion. By this procedure, even for the largest protein tested (6FAB) the conformational space can be reduced to less than one fourth of the logarithm of the original number of possible conformations[12].

3.4 *"Divide and Conquer" (DAC) Strategy*

In spite of the effectiveness of the previous routines, the remaining conformational space is often too large to be sampled by brute force combinatorial techniques. Therefore, additional strategies had to be developed, to further reduce the number of rotamers. We had the idea to divide the set of rotatable side chains into two subsets A and B; the rotamers in set A are (combinatorially) unified into super-rotamers R_A while those in set B are left single. All super-rotamers R_A are then temporarily fixed (transferred to the template) and each time all rotamers of set B are submitted to a DEE-test on basis of Eq. 7. For each R_A-fixation a separate list of dead-ending rotamers is created (see Fig. 2). It can be proved that rotamers which are dead-ending for all temporary R_A-fixations are truely dead-ending.

These manipulations are algorithmically straightforward. The set of super-rotamers $\{R_A\}$ can be created by making a list of all rotamer combinations of single side chains of $\{A\}$. The fixation of each R_A involves the temporary correction of the inherent energies $E(r_i)$ of the single rotamers belonging to set B by the equation

$$E(r_i^{corr}) = E(r_i) + \mathcal{E}(R_A, r_i)\,;\; i \in \{B\} \tag{9}$$

where $\varepsilon(R_A, r_i)$ is defined by Eq. 5. The next step is the screening for dead-ending rotamers r_i by iterative application of Eq. 7 (using the corrected energy values) and the storage of such rotamers in a list. After having fixed all super-rotamers R_A the intersection of all lists yields the dead-ending rotamers which can be eliminated. In view of the combinatorial nature of super-rotamers, this procedure is practically limited to super-residues consisting of only one or two residues.

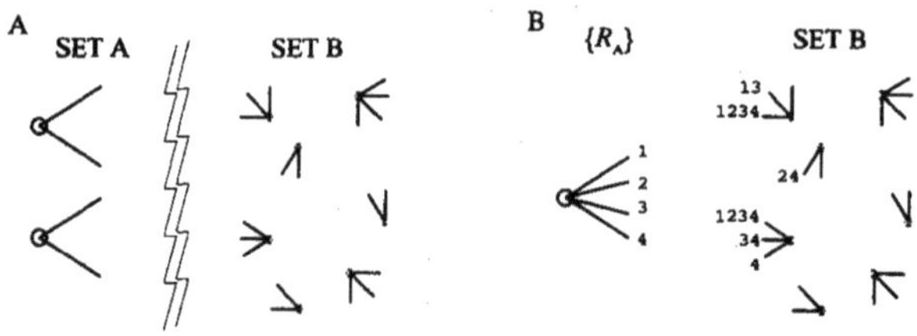

Figure 2: The "divide and conquer" strategy. Rotamers are represented by straight lines. In Fig. 2A the side chains are divided into two sets. Set A contains two side chains, each having two rotamers. In Fig. 2B these rotamers are combined into four super-rotamers, labeled 1 to 4. The temporary fixation of each of them leads to dead-ending rotamers in set B (as labeled accordingly). Rotamers in set B which are dead-ending upon fixation of all super-rotamers R_A (labeled 1234) are truely dead-ending.

The DAC-strategy can be interpreted as a partial solution to the bottom-line DEE-concept. Indeed, according to the bottom-line theorem, a rotamer r_i is dead-ending if a favorable switch-rotamer r_i' can be identified for each conformation of the non-*i* residues. The switch-rotamer r_i' does not need to be the same for each conformation. By systematically sampling part of the conformational space (using super-rotamers) the r_i rotamers may switch each time to a *different* r_i' and remain dead-ending. In the limit, when the A-set would contain all but one of the side chains, the exact bottom-line method would be used. Unfortunately, this is computationally prohibitive, but the DAC-strategy provides a valuable compromise.

The effectiveness of the DAC-approach (and other routines) is illustrated in Fig. 3 on basis of three proteins of different size: pea lectin (2LTN, chains a and b, 189 rotatable residues), wheat germ agglutinin (9WGA, 82 rotatables) and crambin (1CRN, 26 rotatables). The latter protein was selected to monitor the calculation speed for very small or partial proteins. After the initial elimination of template and side chain incompatible rotamers (section 3.2), the convential DEE-routines (section 3.3) managed to further reduce the number of rotamers by 66% (lectin), 77% (agglutinin) and 91% (crambin). With these rotamers, still 10^{94}, 10^{38} and 10^{4} global conformations were possible for the three proteins, respectively. However, in the former two cases, the DAC-routine could further bring these numbers down by about ten orders of magnitude to 10^{82} and 10^{30}, respectively. In the case of crambin, which was already much closer to a unique solution, there were still 216 global conformations possible. The DAC-calculations were extremely fast for crambin (0.2 CPU-sec), fast for agglutinin (35 CPU-min) but slow for lectin (13 CPU-hours).

3.5 Dead-end Elimination Assisted by Local Modeling

We have developed another approach which bears some resemblance to the local-modeling method of Wilson *et al.*[4] We also define local sites of adjacent side-chains (in fact, each residue is selected in turn as the center of a site), determine the lowest energy conformation for each site and keep only the conformation of the central side chain. Likewise, we repeat these actions several times for all side chains, until convergence. However, a major difference is that we determine the lowest energy conformation by applying all afore-mentioned DEE-methods while Wilson *et al.* use combinatorial enumeration. For this reason we can aford to have much larger sites containing, on average, 11 residues in stead of 5 (ref. 4). Another important difference is the fact that we do not just keep the calculated conformations of the central residues but use them as *estimates* of the GMEC-rotamers. These estimates, denoted as g_i, are then utilized in a modified version of the original DEE-criterion (Eq. 3) to which *all* rotamers r_i are submitted:

$$E(r_i)+\sum_{j=1}^{N}\min E(r_i,r_j) > E(r'_i)+\sum_{j=1}^{N} E(r'_i,g_j)\,;\, j\neq i \tag{10}$$

Note that in comparison with Eq. 3 the max-terms have been replaced by the pairwise interactions with the estimated GMEC-rotamers. It is easy to prove the validity of criterion 10, on condition that the g_i rotamers are the true GMEC-rotamers. If this is not the case, then criterion 10 can theoretically lead to erroneous eliminations, although this is in practice very unlikely in view of the min-terms which act as a "safety factor". Also, *a posteriori* comparison of the final results with the conformations resulting from local modeling has never shown any differences until now (which in fact means that local modeling alone is secure enough).

Dead-end elimination on basis of criterion 10 and local modeling has proved to be extremely effective. The number of excess rotamers could be reduced from 590 to 36 (i.e. 10^{10} possible combinations) for lectin, from 224 to 0 (i.e. a unique solution) for agglutinin and from 10 to 7 (72 combinations) for crambin (see Fig. 3). For lectin this was achieved after 5.7 CPU-hours while for agglutinin and crambin the calculation was considerably faster (4.7 CPU-min and 0.4 CPU-sec, respectively).

3.6 Combinatorial Build-up, assisted by Dead-end Elimination

The final routine of the DEE-algorithm is a combinatorial build-up procedure, assisted by dead-end elimination on basis of Eq. 7. This routine is very similar to the DAC-routine described in section 3.4 but the branches of the combinatorial tree are explored "in depth" whereas for the DAC-routine the combinations are made "in width". Each node of the combinatorial tree represents a particular rotamer combination of a sub-set of the remaining rotatable side chains and can also be envisaged as a super-rotamer. At each node all non-combined single rotamers are screened for dead-end cases following the method described in section 3.4. If this does not lead to a unique solution the node is further branched by adding one side chain to the central, growing super-residue. Side chains having the lowest number of rotamers and the highest possible interaction are combined first. The exploration of the complete tree is conveniently done by calling the routine in a recursive way.

Lectin, having still 26 rotatable residues for which 10^{10} global conformations are possible before entering this routine, was the only challenging case. Yet, after only 2 CPU-sec the GMEC was found. This was mainly due to the fact that the deepest level of combination corresponded to a super-rotamer consisting of only 4 single rotamers; at each of these branches the 24 other side chains "immediately" found their optimal solution by application of the DEE-method.

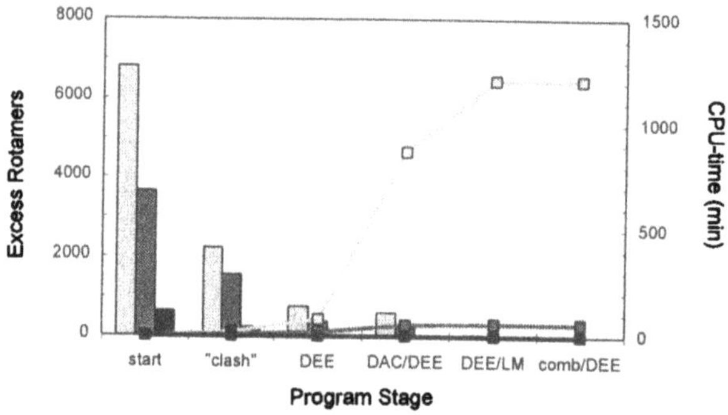

Figure 3: Dead-end elimination by the various routines for three proteins. The number of excess rotamers (the total number of rotamers minus one for each rotatable residue) and the CPU-time is shown as a function of the program stage. The experiments have been performed on a SG Indy R4600PC 100 MHz workstation. Light grey bars/curve is for lectin, dark grey is used for agglutinin and black for crambin. "clash" means the elimination of template and side chain incompatible rotamers (section 3.2). DEE denotes the results after conventional dead-end elimination (section 3.3). DEE/DAC is the situation after rotamer elimination using the DAC strategy (section 3.4). DEE/LM means dead-end elimination assisted by local modeling. comb/DEE corresponds to the final result after the DEE-assisted combinatorial routine. The total computing time for crambin (black curve at the bottom) was 48 sec.

4. Conclusions

In this work we have discussed various DEE-criteria and the way they can be algorithmically arranged in order to optimize computational performance. We have shown that in principle all routines are required to successfully determine the GMEC of large proteins. A specific study on a large set of test proteins (De Maeyer *et al.*, submitted) has shown that actually proteins of any size can be modeled with the current method although the calculation time for the largest proteins may exceed one day. On the other hand, computation is extremely fast for small sets of side chains and not all routines are essential. This opens new perspectives for future developments in protein modeling. For instance, if the determination of the absolute global mimimum is not needed with mathematical rigor, proteins of any size can be split up in overlapping parts of about 30 residues which are modeled individually. Other possible developments are the combination of systematic local main chain sampling with dead-end elimination for the side chains, or ligand docking to a receptor with flexible side chains (ref. 18 and Desmet *et al.*, submitted). Such applications involve repeated cycles of side chain modeling and therefore require very fast and secure methods. With respect to the latter, the DAC-method and other practical solutions to the bottom line theorem may be very helpful.

Acknowledgements

J.D. thanks the Belgian National Fund for Scientific Research (NFWO), the Research Foundation of the K.U.Leuven and the "Vlaams Instituut voor de bevordering van het wetenschappelijk-technologisch onderzoek in de industrie" (IWT) for financial support. I.L. and M.D.M. acknowledge the "Flemish Interuniversity Institute for Biotechnology". J.D. thanks Prof. Jan Spriet for helpful discussions.

References

1. M. Vásquez, *Curr. Opin. Struct. Biol.* **6**, 217 (1996).
2. S. Subbiah *et al, Curr. Biol.* **3**, 141 (1993).
3. L. Holm and C. Sander, *Proteins* **14**, 213 (1992).
4. C. Wilson *et al, J. Mol. Biol.* **229**, 996 (1993).
5. J. Desmet *et al,* in *The protein Folding Problem and Tertiary Structure Prediction*, eds. K. Merz Jr. and S. LeGrand, pp. 307-337 (Birkhäuser, Boston, 1994).
6. C.A. Laughton, *J. Mol. Biol.* **235**, 1088 (1994).
7. S.Y. Chung and S. Subbiah, *Prot. Sci.* **4**, 2300 (1995).
8. F. Eisenmenger *et al, J. Mol. Biol.* **231**, 849 (1993).
9. J. Desmet *et al, Nature* **356**, 539 (1992) .
10. I. Lasters and J. Desmet, *Prot. Eng.* **6**, 717 (1993) .
11. R.F. Goldstein, *Biophys. J.* **66**, 1335 (1994) .
12. I. Lasters *et al, Prot. Eng.* **8**, 815 (1995) .
13. P. Delhaise *et al, J. Mol. Graph.* **2**, 103 (1984).
14. B.R. Brooks *et al, J. Comput. Chem.* **4**, 187 (1983).
15. D.A. Keller *et al, Prot. Eng.* **8**, 893 (1995).
16. B.I. Dahiyat and S.L. Mayo *Prot. Sci.* **5**, 895 (1996).
17. F.C. Bernstein *et al, J. Mol. Biol.* **112**, 535 (1977).
18. A.R. Leach, *J. Mol. Biol.* **235**, 345 (1994).

USING VIEWS FOR RETRIEVING DATA FROM EXTREMELY HETEROGENEOUS DATABANKS

T. Etzold, G. Verde

EMBL, Meyerhofstrasse 1, 69112 Heidelberg, Germany

Information in molecular biology or biology in general is contained in a multitude of different databanks each specializing in a certain area. This specialization is useful since it improves the maintainability of the data and the flexibility of the overall structure which until now manages to exist without almost any standards. However, information gathering from these extremely heterogeneous sources is difficult since the desired data may be scattered over many databanks. This paper presents the concept of views implemented in the retrieval system SRS[1,2] that uses links between databanks and a sophisticated parsing engine for information extraction to provide a flexible way of searching and obtaining data across databank boundaries. The implementation provides homogeneous access to all databanks using two types of views: the list-view which displays selected data-fields in their original format and the table-view available for HTML and plain ASCII text which tries to represent the data in a format independent from that of the source databank.

1 Introduction

Information in molecular biology is available in a growing number of databanks that specialize on one single aspect such as promoters of eukaryotic genes (EPD[3]), known tertiary structures of proteins (PDB[4]) or all known enzymatic activities (ENZYME[5]) to name only a few. Each databank defines an information domain. Its boundaries to other databanks are outlined by the object it wants to characterize but also by practical judgment. An important goal is to have as little overlap as possible with other databanks and instead of duplicating information provide links to corresponding entries in other databanks. In general the domain defined by a databank does often not fully accommodate real life objects such as a gene, a promoter or an enzyme. To get a full picture of these objects one must often consult many different databanks and carefully extract relevant information from each. For instance, to collect all available information about a specific eukaryotic promoter one could start with an entry in EPD, then move on to the cross-referenced entry in the EMBL[6] databank of nucleotide sequences to obtain the location of the promoter within the gene and its DNA sequence, and finally follow links to the TRANSFAC[7] databank of transcription factors and binding sites in order to find out if any transcription factor binding sites are known.

Today almost every databank can be accessed with retrieval systems of various kinds that allow fast searching and inspection of the found data. Since most of these systems are made available for the use through the World Wide Web (WWW) the data before being displayed can be enriched with hypertext links that will directly lead to corresponding information in other databanks. This is already an enormous improvement and helps to raise individual databanks out of their isolation but on the other side introduces the danger of 'drowning' in data since often only a fraction of the displayed information is of interest. Only few retrieval systems allow hiding of undesired information and none of them can automatically extract and compile selected information from more than one databank source.

The retrieval system SRS allows installation of several dozen databanks on a single site and provides homogenous access to their contents. Until now the retrieved information was always a set of entries each from a single databank. We added the specification of views so that the user can define virtual entries that may include information from many sources. It will be demonstrated in this paper that views can be used to treat the sum of all installed databanks as a single structure where user defined entities can freely span databank boundaries.

2 Links

The implementation of the views relies heavily on the link indices which are an important and unique feature of the SRS system[8]. To create a link index all cross-references in a databank are read and compiled into a list of all pairs of referencing and referenced entries. All link indices are duplicated so that referenced as well as referencing entries can be looked up. In fact, once the link index is compiled it is of no importance anymore which of the two linked entries is referenced and which is referencing and thus the link becomes bi-directional.

Link indices can be used by the two link operators of the SRS query language which are '>' (link right) and '<' (link left). The operands can be sets of entries created by a previous query or entire databanks. The expression

```
embl > swissprot
```

retrieves all SWISS-PROT entries that are linked to EMBL entries and

```
embl < swissprot
```

retrieves all EMBL entries that are linked to SWISS-PROT. The link operator can be seen as an arrow that points to the set where the result will be taken from. In other words the link operations yields a subset of the left ('<') or the right ('>') operand.

Typically an SRS installation has several dozen databanks where most have links to others. Within such an installation all databanks and all pair wise links define a graph where the databanks are the nodes and the links the edges. In a graph all the nodes are connected through paths consisting of one or more edges. This means that also indirect links can be carried out. The expression

```
embl > pdb
```

is such an example where two operands are only indirectly linked, in this case through SWISS-PROT which maintains links to both EMBL and PDB. The link operation is carried out by first finding the shortest path through the graph from EMBL to PDB which the succession of the two links EMBL to SWISS-PROT and then SWISS-PROT to PDB.

A recent extension allows internal links or links among entries of the same databank. Examples of such links are references to the parent node or higher level taxon in entries of the TAXONOMY[9] databank which contains a taxonomic tree spanning all organisms represented by entries in the nucleotide databank GENBANK[10] entries. The query

```
[taxonomy-name:bos taurus] > taxonomy_up > taxonomy_down
```

returns all entries of the same family as "bos taurus". The artificial names "taxonomy_up" and "taxonomy_down" need to be used instead of the databank name since the operation returns entries of TAXONOMY. Here, The link is used to model hierarchic structures which can be further exploited by two extensions of the SRS query language: The operator ">^" returns all nodes in the subtrees represented by the nodes in a set whereas operator ">^" returns only the leaf entries of those subtrees.. The query

```
[taxonomy-name:bovinae] >_ taxonomy_down > genbank
```

first collects all species in the family "bovinae" and by linking these to GENBANK finds all nucleotide sequences which exist for these species.

The information used to build the link indices originates from the databanks themselves and is thus under the control of the databank provider. However, it is possible to create a user defined link simply by adding a new databank where each entry associates entries from two other databanks so that it can be used as an intermediate step for linking. Such databases of links already exist. For instance, HSSP[11] lists all proteins in SWISS-PROT that are similar to protein chains in PDB. So the query

```
pdb > hssp > swissprot
```

gives all SWISS-PROT entries that are similar to chains in PDB as defined by the information in HSSP. Note that the direct link between PDB and SWISS-PROT has a different meaning; the query

```
pdb > swissprot
```

returns all SWISS-PROT entries for which the tertiary structure has been solved. Another example of such a databank is VIRGIL[12] which links GENBANK and OMIM[13], a databank of human genetic disorders. In theory one could make these new links even more powerful by adding information about the quality of the links. Each link in the link database could have a score so that

```
a > [linkab-score#0.5:] > b
```

returns all entries in "b" that are linked to "a" by information in "linkab" where the score of a link must be 0.5 or higher. Databanks of links are presently scarce but they will become more abundant once their importance and usefulness is better understood.

3 Views

SRS regards an entry as a list of data-fields. The simplest form of a view acts as a filter and allows only selected fields to be displayed. For instance, a view could be defined to display only the ID, the description and the line containing the sequence

```
ID   ACHA_HUMAN      STANDARD;        PRT;    482 AA.
DE   ACETYLCHOLINE RECEPTOR PROTEIN, ALPHA CHAIN PRECURSOR.
SQ   SEQUENCE    482 AA;   54545 MW;   E050B513 CRC32;
```

Figure 1. A SWISS-PROT entry viewed by a list-view.

length for SWISS-PROT entries as shown in Figure 1. This type of view, the list-view, displays the selected data-fields in the order they occur within the entry and in their original format which includes line codes or fields labels. It is mostly useful for 'turning off' undesired information during browsing large sets of entries.

The table-view provides more sophistication and possibilities. The entry in the table-view is displayed as a single row. The information displayed is in a different format in the sense that it is shown without the field identification (line codes or field labels). On top of that other conversions can take place to render the information into a more standardized format, e.g., all author names from all data-banks can be converted into the form surname-comma-initials (eg, "Jones, D.G."). The extraction and conversion of the information is accomplished by a parser that is tightly linked to the SRS system and which can be programmed in the Icarus language[14]. Alternative productions can be specified for data-fields displayed in list and table-views. Figure 2 shows the same information as in Figure 1 using a table-view.

SWISSPROT	*Description*	*SeqLength*
ACHA_BOVIN	ACETYLCHOLINE RECEPTOR PROTEIN, ALPHA CHAIN PRECURSOR.	457
ACHA_CHICK	ACETYLCHOLINE RECEPTOR PROTEIN, ALPHA CHAIN PRECURSOR.	456
ACHA_ELEEL	ACETYLCHOLINE RECEPTOR PROTEIN, ALPHA CHAIN (FRAGMENT).	24

Figure 2. A list of SWISS-PROT entries shown in a table-view

The output format of the table-view can be HTML code using the HTML3 table specification or plain ASCII which can be directly loaded into spreadsheet programs or relational database systems. Other formats can be easily added since the table is constructed by using a template. The HTML implementation makes use of the various options to display text within cells which can be left or right aligned, centered or preformatted.

A view in SRS is independent from queries and can be applied to any set of entries provided they are from the databank for which the view was specified. It is possible to specify a view for multiple databanks so that a single view can be applied to sets generated by querying several databanks at the same time. However, one needs to be careful since particular data-fields may not be shared by all databanks for which the view is defined.

Views become particularly useful when combined with links. Each entry displayed can be individually linked with entries from other databanks from which again only selected information is displayed. Since the linked entries in turn can be displayed by a view that specify further links, the overall structure can be seen as a tree where the databanks for which the view is defined are root databanks and the databanks supplying the linked entries leaf-databanks. Figure 3 shows SWISS-PROT entries together with linked entries from ENZYME.

SWISSPROT	*Description*	**ENZYME**	*CatalyticActivity*
MDH_HALMA	MALATE DEHYDROGENASE (EC 1.1.1.37).	1.1.1.37	(S)-MALATE + NAD(+) = OXALOACETATE + NADH.
ODPA_ASCSU	PYRUVATE DEHYDROGENASE E1 COMPONENT, ALPHA SUBUNIT, TYPE I PRECURSOR (EC 1.2.4.1) (PDHE1-A).	1.2.4.1	PYRUVATE + LIPOAMIDE = S-ACETYLDIHYDROLIPOAMIDE + CO(2).

Figure 3. Two SWISS-PROT entries shown with the Description together with their linked entries from ENZYME for whch "CatalyticActivity" field is included.

An Individual data-field may have a list of format options. The Sequence field of protein sequence databanks for example, can be displayed as the plain sequence of characters, in GCG, PIR or FASTA format, or as a Java applet which shows the sequence along with a plot for various amino acid characteristics such as the Kyte-Doolittle hydropathy[15] values.

Figure 4 shows a SWISS-PROT entry with the sequence displayed by a Java applet. Displaying Java applets within views is an elegant way of linking data with analy-

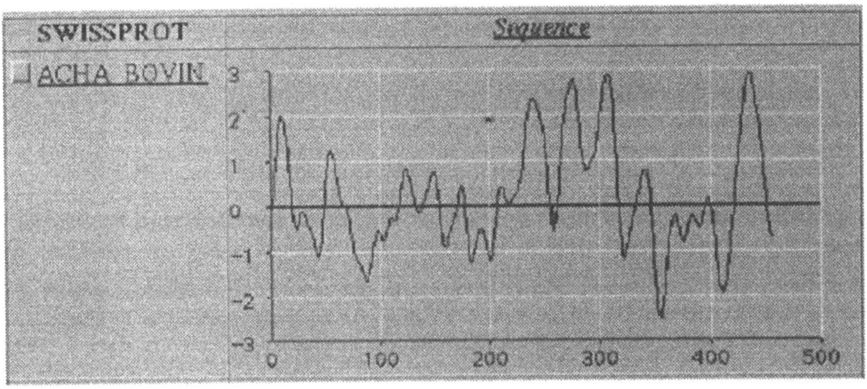

Figure 4. A SWIS-PROT entry with its sequence shown by a Java applet as a hydropathicity plot. The applet can be controlled to display other amino acid properties or to show the curve with an enlarged scale

sis methods and is straightforward since HTML provides tags for calling applets and for specifying their input.

Since a single root entry can be linked to many leaf entries it is sometimes useful to have only the number of linked entries displayed. The SRSWWW server shows this number as a hypertext link that when clicked retrieves the list of entries. The number is of value itself and can be used for statistics. For instance, using the previous example of the link from TAXONOMY to GENBANK one could obtain a table of taxa together with the number of GENBANK entries that exist for all organisms each taxon represents.

By default SRS uses the shortest path to link root and leaf entries. If another link is desired it must be explicitly specified by as a query expression in which the root-entry to be linked is represented by the reserved word "entry". For instance to obtain the view with the number of GENBANK entries for a list of taxa one must specify the query

```
entry >_ taxonomy_down > genbank
```

Working with Views

SRS offers different ways of working with views. The SRSWWW server provides two pages for first selecting root and leaf databanks and then selecting data-fields for each. An additional page displays all defined views. For each databank a number of predefined views exist that can be modified by the user. Views can be applied to entire sets returned by queries or to single entries selected in an entry list.

The command line program "getz" allows definition of simple views on the command line as in

```
% getz -vf description '[embl-description:kinase]'
```

which prints for all kinase sequences in the EMBL databank the description lines. The entry name itself will always be displayed and needs not to be specified. The predefined views of the SRSWWW server are specified in the Icarus language and are available to all SRS programs. More views can be easily added and selected for display by the associated name as in the "getz" command line

```
% getz -view myview '[embl-description:kinase]'
```

that uses the view with the name "myview" to display the result of the query.

Discussion

Views or external schemas are commonly used in databank systems, but until now were not applied within retrieval systems. The views described in this paper are restricted since they must always select entire data-fields which can be large and complex entities themselves. To get a finer granularity in selecting information a system must be used that supports real data schemas (relational databank systems) or object class specifications (object oriented databank systems). However, the simplicity of viewing on the level of data-fields has the advantage that implementation and maintenance is much easier. Databanks can be incorporated into the system without the need of having full knowledge of their organization which allows the integration of extremely heterogeneous databanks. Also, most databanks have a very simple structure and often selection from a list of data-fields is sufficient.

SRS accesses the databanks directly on the flat file level. Its parser makes it completely independent from the format of these files which can range from relational tables to, for instance, PDB files. The table-view gives further independence since it can convert the data into a standard format, e.g., the sequence length will always be displayed as a single number within a table column and more complex items such as a date or an author can share a common format across all databanks.

If the views will be accepted by the community the immediate effect will be that databank links or cross-references will become much more important as they are now which will improve and extend the cross-reference information available.

1. T. Etzold and P. Argos, *Comput. Appl. Biosci.* **9**, 49 (1993).
2. T. Etzold, A. Ulyanov and P. Argos, Methods in Enzymology **266**, 114 (1996).
3. P. Bucher and E.N. Trifonov, Nucleic Acid Res. **14**, 10009 (1986).
4. The Protein Databank, http://pdb.pdb.bnl.gov/.
5. A. Bairoch, *Nucleic Acids Res.* **24**, 221 (1996).
6. The EMBL Nucleotide Databank, http://www.ebi.ac.uk/.
7. E. Wingender, P. Dietze, H. Karas, R. Knueppel, *Nucleic Acids Res.* **24**, 238 (1996).
8. T. Etzold, P. Argos, *Comput. Appl. Biosci.* **9**, 59 (1993).
9. D. Leipe and V. Soussov, http://www3.ncbi.nlm.nih.gov/Taxonomy/taxonomyhome.html.
10. D.A. Benson, M.S. Boguski, D.J. Lipman, J. Ostell, *Nucleic Acids Res.* **24**, 1 (1996).
11. R. Schneider R. and C. Sander, *Nucleic Acids Res.* **24**, 201 (1996).
12. F. Achard, http://www.infobiogen.fr/virgil/home.html.
13. K.H. Fasman, S.I. Letovsky, R.W. Cottingham and D.T. Kingsbury, *Nucleic Acids Res.* **24**, 57 (1996).
14. Interpreter of Commands and RecUrsive Syntax, http://kappa.embl-heidelberg:8000/srs/.
15. J. Kyte and R.F. Doolittle, *J. Mol. Biol.* **157**, 105 (1982).

LENGTH SCALES OF LIPID DYNAMICS AND MOLECULAR DYNAMICS

SCOTT E. FELLER and RICHARD W. PASTOR
Biophysics Laboratory, Center for Biologics Evaluation and Research, FDA
1401 Rockville Pike
Rockville, MD 20852-1448, USA

Following a brief overview of length scales and system size in computer simulation, it is demonstrated that a simulation sized lipid bilayer (typically a 50x50 Å^2 patch) is in the regime where stretching dominates undulation, while the reverse holds for a flaccid macroscopic membrane. Then it is estimated that current system sizes of membrane simulations must be increased by at least a factor of 10 before thermodynamic limits are approached for quantities such as surface tension.

1 Introduction

At any point in the growth of a research area, technical questions can be classified as resolved, pressing, depressing, or ignored. These are not static and the same general issue is often revisited. In computer simulations, for example, algorithms for molecular dynamics at constant number, volume, and energy were discussed extensively before Verlet's method was adopted in the late 1960's. The algorithm issue lay fallow until the early 1980's, when it became necessary to deal with simulating at constant pressure and temperature. Currently, the calculation of free energy and introduction of quantum effects can be considered pressing. Likewise, there has been cyclical interest in the form of potential energy functions and the precise values of parameters, as might be typified by water models. Two other important technical issues are the length of the trajectory, and the size of the system. These are especially linked with computer advances: 100 picoseconds was acceptable for large systems in the 1980's, but a nanosecond is now considered a reasonable standard. (A nanosecond simulation of a 15-20,000 atom system currently takes several months using a supercomputer or a cluster of workstations.) Concern with system size was high in the early days of liquid state simulations. When systems of only 64 or 125 particles were studied, it was clear that sound waves could propagate through the primary cell during the course of the simulation, and size related artifacts in distribution functions were evident; a consensus of at least 300-500 particles for liquid state work gradually emerged.[1] Presently, the upper limit on system size tends to be determined by the required trajectory length and computer speed, rather than by independent physical arguments.

This paper discusses system size from the viewpoint of length scales, with an emphasis on membranes. Physically, a system contains a variety of dynamical modes on different length scales, and some of these couple with each other. In the thermodynamic limit (i.e., infinite particle number and infinite time), all motions are accessible, and a calculated quantity corresponds to a macroscopic observable. With simulations the possibility clearly exists that, because of computer limitations, a system is missing dynamics on an important length scale.

Our central example is a fully hydrated phospholipid bilayer. Simulations of pure bilayers are becoming increasingly common,[2] and proteins have recently been added.[3] A difficulty of these studies is that with all heavy atoms and hydrogens represented, a 15-20,000 particle system corresponds to only about 36 lipids per leaflet, or a patch of approximately 50 Å on a side. In the following sections we estimate some of the errors inherent in modeling a nearly macroscopic system with such a small patch. Three different formalisms will be utilized. In Section 2, we follow the treatment of undulations described in Safran's elegant monograph,[4] and estimate surface roughness, fluctuations of the projected surface area, and the system size dependence of surface tension. As we have recently discussed,[5] the value of the applied surface tension is an important consideration when simulating bilayers with flexible dimensions. Section 3 takes the fluctuations in surface area per lipid explicitly into account. First, using standard statistical mechanical formulas[1] and the experimental lateral compressibility, we estimate the fluctuations in surface area that would be observed in a simulation sized system. We then comment on the theory of Brocchard, DeGennes and Pfeuty,[6] where undulations and stretching are treated together. Section 4 presents arguments (and related cautions) for increasing current system sizes by a factor of 10.

2. Undulation

2.1 Surface roughness

As a first approximation, we can describe the interface as lying in the xy plane, i.e., no spontaneous curvature, with a surface roughness which depends on the magnitude of the undulatory vibrational modes of the system.[4] The system can be described by the amplitude of these modes, u(**q**), which are functions of the wavevector **q**,

$$\left\langle u_{\mathbf{q}}^{2}\right\rangle = \frac{k_B T}{K_c q^4 + \gamma q^2} \qquad (1)$$

where K_c is the bending modulus, γ is the surface tension, k_B is the Boltzmann constant and T is the absolute temperature. The mean squared, real-space fluctuation of the surface is then expressed by converting the sum over wavevectors to an integral:

$$\langle u^2\rangle = \frac{1}{A}\sum_{\mathbf{q}}\langle u_{\mathbf{q}}^2\rangle = \frac{1}{(2\pi)^2}\int d\mathbf{q}\langle u_{\mathbf{q}}^2\rangle \qquad (2)$$

Now consider two different types of interfaces: octane/water, where the roughening of the surface is determined by the large free energy of creating a hydrophillic/hydrophobic surface (i.e., the surface tension, γ), and membrane/water, where γ is very small and the roughening is controlled by the energy cost for bending (K_c). For comparison, we assume that simulations of these two systems are carried out using periodic boundary conditions with the same size primary cells: an area of 50x50 $Å^2$, and a height of 65 Å (the repeat spacing of a typical phospholipid multilayer).

We begin with octane/water. Substituting eq 1 into eq 2, setting the bending modulus to zero, and carrying out the angular integration leads to

$$\langle u^2\rangle = \frac{k_BT}{2\pi\gamma}\int\frac{dq\, q}{q^2} \qquad (3)$$

To avoid the divergences, limits are specified on the maximum ($q_{max} = \pi/a$) and minimum ($q_{min} = \pi/L$) values of q. The roughness of the simple interface is then

$$\langle u^2\rangle = \frac{k_BT}{2\pi\gamma}\ln\frac{L}{a} \qquad (4)$$

Typically, a is assumed to be the molecular diameter. Gravity limits the size of the undulations for liquid/vapor or liquid/liquid interfaces; an estimate of this effect places an upper limit on $L=(\gamma/\Delta\rho g)^{1/2}$, where $\Delta\rho$ is the density difference between phases and g is the gravitational constant. For octane/water, $\Delta\rho$=0.3 g cm^{-3}, yielding L=0.4 cm. Using this value of L, with a = 3 Å (the diameter of a water molecule) and γ = 50 dyn/cm, we obtain $\langle u^2\rangle^{1/2}$ = 4.7 Å at 300 K. Repeating the calculation with L = 50 Å (the largest wavelength which would be possible in a computer simulation employing periodic boundary conditions with a 50 Å box length), yields $\langle u^2\rangle^{1/2}$ = 1.9 Å. Thus, the height of the fluctuations in the simulation cell is comparable to that of the real system.

Now consider the membrane. Under stress free conditions, the surface tension of an isolated bilayer is zero, or close to zero.[6,7] With this assumption, inserting eq 1 into eq 2 yields

$$\langle u^2\rangle = \frac{k_BT}{2\pi K_c}\int\frac{dq\, q}{q^4} = \frac{k_BT}{4\pi^3K_c}\left(L^2 - a^2\right) \qquad (5)$$

Notice the dependence on L^2 rather than ln L as was obtained for the simple interface. The lateral correlation length, i.e. the longest undulation wavelength which the membrane can support, is approximately 1 micron for fluid phase bilayers.[8] Sackmann and coworkers[9] have studied the fluctuations of stearoyloleoyl phosphatidylcholine (SOPC) bilayer vesicles and found a surface roughness amplitude of approximately 100 Å. Assuming a = 8 Å (molecular areas of PC bilayers are typically 60-70 Å^2), K_c=35k_BT, and L = 0.75 μm (the values for SOPC bilayers), we obtain $\langle u^2\rangle^{1/2}$ = 114 Å, in agreement with the experimental observations. Thus, transverse fluctuations in a macroscopic stress free lipid bilayer are 25 times greater than a simple oil/water interface, and are nearly twice the height of the typical simulation cell! Returning to the simulation sized bilayer, inserting L = 50 Å into eq 5, yields $\langle u^2\rangle^{1/2}$ = 0.75 Å.

In addition to surface roughness associated with undulations is what might be termed "microscopic roughness". This arises from molecular packing in the interface, and is present even in "undulation free" bilayers; i.e., the water/bilayer interface is not an infinitely flat sheet but, rather, $\langle u^2\rangle^{1/2}$ = 3-5 Å.[10,11] Consequently, undulations are difficult to discern at the 50 Å length scale.

2.2 *Projected surface area*

The excitation of undulatory modes guarantees that the surface area of the membrane will be greater than the area of the membrane projected onto the xy plane. This increase in area can be quantified in terms of the wavevector amplitudes

$$\Delta A = \frac{1}{2}\sum_{\mathbf{q}} q^2 \langle u_{\mathbf{q}}^2 \rangle \tag{6}$$

Substituting eq 1 into eq 6 and integrating

$$\Delta A = \frac{1}{2}\sum_{\mathbf{q}} q^2 \frac{k_B T}{K_c q^4 + \gamma q^2} = \frac{A k_B T}{4\pi} \int_{q_{\min}}^{q_{\max}} \frac{q\ dq}{K_c q^2 + \gamma} \tag{7}$$

or

$$\frac{\Delta A}{A} = \frac{k_B T}{8\pi K_c} \ln\left[\frac{(K_c \pi^2 / a^2) + \gamma}{(K_c \pi^2 / L^2) + \gamma}\right] \tag{8}$$

For the case of a stress free bilayer (γ=0)

$$\frac{\Delta A}{A} = \frac{k_B T}{4\pi K_c} \ln\frac{L}{a} \tag{9}$$

From eq. 9, K_c=35k_BT and L/a=1000, the difference between the total and projected surface area of a macroscopic (≈1 μm) patch of bilayer membrane is approximately 1.6%. This estimate is in accord with the experimental observations of Evans and coworkers[8,12] who find that large unilamellar vesicles can have their projected areas increased by up to a few percent before expansion of the area per molecule and eventual rupture of the membrane. For a simulation sized patch (L/a=6.2), ΔA/A is only 0.42%

2.3 *Surface tension*

So far we have demonstrated that reducing the size of the lipid system to simulation sized dimensions leads to a significant reduction in the amplitude of undulations, which, in turn leads to nearly identical values of the total and projected surface area. We may expect that the surface tension, which is the conjugate variable to the projected area, would be also be altered.

An estimate of the size of the effect can be obtained by calculating the surface tension of a *macroscopic* membrane where $\Delta A/A = 0.42\%$ (i.e., the value in the simulation cell). Setting the left-hand-side of eq 8 to 0.0042 and solving for γ yields γ between 30 and 60 dyn/cm for the experimentally determined range of K_c. Thus, although the simulation cell is infinitely replicated by periodic boundary conditions so as to model a macroscopic patch of membrane, we are not modeling a flaccid membrane (where $\gamma \approx 0$), but rather one which has been flattened by an applied tension of 30-60 dyn/cm.

We have arrived at similar conclusions from simulations of dipalmitoyl phosphatidylcholine (DPPC) lipid bilayers,[5,11,14] where the calculated surface tensions of 50 Å patches are approximately 35-40 dyn/cm/side. We have also explicitly demonstrated system size dependence:[5] a series of simulations carried out at the identical area per molecule and decreasing number of lipids per side (36, 16 and 9) showed the expected increase in surface tension. These results point towards the existence of a "microscopic" surface tension; i.e., there is residual anisotropy in the pressure tensor on the simulation sized, but not on the macroscopic, length scale.

From the estimates of $\langle u^2 \rangle$ in Section 2.1, the system size dependence of surface tension for liquid/liquid interfaces is expected to be significantly smaller. Our own simulation results for octane/water[13,14] indicate that any constraints due to the length scale of the simulation cell (which had lateral dimensions of 25.6 Å) are small compared with the differences between potential energy parameters and force truncation methods commonly used in simulations. The effect was also recently investigated by Chen,[15] who showed that for a Lennard-Jones fluid the size dependence is negligible above 10 molecular diameters.

3. Stretching

3.1 *Fluctuations in the surface area per lipid*

The preceding treatment of undulations is based on the assumption that the surface area per lipid remains constant along the membrane; i.e., stretching is negligible.

Fluctuations in the surface area associated with local stretching can be estimated from the area compressibility modulus, K_a, using standard formulas:

$$\langle \delta A^2 \rangle = k_B T \left(\frac{\partial A}{\partial \gamma} \right)_T = k_B T \frac{A}{K_a} \quad (10)$$

$$\frac{\langle \delta A^2 \rangle^{1/2}}{A} = \left(\frac{k_B T}{K_a A} \right)^{1/2} \quad (11)$$

Assuming K_a = 140 dyn/cm (the experimental value for many lipids[8]), it follows from eq. 11 that the relative area fluctuation arising from stretching in a flat (i.e., undulation free) 0.8 μm patch is only 0.02%. This is two orders of magnitude less than the 1.6% difference between the total and projected area associated with undulations (cf. Section 2.2, eq 9), and makes it clear why treatments based on undulations alone[4,8,9,16] reasonably model many macroscopic phenomena. Now consider the 50 Å patch: the relative area fluctuations from stretching are 3.6%, and dominate those from undulation (0.42%). Dynamics in 50 Å and 0.8 μm patches are qualitatively different.

Additional insight to this "small system" effect may be obtained by recalling that volume fluctuations in fluids are described similarly to eq. 11,

$$\frac{\langle \delta V^2 \rangle^{1/2}}{V} = \left(\frac{k_B T \chi}{V} \right)^{1/2} \quad (12)$$

where χ is the isothermal compressibility. For a simulation of liquid water (χ = 4.65×10^{-5} atm^{-1} at 293 K) to exhibit relative volume fluctuations of 3.6%, the system would consist of only 48 molecules.

3.2 Undulation and stretching

Brochard et al.[6,16] have emphasized the fundamental difference between the surface tensions of flaccid (undulating) and swollen (undulation free) membranes when describing the dynamics of cell membranes. Their model for unswollen closed membranes begins with the ansatz that the macroscopic surface tension is zero, and incorporates both the bending modulus and the area compressibility modulus. They use an ingenious construction: an absolutely flat bilayer whose surface area is the same as the projected surface area of an undulating bilayer; i.e, the membrane is squeezed into an unphysical state, and seeks to distribute its compression energy into other modes. The surface tension of the macroscopic free energy minimum is written as a sum of a "bare surface tension", γ_0, and a term which takes into account fluctuation effects, $\delta\gamma$; i.e., $\gamma = \gamma_0 + \delta\gamma = 0$, where

$$\delta\gamma \approx \frac{K_a k_B T}{4\pi K_c} \ln \frac{L}{a} \quad (13)$$

Substituting in values of physical constants and lengths similar to those used so far, values of $\delta\gamma$ in the 40 dyn/cm range are obtained. This implies that to suppress undulations (i.e., create a membrane flat on the macroscopic scale), a surface tension of this magnitude would have to be applied.

This formalism might better treat the coupling of undulation and stretching, which is neglected in eq. 5. It is possible however, that bending and compressibility moduli measured for macroscopic systems are not directly applicable in the small wavelength limit studied by simulation (e.g., higher order terms are required).

4. Discussion and Summary

The treatments of undulations we have used here are approximate, yet still provide reasonable estimates of the difference between the simulation and the object of ultimate interest. These differences, which arise from the omission of wavelengths longer than the box length, are small for liquid/liquid systems such as octane/water as they are currently simulated. They are significant however, for lipid bilayers, and should be taken into account when modeling these systems. In particular, quantities which are coupled to undulatory modes, such as the surface tension, might require adjustment from their thermodynamic (i.e., macroscopic) values in order to obtain surface areas per lipid that correspond with experiment (this argument is presented in detail in reference 5). Additionally, undulatory contributions to surface roughness in a simulation cell of 50 Å dimensions will be difficult to separate from the microscopic roughness, and most of the fluctuations in surface area will be associated with stretching.

What is the simulation length scale for lipid bilayers where the effect of periodic boundary conditions becomes negligible (or at least as small as exists in the current octane/water simulations)? The simplest estimate is obtained by using the results of Section 3.1, where the area fluctuations in the 50 Å patch of membrane (36 lipids on a side) were shown to be comparable to the volume fluctuations of 48 waters. Given that a respectable simulation of liquid water currently contains about 500 molecules (volume fluctuations of approximately 1%), we may guess that the size of the lipid simulation should be increased by a factor of 10.

The treatment of Section 2 provides another route. Let us calculate the size of a simulation cell which could support undulations consistent with a macroscopic membrane under a tension of 3 dyn/cm (we arbitrarily choose this as the accuracy at which we might be able to calculate a tension). Setting $\gamma = 3$ dyn/cm in eq 8, the difference between total and projected area is 0.71%. Thus, a very small tension will remove over half the difference between total and projected area. From eq 9, a simulation box of length 181.5 Å will support this level of undulation. Equation 6 predicts an rms undulation amplitude of 2.75 Å, implying that the membrane roughness would have approximately equal contributions from undulations and microscopic roughness. The area of this patch is 13 times greater than the current 50 Å patch, and the system would include approximately 250,000 atoms (not including additional waters required for any increase in the box height).

Clearly a simulation of a system of this size would be a large undertaking. Even assuming a scale-up proportional to $N \ln N$ (this can be obtained with some of the more sophisticated force evaluations, such as particle mesh Ewald[17]), over a 20-fold increase in cpu time would be required for the same length simulation. While such a simulation is plausible in the near future assuming several doublings of computer speed, the time scale issue must be revisited: to obtain a reasonably converged trajectory, the new modes should be sampled over several (ideally many) cycles. The time scale of collective modes is significantly longer than many of the "single molecule" properties that are presently studied in simulations, and the longest can extend out to seconds (see reviews in chapters 1 and 7 of reference 3, and the discussions of director fluctuations presented in reference 18). To the extent that the undulations are faster than 10^{-5} s (the time scale of the deuterium magnetic resonance experiment), the deuterium order parameter, S_{CD}, commonly reported in simulation studies will be reduced as the length scale is increased.

It is not, in fact, unreasonable to extend simulations out to the 100 ns time scale. In our analysis of the time scale of lipid bilayers (chapter 1 of reference 3) we estimated that a simulation of 72 lipids must be 170 ns to obtain a minimal level of translational diffusion (each lipid undergoing, on average, a single jump to a new position one molecular diameter away).

These considerations make the goal of simulating a patch of cell membrane (i.e., a heterogeneous lipid bilayer with a variety of proteins) a worthy theoretical and computational challenge.

Acknowledgments

This research is supported in part by: the Phillips Laboratory, Air Force Material Command, USAF, through the use of the IBM SP2 at the Maui High Performance Computing Center; and the Laboratory of Computational Biosciences, Division of Computer Research and Technology, NIH, through the use of the Intel Gamma.

References

1. M.P. Allen and D.J. Tildesley, *Computer Simulation of Liquids*; (Clarendon: Oxford, 1987). In addition to containing a clear exposition of simulation techniques, this monograph reviews much of the pioneering work in the field.

2. R.W. Pastor, "Molecular dynamics and Monte Carlo simulations of lipid bilayers" *Current Opinion in Structural Biology*, **4**, 486 (1994).
3. K.M. Merz and B. Roux, *Biological Membranes: A molecular perspective from computation and experiment*, (Birkhauser, Boston, 1996).
4. S.A. Safran, *Statistical Thermodynamics of Surfaces, Interfaces, and Membranes*, (Addison-Wesley, Reading MA, 1994)
5. S.E. Feller and R.W. Pastor, "On simulating lipid bilayers with an applied surface tension: periodic boundary conditions and undulations" *Biophys. J.*, **71**, 1350-1353 (1996).
6. F. Brochard, P.G. de Gennes, and P. Pfeuty, "Surface tension and deformations of membrane structures" *J. Physique* **37**, 1099 (1976).
7. F. Jahnig, "What is the surface tension of a lipid bilayer membrane?" *Biophys. J.*, **71**, 1348-1349 (1996).
8. E. Evans and W. Rawicz, "Entropy-driven tension and bending elasticity in condensed-fluid membranes" *Phys. Rev. Lett.* **64**, 2094 (1990).
9. J.A. Radler, T.J. Feder, H.H. Strey, and E. Sackmann, "Fluctuation analysis of tension-controlled undulation forces between giant vesicles and solid substrates" *Phys. Rev. E.* **51**, 4526 (1995).
10. M.C. Weiner and S.H. White, "Structure of a fluid dioleoylphosphatidylcholine bilayer determined by joint refinement of x-ray and neutron diffraction data. III. Complete structure" *Biophys. J.* **61**, 434 (1992).
11. S.E. Feller, Y. Zhang, and R.W. Pastor, "Computer simulation of liquid/liquid interfaces. II. Surface tension-area dependence of a bilayer and monolayer" *J. Chem. Phys.* **103**, 10267 (1995).
12. E.A. Evans and R Skalak, *Mechanics and Thermodynamics of Biomembranes* (CRC Press, Boca Raton, FL, 1980).
13. Y. Zhang, S.E. Feller, B.R. Brooks and R.W. Pastor, "Computer simulation of liquid/liquid interfaces I: Theory and application to octane/water" *J. Chem. Phys.* **103**, 10252 (1995).
14. S.E. Feller, R.W. Pastor, A. Rojunuckarin, S. Bogusz, and B.R. Brooks, "The effect of electrostatic force truncation on interfacial and transport properties of water" *J. Phys. Chem.*, in press.
15. L. Chen, "Area Dependence of the Surface tension of a Lennard-Jones fluid from molecular dynamics simulations" *J. Chem. Phys.* **103**, 10214 (1995).
16. F. Brochard and J.F. Lennon, "Frequency spectrum of the flicker phenomenon in erythrocytes" *J. Physique* **36**, 1035 (1975).
17. U. Essmann, L. Perera, M.L. Berkowitz, T. Darden, H. Lee, L.G. Pedersen, "A smooth particle mesh Ewald method" *J. Chem. Phys.* **103**, 8577 (1995).
18. G.R. Luckhurst and C.A. Veracine, *The Molecular Dynamics of Liquid Crystals* (Kluer, Dordrecht, 1994).

SPECIFIC MODELLING OF REGULATORY UNITS IN DNA SEQUENCES

K. FRECH, T. WERNER

GSF - National Research Center for Environment and Health, Institute of Mammalian Genetics, Ingolstädter Landstraße 1, D-85764 Neuherberg, Germany

Transcriptional control regions are usually composed of a complex arrangement of individual transcriptional elements like protein binding sites. This modular structure allows generation of enormous functional diversity of regulatory regions with a limited set of individual elements. We implemented simple formal representations of these general features of regulatory regions into an algorithm capable of developing complex models reflecting both the element composition and the functional organization of individual elements. Our method (ModelGenerator) requires a training set of at least 10 sequences containing the regulatory regions to be modelled and a very simple initial model which may consist of just two characteristic transcription factor binding sites. We show the capability of our algorithm to expand the initial model solely by comparative sequence analysis leading to complex, biologically meaningful models. A second program (ModelInspector) is capable to scan new sequence data for matches to models defined by ModelGenerator. We show two models for retroviral transcriptional control regions to be highly specific. A search against GenBank using one of the models is shown to be free of false negatives and to produce less than 2 false positives / million nucleotides. Thus, our algorithms appear to be useful tools for the analysis of extremely long genomic sequences which are now becoming available as results of various genome sequencing projects.

1 Introduction

The timely appearance of proteins at correct locations is crucial for development as well as functionality of higher organisms. Transcriptional regulation plays a major role in expression control. It has been shown for the role of engrailed-1 and engrailed-2 genes in mouse brain development that correct transcriptional regulation can be even more important than the protein itself [1]. Transcription is regulated by the interaction of proteins with their cognate DNA binding sites. These DNA elements are organized into regulatory units known as promoters, enhancers or silencers (including scaffold attachment regions, SARs and locus control regions, LCRs). Individual regulatory units are usually determined by the spatial organization of binding sites for common and cell- or tissue-specific transcription factors (TF-sites). These sites are separated by spacer-DNA which is usually not conserved precluding global alignment strategies for identification of regulatory units. At least promoters of functionally related gene families appear to have a detectable common organization of TF-sites as has been shown for saccharomyces cerevisiae [2,3].

Several methods for identification of individual TF-sites have already been developed and are available as programs [4,5,6,7]. However, transcriptional regulation is not an inherent property of individual binding sites but is determined by the context of binding sites. A simple statistical model of limited specificity based on the frequency profile of TF-sites in promoter and non-promoter sequences has been successfully implemented in a program to locate polymerase II promoters (PromoterScan, [8]). The program FunsiteP [9] uses the uneven distribution of TF-sites in promoter subregions for promoter recognition. A model free approach to assess the context by distance correlation of different TF-sites was shown to yield some basic organizational features of yeast promoters [2,3]. However, these basic patterns are not sufficiently specific for an unambiguous definition of promoters.

Other model-building approaches like GeneLang [10], GeneParser [11], or GRAIL [12] focus on gene prediction. Only GRAIL includes few basic features of the promoter regions in the last release.

Here, we present a new method for definition (ModelGenerator) and recognition (ModelInspector) of regulatory regions based on the concept of a strictly modular design of such units. ModelGenerator develops a model by combining several types of individual elements with their overall spatial organization within the regulatory unit. One of the hallmarks of the method is development of a complex model by sequence analysis which can reveal new unknown features not present in the initial model. ModelInspector is capable to scan unlimited sequences with such a model and showed an extraordinary high specificity for the models tested.

2 System and Algorithm

2.1 *Basic requirements for model generation*

ModelGenerator requires a set of at least 10 sequences (with moderate or low overall similarity) containing a single type of regulatory unit. This can be a set of promoter sequences of a gene family that shows common regulation or a set of homologous promoters from different species (e.g. within higher eukaryotes). In addition to the sequence set a very simple initial model (e.g. two characteristic TF-sites and their sequential order) is required.

2.2 *Generation of a model*

ModelGenerator defines two types of individual elements. *Determining elements* are part of the basic organizational framework of the regulatory unit (e.g. TATA box and/or initiator for TATA box containing promoters). They have to be present in almost all of the sequences (few exceptions are allowed) and can be detected with a tolerable number of false positive matches, e.g. by one of the TF-site search programs. *Non-determining* elements are not *per se* clearly associated with the regulatory unit and are distinguished solely by association with other elements. Examples of such elements include poorly defined TF-sites or low energy hairpin structures.

The first step of the model development process is the location of all elements which are part of the initial model in all sequences. These elements are by definition determining elements. This allows to define a basic framework in the individual sequences which is composed of the sequential order of the initial elements and the regions in between. A region is the sequence from one determining element to another (or the sequence before the first or after the last determining element). This also allows the definition of a consistency criterion. An element is considered consistent with the basic framework if it occurs in all or almost all sequences in the same region. Further potential consensus elements are then identified by analysis of the sequence set by the program CoreSearch [13]. Elements found consistently in the majority of sequences are selected for the model as determining elements, whereas new elements not consistent with the basic framework are discarded.

All potential determining elements are located either by a consensus search [5,7] or by other search routines included in ModelGenerator (e.g. secondary structure elements, or direct repeats). Potential matches are rated according to their score assigned by the search program. For each sequence of the training set ModelGenerator then identifies all possible combinations of determining elements which reach the user-defined thresholds and occur in the same sequential order (D-sets). At this point, more than one potential D-set is still possible in a single sequence. The *basic set* is build of all sequences with a single D-set (at least 6 sequences are required). Distance histograms for adjacent elements are then generated from the basic set. A single D-set within sequences with more than one potential D-set can then be selected by the maximum element score and the maximum distance score based on the distance histograms. These sequences are added to the basic set. The determining elements and the regions define the basic framework of the regulatory unit model.

Analysis of individual sequences for non-determining elements is restricted to the regions as defined above. Elements within one region are selected if present in at least a significant subset of the sequences. Thus, all non-determining elements compatible with the basic framework are defined.

Finally, a complete set of distance histograms is calculated for all elements. The complex regulatory unit model consists of descriptions of all individual elements, their mean scores, their sequential order and the distance distributions observed in the training set.

2.3 Detection of matches to the generated model

Another program designated ModelInspector utilizes these models to scan any sequence for unknown regulatory units matching the model. First all matches for individual determining elements which score above the thresholds defined by the model are located in the new sequence. These individual elements are combined to match the organization of the D-set characteristic of the model. If the sum of scores of determining elements exceeds a given threshold (default: 50% of the average sum of the training set), non-determining elements are identified and the sum of scores of all elements is calculated. This total element score and the score for element distances are then used to evaluate the fit of complex elements to the model. Score thresholds are expressed in percent of the mean scores of the model (defaults are: 50% of average element score, and 30% of average distance score). An extensive description of the algorithm and the programs ModelGenerator and ModelInspector will be presented elsewhere (Frech *et al.*, in preparation).

3 Results

We selected retroviral transcriptional control regions in order to test the abilities of ModelGenerator and ModelInspector for several reasons. Retroviruses are expressed under the control of viral control regions designated long terminal repeats (LTRs), which contain all signals for transcriptional initiation as well as transcriptional termination. These LTRs contain both enhancer and promoter regions and are experimentally very well defined. Though retroviral LTRs are homologous in function, LTRs from different groups of retroviruses do not show significant overall sequence homology. Even LTRs from a single group like the Lentiviruses (e.g. HIV, SIV or VISNA) are very different in their overall sequences [14].

3.1 Generation of models for C-type and Lentivirus LTRs

We had two well defined training sets of sequences for generation of these models. The training set for the C-type LTRs contained the 17 LTRs that have already been analyzed by CoreSearch [13] plus one additional sequence (musergln1). The Lentivirus LTR training set consisted of 20 different LTRs (more details are described in [14]). The initial model used in both cases was presence of a TATA box followed by a polyA signal (AATAAA). We first analyzed the TATA boxes present in the training sets and established individual consensus profiles for C-type and Lentivirus TATA boxes with the program ConsInd [5]. The derived consensi are remarkably different in details as shown in Figure 1. Especially the region between

a)

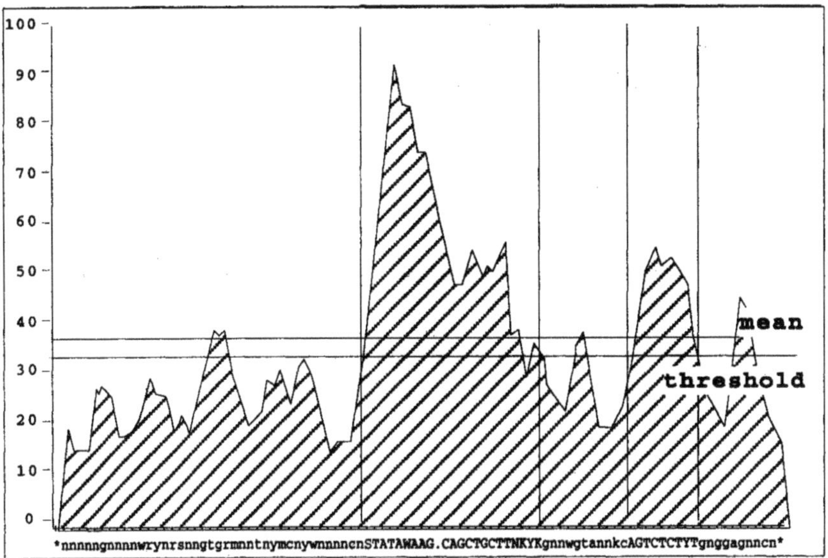

b)

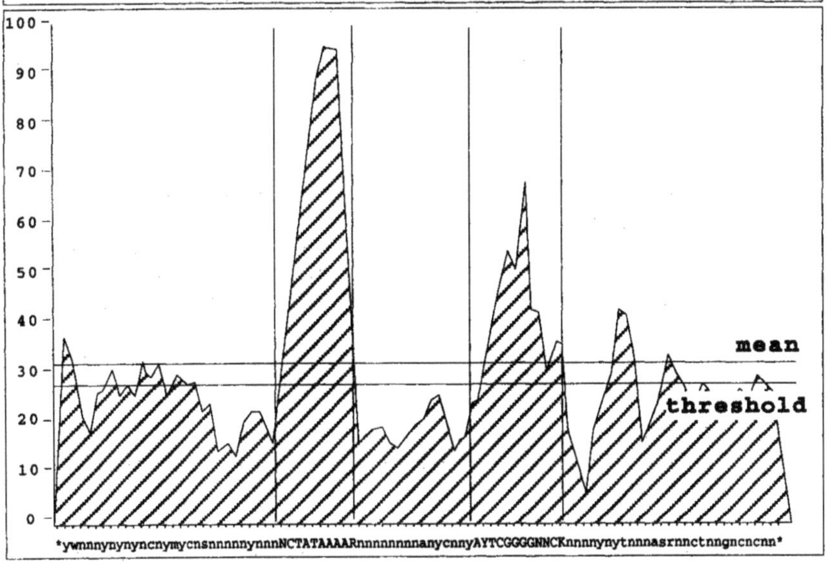

Figure 1: Consensus index profiles. The sequence regions determined to be significant are printed in upper case and marked by two vertical lines. The average consensus index and the threshold used to define the conserved regions are represented by horizontal lines.

a) Consensus index profile of Lentivirus LTR TATA box

b) Consensus index profile of C-type LTR TATA box

the TATA box and the cap-site is much better conserved in Lentivirus LTRs. We suspected these consensi to be specific for the respective LTR type and scored all TATA boxes of both sets against both consensi with ConsInspector [5].

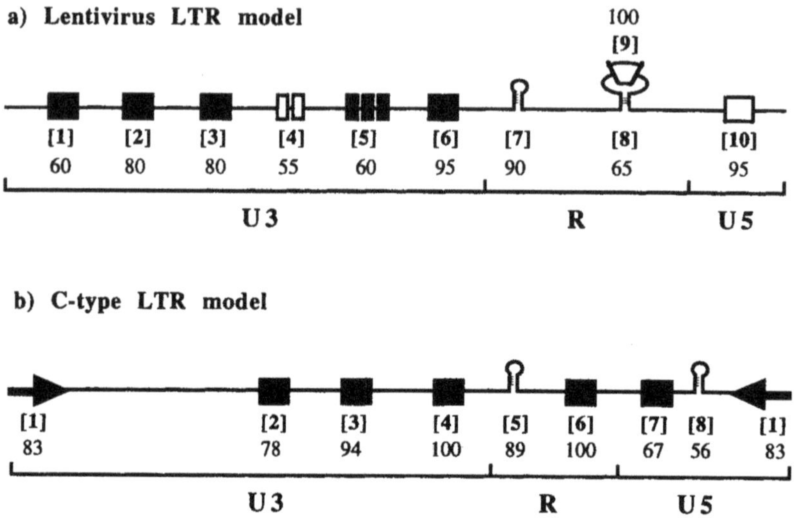

Figure 2: Graphical representations of the Lentivirus and the C-type LTR models
Consensus elements identified by ConsInspector are shown as black boxes. Elements found by MatInspector are shown as white boxes. Hairpins are indicated by a simple hairpin symbol regardless of their true structure. Inverted repeats are shown as black arrows. Bold numbers in brackets **[#]** identify individual elements and numbers below these identifiers show the frequency of the respective elements (in % of sequences containing the elements).
a) Lentivirus LTR model: **[1]** primate element block, **[2]** TATA upstream element, **[3]** Bel-1 similar region, **[4]** NF-κB sites, **[5]** SP-1 sites, **[6]** TATA box, **[7]** TAR region, **[8]** polyA signal hairpin, **[9]** polyA signal, **[10]** polyA downstream element.
b) C-Type LTR model: **[1]** terminal inverted repeat, **[2]** upstream signal, **[3]** CCAAT box, **[4]** TATA box, **[5]** R-region hairpin, **[6]** polyA signal, **[7]** polyA downstream element, **[8]** U5 hairpin.

We chose a cutoff score of 50% of the mean consensus score calculated by ConsInd. None of the C-type TATA boxes reached the cutoff score of the Lentivirus TATA box consensus (1.81) while all were above the cutoff score of the C-type TATA box consensus (1.48). However, three Lentivirus TATA boxes scored above C-type cutoff (sivcps, fivltr, pumaltr) and one Lentivirus TATA box did not reach the Lentivirus cutoff score (bimpevpp). This indicated that even the most specific single element was not sufficient to identify the LTRs. A similar analysis carried out with the polyA signal was even less discriminative for C-type and Lentivirus LTRs (data not shown). However, a combination of both signals yielded better results. There was no TATA/polyA combination in Lentivirus LTRs for which both elements exceeded the thresholds for C-type specific elements and vice versa.

The CoreSearch and ModelGenerator analysis of the LTR training sets revealed additional elements for both LTR types yielding a total of 8 elements for the C-type model (Frech *et al.*, in preparation) and 10 elements for the Lentivirus model [14]. The complete structure of the two LTR models is depicted in Figure 2.

As mentioned in the System and Algorithm section we used distance histograms rather than assuming Gaussian distribution of the distances which would allow calculation of the average value and the standard deviation. The reason for this is shown in Figure 3 which represents the distance histogram derived from the analysis of the distances between the Lentivirus TATA box and the Lentivirus polyA signal. As can be clearly seen there were three preferred distance regions and the average value of the distance distribution (129 bp) would have been totally misleading since it occurred only in 2 of 19 sequences.

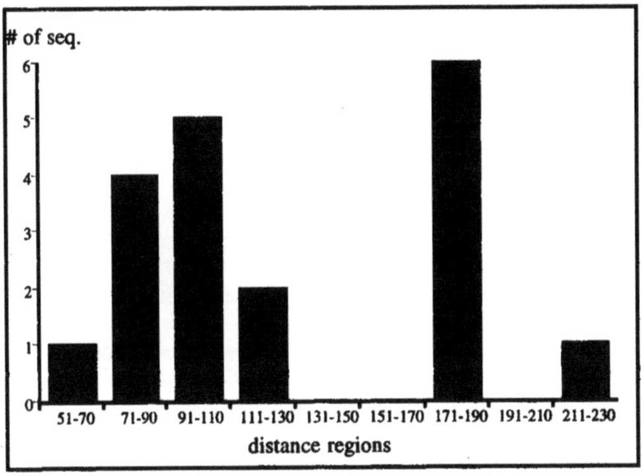

Figure 3: Distance distribution between Lentivirus TATA box and polyA signal
The distance histogram is determined from the training set of Lentivirus LTR sequences.The minimum distance is 64 bp, the maximum distance 214 bp.

3.2 Evaluation of the LTR models

Both LTR models developed by ModelGenerator were used with the program ModelInspector in order to assess the specificity of the models. We already showed that each of the 20 Lentivirus LTR sequences is recognized by a model build from the other 19 sequences [14]. First we analyzed which LTRs were recognized by each model. For that purpose we matched all LTRs from both training sets against both models. Table 1 shows the results of this test. Both models fully recognized their respective training set and clearly discriminated against the other LTR type. Moreover, both models were sensitive to the differences of subgroups within their own training set (Table 1). The different scoring ranges correlated with the biologically defined subgroups with only a very small overlap (0.1) in case of primate and non-primate Lentiviruses. This overlap was solely due to sivsyk which lacked three elements present in all other primate Lentiviruses. These results suggested that both LTR models were very specific. However, in order to verify this it was not sufficient to test the models only with the training set. Therefore, we analyzed all mammalian sequences of GenBank Release 92.0 (sections primate, rodent, and other mammalian, altogether 88,029,873 nucleotides in 89,592 sequences) with ModelInspector and the Lentivirus LTR model. In addition the 1994 Release of the Human Retroviruses and AIDS database [15] containing more than 100 Lentivirus sequences including the LTRs was analyzed in order to determine the number of false negative matches.

Table 1: Cross-validation of LTR models

	primate Lentivirus LTRs			non-primate Lentivirus LTRs			C-type LTRs
	min.	max.	mean	min.	max.	mean	
Lentivirus LTR	5.3	8.6	7.5	4.2	5.4	4.8	0

	exogenous C-type LTRs			endogenous C-type LTRs			Lentivirus LTRs
	min.	max.	mean	min.	max.	mean	
C-type LTR	7.2	7.9	7.4	3.8	5.3	4.6	0

ModelInspector correctly identified all known Lentivirus LTRs in the HIV database (identified in the annotations) indicating that the program produced no false negative matches. It is remarkable that the HIV database also included a number of partial LTRs (usually missing U5 region) which were nevertheless correctly identified. However, presence of less than half of the elements impairs detection excluding small LTR fragments. Table 2 shows the average scores for LTRs from the HIV-1, HIV-2, SIV, AGM, MND, SYK, and RELATED Lentiviruses subgroups as determined from the HIV database search. ModelInspector detected 179 new candidate LTRs on both strands in the mammalian sequences of GenBank in addition to the already known LTRs. Even if all of these new matches would be regarded false positives this would be a false positive rate of about 1 / million nucleotides (exact: 1 / 983,574 nucleotides). This GenBank database search took more than a month on a DEC Alpha 3000/600, but the search time can be reduced to less than one hour by a modified approach involving sequence preanalysis (Frech *et al.*, in preparation).

Table 2: ModelInspector ratings (element score) for Lentivirus LTRs from HIV database

	# of LTRs (partial LTRs)		min. score	max. score	mean score
HIV-1	37	(12)	4.5	7.8	6.6
HIV-2	13	(4)	4.8	7.2	6.5
SIV	21	(6)	5.8	8.5	7.6
AGM	17	(2)	5.1	8.1	6.9
MND	1	(1)	6.7	6.7	6.7
SYK	2	(1)	4.6	5.2	4.9
RELATED	16	(2)	3.5	5.4	4.2

4 Discussion

We described a new algorithm to model transcriptional regulatory regions implemented into a program package consisting of the ModelGenerator program to develop the model and the ModelInspector program capable of searching whole databases for matches to predefined models. ModelInspector has no limit for sequence length allowing the analysis of sequences of several million nucleotides in length such as complete yeast chromosomes. A set of at least 10 sequences and a simple initial model are required as input for ModelGenerator. Most of the model is generated by sequence analysis allowing the development of complex models revealing unknown elements which are part of the organizational framework of the final model. We showed this to work for two groups of retroviral LTRs and demonstrated the discriminative power of the models by cross-validation of the training sets as well as by database searches with one of the models.

ModelGenerator and ModelInspector are using a much more detailed model for regulatory sequences than PromoterScan [8], e.g. our methods use matrix-based TF-site searches in contrast to IUPAC searches employed by PromoterScan. This might explain part of the higher specificities. We have also already shown that the C_i-scores assigned by ConsInspector apparently correlate to some extent with biological functionality [16]. Thus, our approach might also directly benefit from the higher specificity of matrix-based element descriptions as compared to IUPAC searches. The promoter models used by FunSiteP [9] account for the element composition of promoters but do not include detailed organizational features as the models generated by ModelGenerator. We decided to use distance histograms as empirical measures derived from the training set because especially short distances are crucially influenced by sterical restrictions like mutual orientation of adjacent elements with respect to the helix axis. This restriction should be less effective for longer distances which is exactly what we observed.

Although LTRs include polymerase II promoters the models involved more elements in addition to the promoter. These additional elements will most likely contribute to the significant increase in specificity. We showed the LTR models to produce no false negative matches (as far as could be tested). We obtained some preliminary data in the meantime indicating that at least one LTR candidate extracted by ModelInspector from the database has promoter activity which is one of the hallmarks of functional LTRs. Therefore, the number of false positives is lower than the number of additional matches, although we could not yet determine to what extent.

ModelGenerator develops the model from a set of sequences and is not restricted to promoters or LTRs. Any detectable organization of elements within a set of sequences can therefore provide the basis for model development (examples could be enhancers, scaffold attachment regions or even gene models). The ability to construct models for quite different genetic units is one of the main difference to other model based approaches like GeneParser [11], and GRAIL [12] which are special-purpose gene prediction programs. Model generation with GeneLang [10] requires designing a grammar for a completely known model.

A clear advantage of all multi component models over detection of individual elements (e.g. TATA box) is the ability to tolerate missing individual elements without impairing recognition of the sequence by the model. The high specificity of our LTR models suggested that multi component ModelGenerator models might be suitable to distinguish between different promoter classes, e.g. identify promoters responding to a common pathway as a group. Analysis of the promoter regions of glycolytic enzymes in saccharomyces cerevisiae [2,3] indicated that this is possible in principle.

The general design of ModelGenerator also allows to use predefined models as elements for the construction of even more complex models. For example, the described LTR models could be used to develop a model for a complete provirus consisting of a 5'-LTR, a leader region, at least three reading frames for the common retroviral proteins (gag, pol, and env) and a 3'-LTR. Alternatively, a promoter model could be combined with a gene model derived by another method like GRAIL, GeneLang or GeneParser to create a more complex gene model. Of course, ModelGenerator promoter models could be implemented into one of the above methods using ModelInspector as search engine as well.

ModelGenerator integrates a variety of methods which allows extension of the basic model without further *a priori* knowledge or the necessity to alter the program. Thus, new information can be derived directly from the final model which may be a useful prospective analysis facilitating experimental design.

Acknowledgements

We thank Kerstin Quandt for critically reading the manuscript. This work was supported in part by the BMBF Verbundprojekt GENUS 413-4001-01 IB 306 D (Förderschwerpunkt Bioinformatik) and by EU grant BI04-CT95-0226 (TRADAT).

References

1. Hanks, M., Wurst, W., Anson-Cartwright, L., Auerbach, A.B., and Joyner, A.L., *Science* **269**, 679 (1995).
2. Quandt, K., Grote, K., and Werner, T., *Genomics* **33**, 301 (1996).
3. Quandt, K., Grote, K., and Werner, T., *Comp. Appl. Biosci.*, in press (1996).
4. Chen, Q.K., Hertz, G.Z., and Stormo, G.D., *Comp. Appl. Biosci.* **11**, 563 (1995).
5. Frech, K., Herrmann, G., and Werner, T., *Nucleic Acids Res.* **21**, 1655 (1993).
6. Prestridge, D.S. and Stormo, G., *Comp. Appl. Biosci.* **9**, 113 (1993).
7. Quandt, K., Frech, K., Karas, H., Wingender, E., and Werner, T., *Nucleic Acids Res.* **23**, 4878 (1995).
8. Prestridge, D.S., *J. Mol. Biol.* **249**, 923 (1995).
9. Kondrakhin, Y.V., Kel, A.E., Kolchanov, N.A., Romashchenko, A.G., and Milanesi, L., *Comp. Appl. Biosci.* **11**, 477 (1995).
10. Dong, S. and Searls, D.B., *Genomics* **23**, 540 (1994).
11. Snyder, E.E. and Stormo, G.D., *J. Mol. Biol.* **248**, 1 (1995).
12. Uberbacher, E.C. and Mural, R.J., *Proc. Natl. Acad. Sci. USA* **88**, 11261 (1991).
13. Wolfertstetter, F., Frech, K., Herrmann, G., and Werner, T., *Comp. Appl. Biosci.* **12**, 71 (1996).
14. Frech, K., Brack-Werner, R., and Werner, T., *Virology*, in press (1996).
15. Myers, G., Wain-Hobson, S., Henderson, L.E., Korber, B., Jeang, K.-T., and Pavlakis, G.N., Database by Los Alamos National Laboratory (1994).
16. Quandt, K., Frech, K., Herrmann, K., and Werner, T. in *Bioinformatics: From Nucleic Acids and Proteins to Cell Metabolism* (Eds. D. Schomburg; U. Lessel), 47, (1995).

TEST TUBE SYSTEMS WITH CUTTING/RECOMBINATION OPERATIONS

Rudolf FREUND
Institut für Computersprachen, Technische Universität Wien
Resselgasse 3, 1040 Wien, Austria
email: rudi@logic.tuwien.ac.at

Erzsébet CSUHAJ-VARJÚ
Computer and Automation Institute, Hungarian Academy of Sciences
Kende u. 13-17, 1111 Budapest, Hungary
email: csuhaj@luna.aszi.sztaki.hu

Franz WACHTLER
Institut für Histologie und Embryologie, Universität Wien
Schwarzspanierstr. 17, 1090 Wien, Austria
email: franz.wachtler@univie.ac.at

We introduce test tube systems [1,2,3,9] based on operations that are closely related to the splicing operation[8], i.e. we consider the operations of *cutting* a string at a specific site into two pieces with marking them at the cut ends and of *recombining* two strings with specificly marked endings[7]. Whereas in the splicing of two strings these strings are cut at specific sites and the cut pieces are recombined immediately in a crosswise way, in CR(cutting/recombination)-schemes cutting can happen independently from recombining the cut pieces. Test tube systems based on these operations of cutting and recombination turn out to have maximal generative power even if only very restricted types of input filters for the test tubes are used for the redistribution of the contents of the test tubes after a period of cuttings and recombinations in the test tubes.

1 Introduction

Test tube systems were introduced as biological computer systems based on DNA molecules[1,2,3,9], the practical solution of NP problems with such systems was described, and the theoretical features of test tube systems based on the splicing operation were investigated[4]. In this paper we are going to explore test tube systems based on the operations of cutting and recombination[7] and with input filters which only allow specific parts of the contents of the other test tubes to pass (such filters, for example, are conceivable for DNA molecules by combining the principles of affinity chromatography and in-situ-hybridization). As we shall show even very restricted kinds of such filters testing for the existence respectively non-existence of specific markings allow for reaching the generative power to generate any recursively enumerable language.

The computational universality of specific variants of H systems [5,10] and for test tube systems based on the splicing operation[4] has been proved recently. In this paper we shall show that universal test tube systems based on cutting and recombination rules exist for different variants of input filters.

In the second section of this paper we define the notions from formal language theory needed in this paper and introduce the formal definitions of cutting/recombination schemes (CR-schemes). In the third section of this paper we introduce test tube systems with cutting/recombination rules (CRTTS) and we prove that CRTTS can generate every recursively enumerable language. This result also implies the existence of universal CRTTS. A short summary of the results obtained in this paper and an overview of future research topics conclude the paper.

2 Definitions and Examples

In this section we only define some notions from formal language theory that we shall need in this paper. Moreover we recall the definitions for CR-schemes[7] and give some explanatory examples.

The free monoid generated by the alphabet V is denoted by V^*, its elements are called *strings* or *words* over V; λ is the empty string, $V^+ = V^* - \{\lambda\}$. The length of a string w in V^* is written as $|w|$.

A *grammar scheme* γ is a triple (V_N, V_T, P), where V_N is a (finite) set of symbols, i.e. the alphabet of *non-terminal symbols;* V_T is a (finite) set of symbols with $V_N \cap V_T = \emptyset$, i.e. the alphabet of *terminal symbols*; P is a (finite) set of *productions* of the form (α, β), where $\alpha \in (V_N \cup V_T)^+$ and $\beta \in (V_N \cup V_T)^*$. For two words $x, y \in (V_N \cup V_T)^*$, the *derivation relation* $\vdash_\gamma$ is defined if and only if $x = u\alpha v$ and $y = u\beta v$ for some production $(\alpha, \beta) \in P$ and two strings $u, v \in (V_N \cup V_T)^*$; we then also write $x \vdash_\gamma y$. The reflexive and transitive closure of the relation $\vdash_\gamma$ is denoted by $\vdash_\gamma^*$.

A *grammar* G is a quadruple (V_N, V_T, P, S), where $\gamma = (V_N, V_T, P)$ is a grammar scheme and $S \in V_N$; in a more general way, we can also take $S \in (V_N \cup V_T)^+$. The λ-free language generated by G is

$$L(G) = \{w \in V_T^+ \mid S \vdash_\gamma^* w\}. \tag{1}$$

A subset L of V_T^+ is called *recursively enumerable* if and only if there exists a grammar G that generates L, i.e. $L(G) = L$. Moreover, L is called *recursive* if and only if both L and its complement, $V_T^+ \setminus L$, are recursively enumerable. The family of (λ-free) recursively enumerable languages and the family of (λ-free) recursive languages over the alphabet V_T shall be denoted by $ENUM(V_T)$ and $REC(V_T)$, respectively.

A *grammar scheme* γ_U with $\gamma_U = (V_N, V_T, P)$ is called *universal (for V_T)* if for every $L \in ENUM(V_T)$ there exists a word A_L such that the grammar G_L with $G_L = (V_N, V_T, P, A_L)$ generates L. One of the important results of formal language theory is that for every V_T such a universal grammar γ_U exists.

Definition 1. A *cutting/recombination scheme* (or a *CR-scheme*) is a quadruple $\sigma = (V, M, C, R)$, where V is a finite alphabet; M is a finite set of *markings;* V and M are disjoint sets; C is a set of *cutting rules* of the form $u\#l\$m\#v$, where $u \in V^* \cup MV^*$, $v \in V^* \cup V^*M$, and $m, l \in M$, and $\#, \$$ are special symbols not in $V \cup M$; $R \subseteq M \times M$ is the recombination relation representing the *recombination rules.*

Cutting and recombination rules are applied to objects from $O(V, M)$, where we define

$$O(V,M) = V^+ \cup MV^* \cup V^*M \cup MV^*M, \tag{2}$$

i.e., as the empty word has no meaningful representation in nature, λ is not considered to be an object we have to deal with.

For $x, y, z \in O(V, M)$ and a cutting rule $c = u\#l\$m\#v$ we define $x \vdash_c (y, z)$ if and only if for some $\alpha \in V^* \cup MV^*$ and $\beta \in V^* \cup V^*M$ we have $x = \alpha uv\beta$ and $y = \alpha ul$, $z = mv\beta$. For $x, y, z \in O(V, M)$ and a recombination rule $r = (l, m)$ from R we define $(x, y) \vdash_r z$ if and only if for some $\alpha \in V^* \cup MV^*$ and $\beta \in V^* \cup V^*M$ we have $x = \alpha l$, $y = m\beta$, and $z = \alpha\beta$. For a CR-scheme $\sigma = (V, M, C, R)$ and any language $L \subseteq O(V, M)$ we write

$$\begin{aligned} \sigma(L) &= \{y \mid x \vdash_c (y,z) \text{ or } x \vdash_c (z,y) \text{ for some } x \in L,\ c \in C\} \cup \\ &\quad \{z \mid (x,y) \vdash_r z \text{ for some } x, y \in L,\ r \in R\}, \end{aligned} \tag{3}$$

and we define $\sigma^*(L) = \bigcup_{i \geq 0} \sigma^i(L)$, where $\sigma^0(L) = L$ and $\sigma^{i+1}(L) = \sigma^i(L) \cup \sigma(\sigma^i(L))$ for all $i \geq 0$. □

Thus $\sigma(L)$ contains all objects obtained by applying one cutting or one recombination rule to objects from L; $\sigma^*(L)$ is the smallest subset of $O(V, M)$ that contains L and is closed under the cutting and recombination rules of σ.

There is a close relationship between CR schemes and *splicing schemes (H schemes):* For short, a *splicing rule* $u_1\#v_1\$u_2\#v_2$ being applied to two strings $x_1u_1v_1y_1$ and $x_2u_2v_2y_2$ yields the two strings $x_1u_1v_2y_2$ and $x_2u_2v_1y_1$ which corresponds to cutting the strings $x_1u_1v_1y_1$ and $x_2u_2v_2y_2$ into the strings $x_1u_1[m]^+$, $[m]^- v_1y_1$ and $x_2u_2[m]^+$, $[m]^- v_2y_2$ by using the cutting rules $u_1\#[m]^+\$[m]^-\#v_1$ and $u_2\#[m]^+\$[m]^-\#v_2$ and recombining them immediately by applying the recombination rule $\left([m]^+, [m]^-\right)$ in a crosswise way.

In the following we shall restrict ourselves to cutting rules of the form $u\#[m]^{+}\,\$\,[m]^{-}\,v$, i.e. the markings generated by the cutting rule are the *positive* $\left([m]^{+}\right)$ and the *negative* $\left([m]^{-}\right)$ version of $[m]$. In this case the derivation of the two parts $xu\,[m]^{+}$, $[m]^{-}\,vy$ from the object $xuvy$ by the cutting rule $u\#[m]^{+}\,\$\,[m]^{-}\,\#v$, i.e. the derivation $xuvy \vdash_{u\#[m]^{+}\$[m]^{-}\#v} \left(xu\,[m]^{+}, [m]^{-}\,vy\right)$ in a more depictive way can be expressed by $xu \underset{[m]}{|} vy \vdash \left(xu\,[m]^{+}, [m]^{-}\,vy\right)$.

The following example shows the chemical background of the notations introduced above, i.e. the markings $[m]^{+}$ and $[m]^{-}$, respectively, correspond to the positive and negative charges of ions:

Example 1. Consider the salt molecule $NaCl$, which in water dissipates to the ions $Na+$ and $Cl-$. This reaction corresponds to applying the formal cutting rule $Na\#[m]^{+}\,\$\,[m]^{-}\,\#Cl$ to the molecule string $NaCl$, which yields the formal derivation step $Na \underset{[m]}{|} Cl \vdash \left(Na\,[m]^{+}, [m]^{-}\,Cl\right)$. Obviously the two parts $Na\,[m]^{+}$, $[m]^{-}\,Cl$ can be recombined to $NaCl$ by the recombination rule $\left([m]^{+}, [m]^{-}\right)$, i.e. $\left(Na\,[m]^{+}, [m]^{-}\,Cl\right) \vdash NaCl$. □

3 CR Test Tube Systems

In this section we introduce test tube systems [1,2,3,9] that are based on the formal operations of cutting and recombination rules as introduced in the previous section. The idea of test tube systems is to describe computational devices where the computations in each test tube are based on specific operations and any computation is done in a distributed way. As a communication step the resulting contents of the test tubes then is redistributed according to specific constraints, i.e. the contents of each test tube is distributed to all test tubes according to specific input filters again, whereas the rest remains in the test tube. These ideas have already been formalized for the splicing operation [4]; in the following we define test tube systems where the operations that can take place in one test tube are cuttings and recombinations and investigate the generative power of these systems with the operations of cuttings and recombinations. We shall show that every recursively enumerable language can be generated by such a test tube system which only needs a very special restricted kind of input filters. Moreover, this result also guarantees the existence of a universal test tube system with cuttings and recombinations.

Definition 2. A *test tube system with cuttings and recombinations* (a *CRTTS* for short) σ is a quintuple (V, M, A, n, ρ, I), where

1. V is a (finite) set of *symbols;*
2. M is a (finite) set of *markings;* M and V are disjoint sets;
3. A is a (finite) set of *axioms,* which are elements from $O(V, M)$;
4. n, $n \geq 1$, is the number of test tubes;
5. ρ is a (finite) sequence $(\rho_1, ..., \rho_n)$, where $\rho_i = (C_i, R_i)$ is a finite set of *test tube operations of cuttings and recombinations,* respectively, in the test tube T_i, i.e. C_i is a (finite) set of cutting rules over (V, M) and R_i is a (finite) set of recombination rules over (V, M); $\sigma_i = (V, M, C_i, R_i)$ is the corresponding CR-scheme;
6. $I = (I_1, ..., I_n)$, where $I_i \subseteq O(V, M)$ is the *input filter* for the test tube T_i, $1 \leq i \leq n$.

The computations in the system σ run as follows: At the beginning of the computation the axioms are distributed over the n test tubes T_i according to the corresponding input filters I_i, i.e. T_i starts with $A \cap I_i$. Now let L_i be the contents of T_i at the beginning of a derivation step. Then in each test tube the CR-scheme σ_i operates on L_i, i.e. we obtain $\sigma_i^*(L_i)$. The next substep is the redistribution of $\sigma_i^*(L_i)$ over all test tubes according to the corresponding input filters. From $\sigma_i^*(L_i)$ only the part $\sigma_i^*(L_i) \cap I_j$ that passes the input filter I_j is distributed to the test tubes T_j, $1 \leq j \leq n$, whereas the rest $\sigma_i^*(L_i) \setminus \left(\bigcup_{1 \leq j \leq n} (\sigma_i^*(L_i) \cap I_j)\right)$ remains in T_i. The final result of the computations in σ consists of all strings from V^+ that can be extracted from the *final test tube* T_1.

More formally, an *instantaneous description* (ID for short) of the system σ is an n-tuple $(L_1, ..., L_n)$ with $L_i \subseteq O(V, M)$, $1 \leq i \leq n$, where L_i describes the contents of test tube T_i at the beginning of a derivation step. The initial ID is $(A \cap I_1, ..., A \cap I_n)$, i.e. at time $t = 0$ the test tubes T_i contain the axioms $A \cap I_i$. Let $(L_1(t), ..., L_n(t))$ denote the ID at time t; then one derivation step with the system σ yields the ID $(L_1(t+1), ..., L_n(t+1))$, where

$$\begin{aligned} L_i(t+1) &= \left(\bigcup_{1 \leq j \leq n} (\sigma_j^*(L_j(t)) \cap I_i)\right) \cup \\ &\quad \left(\sigma_i^*(L_i(t)) \setminus \left(\bigcup_{1 \leq j \leq n} (\sigma_i^*(L_i(t)) \cap I_j)\right)\right) \\ &= \left(\left(\bigcup_{1 \leq j \leq n} \sigma_j^*(L_j(t))\right) \cap I_i\right) \cup \\ &\quad \left(\sigma_i^*(L_i(t)) \setminus \left(\sigma_i^*(L_i(t)) \cap \bigcup_{1 \leq j \leq n} I_j\right)\right). \end{aligned} \tag{4}$$

We also write $(L_1(t),...,L_n(t)) \vdash_\sigma (L_1(t+1),...,L_n(t+1))$. The language generated by σ, $L(\sigma)$, is defined by $L(\sigma) = \bigcup_{t=0}^{\infty}(L_1(t) \cap V^+)$. □

A minimal requirement on the feasability of the input filters I_i is their recursiveness, i.e. we demand that it is decidable whether a string can pass the filter or not. Yet in order to obtain more interesting results we have to put restrictions on the input filters:

Definition 3. A subset of $O(V, M)$ is called a *simple* $(V, M)_2$*-filter* if it equals

1. V^+ or
2. $\{m\} V^*$ for some $m \in M$ or
3. $V^* \{m\}$ for some $m \in M$ or
4. $\{m\} V^* \{n\}$ for some $m, n \in M$.

A simple $(V, M)_2$-filter is called a *simple* $(V, M)_1$*-filter*, if it is not of the form $\{m\} V^* \{n\}$. Any finite union of simple $(V, M)_i$-filters, $i \in \{1, 2\}$, is called a $(V, M)_i$*-filter*. □

In the following example we show how the language $\{a^{2^n} \mid n \geq 1\}$ can be generated by a CRTTS with $(V, M)_1$-filters:

Example 2. Let $\sigma = (V, M, A, 8, \rho, I)$ be the CRTTS with

$$V = \{a, B, F, X, Y\},\ M = \left\{[x]^+, [x]^- \mid x \in \{b, c, d, e, f, l, n, r, s, t\}\right\},$$
$$A = \{XaaBY, XaaY, XBY, F\},$$
$$\rho = (\rho_1, \rho_2, \rho_3, \rho_4, \rho_5, \rho_6, \rho_7, \rho_8),\ I = (I_1, I_2, I_3, I_4, I_5, I_6, I_7, I_8),$$
$$\rho_1 = \left(\emptyset, \left\{\left([s]^+, [e]^-\right)\right\}\right),$$
$$\rho_2 = \left(\left\{X\#[e]^+\$[e]^-\#aa, \#[s]^+\$[s]^-\#F\right\}, \left\{\left([f]^+, [t]^-\right)\right\}\right),$$
$$\rho_3 = \left(\left\{aa\#[f]^+\$[f]^-\#BY, F\#[t]^+\$[t]^-\#\right\}, \emptyset\right),$$
$$\rho_4 = \left(\left\{aa\#[b]^+\$[b]^-\#BY, XB\#[c]^+\$[c]^-\#Y\right\}, \emptyset\right),$$
$$\rho_5 = \begin{pmatrix} \left\{X\#[d]^+\$[d]^-\#aaa, X\#[d]^+\$[d]^-\#aaY\right\}, \\ \left\{\left([b]^+, [c]^-\right), \left([c]^+, [d]^-\right)\right\} \end{pmatrix},$$
$$\rho_6 = \begin{pmatrix} \left\{w\#[r]^+\$[r]^-\#aY \mid w \in \{aa, aB, Ba\}\right\} \cup \\ \left\{Xaa\#[n]^+\$[n]^-\#Y\right\}, \emptyset \end{pmatrix},$$
$$\rho_7 = \left(\left\{X\#[l]^+\$[l]^-\#v \mid v \in \{aaa, aaB, BaY\}\right\}, \left\{\left([r]^+, [n]^-\right)\right\}\right),$$

$\rho_8 = \left(\emptyset, \left\{\left([n]^+, [l]^-\right)\right\}\right)$;
$I_1 = V^* \left\{[s]^+\right\} \cup \left\{[e]^-\right\} V^*, I_2 = V^* \left\{[f]^+\right\} \cup \left\{[t]^-\right\} V^* \cup V^* \left\{[t]^+\right\}$,
$I_3 = I_4 = I_6 = V^+$, $I_5 = V^* \left\{[b]^+\right\} \cup V^* \left\{[c]^+\right\} \cup \left\{[c]^-\right\} V^*$,
$I_7 = V^* \left\{[r]^+\right\} \cup \left\{[n]^-\right\} V^*$, $I_8 = V^* \left\{[n]^+\right\} \cup \left\{[l]^-\right\} V^*$.

The generation of the words a^{2^n} in this CR test tube system briefly can be described in the following way:

In general, let us assume we have already obtained the word $Xa^{2^n}BY$ for some $n \geq 1$ in test tube T_4 (originally we start with the axiom $XaaBY$), where the following cuttings can take place: $Xa^{2^n} \underset{[b]}{|} BY \vdash \left(Xa^{2^n} [b]^+, [b]^- BY\right)$ and $XB \underset{[c]}{|} Y \vdash \left(XB [c]^+, [c]^- Y\right)$. In T_5 we then obtain $\left(Xa^{2^n} [b]^+, [c]^- Y\right) \vdash Xa^{2^n}Y$ by the recombination rule $\left([b]^+, [c]^-\right)$, and by cutting with one of the rules $X\# [d]^+ \$ [d]^- \#aaa, X\# [d]^+ \$ [d]^- \#aaY$ we get $X \underset{[d]}{|} a^{2^n}Y \vdash \left(X [d]^+, [d]^- a^{2^n}Y\right)$. The recombination rule $\left([c]^+, [d]^-\right)$ then yields $\left(XB [c]^+, [d]^- a^{2^n}Y\right) \vdash XBa^{2^n}Y$. In sum, we have rotated the symbol B from the end to the beginning of the block of symbols a.

The rules in the test tubes T_6, T_7 and T_8 have the effect that a symbol a at the end of the word to the left of the symbol Y is eliminated, yet instead two symbols a are added at the beginning, i.e. from Xa^kBa^mY we obtain $Xa^{k+2}Ba^{m-1}Y$. A full cycle of rotations therefore doubles the number of symbols a, i.e. from $XBa^{2^n}Y$ we obtain $Xa^{2^{n+1}}BY$.

The test tubes T_3, T_2, and T_1 finally allow us to obtain the terminal strings a^{2^n} : In T_3 we get $Xa^{2^n} \underset{[f]}{|} BY \vdash \left(Xa^{2^n} [f]^+, [f]^- BY\right)$ and $F \underset{[t]}{|} F [t]^+, [t]^-$. The objects $Xa^{2^n} [f]^+$, $F [t]^+$, and $[t]^-$ are passed to T_2, where we have $\left(Xa^{2^n} [f]^+, [t]^-\right) \vdash Xa^{2^n}$, $X \underset{[e]}{|} a^{2^n} \vdash \left(X [e]^+, [e]^- a^{2^n}\right)$, as well as $\underset{[s]}{|} F [t]^+ \vdash \left([s]^+, [s]^- F [t]^+\right)$. Passing the objects $[e]^- a^{2^n}$ and $[s]^+$ to T_1, we finally obtain the terminal word a^{2^n} by $\left([s]^+, [e]^- a^{2^n}\right) \vdash a^{2^n}$. □

Remark 1. In general, the formal definitions allow an infinite number of objects to be generated in one derivation step, which is an unnatural situation for practical implementations. A more practical assumption would be that instead of $\sigma_i^*(L_i)$ any arbitrary (finite) subset of $\sigma_i^*(L_i)$ can evolve in the test tube T_i during a computation period. Then only this subset is distributed to all test tubes according to the input filters. In fact, for all examples and all constructions in the proofs of this paper such an interpretation of the computations in the test tubes still would allow us to generate all desired objects, although it would never be clear, when these objects would evolve. In a practical environment the number and the size of objects that can be generated also depends on the amount of original material of axioms we take at the beginning. Moreover, if parts of (the subset of) $\sigma_i^*(L_i)$ are to be redistributed over different test tubes it is only necessary to assume that any allowed distribution of the whole material will possibly happen; in practical implementations of test tube systems an intermediate amplification [2,9] of the material may already guarantee that enough material is distributed to all the possible test tubes.

Similar ideas as for the construction of the CRTTS in the preceding example can be used for proving the general result established in the following theorem:

Theorem 1. *For every recursively enumerable language L, $L \subseteq V_T^+$, we can construct a CRTTS σ_L with $(V,M)_1$-filters which generates L.*

Proof. Let L be given by a grammar $G'_L = (V'_N, V_T, P', S')$, i.e. $L(G'_L) = L$. Without loss of generality we can consider the language $L\{h\}$ instead of L, where $h \notin (V'_N \cup V_T)$ is a new symbol; let $G_L = (V_N, V_T, P, S)$ be a grammar such that $L(G_L) = L\{h\}$ and moreover for each derivation of any word $wh \in L\{h\}$ the symbol h is generated in the last step of this derivation and does not occur in another sentential form of this derivation. The effective construction of G_L from G'_L is obvious by using common proof techniques from the theory of formal languages and therefore omitted. Moreover, for each $(\alpha,\beta) \in P$ without loss of generality we can assume $1 \leq |\alpha| \leq 2$ and $0 \leq |\beta| \leq 2$. Now let $P_0 = P \cup \{(U,U) \mid U \in (V_N \cup V_T)\} = \{(\alpha_i,\beta_i) \mid 1 \leq i \leq m\}$ and σ_L be the CRTTS $\sigma_L = (V, M, A, 3m+5, \rho, I)$ with

$$V = V_N \cup V_T \cup \{h\} \cup \{B, F, X, Y\},$$

$$M = \left\{[x]^+, [x]^- \mid x \in \{b,c,d,e,f,h,s,t\} \cup \{i_l, i_n, i_r \mid 1 \leq i \leq m\}\right\},$$

$$A = \{XSBY, F, XBY\} \cup \{X\beta_i Y \mid 1 \leq i \leq m\},$$

$$\rho = (\rho_1, \rho_2, \rho_3, \rho_4, \rho_5, \rho_6, \rho_7, \ldots, \rho_{3m+4}, \rho_{3m+5}),$$

$$\rho_1 = \left(\emptyset, \left\{\left([s]^+, [e]^-\right)\right\}\right),$$

$$\rho_2 = \begin{pmatrix} \left\{X\#[e]^+\$[e]^-\#a \mid a \in V\right\} \cup \left\{\#[s]^+\$[s]^-\#F\right\}, \\ \left\{\left([f]^+, [t]^-\right)\right\} \end{pmatrix},$$

$$\rho_3 = \left(\left\{a\#[f]^+\$[f]^-\#hBY \mid a \in V\right\} \cup \left\{F\#[t]^+\$[t]^-\#\right\}, \emptyset\right),$$

$$\rho_4 = \left(\begin{array}{l} \left\{ w\#\,[b]^+\,\$\,[b]^-\,\#BY \mid w \in V^2 \cup \{X\}\,V \right\} \cup \\ \left\{ XB\#\,[c]^+\,\$\,[c]^-\,\#Y \right\}, \emptyset \end{array} \right),$$
$$\rho_5 = \left(\begin{array}{l} \left\{ X\#\,[d]^+\,\$\,[d]^-\,\#v \mid v \in V^3 \cup V^2\,\{Y\} \cup V\,\{Y\} \right\}, \\ \left\{ \left([b]^+, [c]^-\right), \left([c]^+, [d]^-\right) \right\} \end{array} \right),$$
$$I_1 = V^* \left\{ [s]^+ \right\} \cup \left\{ [e]^- \right\} V^*,\ I_2 = V^* \left\{ [f]^+ \right\} \cup \left\{ [t]^- \right\} V^* \cup V^* \left\{ [t]^+ \right\},$$
$$I_3 = I_4 = V^+,\ I_5 = V^* \left\{ [b]^+ \right\} \cup V^* \left\{ [c]^+ \right\} \cup \left\{ [c]^- \right\} V^*,$$

and for all i with $1 \leq i \leq m$,

$$\rho_{3i+3} = \left(\begin{array}{l} \left\{ w\#\,[i_r]^+\,\$\,[i_r]^-\,\#\alpha_i Y \mid w \in \{XB\} \cup V^2 \cup \right. \\ \left. \{uB, Bu \mid u \in V\} \right\} \cup \left\{ X\beta_i\#\,[i_n]^+\,\$\,[i_n]^-\,\#Y \right\}, \emptyset, \end{array} \right)$$
$$\rho_{3i+4} = \left(\begin{array}{l} \left\{ \begin{array}{l} X\#\,[i_l]^+\,\$\,[i_l]^-\,\#v \mid v \in V^3 \cup V^2\,\{B\} \cup V\,\{B\}\,V \cup \\ \{B\}\,V^2 \cup V\,\{BY\} \cup \{B\}\,V\,\{Y\} \cup \{BY\} \end{array} \right\}, \\ \left\{ \left([i_r]^+, [i_n]^-\right) \right\} \end{array} \right),$$
$$\rho_{3i+5} = \left(\emptyset, \left\{ \left([i_n]^+, [i_l]^-\right) \right\} \right),$$
$$I_{3i+3} = V^+,\ I_{3i+4} = V^* \left\{ [i_r]^+ \right\} \cup \left\{ [i_n]^- \right\} V^*,$$
$$I_{3i+5} = V^* \left\{ [i_n]^+ \right\} \cup \left\{ [i_l]^- \right\} V^*.$$

Any sentential form w occuring in a derivation in G_L is represented by a rotated version of the form $XvBuY$, where $w = uv$, in σ_L; the symbol B marking the beginning of the word w in its rotated version in $XvBuY$ can be rotated in the test tubes T_4 and T_5 as it was already explained in the previous example. The final extraction of the terminal words in Lh is done in the test tubes T_3, T_2, and T_1 in a similar way as in the previous example. In the test tubes T_{3i+3}, T_{3i+4}, and T_{3i+5} the application of a production (α_i, β_i) is simulated in that way that α_i is eliminated at the right end and β_i is inserted at the left end, i.e. from $XvBu\alpha_iY$ we obtain $X\beta_ivBuY$: By the cutting rules in T_{3i+3} we obtain $Xz \underset{[i_r]}{\mid} \alpha_iY \vdash \left(Xz\,[i_r]^+, [i_r]^-\,\alpha_iY\right)$ and $X\beta_i \underset{[i_n]}{\mid} Y \vdash \left(X\beta_i\,[i_n]^+, [i_n]^-\,Y\right)$, in T_{3i+4} the cutting and recombination rules yield $\left(Xz\,[i_r]^+, [i_n]^-\,Y\right) \vdash XzY$, $X \underset{[i_l]}{\mid} zY \vdash \left(X\,[i_l]^+, [i_l]^-\,zY\right)$, and in T_{3i+5} we obtain $\left(X\beta_i\,[i_n]^+, [i_l]^-\,zY\right) \vdash X\beta_izY$. By simulating the additional unit productions (U, U), every symbol $U \in (V_N \cup V_T)$ can be rotated, i.e. from

$XvBuUY$ we obtain $XUvBuY$. In this way we can rotate the sentential form $u\alpha v$ represented by a string of the form as $Xv_2Bu\alpha v_1Y$, $v = v_1v_2$, until the position where we want to apply a production (α, β) is just at the left of the symbol Y, i.e. until we have obtained $XvBu\alpha Y$. □

When using $(V, M)_2$-filters, all the test tubes T_{3i+3}, T_{3i+4} and T_{3i+5}, $1 \leq i \leq m$, as well as T_4 and T_5 constructed in the proof of Theorem 1 can be merged into only two test tubes T_2' and T_3', respectively:

Theorem 2. *For every recursively enumerable language L, $L \subseteq V_T^+$, we can construct a CRTTS σ_L' with $(V, M)_2$-filters and only three test tubes which generates L.*

Proof. Let L be given by the grammar G_L and let P_0 be defined as in the proof of Theorem 1.

We now consider the CRTTS $\sigma_L' = (V, M, A, 3, (\rho_1', \rho_2', \rho_3'), (I_1', I_2', I_3'))$, where M, A are defined as in the proof of Theorem 1 and

$$\begin{aligned}
\rho_1' = \Big(&\emptyset, \Big\{\left([s]^+, [e]^-\right), \left([f]^+, [t]^-\right)\Big\}\Big),\\
\rho_2' = \Big(&\Big\{X\#\, [i_l]^+\, \$\, [i_l]^-\, \#v \mid v \in V^3 \cup V^2\{B\} \cup V\{B\}V \cup \{B\}V^2 \cup \\
&V\{BY\} \cup \{B\}V\{Y\}, 1 \leq i \leq m\Big\} \cup \Big\{w\#\, [i_r]^+\, \$\, [i_r]^-\, \#\alpha_i Y \mid \\
&\{w \in \{B\} \cup \{Bu \mid u \in V\} \cup V^2, 1 \leq i \leq m\}\Big\} \cup \\
&\Big\{X\beta_i\#\, [i_n]^+\, \$\, [i_n]^-\, \#Y \mid 1 \leq i \leq m\Big\} \cup \Big\{\#\, [s]^+\, \$\, [s]^-\, \#F\Big\} \cup \\
&\Big\{X\#\, [d]^+\, \$\, [d]^-\, \#v \mid v \in V^3 \cup V^2\{B\} \cup V\{BY\}\Big\} \cup \\
&\Big\{w\#\, [b]^+\, \$\, [b]^-\, \#BY \mid w \in V\Big\} \cup \Big\{XB\#\, [c]^+\, \$\, [c]^-\, \#Y\Big\} \cup \\
&\Big\{X\#\, [e]^+\, \$\, [e]^-\, \#w \mid w \in V^3 \cup V^2\{h\} \cup V\{hB\}\Big\} \cup \\
&\Big\{a\#\, [f]^+\, \$\, [f]^-\, \#hBY \mid a \in V\Big\} \cup \Big\{F\#\, [t]^+\, \$\, [t]^-\, \#\Big\}, \emptyset\Big),\\
\rho_3' = \Big(&\emptyset, \Big\{\left([i_n]^+, [i_l]^-\right), \left([i_r]^+, [i_n]^-\right), \left([c]^+, [d]^-\right), \left([b]^+, [c]^-\right)\Big\}\Big);\\
I_1' = &\Big\{[e]^-\Big\}V^*\Big\{[f]^+\Big\} \cup V^*\Big\{[s]^+\Big\} \cup \Big\{[t]^-\Big\}V^*,\ I_2' = V^+,\\
I_3' = &\Big\{[d]^-\Big\}V^*\Big\{[b]^+\Big\} \cup V^*\Big\{[c]^+\Big\} \cup \Big\{[c]^-\Big\}V^* \cup \\
&\textstyle\bigcup_{1 \leq i \leq m}\left(\Big\{[i_l]^-\Big\}V^*\Big\{[i_r]^+\Big\} \cup V^*\Big\{[i_n]^+\Big\} \cup \Big\{[i_n]^-\Big\}V^*\right).
\end{aligned}$$

By the cutting rules in T_2' we obtain $X \underset{[i_l]}{\mid} uBv\alpha_i Y \vdash \left(X\, [i_l]^+, [i_l]^-\, uBv\alpha_i Y\right)$ and $[i_l]^-\, uBv \underset{[i_r]}{\mid} \alpha_i Y \vdash \left([i_l]^-\, uBv\, [i_r]^+, [i_r]^-\, \alpha_i Y\right)$, as well as in addition

$X\beta_i \underset{[i_n]}{|} Y \vdash \left(X\beta_i [i_n]^+, [i_n]^- Y\right)$; by the recombination rules in T_3' we get $\left(X\beta_i [i_n]^+, [i_l]^- uBv [i_r]^+\right) \vdash X\beta_i uBv [i_r]^+$ and $\left(X\beta_i uBv [i_r]^+, [i_n]^- Y\right) \vdash X\beta_i uBvY$, i.e. in sum from $XuBv\alpha_i Y$ we derive $X\beta_i uBvY$ thus simulating the application of the production (α_i, β_i). Rotating the symbol B works in a similar way, thus yielding $XBwY$ from $XwBY$, and terminal strings $w \in V_T^+$ are obtained in T_1' by passing the objects $[e]^- w [f]^+$ as well as $[s]^+$ and $[t]^-$ from T_2' to T_1'. The use of the $(V, M)_2$-filters $\left\{[e]^-\right\} V^* \left\{[f]^+\right\}$ in I_1' as well as of the $(V, M)_2$-filters $\left\{[d]^-\right\} V^* \left\{[b]^+\right\}$ and $\left\{[i_l]^-\right\} V^* \left\{[i_r]^+\right\}$, $1 \le i \le m$, respectively, which are not $(V, M)_1$ -filters, guarantees that only objects with corresponding markings on the left-hand side and on the right-hand side can pass from T_2' to T_1' and T_3', whereas objects with markings that do not fit together remain in T_2'. □

The existence of universal grammar schemes now implies the existence of universal CRTTS with $(V, M)_i$-filters, $i \in \{1, 2\}$:

Corollary 1. *For every alphabet V_T and every universal grammar scheme γ_U for V_T, $\gamma_U = (V_U, V_T, P_U)$, we can effectively construct a universal CRTTS $\sigma_{U,i}$, $\sigma_{U,i} = (V_i, M_i, A_i, n_i, \rho_i, I_i)$, with $(V, M)_i$-filters, $i \in \{1, 2\}$, such that any $L \in ENUM(V_T)$ is generated by the CRTTS $\sigma_{L,i}$ with $(V, M)_i$-filters with $\sigma_{L,i} = (V_i, M_i, A_i \cup \{XA_L BY\}, n_i, \rho_i, I_i)$, where A_L is the axiom for which the grammar $G_L = (V_N, V_T, P, A_L)$ generates L; in the case $i = 2$, $n_2 = 3$, i.e. ρ_2 consists of only three components.*

Proof. We just have to apply the constructions in the proofs of Theorem 1 and Theorem 2, respectively, to the universal grammar scheme γ_U for V_T with the only exception that we do not take $XSBY$ as an axiom in A. Instead of this, in every special CRTTS $\sigma_{L,i}$ with $(V, M)_i$-filters the starting axiom A_L is taken. □

4 Summary and Future Research

The construction of molecular computers based on test tubes has been considered by using different operations on the test tubes [1,2,3,9]. Test tube systems based on the splicing operation were shown to allow the construction of universal mechanisms [4]. In the preceding section we have shown the (theoretical) possibility how to obtain universal biological molecular computers based on test tube systems with cutting and recombination rules. Our definitions can easily be extended in order to cover a large variety of such test tube sytems [6]; hence our results should also be true for various possible practical implementations of such systems. On the other hand, we only provide a kind of programming language for molecular computers; feasible solutions for specific problems should take advantage of the specific features of CRTTS without only relying on the general methods used in the proofs of the results given in this paper.

Acknowledgements

The first two authors want to gratefully thank Gheorghe Păun for days (and nights) of intensive discussions on the topics related with splicing and test tube systems and they also appreciate fruitful discussions with Lila Kari on some of the topics considered in this paper. The work of the second author was supported by Hungarian Scientific Research Fund OTKA No. T017105.

References

1. L. M. Adleman, Molecular computation of solutions to combinatorial problems, *Science* **226**, 1021 – 1024 (1994).
2. L. M. Adleman, On constructing a molecular computer, *manuscript* (1995).
3. D. Boneh, C. Dunworth, R.J. Lipton, and J. Sgall, On the computational power of DNA, *to appear* (1996).
4. E. Csuhaj-Varjú, L. Kari, and Gh. Păun, Test tube distributed systems based on splicing, *Computers and Artificial Intelligence*, Vol. **15** (2), 211-232 (1996).
5. R. Freund, L. Kari, and Gh. Păun, DNA computing based on splicing: The existence of universal computers, Techn. Report 185-2/FR-2/95, TU Wien, Institute for Computer Languages (1995).
6. R. Freund and F. Freund, Test tube systems or How to bake a DNA cake, Proc. Workshop Grammar Systems: Recent Results and Perspectives, *to appear* (1996).
7. R. Freund and F. Wachtler, Universal systems with operations related to splicing, *Computers and Artificial Intelligence*, Vol. **15** (4), 273-294 (1996).
8. T. Head, Formal language theory and DNA: An analysis of the generative capacity of specific recombinant behaviors, *Bull. Math. Biology* **49**, 737 – 759 (1987).
9. R. J. Lipton, Speeding up computations via molecular biology, *manuscript* (1994).
10. Gh. Păun, Regular extended H systems are computationally universal, *J. Automata, Languages and Combinatorics*, Vol. 1 (1), 27 - 36 (1996).

ORGANIZING AND COMPUTING METABOLIC PATHWAY DATA IN TERMS OF BINARY RELATIONS

S. GOTO, H. BONO, H. OGATA, W. FUJIBUCHI, T. NISHIOKA,[a] K. SATO,[b]
M. KANEHISA
Institute for Chemical Research, Kyoto University,
Uji, Kyoto 611, Japan

A new database system named KEGG is being organized to computerize functional aspects of genes and genomes in terms of the binary relations of interacting molecules or genes. We are currently working on the metabolic pathway database that is composed of three interconnected sections: genes, molecules, and pathways, which are also linked to a number of existing databases through our DBGET retrieval system. Here we present the basic concept of binary relations and hierarchical classifications to represent the metabolic pathway data. The database operations are then defined as an extension of the relational operations, and the path computation problem is considered as a deduction from binary relations. An example of using KEGG for the functional prediction of genomic sequences is presented.

1 Introduction

The first complete genome of an organism, $\phi x174$, was determined in 1977,[1] which was followed by the explosion of DNA sequence data for specific genes, as well as for small genomes of viruses and organelles. The first complete genome of a free-living organism, *Haemophilus influenzae*, was determined in 1995,[2] which would certainly be followed by the explosion of complete genomic sequences and complete gene catalogs of a number of organisms from bacteria to eukaryotes. Whereas the experimental technologies have been refined to systematically analyze a whole genome, the computational methods for deciphering functional implications are still based on the analysis of each gene or gene product at a time. A systematic computational analysis is required for functional prediction of a whole genome.

At present, the functional data is computerized as an attribute of each sequence, for example, in the features tables of the sequence databases and in the motif libraries such as PROSITE.[3] Thus, the basic idea for functional prediction is to search similarities of each sequence in the sequence databases or in the motif libraries and then to extend sequence similarities to functional

[a]Present address: Graduate school of Agriculture, Kyoto University, Sakyo-ku, Kyoto 606-01, Japan
[b]Permanent address: Cray Research Japan LTD., 12-25 Hiroshiba-cho, Suita-shi, Osaka 564, Japan

similarities. The problem here is the lack of a suitable measure for the correctness of functional assignment, especially for the similarities in the so-called twilight zone. The sequence-function relationships of single molecules represent how individual components of a biological system work, and they do not contain higher level information of how components are connected to form a functional unit, such as a metabolic pathway, a signal transduction and an operon. As long as the assignment is made for each component separately, it will be difficult to check if such a functional unit is properly formed.

We have initiated a project named KEGG,[c] Kyoto Encyclopedia of Genes and Genomes, to computerize current knowledge of the information pathways of genes and gene products, which may be considered as wiring diagrams of biological systems. KEGG consists of three types of data, pathways, genes, and molecules, that are linked with each other and with the existing databases through our DBGET [d] integrated database system.[4] Currently, we focus our attention to the metabolic pathways and enzyme genes. The database project LIGAND [5] for enzyme reactions, enzymes, and metabolic compounds is also tightly coupled with the KEGG project. In this paper, we present the basic concept of the binary relation between two interacting molecules or genes as a fundamental element to represent the pathway, the manipulation of binary relations based on relational operations, and the path computation as a deduction from binary relations. We also briefly mention how the pathway data can be utilized to make a functional assignment from a gene catalog.

2 Data Representation

2.1 Basic Data Item

The basic data item in KEGG is a gene, a gene product, a metabolic compound, or any other molecule in a cell, which may be identified in the form:

database:entry

or

organism:gene

where 'database' is the database name such as genbank and swissprot, 'entry' is the entry name or the accession number, 'organism' is the organism name, and 'gene' is the gene name. This is the uniform identifier both in KEGG and DBGET. For example,

EC:6.3.2.3

and

[c] http://www.genome.ad.jp/kegg/kegg.html
[d] http://www.genome.ad.jp/dbget/dbget.links.html

Table 1: Examples of binary relations

Data item 1	Data item 2	Type of relation
genbank:DROALPC	medline:93273796	factual data and reference
embl:DMALPC	sp:CTNA_DROME	translation from nucleotides to amino acids
genbank:DROALPC	embl:DMALPC	same accession
cpd:C00118	cpd:C00111	substrate and product
EC:4.2.1.1	EC:5.3.1.1	two consecutive enzymes in the metabolic pathway
D.melanogaster:dpp	D.melanogaster:sax	two interacting genes (ligand and receptor)
E.coli:tpiA	sp:TRIS_ECOLI	gene product as stored in public database
E.coli:tpiA	EC:5.3.1.1	gene and function
B.subtilis:tpi	EC:5.3.1.1	gene and function
E.coli:tpiA	B.subtilis:tpi	orthologous genes

cpd:C00051

represent glutathione synthase and glutathione, respectively, in the LIGAND database, and

E.coli:tpiA

represents triosephosphate isomerase gene in *E. coli*.

2.2 Binary Relations

To represent the data of interacting molecules or genes, we use the simplest form of representation: the binary relation that corresponds to the pairwise interaction. Any higher level interactions involving more than two components at a time will be approximated by the collection of pairwise interactions. The concept of binary relations has already been utilized in the LinkDB database[6] of the DBGET system. For example, the link between two database entries:

database1:entry1 ⇒ database2:entry2

and the link between a database entry and a gene name:

database:entry ⇒ organism:gene

are usually provided by each database and implemented in LinkDB/DBGET. Examples of these and other types of binary relations are shown in Table 1.

KEGG incorporates the links that exist in LinkDB/DBGET (Fig. 1(a)) and, in addition, contains more biological links of two interacting molecules

DBGET →

Database:Entry	Enzyme
sp:TYRB_ECOLI	2.6.1.57
sp:PHHC_PSEAE	2.6.1.57
pir:XNECY	2.6.1.57
⋮	⋮
genbank:BACGTPBP	4.2.1.51

(a) Relation between a database entry and an enzyme. This relation is extracted from LinkDB[6] in the DBGET system.[4]

LIGAND →

Enzyme	Substrate	Product
2.6.1.57	Prephenate	Pretyrosine
4.2.1.51	Prephenate	Phenylpyruvate
4.2.1.51	Chorismate	Prephenate
⋮	⋮	⋮

(b) Binary relation between chemical compounds (substrate and product) that participate in a chemical reaction. This relation is extracted from LIGAND Chemical Database for Enzyme Reaction.[5]

KEGG Pathway →

(c-1)

Map	Enzyme
Phe, try and trp biosynthesis	2.6.1.57
Phe, try and trp biosynthesis	4.2.1.51
⋮	⋮
Terpenoid biosynthesis	2.5.1.10

(c-2)

Map	Enzyme1	Enzyme2
Phe, try and trp biosynthesis	4.6.1.4	4.2.1.51
Phe, try and trp biosynthesis	4.2.1.51	2.6.1.57
⋮	⋮	⋮
Terpenoid biosynthesis	2.5.1.1	2.5.1.10

(c) Relationship between an enzyme and its location (map) in the metabolic pathways (c-1). Binary relation between two enzymes that appear consecutively in the pathway (c-2). These relations are extracted from the pathway diagrams of KEGG.

KEGG Genes →

Organism:Gene	Enzyme
H. influenzae:HI1145	4.2.1.51
H. influenzae:HI0196	4.6.1.3
⋮	⋮
H. sapiens:ADCY1	4.6.1.1

(d) Relation between a gene and an enzyme. It is extracted from the KEGG hierarchical text data in the genes section.

Figure 1: Relational tables used in the computation of pathways

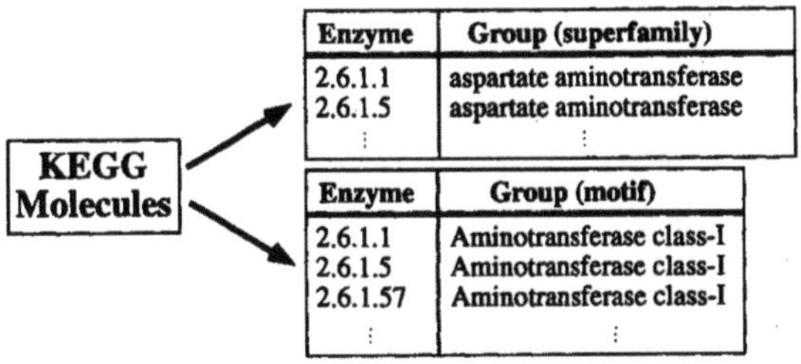

(e) Relation between an enzyme and the group to which it belongs. This relation is derived from the KEGG hierarchical text data in the molecules section. Currently, there are four classifications based on EC numbers,[7] PIR superfamilies,[8] SCOP 3D-folds[9] and PROSITE motifs.[3]

Figure 1: Relational tables used in the computation of pathways (contd.)

or genes. For the metabolic pathways, the two types of binary relations are identified. One is the substrate-product relation in the form of

cpd:C00118 ⇒ cpd:C00111

which is extracted from the LIGAND database (Fig. 1(b)). The other is the relation of two consecutive enzymes appearing in the known pathways, such as

EC:4.2.1.1 ⇒ EC:5.3.1.1

This relation is extracted from the pathway diagrams of KEGG (Fig. 1(c)).

2.3 Hierarchical Classifications

A hierarchy is often used to represent functional and structural similarities of genes and molecules. The hierarchical classification of EC numbers is based on the nature of chemical reactions catalyzed by enzymes. The degree of similarity in sequences and 3D structures of proteins is used for classifying superfamilies and folds. The taxonomy is the classification of organisms, which is important for extending sequence and 3D structural similarities to functional similarities. In the current version of KEGG, we construct enzyme classification tables according to EC numbers,[7] PIR superfamilies,[8] SCOP 3D-folds,[9] and PROSITE motifs[3] (Fig. 1(e)).

Once the entire genome is sequenced and the complete catalog of genes is obtained, it is natural to attempt to classify all genes according to their functions. Riley's hierarchical classification and categorization of *E. coli* genes[10] is an example of such an attempt. In KEGG, the functional classification is based on the actual pathway data which we consider as an objective criterion for categorization of functional units. In the WWW implementation of KEGG, the classification tables can be viewed and manipulated as what we call hierarchical text data, where branches of the tree may be expanded or collapsed by simply clicking on the headings and subheadings.

2.4 Pathway Diagrams

The metabolic pathway diagrams such as by Boehringer[11] and by the Japanese Biochemical Society[12] represent a consensus view of known metabolic pathways for humans to understand. Starting from these two compilations, we have computerized the metabolic pathway data in the form of about 80 graphical diagrams. Each diagram contains enzyme objects that can be manipulated together with the relational operations. The diagram is intended as a drawing of all chemically feasible pathways, rather than a consensus of known pathways. Thus, although the reference diagram has to be drawn and continuously updated manually, the organism-specific pathways are automatically generated by matching the enzymes in the gene table with the enzymes on the pathway diagrams. For example, Figure 2 shows the phenylalanine, tyrosine and tryptophan biosynthesis pathway for *H. influenzae*, where each box represents an enzyme with the EC number inside and those enzymes found in *H. influenzae* are marked for easy recognition. Thus, the organism-specific pathway can be seen by following the connection of marked enzymes.

In the WWW implementation of KEGG, the subsets of enzymes stored in the public databases including PDB,[13] PIR,[8] SWISS-PROT,[14] GenBank,[15] and OMIM,[16] can also be viewed as marked boxes on each pathway diagram. The process of marking these enzyme subsets and the organism-specific pathways is automatic and daily updated in KEGG. In all the pathway diagrams, marked or unmarked, an enzyme in the box is a clickable object (see Fig. 2) to retrieve the corresponding entry in the LIGAND database, and then related entries can be obtained from a number of databases through DBGET. The boxed enzyme is also a searchable object; the enzymes as they appear in the known pathways can be searched and viewed graphically.

3 Computation

3.1 Partial Join Operation

The process of marking organism-specific pathways is based on the matching of the gene catalog (Fig. 1(d))

$$\text{organism:gene} \Rightarrow \text{EC:number}$$

and the list of enzymes on each pathway diagram (Fig. 1(c))

$$\text{map:accession} \Rightarrow \text{EC:number}$$

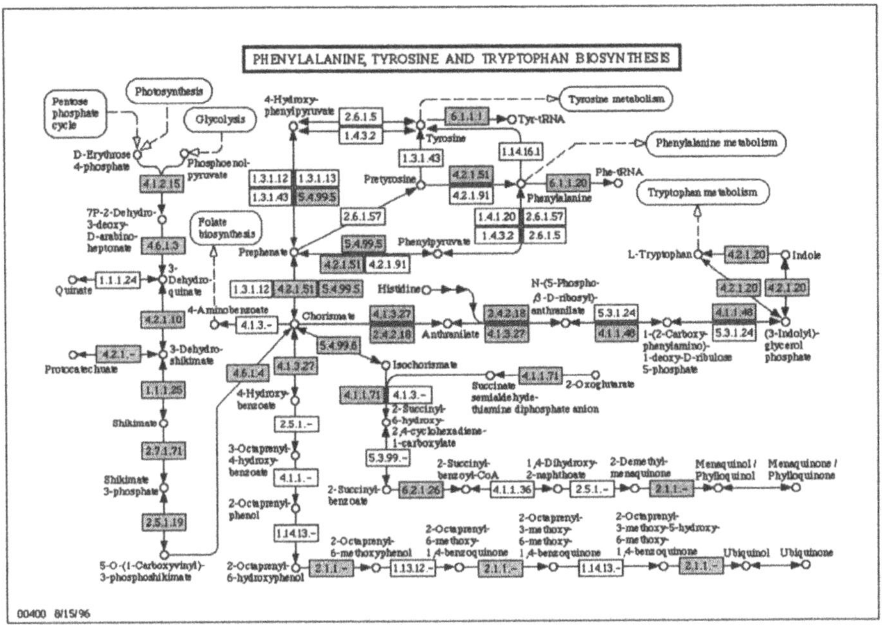

Figure 2: Phenylalanine, tyrosine and tryptophan biosynthesis pathway for *H. influenzae*

where 'map' is the database name for the pathway diagrams and 'accession' is the accession number of each diagram. The matching process is made by a join operation on EC:number. In the standard relational database the join is made by exactly matching the values in two columns, but the join here contains an interpretation of the EC number classification where a wild card is permitted for the lowest levels of the numbering scheme.

By applying this partial join operation in a more organized way, the process of query relaxation [17] in the deductive database can be implemented. Suppose an enzyme is found to be missing after examining the connectivity of the pathway. Because the EC number assignment is usually made by sequence similarity, it is necessary to check if other enzymes belong to the same superfamily of similar sequences. This can be done by going up the hierarchy of the superfamily (Fig. 1(e)):

$$\text{EC:number} \Rightarrow \text{SF:number}$$

and then examining all EC numbers in the superfamily (going down the hierarchy).

3.2 Path Computation

When no appropriate enzymes are found even by going up the hierarchy, the next step is to examine if alternative reaction paths can be found, given two compounds as the initial substrate and the final product. Suppose enzyme E catalyzes a chemical reaction with substrate X and product Y. Then the reaction is represented by the following form in the deductive database.

$$reaction(E, X, Y).$$

When the conversion of compound X to compound Y is a multistep process consisting of a number of enzymes, the enzymatic pathway is represented by:

$$path(X, Y, [E]) \leftarrow reaction(E, X, Y).$$
$$path(X, Y, [E \mid EL]) \leftarrow reaction(E, X, Z), path(Z, Y, EL).$$

This is a simple deduction from a collection of binary relations of substrates and products or, equivalently, a list of enzymes. We have been experimenting this path computation by the deductive database CORAL.[18] However, when we actually provide the path computation capability in KEGG we will use the C++ library that we are currently developing for efficient manipulation of binary relations and hierarchies.

Another type of problem in path computation is to compute from a given list of enzymes all possible pathways starting and ending at all possible compounds. This will become necessary for analyzing a collection of enzymes that have not matched on any of the known metabolic pathways. Apparently, there are still a number of unknown pathways, especially for secondary metabolisms and metabolisms that are turned on under stressful conditions. This type of computation may help understand such additional pathways.

4 An Example

4.1 Identifying Missing Enzymes

As shown in Fig. 2, the connectivity of marked enzymes can be used as a criterion to assess the accuracy of gene finding and functional prediction from genomic sequences. Especially, missing enzymes in each organism can be found immediately by just looking at the connectivity. In the case of the phenylalanine biosynthesis for *H. influenzae*, the enzymes missing are, among others, tyrosine transaminase (EC 2.6.1.5), aromatic amino acid transaminase (EC 2.6.1.57), phenylalanine dehydrogenase (EC 1.4.1.20), and cyclohexadienyl dehydrogenase (EC 1.3.1.43).

According to the current knowledge in the map, the lack of these enzymes results in the incompletion of the biosynthesis, which may be fatal to the organism. There are basically two possibilities that we need to examine to resolve this problem. The first case is that the genes coding for the missing enzymes have not been identified in the gene finding process, even though the organism actually has them. If the complete genome is already sequenced, the gene finding and functional assignment have to be repeated more carefully.

The second case is that the organism does not have the genes coding for those enzymes, and it uses other chemical reactions (enzymes) to produce phenylalanine. In this case, we need to search for alternative pathways from the source chemical compound to the target chemical compound, starting from the list of all enzymes identified or predicted in the genome.

4.2 Searching Alternative Assignments Using Hierarchies

As a way to re-examine the functional assignment of genes, the superfamily, motif and 3D-fold classifications and partial join operations can be used. Using the CORAL system we searched alternative assignments of enzyme genes for the three possible pathways from prephenate to phenylalanine in Fig. 2. The EC numbers of the missing (unmarked) enzymes were given to the system, and it returned the result shown in Table 2. If the enzyme 2.6.1.57 had been assigned to 2.6.1.1, or the enzyme 1.4.1.20 had been assigned to 1.4.1.4, the pathway from prephenate to phenylalanine would have been formed. In fact, two genes HI0286 and HI1617 are given the same EC numbers 2.6.1.1 according to the result of the sequence similarity search. They may require more careful analysis. The enzyme 1.4.1.4 was, however, correctly assigned and utilized in the other sections of our pathway database. We will probably need to search hypothetical proteins and unassigned genes in the *H. influenzae* genome for this missing enzyme.

4.3 Computing Alternative Paths

The path computation becomes necessary when we cannot find appropriate enzymes. Unfortunately, the current version of our database is not adequate to systematically perform the computation. For the example of Fig. 2, the LIGAND database describes the chemical reaction of enzyme 2.6.1.57 as the conversion between an aromatic amino acid and an aromatic oxo acid. It does not specify pretyrosine and prephenate, and we do not currently have a hierarchy of compound names. The reaction between prephenate and phenylpyruvate by enzyme 5.4.99.5 is not included at all in the current version of LIGAND.

Table 2: Result of the search of alternative enzymes for those participate in the phenylalanine biosynthesis for *H. influenzae*

Missing	Alternative	Classification used
2.6.1.57	2.6.1.1	motif (Aminotransferases class-I pyridoxal-phosphate attachment site)
2.6.1.5	2.6.1.1	motif (Aminotransferases class-I pyridoxal-phosphate attachment site) superfamily (aspartate aminotransferase)
1.4.1.20	1.4.1.4	motif (Glu / Leu / Phe / Val dehydrogenases active site)
1.4.3.2	1.4.3.5	EC number classification

In any case, we tried to compute alternative paths from phenylpyruvate to phenylalanine, but no paths were found. We believe, however, as we add more reactions and more compounds to LIGAND, which are then converted to relational tables in KEGG, and work out a hierarchy of compound names, the path computation will become a practical tool for biologists.

5 Discussion

The complete genome sequences of at least five free-living organisms, *H. influenzae*,[2] *M. genitalium*,[19] *M. jannashii*,[20] *Synechocystis sp.*[21] and *S. cerevisiae*, are already available via WWW or FTP servers of the original sequencing groups. They also provide the list of predicted coding regions and predicted gene functions. The major purpose of the KEGG metabolic pathway database is two-fold. First, we wish to establish an integrated view of higher functional aspects of gene products, namely, how they are interacting, for an increasing number of organisms. Second, we will provide a practical tool for making assignments of enzyme genes from genomic sequences.

For the first purpose, there are also other metabolic pathway databases, such as EcoCyc,[22] HinCyc,[23] EMP,[24,25] which often contain more detailed information of specific pathways and specific organisms than KEGG. Perhaps, the major feature of KEGG is its link capabilities, both in terms of the linking to the existing databases and different organisms and in terms of the linking to compute a pathway from binary relations. Because of these links we expect KEGG can be used to extract different information from the other metabolic pathway databases.

In KEGG the binary relations in the relational tables are effectively utilized for path and other computations using logic. Of course, we are well aware of the complications of biological problems, which may sometimes be better treated by object-oriented technologies. However, a complex data representation may result in an ineffective computation. It remains to be seen whether the simple representation and efficient computation in KEGG can result in biologically significant observations. Toward that end, we are in the process of manually extracting main substrates, products, and cofactors for each of the enzymatic reactions of all known metabolic pathways. By representing each reaction as a collection of binary relations, we will try to reproduce the known pathways. At the same time, we need to computerize the synonyms and hierarchies of compound names. We are working on this in conjunction with the COMPOUND section of the LIGAND database.

The DBGET/LinkDB system is based on the model of loosely-coupled integration, where different databases with different schemas are integrated at the level of data entries. Thus, entries in different databases can be retrieved uniformly and links are made between related entries in different databases. This approach has been successful in view of the proliferation of WWW and the rapid progress of genome projects. The text-based DBGET system has been extended to the multimedia environment, and DBGET has been and will continue to be able to cope with the ever increasing number and volume of daily updated databases. Since KEGG inherits and shares DBGET/LinkDB capabilities, it will also be able to provide the most up-to-date metabolic pathways for a number of organisms including all organisms with complete genomes known.

The algorithm used in computing pathways between two compounds is based on Mavrovouniotis's algorithm.[26] Here it is implemented in a simpler way by representing reactions as binary relations, which enables us to treat the path computation as a logical derivation. Using various hierarchies and the framework of query relaxations,[17] the computation of alternative pathways can be accomplished. For example, Gaasterland and Selkov [25] adopted the taxonomy of *Mycoplasma* as a measure of proximity between organisms for use in the query relaxation. As a next step it will be necessary to combine different types of hierarchies, such as taxonomy, sequence similarity, and compound similarity, to compute alternative pathways.

Acknowledgement

This work was supported in part by a Grant-in-Aid for Scientific Research on Priority Areas 'Genome Science' from the Ministry of Education, Science, Sports and Culture in Japan. The computation time was provided by the

Supercomputer Laboratory, Institute of Chemical Research, Kyoto University.

References

1. F. Sanger *et al*, *Nature* **265**, 678 (1977).
2. R.D. Fleischmann *et al*, *Science* **269**, 496 (1995).
3. A. Bairoch *et al*, *Nucleic Acids Res.* **24**, 189 (1996).
4. Y. Akiyama *et al*, in *Proceedings of the 1995 Meeting on the Interconnection of Melecular Biology Databases* (P. Karp *et al* eds) ⟨http://www.ai.sri.com/~pkarp/mimbd/95/abstracts.html⟩.
5. M. Suyama *et al*, *Comput. Appl. Biosci* **9**, 9 (1993).
6. S. Goto *et al*, in *Proceedings of the 1995 Meeting on the Interconnection of Melecular Biology Databases* (P. Karp *et al* eds) ⟨http://www.ai.sri.com/~pkarp/mimbd/95/abstracts.html⟩.
7. Enzyme Nomenclature, Academic Press Inc. (1992).
8. D.G. George *et al*, *Nucleic Acids Res.* **24**, 17 (1996).
9. A.G. Murzin *et al*, *J. Mol. Biol.* **247**, 536 (1995).
10. M. Riley *et al*, *Escherichia coli and Salmonella: Cellular and Molecular Biology 2nd Ed.*, 2118–2202, ASM Press (1996).
11. M. Gerhard ed., Biological Pathways, Third Edition. *Boehringer Mannheim* (1992).
12. T. Nishizuka ed., Metabolic Maps. *Biochemical Society of Japan* (1980) (in Japanese).
13. F.C. Bernstein *et al*, *J. Mol. Biol.* **112**, 535 (1977).
14. A. Bairoch and R. Apweiler, *Nucleic Acids Res.* **24**, 21 (1996).
15. D.A. Benson *et al*, *Nucleic Acids Res.* **24**, 1 (1996).
16. P. Pearson *et al*, *Nucleic Acids Res.* **22**, 3470 (1994).
17. T. Gaasterland *et al*, *J. Intelligent Information Systems* **1**, 293 (1992).
18. R. Ramakrishnan *et al*, The CORAL Manual: A tutorial introduction to CORAL (1993).
19. C.M. Fraser *et al*, *Science* **270**, 397 (1995).
20. C.J. Bult *et al*, *Science* **273**, 1058 (1996).
21. T. Kaneko *et al*, *DNA Res.* **3**, 109 (1996).
22. P.D. Karp *et al*, *Nucleic Acids Res.* **24**, 32 (1996).
23. P.D. Karp *et al*, *Ismb* 4, 116 (1996).
24. E. Selkov *et al*, *Nucleic Acids Res.* **24**, 26 (1996).
25. T. Gaasterland and E. Selkov, *Ismb* **3**, 127 (1995).
26. M.L. Mavrovouniotis, in *Artificial Intelligence and Molecular Biology* (L. Hunter ed.), 325 (1993).

Development of a Cell Signaling Networks Database

TAKAKO IGARASHI and TSUGUCHIKA KAMINUMA
Division of Chem-Bio Informatics, National Institute of Health Sciences, 1- 18-1 Kami-Yoga, Setagaya-ku, Tokyo 158, JAPAN

Abstract

In multicellular organisms cell signaling networks play important roles in wide range of biological phenomena, such as development, differentiation, reproduction, morphogenesis, carcinogenesis, apoptosis, and even learning. In order to explain biological phenomena based on cell signaling models, we have developed a database for cell signaling networks. The system contains mechanisms of signal transduction and structure and functional data and references of extracellular chemicals and biomolecules. CSNDB is constructed using ACEDB system, and includes various graphical representations such as pathway diagrams, map diagrams, 3-D images, pictures, and VRML environment. The system will be useful for modeling cells and their information processing, and to explain important biological phenomena based on these models.

1 Introduction

In living organisms biological reactions occur in order producing cascades, or biological pathways. There are two major pathways in cells of multicellular organisms; metabolic pathways and cell signaling pathways. Metabolic pathways had been studied by biochemists before the rise of molecular biology, and detailed knowledge of pathways had been accumulated and depicted on paper. Biochemical pathways provided from Boehringer Mannheim Co.[1] is a such example. Computerized databases for metabolic pathways have also been developed. EcoCyc[2] and Soybase[3] are such examples.

In 1980s however, the cell signaling mechanisms have been unveiled at molecular level in various multicellular organisms. It was found that cell signaling networks play important roles in wide range of biological phenomena that characterize multicellular animals. These phenomena include development, differentiation, reproduction, morphogenesis, carcinogenesis, apoptosis, and even learning.

Since two years ago, we have started to develop a database for cell signaling networks (CSNDB)[4,5]. The eventual goal of this project is to catalog all the cell signaling networks in living organisms in order to make more realistic and quantitative models for biological phenomena. The system will be useful for modeling cells and their information processing, and to explain important biological phenomena based on these models. The system may also be useful for interpreting molecular diseases and also for designing new drugs, because the disorder of cell signaling networks has close relation with molecular disease. In this paper we shall introduce the first prototype of the system.

2 System and methods

2.1 System environment

The CSNDB was implemented using ACEDB[6] system, which was originally developed by Dr. Jean Thierry-Mieg and Dr. Richard Durbin in order to manage C. elegans genome data. It is now used for wide range of other applications including various genome projects.

CSNDB was developed on workstations of Silicon Graphics Indigo. These workstations are connected to the Internet by a dedicated communication line (256Kbps).

2.2 Data sources

Knowledge on cell signaling networks was classified from a standard text book[7], reviews, and original papers. In addition we referred molecular databases on the Internet; SwissProt[8] for protein data, PDB[9] for three dimensional structures of protein, and Online Mendelian Inheritance in Man (OMIM)[10] for molecular disease.

3 Results

3.1 Representation of signal pathways

The system provides the knowledge of signal transduction pathways and of signal molecules. In CSNDB the pathways are designed to present the mechanisms of cellular signal transduction, which is the basic knowledge of the system. We considered six points regarding representation of signaling pathways;

1. diagram representation of pathway
2. hypertext link between diagram and molecular data
3. layer structure of pathway representation
4. connection between disorder of pathway and molecular disease
5. effects of external chemicals, such as toxins and drugs
6. comparison of pathways among species.

According to these points, we designed the pathway representation of CSNDB.

In CSNDB the signaling pathways are represented as flow diagrams that consist of nodes and arrows (Figure 1). A node represents a signaling molecule and an arrow represents a molecular interaction that transfers the signal. The facility of diagram depiction is provided by ACEDB, and there exist hypertext links between flow diagrams and molecular information. If one clicks a node, the next window that contains deeper information about this signal molecule is displayed, and if one clicks an arrow, then the detail modes of molecular interactions are presented as a new window. The information of molecular interaction includes following properties;

1. the mode of signal transduction; phosphorylation, ligand receptor binding, SH2 recognition, GTP/GDP exchange, and so on
2. protein sites or motifs used for signal transduction
3. character of the signal transduction; activation, suppression, perception, transduction, propagation, amplification, integration, adaptation, and response
4. cellular localization of signal transduction.

The living organisms prepare not single but plural pathways for response to stimuli. In multicellular organisms communications of pathways would be necessary to regulate complex biological mechanisms. Pathways in the cells communicate with one another in order to control biological responses as whole. Theses communications are called as cross-talk or feed-back regulations. In order to represent communications of pathways, we included the higher level pathways in CSNDB. Figure 2 shows an example of the higher level pathway. In this diagram the relation of pathways are depicted, and each node links to the individual pathways described in molecular level. In this way CSNDB contains the dynamic character of signal pathways.

Regarding as differences of pathways between species, some pathways are conserved, the others are not. Generally the higher animals possess the larger number of pathways as well as signal molecules. It seems that the diversity of pathways would be one of the driving forces of evolution from unicellular organisms to multicellular organisms. For the purpose of evolutionary analysis of pathways, we started to include information on comparisons of pathways between different species. It is still under preparation.

At present 29 pathways are included in the system.

3.2 Representation of signal molecules

Signal molecules are individual components of signal pathway. Signal molecules are grouped into eight; hormones, cytokines, receptors,

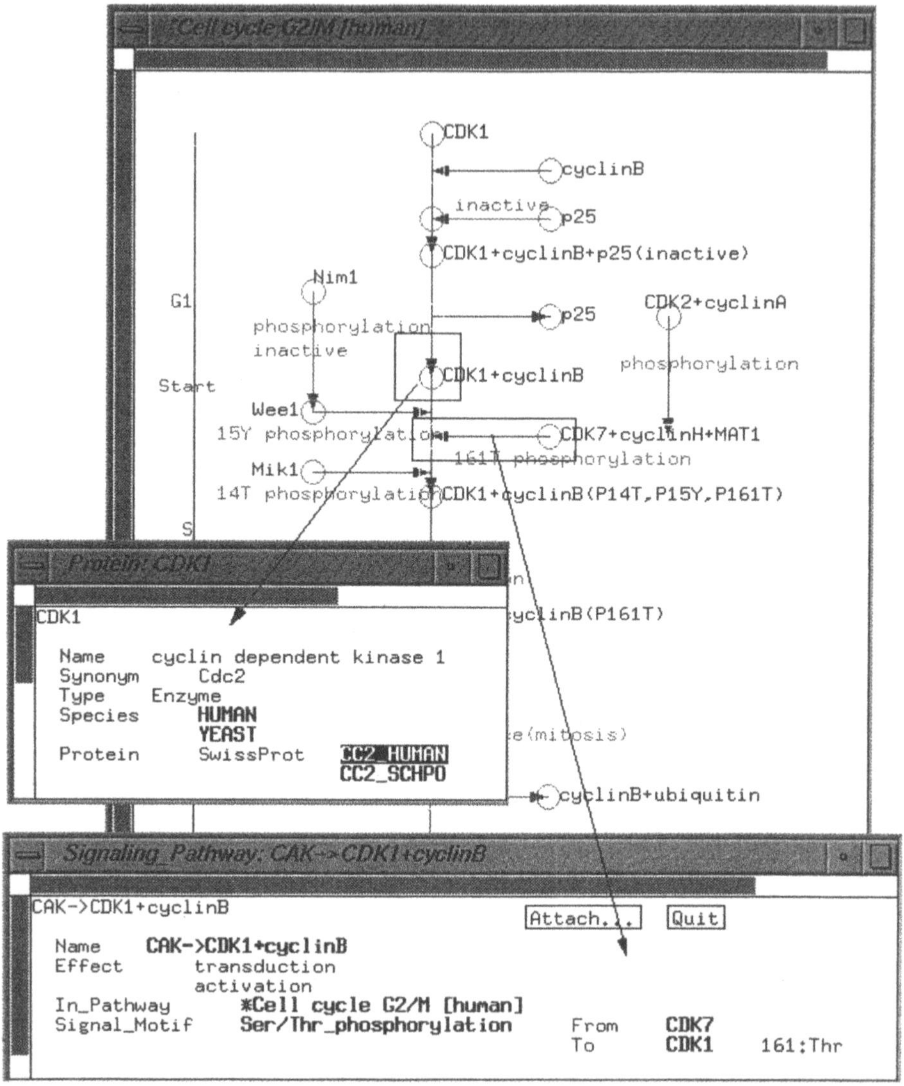

Figure 1: Representations of pathway diagrams. Left arrow indicates hypertext link between the node object and the molecular data, and right arrow indicates hypertext link between the arrow object and the modes of signal transduction.

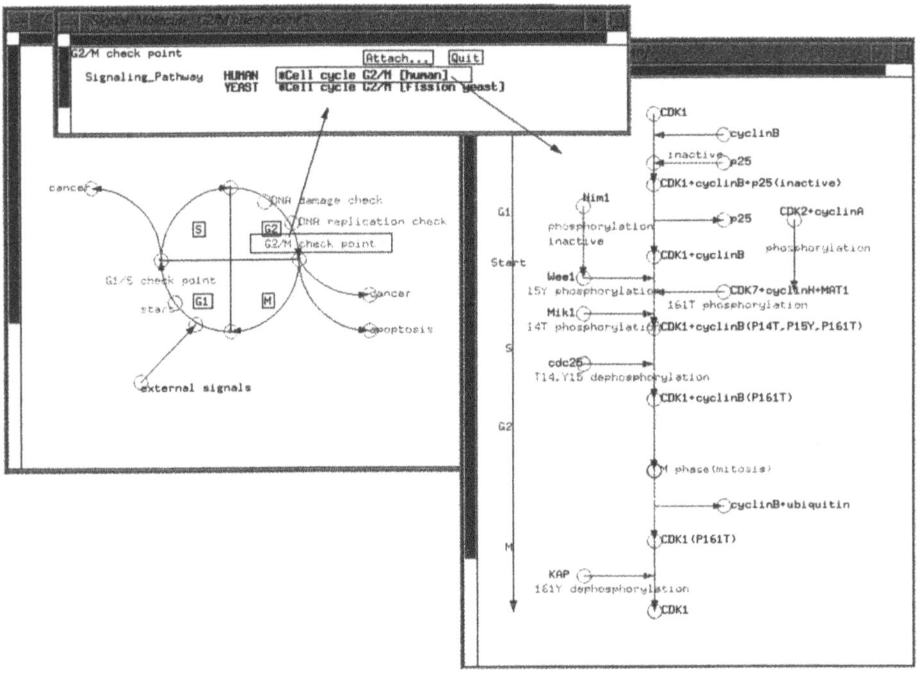

Figure 2: Representation of higher level pathways. The arrows indicate hypertext links between the node in the diagram and the component pathway described in molecular level.

ion channels, effectors, enzymes, messengers, and transcriptional factors. Each signal molecule is characterized by the following biological attributes;

1. Biochemical Data : chemical name, synonyms, cellular location, organism location, functions, isozymes, and homologues in other species.
2. Structural Data : domain structures, functional motifs, 3-D structures, and ligand bindings.
3. Genomic Data : exon and intron structures, DNA sequences, and protein sequences.
4. Associated Chemicals : activators, inhibitors, agonists, antagonists, toxins, and drugs.
5. Bibliographical Data : papers, and the date of the last update.

The ACEDB system is able to contain not only the character data but also the computer commands to invoke external programs. Using this facility we implemented appropriate external viewer programs on CSNDB. We implemented RasMol[11] for three dimensional structure, XV[12] for figure, and Netscape[13] for the connection to the Internet

Figure 3 shows examples for representations of molecular data. The chemical structure of xenobiotic ligand is displayed by XV. The three dimensional structure of protein is displayed by RasMol. This graphical model can be freely rotated and magnified. The original data provided from SwissProt is displayed by Netscape through the Internet connection.

The present CSNDB contains the following information; 281 signal molecules, 1147 sequences, 210 chemicals, 114 3-D structures, 151 pictures, and 1328 papers.

3.3 Molecular disease representation

CSNDB also contains molecular disease data. The key idea is that cell signaling networks are constructed with many oncogenes. We consider that the disorder of cell signaling networks has close relation with molecular diseases. Then we contained the information on mutational changes of signal molecules and on caused diseases.

We obtained the data of mutation sites of proteins, base changes on DNA, and molecular diseases from OMIM. In addition, we entered structural knowledge of protein. This is for the purpose of structural analysis of molecular disease. We added a functional motif or domain to each mutation site. (Figure 4). Three dimensional structures of proteins were also added (Figure 4). This structure are represented with VRML[14] model in which the mutated amino acids are particularly depicted by space fill models. Using VRML facility, we contained hypertext links

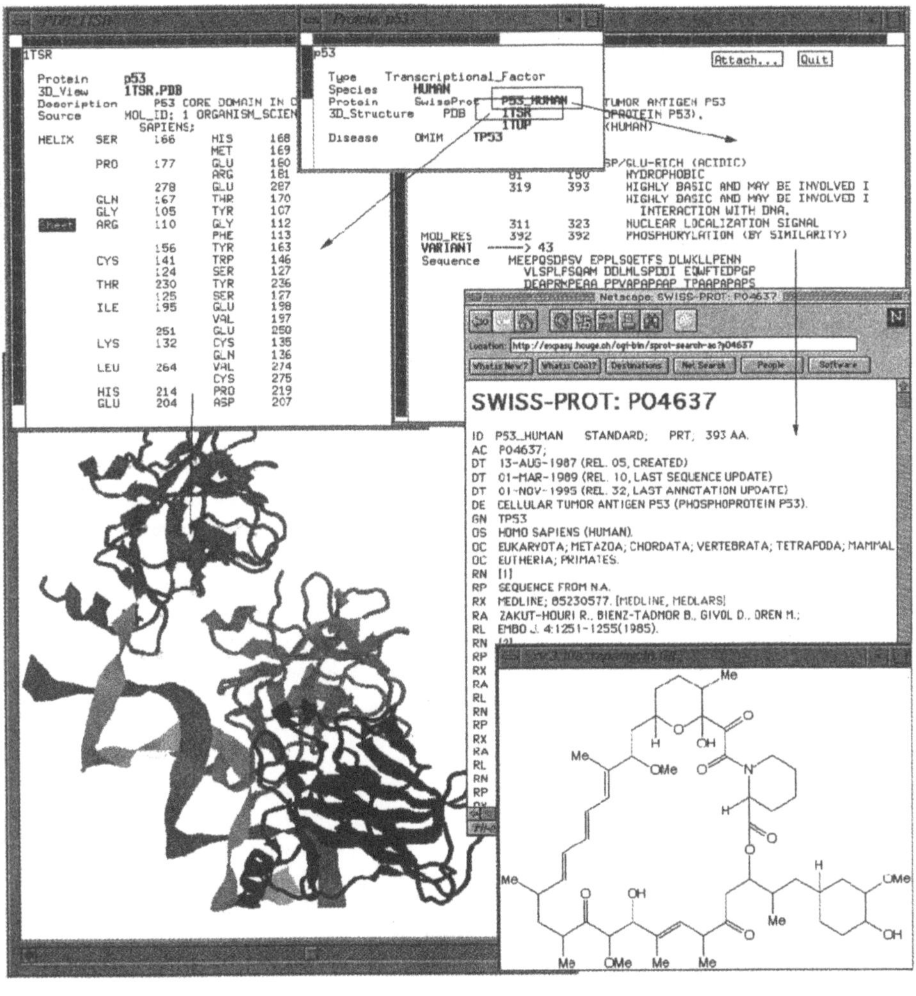

Figure 3: Presentations of molecular information of p53 (for example). Molecular data taken from original papers, SwissProt, crystal structure of p53 binding with DNA, the original data of SwissProt presented by Netscape, and chemical structure of rapamycin which inhibits progression of cell cycle within G1 phase are shown.

between individual mutated amino acids and the molecular disease data. Mutation maps were also added. They represent positions of mutated amino acid corresponding to protein sequences and functional domains (Figure 4). Since in mutation maps we utilize the same technique as pathway diagrams , there exist hypertext links between the descriptions in the maps and the disease data. Then in CSNDB, one can refer molecular disease data, three dimensional mutation sites, and mutation site maps simultaneously.

At present 18 signal molecules include molecular disease information.

3.4 Network environment

The WWW interface of CSNDB was produced using the program developed at National Agricultural Library[15]. All the facilities of CSNDB are available from the Internet (http://geo.nihs.go.jp/csndb.html).

4 Discussion

In the past decades a lot of features of biological mechanisms have been elucidated, and various biological databases have been developed. PIR[16], GenBank[17], EMBL[18], PDB, SwissProt, and OMIM are such examples. These databases have become the standard references for molecular scientists. However all these databases target the attributes of individual molecule. Novel databases for not an individual molecule but molecular interactions are required for more realistic representation of living organisms. CSNDB will be one of such examples. We consider that this kind of knowledge base for molecular interactions will be more important.

We used ACEDB for the base system of CSNDB. ACEDB is the database system originally for integrating C. elegans genome data. It is now widely used for various genome projects. ACEDB has some object oriented features, and theses features have been proved to suite for implementing various genome data. In this work we found that ACEDB was also suitable for integrating the cell signaling knowledge. Because biological data are very often incomplete and sometimes are drastically revised when new experimental facts are discovered, we consider that the flexibility of object oriented features of ACEDB are appropriate for integration of biological knowledge.

At present we included the pathways of human and yeast (fission and budding yeast). We are planing to expand the system to other species such as Drosophila and C. elegans. We are interested in the evolution of pathways, especially in the evolution from the unicellular organisms to multicellular organisms. CSNDB is expected to give good insight into this issue.

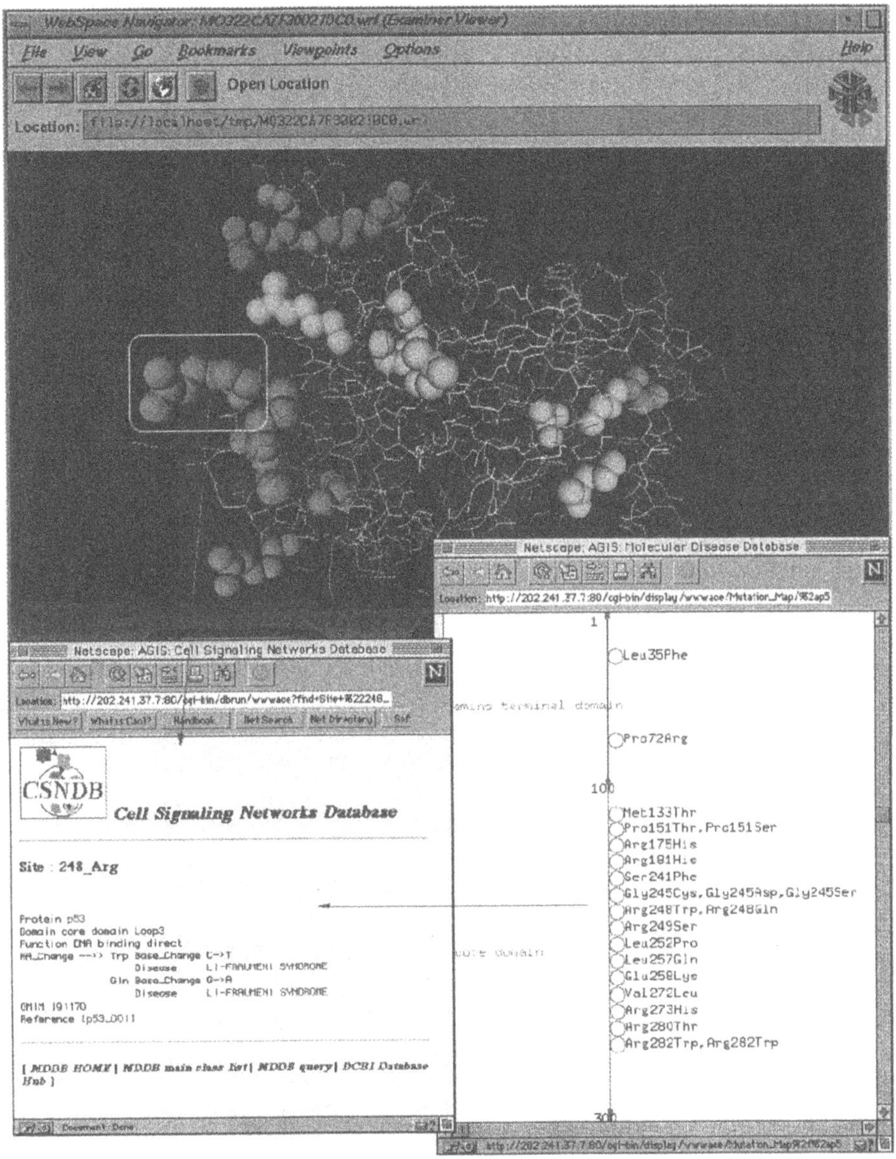

Figure 4: Representations of molecular disease data. The three dimensional image is presented using VRML environment. The arrows indicate hypertext links between the mutation site in VRML model, map presentation, and molecular disease data.

We also consider the necessity of classification of pathways in CSNDB. We need to produce hierarchical classification of entire sets of pathways in living organisms. This classification will be important for simulation of biological responses in computer system.

Though the CSNDB was originally designed to be a basic and common tool for wide range of researchers, it could also be used as personal systems by experimentalists who are studying specific receptors, cell signal transduction and other proteins. They may add their own data to the system or fill in their own data to the empty CSNDB.

Acknowledgments

The authors thank to Dr. J. Thierry-Mieg and Dr. R. Durbin who have helped us to use ACEDB, and Dr. M. Smith who let us use OMIM data. The authors also thank to Ms. M. Yukawa and Ms. S. Hasegawa who helped for data input. This work was partly supported by Japanese Human Science Foundation Research Aid Program and by Science Research Promotion Fund from Science and Technology Agency.

5 References

1. Michal, G. Biochemical Pathways Wall Chart. Boehringer Mannheim GmbH Biochemica, 1892.
2. Karp, P. and Riley, M. and Paley, S. and Pellegrini-Toole, A., EcoCyc: Electronic Encyclopedia of E. coli Genes and Metabolism, Nucleic Acids Research, 24, 32-40, 1996.
3. Grant, D. et al. http://probe.nalusda.gov:8000/plant/aboutsoybase.html
4. Igarashi, T., Nadaoka, Y., and Kaminuma, T. A Data and Knowledge Base for Cell Signaling Networks, Proc. IPCAT95, 188-198, 1995.
5. Igarashi, T., Nadaoka, Y., and Kaminuma, T. A Data and Knowledge Base for Cell Signaling Networks, Genome Informatics Workshop 1995, 49-56, 1995.
6. Thierry-Mieg, J. and Durbin, R. http://probe.nalusda.gov:8000/acedocs/index.html.
7. Hunter, T., Cell, 50, 823-829, 1987.
8. http://expasy.hcuge.ch/sprot/sprot-top.html.
9. http://www.pdb.bnl.gov/index.html.
10. McKusick, V.A.: Mendelian Inheritance in Man. Catalogs of Human Genes and Genetic Disorders. Baltimore: Johns Hopkins University Press, 1994 (11th edition).

11. Bradley, J. ftp://ftp.cis.upenn.edu/pub/rasmol.

12. Sayle, R. ftp://colonsay.dcs.ed.ac.uk/pub/xv.

13. Netscape is a product from Communication Corporation (http://www.netscape.com/).

14. VRML is a extension of HTML which allows us virtual reality environments on WWW (http://vrml.wired.com/).

15. Barnett, J. and Bigwood, D. , http://probe.nalusda.gov:8000/acedocs/ace95//nalwww.html.

16. Sidman KE. George DG. Barker WC. Hunt LT. The protein identification resource (PIR), Nucleic Acids Res., 16, 1869-1871, 1988.

17. Benson, D., Boguski, M., Lipman, D.J., and Ostell, J. Nucleic Acids Research, 22, 3441-3444, 1994.

18. http://www.embl-heidelberg.de/.

THE NATIVE SEQUENCE DETERMINES SIDECHAIN PACKING IN A PROTEIN, BUT DOES OPTIMAL SIDECHAIN PACKING DETERMINE THE NATIVE SEQUENCE ?

P. KOEHL
UPR 9003 du CNRS, Boulevard Sebastien Brant, 67400 Illkirch Graffenstaden, France.

M. DELARUE
Laboratoire d'Immunologie Structurale, Institut Pasteur, 25 rue du Docteur Roux, 75015 Paris, France.

Globular proteins have highly compact structures and the corresponding packing interactions are widely considered as the principal determinant of the native structure. It is therefore important that theoretical approaches to protein design explicitly take in account packing, which requires that a full atomic representation of the designed protein is maintained. As a first step towards this goal, we have developed in this report an inverse folding algorithm with the aim of specifically designing amino acid sequences which optimise sidechain packing for a given protein fold. The design is performed by a global Monte Carlo optimisation in sequence space, with constant amino acid composition and a full-atom representation of the various protein models. Packing is defined by a Lennard-Jones potential. The program was tested by designing stable sequence variants for the chymotrypsin inhibitor fold. The final protein models showed an increase in intramolecular atomic contacts and a decrease in the overall volume compared to the native structure. Starting from the backbone only of the target structure, the algorithm did gradually retrieve reliable though limited sequence information. Higher compatibility might be achieved by improving the potential, however our results suggest that packing interactions are an essential element of a yet-to-be-defined successful energy function for protein design.

1. Introduction

It is the ability of proteins to fold into unique three dimensional structures that allows them to exert their biological function. Hence, comprehending how the amino acid sequence is related to the 3D conformation in the native state is essential to an understanding of biological processes. The direct approach to this problem consists of finding the folded conformation of a protein based on its sequence. Although considerable theoretical as well as experimental efforts have been made in recent years, the attainment of this ultimate goal does not appear imminent. An alternative approach is the inverse protein folding problem, which consists in identifying which sequences are compatible with a given fold[1] (for recent reviews see [2-4]). Elaboration of this alternative view is not only theoretically interesting but is also important for protein design and engineering. This paper focuses on sequence design.

Several global protein sequence design methods have been developed either using lattice models[5-7] in which a systematic search of all possible sequences is tractable (see for example [8]), or only considering mainchain and Cß atoms[9-11] using simplified pairwise potentials in order to compensate (to a certain extent) for the missing information, such as packing. However, none of these methods can capture detailed atomic interactions and need to be expanded such that they maintain a complete all-atom representation of the designed protein structure. In the early work on sequence design, Ponder and Richards[12] provided the first step towards this goal. Under the assumption that residues in the interior of a protein are the most important in determining its fold, they tested systematically combinations of sidechains fitting in the cores of small proteins, based on steric overlaps, hydrogen bonding and packing density criteria. The number of residues included in the combinatorial search was however limited for practical computing reasons. The same problem was encountered in more recent applications which limited the search in sequence space to residues in the core of the protein[13-16].

Because exposed residues also contribute to the structure and activity of native proteins, they ought to be included in the sequence design process. In this paper, we propose a global protein sequence design algorithm which maintains an all-atom representation. The optimisation procedure is based on a Monte Carlo procedure is sequence space, where random moves are either accepted or rejected using the Metropolis criterion[17]. At each step of the calculation, a chimeric protein based on the known backbone structure and the current designed sequence is built, using our recent fast method for sidechain placement[18]. The internal Van der Waals' energy of this model protein is used to evaluate the compatibility of the sequence with the desired protein fold. As such the strategy is set up to select sequences with optimised sidechain packing within a given 3D framework. It was tested on the compact structure of the chymotrypsin inhibitor of barley seed, PDB[19] code 2CI2. We compared the properties of the corresponding designed sequences with properties of the native sequence, in order to assess the extent to which protein sequences are determined by VdW packing interactions.

Optimisation in sequence space such as that proposed here requires special care, since the only physical competition existing in the actual folding process is between different structures for one sequence. In the procedure described here, we try in fact to mimic natural evolution, which explores different sequences in the framework of one 3D structure, with the difference that this exploration is done at the DNA level, and not directly at the 3D structure level. This difference between folding and sequence design raises the problem of specificity, i.e. the incompatibility of the designed sequences with folds different from the specified one. This is discussed below.

2. Methods

A good strategy for protein design requires that the designed sequence shows a high compatibility with the desired structure while at the same time exhibiting low compatibility with alternative structures, i.e. the "design in" and "design out" procedures proposed by Yue and Dill[5]. A thorough discussion on this issue was recently presented by Jones[3]. To alleviate this problem we use in this study the approach described by Shakhnovich and Gutin[20] in which the sequence composition is maintained during the sequence optimisation. This sequence constraint was also added to account for the fact that the amino acid composition of a protein is known to be highly dependent on its folding class[21].

Most methods which try to solve the protein folding problem or inverse protein folding problems have two components, i.e. an optimisation algorithm, and a procedure that measures sequence-structure fitness:

2.1 Monte Carlo optimisation in sequence space

Optimal sequences with a given amino acid composition can be obtained through a Monte Carlo simulation in sequence space, following the strategy described by Shakhnovich and Gutin[20]. Starting from a random sequence S0 with the required composition, whose energy is E0, two positions are chosen at random, and the corresponding amino acid types are exchanged. The energy E1 of the new sequence S1 is calculated, and the move is accepted or rejected according to the Metropolis acceptance probability given by[17] :

$$P\{S0 \rightarrow S1\} = \begin{cases} e^{-\frac{E1-E0}{Tmc}} & if \quad E1 - E0 > 0 \\ 1 & otherwise \end{cases} \qquad (1)$$

where Tmc is a parameter usually referred to as the temperature of the Monte Carlo simulation.

2.2 Sequence structure fitness

The coordinates of the backbone atoms (including Cß) of the desired target structure are given as input to our programs. For residue positions occupied by glycine in the target structure, a Cß is built using standard geometry when required. The current sequence during the Monte Carlo simulation is threaded on this backbone, and sidechains are positioned using our approach based on an iterative self consistent mean field theory[18]. Sidechain conformations are selected from a fixed set of rotamers[22], and the selection is based solely on a Lennard Jones potential for VdW interactions; no full energy minimisation is performed at the end to remove possible clashes between rotamers, for sake of computing efficiency. The Lennard-Jones potential of the final model is used to score the compatibility of the corresponding sequence with the target fold.

2.3 Implementation for computing efficiency

Our sidechain placement technique is based on a fixed set of sidechain positions. Since the backbone of the protein is maintained rigid, all possible sidechain-sidechain interactions can be calculated once, for all types of amino acids, yielding a large but efficient energy matrix which can be used at each cycle, both for the mean field optimisation (see [18] for details), as well as for estimating the energy of the model proteins. A complete Monte Carlo simulation over 50000 cycles for a 65 residue protein required 7 hours of CPU time on an IBM 43 P computer.

3. Results

3.1 Designing protein sequences by optimising sidechain packing

The sequence design procedure was tested on the chymotrypsin inhibitor of barley seed (PDB code 2CI2; 65 residues). The Monte Carlo simulation was run over 50000 cycles, with Tmc chosen such that the final acceptance ratio is 20% (Tmc = 1). The initial sequence was chosen to be a random reshuffling of the native sequence. The evolution of the VdW energies of the protein models built from the designed sequences is shown in Figure 1.

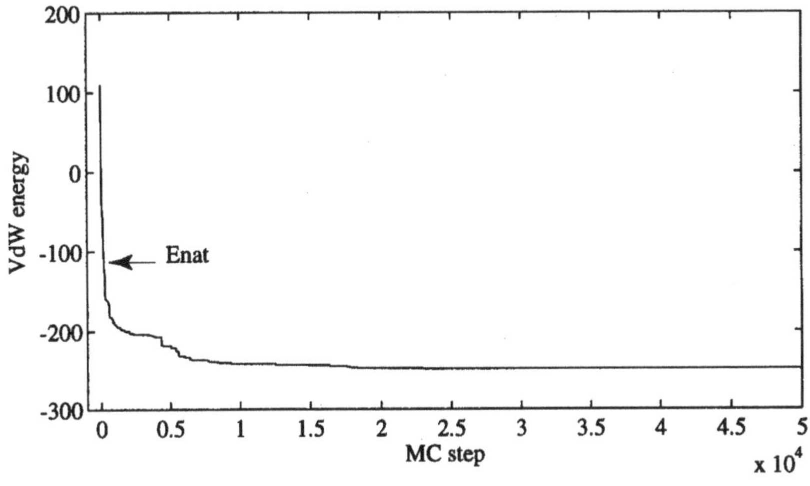

Figure 1 : Evolution of the VdW energies of the various sequences threaded on the backbone of chymotrypsin inhibitor 2CI2 in the course of the Monte Carlo simulation is sequence space. Enat shows the energy (-110 Kcal/Mol) with which the natural sequence of 2CI2 is fitted into its own tertiary structure.

Clearly, the procedure improves packing as defined by Lennard-Jones interactions, yielding proteins with VdW energies much lower than the native protein. It should be mentioned that in all these protein models, the position of the sidechains are approximate, and correspond to discrete conformations derived from a rotamer library. To test the influence of this approximation on our sequence design procedure, protein models were selected in the course of the simulation and energy minimised *in vacuo* using CHARMM[23] version 24b1, based on an all atom force field. A shifted cut-off for non bonded interaction of 13Å and a distance dependent dielectric factor (ε=4R) were used. Results are shown on Figure 2.

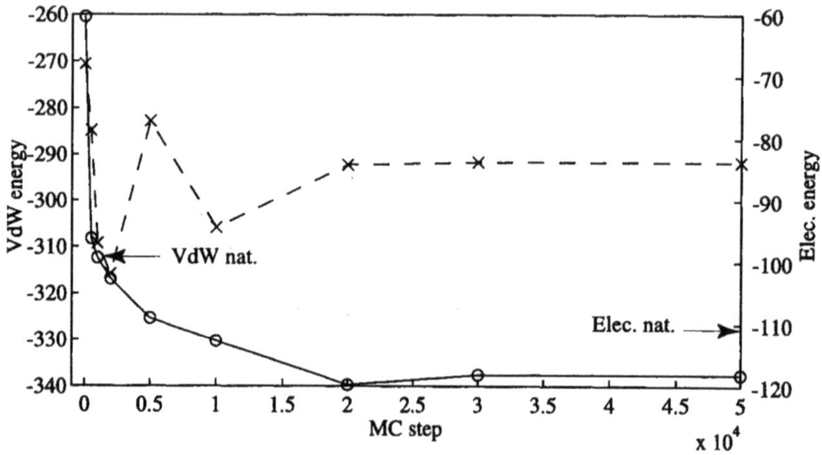

Figure 2 : CHARMM VdW energies (o) and electrostatic energies (x) of protein sequence variants of 2CI2 selected from the full set of structures derived from the Monte Carlo simulation shown in Figure 1 and energy minimized, versus the corresponding Monte Carlo step number. Points were joined by full lines for VdW data and dashed lines for electrostatics data, for sake of clarity. The VdW energy (-313 Kcal/Mol) and electrostatics energy (-112 Kcal/Mol) of the native 2CI2 are shown as arrows.

The total energy of the final protein model (+437 Kcal/Mol) is higher than the total energy of the native protein (+420 Kcal/Mol). However we confirm that our sequence design procedure improved packing as measured by VdW interactions, and even designed proteins with slightly better VdW energies than the native protein (Figure 2). The electrostatic potential, which was not included for sidechain placement or in the scoring function for the Monte Carlo procedure, is not refined but remains negative and reasonable (Figure 2).

Improving sidechain packing yields highly compact protein models. This was monitored by measuring the decrease of the accessible surface areas (ASA) and of the volumes of some of the model proteins generated during the Monte Carlo sequence design. Results are shown on Figure 3.

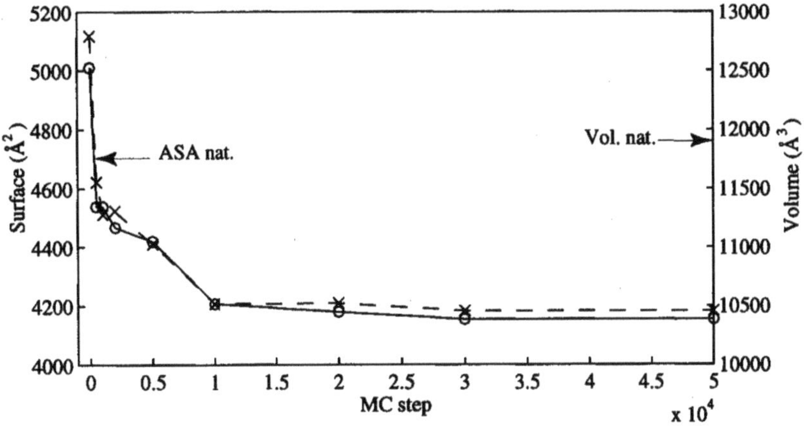

Figure 3 : Evolution of the accessible surface areas (o joined by full lines) and volumes (x joined by dashed lines) of selected protein variants of 2CI2 derived from the Monte Carlo simulation shown in Figure 1, versus the corresponding Monte Carlo step number. ASAnat (4707 $Å^2$) and Vnat (11878 $Å^3$) are the ASA and volume of the native protein, respectively. Surface areas were calculated using the method of Shrake and Rupley[24] implemented in our program ENVIRON[25], and an approximate protein volume was derived from the method proposed by Hao *et al*[26]. The ASA and the volume of the final model protein are 12% lower than the corresponding parameters of the native protein.

3.2 Comparing designed and natural sequences.

An interesting feature of our sequence design procedure is that it succeeds in gradually retrieving information concerning the native sequence (Figure 4). An alignment of the final model sequence (bottom) with the native sequence (top) is given below :

```
NLKTEWPELVGKSVEEAKKVILQDKPEAQIIVLPVGTIVTMEYRIDRVRLFVDKLDNIAEVPRVG
     |   ||         | |  |       | |           |
AGRLIWVIEVGETDLIDLLEIRQFEPVTVDKRNPEGKANVPVVLPVEVIEKKVATMLSKIKDYRQ
```

9 residues are identical between the two sequences : W6, V10, G11, I21, Q23, P26, P34, G36 and V48, all located within secondary structures of the protein except for the first tryptophan. Surprisingly, both core and exposed residues are present : W6, I21 and V48 are buried, while all six others have a high fraction of their surface area accessible to solvent. Most of the exposed conserved residues are small. Both

G11 and G36 have positive phi values. Interestingly, L2, which has a positive phi value of 155° in the native structure of 2CI2, has been replaced by a glycine in the optimised model protein.

If the Monte Carlo simulation is repeated at infinite temperature (i.e. all mutations are accepted), the generated sequences are on average 8% identical to the native sequence, which corresponds to the information contained in the constraint of constant amino acid composition.

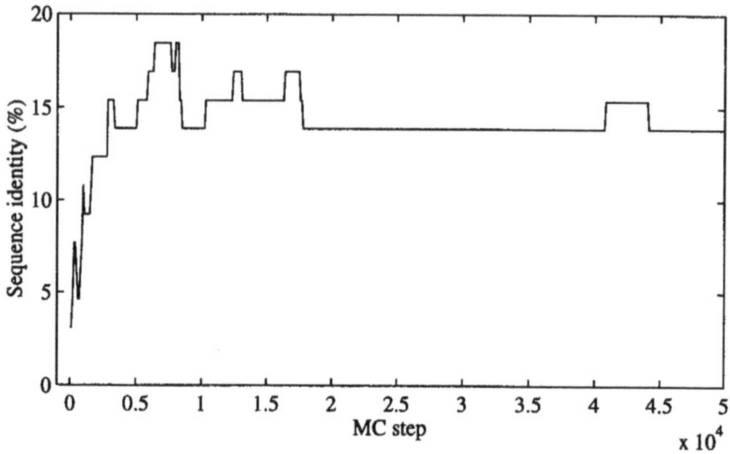

Figure 4 : Sequence identity between the native sequence of 2CI2 and the sequences optimized in the course of the Monte Carlo simulation shown in Figure 1. This information was calculated every 100 cycles, for computing efficiency.

3.3 Specificity of the designed sequence

With our definition of the energy, the sequences we designed are the most stable for the given chymotrypsin inhibitor fold. But will these sequences fold to this structure, i.e. are they incompatible with other protein folds ? To address this question"hide-and-seek" computer experiments were performed[27,28]. In this procedure, the target structure X for a given sequence S is hidden among a large number of non-native folds C, and the task is to retrieve X using an energy criteria. Success is achieved if the energy of S threaded on X, E(S,X), is lower than any E(S,C). A measure of this success is provided by a z-score[29, 30]:

$$z = \frac{E(S,X) - \langle E(S,C) \rangle}{\sigma} \qquad (2)$$

where <> stands for the average over all conformations C, and σ is the corresponding standard deviation.

In the first group of experiments, E was set to the VdW energy. Alternative structures were derived from a database of 101 protein chains selected by Jones et al[31]. The sequence S was shifted along each of these chains. Sidechains were added on each corresponding backbone, using our self-consistent mean field approach[18]. The corresponding z-score is referred to as z_{vdw}.

In the second group of experiments, the sequence S was directly given as an input to the PROSA II program. PROSA II follows the same scheme presented above, with the difference that E is set to be a combination of potentials of mean force based on amino acid contact preferences and a solvation term[32, 33]. The corresponding z-score is referred to as z_{pro}.

Both experiments were performed on the native sequence of 2CI2 as well as on a subset of sequences selected during the Monte Carlo sequence design of the chymotrypsin inhibitor fold 2CI2. Results are shown in Figure 5.

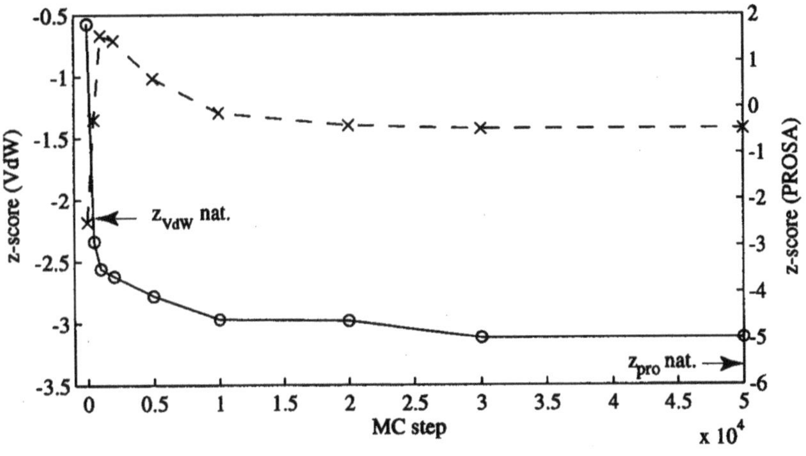

Figure 5 : Evolution of z_{VdW} (o and full lines) and z_{Pro} (x and dashed lines) for selected sequences derived from the Monte Carlo simultation shown in figure 1, versus the corresponding Monte Carlo step number. Hide-and seek experiments on the native sequence of 2CI2 yielded z_{VdW} of -2.12 and z_{Pro} of -5.65. These values are shown for reference as arrows.

The sidechain modelling procedure, the Monte Carlo optimisation in sequence space and the hide-and-seek experiment based on VdW energy are consistent in that they are all based on VdW interactions only. Figure 5 shows that optimising the stability of a sequence for a given fold while keeping the amino acid composition is correlated with an increase of the specificity of the designed sequences. This supports the sequence design scheme proposed by Shakhnovich and Gutin[20]. The z_{vdw} of the optimised sequence (-3.12) is even lower than the corresponding z-score for the native sequence (-2.12).

VdW interactions however only describe one aspect of protein structures. Using a more general energy function such as the potentials of mean force of PROSAII, we observe that the sequences designed to increase packing density within the framework of 2CI2 are not specific to this structure.

4. Discussion

Considerable experimental and theoretical efforts have been directed toward de novo protein design. Though most experimentally designed proteins contain significant amounts of secondary structures and appear to fold into an approximately correct topology, they generally lack a well-defined and uniquely structured folded state. A common suspicion is that these designed proteins lack the specific dense packing interactions observed in structures of natural proteins. Hence it is important that theoretical approaches to protein design explicitly take in account packing, which requires that a full atomic representation of the designed protein is maintained. As a first step towards this goal, we have developed in this study an all-atom inverse folding algorithm with the aim of specifically designing amino acid sequences which optimise sidechain packing for a given protein fold. The design is performed by a Monte Carlo optimisation in sequence space, with constant amino acid composition. Packing is defined by a Lennard-Jones potential. Using this program, we have designed highly compact variants of the chymotrypsin inhibitor 2CI2. The final protein model had better van der Waals packing interactions than the native structure. Its density was higher, as observed by smaller total accessible surface areas, as well as by a smaller overall volume, when compared with the native fold. Similar results (not shown) were obtained with chicken triosephosphate isomerase (PDB code 1TIM; 245 residues).

At this stage, our algorithm succeeded in optimising sidechain packing. Can this be of some use for protein design ? Starting from the backbone only of the target structure, the algorithm gradually retrieved sequence information. In the case of 2CI2, the final optimised sequence was only ≈14% identical to the native sequence. Interestingly, the algorithm imposed glycines in position where they are favoured due to steric hindrance. No constraints were imposed on the phi angle of prolines, hence distorted prolines were certainly constructed. This could easily be corrected by adding an energy term to constrain prolines. These two remarks illustrate the positive aspects of working with an all-atom representation of the protein. Though it was not expected that the algorithm would predict the native sequence exactly (proteins are known to be tolerant to mutations[34], we did expect to

find sequences bearing significant resemblance to the native sequence, and this was not found to be the case. It is not clear however that we could expect much better :
-first, the potential energy function which measures the fitness of a sequence with a given structure is based on VdW interactions only and is clearly incomplete for a reliable sequence design algorithm. It does not include for example electrostatics, nor a potential to estimate hydrophobic interactions. These extra terms might not be required if the core only of the protein was considered, but are compulsory for a global sequence design procedure, if we want to maintain patterns of hydrophobic residues in the core, and hydrophilic residues at the surface of the protein.
- second, native structures do not always privilege sidechain packing : it was shown recently that local packing in the vicinity of ß-sheets are not optimal in order to preserve the backbone-to-backbone hydrogen bond patterns within the secondary structures[35]. It should be mentioned that even if we had used the (yet unknown) true complete potential, we might not have achieved the native sequence since nature designs sequences not only for stability but also for function. Natural proteins are usually not optimal : their stability can be improved when for example buried polar groups are replaced by hydrophobic residues or when exposed hydrophobic residues are made polar[34]. These considerations will be difficult to include in any protein design scheme.
- finally our procedure may not infer specificity to our sequences. A sequence is optimal for a given fold if, in addition to being fit to the target fold, it is incompatible with all other possible folds. A commonly used approach consists in maximising the so-called 'energy gap', defined as the difference in energy between the native state and either the best non native conformation[36, 37], or the mean energy of all non native states[38, 39]. The energy gap condition was found to be necessary and sufficient for a 27 mer HP model[40]. It can be included explicitly[39], or implicitly by imposing the amino acid composition[20]. Our approach is based on the latter, and we have shown that by considering VdW interactions only, it did improve specificity (figure 5). The fact that the sequences we designed reached levels of specificity better than the native sequence within the framework of VdW interactions, but were shown to bear no specificity when using another more complete potential may be related to the problem of the definition of the energy function mentioned above. This is in agreement with the conclusion reached by Behe et al[41], i.e. that packing is not the principal cause of conformational specificity. The procedure itself might be questioned : it was shown to fail in the process of designing large HP sequences[42]. Imposing the amino acid composition introduces another limitation : a given protein may not include all twenty amino acids, and the missing ones will never be considered in the sequence design procedure.

The method proposed here can be seen as a framework for a global sequence design procedure based on a full atom representation of proteins. There is room for improvement, including the testing of various potential energy functions that would provide better estimates of structure-sequence fitness than VdW interaction alone.. Other limitations of our method are related to the constraint of using an overly precise structural template. Crystallographic studies have shown that both backbone and sidechain adjustments occur when residues within protein cores are mutated (for review, see [34]). We are currently working on including backbone flexibility, using multiple copies of the backbone, as described in our earlier work[43]. The self consistent mean field approach itself can be improved to include dynamics[44].

5. Acknowledgements

We thank M. Sippl for making his program PROSAII available to us.

6. References

1. Drexler, K. E. (1981). Proc. Natl. Acad. Sci. (USA) 78:5275-5278.
2. Bowie, J. U. & Eisenberg, D. (1993). Curr. Opin. Struct. Biol. 3:437-444.
3. Jones, D. T. (1995). Curr. Op. Biotechnology 6:452-459.
4. Desjarlais, J. & Handel, T. (1995). Curr Opin. in Biotechnology 6:460-466.
5. Yue, K. & Dill, K. A. (1992). Proc. Natl. Acad. Sci. (USA) 89:4163-4167.
6. Shakhnovich, E. I. & Gutin, A. M. (1993). Proc. Natl. Acad. Sci. (USA) 90:7195-7199.
7. Deutsch, J. M. & Kurosky, T. (1996). Phys. Rev. Lett. 76:323-326.
8. Chan, H. S. & Dill, K. A. (1991). J. Chem. Phys. 95:3775-3787.
9. Jones, D. T. (1994). Prot. Sci. 3:567-574.
10. Sun, S., Brem, R., Chan, H. S. & Dill, K. A. (1995). Prot. Eng. 8:1205-1213.
11. Hinds, D. A. & Levitt, M. (1996). J. Mol. Biol. 258:201-209.
12. Ponder, J. W. & Richards, F. M. (1987). J. Mol. Biol. 193:775-791.
13. Hellinga, H. W. & Richards, F. M. (1994). Proc. Natl. Acad. Sci. (USA) 91:5803-5807.
14. Kono, H. & Doi, J. (1994). Proteins: Struct. Funct. Genet. 19:244-255.
15. Desjarlais, J. & Handel, T. (1995). Protein Sci. 4:2006-2018.
16. Dahiyat, B. & Mayo, S. (1996). Protein Sci. 5:895-903.
17. Metropolis, N., Rosenbluth, A. W., Rosenbluth, M. N., Teller, A. H. & Teller, E. (1953). J. Chem. Phys. 21:1087-1092.
18. Koehl, P. & Delarue, M. (1994). J. Mol. Biol. 239:249-275.
19. Bernstein, F. C., Koetzle, T. F., Williams, G., Meyer, D. J., Brice, M. D., Rodgers, J. R., Kennard, O., Shimanouchi, T. & Tasumi, M. (1977). J. Mol. Biol. 112:535-542.
20. Shakhnovich, E. I. & Gutin, A. M. (1993). Protein Eng. 6:793-800.

21. Nakashima, H., Nishikawa, K. & Ooi, T. (1986). J. Biochem. 99:153-162.
22. Tuffery, P., Etchebest, C., Hazout, S. & Lavery, R. (1991). J. Biomol. Struct. Dynam. 8:1267-1289.
23. Brooks, B., Bruccoleri, R., Olafson, B., States, D., Swaminathan, S. & Karplus, M. (1983). J. Comput. Chem. 4:187-217.
24. Shrake, A. & Rupley, J. (1973). J. Mol. Biol. 79:351-371.
25. Koehl, P. & Delarue, M. (1994). Proteins: Struct. Funct. Genet. 20:264-278.
26. Hao, M., Rackovsky, S., Liwo, A., Pincus, M. & Scheraga, H. (1992). Proc. Natl. Acad. Sci. (USA) 89:6614-6618.
27. Hendlich, M., Lackner, P., Weitckus, S., Floeckner, H., Froschauer, R., Gottsbacher, K., Casari, G. & Sippl, M. J. (1990). J. Mol. Biol. 216:167-180.
28. Sippl, M. & Weitckus, S. (1992). Proteins: Struct. Funct. Genet. 13:258-271.
29. Bowie, J. U., Lüthy, R. & Eisenberg, D. (1991). Science 253:164-170.
30. Sippl, M. (1993). Proteins: Struct. Funct. Genet. 17:355-362.
31. Jones, D. T., Taylor, W. R. & Thornton, J. M. (1992). Nature (London) 358:86-89.
32. Sippl, M. (1993). J. Comput. Aided. Mol. Des. 7:473-501.
33. Sippl, M. J. & Jaritz, M. (1994) in *Distance based approaches to Protein Structure Prediction*, H. Bohr and S. Brunak eds, 113-134.
34. Baldwin, E. P. & Matthews, B. W. (1994). Curr. Opin. Biotech. 5:396-402.
35. Schultz Beardsley, D. & Kauzmann, W. (1996). Proc. Natl. Acad. Sci. (USA) 93:4448-4453.
36. Bryngelson, J. D. & Wolynes, P. G. (1987). Proc. Natl. Acad. Sci. (USA) 84:7524-7528.
37. Shakhnovich, E. I. & Gutin, A. M. (1990). Nature (London) 346:773-775.
38. Reva, B. A. & Finkelstein, A. V. (1992). Prot. Eng. 5:625-628.
39. Godzik, A. (1995). Prot. Eng. 8:409-416.
40. Sali, A., Shakhnovich, E. I. & Karplus, M. (1994). J. Mol. Biol. 235:1614-1636.
41. Behe, M. J., Lattman, E. E. & Rose, G. D. (1991). Proc. Natl. Acad. Sci. (USA) 88:4195-4199.
42. Yue, K., Fiebig, K. M., Thomas, P. D., Chan, H. S. & Shakhnovich, E. I. (1995). Proc. Natl. Acad. Sci. (USA) 92:325-329.
43. Koehl, P. & Delarue, M. (1995). Nature Struct. Biol. 2:163-170.
44. Huber, T., Torda, A. & Van Gunsteren, W. (1996). Biopolymers 39:103-114.

DESIGN OF HYDROPHOBIC CORE OF *E.coli* MALATE DEHYDROGENASE BASED ON THE SIDE-CHAIN PACKING

H. KONO

Tsukuba Life Science Center, The Institute of Physical & Chemical Research (RIKEN), Tsukuba, Ibaraki 305, Japan

M. NISHIYAMA, M. TANOKURA

Biotechnology Research Center, The University of Tokyo, Tokyo 113, Japan

J. DOI

Bioinformation Engineering Laboratory Department of Biotechnology, The University of Tokyo 1-1-1, Yayoi, Bunkyo-ku, Tokyo 113, JAPAN

We have developed computational programs for the de novo design of hydrophobic cores of proteins. The first program optimizes side-chain conformations using an updated rotamer library for potential hydrophobic residues, based on the backbone structure of the protein of interest. The second program selects candidates to be engineered among the sequences by estimating changes in Gibbs free energy between the folded and unfolded structure of the proteins with new sequence. Using these programs, we constructed several variants of *E. coli* malate dehydrogenase (eMDH) which could have increased stability at 25°C, compared to the wild type enzyme. To quantitate stability change between variants and the wild type, circular dichroism spectra were measured as a function of guanidine hydrochloride concentration at 25°C, pH 7.0. This analysis showed that three variants constructed in this study were stabilized more than or equal to the wild type. This demonstrated that our programs may be powerful tools to design new proteins with high stability.

1 Introduction

The de novo design of protein is one of the ultimate purposes in protein engineering. Many efforts have been made in the creation of a new amino acid sequence that folds into a predetermined three dimensional topology [1,2,3]. Empirical knowledge obtained so far has been tested in the design of a sequence from a given structure.

Protein folding problem is not only essential for understanding of the nature of protein structure, but also has immediate importance to many aspects of biology and biotechnology. There has been increasing interest in design of more stable variants of existing proteins. Godzik [4] tried to find out ideal sequences for a plastcyanin from 20^{99} sequence space using a threading algorithm. However, the obtained sequences showed a poor similarity to the native sequence. Also, using a genetic algorithm as well as the threading potential, Jones *et al*[5] tried to design a new α-helical protein from the sequence giving all β-structure. The designed protein, however, exhibited little helical property in water containing ethylene glycol or methanol. Thus, no success have been achieved in design of a whole protein, although the threading method has been claimed to be potentially capable of sequence design.

In addition, Hellinga and Richards [6] designed a hydrophobic core of λ repressor using a simulated evolution algorithm. They succeeded in obtaining the sequences with biological activity in the higher rank of the calculation. But, the relationship of the energetics they used and biological activity of these sequences was not clear. Desjarlais and Handel [7] also successfully engineered a hydrophobic core of phage 434 cro protein. The sequences for the core were designed to achieve only a tight packing using a genetic algorithm. Although the order of protein stability obtained by their calculation did not always agree with that by the experiments, the results showed that tight packing is one of the important factors in de novo design of stable protein. Based on the side chain packing, Lee & Levitt [8] and Lee [9] predicted the energetics of protein thermostability and Wilson *et al*[10] carried out the energetic analysis of substrate binding. The packing contribution to the protein stability was well reviewed by Lim & Richards [11].

In this paper, we describe two computational programs, which produce protein sequences with increased thermostability by optimizing side-chain packing of hydrophobic core. And the calculated thermostability using these programs was compared with that of biologically engineered proteins.

2 Materials and Methods

2.1 Design of sequences

Two programs were used in the prediction of amino acid sequence for a core and the first one was based on the automata network method [12] as previously described. Using this program, a set of amino acid sequences and their side chain conformations which could achieve a tight side chain packing were predicted by random jumps in the sequence and conformational space of hydrophobic amino acids such as Ala, Val, Leu, Ile, Met and Phe. As for side-chain conformation of each residue site, an updated rotamer library [13] was used together with the rotamer derived from the crystal structure of *E. coli* malate dehydrogenase. Consequently, 123 sets of sequences were obtained after 1,000 runs at various initial states of the network.

Then the second program was used to estimate Gibbs free energy changes

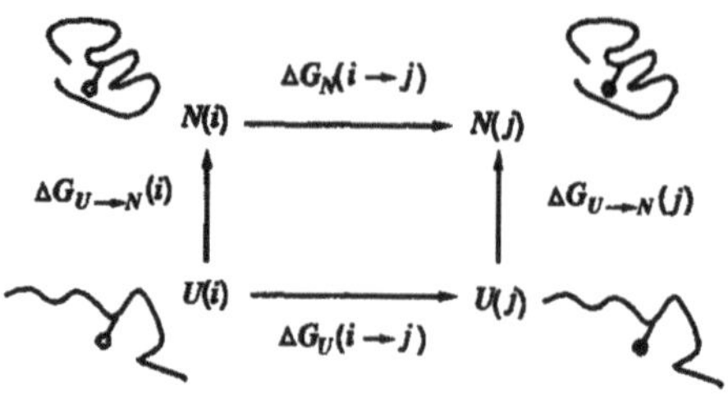

Figure 1: The thermodynamic cycle between wild type (i) and its variant (j).

of the sequence produced by the first program. In estimation of Gibbs free energy changes, hydration, side-chain entropy, bond energy and non-bond energy were considered. The stability of a sequence i is given by changes in free energy ΔG^{H_2O} between native state, N, and unfold state, U,

$$\Delta G_{U\Rightarrow N}(i) = \Delta E^{solvation}_{U\Rightarrow N}(i) + \Delta E^{entropy}_{U\Rightarrow N}(i) + \Delta E^{nb}_{U\Rightarrow N}(i) + \Delta E^{bond}_{U\Rightarrow N}(i) \quad (1)$$

where $\Delta E^{solvation}_{U\Rightarrow N}(i), \Delta E^{entropy}_{U\Rightarrow N}(i), \Delta E^{nb}_{U\Rightarrow N}(i), \Delta E^{bond}_{U\Rightarrow N}(i)$ are terms due to changes in the solvation, entropy, non-bonded interactions and covalently bonded structure between the unfolded and native state of the protein, respectively. The energy difference between two sequences i and j is given by the thermodynamic cycle in Figure 1. This thermodynamic linkage allows the difference in the stabilities of two sequences to be described by two equivalent forms: the natural difference of the stabilities

$$\Delta\Delta G_{U\Rightarrow N}(i \Rightarrow j) = \Delta E_{U\Rightarrow N}(j) - \Delta E_{U\Rightarrow N}(i) \quad (2)$$

and a second form that does not reflect chemical reality but is accessible by considering the cycle,

$$\Delta\Delta G_{U\Rightarrow N}(i \Rightarrow j) = \Delta E_N(i \Rightarrow j) - \Delta E_U(i \Rightarrow j). \quad (3)$$

The cycle can be written as the sum of the differences of each component

$$\begin{aligned} \Delta\Delta G_{U\Rightarrow N}(i \Rightarrow j) &= \Delta\Delta E^{solvation}_{U\Rightarrow N}(i \Rightarrow j) + \Delta\Delta E^{entropy}_{U\Rightarrow N}(i \Rightarrow j) \\ &\quad + \Delta\Delta E^{nb}_{U\Rightarrow N}(i \Rightarrow j) + \Delta\Delta E^{bond}_{U\Rightarrow N}(i \Rightarrow j). \end{aligned} \quad (4)$$

Each of these terms is subject to the thermodynamic linkage relationship and can therefore be calculated by equations analogous to either Eqs. 2 or 3.

The contribution of the solvation term to the folding energy of a sequence i with n residues long, can be given as follows,

$$\Delta E^{solvation}_{U\Rightarrow N}(i) = \sum_{k=0}^{n} g_k \frac{A^0_k(i) - A_k(i)}{A^0_k(i)} \quad (5)$$

where g_i is the free energy of transfer between gas and water [14] and A^0 and A are solvent accessible surface areas in the unfolded state and in the folded state, respectively. The free energy of solvation, to be added to the AMBER energy, must correspond only to the additional interactions of the atoms of the solute with water. Consequently, we used the parameters derived from observed free energies of transfer from gas to aqueous solution. The area was calculated using the program developed based on the MSEED algorithm [15]. Since the unfolded protein is assumed to be in an extended form, the contribution of the solvation term to the energy differences of the sequences becomes

$$\Delta\Delta E_{U\Rightarrow N}^{solvation}(i \Rightarrow j) = \sum_{k=0}^{n} g_k \frac{A_k^0(j) - A_k(j)}{A_k^0(j)} - \sum_{k=0}^{n} g_k \frac{A_k^0(i) - A_k(i)}{A_k^0(i)}. \quad (6)$$

The loss of entropy on protein folding causes an important contribution to the stability of a protein. Since neither glycine nor proline was being considered in this study, the main chain entropy was assumed to be unaffected by the sequence changes. Loss of side-chain entropy on the folding is reflected by the degrees of rotational freedom in the native and unfolded state of all side chain. Because all side chains were fully buried in this simulation, the side-chain entropies in the native were assumed to be 0. The entropies in the unfolded were taken from the literature [16]. Then, the change in entropy is

$$\Delta\Delta E_{U\Rightarrow N}^{entropy}(i \Rightarrow j) = \sum_{k=0}^{n}(S_k(j) - S_k(i)). \quad (7)$$

As for non-bonded interaction, only the van der Waals interactions were considered. The coulombic interaction term was ignored, due to the fact that only uncharged residues were used in this calculation. The differences in stabilities of the sequences due to the non-bonded interactions were determined using

$$\Delta\Delta E_{U\Rightarrow N}^{nb}(i \Rightarrow j) = \Delta E_N^{vdw}(i \Rightarrow j) - \Delta E_U^{vdw}(i \Rightarrow j). \quad (8)$$

$\Delta E_N^{vdw}(i \Rightarrow j)$ is obtained directly from the calculation by evaluating a 6-12 potential function with parameters obtained from the AMBER 3A force field [17]. $\Delta E_U^{vdw}(i \Rightarrow j)$ could be ignored due to the same reason described for the solvation term. Since the energy of covalent bonding should be unchanged in respect of the the folding state, $\Delta\Delta E_{U\Rightarrow N}^{bond}(i \Rightarrow j) = 0$.

2.2 Selection of hydrophobic core

E.coli malate dehydrogenase (eMDH) consists of 312 amino acids with nine helices and eleven strands, which form into a homo-dimer. Its structure has

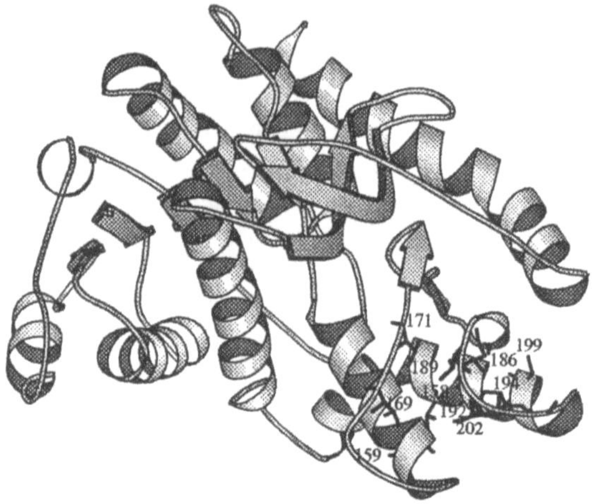

core : 158A, 159A, 169V, 171V, 186L, 189V 192V, 194F, 199V, 202L

Figure 2: eMDH structure. Residues composing the core we focused in this study are denoted by thick line. This drawing was produced by MOLSCRIPT[20].

been determined by X-ray at 1.9Å with an R-value 0.195 [18]. Using a computer graphics system [19], we searched hydrophobic core of the enzyme by manually clipping the molecular and found four by monomer. We selected one out of the four (shown in Figure2) as the target in this study because it corresponds to the core of *Thermus flavus* malate dehydrogenase, a site experimentally shown to be one of determinants of the high thermal stability (unpublished data). The core consists of 10 hydrophobic residues at 158, 159, 169, 171, 186, 189, 192, 194, 199 and 202.

2.3 Mutagenesis

We conducted mutagenesis with a PCR method [21]. The nucleotide sequences of mutation points were confirmed by the M13 dideoxy chain termination method [22,23] with a DSQ-1000 (Shimadzu Co., Kyoto) DNA sequencer. The mutated gene was expressed in *E.coli* 5131-5 [24] using pUC18 as the expression plasmid. The cells were disrupted by sonication and eMDH variants were purified by Blue Sepharose CL-6B affinity column chromatography.

2.4 Circular dichroism

All circular dichroism (CD) spectra were measured with JASCO J-720 spectropolarimeters between 200 and 250 nm using proteins of about 100 μg/ml in 20 mM phosphate buffer (pH 7.0) at 25°C.

The changes in the CD spectra at θ_{222} nm of the proteins were compared by normalizing each transition curve to the apparent fraction of the unfolded form. Thermodynamic parameters, ΔG^{H_2O} and m, were extracted from the denatured curves by assuming that the unfolding reaction follows a two-state model $D \rightleftharpoons 2U$ [25]. ΔG is the change in free energy between D and U at a given GuHCl concentration, ΔG^{H_2O} is the value in the absence of denaturant and m is a fitting parameter that reflects the cooperativity of the unfolding transition.

2.5 Assay for the enzyme activity

Steady-state kinetic analyses were carried out by measuring the decrease in absorbance at 340 nm in reaction mixtures which contains 4 nM of the purified enzymes and 167 μM of oxaloacetate in 33 mM potassium phosphate buffer (pH 7.0) at 30°C as described previously [26].

3 Results

3.1 Designed sequences and their stability

Our programs produced eMDH variants with new amino acid sequences giving various free energy. The highest score of the free energy (14.17 kcal/mol) was obtained in can35 which had 5 amino acid replacements of Val158Leu, Val169Leu, Val189Ala, Phe194Leu and Val199Ile. This and other seven variants with various level of free energy (stability) were chosen for site-directed mutagenesis as described above. The amino acid sequences and their energy components are shown in Table 1 and 2, respectively. It can be seen from these results that the side-chain conformations of the predicted variant structures is very similar to those of the crystal structure and exhibit more tight packing (Figure 3). Except two variants, V169L/V199I and P_{ref}, other variants appeared to be more stable than the wild type at 25°C. P_{ref} was designed as a reference where 4 valine residues were simultaneously replaced with larger residues, Leu or Ile. For P_{ref}, unfavorable van der Waals contacts should occur because there was no room to contain four larger residues in the backbone structure which was fixed to that of the wild type. As for V169L/V199I, since the sum of the solvation term and the entropic term was a little larger than

Table 1: Designed sequences for eMDH type core region

variant	158	159	169	171	186	189	192	194	199	202
wild	V	A	V	V	L	V	V	F	V	L
V199I	V	A	V	V	L	V	V	F	i	L
V169L/V199M	V	A	*l*	V	L	V	V	F	*m*	L
V169L/V199I	V	A	*l*	V	L	V	V	F	*i*	L
V169L	V	A	*l*	V	L	V	V	F	V	L
can25	*l*	A	*m*	V	L	*a*	V	*l*	*m*	L
can26	*l*	A	*l*	*l*	L	*a*	V	*l*	*i*	L
V199M	V	A	V	V	L	V	V	F	*m*	L
can35	*l*	A	*l*	V	L	*a*	V	*l*	*i*	L
P_{ref}	*l*	A	*l*	*l*	L	V	V	F	*i*	L

Amino acids shown with lowercase are different from wild one.

Table 2: Predicted changes in free energy

protein	$\Delta\Delta H$ (kcal/mol)	$-T\Delta\Delta S$	$\Delta\Delta g$	$\Delta\Delta G^{cal}$
V199I	+1.61	−0.68	−0.22	+0.71
V169L/V199M	+6.18	−2.07	−3.01	+1.10
V169L/V199I	+2.27	−1.36	−1.37	−0.46
V169L	+0.66	−0.68	+0.15	+0.13
can25	+7.70	−3.21	−2.65	+1.85
can26	+11.25	−2.47	+0.53	+9.31
V199M	+7.24	−1.39	−1.99	+3.86
can35	+15.67	−1.79	+0.29	+14.17
P_{ref}	−101.48	−2.72	+0.40	−103.80

T = 298 K. $\Delta\Delta g$ values from Ooi *et al.* $\Delta\Delta G^{cal}$ denotes a calculated $\Delta\Delta G$.

the enthalpic term, the stability was predicted to decrease. In general, replacement of a hydrophobic amino acid with the larger one increases the stability. However, it was not always the case in this study. In the variant V169L/V199I, the introduction of Ile at position 199 protected the surrounding residues from exposure to the solvent and thus caused a decrease in $\Delta\Delta g$.

3.2 Native structure for variants

We constructed the mutated eMDH genes for the expression of the nine variants described above and six variants of nine designed proteins were obtained. The other three mutants with replacement of Phe by Leu at position 194 were not produced with unknown reason. We assume that Phe 194 is an important residue for eMDH for correct folding to a native form. CD spectra of variants proved that all the variants had the same structure as the wild type

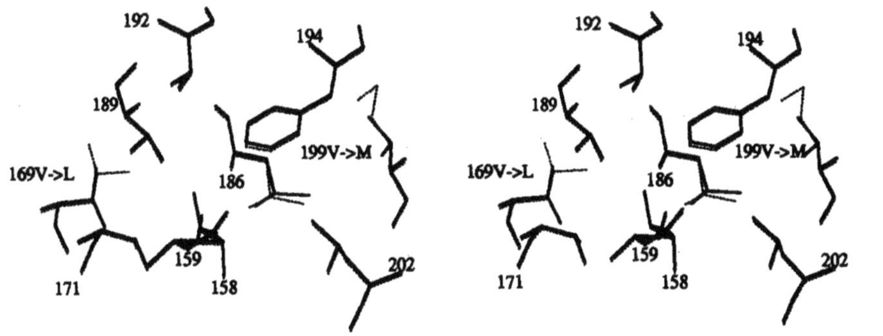

Figure 3: Stereo view of the core of V169L/V199M (dashed line) superimposed on that of the wild (solid line).

(data not shown). When the proteins were denatured with GuHCl and were refolded by dilution of the denaturant, all the proteins completely recovered their secondary structures and the enzyme activities (data not shown).

3.3 Stability

To quantitate the change in stability experimentally, CD spectra of each variant were measured as a function of GuHCl concentration at 25 °C, pH

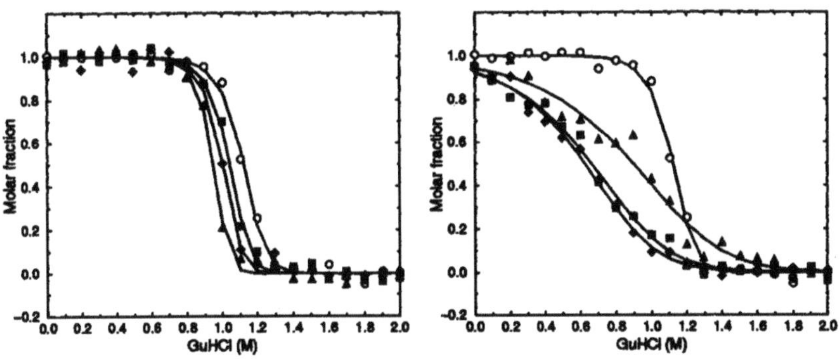

Figure 4: Molar fractions plotted against GuHCl concentration. Left figure shows wild type (circle), V169L (square), V169L/V199I (diamond) and V169L/V199I (triangle). Right figure shows wild type (circle), P_{ref} (square), V199M (diamond) and V199I (triangle).

Table 3: Thermodynamic parameters for eMDH and its variants.

protein	ΔG^{H_2O}	m[1]	$\Delta\Delta G^{exp}$	$\Delta\Delta G^{cal}$	activity[2]
Wild	22.4 ± 1.7	13.2 ± 1.4	–	–	47.2
V169L	22.9 ± 2.7	14.7 ± 2.6	+0.5	+0.13	41.3
V199M	10.2 ± 0.5	4.2 ± 0.6	−12.2	+3.86	8.1
V199I	10.5 ± 0.5	3.3 ± 0.5	−11.9	+0.71	8.6
V169L/V199M	25.6 ± 3.2	19.0 ± 3.3	+3.2	+1.10	40.5
V169L/V199I	23.2 ± 2.7	15.6 ± 2.7	+0.8	−0.46	31.2
P_{ref}	10.1 ± 1.1	3.8± 0.9	−14.9	−103.8	9.8

[1] m : the slope of a denatured curve. $\Delta\Delta G^{cal}$, $\Delta\Delta G^{exp}$: calculated and experimental $\Delta\Delta G$ (kcal/mol), respectively. [2] unit = μmol/min

7.0 (Figure 4). The ΔG^{H_2O} and slope of denaturation curve were estimated by non-linear least-squares fitting. From the estimation, three variants in this study were found to be more stable than or equal to the wild type enzyme.

For V169L, V169L/V199M and V169L/V199I, which have similar denaturation cooperativity (m value) to the wild type, the calculated $\Delta\Delta G$ values between the wild type and variants were consistent with those determined by the experiments within experimental error (Table 3).

4 Discussion

Lee & Levitt predicted mutant stability based only on van der Waals energies of the folded state using a simulated annealing algorithm[8] without the energies of the unfolded state, hydration and entropic contributions. Lee applied a self-consistent ensemble optimization theory for prediction of mutant energetics[9], in which hydration and entropic contributions were also ignored. Although, their calculated energies by these methods appeared to correlate with the experimental thermostabilities of mutants of λ repressor, the energies were not quantitatively identical to those of experiment.

We previously examined with the reliability of our programs using a smaller protein, barnase, with a single domain (submitted) and the calculated $\Delta\Delta G^{H_2O}$ values of this protein and its mutants coincided with the experimental values (correlation coefficient 0.93). In this study, we applied our programs to measure a lager, multi-meric protein, eMDH, by consideration of both folded and unfolded state together with hydration, entropic contributions and van der Waals energy. The method enabled us to estimate the free energy change in between the native and unfolded state. Using this method, we designed a number of amino acid sequences with high stability. For the three proteins, V169L, V169L/V199M and V169L/V199I, which had similar denaturation cooperativity to that of the wild type, the calculated $\Delta\Delta G$ values between the wild type and variants coincided quantitatively with the values determined by the experiments within the experimental errors. In particular, the double mutant V169L/V199M was more stable than the wild type enzyme by 3.2 kcal/mol of $\Delta\Delta G$. This means that hydration and entropic contributions cannot be ignored in quantitative prediction because the stability changes are likely to be overestimated when only enthalpic energies were considered. In comparison with other methods mentioned above, our method can save computational cost because it can predict a set of sequence and their energies in a single run and does not have to sample many conformations for each set of sequences. Therefore our method may be a powerful tool to design new proteins with an increased stability.

However, the calculation was not applicable to estimate an exact $\Delta\Delta G$ value for the variants, V199I, V199M and P_{ref}, which show a different cooperativity pattern from that of the wild type. In consideration of the fact that our program may not be suitable to estimate $\Delta\Delta G$ values induced by replacement which could cause main chain movement, we may assume that the observed difference in $\Delta\Delta G$ values between the calculation and the experiment is partially attributed to the main chain movement in these variants. It is also likely that the decrease of specific activities in the variants may be caused by the slight distortion of the 3D structure. In addition, the specific activity showed that replacements of Val with Met or Ile at position 199 caused conformational change to some extent while the three variants, V169L, V169L/V199M and V169L/V199I, kept the structure similar to that of the wild type (Table 3). Their three dimensional structures must be determined to answer this question.

To be an alternative explanation, the failure in the prediction of $\Delta\Delta G$ for the three variants, V169L, V169L/V199M and V169L/V199I, with smaller $\Delta\Delta G$ than our calculation might be due to the fact that the denatured state of these variants was different from that of the wild type. Studies on staphylococal nuclease[27,28] indicated that the denatured state of variants with larger m value have a less structured denatured state with a greater exposure of nonpolar residues to solvent. This suggests an existence of multiple forms even in denatured state. To clarify these possibilities, determination of further characterization is required.

The loss of stability by more than 10 kcal/mol of $\Delta\Delta G$ for single variants, V199I and V199M, shows that the residue at 199 is a key residue for protein stability. However, there was no difference between each variant and the wild type in CD spectra at a range from 200 to 250 nm in the absence of the denaturant, suggesting that the global structure was not significantly distorted

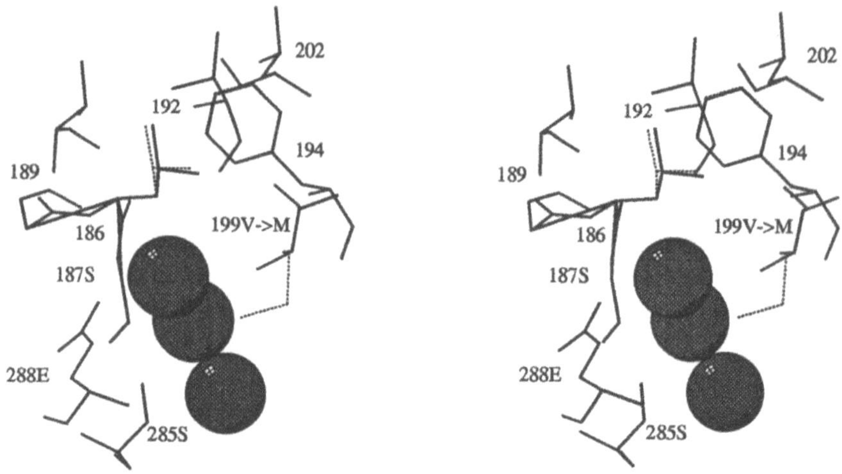

Figure 5: Stereo view of the cleft near the V199. In the crystal structure, three water molecules (sphere) in the cleft formed hydrogen bonds with S187, S285 and E288. Substitution of V199 with M (dashed line) can cause one of three waters push out.

in each variant. Although Val 199 locates at the N-terminus of the seventh helix and participates in the formation of one edge of the hydrophobic core, a cleft containing three water molecules is found in the vicinity of Val 199. We assume that one of the waters forming a hydrogen bond network with Ser 187, Ser 285 and Glu 288, would be pushed out by the substitution of Val 199 with Met or Ile and, hence, their stability of the variants were decreased (Figure 5). When additional substitution of Val 169 with Leu was introduced, the stability of the variants, V199I and V199M, were recovered. Since residue 169 located at a distance more than 15 Å from the residue 199 in the crystal structure, it is unlikely that these residues interact directly with each other. We suggest that some dynamic event may cause a repacking of the core.

Acknowledgments

We would like to thank Dr. T. Fujii for his assistant in measuring CD spectra. We also would like to thank M. Kinoshita, M. Kukimoto, N. Kobashi and N. Kudo for their help in engineering variants. Finally, we would like to thank Dr. Hao for carefully reading the manuscript.

References

1. W. F. DeGrado *et al*, *Science* **243**, 622-628 (1989).
2. C. Sander *et al*, *Proteins:Struct.Funct.Genet.* **12**, 105-110 (1992).
3. M. H. Hecht, *Proc.Natl.Acad.Sci.USA* **91**, 8729-8730 (1994).
4. A. Godzik, *Protein Engineering* **8**, 409-416 (1995).
5. D. Jones *et al*, *Proteins:Struct.Funct.Genet.* **24**, 502-513 (1996).
6. H. W. Hellinga and F. M. Richards, *Proc.Natl.Acad.Sci.USA* **91**, 5803-5807 (1994).
7. J. R. Desjarlais and T. M. Handel, *Protein Science* **4**, 2006-2018 (1995).
8. C. Lee and M Levitt,*Nature (London)* **352**, 448-451 (1991).
9. C. Lee, *J.Mol.Biol.* **236**, 918-939 (1994).
10. C. Wison *et al*,*J.Mol.Biol.* **220**, 495-506 (1991).
11. W. A. Lim and F. M. Richards, *Quarterly Reviews of Biophysics* **26**, 423-498 (1994).
12. H. Kono and J. Doi, *Proteins:Struct.Funct.Genet.* **19**, 244-255 (1994).
13. H. Kono and J. Doi, *J.Compt.Chem.* , in press (1996).
14. T. Ooi *et al*, *Proc.Natl.Acad.Sci.USA* **84**, 3086-3090 (1987).
15. G. Perrot*et al*, *J.Compt.Chem.* **13**, 1-11 (1992).
16. M. J. E. Sternberg and J. S. Chickos, *Protein Engineering* **7**, 149-155 (1994).
17. J. S. Weiner *et al*, *J.Am.Chem.Soc.* **106**, 765-784 (1984).
18. M. D. Hall *et al*, *J.Mol.Biol.* **226**, 867-882 (1992).
19. T. Ishii *et al*, *Transactions of Information Processing Society of Japan* **32**, 590-598 (1991).
20. P. Kraulis, *J.Appl.Cryst.* **24**, 946-950 (1991).
21. W. Ito *et al*, *Gene* **102**, 67-70 (1991).
22. F.S. Sanger *et al*, *Proc.Natl.Acad.Sci.USA* **74**, 5463-5467 (1977).
23. J. Messing and J. Vieira, *Gene* **19**, 269-276 (1982).
24. M. Nishiyama *et al*, *J.Biol.Chem.* **261**, 14178-14183 (1986).
25. M. S. Gittelman and C. R. Matthews, *Biochemistry* **29**, 7011-7020 (1990).
26. M. Nishiyama *et al*, *J.Biol.Chem.* **268**, 4656-4660 (1993).
27. D. Shortle and A. K. Meeker, *Proteins:Struct.Funct.Genet.* **1**, 81-89 (1986).
28. D. Shortle *et al*, *Biochemistry* **29**, 8033-8041 (1990).

LATENT PERIODICITY OF DNA SEQUENCES OF MANY GENES

E.V. KOROTKOV
Center of Bioengineering of the Russian Academy of Sciences, 60-Oktybrya prospect, 7/1, Moscow, Russia

D.A. PHOENIX
University of Central Lancashire Preston PR1 2HE, UK

ABSTRACT

A method of latent periodicity search being developed. Mutual information is used to reveal of DNA or mRNA sequence latent periodicity. The latent periodicity of DNA sequence is a periodicity with low level of homology between any two periods inside DNA sequence. The mutual information between artificial numerical sequence and DNA sequence is calculated. The length of the artificial sequence period is varied from 2 to 150. The high level of the mutual information between artificial a nd DNA sequences alows to find any type of latent periodicity of DNA sequence. The latent periodicity of many DNA coding regions has been found. Potential significance of latent periodicity is discussed.

INTRODUCTION

The search of periodical sequences in DNA is important for understanding of the DNA sequence structure of human and other species genomes. Periodical sequences in human genome are now found as satellite and minisatellite sequences [11, 26, 2]. These sequences contain a short repeated fragment of DNA. Mathematical methods of determining symbolical sequence periodicity are now developed [7, 8, 19, 20, 21, 27]. These approaches are directed to application of mathematical methods advanced for analysis of numerical sequences periodicity to study periodicity of symbolical sequences. A transformation of a symbolic sequence to a numerical sequence is frequently used for such analysis. The investigations have shown a periodicity of amino acid sequences of some genes [18, 19, 20, 21, 25] and a periodicity of some DNA sequences [3, 4, 7, 8, 23].

The study of a periodicity of DNA sequences is mainly based on the analysis of homological periodicity including imperfect [17, 24, 27, 28]. However, hidden periodicity of DNA sequence may exist and this periodicity can not be found by the algorithms developed. For example, there may be observed (A/C/T)(T/G)(G/A)(T/A)(C/G/A)(G/T) period where the first position of a period contains A, C or T, the second position contains T or G and so on. Earlier, a new mathematical method of latent periodicity detection has been developed and the latent periodicity of some human genes has been found [15]. The mathematical approach directed to detecting similar laws in DNA and DNA sequences is improved in the present work. Latent periodicity of some DNA regions is shown. These DNA contain the following genes: albumin gene, farnesyltransferase alpha-subunit gene and plasmogen. Mathematical approach being developed uses the method of enlarged similarity of DNA sequences [13,14].

SYSTEM AND METHODS

A comparison of artificial periodic sequences with the DNA sequence analyzed is used for detection of latent periodicity [15]. The alphabet of artificial sequences contains letters S_i. The sequence $S_1S_2S_1S_2S_1S_2$... is generated for the search of DNA period qual to 2 bases. The sequence $S_1S_2...S_nS_1S_2...S_n$ is generated for study of the DNA period equal to n bases. The length of artificial sequence is equal to the length of the analyzed sequence. The artificial sequences having period from 2 up to 150 are serially compared with the analyzed DNA sequence. Mutual information is chosen as measure of similarity of artificial and DNA sequences. A matrix M is filled in for calculation of the mutual information. Elements of the matrix M are numbers of coincidences of each type between the artificial sequence and the DNA sequence. The dimension of matrix M is 4xn. The value of the matrix M rows are the bases A, U,C and G. Value of the columns of the matrix M are the letters S_i ($i=1,2,\ldots, n$) of the artificial sequence. The sums of row elements are equal to quantity of A, U, C and G bases in the DNA sequence. The sums of elements in each column are equal to the quantity of S_i letters in the artificial sequence. The mutual information is calculated using the formula [16]:

$$I = \sum_{1}^{4}\sum_{1}^{n} m_{ij}\ln m_{ij} - \sum_{1}^{n} x_i \ln x_i - \sum_{1}^{4} y_j \ln y_j + L\ln L \qquad (1)$$

Here m_{ij} is the element of a matrix M; x_i is the quantity of A, U, C and G symbols in the DNA sequence; y_j is the quantity of S_j symbol in the artificial sequence; L is the length of compared sequences. The 2I value is distributed as X^2 with 3(n-1) degrees of freedom. It permits to evaluate the probability of accidental formation of periodicity.

All possible periods can be divided into two classes. The first class (simple periods) includes periods that are equal to simple numbers. The simple numbers are the numbers that can be devided without remainder on one or on itself. The second class (complex periods) contains periods equal to a product of simple numbers. Let us have a compound period A=B*C. B and C are simple periods. Let the period A have the least probability $\alpha= P(X^2 \geq 2I)$ for all periods analyzed. It was shown earlier [29]:

$$I(DNA,B)+I_{DNA}(C,B)+I(DNA,C) = I(C*B,DNA)+I(B,C) \quad (2)$$

Here I(DNA,B) is the mutual information between DNA sequence and the artificial sequence with the period that is equal to B; I(DNA,C) is the mutual information between DNA sequence and the artificial sequence with the period that is equal to A; I(B,C) is the mutual information between two artificial sequences with periods that are equal to B and C; I(B*C,DNA) is the mutual information between DNA sequence and compound artificial sequence with the period that is equal to B*C. For example, let us have B=2 and C=3. We may write the sequences B and C as:

$b_1b_2b_3b_1b_2b_3b_1b_2b_3b_1b_2b_3$

$c_1c_2c_1c_2c_1c_2c_1c_2c_1c_2c_1c_2$

Then we may unite those two sequences and introduce 6 new letters: $a_1=b_1c_1$; $a_2=b_2c_2$; $a3=b_3c_1$; $a_4=b_1c_2$; $a_5=b_2c_1$; $a_6=b_3c_2$. The sequence A = $\{a_1a_2a_3a_4a_5a_6a_1a_2a_3a_4a_5a_6a_1a_2a_3a_4a_5a_6\}$ is a united sequence B*C. The same method is applied if we construct the sequences (DNA*B), (DNA*C) and (DNA*C*B). The mutual information I(B,C) is calculated as:

$$I(B,C) = \{H(B)+H(C)-H(B*C)\}L \quad (3)$$

where H(B), H(C), H(B*C) are the entropies of B, C and B*C sequences and L is the length of sequences. The H(B) is calculated as:

$$H(B) = \Sigma p_i(B)\{\ln p_i(B)\} \quad (4)$$

where $p_i(B)$ is a probability of i letter in B sequence (i=1,2,..B). The entropy H(C) and H(B*C) are calculated by similar way. $I_{DNA}(C,B)$ is conditional mutual information between C and B sequences [29].

$$I_{DNA}(C,B) = H(DNA*B)+H(DNA*C)-H(DNA)-H(DNA*C*B) \quad (5)$$

Here H(DNA*B) is the entropy of the united sequence DNA*B, H(DNA*C) is the entropy of the united sequence DNA*C, H(DNA) is the entropy of the DNA sequence and H(DNA*C*B) is the entropy of the united DNA*C*B sequence. $I_{DNA}(C,B)$ is not negative [29]. If periods of the two sequences B and C are represented by simple numbers, I(B,C)=0. It means that the mutual information I(DNA,B) and I(DNA,C) are independent parts of I(DNA,A). If the mutual information is considered as random value then I(DNA,B) and I(DNA,C) are independent random values. According to [16] 2I(DNA,B) and 2I(DNA,C) is distributed as X^2 with 3(B-1) and 3(C-1) degrees of freedom accordingly.

The mutual information I(DNA,kB), where k = 2,3,4..., may be equal to or exceed I(DNA,B). For example, if we calculate the mutual information between the artificial sequences with the periods of 3,6,9,12... and DNA, then the mutual information for periods 6,9,12... is more or equal to I(DNA,3). This means that the mutual information is accumulated when k is increased. For the compound period A it is conveniently to take value $I_{DNA}(C,B)$ as a measure of the sequence periodicity. This double value has the distribution X^2 with number of degrees of freedom equal to 3(A-1)-3(B-1)-3(C-1). $I_{DNA}(C,B)$ reflects a contribution of the period A to creation of this periodicity by excluding all simple influence. It is conveniently to obtain the $I_{DNA}(C,B)$ spectrum for any period on practice. It may be done by serial deduction of the mutual information of simple periods from the mutual informations of compound periods. It is possible to do a similar subtraction for degrees of freedom, because the mutual information is distributed as X^2 with 3(n-1) degrees of freedom (where n is the period length). Then mutual informations of compound periods are deducted from mutual informations of longer divisible compound periods. For example, the mutual information I(DNA,6) is deducted from I(DNA,12), I(DNA,18) and so on. The spectrum obtained of modified mutual information $I_m(n)$ shows the contribution of each period n to formation of periodicity. The values $2I_m(n)$ are distributed as X^2 with the remaining number of degrees

A contribution of each period in the observed periodicity is convenient to obtain from the spectrum $I_m(n)$. For example, if a DNA sequence has periodicity only in 18 bases, then modified $I_m(n)$ spectrum has only one maximum. If a DNA sequence has periods equal to 3, 6, 9 and 18 bases, then the $I_m(n)$ spectrum has four comparatively small maximums. The modified $I_m(n)$ spectrum may be applied for the detection of enclosed periods.

The modified spectrum $I_m(n)$ must be represented as a spectrum of argument X of the normal distribution for valuation of statistical importance of each period. Using formula (6), transformation $I_m(n)$ is performedd [10]:

$$X(n) = (4I_m(n))^{1/2} - (2t-1)^{1/2} \quad (6)$$

Here t is the number of degrees of freedom for $I_m(n)$. This spectrum X(n) will be shown below for some DNA regions with latent periodicity.

As far as the DNA sequences of coding regions have period equal to 3 bases [28], the search for latent periodicity should be conducted by deducting I(DNA,3) from all divisible periods. It allows to eliminate influence of triplet periodicity on long latent periodicity. The search for DNA regions with I(DNA,3n)-I(DNA,3), which exceed 5,6x is conducted in the present work. 5,6x corresponds to probability 10^{-8} that the found long periodicity is caused by random factors.

RESULTS AND DISCUSSION

The search for regions with latent periodicity was performed in DNA and mRNA clones from the EMBL data bank. The clones with the length less than 1000 bases were not analyzed. An artificial sequence containing 1000 bases was compared with the first 1000 bases of DNA or mRNA clone. Independent variations of the left and right borders were conducted for each artificial sequence with a period from 2 up to 150. The purpose was to find an DNA or mRNA region having the best periodicity and the maximum of I(DNA,3n)-I(DNA,3). If a DNA or mRNA region with latent periodicity was not found then the displacement of the scanned artificial sequence on 100 bases was performed. If a region with latent periodicity was revealed, then the displacement of the artificial sequence on 500 bases was conducted, and the procedure of calculations was repeated. The full length of a clone was analyzed by such a way. After that the next DNA clone from the EMBL data bank was analyzed. The results of the analysis allowed to reveal many DNA and mRNA regions with latent periodicity. More than 30% of human genes (with length more 1000 bases) from EMBL data bank have the regions with latent periodicity. 3 regions with the expressed latent periods are shown on Fig.1 as example. The corresponding X(n) spectrum of that regions is shown in Fig2. The 2I'(n,DNA) on Fig.1 is equal to 2I(DNA,n)-3(n-1). The significance 3(n-1) is an average significance of 2I(DNA,n) when an artificial sequence and an DNA or mRNA sequence are the random sequences. The found sequences with latent periodicity have the significant period equal to 3 bases. These 3 mRNA sequences have the 2I(3,DNA) in the interval of 16,3 up to 62,6. It corresponds to the probability a from less than 10^{-9} up to 10^{-3}.On the background of the period equal to 3 bases (which is characteristic of DNA coding regions) periods of the size divisible by 3 are found. The values 2I'(3n,DNA) for 3 regions from A06977 clone [12]; HSFTA clone [1] and from HSPLASM clone [5] are shown in Fig.1. These regions are components of galactose gene, farnesyltransferase gene and plasminogen. Thosee regions have the latent periods that are equal to 96, 102 and 102 bases. Homology between any pair of periods of these regions has statistically insignificant level.

Earlier the method of searching for a periodicity of a symbolic sequence has been developed [19]. The method is based on writing out the sequence in rows of N columns to detect a period of N. Then the symbols of the sequence are combined in two groups and two letter alphabet is introduced (A and B letters). The amalgamation of symbols in the two groups is performed on the bases of some common characteristics of the symbols. For amino acid sequence those qualities may be hydrophobic of amino acids, charges of amino acids and some others qualities [19]. However, the introduction of two letter alphabet limits the types of periodic sequences that may be found. For example, if we have the period {(a/t)(t/g/c)(c/a)} then a new alphabet A={a,t}, B={c,g} permits to reveal a period in the first column, but periodicity is not revealed in the second and third columns. If we introduce a new alphabet A={t,g,c}, B={a}, then we may find a periodicity of the second column only. An analysis of periodicity by introduction of a new two letter alphabet is effective, if there is a similar distribution of the base types in the columns. Moreover, if we consider triplet periodicity, there are many types of junctions of triplets in two letters and for it is very hard to test all types of junctions.

The regions of DNA or mRNA sequences of some genes with latent periodicity were found earlier [15]. Results of this work and earlier work show that no less than 30% of human genes from the EMBL data bank have regions with latent periodicity. Latent periodicity is not similar to a homological altenation of DNA or mRNA bases and can heavily influences on codon usage. It is possible to assume that latent periodicity is a typical sign of some genes and it can be related to evolutionary origin of genes by process of multiple duplications. Then latent periodicity is a reflection of ancient evolutionary events in gene sequences.

It is also possible to assume that the latent periodicity can also have a certain function in a cell. The latent periodicity can provide certain bends of DNA coding regions [6, 9, 22].

The computer data bank of the regions with latent periodicity is created now. This data bank will be based on computer in Lancashire University.

REFERENCES.

1. D.A.Andres, A.Milatovich, T.Ozcelik, J.M.Wenzlau, M.S.Brown, J.L.Goldstein, U.Francke "CDNA cloning of the two subunits of human CAAX farnesyltransferase and chromosomal mapping of FNTA and FNTB loci and related sequences" Genomics. 18,105 (1993)

2. V.V.Bliskovsky "Tandem DNA repeats in vertebrate genomes: structure, possible mechanisma of creation and evolution" Mol.Biol. (Russian). 25, 965 (1991)

3. M.Bina "Periodicity of dinucleotides in nucleosomes derived from Simian virus 40 chromatin" J.Mol.Biol. 235, 198 (1994)

4. B.Borstnik, D.Pampernik, D.Lukman, D.Ugarkovic. and M.Plohl. "Tandemly repeated pentanucleotides in DNA sequences of eucaryotes" Nucl.Acids Res., 22, 3412 (1994)

5. M.J.Browne, C.G.Chapman, I.Dodd, J.E.Carey, G.M.Lawrence, D.Mitchell, J.H.Robinson "Expression of recombinant human plasminogen and aglycoplasminogenin HeLa cells" Unpublished.

6. P.Carrera and F.Azorin "Srtuctural characterization of intrinsically curved AT-rich DNA sequences" Nucl. Acids Res. 22, 3671 (1994)

7. V.R.Chechetkin, L.A.Knizhnikova and A.Yu.Turygin "Three-quasiperiodicity, mutual correlatuions, ordering and long modulations in genomic nucleotide sequences viruses" J.of Biomol. Str. & Dynamics. 12, 271 (1994)

8. E.A.Cheever, G.C.Overton and B.B.Searls "Fast fourier transform-based correlations of DNA sequences using complex plane encoding" CABIOS. 7, 143 (1991)
9. D.S.Goodsell and R.E.Dickerson "Bending and curvature calculations in B+DNA" Nucl. Acids Res. 22, 5497 (1994)
10. Handbook of applicable mathematics. Volume IV. (1984). Wiley-Interscience Publication. John Wiley & Sons. New-York-Brisbane-Toronto-Singapore.
11. C.M.Hearne, S.Ghosh and J.A.Todd "Microsatellites for linkage analysis of genetic traits" Trends in Genetics. 8, 288 (1992)
12. E.Hinchliffe "Induction of galactose regulated gene expression in yeast" Patent number EP0248637 (1987)
13. E.V.Korotkov E.V. "Fast method of homology and purine-pirimidine mutual relations between DNA sequences search" DNA Sequence. 4, 413 (1994)
14 E.V.Korotkov and M.A.Korotkova "Enlarged similarity of nucleic acids sequences" DNA Research. 3, N.3, 1 (1996)
15. E.V.Korotkov and M.A.Korotkova "Latent periodicity of DNA sequences of some human genes" DNA Sequence. 5, 353 (1995)
16. S.Kullback "Information theory and Statistics" John Wiley & Sons, Inc. New-York, London (1959)
17. V.Yu.Makeev and V.G.Tumanyan "On link between the distance and correlation analysis of various types and Fourier transformation used for the search of the periodical patterns in the primary structures of the biopolymers" Biophysics (Russian). 39, 294 (1994)
18 A.D.McLachlan "Repeated helical pattern in apolipoprotein A-I" Nature. 267, 465 (1977a)
19. A.D.McLachlan "Analysis of periodic patterns in amino acid sequences: collagen" Biopolymers. 16, 1271 (1977b)
20. A.D.McLachlan "Multichannel Fourier analysis of patterns in protein sequences" J.Phys.Chem. 97, 3000 (1993)
21. A.D.Mclachlan and M.Stewart "Analysis of repeated motif in the talin rod" J.Mol.Biol. 235, 1278 (1994)
22. P.T.McNamara, A.Bolshoy, E.N.Trifonov and R.E.Harrington "Sequence-dependent kinks in curved DNA" J.Biomol. Str. & Dyn. 3, 529 (1990)
23. E.Pizzi, S.Linni and C.Frontali "Detection of latent sequence periodicities" Nucl. Acids Res. 18, 3745 (1990)
24. B.D.Silverman and R.Linsker "A measure of DNA periodicity" J.Theor. Biol. 118, 295 (1986)
25. M.Stewart and A.D.Mclaclan "Fourteen actin-binding sites on tropomiosin?" Nature. 257, 331 (1975)
26. J.A.Todd "La carte des microsatellites est arrivee" Human Molecular Genetics 1, 663 (1992)
27. R.F.Voss "Evolution of long-range fractal correlations and 1/f noise in DNA base sequences" Phys. Rev. Letters. 68, 3805 (1992)

28. G. Von Heijne "Sequences analysis in molecular biology" Academic Press, Inc. San-Diego-New-York-London (1987)
29 A.M.Yaglom and I.M.Yaglom "Probability and Information" Nauka Press, Moscow (1960)

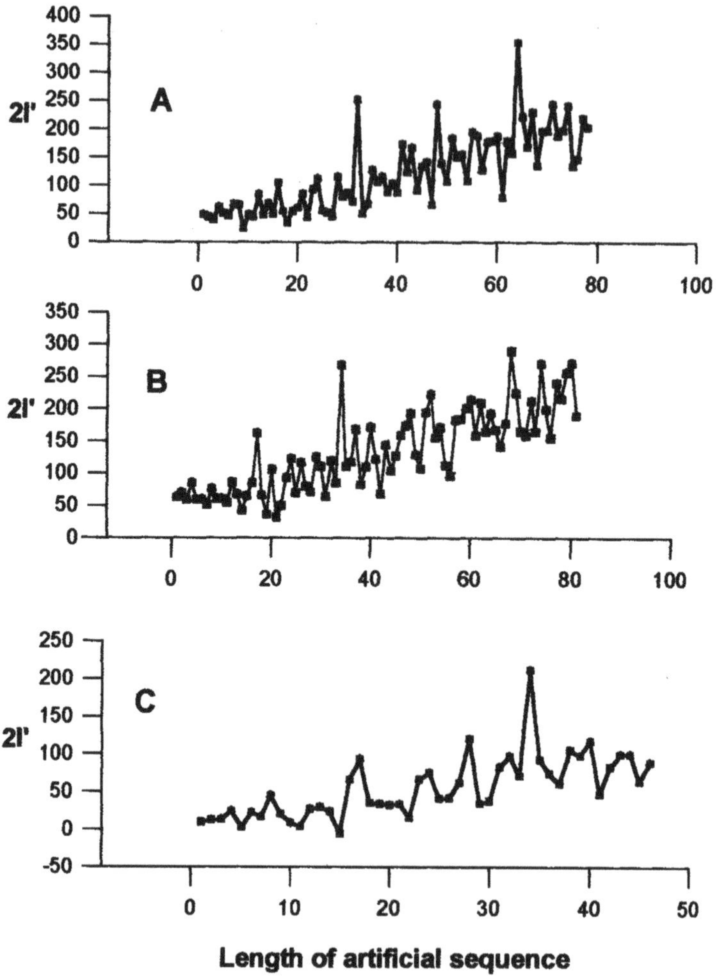

Fig. 1 The dependence 2I upon period of artificial sequence. The length of period is shown as divisible by 3.
A-DNA region (1022-1771 bases) from A06977 clone [12].
B-DNA region (1101-1797 bases) from HSFTA clone [1].
C-DNA region (2725-3454 bases) from HSPLASM clone [5].

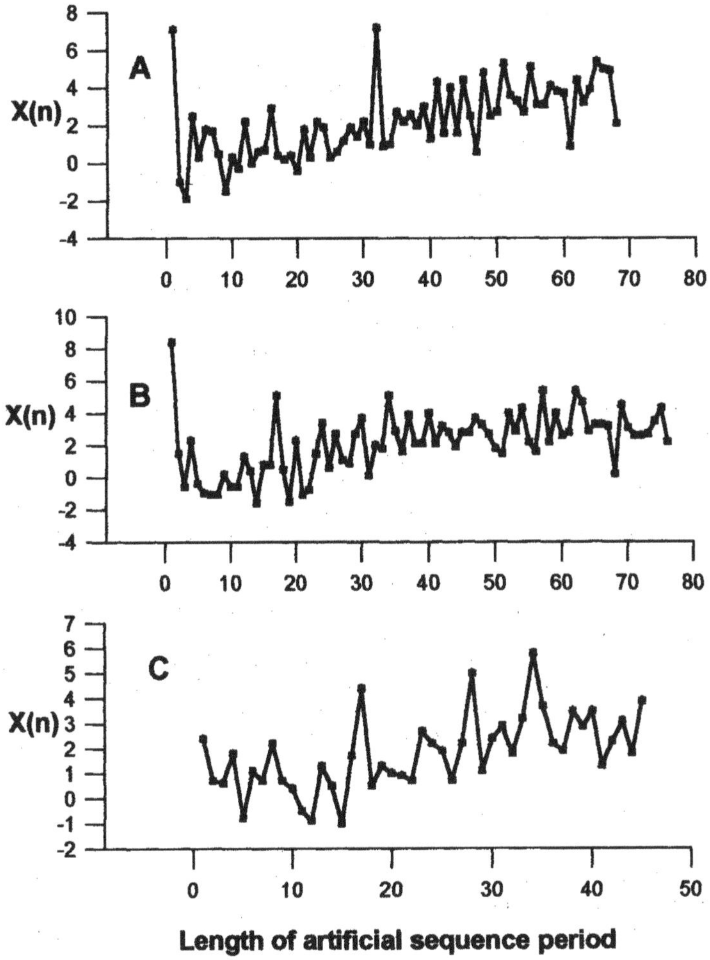

Fig.2 The dependence X(n) upon period of artificial sequence. The length of period is shown as divisible by 3.

A-DNA region (1022-1771 bases) from A06977 clone [12].

B-DNA region (1101-1797 bases) from HSFTA clone [1].

C-DNA region (2725-3454 bases) from HSPLASM clone [5].

Integrating Database Homology in a Probabilistic Gene Structure Model

David Kulp, David Haussler
Baskin Center for Computer Engineering and Computer Science
University of California, Santa Cruz CA, 95064, USA
dkulp@cse.ucsc.edu, haussler@cse.ucsc.edu

Martin G. Reese, Frank H. Eeckman
Genome Informatics Group
Lawrence Berkeley National Laboratory
1 Cyclotron Road, Berkeley, CA 94720
mgreese@lbl.gov, fheeckman@lbl.gov

We present an improved stochastic model of genes in DNA, and describe a method for integrating database homology into the probabilistic framework. A generalized hidden Markov model (GHMM) describes the grammar of a legal parse of a DNA sequence. Probabilities are estimated for gene features by using dynamic programming to combine information from multiple sensors. We show how matches to homologous sequences from a database can be integrated into the probability estimation by interpreting the likelihood of a sequence in terms of the bit-cost to encode a sequence given a homology match. We also demonstrate how homology matches in protein databases can be exploited to help identify splice sites. Our experiments show significant improvements in the sensitivity and specificity of gene structure identification when these new features are added to our gene-finding system, Genie. Experimental results in tests using a standard set of annotated genes showed that Genie identified 95% of coding nucleotides correctly with a specificity of 91%, and 77% of exons were identified exactly.

1 Introduction

Our research is born out of the need for complete, automated, genefinding systems for long unannotated sequences, now being produced at a very high volume. Such genefinders attempt to synthesize statistical and database information. Our genefinding system, called Genie, is a generalized hidden Markov model (GHMM) – a hidden Markov model[1] whose states are arbitrary sub-models emitting variable length sequences. The basic methodology used in the Genie system is described more completely in previous work by Kulp, *et al.*[2] This paper expands on this work and introduces three new additions: an improved probability estimation scheme that combines evidence from multiple sources, a general sensor class to interpret database matches probabilistically, and a simple method to aid in splice site identification by using protein database homology. Our system is similar in design to GeneParser,[3] but is based on a rigorous probabilistic framework.

We first present a brief overview of the general methodology, including the use

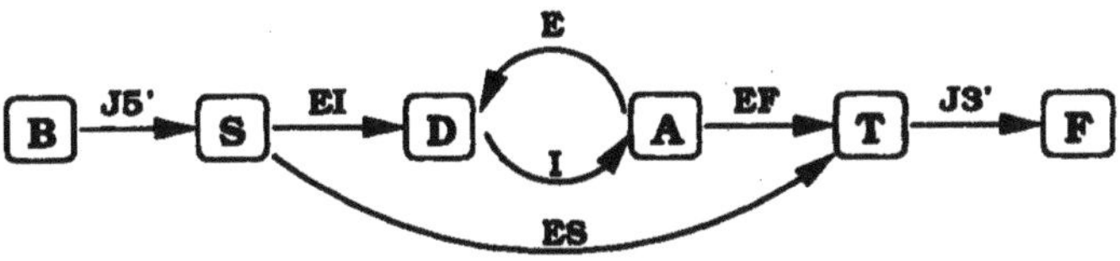

Figure 1: A simple GHMM for a sequence containing a multiple exon gene. The arcs represent multi-symbol states and nodes represent transitions between states. The state labels are J5' : 5' UTR, EI : Initial Exon, E : Exon, I : Intron, E : Internal Exon, EF: Final Exon, ES : Single Exon, and J3' : 3' UTR. The node labels are B : Begin, S : Start Translation, D : Donor, A : Acceptor, T : Stop Translation, F : Final. The arrows imply a generation of bases from 5' to 3'.

of a GHMM to describe the gene structure syntax, signal sensors to identify transitions, and content sensors to "score" candidate regions. A detailed discussion follows describing a simplified method for combining evidence from multiple sources. One such source of evidence is a sequence database. We explain how a database match is interpreted, according to information theory, in terms of encoding cost. Last, we describe an enhancement to the parsing that aids in splice site identification by limiting splice site candidates to those sites that correspond to adjacent hits in a protein database.

2 Methodology

2.1 Basic System Framework

A generalized hidden Markov model is an enhancement to the standard hidden Markov model popularly used in time-sequence pattern recognition such as speech and computation biology. (See, among others, the tutorial from Rabiner and Juang[4] and the introduction to HMMs in biosequence analysis by Krogh, *et al.*[1]) In a standard hidden Markov model, viewed as a generator, each state emits a single symbol. A GHMM describes a more general model in which each state can emit one or more symbols according to an arbitrary distribution. Each state represents an independent sub-model which may, itself, be a hidden Markov model or any statistical model. Figure 1[a] shows a simple model of the eukaryotic gene structure. The states in the model are shown on the arcs of the graph. Nodes in the graph represent transitions between states. Each state corresponds to a sub-model of an abstract gene feature such as an "Internal Exon" (E) or an "Intron" (I). For any candidate sequence, x, and state, q, we can estimate a likelihood of the sequence given the sub-model corresponding to that state's feature, which we denote $P(x|q)$. The method for likelihood estimation is described later in section 2.4.

For any state q, the node that the arc for state q leads to is denoted $node(q)$. Once in this node, a next state is chosen from among the outgoing arcs from this

[a]Figures 1 and 2 used by permission. Copyright 1996, AAAI Press.

node. The probability of choosing the next state r is denoted $P(r|node(q))$. For example, in figure 1, the state I (Intron) leads to the node A (Acceptor). After the acceptor can come either the internal exon state (E) or the final exon (EF). The former is chosen with probability $P(E|A)$ and the latter with probability $P(EF|A)$ where $P(E|A)+P(EF|A) = 1$. These parameters are determined from training data.

Given a complete DNA sequence, we assert that the sequence was derived according to some combination of states, following the syntactic framework of our graph, but the actual ordered set of states is hidden. The predicted gene structure is simply the ordered set of states – the path through the graph – determined to be most likely. We formalize this concept by defining a parse and sequence likelihood. A parse is composed of an ordered set of states, $\{q_1, q_2, \ldots, q_k\}$, and a corresponding ordered set of subsequences, $\{x_1, x_2, \ldots, x_k\}$, where q_1 is a "state arc" coming out of the unique begin node (B), the source of the graph, and q_k is a "state arc" leading to the unique final node (F), the sink for the graph. The likelihood of the sequence $X = x_1, \ldots, x_k$ and the parse $\phi = (q_1, \ldots, q_k; x_1, \ldots, x_k)$, according to a hidden Markov model, is the joint independent probability of the subsequences given the corresponding states and the probability of transitioning between states. That is,

$$P(X, \phi) = P(q_1|\mathrm{B}) \left(\prod_{i=1}^{k} P(x_i|q_i) \right) \left(\prod_{i=1}^{k-1} P(q_{i+1}|node(q_i)) \right). \quad (1)$$

Using a variant of the Viterbi algorithm[4], we can deduce the parse that maximizes equation 1.

While figure 1 represents the basic ordering of gene features, it fails to fully capture the syntactic restrictions of a "legal parse". In an ideal DNA sequence, the parse is "frame consistent", i.e., the total number of coding nucleotides is a multiple of three and the reading frame is consistent from exon to exon. We can add additional states to the model graph such that only frame consistent parses are allowed. Figure 2 shows the model graph representing a frame consistent GHMM. The three levels represent the three frames. Exon lengths are restricted in the various exon transitions in such a way to enforce frame consistency (see Kulp, *et al*[2]).

2.2 *Sensors*

A sensor is an mechanism for recognizing or scoring a subsequence according to a model of an abstract gene feature. There are two types of sensors used in the Genie system: signal sensors and content sensors.

2.3 *Signal Sensor Models*

Signal sensors are used to recognize transitions between states in a GHMM. This type of sensor is used in a pre-processing step to identify candidate sites where state transitions can occur. In the GHMMs shown in figures 1 and 2, the nodes correspond to gene features such as acceptor sites, donor sites, and positions of start

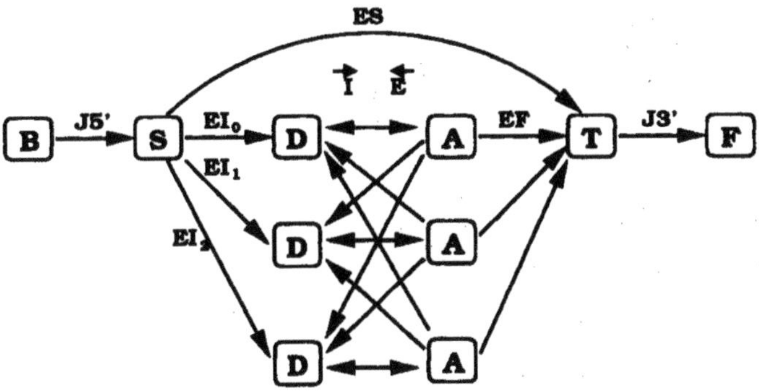

Figure 2: A GHMM including frame constraints. The additional acceptor and donor transition nodes ensure that only syntactically correct parses are considered.

and stop translation. A typical signal sensor might be a neural network to recognize an acceptor site.

2.4 Content Sensor Models

Content sensors are used to estimate the likelihood of a subsequence given a particular state in the GHMM. Typically, the model of a content sensor integrates evidence contributed from multiple sources and estimates a likelihood of a subsequence from the combined information. By applying a simple dynamic program we can estimate the likelihood of a region based on multiple contributions.

Each source of evidence is called a component; a component is trained to recognize a specific feature. For example, an intron content sensor may include a nucleotide component that estimates the likelihood of each nucleotide given an intron nucleotide model. Another component might estimate the likelihood of a subsequence as an intronic repeat given an intron repeat model. The content sensor outputs the likelihood estimation of a subsequence as the maximum likelihood obtained from combinations of components.

Figure 3 shows an example of a fictitious subsequence scored by an internal exon content sensor. It is composed of several components: a nucleotide component, a codon component, end-region components representing the regions adjacent to the acceptor and donor sites, and a database homology match component. A component returns a likelihood for each potential feature occurrence, called an "extent". In the figure, the maximum likelihood is determined by the joint probability of the extents shown in the bottom of the figure, i.e. an acceptor extent, followed by two nucleotide extents, a database match extent, and three codon extents.

Again we use dynamic programming to calculate the joint probability of all extents. The dynamic program used here employs a simpler scheme than that used in the standard Viterbi algorithm for a hidden Markov model as used in our GHMM

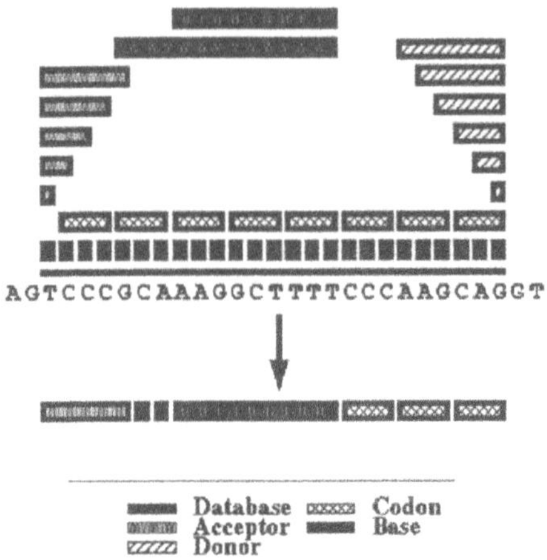

Figure 3: A sample content sensor combines evidence from multiple components to derive a maximum likelihood of the sequence. The arrow shows the combination of component features corresponding to the maximum likelihood.

gene model. Partial extents are prohibited and the transition probabilities between components are assumed to be uniform. The dynamic program is straightforward: the maximum likelihood is memoized at each nucleotide position in the sequence. Let i be the current position, from $1 \dots m$, in the subsequence of length m. For each extent ending at i, the likelihood of the sequence from $1 \dots i$ is calculated as the product of the likelihood of the extent times the maximum likelihood at the starting position of the extent. The extent which produced the maximum likelihood at position i is memoized, and the current position advances to $i+1$. The result, is an $O(m)$ algorithm for estimating the maximum likelihood of the subsequence given the set of components in the content sensor.

This simple, efficient method encourages a modular approach to developing an effective gene-finding system because components can be easily added to or subtracted from a content sensor.

2.5 Integrating Homology Matches

Each component of a content sensor represents a model for a specific gene feature. The component estimates a likelihood for each possible extent. One such component is a database homology match component. Database homology raises the problem of assigning a "fair score" for a match relative to other scoring components such as the codon component. The typical solution is to experimentally weight database scores in an ad-hoc fashion. In the Genie system, the likelihood of a subsequence that is found to be homologous to a subsequence in a database is theoretically interpreted in terms of the bit-cost to encode the subsequence given the database match. Let the "subject" be a database homolog and the "target" be the matching subsequence in the DNA sequence that is being analyzed. We estimate the encoding cost, C, of the target as the sum of the following costs:

- The offset into the database
- Translation Cost – the encoding cost of the target given the subject

The likelihood of the target is calculated as a probability of 2^{-C}.

The offset is described as the encoding cost for uniquely specifying where the match in the database is located. If the number of starting positions for matches in the database is S and assuming that all positions are uniformly likely, then the cost of encoding the offset of the subject in the database is $-\log(1/S) = \log(S)$. The translation cost of the target is database specific, but typically involves a substitution matrix to translate from the subject to the target. We show in section 3.3 how this value is derived for two different types of databases.

2.6 Identifying Splice Sites Using Homology

If two database homology matches are found in a single protein sequence and the two subsequences are adjacent, then we can conclude that the "match pair" implies an insertion in the target sequence of protein coding or non-coding nucleotides. If the insertion is of non-coding nucleotides, then a pair of splice sites can be inferred from a pair of homology matches. To reduce the chance that a match pair is the result of an insertion of coding nucleotides, we only consider those match pairs with suitable splice sites patterns at the match boundaries. To force the splice site to be used in a parse, the dynamic program (Viterbi) mentioned in section 2.1 is modified slightly. If one of the homology matches of a match pair is used to derive the likelihood in a candidate internal exon content sensor, then we infer that the candidate exon must splice to an exon that contains the partner in the match pair. During the dynamic program, if such a condition arises, only parses that conform to the match pair restriction are considered.

Figure 4 shows the situation in which a homology match pair, labeled M_1 and M_2, are found near two candidate splice sites, D_2 and A_2, respectively. The dynamic program disregards all other splice sites, i.e. D_1, A_1, D_3, and A_3, which ensures that *both* splice sites D_2 and A_2 are included or *neither* is included in the parse.

3 Experiments

The GHMM graph used in Genie is as shown in Figure 2. Here, we describe the specific implementation details of the sensors and components used in the Genie system.

Figure 4: A match pair, M_1 and M_2 imply a pair of splice sites, D_1 and A_1. The dynamic program is constrained such that D_1 is used in the final parse if and only if A_1 is used.

3.1 Signal Sensors

Three feedforward neural networks were trained to recognize acceptor sites, donor sites, and the beginning of translation. Each neural network uses a window of nucleotides – four binary inputs per nucleotide. See Kulp, *et al*[3] for more details. The experimental thresholds for these neural networks were set low to ensure that very few false negatives were allowed.

The signal sensor for stop translation is trivial: all occurrences of the three possible stop codons, "TAA", "TGA", and "TAG" are considered as candidates.

Signal sensors serve as an initial pre-processing step to reduce the search space. As such, false negatives will add to the running time of the dynamic program, but are not a serious concern in terms of predictive accuracy because they will likely be discarded as improbable during the parsing step.

3.2 Content Sensors

There are five content sensors used in the Genie system: a non-coding sensor (for J5' and J3'), an intron model, and initial, internal, and final exon sensors. The components used are:

• Nucleotide component – a window of $\pm$ 150 bases estimates the local nucleotide frequency.

• Codon component – a 16-input neural network. The previous three nucleotides are encoded as 12 binary inputs and the local nucleotide frequency are the four remaining real valued inputs. The neural network has 61 outputs corresponding to the estimated likelihood of the 61 possible codons. This feedforward network has a single hidden layer of 17 units; softmax is used as the error function.

• BLASTX[5,6] database component – a homology match component for a protein database described in section 3.3.

• BLOCKS database component – a homology match component for the protein motifs in the BLOCKS database[7] described in section 3.3.

• Exon 5' end-region component – a simple profile trained on the 20 nucleotides downstream of the "AG" consensus.

• Exon 3' end-region component – a profile of the seven nucleotides upstream of the "GT" consensus.

• Intron 5' end-region component – a profile of the six nucleotides downstream of the "GT" consensus.

• Intron 3' end-region component – a profile of the 19 nucleotides upstream of the "AG" consensus.

All of the end-region components allow extents of lengths up to the size of the profile.

Some components are used in multiple sensors. The non-coding sensor contains only the nucleotide component. The intron sensor contains the nucleotide component, and the intron 5' and 3' end-region components. The internal exon sensor contains the codon component, the BLASTX and BLOCKS database components, and the exon 5' and 3' end-region components. The initial and final exon sensors contain the same components as the internal exon, except the 5' end-region and 3' end-region components are not included, respectively.

3.3 Translation Cost for Homology Match Components

The Genie system currently uses two different types of protein databases, the BLOCKS database and a non-redundant sequence database[b].

The BLOCKS database is a collection of over 2000 highly conserved protein motifs without insertions or deletions. We derived a profile for each motif using a nine-component Dirichlet mixture.[8] The translation cost of a target nucleotide sequence given a BLOCKS homology is the combined cost of encoding the target protein product using the BLOCKS motif profile and the cost of translating the target protein product from an amino acid sequence into a nucleotide sequence. The profile cost is simply the product of the probability of each residue in each column. The protein-to-nucleotide cost is computed using the codon component described in section 3.2, but the probability of a codon is normalized to sum to one over all possible codons that translate to the same amino acid.

The other data we use is the non-redundant protein database, "nr". To avoid trivial use of homology in our experiments we remove from nr any sequence with an estimated 50% or greater sequence identity with a protein coded by a sequence in our test set. We use BLASTX with $E = 1$ to identify potential homology matches in the non-redundant protein database. Given a potential match, the translation cost is similar to that used for the BLOCKS database, but the BLOSUM-62 substitution matrix is used instead of the motif profile. We set the BLASTX expectation parameter relatively high, resulting in a large number of false homology matches, but this does not mean that each potential match is actually used in the parse. Most are rejected when evidence from different components is combined during the dy-

[b]The "nr" database supplied by the NIH, available at ftp://ncbi.nlm.nih.gov/blast/db/, includes all protein sequences from GenBank, EMBL, DDBJ, and PDB, but excludes STSs and ESTs.

namic program step. On the other hand, an otherwise weak homology match may be sufficiently strong in a certain context to help identify a true exon.

3.4 Cross-validation Experiments

The data set used during the train/test experiments is a collection of 301 annotated, multiple-exon human DNA sequences from the GenBank sequence database.[c] The data set was randomly partitioned into seven test sets of uniform size to be used in cross-validation experiments. For each test set, the content sensors were trained on the remaining training data and predictions were recorded for the sequences in the test set.

Additional tests were performed on a data set of 570 vertebrate genes. This data set was used by Bursett and Guigo as a benchmark for the comparison of many different gene-finders.[9] The data set is similar to ours, but it includes all vertebrates and similar sequences are not removed.

4 Results

Tables 1, 3, and 2 show the results of running Genie using different configurations on all seven test sets, the average results over the entire data set, and the results using the Bursett/Guigo data set. In accordance with the testing scheme established by Bursett and Guigo, we report sensitivity and specificity with respect to per-base prediction of coding/non-coding and with respect to exact prediction of exons. The per-base sensitivity is the fraction of true coding bases predicted as coding, and the specificity is the fraction of all predicted coding bases that were correct. Similarly, the exon sensitivity is the fraction of true exons predicted exactly, and the specificity is the fraction of predicted exons that were correct. In these tests, correct exon prediction requires identification of the exact position of splice sites. Fully or partially overlapping predictions are not accepted. The approximate coefficient (AC) is described by Bursett and Guigo as a preferred alternative over the correlation coefficient and defined by

$$AC = \frac{1}{2}\left(\frac{\mathtt{TP}}{\mathtt{TP+FN}} + \frac{\mathtt{TP}}{\mathtt{TP+FP}} + \frac{\mathtt{TN}}{\mathtt{TN+FP}} + \frac{\mathtt{TN}}{\mathtt{TN+FN}}\right) - 1$$

where TP, FP, TN, and FN are true positives, false positives, true negatives, and false negatives.

In addition, we also report the fraction of true exons that were not identified either exactly or overlapping (Missing Exons) and the fraction of predicted exons that did not overlap any true exon (Wrong Exons).

[c] The data set is available at ftp://genome.lbl.gov/pub/genesets/.

Table 1: Prediction results on seven test sets and the Bursett/Guigo data set. "Per base" statistics refer to the ability to predict whether a nucleotide is coding or non-coding. "Per exon" statistics refer to the ability to predict a complete exon exactly.

Data Set	*Per Base*			*Exact Exon*				
	Sn	Sp	AC	Sn	Sp	Avg	ME	WE
Part 0	0.92	0.87	0.88	0.75	0.73	0.74	0.05	0.17
Part 1	0.65	0.73	0.63	0.46	0.47	0.46	0.26	0.28
Part 2	0.64	0.82	0.68	0.53	0.57	0.55	0.19	0.21
Part 3	0.73	0.81	0.72	0.56	0.59	0.57	0.19	0.22
Part 4	0.76	0.83	0.75	0.63	0.63	0.63	0.13	0.13
Part 5	0.70	0.83	0.73	0.56	0.55	0.55	0.19	0.20
Part 6	0.78	0.77	0.76	0.66	0.65	0.65	0.21	0.24
Average	0.74	0.81	0.74	0.59	0.59	0.59	0.17	0.21
B/G	0.87	0.88	0.85	0.69	0.70	0.69	0.10	0.15

Table 2: Prediction results on seven test sets and the Bursett/Guigo data set using homology matches and match pairs for splice site identification. In this table, we also include, for comparison, predictive results of GeneID+ and GeneParser3 as reported in Bursett and Guigo. Only sequences of length less than 8000 were tested in the latter data set to provide comparable results with the other genefinders.

Data Set	*Per Base*			*Exact Exon*				
	Sn	Sp	AC	Sn	Sp	Avg	ME	WE
Part 0	0.94	0.95	0.93	0.83	0.83	0.83	0.05	0.09
Part 1	0.73	0.79	0.71	0.55	0.55	0.55	0.23	0.29
Part 2	0.77	0.88	0.79	0.65	0.68	0.67	0.16	0.18
Part 3	0.79	0.82	0.77	0.60	0.61	0.61	0.19	0.28
Part 4	0.83	0.90	0.83	0.68	0.69	0.69	0.14	0.14
Part 5	0.76	0.83	0.76	0.64	0.64	0.64	0.14	0.20
Part 6	0.83	0.74	0.76	0.70	0.63	0.67	0.15	0.32
Average	0.80	0.84	0.79	0.66	0.66	0.66	0.15	0.21
B/G Data Set								
Genie	0.95	0.91	0.91	0.77	0.74	0.76	0.04	0.13
GeneID+	0.91	0.90	0.88	0.73	0.70	0.71	0.07	0.13
GeneParser3	0.86	0.91	0.86	0.56	0.58	0.57	0.14	0.09

Table 3: Prediction results on seven test sets and the Bursett/Guigo data set using homology matches, but no match pair splice site site identification.

Data Set	*Per Base*			*Exact Exon*				
	Sn	Sp	AC	Sn	Sp	Avg	ME	WE
Part 0	0.94	0.90	0.91	0.81	0.78	0.80	0.04	0.17
Part 1	0.72	0.77	0.70	0.50	0.50	0.50	0.21	0.30
Part 2	0.77	0.87	0.79	0.65	0.68	0.66	0.16	0.19
Part 3	0.75	0.80	0.74	0.55	0.58	0.56	0.22	0.28
Part 4	0.83	0.90	0.83	0.68	0.69	0.69	0.14	0.14
Part 5	0.76	0.83	0.76	0.63	0.63	0.63	0.14	0.20
Part 6	0.84	0.74	0.77	0.71	0.64	0.67	0.15	0.32
Average	0.80	0.83	0.78	0.65	0.64	0.64	0.15	0.22

5 Discussion

The work presented here extends the work and results reported in Kulp, *et al*[8]. We have developed a simple probabilistic interpretation of database homology matches and described a means of combining database information and other sources of evidence into an integrated probability estimation. With the addition of information from database homology matches, overall accuracy in predicting exact exons increased by approximately 7%, and the number of missed and wrong exons dropped significantly. Per base sensitivity increased about 7% as well, and specificity rose 3%. The overall performance of Genie compares quite favorably with the other genefinders on the Bursett and Guigo dataset.

Genie appears to perform better on the Bursett and Guigo dataset than on our own dataset. This is especially interesting, since that dataset contains sequences from all vertebrates, whereas Genie was trained on human DNA sequences only, which are all that appear in our dataset. However, this may not be so surprising, given the variance in performance we observe even between different parts of our own dataset. We do not believe that this variance results from the difference in the training sets used for the seven different parts. Rather, it seems there is a wide range of difficulty in genefinding from one sequence to another, depending mostly on the number of exons in the gene and the length of the introns, so some test datasets just end up containing more "hard to parse" sequences than others. For this reason it is especially important to compare the performance of different genefinders on the same benchmark set of test sequences. It would be desirable to also use the same partition of the dataset for cross validation experiments, if possible. For this reason we have made our dataset available with a defined seven part partition.

It is worth noting that no correlation was detected between GC content and predictive accuracy, although additional work is needed in this regard. To illustrate the effectiveness of homology, Figure 5 and 6 show how Genie exploits homology to refine gene structure prediction. In figure 5, a protein fragment from a canine kidney

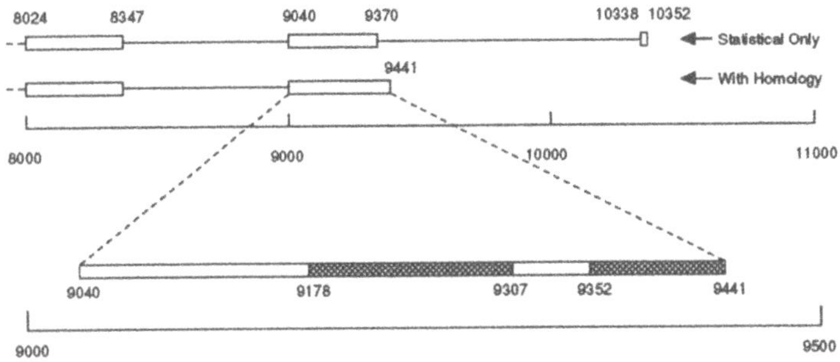

Figure 5: The diagram shows the gene prediction for the final 3000 bases of the 11kb DNA for the human osteopontin six exon gene (GenBank Accession D14813). The first prediction is the result of running Genie without homology information. Genie fails to identify the complete final exon and predicts an additional small final exon. The second prediction includes BLAST searches against the "nr" protein database. Here, two segments from a strong osteopontin-related homolog (PIR Accession A38646) are found, shown shaded, with a small insertion between them.

cell line is used to identify the final exon of an 11Kb DNA sequence. In figure 6, a sheep hypothalamic protein fragment was used by Genie to improve the prediction of a human transcript regulator gene. In the second example, a match pair constrained the parse and ensured correct prediction of the final exon. Homology information does not always improve predictions, however. In some cases, a false match may result in a worse genefinder prediction, but overall performance is improved for the entire test set using homology.

In future work we plan to extend Genie so that it can find multiple genes in a single DNA sequence. We also plan to improve the statistical model used in the intron state of Genie, as well at the model for intergenic DNA. This can be accomplished by incorporating sensors for promoters, the transcription start site, DNA repeat sequences, and the overall structure of 5' and 3' untranslated regions. Further work is also in progress to improve the splice site sensors. Finally, a WWW interface to Genie is also planned.

6 Acknowledgments

We would like thank Kevin Karplus for his contributions to this work, especially the splice site profiles he built, and his valuable discussion. We also extend our gratitude to Gary Stormo, Nomi Harris, Greg Helt, and Richard Hughey for their assistance in the development of Genie. This work was supported in part by DOE grant no. DE-FG03-95ER62112 and DE-AC03-76SF00098. D. Haussler acknowledges support of the Aspen Center for Physics, Biosequence Analysis Workshop.

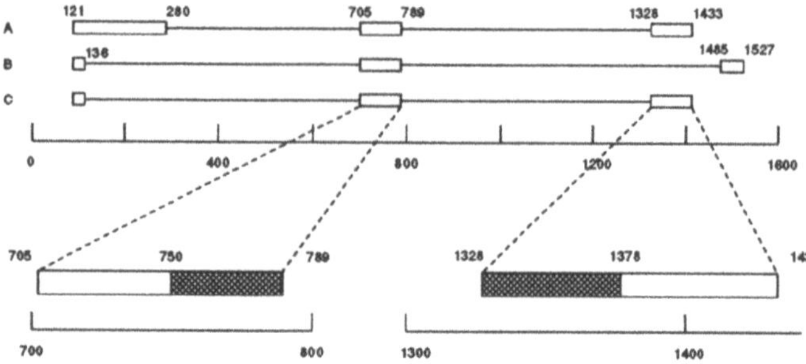

Figure 6: The diagram shows the gene prediction for a small transcription regulation gene (GenBank Accession U20325). (A) shows the correct annotated sequence, (B) is the prediction using statistical methods only, and (C) is the prediction using the "nr" protein database. A homology "match pair" (two adjacent matches in the protein fragment PIR B61322), shown shaded, ensured that the splice sites at positions 789 and 1328 were used in the prediction.

References

1. A. Krogh, M. Brown, I. S. Mian, K. Sjölander, and D. Haussler. Hidden Markov models in computational biology: Applications to protein modeling. *JMB*, 235:1501–1531, February 1994.
2. D. Kulp, D. Haussler, M. Reese, and F. Eeckman. A generalized hidden Markov model for the recognition of human genes in DNA. In *ISMB-96*, St. Louis, June 1996. AAAI Press.
3. E. Snyder and G. Stormo. Indentification of protein coding regions in genomic dna. *JMB*, 248, 1995.
4. L. R. Rabiner and B. H. Juang. An introduction to hidden Markov models. *IEEE ASSP Magazine*, 3(1):4–16, January 1986.
5. S. F. Altshul, W. Gish, W. Miller, Myers E. W., and Lipman D. J. Basic local alignment search tool. *J. Mol. Biol.*, 215, 1990.
6. W. Gish and D. J. States. Identification of protein coding regions by database similarity search. *Nature Genetics*, 3, 1993.
7. Steven Henikoff and Jorja G. Henikoff. Automated assembly of protein blocks for database searching. *NAR*, 19(23):6565–6572, 1991.
8. K. Sjölander, K. Karplus, M. P. Brown, R. Hughey, A. Krogh, I. S. Mian, and D. Haussler. Dirichlet mixtures: A method for improving detection of weak but significant protein sequence homology. *CABIOS*, 12(4), 1996.
9. M. Burset and R. Guigo. Evaluation of gene structure prediction programs. *Genomics*, 34(3):353–367, 1996. Data set and evaluation results can be found at http://www.imim.es/GeneIdentification/Evaluation/Index.html.
10. R. Guigo, S. Knudsen, N. Drake, and T. Smith. Prediction of gene structure. *J. Mol. Biol.*, 226:141–157, 1992.

PACKING AS A STRUCTURAL BASIS OF PROTEIN STABILITY: UNDERSTANDING MUTANT PROPERTIES FROM WILDTYPE STRUCTURE

C. LEE
Dept. of Chemistry, Stanford University, Stanford, CA 94305

M. LEVITT
Dept. of Structural Biology, Stanford University Medical Center, Stanford, CA 94305

Modeling of protein core mutations using sidechain packing can forecast their effects on stability. We have assessed the structural basis of this approach, by evaluating the accuracy of our 1991 model of a three-site mutant of λ repressor (V36L / M40L / V47I), against the recently reported crystal structure. The three mutated residues matched the crystal structure to within 0.89Å (1.11Å for sidechain atoms), giving fairly accurate sidechain placement and packing (81-99th percentile rank in coordinate accuracy). However, the model used different sidechain torsional angles than seen in the crystal structure at residues 36 and 40, apparently to compensate for the backbone shifts present in the actual mutant structure, but not accounted for in our modeling method. To understand the structural basis of stability across a set of λ repressor core mutants, we have analyzed the mutant models, revealing several simple packing effects: V36I, predicted to be stabilized by filling a hydrophobic cavity; M40V, destabilized by a steric clash with the unusual structural demands of a helix-turn transition. These effects illustrate how mutant stability can often be understood directly from scrutiny of wildtype structure. Simply adding the calculated energies of neighboring point mutations predicts the stability effect of the combined mutant relatively well, with little apparent cooperativity, yielding simple rules for each site's amino acid preferences. Our treatment of core packing indicates that it can permit a large fraction of sequences to fit the native fold, as observed experimentally, far more than indicated by rotamer hard-sphere models.

I Introduction

Historically, the complexity of proteins has made it very hard to predict functional properties like stability from the details of three-dimensional structure. Predicting functional properties of mutants adds an extra layer of complexity in that different mutants may change the structure in unknown ways. For this reason, researchers often use non-structural models based on intrinsic properties of amino acids, such as hydrophobicity and packing volume, for explanations of mutant stability. Such models capture important bulk phenomena, without requiring consideration of structural details. For example, burying more hydrophobic surface area can confer increased stability. Similarly, the packing volume model asserts that a change in the overall volume packed inside the core should cause a proportionate loss in stability. Unfortunately, these models give an incomplete and often very poor accounting of protein stability and other functional properties (1-3).

Recently, approaches have been developed that can predict energetic effects like protein stability and binding specificity from high-resolution structural information, by predicting the structural changes caused when a mutation is introduced (4-10). We have developed calculations that predict the minimum packing energy for the mutated sidechain(s) and surrounding sidechains, which correlates well with stability in a set of λ repressor core mutants (1, 11) and T4 lysozyme mutants(12, 13). In this approach, the protein mainchain is held fixed to the wildtype structure, and the mutated sidechain(s) and surrounding sidechains repacked as well as possible in that rigid context. This "best native fit" calculation identifies mutations that cannot fit into the native fold (without significant backbone distortions), but also mutations that improve packing (11).

In this paper we show how these "best native fit" structures can provide insights into the structural basis of the mutants' stability effects. Two types of evidence support the validity of this analysis: **i)** the calculated energies of these models correlate closely with the mutants' stabilities; **ii)** models of a series of T4 lysozyme mutants based on the wildtype structure matched crystal structures to 0.68 - 0.89Å rms on the predicted sidechains (13). This is not unreasonable in light of the extensive evidence showing little backbone shift in mutated proteins (14-16), but would not hold true for large mainchain movements, as observed between globins (17).

II Results and Discussion

Recently, the crystal structure of one of the modeled λ repressor mutants, V36L M40L V47I ("LLI"; we shall refer to the mutants by the amino acid letter codes for residues 36, 40 and 47), has been solved (18), giving a direct test of the accuracy of the original model (fig. 1) (11). The overall RMS of the model vs. the crystal structure was 0.99 Å (1.38 Å for sidechain atoms only), and 0.89 Å for the three mutated residues (1.11 Å for their sidechain atoms). Two of the mutated sidechains (Leu 36, Leu 40) superimpose with reasonable accuracy on the crystal structure (1.27 Å, 1.36 Å sidechain atom RMS, respectively), while the remaining mutated sidechain fits the crystal structure very closely (0.47 Å sidechain RMS). As Lim et al. remarked in their evaluation of the model, the model deviates substantially from the crystal structure in the sidechain torsions at residues 36 and 40 (18). However, these alternative conformations give similar placement of the 36 and 40 sidechains to the crystal structure, and a similar overall space-filling contour. The modeled Leu 36 differs from the crystal structure primarily at the distal, δ-methyls, which are rotated around the sidechain axis. Statistically, this conformation is more accurate (by RMS) than 83% of the possible leucine sidechain conformations at this residue. The modeled Leu 40 superimposes one C^{δ} close to the crystal structure, but has the other reversed. Its statistical rank against all possible leucine conformations at this residue is 81st percentile. These are significantly better than simply choosing the best rotamer (66%), and correspond to quality factors of four to five times better than random (see (13)). Ile 47 matches the crystal structure very closely by both

RMS and sidechain torsional angles; its statistical rank was >99th percentile. The probability of obtaining the observed level of accuracy for the three mutated residues by chance (i.e. by random sidechain rotamers) is 1.9×10^{-4}. Thus, this result is statistically significant.

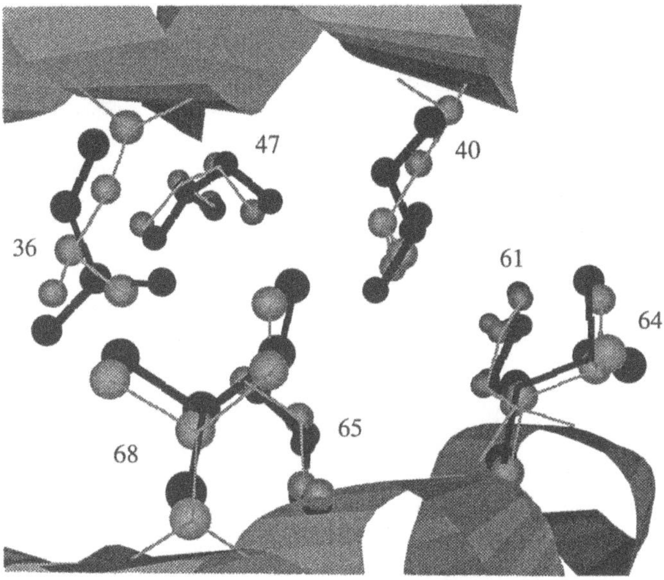

Figure 1: Comparison of the LLI mutant model (dark) vs. crystal structure (light).

To assess the level of error in the model caused by the mutant mainchain shifts, we have repeated our modeling procedure starting from the mutant crystal structure backbone, instead of the wildtype backbone. The resulting model is significantly more similar to the LLI crystal structure at residues 36 and 40 (0.39 Å and 0.66 Å sidechain RMS, respectively), but only marginally better at Ile 47 (0.26 Å RMS). The improved accuracy at 36 and 40 corresponds to statistically near-optimal rankings (>99th, and 98th percentile, respectively). Thus, while our original LLI model was reasonably accurate, its fixed-backbone approximation appears to responsible for nearly all of the error observed versus the crystal structure.

The predictions based on the fixed-backbone approximation appear to compromise between two general trends: **a**) minimal coordinate error: the modeled mutations superimpose well but not precisely on the mutant crystal structure; **b**) minimal strain with the fixed backbone: the predicted conformation is selected based on minimal overall strain, which can actually prevent it from superimposing precisely on the mutant crystal structure coordinates. In the LLI model, Leu 36 and Leu 40 conformations closer to the crystal structure would create steric clashes with surrounding atoms, that could only be relieved by backbone shifts. To extract meaningful energy information about the fit of the mutations within the structure, the model must avoid these anomalous strains as much as possible, by minimizing the structure within the fixed backbone context. These calculations correctly distinguished between mutant LLI (predicted to be slightly more stable than wildtype; experimentally it was the most stable mutant in the set) *versus* mutant FFI (predicted to be much less stable than wildtype; experimentally it was the least stable mutant). By contrast, standard sequence-based measures consider leucine and phenylalanine to be similar, predicting that these mutations should have similar effects on stability (19). The calculations' ability to perceive that leucine has the flexibility to fit the 36 and 40 sites with minimal disturbance, while phenylalanine does not, probably comes at some cost to its accuracy in predicting coordinates, particularly the sidechain torsional angles.

Table 1: Best native fit predictions and analyses for λ repressor core mutants

Mut.	ΔT	ΔE 36	ΔE 40	ΔE 47	ΔEt	ΔVol	Comments (* see text)
LLI	4	-2.4	+2.6	-0.6	-.4	+.+	stabilized by 36, 47 *
Imv	3	-0.8			-.8	+..	stabilized by cavity-filling *
vmv	0					...	(wildtype)
LVI	-2	-2.5	+6.8	-1.2	3.2	+-+	Val40 clash in helix-turn *
IVI	-2	-0.6	+6.8	-1.2	4.9	+-+	Val40 clash in helix-turn *
IVL	-4	-0.6	+6.8	+0.9	7.1	+-+	added torsional strain of Leu 47
vVL	-5		+6.8	+0.9	7.8	.-+	loss of packing stabilization at 36
FLv	-4	+5.1	+2.6		7.7	+..	36 clashes with 42, 65, 68
FFI	-9	+8.8	+5.2	-1.1	13	+++	36, 40 clash with 42, 61, 64, 65, 68
vVI			+6.8	-1.6	5.2	.-+	destabilized vs. IVI by loss of Ile 36
Ivv		-0.6	+6.8		6.2	+-.	destabilized vs. IVI by loss of Ile 47
vVv			+6.8		6.8	.-.	destabilized by loss of Ile 36 & 47

Predicting and Understanding Mutant Stabilities from Wildtype Structure

Table 1 summarizes the "best native fit" models for the 36-40-47 series of λ repressor mutations. Throughout this discussion, we will contrast our predictions with simple packing volume considerations (column **ΔVol** in Table 1), which predict that altering core sidechains' sizes is destabilizing, especially if larger residues than wildtype are introduced.

The packing-volume model, and other astructural models (19), predict that mutating Val 36 $\rightarrow$ Ile should destabilize the protein by overpacking the core with one extra methyl group. However, our model (fig. 2a) indicates that the extra methyl gives *increased* stability, due to a cavity apparent in the wildtype structure, into which the extra methyl can be packed in a good rotamer.

A second mutant, IVI, illustrates complex secondary structural effects on stability. This mutant differs from wildtype by three mutations, two of which (Val 36 → Ile, Val 47 → Ile) each add an extra methyl group, while the mutation at residue 40 (Met → Val) subtracts a methyl. Packing-volume considerations would predict destabilization by overpacking due to the extra methyls.

However, IVI's "best native fit" model indicates an opposite effect (fig. 2b). Residue 40 lies at the boundary between a helix and a turn, and this transitional role disfavors the β-branched sidechain of valine. The helix penalizes the sidechain *gauche+* and *gauche-* rotamers (they collide with the carbonyl of the i-4 residue). Val 40 also lies at the start of a turn, bending its own carbonyl away from the helical conformation, into a position that impinges upon the *trans* rotamer. These contradictory demands create steric strain between the two γ-methyls of the β-branch and the protein backbone. The predicted *trans* conformation, which places its $C^{\gamma 2}$ too close to Ile 68's $C^{\delta 1}$ (2.9Å). 434 repressor (26% identity versus λ repressor; PDB code 1R69 (20)) has valine at the equivalent of position 40, and has a number of structural changes to accommodate it: the carbonyl oxygen of residue 40 bends 20° further away from its sidechain atoms, compared with that in λ repressor; Ile 68 is replaced by Ala; and 64 Leu moves 1.0Å further away from residue 40. This interpretation is supported by the observation that all the mutants with valine at position 40 experimentally have lower T_m than wildtype.

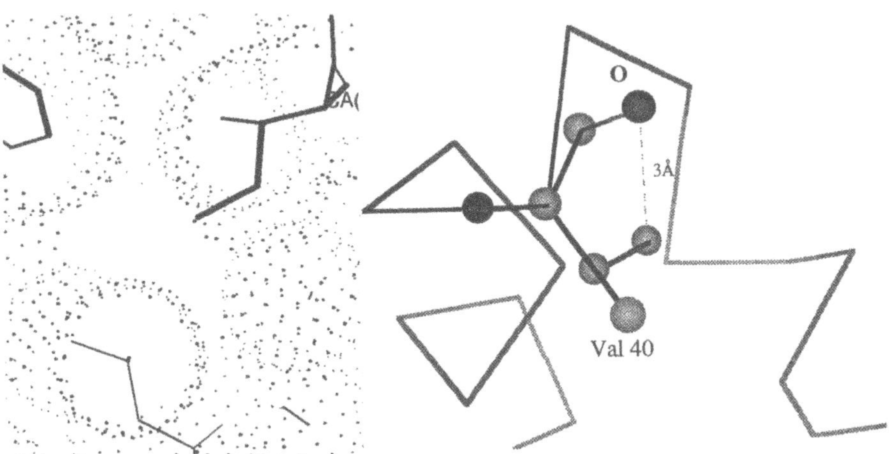

Figure 2: Steric analysis of mutant models **a**. IMV. Ile 36's added methyl group ($C^{\delta 1}$) packs into a cavity present in the wildtype structure. **b**. IVI. Val 40 packs poorly, because the backbone carbonyl (O) is turned away from the helix axis (the helix carbonyls point vertically in this figure), towards the β-branched Val sidechain.

By contrast, the two Val → Ile mutations are predicted to *stabilize* the fold. Ile 47 takes advantage of the cavity created by the shortening of residue 40's sidechain, to pack the "new" methyl group $C^{\delta 1}$ in a good rotamer, while Ile 36 is predicted to fill the same cavity it does in IMV. These predictions could be tested by reverting Ile 36 and Ile 47 to wildtype (see VVI, IVV, VVV, table 1). The packing volume model predicts that relieving the "overpacking" at 36 and 47 should alleviate IVI's destabilization. Intuitively, it makes sense that returning towards the wildtype sequence should move back towards the wildtype stability. However, our calculations indicate that these mutants (VVI and IVV) would be somewhat further destabilized, due to loss of the Ile $C^{\delta 1}$'s attractive van der Waals interactions, with the double mutant VVV least stable.

Analyses of these and other mutants suggested that the unbranched sidechain of Met 40 plays a special role in the stability of λ repressor. We have compared how strongly each of the three sites (36, 40, and 47) are sterically constrained to their wildtype amino acid, by calculating packing energies for all single-site mutants substituted at one of these sites with Leu, Ile, Met, or Val (fig. 3a). These calculations indicate that packing imposes little constraint on sequence at positions 36 and 47--in both cases, some mutants have steric energy as low as wildtype. By contrast, at residue 40 no mutation fits as well as methionine. Leucine, the next best residue, is more than 3 kcal/mol higher in packing energy. The site's helix-turn backbone disfavors β-branched residues. For γ-branches, the χ_2 *gauche+* rotamer position hits Leu 64 C^{β} (2.6 Å) on a neighboring helix, while the *gauche-* position hits 40's own carbonyl oxygen (2.6Å). Thus only one good position (*trans*) is available for a δ-methyl. Since Val and Ile are β-branched, and Leu , His, Phe, Trp and Tyr are γ-branched, Met, a rare amino acid, is the only large hydrophobic that answers this steric prescription well, via the unusual structural virtue of possessing torsional flexibility at each of the atoms in its long sidechain.

Cooperativity and Steric Coupling

In proteins as small as λ repressor, energies do not necessarily correlate closely with melting temperature (T_m); however for these mutants this comparison is possible because the calculated multisite mutant energies correlate well with both the experimental T_m and $\Delta\Delta G_u$ (8). We have calculated the predicted packing effects of point mutations at positions 36, 40 and 47 (fig. 3a). How well can these independent effects predict the multisite mutants' experimental stabilities? These mutants involve overlapping combinations of mutations at three neighboring sites (Table 1), which might be expected to have strongly cooperative effects that would render this simplistic approach invalid. However, simply adding the energy changes of the separate point mutations correlates well with the multisite mutants' experimental stabilities (fig. 3b). Comparison with the regular multisite calculations (arrows in fig. 3b, data from Table 1) shows two cooperative effects. In FLV and FFI, Phe 36 forces neighboring residues (especially 42) into strained conformations that open space for mutation to a larger residue at 40. Second, in the wildtype context, Ile 47 is destabilizing because it clashes with Met 40; when 40 is mutated, however, the regular multisite calculations predict a cooperative effect in which Ile 47 becomes strongly stabilizing (in IVI, LVI, LLI, FFI). Experimentally, Val 36 → Ile raises T_m 3.4°C in the wildtype context (VMV → IMV), but only 2.1°C in VVL → IVL, indicating a cooperative effect, that is only weakly observed in our calculations ($\Delta\Delta E_{calc}$= -0.8 kcal/mol for VMV → IMV, vs. -0.6 for VVL → IVL). To a first approximation, however, it appears multisite stability can be uncoupled to the separate "simple rules" for each site's sequence preferences.

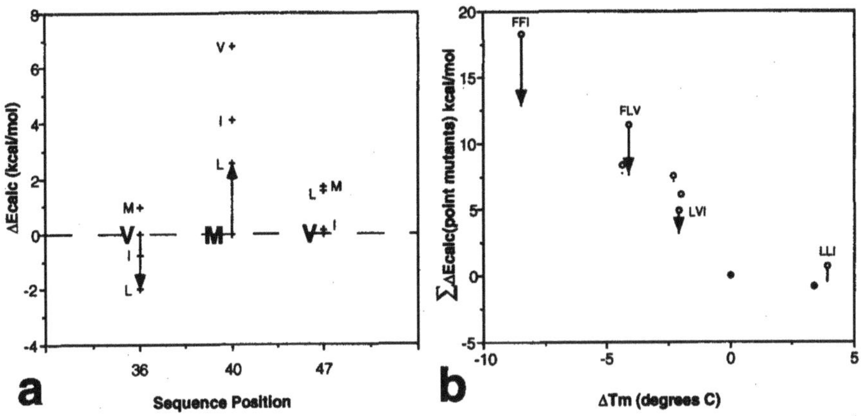

Figure 3: **a**. Comparison of residues 36, 40, and 47's permissiveness to mutation: calculated energies for each of the point mutants. At each position, an arrow indicates the lowest energy mutation. **b**. Cooperativity of neighboring mutations' stability effects. To test the level of energetic coupling between sites 36, 40, and 47, we summed the point mutant energies shown in **a**. for the mutations in each of Lim & Sauer's multisite mutants (o); cooperative effects are shown as vectors between these values and the corresponding multisite calculations (Table 1).

How strongly coupled are the packing arrangements of core sidechains? When core substitutions are made, does packing force significant rearrangements to accommodate the changed group? To address these questions we have examined the optimized-packing predicted structures of the λ repressor mutants for conformational shifts versus the wildtype packing. We have focused on the sidechains neighboring the mutated positions, to assess how their optimal packing conformations change due to the mutations. The predicted rearrangements were slight, typically 0.2 - 0.8Å sidechain RMS shift, and consisted of slight rotations of individual residues contacting a bulky substitution, to make room for it. The degree of predicted rearrangement does not correlate with stability effects; for example, LLI (the most stable of the eight mutants) and FFI (the least stable) were predicted to have nearly equal shifts (0.8Å and 0.9Å respectively). Thus, such shifts can yield a well-packed structure, or merely reduce the strain of a poorly packed mutant. The low level of steric change provides a simple explanation for the relative lack of cooperativity in the calculated energetic effects of the neighboring mutations at 36, 40 and 47. Since each substitution causes little steric change, it produces little alteration in the structural environment of a neighboring mutation, and thus little impact on its energetics.

Comparison with Rotamer Modeling

A key issue for structure prediction methods is the combinatorial problem of finding the global energy minimum out of the essentially infinite set of possible conformations. One strategy that has been widely employed is to reduce the number of possibilities drastically, by limiting consideration to rotamer conformations. In this approach, sidechains are treated not as freely rotatable torsional conformers, but as a small set of rotamers (typically three to five for each sidechain, and more in recent rotamer libraries, especially for aromatic residues) from which one is to be chosen as a best conformation. This reduces the total number of conformational permutations by two to three orders of magnitude per residue in the prediction zone, and yields accurate predictions for sidechain packing on wildtype backbones (5, 21-23). Surveys of high resolution crystal structures have found that about 71% of sidechains fit rotamer angles *gauche+*, *trans* or *gauche-* on χ_1 to within 20° (24), with >90% classifiable as rotamers within an extended library of 67 total conformations for the 20 amino acids (25).

For predicting mutant structures, however, the challenge of mainchain shifts arises. Current methods neglect mainchain movements, and thus are forced to model the mutant sidechains on the "wrong" backbone, derived from the wildtype structure. In this case the inflexibility of the rotamers is a disadvantage, because no sidechain adjustment is allowed to make up for the fact the backbone is held fixed. In non-rotamer based calculations on T4 lysozyme mutants, we observed that packing optimization used sidechain torsional adjustments departing from rotamers to correctly predict the major structural shifts (13). How well can the λ repressor mutants be represented by rotamers?

To assess this question, we have calculated the deviation of their optimal-packing structures from the closest rotamers in the set compiled by Ponder and Richards (25). We have scored each sidechain as fitting a rotamer if its torsional angles are within 20° of a rotamer. For the mutated residues 36-40-47, only 46% of the sidechains over the mutant set fit rotamers. Overall, none of the mutants could be represented by rotamers without at least one major deviation from the optimal packing structure, usually at a substituted position. In contrast, 88% of the neighboring, non-mutated sidechains fit rotamers, over the mutant set, and the only deviations occurred in the highly overpacked mutants FLV and FFI. This contrast may suggest that predicting the best packed structure with rotamers may be more difficult for mutated positions than it has proved to be for fitting wildtype sidechains onto the correct wildtype backbone. Mutant sidechains generally *do* assume standard rotamer conformations within the reference frame of the mutant crystal structure (18, 26). However, in homology modeling based on the wildtype backbone, the inherent mainchain error frequently makes the strict rotamer conformations appear to pack poorly, obscuring the optimal placement of the mutant sidechain atoms and leading to incorrect rotamer selection (13). The lack of backbone movement is the main problem in our calculations; rigid rotamers, used in homology modeling, add to this difficulty by making the sidechains also unable to adjust flexibly in response to mutation. A modeling method for coiled coil proteins has been developed that takes into account both sidechain and mainchain flexibility (27), an important new direction. The occurrence of a non-ideal rotamer conformation in our models appears to be crudely predictive of backbone shifts for the region of that residue.

Packing and Sequence Permissiveness

How strongly does packing constrain sequence within the protein core? The density of packing inside protein cores has long suggested that it may be a very strong constraint (28). Some years ago, Ponder and Richards performed ground-breaking calculations of sequences allowable within protein cores, using exhaustive search of rotamers and assessing packing by hard-sphere cutoffs. These calculations indicated that only a minute fraction (much less than one percent) of possible hydrophobic sequences fit a given protein core well enough to fold, leading to the characterization of this tiny subset as a "template" designating which sequences could adopt its fold (25). However, experimental studies (1, 16, 26, 29-31) have demonstrated that protein cores are surprisingly tolerant to mutation. Fully 70% of Lim & Sauer's hydrophobic sequence variants (mutated at λ repressor residues 36, 40 and 47) possessed detectable biological activity (1). Are these mutations able to fold because the protein backbone can distort significantly to accommodate them, or is a much larger fraction able to pack directly in the wildtype backbone than suggested by previous calculations?

To address this question, we have graphed the calculated "best native fit" energies of all 125 mutants containing Ile, Leu, Met, Phe or Val at residues 36-40-47 (fig. 4), calculated within the unperturbed wildtype backbone. Of these, 4% fit the native core with packing energy lower than that of wildtype, and more than 20% are lower than that of IVI, whose melting temperature is only 2°C lower than wildtype. Overall, 80% were calculated to have better packing energy than FFI, which has a melting temperature 9°C lower than wildtype. Thus, the energetics of steric fit to the native core do not appear to restrict sequence strongly.

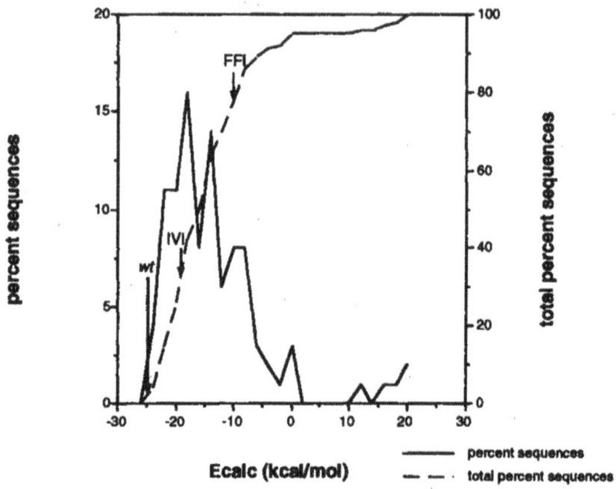

Figure 4: Distribution of packing energies for 36-40-47 Ile-Leu-Met-Phe-Val set

This much greater breadth of acceptable sequences than predicted by previous theory arises primarily in the tools used to locate and assess potential packings. First of all, Ponder and Richards enforced a strict volume requirement: sequences with less total packing volume than wildtype were scored as failing to fold. We simply calculated total packing energy, with no volume constraint. Second, our calculations modeled sidechains with unrestricted structural flexibility, by permitting all torsions to rotate freely (in steps of about 10 degrees), rather than using just a few fixed rotamer conformations. Furthermore, a flexible shell of sidechains surrounding the mutations was included in the molten zone, to allow for structural adjustments in the environment in response to the mutations. Third, to evaluate packing quality we calculated a physically realistic van der Waals potential energy of the system, instead of using a hard-sphere cutoff. Hard-sphere cutoffs neglect the structural adaptability characteristic of proteins, and are unreasonably unforgiving. Furthermore, they don't include attractive van der Waals interactions, which have played a very important role in our calculated stabilization energies. For example, six of the 125 mutants were predicted to be more stable than wildtype, due not to reduced repulsive forces, but to increased attractive interactions. We believe that these new features give a more realistic treatment of core sequence permissiveness. Even with little backbone motion considered, a large number of hydrophobic sequences appear to fit λ repressor core well enough to fold.

III Acknowledgments

We thank Drs. R. Baldwin, P. David, R. Kornberg, P. Padmanabhan, and S. Subbiah for critical reading of this manuscript. C.L. was a Howard Hughes Medical Institute Predoctoral Fellow, and this work was supported by the NIH.

IV Methods

"Best native fit" models and energies were calculated using self-consistent ensemble optimization (SCEO (7, 8, 11, 32)). Coordinates of λ repressor (PDB code 1LRD (33)) were obtained from the Brookhaven Protein Data Bank (34), and sidechain atoms for a molten zone consisting of residues 36, 40, 42, 47, 61, 64, 65 and 68 deleted. The molten zone sidechains were then rebuilt in random conformations, with the desired amino acids at positions 36, 40 and 47. This structure was used as the starting point for 25 cycles of SCEO packing optimization, using linear cooling from 6000K to 298K over the first 15 cycles, followed by ten cycles equilibration at 298K. We followed the standard protocol (8) without modification. The predicted structure for each mutant was generated by selecting each molten zone residue's most frequent conformation in the final, optimally packed ensemble. The packing energy of this final ensemble for each mutant ($\mathbf{E_{calc}}$) was taken as the predictor of its stability, relative to that calculated for wildtype. The energy calculations and parameters were exactly as reported previously (4, 11). To make a crude correction for the mutants' self-energies in the unfolded state, we assumed all χ torsional potentials adopt optimal rotamers in the unfolded state, and subtracted these values from the native packing energies. To model the energetics of a given residue in the unfolded state, we employed a simplistic model of an extended tripeptide chain fragment centered on that residue (8). Models were examined and analyzed using the LOOK software suite (Molecular Applications Group, Palo Alto, CA), and evaluated performed as described in (13).

V References

1. Lim, W. A. & Sauer, R. T. *J. Mol. Biol.* **219,** 359 (1991)
2. Shortle, D., Stites, W. E. & Meeker, A. K. *Biochemistry* **29,** 8033 (1990)
3. Connelly, P., Varadarajan, R., Sturtevant, J. M. & Richards, F. M. *Biochemistry* **29,** 6108 (1990)
4. Lee, C. & Subbiah, S. *J. Mol. Biol.* **217,** 373 (1991)
5. Wilson, C., Mace, J. E. & Agard, D. *J. Mol. Biol.* **220,** 495 (1991)
6. De Filippis, V., Sander, C. & Vriend, G. *Prot. Eng.* **7,** 1203 (1994)
7. Koehl, P. & Delarue, M. *J. Mol. Biol.* **239,** 249 (1994)

FACILITIES FOR EXPLORING MOLECULAR BIOLOGY DATABASES ON THE WEB: A COMPARATIVE STUDY

Victor M. Markowitz, I-Min A. Chen, Anthony S. Kosky, and Ernest Szeto
Data Management Research and Development Group
Lawrence Berkeley National Laboratory, Berkeley, CA 94720

We discuss criteria for evaluating and comparing the main facilities provided by molecular biology databases (MBDs) for exploring (that is, retrieving and interpreting data) on the Web. We use these criteria for examining the facilities supported by typical MBDs such as Genbank, AtDB, GSDB, GDB, and MGD (as of September 5, 1996).

1 Introduction

Molecular biology databases (MBDs) are implemented using different data management systems ranging from file management systems to database management systems (DBMSs). The data in an MBD are structured according to a ***schema*** specified in a ***data definition language*** and are accessed using a ***query language***, where these languages are based on a ***data model*** that defines the semantics of their constructs and queries. For example, the schema of Genome Sequence Data Base (GSDB) [9] and the Mouse Genome Database (MGD) [15] are defined using the data definition language of the Sybase relational DBMS, the structure of the Arabidopsis thaliana database (AtDB) [1] (as well as numerous other MBDs) is defined using ACeDB [5], and the structure of Genome Database (GDB) [7] and the 3DB version of the Protein Data Bank (PDB) [19] are defined using OPM [2] on top of Sybase. For MBDs maintained as flat-files, the data definition languages used for defining their structure are not based on a data model per se and range from generic notations such as the ASN.1 data exchange format used for Genbank [17] to ad-hoc data definition languages such as that employed for EMBL [8].

Exploring MBDs involves examining the structure (metadata) of MBDs, browsing and querying MBDs, and interpreting the results of queries expressed over MBDs. MBDs must provide facilities that would help users to identify an MBD as containing relevant data, formulate queries against the MBD, and to interpret or make use of the data retrieved. Many of these facilities amount to ***documentation*** and query and browsing facilities which are supported to some extent by most MBDs.

In this paper, we discuss criteria for evaluating the main facilities required for exploring MBDs on the Web, that is, retrieving and interpreting MBD metadata and data. We apply these criteria in comparing the main facilities provided by typical MBDs, such as Genbank, AtDB, GSDB, GDB, and MGD. These MBDs were chosen to provide a representative selection of MBDs accessible via the Web, and for illustrating the various levels of support provided for accessing MBDs on the Web. Space limitations do not allow us to provide a comprehensive list of MBDs that can be accessed via the Web nor to discuss their facilities in detail.

The remainder of this paper is organized as follows. In section 2 we discuss the facilities required for exploring and accessing metadata. In section 3 we examine to what extent typical MBDs meet these requirements. In section 4 we discuss criteria for evaluating MBD browsing and querying facilities. In section 5 we apply these criteria in examining the browsing and query facilities of typical MBDs. Section 6 contains concluding remarks.

2 Metadata Support

Ideally, an MBD should provide comprehensive metadata as well as facilities for easy access to and interpretation of this information. MBD metadata would preferably involve descriptions in alternative formats, such as text, Html, and notations, such as diagrams, lists. The need for comprehensive MBD metadata capturing domain knowledge about biology, was discussed extensively at the Meetings on Interconnection of Molecular Biology Databases [14] and in papers such as [10,13]. Comprehensive MBD metadata should include general information regarding MBDs, information on the structure (schemas) of MBDs, alternative MBD views, and information on relationships between MBDs.

General information describes the underlying MBD and should include (i) the MBD name, a brief description of the purpose of the MBD, the physical location and history of the MBD; (ii) information on the data definition language and implementation details for the MBD, including either precise definitions and examples for the data definition language or references to where such information can be found, information on the underlying DBMS and implementation strategy for the MBD; and (iii) keywords to allow high level searches for relevant MBDs.

MBD schemas define the MBD structure in the data definition language of the native data management system underlying the MBD, and perhaps also in alternative data definition languages. Detailed schema definition helps expert users understand certain database design issues and/or choices; it can also be reused in defining similar molecular biology applications. Moreover, schema definitions are essential for users who want to use the *ad hoc* query capabilities provided by some MBDs (see section 4 for more details).

MBD views represent alternative interpretations of the MBD. Metadata on each view should include: (i) an *overview* grouping related components together into higher-level components in order to provide a concise and comprehensible high-level description of the MBD view; and (ii) information on each major construct (class, attribute), including: (a) *semantic definitions* describing the real world or abstract concepts represented by the view construct, and possibly constraints on the values of instances of the construct that cannot be expressed in the underlying data definition language; (b) *design motivation* for the use of a particular construct in representing application data; (c) *synonyms* and *keywords* for identifying differences in terminology and for establishing potential correspondences between the components of different MBDs; and (d) *sample data* providing examples of how the view constructs are used and how typical data might appear. In addition general information on each view should be available, including explanations and motivation for the particular interpretation of the MBD provided by the view.

MBD relationships describe any known relationships (links) with other MBDs, including descriptions of external references stored in the MBD, descriptions of the semantics of the links and information on how to follow the links, and references to metadata for other MBDs.

The ease of locating and accessing MBD metadata is also important to consider. Some MBDs provide explicit metadata information on their Web pages, while others provide metadata in ftp files. The later entails a slow and tedious process of locating and downloading the files, and examining the metadata in these files in whatever format it is provided. A very useful facility is on-line *metadata browsing*, based on hyperlinks between related metadata components.

Maintaining comprehensive MBD metadata can be complex and time consuming if it is not supported by appropriate tools. For example, providing MBD metadata (e.g., schemas, views) in different data definition languages requires *schema conversion* tools; similarly, providing MBD metadata in different formats and notations can be automated by *metadata publishing* tools. Additional tools are needed for revising and/or updating metadata, such as tools for keeping track of MBD changes and for synchronizing the various MBD metadata components mentioned above.

3 Metadata Support: Case Studies

Almost all MBDs provide some metadata support though the level of this support varies greatly. We briefly describe the main metadata support provided by typical MBDs, such as GSDB, MGD, Genbank, AtDB, and GDB, and discuss the main problems of providing such support.

3.1 Case Studies

The GSDB and MGD metadata consist of documentation describing the structure of the relational databases underlying GSDB and MGD in terms of tables and columns. Understanding this documentation requires some familiarity with relational database modeling, for example, in order to understand the role of primary and foreign keys in representing cross-table relationships. No information is provided by GSDB and MGD regarding relational data modeling and its employment in designing GSDB and MGD. MGD provides on-line schema information; users can easily find the schema definition on the Web. The table definitions of the relational MGD schema as well as comments and examples for table attributes can be reviewed (one-level browsing), but cannot be browsed recursively, that is, by following links representing inter-table relationships. The GSDB documentation is available as postscript and Portable Document Format documents. GSDB does not provide on-line schema information nor schema browsing facilities.

The structure of Genbank is defined in ASN.1. ASN.1 is a flexible notation for describing nested file structures but does not constitute a data model per se since it lacks support for integrity constraints and data manipulations. The ASN.1 definition for Genbank requires familiarity with ASN.1, and is not available directly on the NCBI Web site, but can be obtained, together with an ASN.1 tutorial, by ftp. Since NCBI provides large amounts of information via ftp, extra effort is required for locating the files containing metadata. On-line schema information is not available and schema browsing is not supported by Genbank.

The structure of AtDB is defined using ACeDB, which is based on a data model with an object-oriented flavor. The AtDB documentation consists only of the ACeDB schema definition and requires familiarity with the ACeDB flavor of object-oriented constructs; ACeDB documentation is available on line. The AtDB schema is available on the Web and can be recursively browsed online. Furthermore, for each ACeDB class definition one can find a data sample (example) for an instance of that class.

The structure of GDB 6 is defined using OPM, a data model that combines standard object-oriented constructs (object class, attribute) with constructs for modeling scientific experiments (protocols). The structure of GDB databases is available in alternative formats, including OPM and relational formats, and notations, including Html, diagrams, and Ascii. Understanding the OPM or relational schemas for GDB requires familiarity with object-oriented or relational database concepts. A tutorial of object-oriented concepts is available on-line. Descriptive information for GDB 6 is also available for non-database expert users. GDB 6 metadata includes data samples (e.g., map examples in both database and diagrammatic form), and can be browsed on line.

Most MBDs describe relationships to related MBDs merely through links to related Web sites; the semantics of the relationships between related schema components are not provided.

3.2 Discussion

The main problem with providing metadata support is the large number of different data models and DBMSs that are used to implement MBDs, including the relational model, ASN.1, ACeDB and OPM. Understanding and using MBDs requires familiarity with different data models. OPM and ACeDB provide comprehensive metadata support. The object-oriented or type constructs of these models provide more concise and easier to understand database definitions when compared with relational database constructs. Furthermore, ACeDB and OPM schemas can be annotated with descriptions of their various elements. ASN.1 provides a formal and concise notation for data structures, but is not a data model per se and therefore does not support specifying important schema information such as integrity constraints. The relational model is oriented towards the efficient storage and management of data, but does not provide constructs for capturing the semantics of data well: the representation of a single conceptual object in a relational database may be spread over many records in several distinct tables, thus making a relational schema a poor vehicle for communicating the semantics of a database.

Providing MBD metadata in a uniform and consistent way (common data models, formats, and notations) would greatly simplify the task of gathering and interpreting metadata. Uniform metadata representation can be achieved via tools for defining semantically enhanced views for MBDs in a common data model, together with tools for automatically generating alternative representations of these views. An example of such tools are the OPM retrofitting tools that allow constructing OPM views on top of relational or ASN.1 databases[3], and the OPM publishing tools, which allow representing OPM schemas in various formats (Html, LaTeX) and notations (diagrams, lists). Some of these tools have been used for generating the GDB 6 documentation in various formats and notations as part of GDB's metadata support. However effective use of such tools first requires comprehensive metadata and documentation to be available in some form.

4 Browsing and Query Support

Browsing and query facilities supported by MBDs range from fixed-form queries to free-form or ad-hoc queries expressed using a query language.

4.1 Fixed-Form vs Free-Form Querying

Fixed-form or *canned* queries have a fixed structure involving a predetermined set of tables, classes or other database components, and a predetermined set of attributes for each database component. Fixed-form queries can be parameterized on certain values and support some options, allowing the user to control the conditions used in the query or set the values used by the conditions.

Fixed-form queries define *interfaces* through which the underlying MBDs can be examined. These interfaces may not necessarily reflect the structure of the underlying MBD. For example, the list of attributes or fields retrieved by a fixed-form query may be only a subset of the attributes and fields in the underlying MBD.

Unlike fixed-form queries, *free-form* or *ad-hoc* queries do not have a predetermined structure and are usually specified in some query language. The query language, its syntax and its expressive power, depend on the underlying data model and DBMS. Even for the same data model, different DBMSs are likely to support different query languages. For example each major relational DBMS vendor offers their own variant of SQL. Consequently free-form querying requires detailed knowledge of the data model, schema and the particular query language used by the MBD.

SQL is a powerful query language that serves as the underlying standard for the query language of commercial relational DBMSs. Specifying SQL queries, however, requires non-trivial knowledge of the structure and manipulation of relational databases. For example, one needs to understand the meaning of organizing data in tables and of joining tables in order to retrieve related data from tables.

The ODMG-93 standard [16] is followed by most object-oriented query languages, such as the OPM query language (OPM-QL), while systems such as ACeDB have their own brand of object-based query languages. Specifying object queries is simpler than specifying SQL queries mainly because an object query involves higher-level, and therefore fewer elements. For example, a typical OPM-QL query is substantially more concise (in number of its component elements) than an equivalent SQL query. However, specifying object queries still requires understanding the syntax and semantics of the query language, which may be a non-trivial task for non-expert users.

4.2 Formulating, Processing, and Interpreting Queries

The process of querying an MBD involves: (1) formulating a query, which requires understanding how data are represented in the underlying MBD; (2) processing the query, which involves parsing the query, finding an optimized execution plan and retrieving the results of the query; and (3) interpreting the results of the query.

Formulating queries could involve browsing and keyword-search of MBD metadata for identifying MBDs of interest and for determining whether these MBDs contain relevant data. It is important for an MBD to provide support in formulating queries. For fixed-form queries, for example, such support can involve providing the set of allowed attribute values (if this set is not too large), sample (example) attributes values, and help in formulating condition expressions. Free-form queries require additional support in examining the underlying schema, specifying queries involving multiple, not necessarily directly related, elements, managing the query language syntax, and so on.

Fixed-form query processing is relatively simple and can, in certain cases, be provided via information retrieval systems. Indexes can be provided for certain attributes in order to increase the query performance. Free-form query processing is substantially more complex, where the complexity depends on the power of the query language. Commercial DBMSs provide query processing (and various levels of query optimization) for their own brand of SQL. OPM query processing is provided by an OPM query translator that generates equivalent, possibly semantically optimized, SQL queries for the underlying (Sybase or Oracle) database[4].

MBD metadata together with the semantics of the operations underlying MBD query processing can be used for *interpreting* the meaning (semantics) of query results. For example, information on the semantics of objects in a given class can be used for annotating query results, for describing the searching scope of a query, for explaining null query results, for suggesting alternative queries when no results are returned, and so on.

5 Browsing and Query Support: Case Studies

We briefly discuss in this section the query facilities of MBDs such as GSDB, MGD, EMBL, Genbank, AtDB, and GDB, and examine the main problems of these facilities.

5.1 *Case Studies*

EMBL provides a simple sequence retrieval based on accession numbers as well as fixed-form queries via the SRS system [6]: SRS supports browsing and querying multiple MBDs, including EMBL, where querying is restricted to simple conditions of up to four matching expressions involving a limited number of indexes. Forms are linked to explanatory text for assisting users in constructing index matching expressions.

MGD supports fixed-form queries that represent a number of entities of interest (e.g., Probes, PCR Primers, References) which are based on, but do not necessarily reflect the structure of the underlying database. Forms are linked to information on fields and explanatory text for assisting users in constructing query conditions. Sets of allowed values or format information for certain attributes are provided in the query forms together with menu buttons for selecting comparison operators for the query conditions.

Genbank's interface, Entrez [18] is in fact the query interface for a warehouse consisting of Genbank, Medline and several sequence and macromolecular MBDs. Entrez supports a single fixed-form query for the underlying MBD and provides a mechanism of constructing conditions involving a limited number of indexed fields. Help is provided for constructing these conditions. Entrez provides information on the number of data items that may satisfy a given condition, thus assisting users in determining whether the condition is too restrictive or too general (e.g., more than 1000 data items satisfy the condition). Such information allows calibrating conditions.

GDB's Web interface supports only fixed-form queries. Concise queries involving only few fields (e.g., accession number, genome name) support simple searches. More detailed query forms are provided for each class in the underlying databases, where each form reflects the structure of the class. Lists of valid values are provided for attributes associated with controlled vocabularies so that selection conditions for these attributes can be specified easily. Forms are linked to schema information and explanatory text for assisting users in constructing query conditions.

GSDB provides a limited number of fixed-form queries, including a concise 'Sequence and Feature Retrieval' form for retrieval based on accession numbers or sequence names. Sample values are provided for the fields in the query forms, but no other help is provided for constructing or customizing queries. GSDB also supports the specification of free-form queries expressed in the Sybase variant of SQL. Sample SQL queries are provided for main GSDB objects such as genes and products. As mentioned in the previous section, specifying new or customizing existing SQL queries requires non-trivial knowledge of SQL as well as understanding the structure and semantics of the underlying relational database, and therefore is beyond the ability of most casual users.

AtDB can be queried by using both fixed-form and free-form queries supported by ACeDB. The fixed-form queries reflect the structure of AtDB: each ACeDB class underlies a *query-by-example* interface for that class. AtDB supports a different strategy to help users formulating queries. If a query condition is too general (i.e., more than 100 data items satisfy the condition), then the system automatically suggests "sub-selection" conditions for reducing the number of the returned items. Free-form queries in AtDB are expressed in ACeDB's query language, which is a restricted and rather peculiar language: using it requires knowledge of its syntax and semantics and therefore it is not straightforward. AtDB provides on-line schema browsing and a link to ACeDB query language documentation to help users formulating free-form ACeDB queries. However, anecdotal evidence suggests that free-form ACeDB queries are seldom used by ACeDB users.

5.2 Discussion

Fixed-form queries are limited in that they must conform to some predetermined view of the underlying MBD. This limitation can be offset by mechanisms supporting multiple MBD views: that is multiple schemas for a single MBD whose instances are either materialized or computed at run time from the data in the underlying MBD. For example, OPM's support for defining new derived classes allows rapidly extending GDB's query interface by defining new derived classes.

Query interfaces may need to be changed whenever the underlying MBD changes or new features need to be supported. In such cases, schema driven query interfaces, that is, interfaces that are automatically generated from the underlying MBD metadata are easier to extend than manually maintained interfaces. For example, GDB's Web-based query interfaces are easy to maintain since they are automatically generated from the underlying schemas by the Genera tool [11]. We are not aware of similar facilities for other MBD query interfaces.

Since free-form querying requires detailed knowledge of the query language, data model, and MBD structure, some MBDs supporting free-form queries, such as GSDB, try to address these problems by providing sample queries or templates: rather than writing a query from scratch users can adapt or alter the sample queries to suit their needs. However this is only a partial solution: if the query a user wishes to ask diverges significantly from the sample queries provided then significant knowledge of the query language, schema and data model are still required. Consequently, for free-form query facilities to be of use, the query languages and schemas provided must be concise and intuitive, and comprehensive on-line documentation for both must be provided. We are not aware of any MBD that provides such facilities.

Often MBDs do not provide sufficient information for clarifying the semantics of queries specified by users or to interpret the semantics of the query results. For example the Entrez interface provides a number of query forms and various choices of attributes on which to search, but does not offer any description of the extents over which these queries search, or the semantics of the individual attributes. We do not feel that any known MBD supports the level of query interpretation we described in the previous section. These problems are compounded by the extremely large and complex molecular biology nomenclature and by various differences in interpretations of this nomenclature within the molecular biology community.

6 Concluding Remarks

There is a significant disparity between the levels of support provided for online or Web access to various MBDs. Supporting MBD access on the Web requires providing comprehensive metadata and documentation on line. Ideally, such metadata should include schemas in a variety of commonly used data definition languages, semantic descriptions of MBDs and their components, alternative views of MBDs, and sample data. Such metadata should be easy to access and explore, using tools such as Web-based schema browsers.

Many MBDs provide connections to other MBDs via hyperlinks, often embedded in the results of a query. Interpreting and correctly using such links requires documentation describing the semantics of the links, as well as documentation on the linked MBDs. In practice, such documentation is seldom available.

The question of the best way of providing Web-based query facilities for MBDs remains open. A good option is to support fixed-form queries for the most common queries, combined with support for ad hoc queries for flexible data exploration and non-standard queries. Both fixed-form and ad hoc query facilities require comprehensive on-line documentation. In addition, ad hoc query facilities require support for specifying and interpreting queries. It is not clear how best to compromise between expressibility and simplicity/conciseness of a Web-based ad hoc query tool.

Reasons for the lack of comprehensive metadata for some MBDs include the fact that the task of making such metadata available is very labour intensive, and that schemas are revised frequently. Software tools, based on various data models such as OPM and ACeDB, have been shown to make this task substantially easier, and provide a high level of on-line support automatically. A consistent way of documenting MBDs could also facilitate MBD exploration.

The natural extension of exploring individual MBDs is exploring multiple, related, MBDs. Exploring data across multiple MBDs involves coping with the additional problems entailed by the distribution of data among MBDs, the heterogeneity of the systems underlying these MBDs, and the semantic (schema representation) heterogeneity of these MBDs. However, the requirements and facilities for exploring data from individual MBDs apply equally well to exploring data from multiple MBDs.

Acknowledgments

This work was supported by the Office of Health and Environmental Research Program of the Office of Energy Research, U.S. Department of Energy under Contract DE-AC03-76SF00098.

References

1. Arabidopsis thaliana Database, School of Medicine, Stanford University, August 1996; http://genome-www.stanford.edu/Arabidopsis/; see also http://genome-www.stanford.edu/cgi-bin/model/AtDB.
2. Chen, I.A., and Markowitz, V.M. An Overview of the Object-Protocol Model (OPM) and OPM Data Management Tools. *Information Systems*, 20(5), pp. 393-418, 1995.
3. Chen, I.A., and Markowitz, V.M., Constructing and Maintaining Scientific Database Views, Technical Report LBL-38359, 1996.
4. Chen, I.A., Kosky, A., Markowitz, V.M., and Szeto, E., The OPM Query Language and Translator, Technical Report LBL-33706, 1996. Available at http://gizmo.lbl.gov/opm.html.
5. Durbin, R., and Thierry-Mieg, J., Syntactic Definitions for the ACEDB Data Base Manager, 1992; available together with additional documentation at http://probe.nalusda.gov:8000/acedocs/.
6. Etzold, T., and Argos, P. SRS, An Indexing and Retrieval Tools for Flat File Data Libraries. *Computer Applications of Biosciences*, 9, 1, pp.

49-57, 1993. See also http://www.embl-heidelberg.de/srs/srsc.

7. Fasman, K.H., Letovsky, S.I., Cottingham, R.W., and Kingsbury, D. T. Improvements to the GDB Human Genome Data Base. Nucleic Acids Research, Vol. 24, No. 1, pp. 57-63, 1996. See also http://gdbgeneral.gdb.org/gdb/schema.html.
8. The EMBL Nucleotide Sequence Database, European Bioinformatics Institute, http://www.ebi.ac.uk/ebi_docs/embl_db/ebi/topembl.html.
9. Genome Sequence DataBase (GSDB) 1.0. The National Center for Genome Resources, August 1996; http://www.ncgr.org/gsdb/gsdb.html.
10. Karp, P., A Strategy for Database Interoperation, Journal of Computational Biology, Vol 2, No 4, 1995.
11. Letovsky, S., Genera: A Specification-Driven Web/Database Gateway Tool, http://gdbdoc.gdb.org/letovsky/wgen.html.
12. Markowitz, V.M., Chen, I.A., and Kosky, A., Exploring Heterogeneous Molecular Biology Databases in the Context of the Object-Protocol Model. *Theoretical and Computational Genome Research*, (S. Suhai, ed.), Plenum. In press. See also Chen, I.A., Kosky, A., Markowitz, V.M., and Szeto, E., OPM*QS: The Object-Protocol Model Multidatabase Query System, Technical Report LBL-38181, 1995, http://gizmo.lbl.gov/opm.html.
13. Markowitz, V.M., and Ritter, O., Characterizing Heterogeneous Molecular Biology Database Systems, *Journal of Computational Biology*, Vol 2, No 4, 1995.
14. Meeting on Interconnection of Molecular Biology Databases (MIMBD): http://www.sri.ai.com/people/pkarp/mimbd.html.
15. Mouse Genome Database 3.1, The Jackson Laboratory, February 1996; http://www.informatics.jax.org/mgd.html.
16. *The Object Database Standard: ODMG-93*, Cattell, R. G. G. (ed), Morgan Kaufmann, 1994.
17. Programmer's Reference. National Center for Biotechnology Information, Bethesda, Maryland, November 1991.
18. Shuler, G.D., Epstein, J.A., Ohkawa, H., Kans, J.A. Entrez. In *Methods in Enzymology*, (R. Doolittle, ed.). Academic Press, Inc. In press. See also http://www3.ncbi.nlm.nih.gov/Entrez/.
19. 3DB, the Protein Data Bank, Brookhaven National Laboratory, 1996; http://terminator.pdb.bnl.gov:4148/

Towards a Bacteriorhodopsin-Silicon Neuromorphic Photosensor

C. H. Martin, Z. P. Chen and R. R. Birge
W. M. Keck Center for Molecular Electronics and the Department of Chemistry, Syracuse University, Syracuse NY 13244

Abstract

We describe our efforts towards constructing a hybrid protein-silicon neuromorphic photosensor based on the photo-active protein bacteriohodopsin. This protein displays an differential photosensitivity similar to the response of the receptive field of an X-type retinal ganglion cell. Similar bacteriohodopsin photoelectrode arrays display inherent edge detection and motion enhancement. We discuss challenges associated with constructing and understanding the protein-silicon interface and possible chemical solutions for our experimental device.

1 Introduction:

1.1 Visual Computing With Silicon vs. Advanced Materials

VLSI solid state devices dominate computing technologies in every area, including photodetectors (CCDs and CIDs), amplifiers, and processors. In contrast, nature has evolved very different computing architectures, such as in dense and highly parallel neural structures. Briding the gap are the so-called neuromorphic chips–analog VLSI devices which mimic neurological signal processing such as that in the retina [1]. Although current VLSI technology limits the resolution and signal processing capacities of the present devices, the silicon retinas currently under development may one day serve in prosthetic devices for the blind [1].

Advanced materials technology offers the potential for new and improved neuromorphic chips, such as a conducting polymer and our proposed protein-based artificial retina. For instance, a so-called "plastic retina" utilizes conducting polymer in a photosensor architecture to circumvent the expensive analog VLSI components while providing. The conducting polymer simulates the analog VLSI logic circuits which locally correct for global changes in illimuniation. This materials-based artificial retina offer potentially greater spatial resolution with much lower manufacturing costs.

But natural vision also includes inherent motion detection and edge enhancement, and it is here that biotechnology can provides advanced materials suitable for specifically evolved for computation. Natural biomolecular photodetectors consist of highly efficient photo-active proteins such as the rhodopsins [2,3]. In the primate visual system, biomolecular amplification occurs with G-coupled protein receptors. And one particular protein, bacteriorhodopsin (BR), inherently responds to light with a differential photosensitivity common in edge detection and motion enhancement architectures.

The protein BR is especially suited for technological development because of its inherent signal processing capacity, its photochemical properties, and the wealth of scientific knowledge about its function. In particular, the bR photocycle includes a number of distinct photointermediates which make it a highly efficient photochromic material suitable for device applications of bR. Current bR research applications exploit it for holographic optical memories, 2-photon volumetric optical memory, and spatial light modulators. [7]. The transmembrane proton pump also provides a photo-electrical current, however, which can be used to create a novel protein-based photosensor. We propose the further advancements in materials-based artificial retinas may be realized with thin films of the protein bacteriorhodopsin. [4,5,6]

1.2 The Protein Bacteriorhodopsin

Many researchers seek proteins from microorganisms which live in harsh environments, hoping to take advantage of robustness and stability of these biomaterials. The protein bacteriorhodopsin (BR) is the premiere example of this [7]. Bacteriorhodopsin is the light transducing protein of the ancient, salt-loving bacteria *Halobacterium Salinarium* . This bacteria thrives in marshes where salt concentration is six times that of salt water. When deprived of oxygen necessary for respiration, *Halobacterium Salinarium* calls upon on an ancient mechanism for energy production, switching from respiration to photosynthesis by expressing an abundance of the membrane-bound BR. BR transforms light energy into an electrochemical proton gradient which drives ATP synthesis. Additionally, BR comes in an exceptionably stable trimeric form called the purple membrane (PM). Thus, under the most extreme operating conditions, *Halobacterium Salinarium* produces an exceptionally stable, biomolecular photochemical transducer in order to activate an evolutionary vestige for survival.

Bacteriorhodopsin is the best understood protein of the class the rhodopsins visual pigments [3,7], being one of only a few membrane bound proteins with a known crystal structure [8]. Amazingly, bacteriorhodopsin resembles both animal and invertebrate photoreceptors both structurally and functionally, and yet all three evolved independently. As with all rhodopsins, BR consists of seven transmembrane alpha-helical segments and a functional retinal chromophore, a vitamin A derivative. The BR photocycle, the transmembrane proton pump, provides a photo-electrical

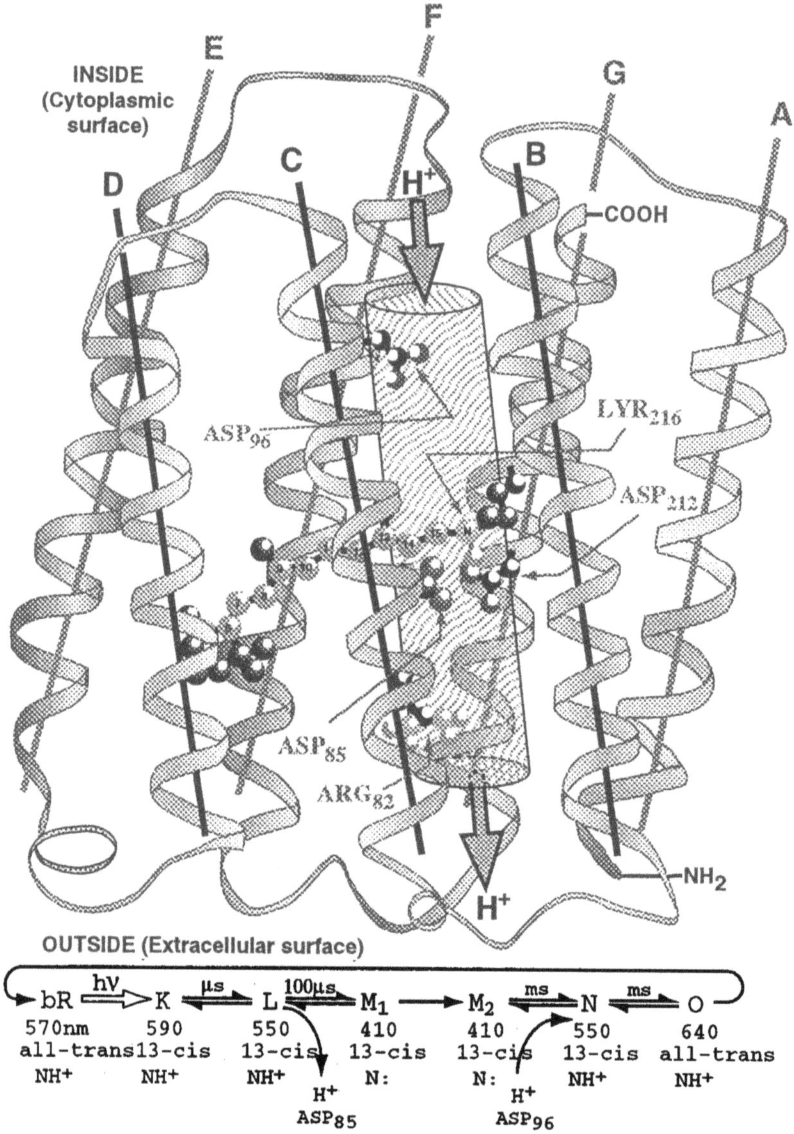

Figure 1: Three dimensional structure and photocycle of the protein bacteriorhopsin. The labels BR_{570} K, L, etc. refer to the spectroscopic intermediates defining the photocyle.

current which can be used to create a protein-based photodetector.

Figure 1 displays the three-dimension structure and the key amino acids involved in the BR photocycle and briefly summarizes the intermediate steps in the photocycle and their lifetimes. Bacteriorhodopsin is the subject of numerous reviews[7,9,10] and current experimental and theoretical research[11,12]. Let us examine the proton motion, key amino acid residues, and protein structural changes through one pass of the photocycle, elucidating the features relevant for device applications. The ground state bR_{570} absorbs green light with an exceptionally high quantum yield (0.65), a desirable property for exploiting this photo-active protein. (Ground state bR_{570} also has an extremely high two-photon absorbtivity and non-linear optical polarizability which distinguishes it as an ideal material in several areas of optical processing[7]) The photoexcited retinal rapidly isomerizes (within 2 ps) to the K form, which can only be trapped at liquid nitrogen temperatures. The fast ($bR_{570} \leftrightarrow K$) interconversion formed the basis of early, cryogenic switches based on BR thin films[7]. The K intermediate thermally relaxes to L, and then, during the $L \rightarrow M_1$ transformation retinal loses its Schiff base proton to Asp85. $M1 \rightarrow M2$ involves an irreversible structural change involving small but significant rearrangements of the alpha-helices. The M forms may be converted back to bR_{570} with blue light – a process important for using BR as holographic recording medium[7] and in a proposed BR-based photosensor (see below)[4]. In the $M_2 \rightarrow N$ interconversion, Asp96 reprotonates retinal. Finally $N \leftrightarrow O \leftrightarrow bR_{570}$ while Asp96 uptakes a new proton from solution. There is also a branched photocycle, $O \leftrightarrow P \leftrightarrow Q$, exploited in BR based volumetric optical memories[7].

The BR photocycle depends on the pH, ionic strength, and detailed amino acid sequence of BR. For example, the mutation D96N dramatically increases the lifetime M state because there is no acidic residue to reprotonate retinal during $M \leftrightarrow N$, thus delaying the second half of the photocycle[7]. Dried BR films yield a smaller photocurrent than wet films because the lower solution proton concentration. The photocycle also may be chemically manipulated by reconsituting BR with a variety of retinal analogs and chemical additives. Below we find that large organic cations can substitute for troublesome BR-bound calcium ions[13].

1.3 Retinal Preprocessing and Neuromorphic Chips

The photocurrent response of BR displays a differential sensitivity common to the X-cell ganglion receptive fields in the primate visual system. Let us first review the X-cell architecture and then compare signal processing features of the primate retina and BR photodetectors.

In contrast to the function of typical solid state photo-detectors, such

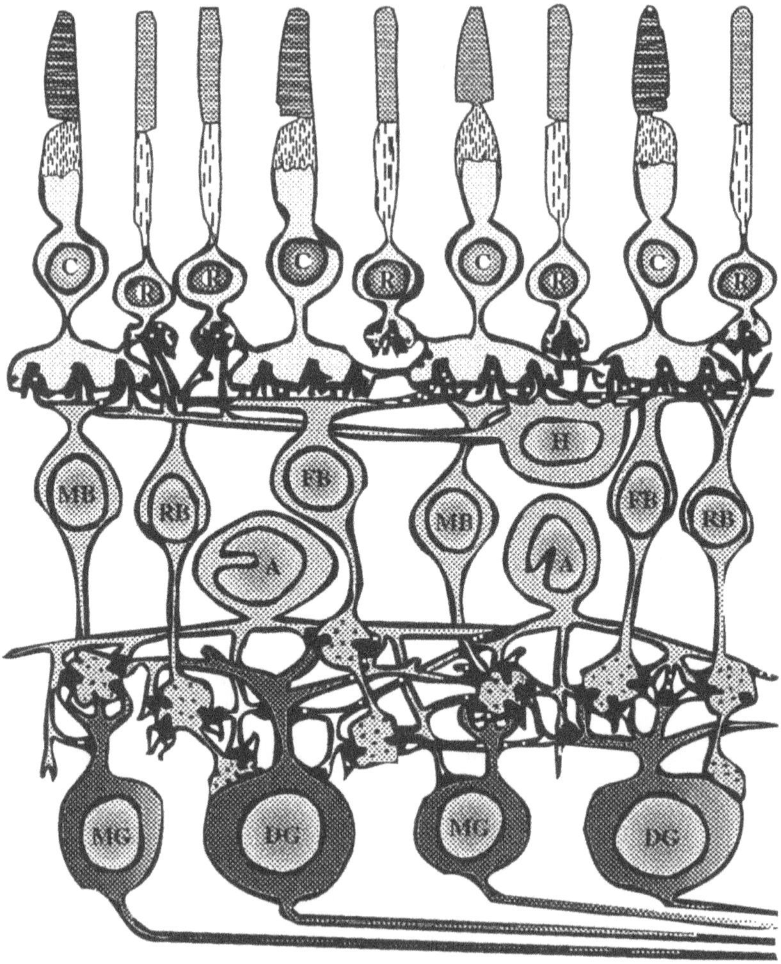

Figure 2: Schematic of the neural components of the primate retina. Depicted are the (R) Rods, (C) Cones, (H) Horizontal, (A) Amacrine, and (MD), (DG) Ganglion cells. Reproduced from Dowling and Boycott.

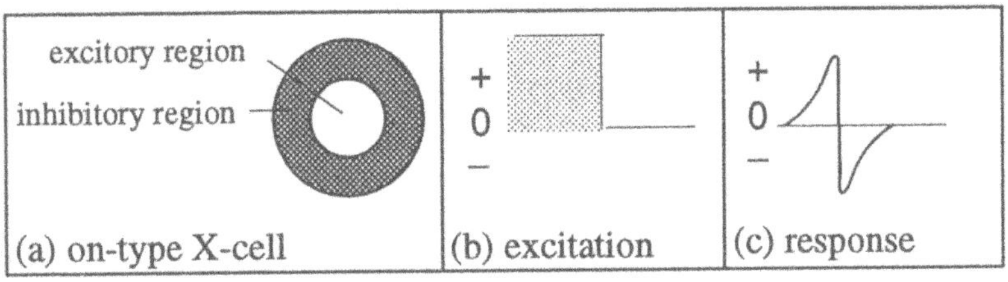

Figure 3: The receptive field and photoresponse of an X-type retinal ganglion cell

as CCD and CID cameras, the vertebrate eye performs edge and motion detection and local contrast control–a result the parallel architecture of retina and the visual processing centers of the brain [14,6]. (In fact, our eyes do not respond to a static image, as evidenced from experiments which project a static image onto the eye, compensating for the continuous and subconscious eye motion.) Here we consider only on the retina, in which a considerable amount of retinal preprocessing takes place. Figure 2 presents the neural components of the primate retina. When light reaches the rod (R) and cone (C) cells, they transmit an electrochemical signal to the overlaying network of Horizontal (H) and Amacrine (A) cells which in turn connect to the neural Ganglion cells (MG, DG) of the optic nerve. This parallel processing network provides initial edge enhancement and motion detection, lumped together as "differential responsivity." The retina also accommodates large scale changes in brightness by with local adjustments to the total contrast (local contrast control) Typical solid state detectors require additional edge and motion enhancement systems and function over a much smaller intensity range [1,15].

The most basic retinal differential responsivity arises in the so-called X-cell receptive field of a single ganglion cell [14]. A receptive field corresponds to the spatial area of the retina which excites that neural cell. [Note that receptive fields overlap extensively, adding an additional layer of parallel processing, however, we consider only one receptive field here] Two types of X-cells exist, on and off, which respond to changes in brightness and darkness, respectively. The receptive field of an on X-cell consists of an circular excitatory region surrounded by a disc-shaped inhibitory region (see Figure 3(a)). When illuminated, the excitatory re-

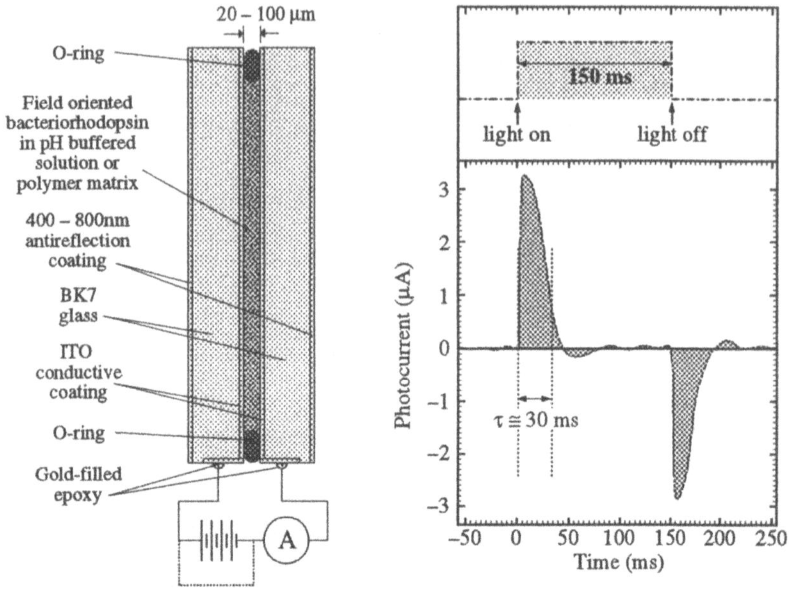

Figure 4: Bacteriorhopdopsin photoelectrode and its photocurrent response

gions produce a positive signal, whereas the inhibitory regions responds negatively. If the entire receptive field is stimulated equally no signal results. When presented with an edge, as in Figure 3(b), the X-cell responds as in Figure 3(c), enhancing the edge through the zero-crossing signal. Hence an X-cell enhances objects passing through its receptive field.

A number of groups have constructed "artificial retinas" which mimic the various image processing features of the retina[1]. By far the most active research occurs in the neuromorphic analog VLSI chips, which utilize traditional semiconductor technologies to implement appropriate parallel signal processing archetectures. Work with organic and biological materials remains comparatively less developed[4,5,15]. The photocycle of BR, however, provides inherent differential responsivity, therefore neuromorphic architectures employing BR films should offer improvements in both resolution and cost over their silicon competitors.

1.4 Earlier Bacteriorhodopsin-based Photosensors

Takei *et. al.* constructed a Bacteriorhodopsin photo-electrode (See Figure 4) with a photo-response that resembles the response of a single X-cell receptive field[4]. They electrodeposited a thin BR-polymer onto a transparent, conducting SnO_2 electrode in order to orient the BR and attach it firmly to the anode. The BR film is dried at high (about 80%) relative humidity to prevent cracking and sandwiched between a second electrodes. Figure 4 depicts this electrode and its photcurrent response . When illuminated with a short laser pulse (150 ms), the BR films yields the differential photocurrent which rises in about 2 ms and with a width of 30 ms. Discontinuing the pulse produces a reverse photocurrent of the similar shape and magnitude. The differential current response apparently arises from proton pump, although the exact details remain unresolved[6]. Never-the-less, the thin BR films respond like the receptive field of a single X-cell, thus motivating the construction of more sophisticated imaging systems based on BR. For example, Lewis *et. al.* propose to recreate the physical architecture of larger receptive fields using BR films oriented to respond in an exhibitory of inhibitory fashion.

A successful BR-based motion sensor has been constructed by Miyaska *et. al.* [5,17]. Instead of creating a dried BR film, as above, they suspended 10 layers of BR Langmuir Blodgett films on top of the $8X8$ array of ITO pixels printed a glass substrate. (Each pixel connects by wire to a separate, external video amplifier). To close the BR-electrode circuit, a layer of aqueous electrolyte gel (1 M KCL, pH 7 to 8) was added on top of the LB films, and a common Au counter electrode was placed on top. The success of the device depends on the use an electrolyte gel between the BR films and the counter electrode, as the wet electrode responds an order-of-magnitude better than dried BR film electrodes. The sensor does not respond to a static image unless the incident light is modulated at a frequency between 20 and 50 Hz. Additonally, it responds to mobile objects, as expected.

The BR photocurrent in these devices, however, remains puzzling [5,17,16,18]. The sensor above employs randomly oriented LB BR films and yet responds in only one direction (the response is said to be rectified). Koyama *et. al.* explain the rectified photocurrent by assuming that the photocurrent results from the voltage difference across the membrane.

Robertson and Lukashev, however, question this model and instead offers that the BR transient photocurrent results from local pH changes at the BR-ITO interface[18]. They prepared wet BR and mutant D96N BR films of two different thicknesses and either random or specific orientation. First, it is found that the highly oriented wild type BR films produce the same photocurrent response as non-oriented films of D96N BR. Since the D96N mutant lack the proton uptake group (see above),

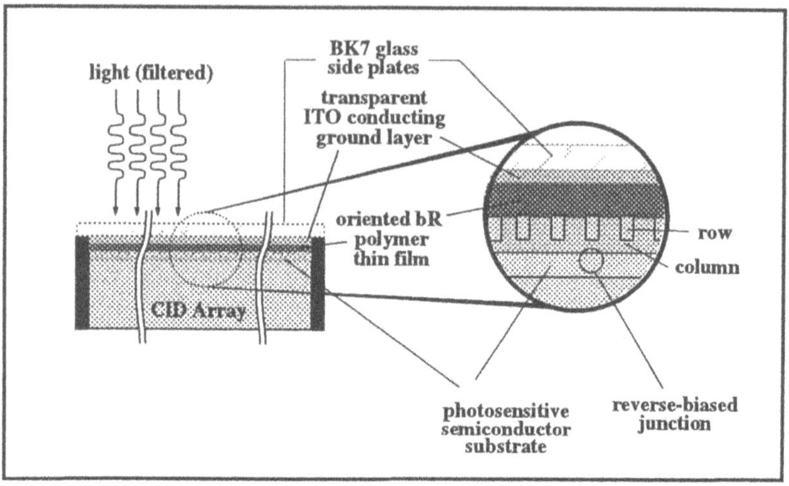

Figure 5: Proposed hybrid protein-semiconductor neuromorphic photosensor

the D96N BR-ITO only experiences the local pH changes associated with proton uptake. Second, the photocurrent D96N BR films shows no volume dependence. Thus, the photocurrent response appears to be solely a surface effect and not associated with the voltage across the membrane. In light of this recent suggestion by Lukashev, we are currently investigating the photocurrent repsonse of a simple BR-silicon interface in an attempt to distinguish between the two possible mechanisms of the BR photoelectric reponse.

1.5 Towards a BR-Silicon Photodetector

Bacteriorhodopsin is the only known material which exhibits differential photoresponsivity. Combined with its high stability, inexpensive and easy production, large quantum yield, etc., it serves as an ideal biocomputing material. The BR-based motion sensor of Miyaska and coworkers is a step in the right direction. In order to compete with the the neuromorphic VLSI devices, however, one requires a higher pixel resolution and integrated silicon architectures (in order to perform additional signal processing).

Our approach to developing a high resolution BR motion sensor is to utilize the on-chip circuitry of a charge injection device (CID) to monitor the photocurrent response of a BR film[6]. The CID provides a high resolution detection silicon grid and the off-the-shelf CID camera provides all of the necessary video amplification circuity– a great simplification for us. We wish to circumvent the substrate photodetector and instead exploit the signal processing circuitry of the CID array (and camera) to create a high-resolution hybrid BR-silicon photosensor. Figure 5 depicts such a device. Future devices may employ a different semiconductor archectecture as the CID is simply the most convenient device to begin research with.

In order to understand how the CID array can detect the BR photocurrent, lets us review the basic CID operation[19,20]. The CID consists of a low band gap semiconductor substrate, the photodetector, coated with thin, transparent polysilicon columns and rows. Thus, the CID is an array of MOS capcacitors. The CID circuitry monitors the photoinduced charge, or electron-hole pairs, in the semiconductor. Before readout, charge transfers to the columns because the column voltage is maintained below the Fermi level of substrate but twice that of the row voltage. Plus the columns are reversed biased with respect to the substrate so they only collect photoinduced (or thermally induced) charge. Readout occurs in two steps. First, the column voltage is brought to zero, thus transferring all stored charge into the rows. The CID circuitry measures the differential current in each row, which is proportional to the stored, photoinduced charge. Second, the row voltages are made zero, thus injecting all stored charge back into the substrate (hence the name Charge Injection Device)

A thin BR-polymer film lies directly on top of the CID detection grid, blocking all light to the CID substrate but providing an BR-silicon interface on which to monitor the BR transient photocurrent. Upon illumination, the BR photocycle transports protons to the surface of the BR-CID, thus changing the surface potential of the gate and driving the MOS junction further into the accumlation region. Thus, the change in surface potential may draw more carries out of the intrinisic semiconductor region below the MOS junction and thus induce charge flow into the MOS capacitor (without generating electron-hole pairs).

The above device faces several other challenges as well. First, the BR film must have a very high optical density and quality in order to completely completely block out the CID photodetector substrate and yet still yield an appreciable photocurrent response at the surface of the CID-BR interface. Second, the CID chips employed lack the standard passivation layer which protects the silicon from free floating ions. Unfortuneately BR-bound Calcium ions seem to poison the CID. To alleviate this problem, our group has synthesized large organic bolaform cations in order replace the detremental Calcium ions[13]. Work is in progress testing the bolaform regenerated BR films in the CID-BR detector. Third, while monolayer wet BR films produce the greatest photocurrent response, a thick wet gel will exhibit more crosstalk between pixels–another consequence of free floating ions. Finally, if the BR photocurrent arises from surface pH changes, the H+ ions may electrochemically degrade the CID detection grid, as in some pH sensitive CHEMFETs[21]. Research continues in our lab towards solving all of these problems.

2 Conclusions

The unique photoelectric properties of the protein bacteriorhodopsin (BR) may be exploited to perform real-time visual processing with a protein-silicon hybrid photodetector. In comparisons to standard analog VLSI neuromorphic chips, a BR-based architecture offers a less expensive, simpler design with higher resolution. Research in this area remains in the initial stages, with many challenges to overcome. Most notably, the protein-silicon interface suffers from crosstalk, ion poisoning and requires extremely high sensitivity using the proposed BR-CID design. The ability to manipulate BR both chemically and genetically, however, opens the door to research a wide range of solutions.

Acknowledgments

This research was supported in part by a grant from the National Institutes of Health (grant number GM-34548). CHM acknowledges the National Science Foundation for a postdoctoral fellowship in Chemistry (grant number CHE 9504697).

References

1. Koch, C., and B. Mathur (1996) Neuromorphic Vision Chips *IEEE Spectrum (special issue: Towards and Artifical Eye)* **May** 38-44
2. Spudich, J. L. (1994) Protein-Potein Interaction Converts a Proton Pump into a Sensory Receptor *Cell* **79** 747-750
3. Skulachev, P. V. (1996) Interrelations of Bioenergetic and Sensory Functions of the Retinal Proteins *Quart. Rev. Biophys.* **26** 177-199
4. Takei, H., A. Lewis, Z. Chen, and I. Nebenzahl (1991) Implementing Receprtive Fields with Excitatory and Inhibitory Optoelectrical Response of Bacteriorhodopsin Films *Applied Optics* **30** 500-508
5. Miyaska, T., K. Koyama, and I. Itoh (1992) Quantum Conversion and Image Detection by a Bacteriorhodopsin-Based Artificial Photoreceptor *Science* **255** 342-344
6. Chen, Z., and R. R. Birge (1993) Protein Based Artificial Retinas *TIBTECH* **11** 292-300
7. R. R. Birge (1990) Photophysics and Molecular Electronic Applications of the Rhodopsins *Ann. Rev. Phys. Chem.* **41** 683-733
8. Henderson, R. and J. M. Baldwin and T. A. Ceska and F. Zemlin and E. Beckmann and K. H. Downing (1990) Model for the

Struture of Bacteriorhodopsin Based On High-Resolution Electron Cryo-micropscopy *J. Mol. Biol.* **213** 899-929

9. Lanyi, J. K. (1992) Proton Translocation and Energy Coupling in the Bacteriorhodopsin Photocycle *J. Bioeng. Biomem.* **24** 169-179
10. Ebry, T. G. (1993) Light Energy Transduction in Bacteriorhodopsin *in Thermodynamics of Membrane Receptors and Channels* Ed. M. B. Jackson CRC Press (Boca Raton)
11. Misra, S., C. H. Martin and T. G. Ebry (1996) *FEBS Lett.* (Manuscript Submitted)
12. Xu, D., C. H. Martin and K. Schulten (1996) Molecular Dynamics Study of Early Picosecond Events in the Bacteriorhodopsin Photocycle: Dielectric Response, Vibrational Cooling and the J, K Intermediate *Biophysical J.* **70**
13. Tan, E. H. L., D. S. K. Govender, R. R. Birge (1996) Large Organic Cations Can Replace Mg^{2+} and Ca^{2+} in Bacteriorhodopsin and Maintain Proton Pumping Ability *J. Am. Chem. Soc.* **110** 2752-2753
14. Dowling, J. E, and B. B. Boycott (1996) *Proc. Roy. Soc. (lond) Ser. B* 166 80
15. Heager, A. J., D. J. Heager, J. Langan, and Y. Yang (1995) *Science* **270** 1642-1645
16. Koyama, K. N. Yamaguchi, and T. Miyaska (1994) Anitobody-Medi ated Bacteriorhdopsin Orientation for Molecular Device Architectures *Scienc e* **265** 762-765
17. Miyaska, T., and Koyama K. (1992) Rectified Photocurrents from Purple Membran Langmuir-Blodgett Films at the Electrode-Electrolyte Interface *Thin Solid Films* **210/211** 146-149
18. Robertson, B., and E. P. Lukashev (1995) Rapid PH Change due to Bacteriorhodopsin Measured with a Tin-Oxide Electrode *Biophys. J.* **68** 1507-1517
19. Michon, G. J. and H. K. Burke (1980) CID Image Sensing *in Charge Coupled Devices* Ed. D. F. Barbe, Springer-Verlag (Berlin)
20. Lunden, J. W., G. J. Michon, and J. Carbone VLSI Solid State Sensors for ENG Camera *Optoelectronic Systems Operation Notes* General Electric Co. (Syracuse, NY)
21. Janata, J. (1985) Chemically Sensitive Field Effect Transistors *Solid State Chemical Sensors* Ed. J. Janata and R. J. Huber Academic Press (Orlando)

AN APPROACH TO DETECTION OF PROTEIN STRUCTURAL MOTIFS USING AN ENCODING SCHEME OF BACKBONE CONFORMATIONS

H. MATSUDA, F. TANIGUCHI, A. HASHIMOTO
Department of Informatics and Mathematical Science,
Graduate School of Engineering Science,
Osaka University,
1-3 Machikaneyama, Toyonaka, Osaka, 560 Japan
e-mail: {matsuda, fumihiro, hasimoto}@ics.es.osaka-u.ac.jp

This paper presents an approach to detection of protein structural motifs. In our approach, first all protein backbone conformations are converted into character strings using an encoding scheme. Then we use the Smith-Waterman local alignment algorithm to detect common structural motifs. By comparing results with the PROSITE regular expression patterns, our method can detect several motifs which the PROSITE patterns fail to detect.

1 Introduction

The amount of protein sequence data has been rapidly increasing due to the progress of DNA sequencing technology. Using those sequence data, a number of methods for investigating the evolutionary process of taxa (biological entities such as genes, proteins, individuals, populations, species, or higher taxonomic units) have been proposed. For example, construction of phylogenetic trees from the sequence data of various organisms has been widely used to clarify the evolutionary histories of those organisms[1,2].

Previous studies on molecular evolution suggested that the evolutionary process of proteins is closely related to their structure and function. For example, when some mutations have a higher chance of causing deleterious effects on the function of the protein than other mutations, the majority of the former mutations will be eliminated from the population by purifying selection. The result will be a reduction in the rate of those mutations compared to that of other mutations.

Recent studies[3,4] revealed that many protein domains adopt the same fold structures even if they have statistically insignificant sequence similarity. In order to understand the relationship among the sequence, structure and function of proteins, it is necessary to infer how the relationship has been emerged in evolutionary process.

In this paper, we focus on locally common substructures, called structural motifs, among related proteins. These motifs are recognized as functionally important sites because they are well conserved in a wide variety of distantly related proteins. We consider those motifs play a role of *building blocks* to establish a variety of functions of proteins.

In order to extract the motifs from proteins, we developed a method for exploring similar protein structure using an encoding scheme of backbone conformations of proteins[5]. In our method, first describe a protein structure as a sequence of vectors obtained by connecting the C_α atoms of consecutive amino acids in the protein, then quantizing each vector to twenty representative by fitting it into one of the normal vectors of the twenty faces in an icosahedron, so that a protein structure is represented by a string of twenty characters. Because the set is limited to twenty representatives, our notation makes it possible to utilize available string matching algorithms.

Previous researches for encoding protein structures into character strings are based on two-dimensional square lattice with two types (nonpolar and other) of amino acids[6], backbone dihedral angles[7,8] or based on the root mean square distance of every seven amino acid segment[9]. Our work relates to researches based on inter-C_α torsion angles[10] and it is an extension of the chain coding scheme in image processing[11,12]. Our method is a general method which is not restricted to describe protein structures but applicable to arbitrary line-drawing objects in three-dimensional space.

The later sections describe the detail of our encoding scheme and its application to detecting protein structural motifs.

2 Encoding scheme

We used three-dimension coordinate data of C_α atoms taken from the Protein Data Bank (hereafter, PDB) Release 72.0.

The method to encode a protein structure into a string is described below. Let n be the number of C_α atoms in a protein. Let p_{i-2}, p_{i-1}, p_i and p_{i+1} $(3 \leq i \leq n-1)$ be successive four C_α atoms in the protein. Place p_{i-2}, p_{i-1} and p_i in the Cartesian coordinates as follows (see Figure 1):

- p_i to the origin of the coordinates,
- p_{i-1} on the z-axis,
- p_{i-2} on the zx-plane.

Here a position vector of p_{i+1} is determined on this coordinates. Then place an icosahedron in the Cartesian coordinates so that the gravity center of the icosahedron is set to the origin of the coordinates. Label each normal vector of twenty faces of the icosahedron twenty letters of the English alphabet as

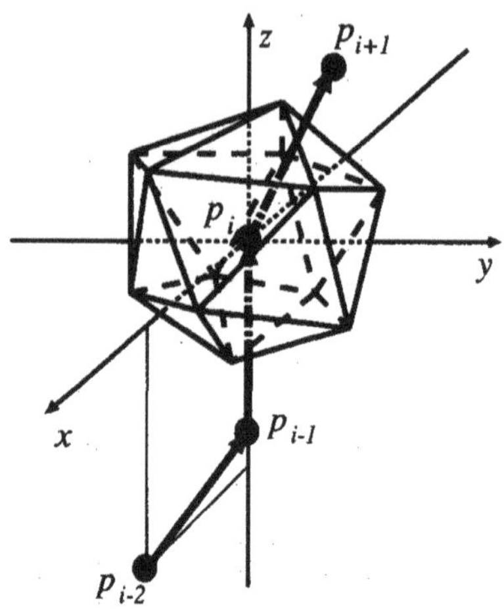

Figure 1: The placement of a protein backbone chain with an icosahedron in the Cartesian coordinates.

shown in Figure 2. `B`, `J`, `O`, `U`, `X` and `Z` are omitted from the alphabet so that it agrees with the one letter code of amino acids.

Using the icosahedron, the position vector of p_{i+1} is quantized by the nearest normal vector in the coordinates, then the position of p_{i+1} is represented by the letter of the normal vector. By this notation, every backbone chain of protein can be denoted to a string of twenty letters.

As a practical matter, there exists ambiguousness for the placement of an icosahedron in the coordinates. We set it so that every amino acid in α-helices is encoded into the same letter (`W` in Figure 2). From the analogy to an encoding method of diagrams in image processing[11,12], we named our notation as *three-dimensional chain code* (hereafter, 3D chain code). Same as the original chain code, the 3D chain code is independent on its position, moving and rotation in any coordinates. Thus the comparison of protein backbone structures can be carried out by some string matching algorithm. Moreover, the method is easily extended to pairwise and multiple alignment.

In the 3D chain code, the letters corresponding to the first two amino acids p_1 and p_2 and the last amino acid p_n cannot be determined since the placements of these points in the coordinates are not defined. However the letter corresponding to p_2 can be decided by restricting the placement of p_1, p_2 and p_3 on the zx-plane (p_1 on the z-axis, p_2 at the origin and p_3 on the zx-plane). Thus the length of the 3D chain code in a protein becomes $m - 2$

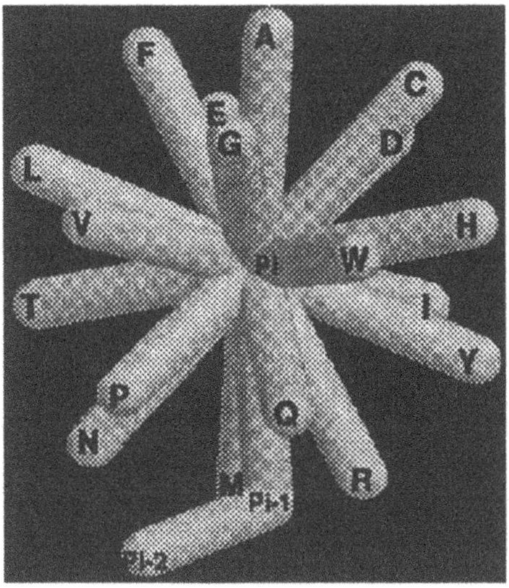

Figure 2: The 3D chain code with the normal vectors of an icosahedron.

where m is the number of amino acids in the protein.

Figure 3 shows the distribution of 3D chain code letters in PDB Release 72.0. As described above, the letter W corresponds to α-helix. The number of occurrences of W amounts to 34.7% of all occurrences. The letters E and D correspond to β-strand. These amount to 17.6% and 12.0%, respectively.

3 Application to searching structural motifs

The PROSITE database[13] contains a large number of entries on motifs. They are mainly classified by using regular expressions which accept amino acid sequence patterns specific to motifs. However even if homology between two amino acid sequences is not so high (such as around 30% of amino acid identities), their tertiary structures are sometimes very similar (within 2.0 Å in the root mean square distance by best-fit superposition method[14]). In this case, it is difficult to detect the candidates of motifs by an analysis only based on sequence similarity. Actually in some case the regular expressions of PROSITE cannot detect motifs.

To cope with this problem, we applied our encoding scheme to detection of motifs. We used the `SSEARCH` and `LALIGN` programs in the version 2.0 of the `FASTA` program package[16]. These programs are based on the Smith-Waterman

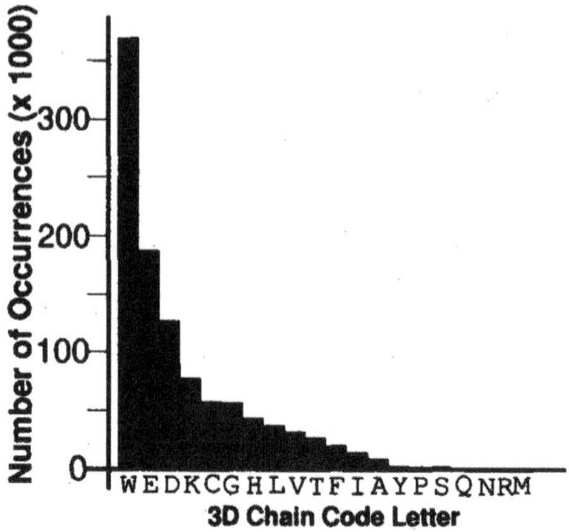

Figure 3: The distribution of 3D chain code letters in PDB Release 72.0

local alignment algorithm[15] and thus suitable for finding local common subsequences.

A similarity score s_{ij} between any two letters c_i and c_j of the 3D chain code $(1 \leq i, j \leq 20)$ is calculated as:

$$s_{ij} = 10 \cos \theta_{ij}$$

where θ_{ij} denotes the angle between two normal vectors corresponding to the 3D chain code letters c_i and c_j (see Figure 2). The penalties for an opening gap and an extension gap are set to -30 and -2, respectively. The opening gap penalty is much higher than the default value (-12) since we intend to find longer common subsequences.

3.1 Helix-turn-helix

Helix-turn-helix motif is specific to the DNA-binding domain of many bacterial transcription regulation proteins. In the PROSITE database, this motif is classified into subfamilies based on sequence similarities. To extract of a pattern for the motif in the 3D chain code, we picked up two regulation proteins; *E. coli* lactose operon repressor LacI (PDB id 1lccA) and *E. coli* catabolite gene activator (PDB id 3gapA). Then we performed the `LALIGN` (local alignment) program with the 3D chain code scoring matrix to find common sequence patterns between them. As the result, we obtained very similar backbone confor-

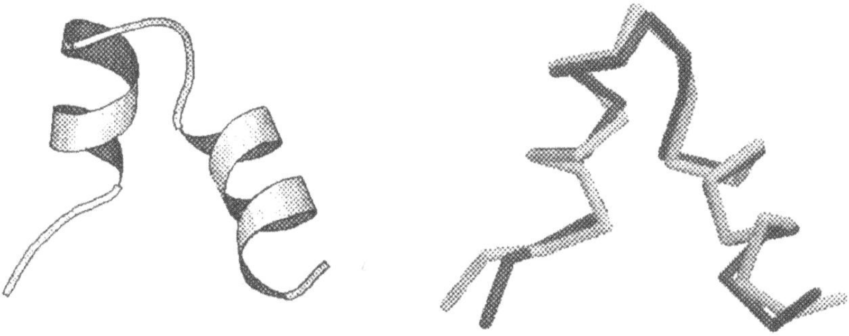

(a) Ribbon model of the extracted helix-turn-helix domain from 3gapA (drawn by MOLSCRIPT[17]).

(b) Superposition of the two extracted domains of 3gapA (dark) and 1lccA (light).

Figure 4: Helix-turn-helix DNA-binding domains extracted from *E. coli* lactose repressor (PDB id 1lccA) and *E. coli* catabolite gene activator (PDB id 3gapA).

mations and confirmed that these correspond to helix-turn-helix DNA-binding domains.

The extracted chain-coded conformations and amino acid sequences of the helix-turn-helix domains are as follows:

```
      3D chain code         Amino acid
1lccA TWWWWWWWKCLKWWWWWWG LYDVAEYAGVSYQTVSRVV
3gapA KWWWWWWGKCFKWWWWWWW RQEIGQIVGCSRETVGRIL
```

In this case, although the identity of amino acids is very low ($5/19 = 26.3\%$), the superposition of these two domains is well overlapped (see Figure 4) and the root mean square distance between them is 0.57 Å.

Then we executed the SSEARCH similarity search program with the 3D chain code scoring matrix between the domain of 1lccA and all chain-coded conformations of PDB Release 72.0. Figure 5 shows the result of SSEARCH sorted by the descending order of S-W score (the similarity score of Smith-Waterman local alignment). The first two proteins are helix-turn-helix DNA-binding domains of other bacterial transcription regulation proteins (1lcdA: another PDB entry for *E. coli* lactose operon repressor, 1trt: *E. coli* tetracycline repressor). The latter two lines are fragments of repressor proteins of bacteriophages (1pra: bacteriophage 434, 4cro: bacteriophage lambda). According to the description of the SWISS-PROT entries (Accession numbers P16117 and P03040, respec-

PDBid	S-W score	3D Chain Code	RMSD	Amino Acid	PROSITE pattern
1lcdA	91	TWWWWWWWKCFKWWWWWWG	0.33	LYDVAEYAGVSYQTVSRVV	HTH_LACI
1trt	88	KWWWWWWWKCFKWWWWWGG	0.73	TTRKLAQKLGIEQPTLYWH	HTH_TETR
1pra	86	TWWWWWWWKCLKWWWWWWW	0.41	QAELAQKVGTTQQSIEQLE	no
4croA	86	TWWWWWWWKCLKWWWWWWW	0.58	GQTKTAKDLGVYQSAINKA	no

Figure 5: Similarity search result for helix-turn-helix DNA-binding domains between *E. coli* lactose repressor (PDB id 1lccA) and PDB using 3D chain coding scheme.

tively), these are also helix-turn-helix DNA-binding domains. But there do not exist motif patterns on these domains in the PROSITE database.

3.2 EF-hand

Many calcium-binding proteins belong to the same evolutionary family and share a type of calcium-binding domain known as the EF-hand. We did the same approach to the detection of helix-turn-helix motifs. First we picked up two proteins known to have the EF-hand calcium-binding domains; *Paramecium tetraurelia* calmodulin (PDB id 1clm) and *Triakis semifasciata* (leopard shark) parvalbumin alpha (PDB id 5pal), then we extracted chain-coded backbone conformations of EF-hand domains by using **LALIGN**. Second similarity search between one of these conformation (the domain of 1clm) and all entries of PDB 72.0.

The extracted chain-coded conformations and amino acid sequences of the EF-hand domains are as follows:

```
        3D chain code                            Amino acid
1clm WWWWWWWWWWWDWKHKCEETWWWWWWWWWW EELIEAFKVFDRDGNGLISAAELRHVMTNL
5pal WWWWWWWWWWHDWKIKAKETWWWWWHWWWW AQVKEVFEILDKDQSGFIEEEELKGVLKGF
```

In this case, the identity of amino acids is also relatively low ($9/30 = 30.0\%$) but the superposition of these two domains is well overlapped (see Figure 6) and the root mean square distance of these domains is 1.72 Å.

Figure 7 shows the result of **SSEARCH**. Although the difference among each S-W score is small, the values of RMSD (the root mean square distance by best superposition) ranges from 0.41 to 1.07 which seems to be due to quantization error by fitting to the normal vectors of the icosahedron. However all domains detected by this search have the pattern of the EF-hand motif described by the regular expression **D-x-[DNS]-{ILVFYW}-[DENSTG]-[DNQGHRK]-{GP}--[LIVMC]-[DENQSTAGC]-x(2)-[DE]-[LIVMFYW]** in the PROSITE database.

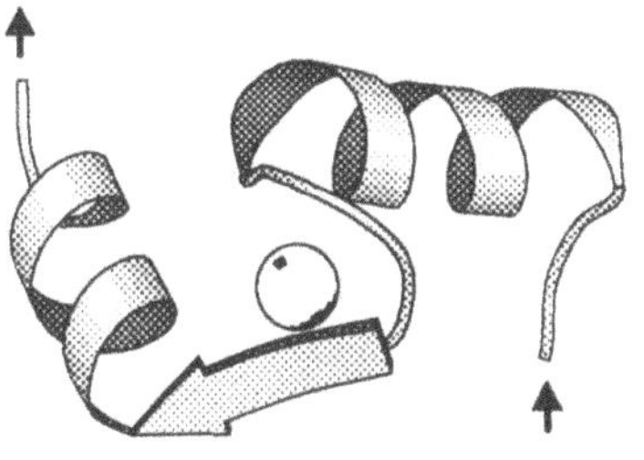

(a) Ribbon model of the extracted EF-hand domain of 1clm (drawn by MOLSCRIPT).

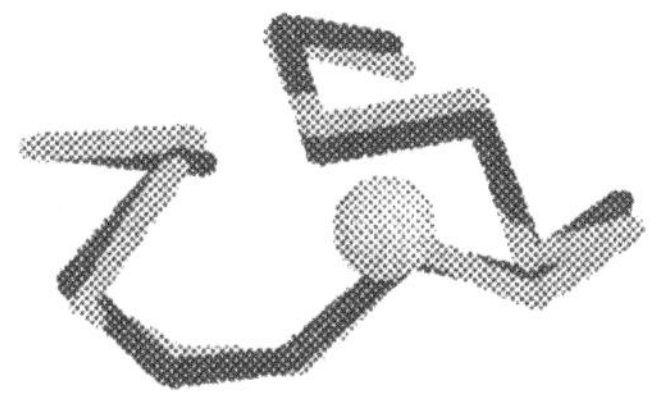

(b) Superposition of the two extracted domains of 1clm (dark) and 5pal (light).

Figure 6: EF-hand calcium-binding domains extracted from *P. tetraurelia* calmodulin (PDB id 1clm) and *Triakis semifasciata* (leopard shark) parvalbumin alpha (PDB id 5pal).

3.3 Greek key

The beta and gamma crystallins (the dominant structural components of the eye lens) form a family of related proteins. Structurally, they consist of two similar domains which are each composed of two similar motifs with the two domains connected by a short connecting peptide. Each motif, which is about forty amino acid residues long, is folded in a distinctive 'Greek key' pattern. The key structure is composed of a β-sheet where two anti-parallel β-strands are connected.

We picked up a gamma-b crystallin (PDB id 4gcr) and a beta crystallin b2 (PDB id 1blbB) from *Bos taurus* (calf) eye lens and extracted Greek Key domains using `LALIGN` as follows:

	3D chain code	Amino acid
4gcr	DEEEKGLWTCGVDEED	ITFYEDRGFQGHCYEC
1blbB	DEEEKGLGTDVWDDEE	IIIFEQENFQGHSHEL

As mentioned in Section 2, the 3D chain code letter for β-strand does not converge to one letter as α-helix but usually takes either `E` or `D`. Thus the identity of chain code in Greek Key decreases compared to those of previous examples. However the chain code identity is still larger than the amino acid identity. For example in the above case, the identity of the chain code is $10/16 = 62.5\%$ whereas that of amino acids is $7/16 = 43.8\%$. The superposition of these two domains is as shown in Figure 8 and the root mean square distance of these domains is 0.58 Å.

PDBid	S-W score	3D Chain Code	RMSD
1top	129	WWWWWWWWWWWWDWKHKCEETWWWWWWWWWW	0.61
1ctr	129	WWWWWWWWWWWWDWKHKCEETWWWWWWWWWW	0.65
3cln	127	WWWWWWWWWWWWDWKHKCEDTWWWWWWWWWW	0.26
1osa	127	WWWWWWWWWWWWDWKHKCEEKWWWWWWWWWW	0.64
1cll	127	WWWWWWWWWWWWDWKYKCEETWWWWWWWWWW	0.65
1cdlC	127	WWWWWWWWWWWWDWKHKCEEKWWWWWWWWWW	0.42
2bbmA	126	HWWWWWWWWWWWDWKHKCEEKWWWWWWWWWW	0.89
5tnc	125	WWWWWWWWWWWWDWKYKAEETWWWWWWWWWW	0.68
4cln	125	WWWWWWWWWWWWDWKHKAEEKWWWWWWWWWW	0.66
2scpB	125	WWWWWWWWWWWWDWKYKCEEKWWWWWWWWWW	1.07
1cdlA	125	WWWWWWWWWWWWDWKYKCEEKWWWWWWWWWW	0.41
2sas	125	WWWWWWWWWWWWIWKHKHEETWWWWWWWWWW	0.62
1cdmA	124	WWWWWWWWWWWHDWKHKCEDKWWWWWWWWWW	0.61
1mysB	123	WWWWWWWWWWWHDWKHKCECTWWWWWWWWWW	0.97

PDBid	Amino Acid	PROSITE pattern
1top	EELANCFRIFDKNADGFIDIEELGEILRAT	EF-hand
1ctr	AEFKEAFSLFDKDGDGTITTKELGTVMRSL	EF-hand
3cln	EEIREAFRVFDKDGNGYISAAELRHVMTNL	EF-hand
1osa	EELIEAFKVFDRDGNGLISAAELRHVMTNL	EF-hand
1cll	AEFKEAFSLFDKDGDGTITTKELGTVMRSL	EF-hand
1cdlC	EEIREAFRVFDKDGNGYISAAELRHVMTNL	EF-hand
2bbmA	EEIREAFRVFDKDGNGFISAAELRHVMTNL	EF-hand
5tnc	EELEDCFRIFDKNADGFIDIEELGEILRAT	EF-hand
4cln	AEFKEAFSLFDKDGDGTITTKELGTVMRSL	EF-hand
2scpB	TMAPASFDAIDTNNDGLLSLEEFVIAGSDF	EF-hand
1cdlA	EEIREAFRVFDKDGNGYISAAELRHVMTNL	EF-hand
2sas	NRIPFLFKGMDVSGDGIVDLEEFQNYCKNF	EF-hand
1cdmA	AEFKEAFSLFDKDGDGTITTKELGTVMRSL	EF-hand
1mysB	QDFKEAFTVIDQNRDGIIDKDDLRETFAAM	EF-hand

Figure 7: Similarity search result for EF-hand calcium-binding domains between *P. tetraurelia* calmodulin (PDB id 1clm) and PDB using 3D chain coding scheme.

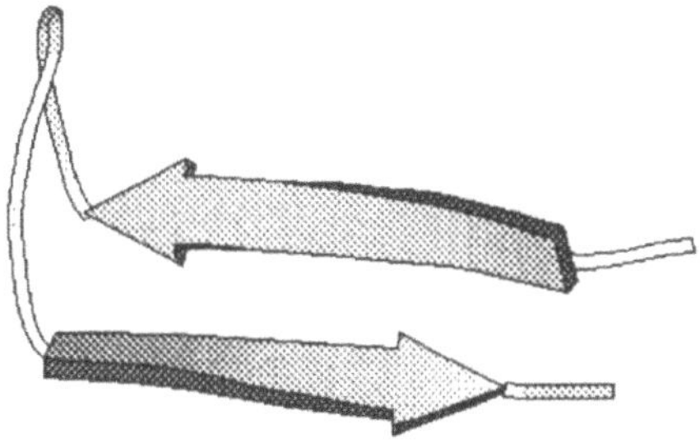

(a) Ribbon model of the extracted Greek key domain of 4gcr (drawn by MOLSCRIPT).

(b) Superposition of the two extracted domains of 4gcr (dark) and 1blbB (light).

Figure 8: Greek key domains extracted from *Bos taurus* gamma-b crystallin (PDB id 4gcr) and *Bos taurus* beta crystallin b2 (PDB id 1blbB).

Figure 9 shows the result of `SSEARCH` (upper 5 lines) and `LALIGN` (lower 4 lines). There are usually four Greek Key motifs in proteins which have this motif. However in a few cases, the PROSITE regular expression pattern for Greek Key (`[LIVMFYWA]-x-{DEHRKSTP}-[FY]-[DEQHKY]-x(3)-[FY]-x-G--x(4)-[LIVMFCST]`) may fail to detect one of four motifs. Thus we tried to detect all four motifs of beta-b2-crystallin in *Bos taurus* lens (PDB id 2bb2) by using `LALIGN` with chain-coded conformations between 4gcr and 2bb2. All motifs including the second one which the PROSITE pattern cannot detect were successfully detected.

4 Analysis of structure evolution

As mentioned in Sect. 3, our encoding scheme can be easily applied to available alignment programs for amino acid sequences by replacing its scoring matrix. Similarly, in principle, it can be applied to available phylogenetic tree construction programs (e.g. our developed system based on the maximum likelihood method [18]). If we construct a tree with our encoding scheme, however, the distances between any two nodes of the tree do not present the evolutionary

PDBid	S-W score	3D Chain Code	RMSD	Amino Acid	PROSITE pattern
1gcs	112	DEEEKGLWTCGGDEED	0.23	ITFYEDRGFQGHCYEC	GreekKey
2gcr	111	DEEEKGLGTCGVEEED	0.39	WMLYEQPNFTGCQYFL	GreekKey
1prr	104	EEDEKGFWTCGLEEED	0.64	ITVFYNEDFQGKQVDL	GreekKey
1prs	101	EEEEEGFWTCGLEEED	0.77	ITVFYNEDFQGKQVDL	GreekKey
1blbC	100	CEDEKGFWLCGGDDEE	0.72	IIIFEQENFQGHSHEL	GreekKey
2bb2-1	108	DEEEKGFWTCGVEEEE	0.27	IIIFEQENFQGHSHEL	GreekKey
2bb2-2	106	DEEEKGLWTCGGEDEE	0.60	WVGYEQANCKGEQFVF	no
2bb2-3	110	DEEEKGLWLCGVEEED	0.33	ITLYENPNFTGKKMEV	GreekKey
2bb2-4	110	DEEEKGLWTCGVEEEE	0.56	WVGYQYPGYRGLQYLL	GreekKey

Figure 9: Similarity search result for Greek Key structure between *Bos taurus* gamma-b crystallin (PDB id 4gcr) and PDB using 3D chain coding scheme.

distances between protein conformations since the change of protein structure highly depends on its function. We will describe structure evolution with our encoding scheme and will analyze frequencies of changes of the code.

5 Conclusion

We have developed a method to detect structural motifs by encoding protein backbone conformations into character strings. The encoding scheme is based on a general encoding scheme for line drawing objects and can give similarity score among each letter of the alphabet so that available string manipulation algorithms can be used for protein structure analysis. By using our method, protein sequences and their tertiary structures can be processed in the same manner except scoring matrices. We hope we will analyze the evolution process of protein structure using our encoding scheme and apply it to reconstruct phylogenetic relationships of protein structures.

Acknowledgement

This work was supported in part by a Grant-in-Aid (08283103) for Scientific Research on Priority Areas from The Ministry of Education, Science, Sports and Culture in Japan.

References

1. M. Nei, *Molecular Evolutionary Genetics* Chap.11 (1987).

2. D.L. Swofford and G.J. Olsen, "Phylogeny Reconstruction," in *Molecular Systematics,* ed. D.M. Hillis and C. Moritz, 411–501 (1990).
3. C. Chothia, "Proteins. One Thousand Families for the Molecular Biologist," *Nature*, **357**, 543–544 (1992).
4. C.A. Orengo, D.T. Jones and J.M.Thornton, "Protein Superfamilies and Domain Superfolds," *Nature*, **372**, 631–634 (1994).
5. H. Matsuda, F. Taniguchi and A. Hashimoto, "A Notation of Amino Acid Conformations for Exploring Similar Protein Structure," *Proc. 1st Pacific Symp. Biocomp.*, 732–733 (1996).
6. K.F. Lau and K.A. Dill, "Theory for Protein Mutability and Biogenesis," *Proc. Natl. Acad. Sci. USA*, **87**, 638–642 (1990).
7. M.J. Rooman, J.-P.A. Kocher and S.J. Wodak, "Prediction of Protein Backbone Conformation based on Seven Structure Assignments: I Influence of Local Interactions," *J. Mol. Biol.*, **221**, 961-979 (1991).
8. R.T. Miller, R.J. Douthart, and A.K. Dunker, "An Alphabet of Amino Acid Conformations in Protein," *Proc. HICSS*, **1**, 689–698 (1993).
9. Y. Matsuo and M. Kanehisa, "An Approach to Systematic Detection of Protein Structure Motifs," *Comp. Appl. Bio. Sci.*, **9**(2), 153–159 (1993).
10. M. Levitt and J. Greer, "Automatic Identification of Secondary Structure in Globular Proteins," *J. Mol. Biol.*, **114**, 181–239 (1977).
11. H. Freeman, "On the Encoding of Arbitrary Geometric Configurations," *IRE Trans. Electronic Computer*, **EC-10**(2), 260–268 (1961).
12. H. Freeman, "Computer Processing of Line-Drawing Images," ACM Comp. Surv., **6**(1), 57–97 (1974).
13. A. Bairoch, P. Bucher and K. Hofmann, "The PROSITE database, its status in 1995," *Nucl. Acids Res.*, **24**(1), 189–196 (1996).
14. W. Kabsch, "A Solution for the Best Rotation to Relate Two Sets of Vectors," *Acta. Cryst.*, **A32**, 922–923 (1976).
15. T.F. Smith and M.F. Waterman, "Identification of common molecular subsequences," *J. Mol. Biol.*, **147**, 195–197 (1981).
16. W.R. Pearson, "Rapid and Sensitive Sequence Comparison with FASTP and FASTA", *Methods in Enzymology*, **183**, 63–98 (1990).
17. P.J. Kraulis, "MOLSCRIPT: A Program to Produce Both Detailed and Schematic Plots of Protein Structuresm," *J. Appl. Cryst.*, **24**, 946–950 (1991).
18. H. Matsuda, "Protein Phylogenetic Inference Using Maximum Likelihood with a Genetic Algorithm," *Proc. 1st Pacific Symp. Biocomp.*, 512–523 (1996).

AN ALGORITHM TO ASSEMBLE PATHWAYS FROM PROCESSES

J. E. MITTENTHAL
Cell and Structural Biology, University of Illinois, 505 S. Goodwin St., Urbana, IL 61801

To understand or to modify a biological pathway, the first step is to determine the patterns of coupling among its processes that are compatible with its input-output relation. Algorithms for this purpose have been devised for metabolic pathways, in which the reactions typically leave the enzymes unmodified. As shown here, one of these algorithms can also assemble molecular networks in which reactions modify proteins, if the proteins are included among the inputs to the reactions. Thus one procedure suffices to assemble pathways for metabolism, cytoplasmic signal transduction, and gene regulation.

1 Introduction

In a molecular pathway or network processes are coupled, with outputs of some processes used as inputs to others. We can discern the coupling and assemble processes into pathways intuitively, for small sets of processes that assemble in a unique way. However, as the number of processes grows, they may form several pathways that can mediate a given input-output relation. Then tools that aid the assembly can be useful. With these tools we can generate an ensemble of alternative pathways, simulate their dynamics, and compare their performance. If knowledge of the real pathway is fragmentary, such an inquiry may point out gaps in our understanding and so may channel further research. If the real pathway is well characterized, study of an ensemble of alternatives can show whether it is an optimum of the evolutionary search (Melendez-Hevia et al., 1994; Mittenthal et al., 1993, 1996). To modify a pathway through bioengineering it is necessary to explore alternatives that more nearly approach a desired performance (Bailey, 1991).

Various algorithms have been used to assemble metabolic reactions into pathways (Seriossis and Bailey, 1988; Happel et al., 1990; Mavrovouniotis et al., 1990, 1992). Typically in metabolism reactions do not modify enzymes, so the enzymes do not appear in the algorithms for constructing pathways. In other networks a process may provide substrates, cofactors, and regulators, as in metabolism, but may also modify proteins. For example, in the signaling net for cytoplasmic signal transduction, reactions modify enzymes and regulatory proteins. Algorithms to synthesize such networks are needed but are not yet available. As illustrated here, the algorithm that Mavrovouniotis et al. (1990) developed for constructing metabolic networks can also be used to construct protein-modifying networks, by including the proteins in the reactions. This algorithm, unlike the others mentioned above, does not depend on stoichiometry, can deal with irreversible reactions, and is complete in that it provides all pathways that meet the constraints.

2 Reactions

The method uses a list of reactions that may participate in the network. The list may include hypothetical reactions, or reactions to be excluded from a particular assembly. A reaction is a unidirectional transformation; the forward and reverse directions of a bidirectional transformation are treated as two reactions. The statement of the reaction includes the reactants and their stoichiometry, the enzymes that catalyze the reaction, and cofactors or regulatory factors that are not transformed in the reaction.

In a reaction molecules may associate and change their conformations without making or breaking covalent bonds. For example, binding an enzyme to a regulatory protein may activate an inactive enzyme, or inactivate an active enzyme. Other reactions may make or break covalent bonds. Examples include phosphorylation of a protein by a kinase or its dephosphorylation by a phosphatase.

3 Steps of the method

Specify the constraints.

- What is the status of each molecule? Is it an admissible participant in the network? Which of its attributes are real, and which hypothetical?

- What are the roles allowed for each molecule? Can it be an input, output, and/or intermediate of the network?

- For each role, is the molecule required, allowed, or excluded?

Make the reaction list.

- For each molecule that may be an intermediate, check that at least one reaction produces it, and at least one reaction consumes it.

- Label the reactions. If the same molecules are involved together in more than one reaction, as in the forward and reverse directions of a bidirectional transformation, it may be useful to give these reactions the same primary index and different secondary indices.

Make the molecule list. For every molecule in the reaction list, enter each form of the molecule separately. Record the indices of all reactions in which it participates, the way it participates in each reaction -- as substrate, product, enzyme, or cofactor -- and the number of these reactions.

Reconstruct the network. Associate with each reaction the reactions that provide its substrates, catalysts, or cofactors. Eliminate each molecule from the molecule list after the reactions that produce it have been associated with the reactions that use it. To simplify recording, eliminate sooner the molecules involved in fewer reactions. A set of coupled reactions identified in this way is a partial pathway. The reactions themselves are the initial, shortest partial pathways. Iterating the association of reactions that produce a molecule with reactions that use it constructs partial pathways of increasing length. After this procedure augments a partial pathway, replace the previous version with the augmented version in the reaction list. When the iteration is complete, the partial pathways can be displayed as directed graphs, and their dynamics can be simulated.

4 Example: Regulation of the breakdown and synthesis of glycogen

We examine the network that regulates the availability of glucose in vertebrate skeletal muscle cells. Two intracellular second messengers, cyclic AMP (adenosine-3',5'-monophosphate) and calcium ion, have partially antagonistic and partially synergistic effects. In response to adrenalin, cyclic AMP stimulates the breakdown of glycogen by glycogen phosphorylase and inhibits the synthesis of glycogen by glycogen synthase. Stimulation of the muscle releases calcium, which transiently increases the activation of glycogen phosphorylase but soon reverses the response to cAMP. Hardie (1991) provided a description of this system that is the basis for the reaction list. Some reactions known to be relevant are not considered, for simplicity. These reactions include phosphorylation of glycogen synthase by casein kinase-1 and glycogen synthase kinase-3, and some regulatory interactions of protein phosphatase-1.

4.1 *The molecule list and the reaction list*

- Molecule list: This list introduces the names and abbreviations for molecules. Reactions of each molecule are taken from the reaction list that follows. + means that the molecule is synthesized through this reaction. - means it is degraded. c means the molecule is a catalyst or cofactor in this reaction. (4) means that the molecule is involved in four reactions.

AMP: adenosine-5'-monophosphate (1)
+: 8.1

Ca: cytoplasmic calcium (6)
+: 2.4; 7.2; 8.2 -: 2.3; 7.1; 8.1

cAMP: cyclic adenosine-3',5'-monophosphate (3)
+: 1.2 -: 1.1; 8.3

PKA: cAMP-dependent protein kinase; protein kinase A; A-kinase (5)
+: 1.1 -: 1.3 c: 2.1; 4.1; 5.2

PKAR2: A-kinase, type 2 regulatory subunit (4)
+: 1.2; 1.5 -: 1.3; 1.4

PKAR2-P: A-kinase, type 2 regulatory subunit, phosphorylated (2)
+: 1.4 -: 1.5

cAMP,PKAR2: complex of cAMP and PKAR2 (2)
+: 1.1 -: 1.2

PKAR2,PKA: complex of PKAR2 and PKA (2)
+: 1.2 -: 1.1

PlaseK: phosphorylase kinase (2)
+: 2.2 -: 2.1

PlaseK-P: phosphorylase kinase, phosphorylated (4)
+: 2.1, 2.4 -: 2.2, 2.3 c: 6.1

PlaseK-P,Ca: phosphorylase kinase, phosphorylated, Ca-activated (3)
+: 2.3 -: 2.4 c: 6.1

PP1: protein phosphatase-1 (5)
+: 3.1 -: 3.2 c: 2.2; 5.1; 6.2

PP1I: protein phosphatase-1 inhibitor-1 (2)
+: 4.2 -: 4.1

PP1I-P: protein phosphatase-1 inhibitor-1, phosphorylated (4)
+: 3.1; 4.1 -: 3.2; 4.2

PP1,PP1I-P: complex of PP1 and PP1I-P (2)
+: 3.2 -: 3.1

PP2B: protein phosphatase-2B (2)
+: 7.2 -: 7.1

PP2B,Ca: protein phosphatase-2B, Ca-activated				(4)
	+: 7.1	-: 7.2	c: 1.5; 4.2	
GlySyn: glycogen synthase				(2)
	+: 5.1	-: 5.2		
GlySyn-P: glycogen synthase, phosphorylated				(2)
	+: 5.2	-: 5.1		
Plase: glycogen phosphorylase b.				(2)
	+: 6.2	-: 6.1		
Plase-P: glycogen phosphorylase a				(2)
	+: 6.1	-: 6.2		
cNMPde: cyclic nucleotide phosphodiesterase				(2)
	+: 8.2	-: 8.1		
cNMPde,Ca: cyclic nucleotide phosphodiesterase, activated				(3)
	+: 8.1	-: 8.2	c: 8.3	

- Reaction list: rxn# = reaction number (index). act = activate. inh = inhibit..

rxn#	effect	reaction		prerequisites
1.1	act PKA	cAMP + PKAR2,PKA	-> cAMP,PKAR2 + PKA	---
1.2	pre-inh PKA	cAMP,PKAR2	-> cAMP + PKAR2	---
1.3	inh PKA	PKAR2 + PKA	-> PKAR2,PKA	---
1.4	act PKA	PKAR2	-> PKAR2-P	PKAR2
1.5	inh 1.3	PKAR2-P	-> PKAR2	PP2B,Ca
2.1	act PlaseK	PlaseK	-> PlaseK-P	PKA
2.2	inh PlaseK	PlaseK-P	-> PlaseK	PP1
2.3	act PlaseK	PlaseK-P + Ca	-> PlaseK-P,Ca	high Ca
2.4	inh PlaseK	PlaseK-P,Ca	-> PlaseK-P + Ca	low Ca
3.1	act PP1	PP1,PP1I-P	-> PP1 + PP1I-P	---
3.2	inh PP1	PP1 + PP1I-P	-> PP1,PP1I-P	---
4.1	act PP1I	PP1I	-> PP1I-P	PKA
4.2	inh PP1I	PP1I-P	-> PP1I	PP2B,Ca
5.1	act GlySyn	GlySyn-P	-> GlySyn	PP1
5.2	inh GlySyn	GlySyn	-> GlySyn-P	PKA
6.1	act Plase	Plase	-> Plase-P	PlaseK-P; PlaseK-P,Ca
6.2	inh Plase	Plase-P	-> Plase	PP1
7.1	act PP2B	PP2B + Ca	-> PP2B,Ca	high Ca
7.2	inh PP2B	PP2B,Ca	-> PP2B + Ca	low Ca
8.1	act cNMPde	cNMPde + Ca	-> cNMPde,Ca	high Ca
8.2	inh cNMPde	cNMPde,Ca	-> cNMPde + Ca	low Ca
8.3	inh cAMP	cAMP	-> AMP	cNMPde,Ca

4.2 *Construct partial pathways*

If reaction r' provides a substrate for reaction r", show this by replacing r" with (r', r") in the reaction list. If reaction r provides a catalyst or cofactor for r", in the molecule list replace r" with (cr, r"). The convention for listing precursors is (cr, r', r"). When this procedure has been followed for all reactions r" for which a given molecule is a prerequisite, it can be eliminated from the molecule list. Eliminate first the molecules involved in fewest reactions.

To begin, note that AMP is involved in only one reaction but is not a prerequisite for any other reactions, so we simply eliminate it. PKAR2-P is a substrate for reaction 1.5, and it is produced in reaction 1.4 ; it is only involved in these two reactions. Therefore we replace reaction 1.5 by (1.4, 1.5) in the reaction list, and eliminate PKAR2-P from the molecule list. We proceed in an analogous way for other molecules. However, reactions that release Ca when the concentration of Ca is low are not used as sources of Ca for reactions that take up Ca when the concentration of Ca is high, because this is logically inappropriate.

After iteration through molecules involved in one or two reactions, the partial pathways (see Fig. 1) are

1.1, 1.2	1.3, 1.1	1.4, 1.5	2.2, 2.1	2.3
2.4	3.2, 3.1	4.2, 4.1	5.1, 5.2, 5.1	6.1, 6.2
7.1	7.2	8.1	8.2	8.3

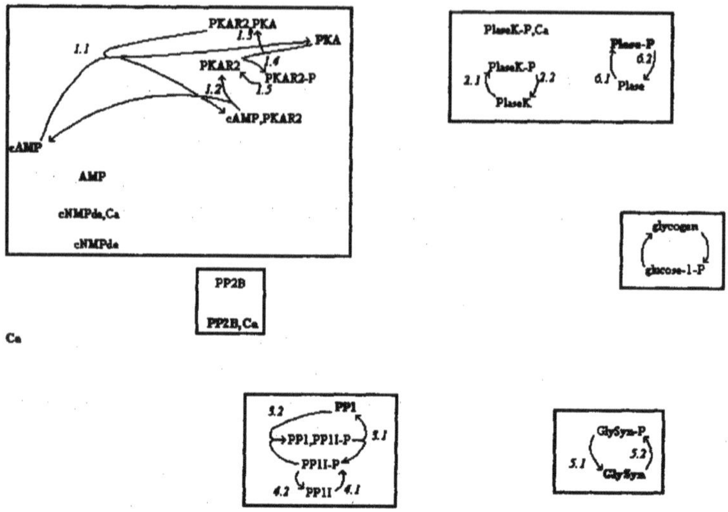

Fig. 1: Partial pathways involving two or more reactions, found after iteration over molecules involved in one or two reactions. All of these partial pathways are localized within functional blocks (rectangles).

After iterating for molecules involved in three or fewer reactions, the list of partial pathways is

1.1, 1.2	1.3, 1.1	1.4, 1.5	2.2, 2.1	2.3, 2.4
3.2, 3.1	4.2, 4.1	5.1, 5.2	6.1, 6.2	
c2.3, 6.2, 6.1	7.1, 7.2	8.1, 8.2	c8.1, 1.2, 8.3	

After iterating for molecules involved in four or fewer reactions, the list of partial pathways (see Fig. 2) is

1.1, 1.2, 1.3	1.1, 1.2, 1.4	1.3, 1.1	1.1, 1.2, (c7.1, 1.4, 1.5)	
1.5, 1.3	1.5, 1.4	2.2, 2.1	2.3, 2.4	3.2, 3.1
4.1, 3.2	c7.1, 4.1, 4.2	c7.1, 3.1, 4.2, 4.1		5.1, 5.2
c2.3, 6.2, 6.1	7.2	8.1, 8.2	c8.1, 1.2, 8.3	

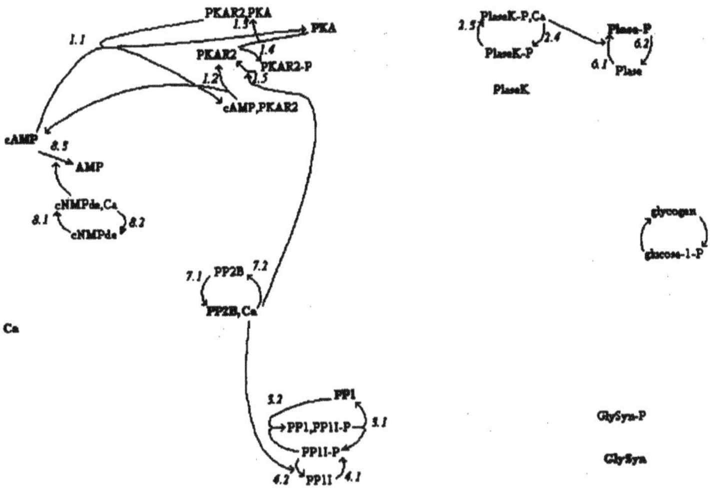

Fig. 2: Partial pathways involving two or more reactions found during iteration over molecules involved in three or four reactions. Most of these partial pathways are within functional blocks, but regulation of two blocks by PP2B,Ca is found.

After iterating for molecules involved in six or fewer reactions the partial pathways, shown in Fig. 3, are

1.1, 1.2, 1.3	1.1, 1.2, 1.4	1.3, 1.1	1.1, 1.2, (c7.1, 1.4, 1.5)
1.5, 1.3	1.5, 1.4	c1.1, 2.2, 2.1	c3.1, 2.1, 2.2
c3.1, 2.4, 2.2	2.1, 2.3	2.3, 2.4, 2.3	3.1, 3.2, 3.1
c7.1, 4.1, 4.2	c7.1, 3.1, 4.2	c1.1, 4.2, 4.1, 3.2	
c1.1, 5.1, 5.2	c3.1, 5.2, 5.1	c3.1, 6.1, 6.2	
c2.1, 6.2, 6.1	c2.3, 6.2, 6.1	7.1, 7.2	8.1, 8.2
c8.1, 1.2, 8.3			

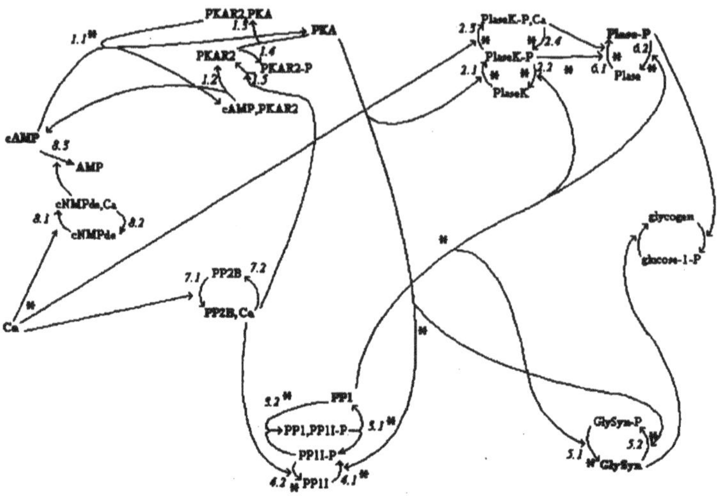

Fig. 3: All partial pathways. Those involving two or more reactions, found during iteration over molecules involved in five or six reactions, are marked *. Pathways of regulation by PKA and PP1 are found.

4.3 *Use the partial pathways to construct responses to elevation of cAMP with low calcium, and to elevation of calcium with low cAMP*

Knowing the partial pathways, one can sketch the consequences of changes in the concentration of cAMP or of Ca. The arguments depend on mass action: If the concentration of a supplied reactant is low, the reaction will proceed at a low rate, as will other reactions dependent on it. To find these reactions one can examine the input (left) sides of reactions in the reaction list, looking for reactants, catalysts, or cofactors that are in low concentration because a supplied reactant is in low concentration.

- Responses to elevation of cAMP with low Ca: When the Ca concentration is low, reactions 2.3, 7.1, 8.1 and their dependent reactions 1.5, 4.2, and 8.3 can be neglected. The remaining partial pathways are

1.1, 1.2, 1.3	1.1, 1.2, 1.4	c1.1, 2.2, 2.1	c3.1, 2.1, 2.2
c3.1, 2.4, 2.2	3.1, 3.2, 3.1	c1.1, 5.1, 5.2	c3.1, 5.2, 5.1
c3.1, 6.1, 6.2	c2.1, 6.2, 6.1		

cAMP acts through reaction 1.1, producing the observed partial pathways:

c1.1, 2.2, 2.1, (c2.1, 6.2, 6.1)	activate phosphorylase
c1.1, 4.2, 4.1, (3.2, 3.1, 3.2)	inhibit PP1
c1.1, 5.1, 5.2	inhibit glycogen synthase

Reactions 1.3 and 1.4 compete for PKAR2, with 1.4 dominant because 1.5 is negligible. Reaction 4.1 promotes 3.2 and so disfavors 3.1, so PP1 is not available to catalyze reactions 2.2, 5.1 and 6.2 .

- Responses to elevation of Ca with low cAMP: When the cAMP concentration is low, reaction 1.1 and its dependent reactions 2.1, 4.1, and 5.2 can be neglected. The remaining partial pathways are

c7.1, 1.4, 1.5	1.5, 1.3	1.5, 1.4	c3.1, 2.1, 2.2
c3.1, 2.4, 2.2	2.1, 2.3	3.1, 3.2, 3.1	c7.1, 4.1, 4.2
c7.1, 3.1, 4.2	c1.1, 4.2, 4.1, 3.2		c1.1, 5.1, 5.2
c3.1, 5.2, 5.1	c3.1, 6.1, 6.2	c2.1, 6.2, 6.1	c2.3, 6.2, 6.1
c8.1, 1.2, 8.3			

Ca acts through reactions 2.3, 7.1, and 8.1, producing the observed partial pathways.

c8.1, 1.2, 8.3	degrade cAMP
(c7.1, 1.4, 1.5), 1.3	release PKAR2, inhibit PKA
1.5, 1.4, 1.5	potentiate PKA activity
3.1, 3.2, 3.1	inhibit PP1
c7.1, 3.1, 4.2	inhibit PP1I
c7.1, 4.1, 4.2	inhibit PP1I
c2.3, 6.2, 6.1	activate phosphorylase
c3.1, 6.1, 6.2	inactivate phosphorylase
c3.1, 5.2, 5.1	activate glycogen synthase
c3.1, 2.1, 2.2	inhibit phosphorylase kinase
c3.1, 2.4, 2.2	inhibit phosphorylase kinase

5 Discussion

As the preceding example illustrates, the algorithm that Mavrovouniotis et al. (1990) devised to assemble metabolic pathways can construct pathways for signal transduction. In this example the reactions assembled in a unique pathway. However, the algorithm can find multiple pathways if they exist (*e.g. loc. cit.*, Appendix B). Mavrovouniotis et al. (1990) implemented their algorithm as a LISP program. The version discussed here is being implemented as a browser to visualize pathways (A. Wozniewicz, personal communication).

The preceding example implies that the algorithm can also assemble other intracellular networks, including pathways mediating gene regulation and cell motility, and multicellular networks, as in the development of an embryo and the operation of endocrine and immune systems. To use the algorithm in these contexts, one keeps track of all precursors for a process, whether they are modified in the process, catalyze it, regulate it, or serve as cofactors. The construction of partial pathways helps one to recognize functional clusters of processes and to appreciate the dynamics of their operation, at first intuitively and then through simulation.

In practice the algorithm is used differently for metabolism than for networks that modify enzymes. Metabolism transmits and transforms matter; the signaling net transmits and processes information. For metabolism the algorithm can provide correct stoichiometry of all metabolites. One can enforce stoichiometry to eliminate intermediate compounds, so that the starting molecules are wholly converted to the final products. In metabolism the forward and reverse reactions of a transformation are not used together, since this is a trivial way to make and remove intermediates. The extent to which the algorithm can provide stoichiometry if enzymes react is unclear. In signaling pathways the molecular inputs elicit changes in the concentrations of the output molecules but can leave intermediates altered in state. The forward and reverse reactions of a transformation may both function in transmitting information through a pathway.

As used here, the algorithm assembled pathways from specified real molecules and reactions. However, it is likely to be most useful in assembling possible pathways from databases of molecules and reactions, including hypothetical candidates. The molecules that participate in a reaction may be specified explicitly by listing them, as was done here. However, a more flexible and powerful way to characterize possible interactions among molecules is implicit specification, in terms of their binding sites. If a molecule has a specified kind of site it can bind to any other molecule in which a complementary site is available, unless steric hindrance or another constraint prevents this. If the algorithm can connect molecules with complementary binding sites, it can assemble a greater variety of less obvious, potentially interesting pathways. At present the data on the identity, specificity, and complementarity of binding sites seem too sparse to use implicit specification, but this situation is changing rapidly.

References

1. J. E. Bailey "Toward a science of metabolic engineering" Science 252, 1668-1675 (1991)

2. J. Happel, P. H. Sellers and M. Otarod, "Mechanistic study of chemical reaction systems" Ind. Engng. Chem. Res. 29, 1057 (1990)

3. D. G. Hardie, Biochemical Messengers. (Chapman and Hall, New York, 1991).

4. M. L. Mavrovouniotis, G. Stephanopoulos, and G. Stephanopoulos, "Computer-aided synthesis of biochemical pathways" Biotechnol. Bioengng. 36, 1119 (1990)

5. M. L. Mavrovouniotis, G. Stephanopoulos, and G. Stephanopoulos, "Synthesis of biochemical production routes" Computers chem. Engng 16, 605 (1992).

6. E. Melendez-Hevia, T. G. Waddell, and F. Montero, "Optimization of metabolism: The evolution of metabolic pathways toward simplicity through the game of the pentose phosphate cycle" J. theor. Biol. 166, 201 (1994)

7. J. E. Mittenthal, B. Clarke, and M. Levinthal, in Thinking About Biology, "Designing Bacteria" Ed. W. D. Stein and F. J. Varela (Addison-Wesley, Reading, MA, 1993)

8. J. E. Mittenthal, A. Yuan, B. Clarke, A. Scheeline "Designing metabolism: Alternative connectivities for the pentose phosphate pathway" in preparation, 1996.

9. A. Seriossis and J. E. Bailey "MPS: An artificially intelligent software system for the analysis and synthesis of metabolic pathways" Biotechnol. Bioengng 31, 587 (1988)

TOWARD A VIRTUAL-LABO-SYSTEM FOR METABOLIC ENGINEERING: DEVELOPMENT OF BIOCHEMICAL ENGINEERING SYSTEM ANALYZING TOOL-KIT (BEST-KIT)

M. OKAMOTO[a], Y. MORITA, D. TOMINAGA, K. TANAKA, N. KINOSHITA, J-I. UENO, Y. MIURA
Department of Biochemical Engineering and Science, Kyushu Institute of Technology, Iizuka-city, Fukuoka 820, Japan

Y. MAKI, Y. EGUCHI
Research Institute, Mitsui Knowledge Industry Co., Ltd., 7-14, 2-Chome, Higashinakano, Nakano-ku, Tokyo 164, Japan

BEST-KIT is an efficient and user-friendly "biochemical engineering system analyzing tool-kit" integrated the following key modules: 1) mathematical modeling and editing of reaction-scheme, 2) automatic derivation of differential equations, 3) numerical calculation, 4) nonlinear optimization, 5) visualization, 6) retrieve the information on reaction mechanism and kinetic parameters from data-base of metabolic pathways. The users of this simulator are assumed to be unfamiliar with computer technology and with computer programming. The integrated interface (UNIX version) is based on Xlib, XToolkit and OSF/Motif Widget.

1 Introduction

True understanding of complexity in bioprocess reaction network requires new approaches to both mathematical modeling and system analysis by using user-friendly computer simulator. Since most biochemical and bioprocess phenomena are the result of synergistic interactions among the components of reaction networks, any viable approach must be based on a nonlinear formalism whose structure permits efficient evaluation, even if the number of components and reaction process is relatively large [1]. One of the pioneers of development of metabolic pathway simulator was David Garfinkel [2]. Since the original development of Garfinkel's BIOSSIM, a number of other metabolic simulators have been written, for example, SCoP [3], MetaModel [4], ESSYNS [5] , SCAMP [6]. On the other hand, a rapid increase in CPU capability of recent prevailing computer enables us to analyze the dynamic property of a large scaled network system. Furthermore, a design of efficient graphical user interface (GUI) can make our interaction with computers easier and more productive. This study aims to the implementation of an efficient and user-friendly "biosimulator for

[a]To whom correspondence should be addressed. (e-mail): okahon@bse.kyutech.ac.jp, (fax): +81-948-29-7801

analyzing a large scaled nonlinear reaction network such as metabolic pathways" integrated the following key modules: 1) mathematical modeling and editing of reaction scheme, 2) automatic derivation of differential equations, 3) estimation of skeletal reaction scheme from several experimental data, 4) numerical calculation, 5) visualization, 6) nonlinear optimization, 7) retrieve the information on reaction mechanism and kinetic parameters from data-base of metabolic pathways. These seven features are integrated in BEST-KIT. We assume the users of this simulator, BEST-KIT, are unfamiliar with computer technology and with computer programming. The integrated interface (UNIX version) is based on Xlib, XToolkit and OSF/Motif Widget [7].

2 Design of BEST-KIT

2.1 Mathematical modeling and editing of reaction scheme

There are two remarkable properties in this module, (i) using the pointing device such as 'mouse', the users can easily design and update an arbitrary reaction scheme in the editing window (working area) through an efficient GUI (Graphical User Interface). The constructed scheme can be saved as a file-style and can be easily loaded to the editing-window. Furthermore, since the graphical pictures of metabolic pathways are saved in the simulator, the users can easily clip a certain reaction scheme or reaction network from given graphical pictures. (ii) a large scaled system consists of a number of small sized sub-systems. The users can easily design a large scaled system by connecting sub-systems each other. We shall describe how to edit the reaction scheme. The following enzymatic reaction system is discussed as an example:

$$\mathrm{E} + \mathrm{S} \underset{k_2}{\overset{k_1}{\rightleftharpoons}} \mathrm{ES_1} \underset{k_4}{\overset{k_3}{\rightleftharpoons}} \mathrm{ES_2} \overset{k_5}{\rightarrow} \mathrm{E} + \mathrm{P}$$

(Scheme 1)

The procedure for editing this scheme is as follows: Selected "put reactant symbol" button in the menu, the users can assign the position of reaction species (reactant) by clicking arbitrary position with the 'mouse' on working area of editing-window. As for the case of scheme 1, since the total number of reactants is 5, five reactant symbols (elements) are arranged in editing-window. Each reactant symbol has four areas such that, i) abbreviated name: this area displays abbreviated reactant's name (changeable), ii) start bottom: this area, displayed "start", indicates 'reactant' or 'substrate', iii) end button: this area, displayed "end", shows 'product', iv) initial concentration: the users have to set

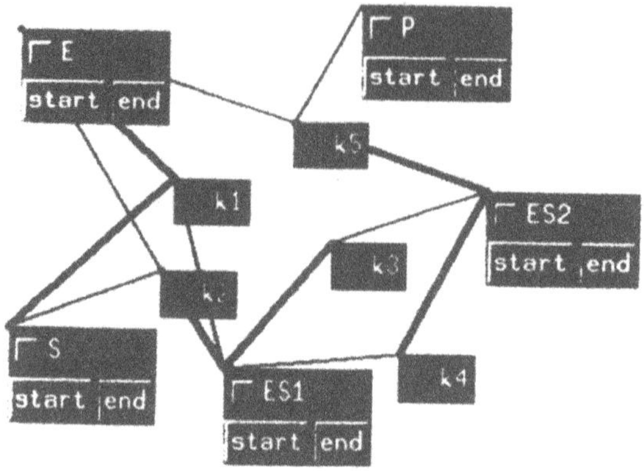

Figure 1: Screen-dump of editing-window for scheme 1.

initial concentration of each reactant in order to solve the numerical solution of a set of simultaneous differential equations. For example, the reaction process $E + S \rightarrow ES_1$, where enzyme E combines substrate S and leading to the inflow of ES_1, can easily be represented as follows: Click the "start" buttons in E and S symbols followed by clicking "end" button in ES_1 symbol. After clicking the mouse in arbitrary position and checking connection condition, connected line between the symbols (E, S, ES_1) is automatically drawn and k1-symbol (symbol for rate constant of its reaction step) is assigned. Fig. 1 is the screen dump of editing-window for scheme 1. The users can modify the scheme by selecting the button of "add substrate", "add product", "cut connection" or "delete symbol". The constructed scheme can be saved as a file-style and can be easily loaded to the editing-window.

We mainly target the dynamic analysis of a large scaled system consisting of a number of interdependent and resource-sharing subnetwork. In the modeling and editing of such a larger scaled system, the assumption that a large scaled system consists of several small-sized subnetwork will save a lot of labor; Fig. 2 shows an example of a large scaled system. The users can divide a large scaled system into arbitrary small-sized subnetwork (subnetwork 1 to 4 in this case). The following procedures represent how to make a large scaled system such as Fig. 2: (1) by clicking the button of "put subnetwork symbol", put the symbols of subnetwork 1 to 4 in editing window, (2) open the window of each subnetwork and make the reaction scheme within the subnetwork, (3) open the every window of subnetwork 1 to 4 and connect the lines among these subnetworks. Fig. 3 is the screen dump of editing-window for the scheme of Fig. 2. By using such procedures to make large scaled system, we can easily

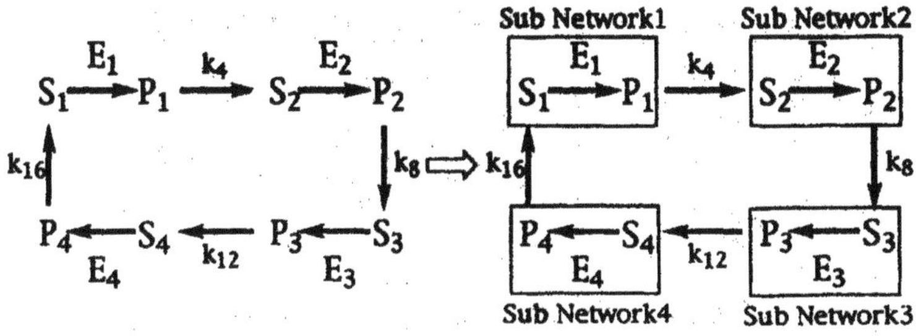

Figure 2: Example of analysis of a large scaled system. Left-hand, whole system; right-hand, dividing into subnetwork.

edit a large reaction network such as pathways of glycolysis.

2.2 Automatic derivation of differential equations

After editing the scheme, cumbersome simultaneous nonlinear differential equations of the scheme based on generalized mass action, can be automatically produced without writing troublesome equations. For the purpose of this, every information with its associated the connected interactions between reaction species (reactants) and rate constants is saved with data-structured style; main parts of these data-structures are shown in Fig. 4. As for reaction species, each part represents as follows: Part a shows the abbreviated name of reaction species, parts b and c represent x- and y-coordinate, respectively, of which value is used in case of drawing in editing-window. Part d shows the number of rate constants related to the inflow of this reaction species, part e is a series of rate constants related to the inflow, part f shows the kinetic order related to part e (n-th ordered reaction). Similar to part d to f, the g shows the number of rate constants related to the outflow of this reaction species, and the h is a series of rate constants related to the outflow, and part i is the kinetic order related to part h. Part j shows the initial concentration of this reaction species. Part k shows the flag on determining whether the value of part j keeps constant or variable with time t.

As for the data structure of rate constants, parts A, B and C are the same notations as part a to c. Parts D and E show the number and a series of reaction species related to the input of this rate constant, respectively; for example, the reaction $E + S \rightarrow ES_1$, supposed k_1 is the rate constant of this reaction step, since this step can be equivalent to the reaction, $E + S \rightarrow (k_1) \rightarrow ES_1$, the reaction species related to the input of rate constant k_1 are E and S, and

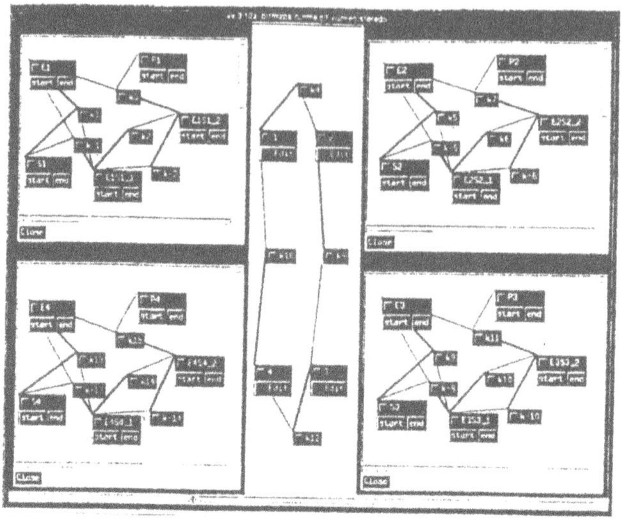

Figure 3: Screen-dump representing the equivalent system to that of Fig. 2 The center part shows the interconnections of subnetwork 1 to 4. The corner windows represent the interconnections of reactants within each subnetwork.

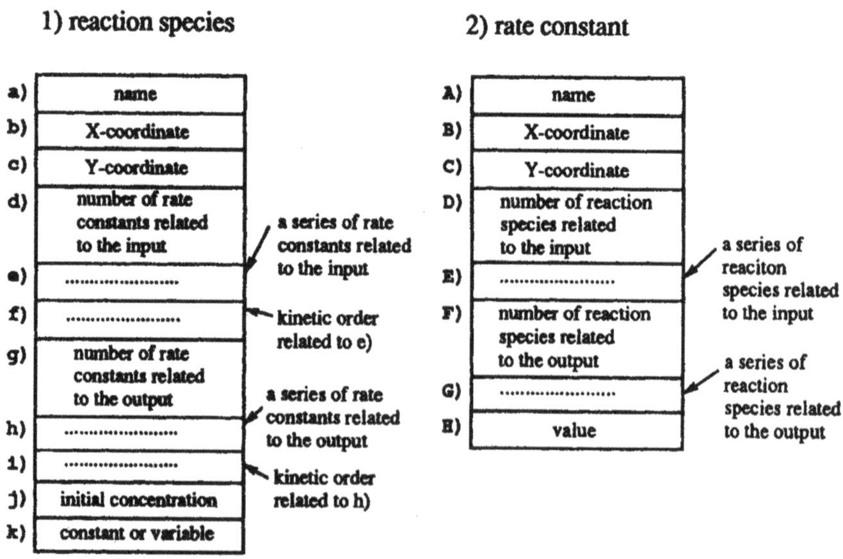

Figure 4: Data-structure of reaction species and rate constants for automatic derivation of rate equations based on generalized mass action.

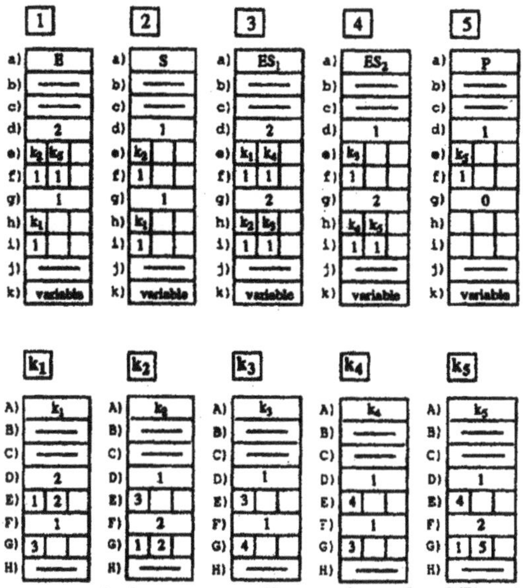

Figure 5: Data-structure of scheme 1 according to the style of Fig. 4. The part a) through k) and A) through H) corresponds to that of Fig. 4.

the reaction species related to the output of the k_1 is ES_1. Parts F and G show the number and a series of reaction species related to the output of this rate constant, respectively. Part H represents the value of this rate constant. According to the style of data-structure shown in Fig. 4, the data-structures for scheme 1 can be represented in Fig. 5, which are automatically saved in disk space after the procedures of "scheme-editing module" described above. The followings represent the procedures of automatic derivation of differential equations of scheme 1: Focused on the reaction step $E + S \rightharpoonup ES_1$ in scheme 1, this step can be divided into 2-steps such that $E + S \rightharpoonup (k_1) \rightharpoonup ES_1$. As for the outflow of the reaction species 1 (denotes E (enzyme)) in Fig. 5, since the value of part g is 1, the data of part h, that is k_1, is assigned, which leads to the reading the value of part D in the data-structure for k_1. The value of this part is 2, which means two kinds of reaction species are related to the input of k_1; in part E, reaction species 1 and 2 are assigned. Considered the kinetic order (part i of both reaction species 1 and 2), the $([E]^1 \cdot [S]^1)$ is the input to the k_1, and the $k_1([E]^1 \cdot [S]^1)$ corresponds to the outflow term of reaction species 1 (E, enzyme); the term $-k_1([E]^1 \cdot [S]^1)$ is automatically added to the rate equation for E ($= dE/dt$). Repeated to this derivation procedure, this module can produce nonlinear simultaneous differential equations of scheme 1 with reference to the data-structures shown in Fig. 5.

2.3 Estimation of skeletal reaction scheme from several experimental data

Organizationally complex systems such as metabolic pathways are comprised of numerous, richly interacting components. The details of the processes that govern expressions and interactions of these components usually are not known, but most of these processes are nonlinear. Consequently, their description requires a representation general enough to capture the essence of the observed response. One approach that satisfies this requirement is the "power-law formalism"[1,8]. The dynamics of a system can be represented by formulating the change in each system component X_i as the difference between all influences that increase X_i and all influences that decrease X_i. Symbolically, the change in X_i can be represented as follows:

$$\frac{dX_i}{dt} = F_i^+(X_1, X_2, \ldots, X_n) - F_i^+(X_1, X_2, \ldots, X_n) \quad (i = 1, 2, \ldots, n) \tag{1}$$

where, X_1 through X_n are the system constituents, F_i^+ and F_i^- are positive-valued differentiable functions of which values can be nonlinearly approximating by a product of power-law functions such that,

$$F_i^+ = \alpha_i \prod_{j=1}^{n} X_j^{g_{ij}}$$

$$F_i^- = \beta_i \prod_{j=1}^{n} X_j^{h_{ij}} \qquad (i = 1, 2, \ldots, n)$$

Thus the equations that describe the dynamics of the system are

$$\frac{dX_i}{dt} = \alpha_i \prod_{j=1}^{n} X_j^{g_{ij}} - \beta_i \prod_{j=1}^{n} X_j^{h_{ij}} \qquad (i = 1, 2, \ldots, n) \tag{2}$$

In a biochemical context, the nonnegative parameters α_i and β_i are called rate constants, and the real-valued exponents g_{ij} and h_{ij} are referred to as kinetic orders. The estimation of these parameter values $(\alpha_i, \beta_i, g_{ij}, h_{ij})$ is many cases the bottleneck and matching the model to experimental data is almost never straightforward and almost always a real challenge. Furthermore, since the number of estimated parameters $(\alpha_i, \beta_i, g_{ij}, h_{ij} (i, j = 1, \ldots, n))$ in Eq.(2) will increase with the number of system constituents (n-value), most nonlinear estimation programs become overwhelmed as soon as models with ten or more

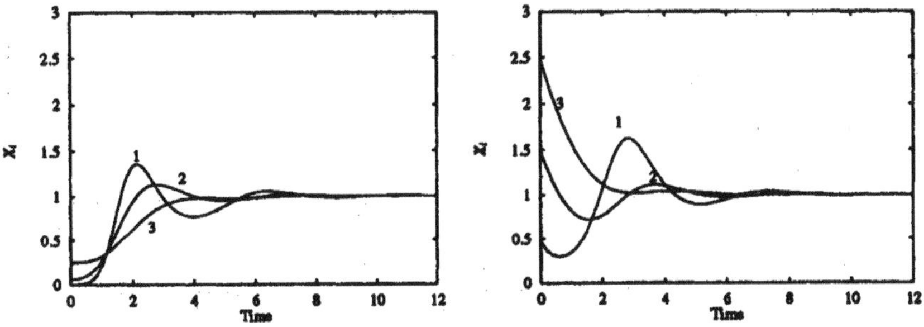

Figure 6: Given time-courses as experimentally observed temporal data. These two time-courses were obtained only by changing the initail concentrations of X_1 to X_3. 1,X_1; 2,X_2; 3,X_3.

parameters are to be fitted to the data; the number of estimated parameters in Eq.(2) is $2n(1+n)$, where n is the number of system constituents. The Genetic Algorithm[9, 10, 11] was introduced as a nonlinear optimization method which is much less likely to be stranded in local minima. Furthermore in this module, in order to find the skeletal structure (small sized system) of power-law formalism (Eq.(2)) matching to the experimental data, some of the parameters of which absolute values are less than a given threshold value are to be removed during the optimization procedures. By introducing this algorithm, optimized essential power-law model matching to experimental data can be discovered.

In order to examine the effectiveness of our proposed procedures, they were applied to the following test case: The observed time-courses of X_1, X_2, X_3 are shown in Fig. 6. Supposed that these time-courses were given as experimental data, we examined whether our proposed optimization procedures could explore and estimate the combination of parameters which can provide the best fitted time-courses shown in Fig. 6. Since the number of n in Eq. (2) is 3, the number of estimated parameters should be 24. We adopted here the effective numerical calculation method for solving a set of simultaneous differentail euqations developed by Irvine and Savageau[12].

The best fitted time-courses to Fig. 6 were found after 100th generations in genetic algorithm. The obtained time-courses are shown in Fig. 7; these are are quite similar to those in Fig. 6.

2.4 Numerical calculation and Visualization

The most difficult problem in application of numerical methods to rate equations had been the "stiffness", but research on the numerical solution of non-linear "stiff" differential equations has been advanced rapidly since the end of

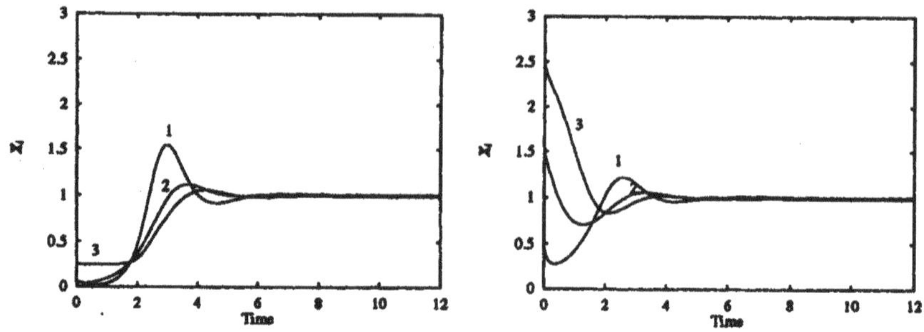

Figure 7: Obtained calculated time-courses by our proposed method. 1,X_1; 2,X_2; 3,X_3.

1960s. We adopt here the Gear method [13], which is accepted as one of the most general and efficient procedures to solve the "stiff" differential equations.

The users can easily get dynamic response (time-course) and phase-plane diagram of given reaction species in X-window space.

2.5 Nonlinear optimization

Optimization is a pure mathematical procedure for evaluation of unknown kinetic parameters from a given model scheme and observed concentration changes in reaction species. As a tool of the nonlinear optimization, we adopt the hybrid numerical optimization technique[10] incorporated the Genetic Algorithm (GA) into the Modified Powell method combined with the Rosenbrock method. Escaped from the trapping in local minimum, this procedure can seek out the global minimum with considerably fast convergence. The estimated value can be minimize the value of the following objective function (F):

$$F = \sum_{i=1}^{i_{max}} \sum_{j=1}^{(Exp_i)_{max}} \left(\frac{Cal_{ij} - Exp_{ij}}{Exp_{ij}} \right)^2 \qquad (3)$$

where, i_{max} is the number of experimentally observed reactants, $(Exp_i)_{max}$ is the total number of experimental data (concentration change) for reactant (Exp_i), and Exp_{ij} shows the j-th experimental data (concentration change) for reactant (Exp_i), Cal_{ij} is the j-th calculated value (concentration change) for reactant (Exp_i). Fig. 8 shows the snap-shot of optimization window.

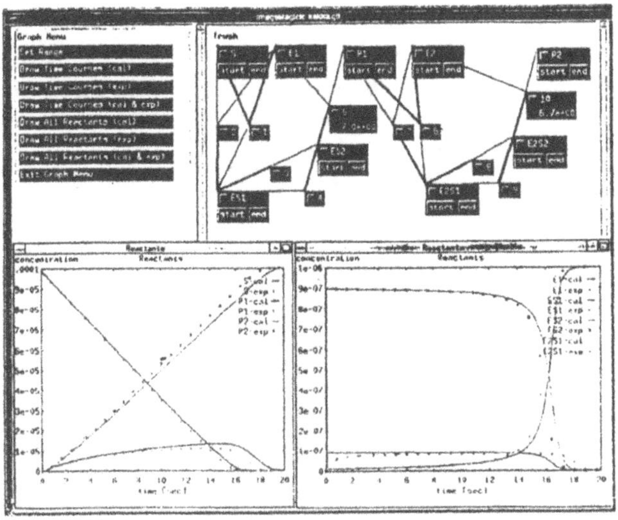

Figure 8: Snap-shot of optimization procedures. After the automatic estimation (optimization) of rate parameters, of which values are best fitted to the experimental data, the comparison between the calculated time-course of every reactant and experimental data can be visualized in the lower windows.

2.6 Retrieve the information on reaction mechanism and kinetic parameters from data-base of metabolic pathways

This module is now under construction, however, by saving the graphical pictures of metabolic pathways in the simulator, the users can easily clip a certain fragment of reaction network from a given graphical picture and can examine the dynamics of that system by using the modules described above. Furthermore, through the graphical pictures and Internet World-Wide-Web (WWW), the users can retrieve and pick up the every information on the reaction mechanism of a given reaction network and reported kinetic parameters from several network-sites of database on metabolic pathways. Dr. Peter Karp and his collaborators have developed a number of powerful and familiar visualizations of metabolic data, such as automatically generated layouts of metabolic pathways (see the location, http://www.ai.sri.com/~ pkarp/pathways.html). Through the graphical pictures and graphical user interface allows the users not only to query the knowledge database on metabolic information (enzyme, regulation mechanism, etc.) but also to analyze the dynamic modeling.

3 Discussion

BEST-KIT is one of general-purpose simulators of metabolic and nonlinear chemical networks. The program is written in C and the user who is not expert in computer technology can nevertheless analyze the dynamics of reaction networks without writing troublesome rate equations even if the number of system constituents is very large. Furthermore even the case that the interaction mechanisms between constituents of the system are not well known, the user can formulate the system's representation based on power-law formalism matching to the experimental data. Most of the modules except data-base module have already developed and they are integrated in BEST-KIT through the integrated interface (UNIX version) based on Xlib, XToolkit and OSF/Motif Widget. We are planning to put BEST-KIT on our Internet WWW server for open usage. Our final goal is the development of virtual-labo-system in metabolic engineering. Without such an efficient tool or system, those who want to analyze the dynamics of the complex system have to look up the references on this system first in order to collect the kinetic data and information on interaction mechanism between constituents, followed by writing the troublesome complex nonlinear rate equations to set up mathematical model of the system. Since the computer programming requires numerous special techniques, those who are unfamiliar with programming are apt to abstaining from theoretical works on metabolic engineering. The development of efficient virtual-labo-system on metabolic engineering will propose a new type of research to many of the experimental biochemists.

Acknowledgment

This study was performed through the Scientific Funds of the Frontier Research in Telecommunications of Ministry of Posts and Telecommunications, Japan, and Tateishi Science and Technology Foundation, Japan, and the Kurata Foundation, Japan.

References

1. E.O. Voit, Canonical nonlinear modeling: S-system approach to understanding complexity (Van Nostrand Reinhold, New York, 1991).
2. D. Garfinkel, A machine-independent language for the simulation of complex chemical and biochemical systems. Comput. Biomed. Res., **2**, 31 (1968).

3. J.M. Kootsey, Future directions in computer simulations. Bull. Math. Biol., **48**, 405 (1986).
4. J.-H.S. Hofmeyr and K.J. van der Merwe, METAMOD: software for steady-state modeling and control analysis of metabolic pathways on the BBC microcomputer. Comput. Applic. Biosci., **2**, 243 (1986).
5. D.H. Irvine, S-systems: efficient solution of nonlinear models expressed in S-system canonical form. Math. Comput. Model., **11**, 123 (1988).
6. H.M. Sauro, SCAMP: a general-purpose simulator and metabolic control analysis program. Comput. Appl. in Biosci., **9**, 441 (1993).
7. Open Software Foundation, OSF/Motif programmer's reference (Rev. 1.1) (Prentice-Hall, New Jersey, 1991).
8. M.A. Savageau, Biochemical system analysis: a study of function and design in molecular biology (Addison-Wesley, Reading, 1976).
9. L. Davis, Handbook of genetic algorithms (Van Nostrand Reinhold, New York, 1991).
10. M. Okamoto, T. Nonaka, S. Ochiai, and D. Tominaga, Nonlinear numerical optimization with use of a hybrid genetic algorithm incorporated the modified Powell method. Proc. Intl. Sympo. on Artificial Life and Robotics (1st AROB, ISBN:4-9900462-6-9), 89 (1996).
11. D. Tominaga, J-I. Ueno, Y. Miura, M. Okamoto, Discovery of a Skeletal Network Describing Complex Nonlinear Dynamics: Optimized Essential Model for Temporal Input-Output Matching, Proceeding of 4th. Intl. Conf. on Soft Computing (World Scientific, New Jersey, *in press*).
12. D.H. Irvine, M.A. Savageau, Efficient solution of nonlinear ordinary differential equations expressed in S-system canonical form, SIAM J. NUMER. ANAL. **27**, 704 (1990).
13. C.W. Gear, Numerical initial value problems in ordinary differential equations (Prentice-Hall, New Jersey, 1971).

METHOD FOR LOW RESOLUTION PREDICTION OF SMALL PROTEIN TERTIARY STRUCTURE

ANGEL R. ORTIZ, WEI PING HU, ANDRZEJ KOLINSKI, JEFFREY SKOLNICK*

Department of Molecular Biology, The Scripps Research Institute,

10666 N. Torrey Pines Rd., La Jolla, CA 92037

A new method for the *de novo* prediction of protein structures at low resolution has been developed. Starting from a multiple sequence alignment, protein secondary structure is predicted, and only those topological elements with high reliability are selected. Then, the multiple sequence alignment and the secondary structure prediction are combined to predict side chain contacts. Such contact map prediction is carried out in two stages. First, an analysis of correlated mutations is carried out to identify pairs of topological elements of secondary structure which are in contact. Then, inverse folding is used to select compatible fragments in contact, thereby enriching the number and identity of predicted side chain contacts. The final outcome of the procedure is a set of noisy secondary and tertiary restraints. These are used as a restrained potential in a Monte Carlo simulation of simplified protein models driven by statistical potentials. Low energy structures are then searched for by using simulated annealing techniques. Implementation of the restraints is carried out so as to take into account of their low resolution. Using this procedure, it has been possible to predict *de novo* the structure of three very diferent protein topologies: an α/β protein, the bovine pancreatic trypsin inhibitor (6pti), an α-helical protein, calbindin (3icb), and an all β- protein, the SH3 domain of spectrin (1shg). In all cases, low resolution folds have been obtained with a root mean square deviation (RMSD) of 4.5-5.5 Å with respect to the native structure. Some misfolded topologies appear in the simulations, but it is possible to select the native one on energetic grounds. Thus, it is demonstrated that the methodology is general for all protein motifs. Work is in progress in order to test the methodology on a larger set of protein structures.

1.- Introduction

Prediction of the three dimensional structure of a protein from its amino acid sequence is still one of the most important unsolved problems in contemporary molecular biology. Although protein structure determination by experimental methods has become more efficient, the ratio between the number of known sequences and the number of known structures is rapidly increasing. An advantage of this fast growth of protein sequence databases is that many sequences can be grouped into structurally conserved families (Sander & Schneider, 1991). This increasing number of protein families for which many homologous proteins are known affords a new opportunity to exploit evolutionary information. When aligned together, such families exhibit features of residue conservation that are directly related to their three dimensional structure. Using this principle, multiple aligned sequences in a family of homologous proteins have been used recently to improve the prediction of secondary structure in proteins (Rost & Sander, 1993). Prediction of contact maps has also been attempted by analyzing correlated mutations in multiple sequence analysis, showing interesting results (Göbel *et al.*, 1994). Combination of predictions based on multiple sequence alignments with structure calculations are starting to emerge aimed at predicting simple protein topologies (Hänggi & Braun, 1994; Numenthaler & Braun, 1995; Aszódi *et al.*, 1995). Along these lines, we investigate the possibilities of predicting low resolution structures of small proteins using restraints derived from multiple sequence alignments and Monte Carlo simulations. Two significant differences can be found with respect to previous studies: firstly, the signal-to-noise ratio of the predicted contacts is increased by means of a new two-step procedure (Ortiz *et al.*, 1996) that first detects pairs of topological elements in contact using correlated mutation analysis and then expands the number of contacts by using inverse folding. Secondly, a robust lattice Monte Carlo simulation, the MONSTER method (Skolnick *et al.*, 1996), is used to generate the protein model. The MONSTER method can efficiently find native-like structures with a RMSD of 3-4 Å using N/5 contact map restraints, where N is the number of residues in the chain. This approach has been applied to a small set of topologically different proteins, and preliminary results of its performance are described here.

2.- Methods

A flow chart of the procedure can be found in figure 1. It can be divided in two separate steps: restraint derivation and structure assembly, which are described in detail in the following paragraphs.

Restraint derivation method

Secondary structure prediction

Multiple sequence alignments for each of the proteins studied were obtained from the HSSP data base (Sander & Schneider, 1991). This alignment was used as input for the PHD method of secondary structure prediction (Rost & Sander, 1993). From the output, all elements predicted as strands were assumed to correspond to a strand in the real secondary structure. For the helices, only those elements with a reliability index higher than 3 were used. Chain reversals were then predicted by using the "U-turn" algorithm (Kolinski *et al.*, 1996). Elements predicted as turns override PHD predictions, as "U-turn" prediction has been proven to be highly reliable (Kolinski *et al.*, 1996).

Side-chain contact prediction

The prediction of residue contacts is performed in two stages (Ortiz *et al.*, 1996): first, a correlated mutation analysis of the multiple sequence alignment is carried out. Then, inverse folding is used to "enrich" the number of contacts. For details about the correlated mutation analysis, see Göbel *et al.* (1994). Briefly, the method is based on defining an exchange matrix or other similarity measure at each sequence position in a multiple alignment and then calculating a correlation coefficient between the exchange matrices at any two positions. In this work, the same multiple alignment used for secondary structure prediction was used, and only correlations between elements to be predicted in secondary structural regions (and not "U" turns) are considered. The rationale is that in this way it is possible to restrict the predictions to rigid elements of the core, for which the assumption of closeness in space for positions showing covariance in their mutational behavior is, in principle, more valid. This analysis delineates predicted secondary structure elements in contact. A relatively high cutoff for the correlation coefficient of 0.5 is used for contact prediction.

Correlated mutation analysis only provides a few points in the contact map, which we call "seeds", and usually do not provide enough restraint information. The set of restraints is then enriched by using inverse folding. This is based on the observation that the pairing of secondary structure elements in proteins is highly

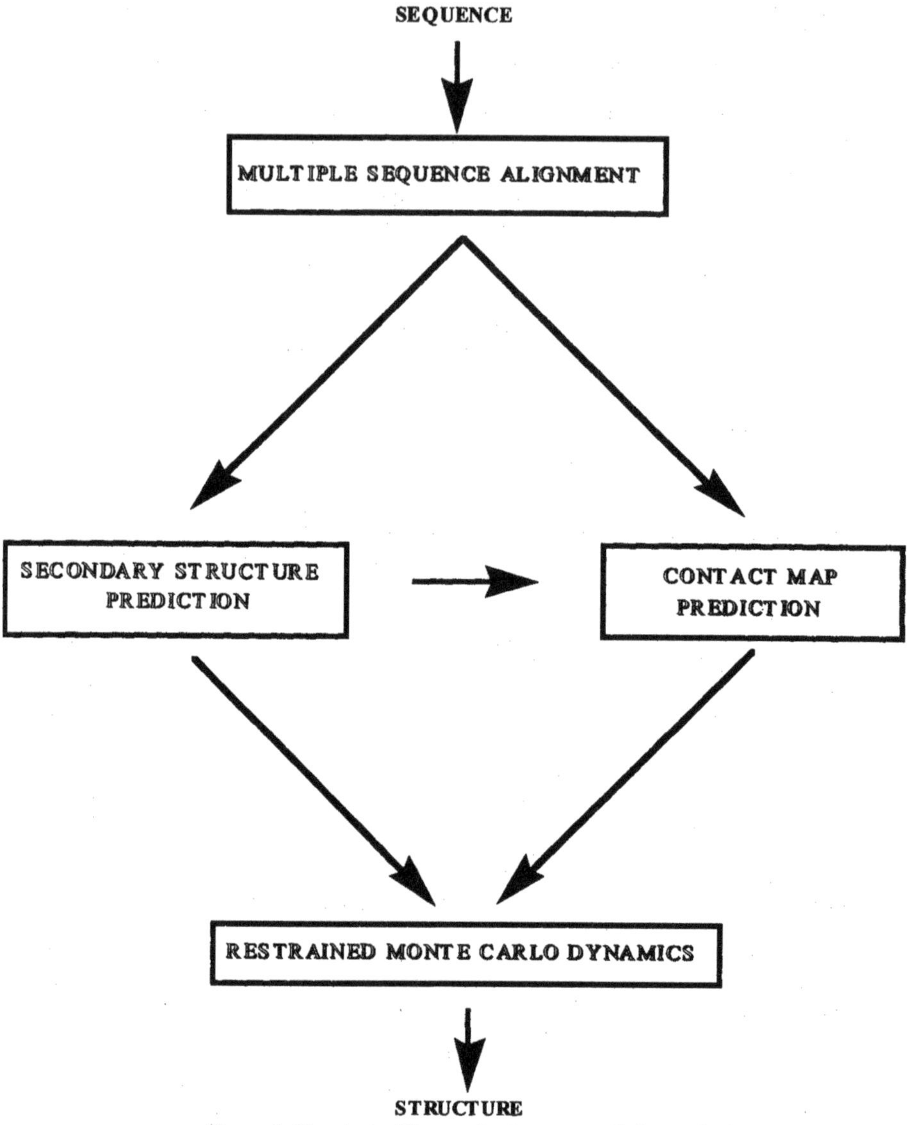

Figure 1. Flowchart of the protein structure prediction method.

degenerate; that is, there is a limited number of ways of pairing secondary structure elements. Thus, pairs of secondary structure elements predicted to be in contact are scanned by using inverse folding, subjected to the constraint that the predicted contact should be present. A tolerance of ± 1 residue shift in each one of the members of the contact pair is allowed in order to take into account the inaccuracies in the correlated mutation analysis. Fragments are then clustered and scored. Fragments are superimposed in space by minimizing their corrdinate RMS deviation, and if they do not show a clear clustering, with an upper limit of 5 Å for the most divergent pair of fragments, the pair of fragments is discarded, and side chain restraints are not derived. On the other hand, if the fragments do cluster, they are scored by the inverse folding potential. The average fragment of the cluster is used as a representative, and a selection is done among the fragments that fulfill the constraints by means of the inverse folding score: the lowest scoring fragment is selected, and then the contact map for the selected fragment is projected onto the query sequence. With this procedure, the number of predicted contacts usually increases by about five times with respect to the number of contacts predicted from the correlated mutation analysis.

The MONSTER Method

The protein model is based on a lattice representation of the Cα-backbone trace. The details of the model have been described previously (see Kolinski & Skolnick, 1996 for a review). Here, we give a brief summary for the reader's convenience. The procedure is divided in two steps: assembly and refinement. Slightly different protein representation is used in each one of the cases. Where appropriate, distinction will be made about the differences in implementation.

Lattice model of protein chain

The Cα backbone is a string of vectors of the type a•v with {v}={(3,1,1),... (3,1,0),... (3,0,0),... (2,2,1),... (2,2,0),....}, with a=1.22 Å. The lattice resolution is about 0.6-0.7 Å RMS (Godzik *et al.*, 1993). Virtual bond angles between successive Cαs are restricted to reproduce a protein-like distribution, and two successive backbone vectors provide the reference frame for the definition of a set of model (single interaction center for each side group) rotamers that cover the conformational space of the side chains with a 1 Å grid. A "rotamer" located at 0.3 Å from the Cα is assumed for glycine.

Force field of the protein model

The force field contains potentials of mean force (predominately of statistical origin) that account for the short range interactions, long range interactions, and hydrogen bond interactions (which could be short or long range). The total energy is given by:

$$E= 0.5E_{14} + 1.5E_{l} + 2.75E_{pair} + E_{H\text{-}bond} + E_{target,14} + V_{long} \quad (1)$$

All contributions to the potential are available via anonymous ftp (Skolnick, 1996), and detailed account of each one of the terms can be found in Skolnick *et al.* (1996a). Here only a brief description is given:

1.- Local conformational propensities (E_{14}) : This is a sequence dependent term divided into six conformational states that roughly correspond to extended right, and extended left handed states, wide right and left turns, and right and left handed helical states respectively. This component depends on the sequence through the pair of neighboring amino acids A_i and A_{i+1} , and controls the local chain geometry.

2.- One-body term (E_1): Centrosymmetric potential which reflects the tendency of some amino acids to be buried and some to be exposed. It is dependent of the expected radius of gyration of a single domain protein consisting of N amino acids in its native conformation ($S_0 = 2.2\ N^{0.38}$ in Å). This potential is applicable only to single domain proteins.

3.- Pairwise tertiary interactions (E_{pair}): The pair interactions beyond the fourth neighbor are derived from the statistics of the database, and neglected between nearest neighbors in sequence, assuming that these interactions are already accounted for by the hydrogen bond potential (see below) and secondary structure preferences.. For residues i and j,

$$E_{ij} = \begin{cases} E^{rep}, & \text{for } r_{ij} < R_{ij}^{rep} \\ e_{ij}, & \text{for } R_{ij}^{rep} < r_{ij} < R^{con}_{ij}, \text{ and } e_{ij} > 0 \\ fe_{ij}, & \text{for } R_{ij}^{rep} < r_{ij} < R^{con}_{ij}, \text{ and } e_{ij} < 0 \\ 0 & \text{Otherwise.} \end{cases} \quad (2)$$

where: r_{ij} is the distance between the side chain centers of mass, R_{ij}^{rep} and are R^{con}_{ij} the cut-off values for hard core excluded volume interactions and for square-well, soft pairwise interactions, respectively. The amino acid pairwise specific parameters, e_{ij} are described elsewhere (Skolnick *et al.*, 1996). In order to facilitate assembly, the magnitude of this interaction for a repulsive pair of residues is decreased by a factor of two. E^{rep} is the repulsive energy associated with the overlap of alpha carbons and side chains, and it is on the order of $5k_BT$. f is an angular factor which weakly favors almost parallel or almost antiparallel orientations of the secondary structure elements such as occur in all beta and mixed α/β proteins (Skolnick *et al.*, 1996).

3.- Hydrogen bonds ($E_{H\text{-}bond}$): It operates only between α-carbons, following an scheme very much in the spirit of Levitt and Greer (Levitt & Greer, 1977). Each α-carbon can participate in at most two hydrogen bonds (the α-carbon of proline is an exception and can participate in only one hydrogen bond), and there is no directionality (donor-acceptor) in the scheme. This scheme reproduces 90 % of the main chain hydrogen bonds assigned to the structure by DSSP Kabsch-Sander algorithm (Kabsch & Sander, 1983). Explicit cooperativity is also introduced. When two neighboring pairs of residues are hydrogen bonded, the system gets an additional favorable energy (cooperativity). Note that we ignore all side chain - side chain and side chain - backbone hydrogen bonding. Hydrogen bond energy is modulated depending upon the hydrophobicity of the residues under consideration. For hydrophobic residues, it also depends on whether or not the residue is buried or exposed. In refinement, a different model for the short range interactions and a different hydrogen bond scheme are used. Here, explicit coordinates for the protein backbone are used, and thus orientational correlations of the peptide bond plates are simulated in the short range term of the potential. The short range interactions are of two types: generic (sequence independent) and sequence specific. The role of sequence independent potentials is to provide a strong bias towards short and intermediate range correlations that mimic conformational regularities in proteins. These include a bias towards the right handed geometry of helix-like fragments, a slight bias toward left handed expanded states, and terms reflecting the conformational stiffness of more regular secondary structure fragments, regarless of amino acid composition. The hydrogen bond scheme takes the form of a simplified Coulombic potential that is moderated by an angular factor. Details of the implementation and relative scaling with respect to the long range term of the potential can be found in Kolinski *et al.* (1995a, 1995b).

Restraint Contributions

Secondary structure restraints and a limited number of tertiary restraints are used. Furthermore, a set of knowledge-based restraints is used. The implementation of each kind of restraint is discussed in turn.

Short range restraints

1. For those residues assigned to be helical, hydrogen bonds beyond the fifth residue along the chain are not allowed. Similarly, a β-assigned residue cannot have a helix hydrogen bond pattern nor can it hydrogen bond to a residue that has been assigned to be in a helical region of the molecule.

2. A given residue can be in one of five conformational states, assigned on the basis of the local chain geometry. For those residues which have an assigned secondary structural type, energetic biases for the various allowed conformational states are assigned. Left handed helices experience a repulsion of 1., in k_BT units. Turns are encoded on a generic basis, i.e., their chirality is not specified. Rather they behave as flexible joints between regular secondary structural elements. See Skolnick *et al.* (1996) for details. The resulting background target local conformational energy is

$$E_{target,14} = \sum_{k=2}^{N-2} 2.5\mu(k) \sum_{j=1}^{5} \sec(k,j) + (1-\mu(k)) \sum_{j=1}^{6} ag(k,j) \quad (3)$$

where $\mu(k)=1$ if the secondary structure is assigned *a priori*, and it is equal to zero otherwise. ag(k,j) is an amino acid pair specific matrix describing local interactions, that depends on the identity of A_k and A_{k+1}. It is defined with respect to the six conformational bins, left and right hand extend/beta states, left and right hand wide turns, and left and right handed helices/tight turns, and acts propagating secondary structure elements. sec(k,j) contains the local energetic bias for a particular conformational bin, as predicted from the secondary structure prediction procedure.

Long range restraints

Long range restraints operate on the level of distances between the centers of mass of the side groups. Due to the fuzzy representation of the side chains in our model and the ambiguity in the restraint derivation, long range restraints are implemented as follows: If residues i and j are predicted to be in contact, then the residue based pair potential of eq.2 is modified so that e_{ij}=-1.25. The long range tertiary restraints are as follows. Let $d_{ij}=r_{ij}-R^{con}_{ij}$

$$
\begin{aligned}
V_{long}(r_{ij}) &= 0 && \text{if } r_{ij} < R^{con}_{ij} \\
&= g\, d_{ij}^{\,2} && \text{If } R^{con}_{ij} < d_{ij} < 34.5\ \text{Å} \\
&= g(34.5)^2 && \text{otherwise.}
\end{aligned}
\tag{4}
$$

Typically, the value of g ranges from 0.5 to 2. In folding from random compact states, the restraints are not implemented simultaneously. Rather, the "sequential growing strategy" is used. This appears to increase the folding efficiency by decreasing the extent of kinetic trapping.

Knowledge-based restraints

Finally, for one of the proteins tested (6pti, see below), knowledge based information about protein topology is used (Skolnick *et al.*, 1996). This knowledge based information acts to reduce the number of misfolded structures. In particular, it helps to eliminate the problem of topological mirror image states, and thereby enhances the folding efficiency. By a topological mirror image, we refer to structures where the chirality of the secondary structure connections is reversed (Pastore *et al.*, 1991).

Conformational sampling

The sampling of conformational space occurs via a standard asymmetric Monte Carlo Metropolis scheme (Metropolis *et al.*, 1953). The conformational updates are composed of several types of local conformational micromodifications of the chain backbone and their associated side groups, side group equilibration cycles, and rare (small distance) motions of larger chain fragments.

Fully extended chains are selected as initial structures in the assembly stage. Each simulation started at a reduced temperature in the range of 2.0, and then the temperature is slowly lowered to 1.0. The final structure obtained from the assemply step is then subjected to refinement, again using simulated annealing with a temperature range of 2.0-1.0. Typically, three kinds of structures result: There are misfolded states of higher energy that can be trivially dismissed; the correct native like folds with various root mean square deviations of the α-carbons from native; and the topological mirror image folds. These pseudo mirror image folds could be identified in two ways. First, they may exhibit an *a priori* violation of the known connectivity handedness rules for some supersecondary connections. Second, the average energies of the mirror image structures are higher than that for the correct folds. The predicted structure is the one which exhibits the lowest average and minimum energies.

Test cases studied

Three different test cases have been studied (Table 1), chosen as small protein representatives of different structural classes, in order to explore the methodology with different protein motifs: an α/β protein, the bovine pancreatic trypsin inhibitor (6pti); an α-helical protein, calbindin (3icb); and an all β-protein, the SH3 domain of spectrin (1shg). In all cases the starting conformation was a fully extended chain, and ten simulations for each protein were carried out.

Table 1. Summary of results of the folding simulations (for the lowest energy structures).

Prot[a]	Nres[b]	Nsq[c]	Npc[d]	Ntc[e]	rms_r[f]	rms_n[g]	E_n[h]	rs_n[i]	rms_w[j]	E_w[k]	rs_w[l]
6pti	56	45	19	92	**4.7**	6.0	-410	19	9.7	-397	18
3icb	75	67	25	154	**4.5**	6.8	-406	21	12.6	-342	11
1shg	57	20	39	109	**4.5**	4.5	-198	19	8.22	-125	17

[a]*Prot* refers to the pdb access number of the protein studied.

[b]*Nres* is the number of residues of the protein in the pdb file.

[c]*Nsq* stands for the number of sequences aligned in the HSSP (Sander & Schneider, 1991) multiple sequence alignment file.

[d]*Npc* corresponds to the number of predicted contacts used in the simulation.

[e]*Ntc* is the number of side chain contacts in the experimental structure.

[f]rms_r is the rms deviation with respect to the experimental structure of the final predicted structure after refinement (measured in Å).

[g]rms_n corresponds to the rms deviation of the computed structure to the experimental structure after the assembly runs for the native-like topology (measured in Å).

[h]E_n is the total energy of the protein after the assembly run for the native-like topology (measured in k_BT units).

[i]rs_n refers to the number of restraints satisfied in the assembled native-like structure.

[j]rms_w corresponds to the rms deviation of the alternative topology of lowest energy with respect to the experimental structure, after the assembly run (measured in Å).

[k]E_w is the total energy of the protein in the lowest energy alternative topology found, after assembly runs (measured in k_BT units).

[l]rs_w stands for the number of restraints satisfied in the alternative topology after assembly runs.

3.- Results and Discussion.

6pti

6pti is a small α/β protein of 57 residues (Table 1). The structure of 6pti (figure 2a) consists of a small α-helix, involving residues 48 to 55, packed against a twisted β-hairpin, associated with residues 18-35. These elements are connected by long loops. There are 3 disulfide bridges in the structure. The secondary structure prediction correctly locates the elements of secondary structure, including the turn in the β-hairpin, altough there is a shift and slight overprediction in the first strand of the β-hairpin, and it misses the C-terminal part of the helix (figure 3a). The prediction accuracy for this protein is 80.4 %. The contact map prediction predicts 19 contacts (Table 1). They locate the strand pairing and the packing of the α-helix against the β-hairpin, although there is a shift in the residues involved in the contact of the secondary structure elements.

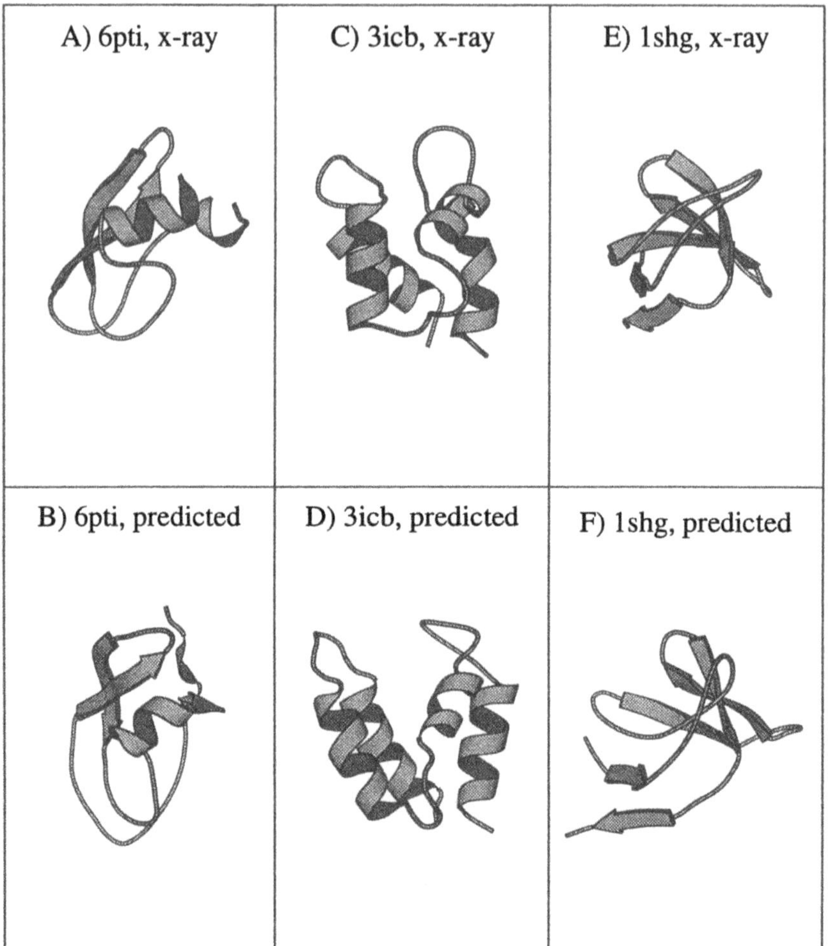
A) 6pti, x-ray
C) 3icb, x-ray
E) 1shg, x-ray
B) 6pti, predicted
D) 3icb, predicted
F) 1shg, predicted

Assembly Monte Carlo simulations locate native-like topologies with an RMSD of about 6 Å with respect to the experimental structure (Table 1). However, another alternative topology appears, corresponding to the topological mirror image of the native structure (Pastore *et al.*, 1991). Distinction between both topologies can be made in this case on the basis of the force field energy and the number of restraints fulfilled (Table 1). Refinement runs allow to obtain structures with an RMSD of 4.7 Å with respect to the experimental structure. Figure 2b shows the predicted structure. The general fold topology is well reproduced. However, there are still wrong details in the predicted structure. The most salient ones are the shift in the helix to hairpin packing and the wrong twist of the β-hairpin. On the other hand, it is worth noting that the simulations are able to correct the wrong prediction of the C-terminal helix as a coil, and thus in the predicted structure, it forms part of the α-helix, as in experiment.

3icb

3icb is a four helix bundle (figure 2c) of 75 residues (Table 1). The secondary structure prediction successfully locates the four helices. However, the PHD method overpredicts the number of residues in helical conformation for the second helix, but the "U-turn" prediction algorithm detects a clear "U-turn" in that region and hence successfully corrects the PHD prediction (figure 3b). The contact map prediction detects 25 side chain contacts (Table 1). They correspond to contacts between helices II and III; III and IV; and I and IV. Assembly runs typically produce structures in the range of 6 Å with respect the experimental structure. The predicted structure of 3icb, after refinement, can be found in figure 2d. The RMSD of the final refined conformation is 4.5 Å with respect to the experimental structure (table I). The main differences with respect to the native structure are the different conformations of the loops, the more open structure in the calcium binding loops face, the more parallel arrangement of the third helix, and the lack of bend in the first helix. The alternative mirror image topology appears frequently in this case, but again can be dismissed on the basis of the number of restraints fulfilled and the force energy (Table 1).

1shg

1shg is a small all β-protein (figure 2e) of 57 residues (Table 1), consisting of 5 strands arranged so as to form a barrel structure. Because of its all beta topology and the presence of bends in the strands in order to configurate the barrel, together with the long loops connecting secondary structure elements, this protein represents a considerable challenge for the methodology. The secondary structure prediction is shown in figure 3c. It is worth noting that in this case the prediction accuracy is only 65 %. There are several differences between the predicted secondary structure and the observed one: the number of residues in the first strand is overpredicted. Furthermore, there is an overprediction of a strand between residues 18 and 20. Aditionally, the small helix between 50 and 52 is not predicted, and the two last strands are considerably shortened. The "U-turn" prediction also shifts the prediction of some turns by about 2-3 residues. The number of predicted contacts in this case is 17 (Table 1). Succesful assembly simulations for this structure provide folds in the order of 6-7 Å RMSD with respect the experimental structure. However, a considerable number of misfolded alternative topologies appear, most cases are trapped intermediates with wrong pairings of strands, or structures with almost parallel angles between between the two β-sheets. In this case the force field energy averaged over short runs does not discrimate between the alternative anwers and the correct topology, perhaps because the structures obtained after assembly are still relatively away from the experimental structure in conformational space, and because of the shifts in the "U-turns" and predicted contacts introduce a considerable distortion in theresidue environment, which reflects in the computed energy. The slightly higher number of restraints satisfied by the correct topology does not provide in this case clear criteria for selecting the right topology unambiguously. However, it was possible to select it on the basis of long isothermal runs. The results are reported in Table I, where can be observed that the correct topology can be identified. The refined structures provide folds with a RMSD of 4.5 Å with respect to experiment. Figure 2f shows the predicted structure. The main differences with the experimental structure come from the positioning of the loops and the angles between the strands. On the other hand, strands are highly "idealized" and they do not show the bend observed in the experimental structure.

```
A)   protein:        6pti             length       56     Q³=80.4

      ....,....1....,....2....,....3....,....4....,....5....,....6
AA | RPDFCLEPPYTGPCKARIIRYFYNAKAGLCQTFVYGGCRAKRNNFKSAEDCMRTCG |
OB |   HHHH            EEEEEEE    EEEEEEE              HHHHHHHH  |
PR | 5555555555555334444444444433344444445555555555555222222555 |

B)   protein:        3icb             length       75     Q³=89.3

      ....,....1....,....2....,....3....,....4....,....5....,....6
AA | KSPEELKGIFEKYAAKEGDPNQLSKEELKLLLQTEFPSLLKGPSTLDELFEELDKNGDGE |
OB |   HHHHHHHHHHHH              HHHHHHHHHHHH        HHHHHHHH    |
PR | 552222222222225551111111122222222222223333355522222222222255333336 |

      ....,....7....,....8....,....9....,....10...,....11...,....12
AA | VSFEEFQVLVKKISQ |
OB |   HHHHHHHHHHHH  |
PR | 552222222222255 |

C)   protein:        1shg             length       57     Q³=64.9

      ....,....1....,....2....,....3....,....4....,....5....,....6
AA | KELVLALYDYQEKSPREVTMKKGDILTLLNSTNKDWWKVEVNDRQGFVPAAYVKKLD |
OB |   EEEE                    EEEEEE      EEEEEE    EEEEEEHHHEEEEE |
PR | 554444444455533335444553344444553333554455553544455554455 5 |
```

Figure 3. A) Secondary structure assignment for 6pti; B) Secondary structure assignment for 3icb; C) Secondary structure assignment for 1shg. "AA" refers to the aminoacid sequence of the protein; "OB" is the observed secondary structure in the experimental conformation, according to the DSSP assignment; "PR" is the assigned secondary structure state in the folding simulations, according with the prediction results (see Methods). In the numeration scheme adopted, "1" stands for coil assignment; "2" for helix assignment; "3" for turn assignment"; "4" for strand assignment and "5" correspond to no assignment of secondary

4.- Conclusions.

Low resolution folds of small proteins have been obtained using a hierarchical approach that starts from multiple sequence alignments. For the test cases presented, the method is able to predict reliably the correct fold with an accuracy of 4.5-5.5 Å. Certainly, a larger test set of proteins is needed in order to correctly assess the methodology. Such work is now in progress. Still, even demonstrating the generality of the method, considerable improvements are required. It is important is to achieve a higher yield of successful simulations, which currently is in the order of 30 % for the cases studied. It is also crucial to select the correct topology from the misfolded alternatives. The results with 1shg suggest that long isothermal runs may be required to obtain an adequate energy spectrum that allows reliable identification. In any event, the approach presented here seems to be a promising one for predicting protein structure from sequence.

References

Aszódi, A., Gradwell, M. J. & Taylor, W. R. (1995). *J. Mol. Biol.* **248**, 308-326.
Göbel, U., Sander, C., Schneider, R. & Valencia, A. (1994). *Proteins*, 18, 309-317.
Godzik, A., Kolinski, A. & Skolnick, J. (1993) *J. Comp. Chem.* **14**, 1194-1202.
Hänggi, G. & Braun, W. (1994). *FEBS Letters* 344, 147-153.
Kabsch, W. & Sander, C. (1983). *Biopolymers* **22**, 2577-2637.
Kolinski, A. *et al.* (1995). *J.Chem.Phys.* **103**, 4312-4323.
Kolinski, A., Galazka, W., Skolnick, J. (1995). *J.Chem.Phys.* **103**, 10286-10297.
Kolinski, A. & Skolnick, J. (1996). *Lattice Models of Protein Folding, Dynamics and Thermodynamics*, R. G. Landes Company, Austin, TX.
Kolinski, A., Skolnick, J. & Godzik, A. (1996). *Proteins* (submitted).
Kraulis, P. (1991) *J. Appl. Cryst.* **24**, 946-950.
Levitt, M. & Greer, J. (1977). *J. Mol. Biol.* **114**, 181-293.
Metropolis, N. *et al.* (1953). *J.Chem.Phys.* **51**, 1087-92.
Numenthaler, C. & Braun, W. (1995). *Prot. Science* 4, 863-871.
Rost, B. & Sander, C. (1993). *J. Mol. Biol.* **232**, 584-599.
Sander, C. & Schneider, R. (1991). *Proteins* 9, 56-68.
Skolnick, J., Kolinski, A. & Ortiz, A. R. (1996). *J. Mol. Biol.*. (submitted).
Skolnick, J. (1996). ftp.scripps.edu in directory /pub/skolnick/nmr.
Skolnick, J. *et al.* (1996). *Prot. Engn.*, (submitted).
Smith-Brown, M. J., Kominos, D. & Levy, R. M. (1993). *Prot. Engn.* **6**, 605-614.
Ortiz, A. R., Hu, W. P. & Skolnick, J. (1996). *Unpublished results.*
Pastore, A. *et al.* (1991). *Proteins*, 10, 22-32.
Wlodawer, A. *et al.* (1987). *J. Mol. Biol.* **198**, 469-480.

MULTIPLE MODEL APPROACH — DEALING WITH ALIGNMENT AMBIGUITIES IN PROTEIN MODELING

K. PAWŁOWSKI
Institute of Biochemistry & Biophysics, Polish Academy of Sciences, Warszawa, Poland

Ł. JAROSZEWSKI
Department of Chemistry, Warsaw University, Warszawa, Poland

A. BIERZYŃSKI
Institute of Biochemistry & Biophysics, Polish Academy of Sciences, Warszawa, Poland

A. GODZIK
The Scripps Research Institute, 10666 N.Torrey Pines, La Jolla, CA 92037, USA

Sequence alignments for distantly homologous proteins are often ambiguous, which creates a weak link in structure prediction by homology. We address this problem by using several plausible alignments in a modeling procedure, obtaining many models of the target. All are subsequently evaluated by a threading algorithm. It is shown that this approach can identify best alignments and produce reasonable models, whose quality is now limited only by the extent of the structural similarity between the known and predicted protein. Using a similar approach structure prediction for the oxidized dimer of S100A1 protein, for which the structure is not known, is presented.

1. Introduction

Despite intense efforts we are not able to predict the three dimensional structure of a protein from its amino acid sequence alone. Comparative modeling, the only consistently successful prediction method, is based on a simple observation that proteins with similar sequences fold to similar structures. In this technique, an unknown structure of a new protein (the target) is predicted on the basis of a sequentially related known structure (the template).[1, 2]

The modeling process consists of template identification, creation of an alignment and building of a model. For homology modeling the first step is trivial, or at least much easier than others. The creation of the alignment is the most crucial step. Any errors made at this stage are usually impossible to correct later and lead to significant errors in final models.[3] At the same time, inherent problems with the alignment preparation are often unappreciated.[4] In this contribution we will focus on this stage in the modeling process.

Efficient algorithms for sequence alignments were developed many years ago [5] and are now widely available. They require two groups of parameters: a scoring matrix and penalties for introducing gaps into the alignment. Unfortunately no optimal set of parameters has been identified to work well for different proteins. [4]

If the target and the template proteins have over 50% of identical amino acids, the alignment is trivial. With protein sequence similarity between 50 and 30% significant differences between different alignments emerge in some regions. But in the protein core the alignment is still well defined and doesn't depend on parameters used. The situation changes again, when the sequence similarity drops below 30%. Alignments become very ill defined, changing dramatically with scoring matrices and gap penalties.[4] Ambiguities are no longer confined to loops, but involve protein core. In such situations, although comparative modeling in principle could work properly, models can be useless due to alignment errors.

For protein pairs where both structures are known, alignment strategies could be investigated with the help of structural alignments.[4, 6] Unfortunately, while some sets of parameters are better than others, this is true only on the average.[4] For any single case we cannot be sure that strategy which is statistically the best would actually produce the „true" alignment. At the same time, the approach suggested in modeling packages' manuals is to prepare the „best possible alignment" and to stake everything on the resulting model. In this contribution we propose a simple method, the multiple model approach, which intends to improve on this strategy. It consists of the following steps:

1. exploration of the alignment diversity, by using various alignment protocols
2. elimination of alignments contradicting our knowledge of the target.
3. construction of full-atom models using all the remaining alignments
4. choice of the best model

In this contribution quality of the models (point 4 above) is evaluated by a threading algorithm.[7] Similar strategy was used by other groups to assess quality of crystallographical models.[8] Self-threading energy of a full atom protein model was used in evaluating alignment strategies for threading alignments [9] and to analyze interactions in a family of structurally divergent homologous proteins.[10] A related approach based on the measurement of core volume and packing pair potential was used to compare suboptimal sequence alignments for difficult to align protein pairs.[11]

2 Methods

The multiple model method. The accuracy of sequence alignment depends strongly on the substitution matrix used and vary significantly for different gap penalties.[4] If the real structure of the target is not known, the selection of the correct alignment is not trivial. Several methods have been suggested to identify a part of the alignment one could be certain about,[6] but such methods focus only on a small fraction of the alignment.

Here, to explore the range of possible alignments, we use five different scoring matrices, judged to be among the best in a comprehensive test.[4]

The test case 1: EETI and PCI. The two small disulfide-rich proteins, trypsin inhibitor (EETI, 2ETI), and potato carboxypeptidase inhibitor (PCI, 4CPA) have weak, but detectable homology, although they inhibit different proteases. Although, as expected, the proteins share similar structural scaffold, the binding sites are located at different positions in the structures. In EETI the trypsin-binding loop consists of residues Gly1- Met7 and the scissile peptide bond is situated between Arg4 and Ile5. In PCI the active site of carboxypeptidase is blocked by the last four residues. Early alignments of this protein pair were partly in error since only two of three disulfide bridges are structurally conserved between the two proteins.[12]

The test case 2: Calbindin and parvalbumin. Calbindin (4ICB) and parvalbumin (5CPV) belong to the EF-hand calcium binding protein family.[13] These all-alpha proteins are built of ion binding motifs named EF-hands, usually combined in pairs to form a functional unit. Calbindin contains one such unit, even that the first EF-hand motif differs significantly from other such motifs, with a two residue insertion and a missing aspartic acid (conserved in all other proteins from this family) at the N-terminal end of the calcium binding loop. Prior to calbindin structure determination it was speculated [14] than the organization of both motifs might be significantly different that the one in parvalbumin, which was the first known protein from this family. Parvalbumin has three motifs, because apart from the typical EF-hand unit it contains an additional motif at the N-terminus. This motif is inactive due to several mutations, but significant sequence similarity between it and other motifs is retained. It is widely believed that both proteins evolved by gene duplication, with two copies present in calbindin and three in parvalbumin. Differences between disparate alignment procedures in this case arise from attempts to align the inactive motif 1 of parvalbumin with modified motif 1 of calbindin, instead of the structurally correct alignment: motif 2 of parvalbumin with motif 1 of calbindin.

Calculation of the alignments. Four substitution matrices were selected from the best scoring substitutions matrices recommended by Argos and co-workers.[4] The Dayhoff matrix as modified in the GCG package,[15] was also included, identified as GCG. Notation for the substitution matrices as well as the optimal parameter values were adapted from.[4] The alignments were determined using the GAP program from GCG package.[15]

Structure prediction: S100A1 protein. S100A1 is a homodimer containing a pair of EF-hand motifs in every chain.[13] S100A1 contains one cysteine residue per chain and occurs in oxidized and reduced forms. The three-dimensional structures of only two proteins closely homologous to S100A1 are known so far: calbindin [16] and calcyclin.[17] Neither of these structures can be used as a template for the oxidized S100A1. Calbindin is monomeric while in calbindin the residues corresponding to S100A1 cysteines are far away from each other, what makes formation of a disulfide bridge impossible without much structural change. This is supported by experimental data on cysteine oxidation [18] and ion binding [Goch and Bierzynski, unpublished data]. In such a situation other structural templates from the EF-hand family are sought. In this case alignment ambiguity stems from the possibility of changing the order in which four EF-hand motifs from a S100A1 dimer are threaded into the template structures (see below).

Structure prediction: modeling templates and sequence - structure alignments For modeling of the oxidized S100A1 dimer structures of bovine recoverin (PDB code 1REC) and SCaBP (sarcoplasmic Ca^{2+}-binding protein from sandworm; PDB code 2SCP) were chosen as templates. Only these two structures contain four EF-hand motifs (as S100A1 dimer) and at the same time have compact conformations allowing the formation of the interchain disulfide bridge without much structural rearrangement. Other known four motif EF-hand calcium proteins have extended conformations with little or no interactions between units.

Structures of all the four EF-hand units present in the templates are very similar, with C_α RMSD on the order of 2-3 Å. Still, due to different unit packing, the overall structures are completely different.[10] Therefore the two structures could be used as distinct templates for modeling. Only the EF-hand motifs were used as templates, because inter-motif linkers and terminal segments vary in length. In the modeling studies the sequence of the bovine S100A1 [19] was used.

At first, all the possible orders in which four EF-hand motifs from S100A1 can be threaded into the template structures were taken into account. Then only these alignments were retained that allowed EF-hand motifs from one S100A1 chain form a standard EF-hand unit. Given this condition there are four non-equivalent alignments of S100A1 dimer within a four-motif template (see Table 2). In order to account for the fact that S100A1 homodimer should be symmetric, only those alignments were used that allowed for symmetry on the level of motif - motif contacts, if not on the level of contacts between individual residues.

The alignments of S100A1 sequence to the recoverin and SCaBP template structures were done in three steps: 1° S100A1 chain sequence was aligned with the calbindin sequence using the Dayhoff PAM 250 matrix. Given the high sequence identity, other scoring matrices gave almost identical alignments. 2° a contact map overlap algorithm [20] was used to produce structural alignments of all the EF-hand motifs from recoverin and SCaBP with both EF-hand motifs of calbindin. 3° the results of the first two steps were combined to obtain alignments of an S100A1 dimer with the templates' structures.

Since modeling the N- and C- terminal segments outside the EF-hand motifs would be arbitrary, only residues Thr 10 - Cys 85 were modeled. The chain segments linking the N- and C-terminal motifs were allowed to relax the strains caused by different alignments. The alignments used are schematically shown in Table 2.

Automated modeling, analysis of models' energy and structural similarity One of recent automated modeling methods was used, implemented in MODELLER.[21] Standard MODELLER routine 'homol' was used. Oxidized structures were modeled with additional disulfide restraint.

The energy parameters, developed for the topology fingerprint threading algorithm [7] were used. The structures of proteins that were modeled in this study were not used for the derivation of energy parameters. The term „energy" is often used here instead of „score", which does not mean that scores can be rigorously treated as real physical energies. The „energy" units roughly correspond to the value of one kT in room temperature.[22]

Two measures of structural similarity are used: root mean square deviation between equivalent C_α positions (RMSD) and the contact map overlap.[20, 23]

For pairs of two native protein structures final RMSD was calculated after superposing the two structures by minimization of C_α RMSD whereas equivalent pairs of C_α atoms were defined by the given sequence alignment.

The quality of sequence alignments was measured by calculating the structural similarity (measured as contact map overlap), between the target and the template according to each alignment. This strategy was used, because it was recently discovered [23, 24] that structural alignments are very ill-defined, with very high density of high-scoring, alternative alignments. Therefore, comparing the alignment to a single „standard of truth" alignment would bias the procedure to an arbitrary alignment chosen from the group of high scoring alignments. This problem becomes serious only for very distant homologues, therefore it is unlikely to change the results of the gap parameters optimization [4] which was primarily done on highly homologous proteins.

3 Results

3. 1 Test cases: alignments

For both pairs of proteins studied here, several different alignments were obtained (see Figures 1, 2). The differences between the alignments were quite high: sequence identity reported by various methods ranged from 21 to 32 % for the EETI / PCI pair and from 26 to 34 % for calbindin and parvalbumin. Alignment ambiguity is even more striking on the structural level: various sequence alignments imply structural alignments ranging from 19 to 44% contact map overlap for EETI and PCI and from 26 to 39 % for calbindin and parvalbumin (see Table 1). It means that the number of conserved inter-residue contacts can change by the factor of 2 depending on the alignment procedure used. Also the more commonly used measure of structural similarity, C_α RMSD, shows variation (see Table 1) corresponding to a broad range of structural alignments - from acceptable values to practically meaningless 8 Å in the case of calbindin and parvalbumin. The latter value indicates that while some regions might have been aligned correctly, some gross misalignments occurred (see below).

```
A)
EETI residues 1-28
..GCPRIL.MRCKQDSDCLAGCVC....GPNGFCG... b_74, str
..GCPRIL.MRCKQDSDCLAGCVCGP..NG..FCG... b_62
..GCPRIL.MRCKQDSDCLAG..C.VC.GPNGFCG... gonnet
..GCPRIL.MRCKQDSDCLAGCVCGPNGFCG......        GCG
..G.CPRILMRCKQDSDC.LAG..CVCGPN.GFCG... [12]

PCI residues 1-37
EHADPICN.KPCKTHDDCSGAWFCQACWNSARTCGPYV


B)
calbindin, residues 1-26
....................................MKSPEELKGIFEKYAAKEGDPNQLSK  b_74,GCG
.................MKSPEEL..KGIFEK..YAAKEGDP..........NQ.....LSK  b_62
.................MKSPEEL..KGIFEK..............YA..AKEGDPNQ.LSK  gonnet
...................MKSPEELKGIFEKYAAKEGDPNQLSK.................  str

parvalbumin, residues 1-60
AFAGVLNDADIAAALEACKAADSFNHKAFFAKVGLTSKSADDVKKAFA..IIDQDKSGFIEE


calbindin, residues 27-76
EELKLLLQ...TEFPSLLKGPSTLDELFEELDKNGDGEVSFEEFQVLVKKISQ      b_74, GCG
EELKLLLQ...TEFPSLLKGPSTLDELFEELDKNGDGEVSFEEFQVLVKKISQ      b_62
EELKLLLQ...TEFPSLLKGPSTLDELFEELDKNGDGEVSFEEFQVLVKKISQ      gonnet
EELKLLLQT.EFPSLLKGPSTL..DELFEELDKNGDGEVSFEEFQVLVKKISQ      str

parvalbumin, residues 61-108
DELKLFLQNFKADARALTDGET..KTFLKAGDSDGDGKIGVDEFTALVKA...
```

Figure 1: Sequence alignments obtained using different substitution matrices.
For both cases the first lines contain the shorter sequence as aligned using the substitution matrix indicated on the right. The template sequence is shown below. A) EETI/PCI; B) calbindin/parvalbumin.

The differences in alignments are not limited to outside loops, but extend to the core regions (see Figure 2). This is well documented by another quantity, the buried contact map overlap (see Table 1). It is calculated as the ordinary contact map overlap, but only contacts between buried residues are included. Different values of buried contact map overlap obtained for various alignments mean that those different fractions of protein cores were aligned correctly.

The benner74 (denoted b_74 in the Figure 1) and str substitution matrices produced identical EETI/PCI alignments, however different from the optimal one. The mere fact that two different substitution matrices give identical alignment does not imply this is the best one. All the alignments of these proteins agree in the N-terminal part of the sequence (residues 1-20; see Figures 2 A, B). In the C-terminal part of the sequence for every position at least three different alignments were obtained. Although these differences didn't involve more than a shift of four residues, they were sufficient to generate erroneous models with visibly higher energy.

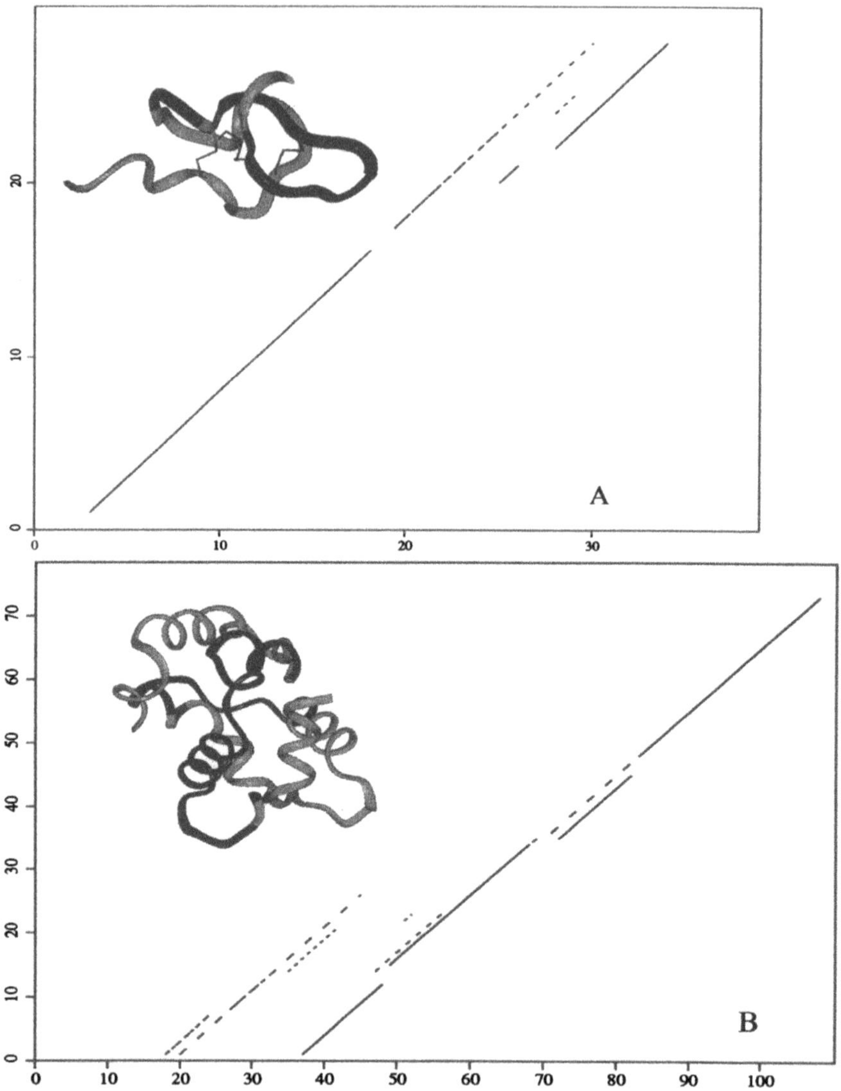

Figure 2: Regions where alignments diverge
Dot-matrix representations of alignments for the EETI/PCI [A] and calbindin/parvalbumin [B] pairs. Best alignments are shown as continuous lines. Other alignments, where different from the best ones, are shown as dashed lines. Ribbon representations of PCI and parvalbumin structures are shown in the insets. The regions where differences in alignments occur are shown in black.

Table 1: Model characteristics. t/t: target/template comparison; t/m: target/model comparison For target/template contact map overlap the values in parentheses were calculated for the buried residues only.

Substitution	sequence	model	MODE-	C_α RMSD [Å]		contact map overlap	
matrix	identity	energy	LLER score	t/t	t/m	t/t	t/m
EETI/PCI							
benner74	28.6	-0.4	244	3.6	3.2	33 (47)	39
blosum62	32.1	5.7	288	4.0	3.8	27 (47)	34
gonnet	32.1	-2.2	200	3.1	2.9	44 (56)	58
GCG	21.4	11.7	197	5.3	5.3	19 (28)	23
str	28.6	-0.4	244	3.6	3.2	33 (47)	39
structural [12]	28.6	-2.0	164	2.6	2.5	33 (44)	62
calbindin / parvalbumin							
benner74	30.4	-18.5	420	4.4	4.2	39 (54)	51
blosum62	33.8	-16.1	595	8.9	8.2	32 (49)	41
gonnet	32.4	-12.4	680	8.1	7.4	34 (50)	49
GCG	30.4	-18.5	420	4.4	4.2	39 (54)	51
str	26.0	-12.3	554	8.8	8.9	26 (26)	36

In the case of calbindin and parvalbumin identical alignments were produced using benner74 and GCG substitution matrices. The calbindin / parvalbumin alignments differ, as expected, mostly in the 1-40 region (the inactive EF-hand motif) in parvalbumin sequence (see Figure 2), which is erroneously aligned by most substitution matrices with parts of the first EF-hand motif of calbindin (with a shift of ca. 20 residues relative to the best alignment). This error had to propagate, so large gaps are aligned with the second parvalbumin EF-hand motif (region 40-80; see Figure 1B) and differences end only at the beginning of the third motif. Only the 26 positions at the C-terminus are aligned in the same manner by all the substitution matrices used. This case may seem to be more trivial than the first one since some knowledge on sequence patterns of EF-motifs could allow to discard the wrong alignments. Such knowledge is not possible however without first knowing the target calbindin structure.

3. 2 Test cases: models

Protein models obtained starting from alignments as divergent as described above, are not surprisingly very different one from another. It is very encouraging that in both test cases the models picked up by the energy score criterion are those that are closest to the native target structure (see Table 1). Moreover, the models judged to be worst by this criterion are those that differ most from the native structure. It was checked that all the energy terms used here are important for selection of the most correct model.

The differences in energies between the models are largest for those residues that are misaligned relative to the best alignment (data not shown). In „bad" EETI models residues with high energy are found mostly in the C-terminal region, where alignments differ. Interestingly, residues with high energy are found also in the N-terminal part of some bad EETI models. In this region all the alignments are identical, so differences in energy of a residue reflect propagation of alignment errors. Similar observations can be made for calbindin models.

In the two test cases studied, different mutation matrices gave good and bad alignments. In the case of EETI and PCI the gonnet substitution matrix produced the best alignment while the GCG gave the worst. In the case of calbindin and parvalbumin the best alignments were obtained using the benner74 and GCG substitution matrices, and the worst one using the str matrix.

The best model of EETI, built without the knowledge of the native structure, is nearly as accurate as the model based on the previously published alignment that was prepared using the EETI structure [12] (See Table 1).

An internal measure of model quality supplied by the MODELLER program,[21] did not always allow to distinguish the most correct model (see Table 1). In one case (calbindin model) it selected the best one, while in the other case (EETI model) - the worst. It is not surprising though, since this function doesn't describe physical quality of the model, only degree of satisfaction of the restraints imposed.

There is a difference in sensitivity between contact map overlap and C_α RMSD. In case of calbindin models compared to the native structure RMSD varies from 4.4 to 8.9 Å whereas contact map overlap varies only from 36 to 51 %. This reflects the fact that the former measure is more global - it is not sensitive to regions of weak structural similarity and changes of relative positions of otherwise similar protein segments.

3. 3 Predicted structure of the oxidized S100A1 protein

Energies of models (see Table 2) suggest that the oxidized S100A1 dimer prefers the recoverin fold. Some of the scores however may be partly affected by the difficulty of modeling the segments linking the EF-hand motifs and the terminal „tails".

The best model of the oxidized S100A1 follows the general fold of recoverin, and the two chains occupy place of recoverin EF-hand motifs. S100A1 chains are linked by the disulfide bridge and stabilized by hydrophobic interactions between several interface residues. The placement of chain segments linking the motifs, which is different than in recoverin, does not distort the recoverin-like structure.

The model proposed here represents S100A1 in the calcium-loaded state. Although calcium ions were not present in the modeling process, they were included *implicite* since the templates were structures with ion-binding sites occupied.

Table 2: Energy for the models of S100A1 dimer. Different alignment modes are represented in column 1. EF-hand motifs from templates are numbered from the N-terminal. For the S100A1 dimer N1 denotes N-terminal motif from first S100A1 chain, etc. Empty cells represent models that were not considered due to the symmetry requirement (see the „Methods" section).

Alignment of EF-hand motifs		Template	
		Recoverin	SCaBP
S100A1 motifs template motifs	N1 C1 N2 C2 1 2 3 4		+4.1
	N1 C1 C2 N2	**-17.6**	
	C1 N1 N2 C2	-6.1	
	C1 N1 C2 N2		+22.6

4 Discussion

In this work we proposed a novel approach to the problem of alignment ambiguities which is encountered in the initial stages of comparative protein modeling. The importance of the alignment choice can be seen in some of the wrong models obtained in this study. These models, although prepared using state-of-the art alignment methods that statistically perform well, contain errors as severe as completely incorrect ion binding site in the case of calbindin. It was shown, that in both test cases studied, our criterion of model energy can correctly recognize the best model. Using an automated modeling procedure and analyzing resulting models with the statistical potential allows one to worry less about quality of the alignment. This approach can be extended, as presented on the example of S100A1 structure prediction, to using different structural templates if it is not clear a priori, which is the most appropriate for modeling.

The manuals of comparative modeling programs stress the importance of the sequence alignment and ask the user to prepare it with utmost care. The author of the MODELLER package goes even further and suggests an iterative approach, i. e. careful analysis of a model produced using an initial alignment, reexamination and correction of the alignment and producing an improved model.[21] The approach presented here can be viewed as a practical realization of these suggestions, but construction of many alignments and models can be done simultaneously what allows for partial automation of the process.

At the stage of alignment construction separated fragments of target sequence are equivalenced to fragments of template structure. The construction of the model can be regarded as a test of geometric feasibility of the connectivity between aligned target sequence fragments. At this point one may wonder, what actual characteristics of the model give raise to good/bad self-threading score and if it would be possible to incorporate them into the threading program itself. The search for such features was an initial objective of the research described here and it remains our ultimate goal. Unfortunately, so far we were not able to identify the high energy fragments of the model in a way which could be utilized on the alignment stage. Thus, model building remains a slow, but necessary ultimate test for the accuracy of the alignment. It should be stressed, that even if a relatively small number of alignments can be tested and compared, each of these alignments come from the well optimized alignment procedure.

The approach described here attempts to explore the conformational space more widely than standard modeling techniques, in recognition of the fact that constructing just one model requires one to be able to formulate very decisive assumptions about the modeled structure. Proposing a number of models for subsequent theoretical evaluation and experimental verification is a step towards more reliable modeling in situations, where substantially homologous structures can be identified, but it is not clear which of them to use and how to use them. Still, this approach is limited to testing and comparing models, which all come from within the space of already known protein topologies.

Acknowledgments

We thank A.Koliński for stimulating discussions. We thank Dr. W. Chazin for making the calcyclin structure available to us prior to its release. We thank Dr A. Šali for kindly providing us with his MODELLER program. Support by the following grants is acknowledged: NIH GM-48835 (AG), Howard Hughes Medical Institute grant 75195-53402 (£J), Polish Committee for Scientific Research grant KBN-4111789101 (AB and KP).

References

1. Thornton, J.M. and M.B. Swindells, in *Molecular Structures in Biology*, R. Diamond, Editor. 1993, Oxford Univerity Press: Oxford.
2. Johnson, M.S., *et al. Crit. Rev. Biochem. & Mol. Biol.* **29,** 1 (1994)
3. Karplus, M. and A. Sali. *Current Opinion Struct Biol.* **5,** 58 (1995)
4. Vogt, G., T. Etzold, and P. Argos. *J. Mol. Biol.* **249,** 816 (1995)
5. Needelman, S.B. and C.D. Wunsch. *J. Mol. Biol.* **48,** 443 (1970)
6. Vingron, M. and P. Argos. *Prot. Engineer.* **3,** 565 (1990)
7. Godzik, A., J. Skolnick, and A. Kolinski. *J. Mol. Biol* **227,** 227 (1992)
8. Luethy, R., J.U. Bowie, and D. Eisenberg. *Nature* **356,** 83 (1992)
9. Jaroszewski, L. and A. Godzik. *Prot. Engineer.* submitted (1996)
10. Pawlowski, K., A. Bierzynski, and A. Godzik. *J. Mol. Biol.* **258,** 349 (1996)
11. Saqi, M.A., P.A. Bates, and M.J. Sternberg. *Prot. Engineer.* **5,** 305 (1992)
12. Chiche, L., *et al. Prot. Engineer.* **6,** 675 (1993)
13. Kawasaki, H. and R. Kretsinger. *Protein Profile* **1,** 343 (1994)
14. Kretsinger, R.H. *CRC Crit. Rev. Biochem.* **8,** 119 (1980)
15. Genetic Computer Group. Program Manual for the GCG Package, Version 7 (1991)
16. Svensson, L.A., E. Thulin, and S. Forsen. *J. Mol. Biol.* **223,** 601 (1992)
17. Potts, B.C., *et al. Nature Str. Biol.* **2,** 790 (1995)
18. Mely, Y. and D. Gerard. *J. Neurochem.* **55,** 1100 (1990)
19. Bairoch, A., *SwissProt*, . 1994.
20. Godzik, A., J. Skolnick, and A. Kolinski. *Prot. Engineering* **6,** 801 (1993)
21. Sali, A. and J.P. Overington. *Protein Science.* **3,** 1582 (1994)
22. Godzik, A., A. Kolinski, and J. Skolnick. *Protein Science* **4,** 2107 (1995)
23. Godzik, A. *Protein Science* **5,** 1325 (1996)
24. Zu-Feng, F. and M. Sippl. *Folding & Design* **1,** 123 (1996)

SEARCH FOR DNA CONFORMATIONAL FEATURES FOR FUNCTIONAL SITES. INVESTIGATION OF THE TATA BOX

M.P. PONOMARENKO, J.V. PONOMARENKO, A.E. KEL, N.A. KOLCHANOV
Institute of Cytology and Genetics, 10 Lavretyev Ave, 630090 Novosibirsk, Russia.

A method for search of DNA conformational features significant for functional sites is developed. The method uses helical angles averaged for known X-ray structures. Nucleotide sequences are assigned mean angles in a given region. Choice of the significant angles is based on their capabilities to discriminate functional sites from random sequences. The yeast, invertebrate and vertebrate TATA boxes are analyzed using this method. Regions neighboring the TATA boxes are found to have smaller helical twist and roll angles. The results agree with the experimental data on Dickerson-Drew dodecamers. There is a significant decrease in the length of a small roll angle region with increasing complexity of taxon organization.

1. INTRODUCTION

The problem of transcription regulation has become pivotal in structural molecular biology. There is a growing body of experimental information on the molecular mechanisms of transcription [1]. Attention has been focused on the TATA box because it is utilized to anchor transcription complexes [2]. X-ray structures for Dickerson-Drew dodecamers [3] and the TATA binding protein (TBP) complex with the TATA box [4] have been determined; the equilibrium dissociation constant of the complex has been measured [5]; nonspecific TBP-binding to DNA and its stable sliding along the DNA is now known to precede the formation of the TBP-TATA complex [2]. All this strongly suggests that a region in the neighborhood of the TATA box may be involved in the TBP-TATA recognition [2].

The theoretical approaches used to analyze the TATA box sequences have included consensus [6], long consensus pattern [7], information content [8], weight matrix [9, 10], statistical mechanics [11], neural network [12], recursive systems [13], and mathematical statistics [14]. These approaches have provided new insights into the structure and function of the TATA box. However, based on the structural results the TATA box has not been, as yet, accurately predicted. The question is raised: Are there conformational features in the neighborhood of the TATA-box that can be used to increase prediction accuracy ?.

Interest in the effect of nucleotide context on the helical configuration of B-DNA has been stirred by Dickerson and Drew [3, 15] and Calladine [16]. Subsequent analysis of sequence-dependent DNA structure relied on the Calladine rules [17]. The number of unraveled X-ray structures of B-DNA and DNA-protein complexes is increasing [1, 2, 4, 18, 19, 20, 21, 22, 23].

A method using a library of low energy conformation theoretically calculated for B-DNA hexanucleotides [24] has been developed [25]. It is improved here by introducing experimental data on averaged helical angles for dinucleotides [18, 21, 22, 23]. The yeast, invertebrate and vertebrate TATA boxes were analyzed using the combined method. It was determined that the mean values for the roll and helical twist angles of a TATA box are smaller than those for a random sequence. Closer examination revealed that the length of the region with a small roll angle decreases with increasing complexity of evolutionary organization.

2. MATERIALS AND METHODS

The conformational angles X_1, X_2, X_3, X_4, X_5, X_6, X_7, X_8, X_9 for dinucleotides are given in Table 1. Angles X_1, X_2, X_3 were taken from [18, 21, 22]; their values were averaged from known X-ray structures of DNA. Angles X_4, X_5, X_6, X_7, X_8, X_9 were

Table 1. The helical angles were averaged for known X-ray structures of DNA (degrees)

Dimer	Direction	Wedge	Helical twist			Roll		Tilt	
	Free	**Free**	**Free**	**Both**	**Comp**	**Both**	**Comp**	**Both**	**Comp**
s_1s_2	X_1	X_2	X_3	X_4	X_5	X_6	X_7	X_8	X_9
AA	-154	7.2	35.6	35.5	35.5	0.5	1.0	1.0	1.5
AT	0	2.6	31.5	29.5	29.0	0	0	0	0
AG	2	8.4	27.7	35.5	35.0	5.0	5.0	1.0	1.0
AC	143	1.1	34.4	31.0	30.5	1.5	0	0.5	0
TA	0	0.9	36.0	37.5	39.5	4.0	2.5	0	0
TT	154	7.2	35.6	35.5	35.5	0.5	1.0	1.0	1.5
TG	64	3.5	34.5	36.0	36.0	5.0	6.5	-0.5	0.5
TC	-120	5.3	36.9	36.5	35.5	2.5	2.5	1.0	1.5
GA	120	5.3	36.9	36.5	35.5	2.5	2.5	1.0	1.5
GT	-143	1.1	34.4	31.0	30.5	1.5	0	0.5	0
GG	57	2.1	33.7	35.0	36.0	5.0	3.0	0	1.0
GC	180	5.0	40.0	35.0	34.5	-3.0	-2.5	0	0
CA	-64	3.5	34.5	36.0	36.0	5.0	6.5	-0.5	0.5
CT	-2	8.4	27.7	35.5	35.0	5.0	5.0	1.0	1.0
CG	0	6.7	29.8	34.5	34.5	5.0	6.5	0	0
CC	-57	2.1	33.7	35.0	36.0	5.0	3.0	0	1.0
Ref.	[18, 21, 22]			[23]					

<u>Notes</u>: **Free** is for the angles X_1, X_2, X_3 averaged from free DNA; **Comp** is for the angles X_5, X_7, X_9 from DNA-protein complexes; **Both** is for the angles X_4, X_6, X_8 from the complexes and from free DNA

taken from [22]; X_5, X_7, X_9 were averaged from DNA-protein complexes; and X_4, X_6, X_8 from the complexes and from free DNA.

The definitions of the direction and wedge angles, X_1 and X_2, and their geometrical implications have been given in [22]. The helical twist (X_3, X_4, X_5), roll (X_6, X_7) and tilt (X_8, X_9) angles have been recommended as nomenclature for description of DNA conformations by the EMBO Workshop [20]. As shown in Table 1, the helical twist angles averaged for different data sets (X_3, X_4, X_5) differ from one another. It was not clear which angle set would provide significant

Table 2. Sets of nucleotide sequences

no	Set		Sequences			TATA-pattern	
	promoters	type	number	length	margins	start	aligned by
1	Yeast	S^+	75	70 bp	[-30; +39]	0	subsequence TATAT
2	Invertebrate	S^+	158	70 bp	[-30; +39]	0	weight matrix [10]
3	Vertebrate	S^+	486	70 bp	[-30; +39]	0	weight matrix [10]
4	*E.coli*	S^+	135	70 bp	[-39; +30]	0	consensus, TATAAT [6]
5	Random	S^-	500	70 bp	by $\{S^+\}$	none	none

<u>**Note:**</u> sets 1 and 4 are compiled on the basis of EMBL Data Library, sets 2 and 3 on the basis of EPD

conformational features of the TATA box. Therefore, each single set was analyzed one by one. Two data sets for the roll angle (X_6, X_7) and two data sets for the tilt angle (X_8, X_9) were also analyzed for the same reason.

Table 2 presents the nucleotide sequences used in analysis. There were 5 sequence sets. Set 1, 75 yeast promoters aligned by their subsequence TATAT. Sets 2 and 3, 158 invertebrate and 486 vertebrate promoters. The TATA box weight matrix [10] was used to align these promoters. Set 4, 135 *E.coli* promoters. The TATA pattern of these promoters, Pribnow box, was identified by the consensus TATAAT [6]. Sets 1 and 4 were compiled on the basis of EMBL Data Library (release 42) with keywords «promoter» and «primary transcript»; and sets 2 and 3 were taken from the database EPD (release 45). Set 5, 500 random sequences with the same nucleotide frequencies. This set served to search for significant differences between the promoters and the random sequences. All the sequences were 70 b.p. long. The start of the TATA pattern was taken as 0. Sequence position was numbered in this way to pinpoint the TATA pattern whose position varied with respect to transcription start.

Sequence regions $\{s_a...s_i...s_b\}$ located from a to b and of length (b-a+1) were examined. All the possible sequence regions not smaller than one dinucleotide were taken into account. Their number for a sequence L long was n(L)=L×(L-1)/2. The total number of sequence regions was n(70)=70×(70-1)/2=2415.

Each region a, b with the sequence $S=\{s_a...s_i...s_b\}$ was assigned a mean value of a conformational angle X_k:

$$X_{k,a,b}(S) = \frac{1}{b-a}\sum_{i=a}^{b-1} X_k(s_i s_{i+1}), \qquad (1)$$

where X_k is any one of the angles given in Table 1.

Let formula (1) be applied to the sequence S={TATA}. The mean value $X_{7,1,4}$(TATA) for the roll angle X_7 was calculated as: $X_{7,1,4}$(TATA) = [X_7(TA) + X_7(AT) + X_7(TA)] / (4 - 1) = [2.5° + 0.0° + 2.5°] / 3 = 5° / 3 = 1.67°.

Formula (1) was applied to each of the 9 angles given in Table 1. A number of angles $X_{k,a,b}$ can be calculated N(L)=9×n(L) for a sequence L long. Thus, a total number of N(70)=9×2415=21735 angles was tested.

The SITEVIDEO system [26, 27] was used to analyze the conformational angles $X_{k,a,b}$. The system allows to test for significance various physicochemical, statistical, contextual and conformational properties defined theoretically or experimentally. In a previous analysis [25], we have modified SITEVIDEO by using Sklenar's theoretical parameters for B-DNA [24]. In the present study, the SITEVIDEO was further modified by introducing experimental parameters for B-DNA [18, 21, 22, 23].

Fig.1 illustrates how the significant angles for the TATA patterns are identified by the current version of SITEVIDEO. Two sequence sets S^+ and S^- were initial, with S^+ containing the TATA patterns and S^- random sequences. SITEVIDEO treats S^+ and S^- in four steps.

Step 1, calculation of all the 21,735 angle values $X_{k,a,b}(S)$ for all the sequences from S^+ and S^- by formula (1). This yields the sets $X_{k,a,b}(S^+)$ and $X_{k,a,b}(S^-)$ for the TATA and random sequences, respectively.

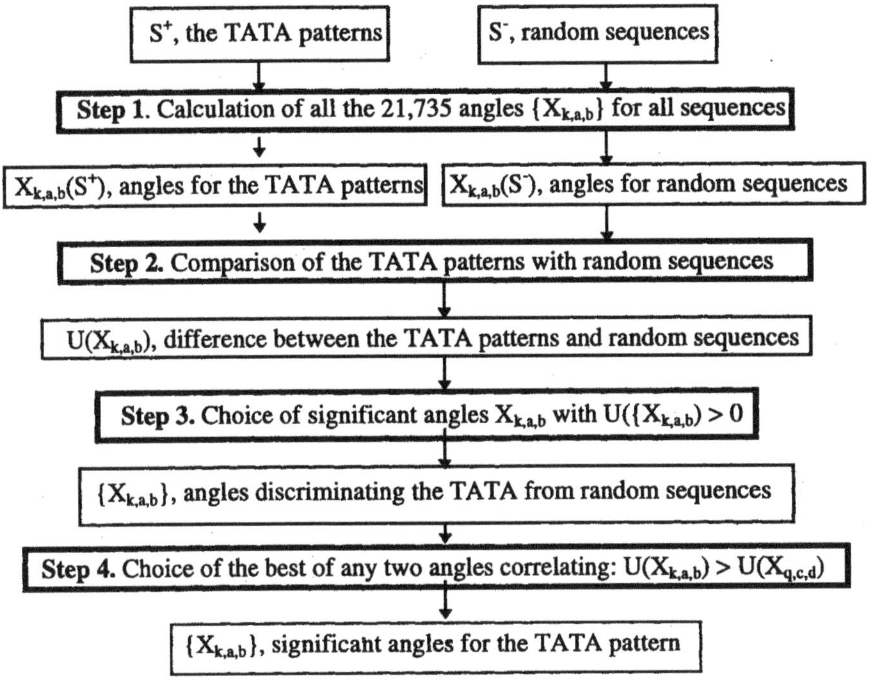

Fig. 1. A search for significant conformational angles in the TATA pattern.

Step 2, pairs $X_{k,a,b}(S^+)$ and $X_{k,a,b}(S^-)$ are analyzed. This yields an estimate $U(X_{k,a,b})$ of the difference between $X_{k,a,b}(S^+)$ and $X_{k,a,b}(S^-)$. The algorithm [27] was used to test for significance as mean, variance, range and other statistics. A positive weight from 0 to 1 was assigned to each significant difference, and a negative weight from -1 to 0 to each insignificant difference, and the mean value of the weights is the estimate $U(X_{k,a,b})$ of the differences between $X_{k,a,b}(S^+)$ and $X_{k,a,b}(S^-)$. According to the decision making theory [28], the U value varies from -1 to 1; insignificant differences predominate at $U<0$, and significant at $U>0$; and the greater the U, the larger are the number of significant differences.

Step 3, all the conformational angles $X_{k,a,b}$ with $U(X_{k,a,b})>0$ are taken for further analysis so that only angles in which the TATA patterns differ from random sequences are chosen.

Step 4, when any angles $X_{k,a,b}$ and $X_{q,c,d}$ correlate, the angle $X_{q,c,d}$ with the smaller $U(X_{q,c,d})$ value is discarded, the other $X_{k,a,b}$ with the greater $U(X_{k,a,b})$ is fixed. A list of significant angles $X_{k,a,b}$ for the TATA pattern is thus generated.

3. RESULTS AND DISCUSSION

The yeast, invertebrate, vertebrate TATA boxes (Table 1) were analyzed using the developed method. Analysis was based on a set of 500 random sequences. Table 3 summarizes the obtained results. Two independent conformational angles were found for the yeast TATA box. One was a mean helical twist angle in the region from -2 to 9 with U=0.95. The mean helical twist angle was 33.1°±0.3° for the TATA box and 34.7°±0.4° for the random sequences. The occurrence probability

Table 3. Significant conformational angles for the TATA box

Promoters	Angle				Value, (degrees)		Sig-nifi-cance
	name	X_k	region, [a; b]	$U(X_{kab})$	promoters mean ± s.d.	random mean ± s.d.	
Yeast	twist	X_4	[-2; 9]	0.95	33.1±0.3	34.7±0.4	10^{-7}
	twist	previous*	[-10; 9]	0.81	32.2±0.9	35.6±0.8	10^{-9}
	roll	X_7	[-13; 7]	0.93	1.97±0.26	2.53±0.28	10^{-7}
Invertebrate	twist	X_4	[0; 6]	0.91	33.8±0.4	34.7±0.6	10^{-13}
	twist	previous*	[-3; 5]	0.78	33.7±0.7	36.3±1.3	10^{-8}
	roll	X_7	[-7; 7]	0.90	1.93±0.23	2.67±0.27	10^{-40}
Vertebrate	roll	X_7	[0; 6]	0.99	0.88±0.25	2.22±0.57	10^{-40}
E.coli	roll	X_7	[-30; 10]	0.72	2.35±0.22	2.60±0.16	10^{-7}

*) Asterisks, our previous results [25] based on Sklenar's parameters [24]

for the difference between the mean values was less than 10^{-7}. The mean helical twist angle for the invertebrate TATA box in the region from 0 to 6 is 33.8°±0.4°, significantly smaller than for the random sequences (34.7°±0.6°).

Thus, a small helical twist angle in the neighborhood of the TATA box was found. Based on Sklenar's parameters [24], we have obtained [25] a small helical twist angle in the neighborhood of the yeast and invertebrate TATA boxes (Table 3). The previous results are in agreement with our present and also with the X-ray structure of Dickerson-Drew dodecamers [3].

A mean roll angle in the region from -13 to 7 was the other significant angle found in the neighborhood of the yeast TATA box (Table 3). Angle value was 1.97°±0.26° for the TATA box and 2.53°±0.28° for the random sequences, the difference between the two mean values being significant ($\alpha<10^{-7}$). The roll angle is also smaller for the invertebrate and vertebrate TATA boxes than for the random sequences (Table 3).

It is of interest that the roll angles were equally small for the TATA and Pribnow boxes (Table 3), and also for the Dickerson-Drew dodecamers [3]. Moreover, the conformational invariant in the neighborhood of the TATA box is consistent with the experimental data indicating that TBP stably sliding along the DNA precedes the formation of the TBP-TATA complex [2].

The roll angle for the TATA patterns (black) and for the random sequences (white) are given in Fig.2. The increasing difference between the TATA and random sequences may be ordered as *E.coli* → yeast → invertebrate → vertebrate. The significance of the order was tested by assigning rank values to each of the taxon according to the increasing complexity of organization (Fig.3, the vertical scale). The length of the region with a small roll angle was also scaled. The linear correlation coefficient r between the rank and the length was -0.96 ($\alpha<0.05$).

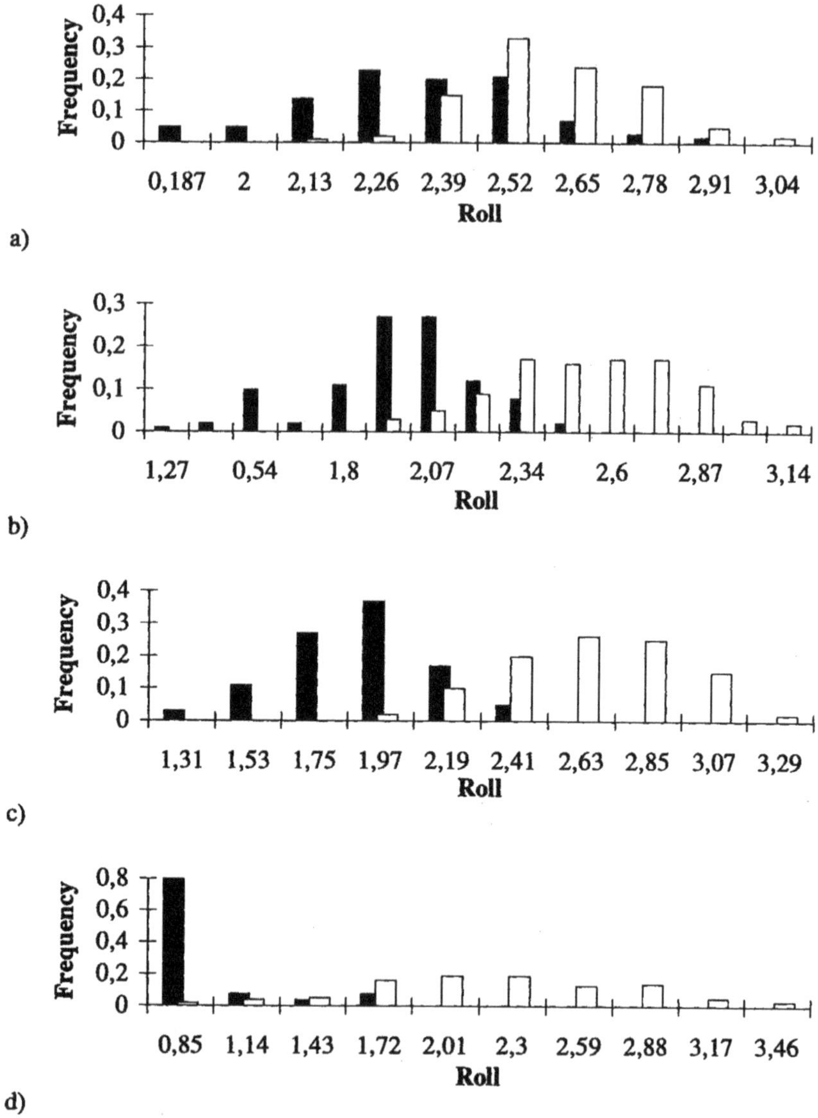

Fig. 2. Frequency histograms of the roll angle for the TATA (black) and random (white) sequences. Taxa: a) *E.coli*; b) yeast; c) invertebrate; d) vertebrate.

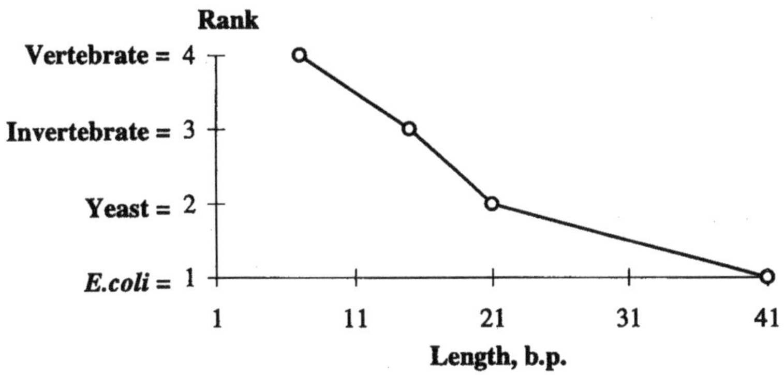

Fig. 3. Reduction of the promoter region with a small roll angle with increasing complexity of taxa organization. The linear correlation coefficient $r=-0.96$ ($\alpha<0.05$).

Thus, the promoter region with a small roll angle reduces with increasing complexity of taxon organization. The reduction might have resulted from an increase in the number of transcription factors associated with increasing complexity of taxon organization. The *E.coli* transcription machinery is simplest because RNA-polymerase recognizes the Pribnow box and performs all the other functions. Consequently, an error admitted by RNA-polymerase in the false recognition cannot be corrected. For this reason, the Pribnow box must be safeguarded by other signals necessary for the *E.coli* transcription machinery. Thus, the *E.coli* region with a small roll angle were expected to be longest. This was, indeed, the case.

The formation of an eukaryotic transcription complex is multistep. For the majority of genes, the TBP-TATA recognition initiates the complex formation. In a cascade, other transcription factors bind to the DNA sites proximal to or distant from the TATA box. Hence, a false TBP-TATA recognition would not lead to the formation of the transcription complex, because they have no transcription factor binding sites providing recognition around the false TATA box. Therefore, the role of the TATA box in the transcription machinery is restricted compared to the Pribnow box. The regression may possibly result in a reduction of the promoter region with a small roll angle in the neighborhood of the TATA box. For this reason, the reductions were expected in the passages from unicellular (yeast) to multicellular (invertebrate, vertebrate) and from the invertebrate to the vertebrate. These expectations were met (Fig.3).

Taken together, the obtained data evidence that analysis of "sequence-conformation" relationships allows to reveal conformational features maintained unaltered during evolution. There is a good agreement between our previous results [25] based on Sklenar's theoretical parameters [24] and our present using experimental parameters [18, 21, 22, 23]. Thus, the Sklenar's parameters for the B-DNA [24] offers promise in structural molecular biology.

ACKNOWLEDGMENTS

The authors are grateful to A.Fadeeva for translating this paper into English. This research was supported by the Russian Foundation of Fundamental Investigation.

REFERENCES

1. S. Neidle, DNA structure and recognition, IRL Press, New York (1994)
2. R.A. Coleman and B.F. Pugh, J. Biol. Chem., 270, 13850 (1995)
3. R.E. Dickerson and H.R. Drew, J. Mol. Biol., 149, 761 (1981)
4. Y. Kim et al, Nature, 365, 512 (1993)
5. S. Hahn et al, Proc. Nath. Acad. Sci. U.S.A., 86, 5718 (1989)
6. R. Staden, Comput. Appl. Biosci., 5, 89 (1989)
7. P. Taylor et al, Comput. Appl. Biosci., 7, 495 (1991)
8. T.D. Schneider et al, J. Mol. Biol., 188, 415 (1986)

9. D.K. Hawley and W.R. McClure, Nucleic Acids Res., 11, 2237 (1983)
10. P. Bucher, J. Mol. Biol., 212, 563 (1990)
11. O.G. Berg and P.H. von Hipple, J.Mol.Biol., 193, 723 (1987)
12. M.C. O'Neill, Nucleic Acids Res., 19, 313 (1991)
13. L. Milanezi et al, in Guide to human genome computing, Ed. M. Bishop, Academic Press, London, 249 (1994)
14. Y.V. Kondrakhin et al, Comput. Applic. Biosci., 11, 477 (1995)
15. R.M. Wing et al, Nature, 287, 755 (1980)
16. C.R. Calladine, J. Mol. Biol., 161, 343 (1982)
17. C.R. Calladine and H.R. Drew, J. Mol. Biol., 178, 773 (1984)
18. W. Kabsh et al, Nucleic Acids Res., 10, 1097 (1982)
19. R.E. Dickerson, J. Mol. Biol., 166, 419 (1983)
20. R.E. Dickerson et al, EMBO J., 8, 1 (1989)
21. A. Bolshoy et al, Proc. Nath., Acad. Sci. U.S.A, 88, 2312 (1991)
22. E.S. Shpigelman et al, Comput. Applic. Biosci., 9, 435 (1993)
23. M. Suzuki and N. Yagi, Nucleic Acids Res., 23, 2083 (1995)
24. H. Sklenar, in Proceedings of the International Workshop on Computational analysis of eukaryotic transcriptional regulatory elements, Heidelberg, 44 (1996)
25. N.A. Kolchanov et al, in Proceedings of the International Workshop on Computational analysis of eukaryotic transcriptional regulatory elements, Heidelberg, 40 (1996)
26. A.E. Kell et al, Comput. Applic. Biosci., 9, 617 (1993)
27. M.P. Ponomarenko et al, in Computer analysis of genetic macromolecules. Eds. N.A. Kolchanov and H. Lim, World Sci. Pub., Singapore, 35 (1993)
28. P.C. Fishburn, Utility theory for decision making, Wiley, New York (1970)

ALGORITHMIC COMPLEXITY OF GROWTH HORMONE RELEASE IN HUMANS

K. PRANK, M. WAGNER, G. BRABANT
Department of Clinical Endocrinology, Medical School Hannover,
D-30623 Hannover, Germany

Most hormones are secreted in an pulsatile rather than in a constant manner. This temporal pattern of pulsatile hormone release plays an important role in the regulation of cellular function and structure. In healthy humans growth hormone (GH) secretion is characterized by distinct pulses whereas patients bearing a GH producing tumor accompanied with excessive secretion (acromegaly) exhibit a highly irregular pattern of GH release. It has been hypothesized that this highly disorderly pattern of GH release in acromegaly arises from random events in the GH-producing tumor under decreased normal control of GH secretion. Using a context-free grammar complexity measure (algorithmic complexity) in conjunction with random surrogate data sets we demonstrate that the temporal pattern of GH release in acromegaly is not significantly different from a variety of stochastic processes. In contrast, normal subjects clearly exhibit deterministic structure in their temporal patterns of GH secretion. Our results support the hypothesis that GH release in acromegaly is due to random events in the GH-producing tumorous cells which might become independent from hypothalamic regulation.

1 Introduction

In endocrine systems information is encoded in the temporal pattern of pulsatile hormone release. This temporal pattern of secretion has been demonstrated in most endocrine systems with pulse frequencies ranging from approximately 6 to 140 pulses in 24 hours (Brabant *et al.*[1]). This pulsatile mode of hormone release has important effects on the regulation of target cell function and structure (Weigle and Goodner[2], Haisenleder *et al.*[3], Shupnik[4]). A classification of the temporal patterns of pulsatile hormone secretion as stochastic or deterministic is of major importance for the understanding of diseases caused by the disruption of the physiological pattern.

Time series of growth hormone (GH) concentration in the blood of healthy adult subjects are characterized by 6 to 12 distinct pulses of GH release within 24 hours (Ho *et al.*[5], Hindmarsh *et al.*[6], Fig. 1a). In contrast to this orderly pattern of GH release, patients bearing a GH-producing tumor within the pituitary gland (acromegaly) exhibit an irregular pattern of GH concentration fluctuations in the blood accompanied with excessive mean levels of GH (Hartman *et al.*[7], Riedel *et al.*[8], Fig. 1b). This highly disorderly pattern of excessive concentrations of GH has important pathophysiological effects such as the stimulation of connective tissue growth, cardiovascular and cerebrovascular disease, diabetes mellitus, and arthritis (Daughaday[9]).

Normal pulsatile GH secretion from the pituitary gland is regulated by growth hormone-releasing hormone (GHRH) and growth hormone-inhibiting hormone (somatostatin) which are secreted from the hypothalamus. It has been hypothesized that that the irregular pattern of GH release in acromegaly arises from random episodic GH secretion from the GH-producing pituitary tumor which operates under reduced control of the hypothalamus.

To investigate this hypothesis 24-h time series of GH concentration in blood were measured in five healthy controls and six patients with acromegaly. To classify the temporal pattern of the GH concentration time series as random or deterministic is of major importance for the understanding of acromegaly and the development of the specific symptoms. The time series of GH concentration were analyzed by computing the algorithmic complexity as a context-free complexity measure and comparing the results for the measured GH time series with those obtained for the statistically matched random surrogate data sets.

2 Subjects and Methods

2.1 Subjects and Patients

Five young male subjects (aged 22-33 years, body mass index (BMI) 23.8 kg/m^2) and six patients (three males and three females) with clinical and biochemical diagnosis of acromegaly (aged 27-54 years) and not cured by previous therapies took part in this study. The studies were approved by the local Committee on Medical Ethics, and all subjects and patients gave their informed written consent. All healthy controls were carefully examined to exclude underlying diseases. The healthy controls and the acromegalic patients were admitted to our endocrine unit
at noon, and a central venous catheter was placed. Blood samples were taken every 10 min over 24 h, starting at 1800 h. Sleep was allowed between 2300 h and 0600 h. The 24-h GH secretory profile in the acromegalic group was studied without any medication.

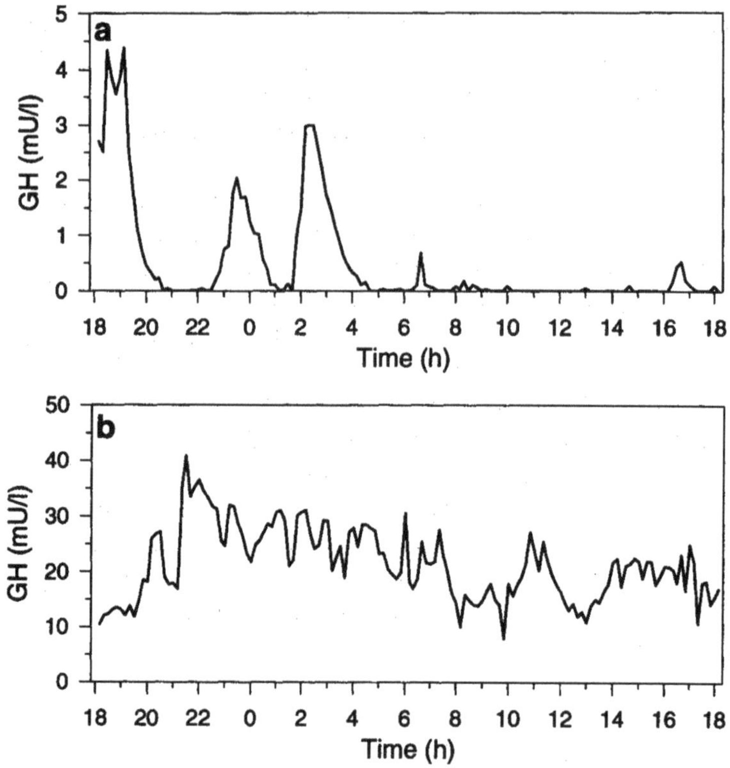

Figure 1: Measured 24-h time series of GH blood concentrations in a healthy subject (a) and (b) in a patient with excessive GH secretion (acromegaly). Blood samples were taken at 10-min. intervals.

2.2 Hormone Determination

The hormone concentrations of all serum samples were measured in duplicate. Commercially available immunoradiometric assays with a sensitivity of 0.2 mU/liter were used. Serum samples below the detection limit were set to 0.01 mU/liter. Intra- and interassay coefficient of variation ranged from 2.5% and 7.1% for low hormone concentration values to 6.0% and 8.0% for high values.

2.3 Algorithmic Complexity

Context-free grammar complexity (Ebeling *et al.*[10]) has recently been demonstrated to quantify the degree of non-random internal structure in experimental spike trains of spontaneously active neurons (Rapp *et al.*[11]). Using this algorithmic complexity measure in conjunction with statistically matched surrogate random data sets it is possible to classify neurons based on the sequence-sensitive structure of their interspike interval trains. Applying conventional distribution-determined measures such as the mean interval, the standard deviation, skewness, or kurtosis this classification has not be possible (Rapp *et al.*[11]). This definition of algorithmic complexity is based on Kolmogorov's and Chaitin's definitions of complexity (Kolmogorov[12], Chaitin[13]). To quantify the complexity of a message one has to determine the length of a program necessary to generate the message. The complexity of an experimental time series of a continuous variable can be determined by reducing the time series first to a sequence consisting of a finite number of different symbols, e.g. a binary symbol sequence. Such a binary sequence is generated from an experimental time series by assigning values equal to the median (alternatively mean or midpoint) or larger to the symbol *1* and values smaller than the median are assigned to the symbol *0*. It has been demonstrated that partitioning asymmetrically distributed data about the midpoint can give misleading indication of structure (Rapp *et al.*[11]). To determine the measure of algorithmic complexity one might consider the following sequence of binary symbols:

$$S = 1\,0\,1\,0\,1\,0\,0\,1\,1\,0\,1\,0\,0\,1\,0\,0\,1\,0\,0$$

The algorithm to compute algorithmic complexity tries to reduce the current message into a sequence by minimizing the number of symbols. In the first step repeated pairs are determined in the binary sequence. In the message *S* the pair *1,0* occurs seven times. This pair is replaced by the symbol *a*, so that the message *S* becomes:

$$S = a\,a\,a\,0\,1\,a\,a\,0\,a\,0\,a\,0$$

The pair *a, 0* is repeated four times in *S* and replaced by the symbol *b*.

$$S = a\,a\,b\,1\,a\,b\,b\,b$$

At this point the only pair remaining in the message is *a,b* which is repeated only twice. It can be easily shown that replacing a pair which is repeated only twice by introducing a new symbol will not reduce the complexity so that we stop here to look for repeated pairs. Now the search for higher order repetitive sequences such as triples begins. However, the sequence S does not contain any triple or higher order repetitive sequences, so that the final reduced message reads as:

$$S = a^2\, b\, 1\, a\, b^3$$
$$a = 1\, 0$$
$$b = a\, 0$$

In the procedure presented here an upper bound for the measure of algorithmic complexity is determined using the following rules: each symbol in the final sequence S contributes 1 to the complexity estimate whereas exponentials contribute logarithmically.

The reduced sequence S contains 5 symbols, the exponent 2 occurs once as well as the exponent 3. Thus S contributes $5 + \log_2 2 + \log_2 3$ to the total complexity measure. The symbols a and b contribute 2 respectively. The total complexity estimate is:

$$complexity(S) = [5 + log\_2\ 2 + log\_2\ 3 + 2 + 2] = 11$$

where the square brackets indicate that the integer part of the complexity estimate is calculated. Other measures of complexity have been proposed and applied to the analysis of the electroencephalogram (EEG) data and to animal behavior (Xu and Wu[14], Paulus *et al.*[15]). To determine the algorithmic complexity the 24-h GH concentration time series from both groups were transfered first into binary sequences by partioning the respective time series into values above and below the median. The same procedure to determine algorithmic complexity was applied onto three different types of random surrogate data sets.

2.4 Surrogate Data

We generated surrogate data as statistical controls for our experimental data to test the null hypothesis that the experimental data could be accounted for by a linear stochastic process. Surrogate data are randomized versions of the original data sets preserving certain statistical features of their originals. For each original time series we generated ten surrogate data time series by three different procedures (Theiler *et al.*[16], Change*t al.*[17]).

2.5 Phase Randomized Surrogate Data

In this procedure the original time series is Fourier transformed to obtain phase and amplitude spectra. The phases are randomized using i.i.d. (independent identically distributed) random numbers from an [0, 2π] interval and after transforming back to the time domain one gets a randomized version of the original time series which preserves the power spectrum, the mean, the standard deviation, and the autocorrelation. This sort of surrogate data is used to test the null hypothesis that the results can be explained by using data from a Gaussian linear stochastic process. Other types of surrogate data are necessary since this procedure does not preserve the histogram of the signal amplitudes.

2.6 Gaussian Scaled Surrogate Data

Gaussian scaled surrogate data are generated by shuffling the original data in such a way that the amplitude distribution of the original is preserved and that the power spectrum remains very similar but not identical as in the case of the phase randomized surrogates. Using this sort of surrogates we can test the null hypothesis that our results can be explained by testing data from a nonlinear static transformation of a linear stochastic process.

2.7 Fourier Shuffled Surrogate Data

This third type of surrogate is used to overcome some of the difficulties arising with the Gaussian scaled surrogates. The surrogate is agian contructed from the original experimental time series. However, one tries to approximate as closely as possible the linear correlation or smoothness found in the original data set. This type of surrogate is created by generating a phase randomized surrogate of the measured time series, and then rank ordering the original data values in the rank order of thsi phase randomized surrogate.

2.8 Statistical Significance

To measure the amount of deterministic structure that might have been destroyed by the randomization techniques we used the significance level L defined as:

$$L = | M_{orig} - \langle M_{surr} \rangle | / \sigma_{surr}$$

where M_{orig} is the complexity estimate for the measured time series, $\langle M_{surr} \rangle$ denotes the average complexity estimate of ten surrogate data sets, and σ_{surr} is the standard deviation (SD) of the complexity estimates for the surrogate data. Thus L indicates the amount of deterministic non-random structure in the original time series which has been destroyed by applying the respective surrogate technique. The significance level L is given in *SDs* separating the complexity estimate for the measured time series from that for the surrogate random data sets. Assuming Gaussian statistics, $L \geq 2$ corresponds to a confidence level of greater than 95%.

3 Results

The group of patients with acromegaly exhibited a significantly ($p < 0.01$, unpaired t-test) larger value for the algorithmic complexity of 51.2 ± 7.6 compared to the healthy controls with 35.8 ± 4.5 (Table 1). Applying the significance level L as defined above we found that in the group of acromegalic patients the algorithmic complexity estimates for the three different types of random surrogate data were not significantly different from those obtained for the original measured GH concentration time seriesv (Table 2). In contrast to the results found for the acromegalic patients, the algorithmic complexity values obtained for the experimental time series in the group of healthy controls was significantly different from the values obtained for the Gaussian scaled and phase randomized surrogate data sets (Table 1).

Table 1: Algorithmic complexity (M) of measured original GH-concentration time series and three different types of surrogate random data sets (values are given as mean ± stdev).

	Controls	Acromegaly
Original Data	35.8 ± 5.1	51.2 ± 8.4
Phase Randomized	46.5 ± 3.1	54.5 ± 6.0
Gaussian Scaled	43.8 ± 3.6	54.5 ± 6.0
Fourier Shuffled	43.8 ± 3.6	54.2 ± 5.6

Table 2: Level of statistical significance (L) for differences in algorithmic complexity between measured original GH-concentration time series and three different types of surrogate random data sets (values are given as mean ± stdev).

	Controls	Acromegaly
Phase Randomized	4.6 ± 2.9	1.4 ± 1.6
Gaussian Scaled	2.6 ± 1.6	1.0 ± 0.6
Fourier Shuffled	1.7 ± 1.1	1.0 ± 0.6

4 Discussion

Applying the measure of algorithmic complexity as a context-free complexity estimate in conjunction with random surrogate data as statistical controls we clearly demonstrate non-random internal structure in the temporal dynamics of GH secretion in healthy controls. Using this approach our findings support the suggestion of random secretion of GH in acromegalic patients as indicated by significantly indistinguishable estimates for the algorithmic complexity compared to the three different types of random surrogate data. Whether the regulatory mechanism controlling GH secretion operate stochastically or deterministically in the normal and diseased situation must be a fundamental feature of any theoretical model that can explain how this hormonal subsystem processes information. The technique presented in this study might allow for the evaluation of non-random deterministic structure in other experimental systems in biology and medicine where currently available methods of nonlinear analysis fail due to nonstationarity or the limited amount of data available for analysis.

Acknowledgments

This work was supported by Deutsche Forschungsgemeinschaft under grant Br 915/4-1.

References

1. G. Brabant *et al*, *Trends Endocrinol. Metab.* **3**, 183 (1992).
2. A. S. Weigle and C. J. Goodner, *Endocrinology* **118**, 1606 (1986).
3. D. J. Haisenleder *et al*, *Endocrinology* **130**, 2917 (1992).
4. M. A. Shupnik, *Mol. Endocrinol.* **4**, 1444 (1990).
5. K. Y. Ho *et al*, *J. Clin. Endocrinol. Metab.* **64**, 51 (1987).
6. P. C. Hindmarsh *et al*, *Clin. Endocrinol. (Oxf.)* **32**, 739 (1990).
7. M. L. Hartman *et al*, *J. Clin. Invest.* **94**, 1277 (1994).
8. M. Riedel *et al*, *Clin. Endocrinol. (Oxf.)* **37**, 233 (1992).
9. W. H. Daughaday in *Endocrinology*, ed. L. J. DeGroot (Saunders, Philadelphia, 1995).
10. Ebeling *et al*, *Math. Biosci.* **52**, 53 (1980).
11. P. E. Rapp *et al*, *J. Neurosci.* **14**, 4731 (1994).
12. A. N. Kolmogorov, *IEEE Trans. Inform. Theory* **IT14**, 662 (1965).
13. G. J. Chaitin, *IEEE Trans. Inform. Theory* **IT20**, 10 (1974).
14. J. H. Xu and X. B. Wu in *Biomedical modeling and simulation*, eds. J. Eisenfeld, D. S. Levine, M. Witten (Elsevier, Amsterdam, 1992).
15. M. P. Paulus *et al*, *Proc. Natl. Acad. Sci.* **87**, 723 (1990).
16. J. Theiler *et al*, *Physica* **58D**, 77 (1992).
17. T. Chang *et al*, *Biophys. J.* **67**, 671 (1994).

EXPLORING THE FITNESS LANDSCAPES OF LATTICE PROTEINS

ALEXANDER RENNER[a] and ERICH BORNBERG-BAUER[b c d]
(b) Abt. Theoretische Bioinformatik, Deutsches Krebsforschungszentrum
Im Neuenheimer Feld 280, D - 69 120 Heidelberg

We present methods to investigate the sequence to structure relation for proteins. We use random structures of HP-type lattice models as a coarse grained model to study generic properties of biopolymers. To circumvent the computational limitations imposed by most lattice protein folding algorithms we apply a simple and fast deterministic approximation algorithm with a tunable accuracy. We investigate ensemble properties such as the conditional probability to find structures with a certain similarity at a given distance of the underlying sequence for various alphabets. Our results suggest that the structure landscapes for lattice proteins are generally very rugged, while larger alphabets fine tune the folding process and smoothen the map. This implies a simplification for evolutionary strategies. The applied methods appear to be helpful in the study of the complex interplay between folding strategies, energy functions and alphabets. Possible implications to the investigation of evolutionary strategies or the optimization of biopolymers are discussed.

1 Introduction

Under physiological conditions *in vitro* biopolymers generally fold to a unique structure. It is often assumed that only the sequence determines this "native" state and that it corresponds to the MFE (equilibrium minimum free energy) state (the *thermodynamic hypotheses*). The search space is astronomically large, yet proteins fold in seconds. Many mechanisms were proposed to understand protein folding, but there is no consensus yet [1]. Folding *in vivo* is even more involved since several agents prevent misfolds, aggregation etc. During the last decades several highly simplified models, among them lattice proteins have been derived to investigate the basic principles that govern the folding process of biopolymers and enable natural proteins to evolve under the constraints of functional adaptation and natural foldability [e]. In the **HP** model [2,3] (where **H** stands for a hydrophobic residue and **P** for a polar one) it is assumed that the non specific *hydrophobic force* is the dominant contribution to stability. It therefore to a large extent determines the 3D structure of the backbone [4,3,2]. In this framework side-chain packing selects structures within this relatively small set of compact states and hence allows for detailed functional fine tuning. For an excellent review of current methods the reader is referred to Dill *et al.* [3].

[a]Institut für Theoretische Chemie, Universität Wien, Währingerstraße17, A-1090 Wien
[c]Inst. für Mathematik, Universität Wien, Strudlhofg. 4, A-1090 Wien (Austria ⊂ Europe)
[d]correspondence: bornberg@dkfz-heidelberg.de , http://www.dkfz-heidelberg.de/tbi
[e]i.e. the ability to also attain the functional state within a reasonable time.

For our investigations we will use a sequential folding procedure and apply it to **HP**-type lattice proteins. Sequential folding may be relevant within several frameworks e.g. for the folding of sub-domains *in vitro* and the early steps of forming a nucleus or locally ordered structures. It may also account for the case of unguided folding of a nascending chain [f] *in vivo* being extruded from the ribosome to the lumen. This was proposed by Levinthal [5]. Some evidences for the relevance of sequential folding were recently summarized [6].

There is a promising strategy to construct biopolymers without disposing of details about folding: applied molecular evolution is intended to complement or even replace rational design. There, starting from an initial pool of random sequences, the principles of evolutionary optimization, error prone replication and selection of fitter offsprings, are applied in a test tube system. This illustrates the importance of studying not only the foldability of single sequences but the sequence structure relation of ensembles of random ensembles as well. To understand and describe at a molecular level how the principles of Darwinian evolution act in shaping biopolymers is also crucial for the understanding of prebiotic evolution. These principles can be exploited for biotechnology. Evolving entities must in principle accomplish two tasks: to *conserve* acquired features in their genotype and to *adapt* to new requirements on the phenotypic level as well. Since there is a tradeoff between these tasks, it is crucial to understand roles, interdependencies and interrelations between genotype and phenotype.
Early concepts (developed in the thirties by S. Wright and R. Fisher) coined the term of *fitness landscapes*. Evolution is viewed as an adaptive walk over the set of genotypes preferring "fitter" offsprings by selecting for some functional criterion, a phenotype property. Later considerations focused on influence and importance of phenotypically neutral mutations. Only few mutations can be advantageous but a continuous gradient of fitness must be maintained so that mutated offsprings survive [7,8]. Applied to biopolymers, this implies that residues essential for function will be rather conserved and non-essential ones will be replaced by evolutionary diverse sequences [g].
Since it is difficult to define fitness *a priory* and it is generally assumed that structure largely determines function [h], we are primarily interested in the *sequence to structure map*. "Simple exact models" [3] such as lattice proteins or RNA secondary structures are an ideal playground to explore these issues on large ensembles of biopolymers. The impact of parameters on structure formation can be studied in full detail and computational demands are reduced to a manageable level. Since in principle the structure prediction problem is of comparable complexity for real proteins and (fully represented) RNA, we were motivated by the recent success in characterizing the sequence to structure map-

[f] i.e. a chain under construction
[g] For the **HP** representation one would expect **HH** contacts in the core to be conserved.
[h] in the sense that it is a *conditio sine qua non* [9]

ping for RNA secondary structures[10,11,12,13,14]. This problem is, however, more involved for real proteins: 1) in contrast to RNA, proteins do not comprise genotype and phenotype in one molecule 2) there is a level of neutrality that arises from the redundancy of the genetic code at the genotype level *and* from structural robustness of folding at the phenotype level 3) structure representations simpler than the lattice approximation are not available. This in turn implies the need for computationally demanding almost-exhaustive or approximation algorithms.

In this work we are not so much interested in folding single instances. This has been solved at a reasonable level for the **HP** model[3,15]. For a different lattice model, a 3x3x3 cube with a broad spectrum of interactions the thermodynamic property of a pronounced energy gap between the ground state and other states was proposed to be a necessary and sufficient condition for fast folding in a Monte Carlo run [16,17,18]. We will also not discuss evolutionary issues any further (such as the nature of a possible primordial alphabet and the number of possible structures [19,20,21] that can be realized). It is our goal to present some techniques to give an idea how questions that we consider as relevant to understand limits and possibilities of biopolymer evolution can be addressed at different levels of simplification. Some recent results that we hope will clarify some aspects of the complex interplay of folding mechanisms, alphabets, and potentials will be presented.

2 Methods

2.1 "Generic" Lattice Proteins

The HP model: Here we refer to one of the most popular models of lattice proteins, the subclass of **HP**-models, introduced by Dill *et al.* [2,3]. All residues have the same size. The peptide chain is constructed by placing residues sequentially on the beads of a regular lattice. The resulting chain has identical bond lengths and discrete bond angles. We use relative moves for storing and comparing structures: the structure is represented as a self avoiding walk on a regular lattice and the movement of the chain is represented as a sequence of moves where each is encoded relative to the prior. The method is well known (see e.g. [2]); our version has been adapted to apply to any regular lattice (a detailed description will be given [22]). The algorithm has several advantages over representing structures by absolute moves or integer coordinates: 1) lattice independent programming of folding algorithms and structure comparison is possible 2) point mutations are pivot moves [23] 3) concatenation of strings corresponds to elongation of the walks 4) storage requirements are kept small and 5) structures can be compared utilizing classical string comparison methods[24].

Potentials: The generalized energy function for a sequence with n residues $S = (s_1, s_2, ..., s_n)$ with $s_i \in \mathcal{A} = \{a_1, a_2, \ldots, a_b\}$, the alphabet of b residues and an overall configuration $X = (x_1, x_2, ..., x_n)$ on a lattice $\mathcal{L}$ can be written as the sum of all pairwise inter-residue interactions:

$$E(S,X) = \sum_{i}^{n} \sum_{j>i+1}^{n} \mathcal{E}(s_i, s_j) d_{ij}^{\alpha} f(s_i, s_j, |i-j|) \tag{1}$$

where $d_{ij} = ||x_i - x_j||$ is the Euclidian distance, $\mathcal{E}_{ij} = \mathcal{E}(s_i, s_j)$ a pair-potential retrieved from the energy matrix. In our implementation, contributions are considered up to a certain cutoff distance: $d_{ij}^{\alpha} = 0$ if $d_{ij} >$ cutoff. For consistency we used $cutoff = 1$ whenever direct comparison to Dill's model was considered and $f = 1$ throughout this work.
We implemented three different potentials: In the "classical" **HP**-model (random) heteropolymers are composed from $\mathcal{A} = \{\ \mathbf{H}, \mathbf{P}\ \}$ with only one stabilizing interaction if and only if hydrophobic residues (**H**) are neighbors on the lattice but not along the chain. Polar residues (**P**) do not explicitly contribute to the energy. The salient features of real protein structures are implicitly considered: the hydrophobic effect comprises solvent-driven collapse to a native state, the self-avoiding walk constraint accounts for the excluded volume effect. The **HP**' set includes a strong overall interaction as well. The **HPNX**-model is a generic extension of the **HP** model and mimics "electrostatic" interactions between negative residues (**N**) and those with a positive charge (**P**) as well as repulsions within these classes. A third class of apolar residues is "neutral" (**X**)[i].

$\mathcal{E}_{ij}$	H	P
H	-1	0
P	0	0

$\mathcal{E}_{ij}$	H	P
H	-3	-1
P	-1	-0

$\mathcal{E}_{ij}$	H	P	N	X
H	-4	1	1	0
P	1	0	-1	0
N	1	-1	0	0
X	0	0	0	0

Table 1: Energy potentials for alphabets HP, HP' and HPNX.

Lattice Protein Folding is NP-hard [25]. A large variety of approximation algorithms was therefore developed [15,26,27]. Most of these are not fast enough to investigate large ensembles of structures and stochastic optimization techniques (see e.g. [28]) are not useful either to study ensemble properties of specifically folded single chains[j]. Hart and Istrail [29] recently presented an algorithm for the **HP** model that guarantee folding within at least 3/8 of the optimum energy. It

[i]The frequency of **H**s is the same as in the **HP** model, such that a random distribution of the **HX** subset corresponds exactly to the **HP** model.

[j]another reasons is given in the next section 2.2

is deterministic, works in $\mathcal{O}(n)$, but does not consider different potentials and cross-space interactions. It will be compared in future work.
Here we use a straightforward deterministic algorithm, termed the *greedy Chain Growth Algorithm* (gCGA) [30]. In its simplest version the algorithm is fast but there is, of course, a trade-off between accuracy and speed. Starting with an initial move, it proceeds along the chain. The next m residues in the sequence are added without consideration of the following residues. Energy contributions, retrieved from $\mathcal{E}_{IJ}$, are evaluated for all neighbors. The next move is determined by sorting these configurations with respect to energies, selecting the best and appending the first move of this chosen configuration to the "frozen" core. The gCGA was shown [30,24] to yield good results for short chains on a square lattice.

2.2 *Landscapes*

Sequence Space $\mathcal{S}^{(n)}$ is defined as the set of all b^n sequences $S_i(n)$ of a given length n that can be converted by well defined string-edit operation; we regard only point mutations. For two strings of equal length n, the number of positions by which they differ is known as *Hamming distance* h and defines a metric in *Sequence Space* $\mathcal{S}^{(n)}$. The probability $P[h]$ that two randomly chosen sequences have distance h is given by:

$$P[h] := P[d_S(S_1(n), S_2(n)) = h] = (b-1)^h \binom{n}{h} b^{-n} \tag{2}$$

The *Shape Space* $\mathcal{X}^{(n')}$ is defined as the set of all possible structures X_i for sequences of length n. Following Guttman *et al.* [31,32] the number of *self avoiding walks* (SAWs) on a lattice is $\#(SAWs) = a\hat{c}_{eff}^{n-2} n^{\beta}$ where β is a scaling exponent and c_{eff} the effective connectivity of the lattice [k].

Our description of *landscapes* follows that of Fontana *et al.* [10,11] on RNA secondary structures. A general notion starts with the definition of *Combinatory Maps* (**CM**) which are maps from one metric space $(\mathcal{G}, d_G)$ into another metric space $(\mathcal{F}, d_F)$. If a scalar quantity is assigned, the mapping $\phi : (\mathcal{G}, d_G) \rightarrow \mathbb{R}^1$ was also termed a *combinatorial landscape* (**CL**).
For reasons mentioned above we are interested in the sequence to structure map and functional properties associated with the structure. CMs are then viewed as generalizations of mappings from genotype (*sequence space* $(\mathcal{S}, d_S = h)$) to phenotype (*shape* or *structure space* $(\mathcal{X}, d_x = t)$), CLs are generalizations of mappings from genotype into fitness values. Biopolymer folding can now be understood as a mapping Φ from one space into another: $\Phi : (S, h) \Longrightarrow (X, t)$.

[k] For a square lattice $\hat{c}_{eff} = 2.63$ and $\beta = 0.33$ for the cubic lattice 4.68 and 1.16 respectively.

Scalar phenotype characteristics f_i for biopolymers are, for example, the radius of gyration $F_i := G_i(S_i, X_i)$ or the minimum free energy $F_i := E_i(S_i, X_i)$. A metric is simply $d_F(i,j) = |F_i - F_j|$. We define *neighbors* of a genotype G_i as the set of genotypes G_j with the smallest possible distance in genotype space $\mathcal{G}$: $N(G_i, d_G) = \{G_j | d_G(i,j) = 1\}$. *Neutral Neighbors* $NN(G_i)$ in a CL or a CM are the set $N(G_i)$ of neighbors that fall into the same phenotype with respect to the chosen d_F and Φ: $NN(G_i, d_G, d_F) = \{N(G_j) | d_F(i,j) = 0\}$. An instance (G_i, F_i) is called a *local optimum* if all neighbors $N(G_i)$ have fitness values lower than $F(G_i)$.
Landscapes have a characteristic topology. If there is a large number of local optima near any point, the landscape is called *rugged* and global optimization strategies may fail. Most descriptions are based on the definition of an autocorrelation function where $\langle . \rangle$ denote expectation values:

$$\rho(h) := \rho(d_G = h) = 1 - \frac{\langle d_F^2 | h \rangle}{\langle d_F^2 \rangle} \tag{3}$$

This expression can be viewed as a measure of the average similarity d_F of phenotype properties (energies, radius of gyration, structures etc.) for a fixed genotype distance h of the underlying genotype (sequence) [l]. It is obvious that for $h = 0$ (i.e. two identical sequences) a deterministic procedure (but not necessarily a stochastic one) will yield the same structure. Consequently, the autocorrelation function yields 1 at $h = 0$ and decays to a value of $\rho(h) = 0$ when all similarity is destroyed. A suitable *characteristic length* is the *correlation length* l_{d_F}. It is defined as the solution of $\rho_F(h) = 1/e$ [m]. As analytical solutions are not available for most landscapes we use large statistical ensembles of computationally folded biopolymers to compute $\rho(h)$. A two-dimensional probability density surface $P[d_F = t | d_G = h]$ was proposed for easier visualization [10,11]. It expresses the joint probability of two genotypes $G_i(n), G_j(n)$ having phenotype distance $d_F(i,j)$ at a given genotype distance $d_G(i,j) = h$.

Structure representation: We use the string of relative moves $\mathcal{R}_i := R(X_i) = (r_1, r_2, \ldots, r_i), r_i \in R$ (where R is the alphabet of relative moves), the distance matrix $DM^{(n \times n)}$ (which is symmetric and contains the Euclidian distances between two residues) [n] and the contact matrix $CM(X_i)$, which contains a 1 where the entries $d_{ij} = 1$ and 0 else. Scalar measures of compactness are the *radius of gyration*, and the number of contacts C_C, defined for all $(\frac{b(b+1)}{2})$ pairs of interactions as: $C_C^{(a_i,a_j)}(X_I) = |\{C_{ij} | (a = i, b = j)\}|$.
Defining *distance measures* is essential for comparing structures and to characterize landscapes: the number of identical contacts is defined as $D_C^{a_i,a_j}(X_1, X_2) =$

[l] When e.g. structure distances are correlated to sequence differences, measured by h, we obtain a characteristics of the sequence to structure mapping.

[m] where e denotes Euler's constant

[n] All information except the nature of the bonds and the chirality are retained.

$|\{i,j \in N, i < j | c_{ij}(X_1) = c_{ij}(X_2) = 1\}|$ and can be normalized e.g. as $\hat{D}_C^{a_i,a_j}(X_1,X_2) = \frac{2D_C(X_1,X_2)}{C_C(X_1)+C_C(X_2)}$ such that only contact regions in two structures are taken into account. Comparing two structures R_i, R_j is simple: the Hamming distance counts the number of pairs of identical directions at identical positions $D_{R_h} = (n - h(R_1, R_2))$. R_i-s can also be aligned using standard dynamic programming procedures defining gap-penalties and edit costs for the exchange of directions [24].

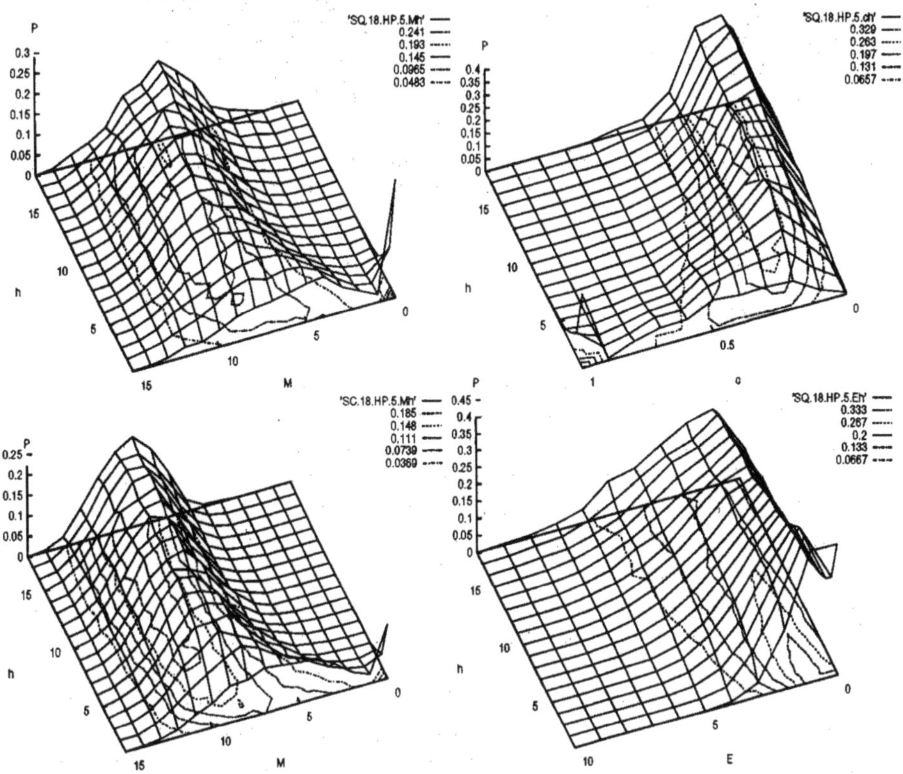

Figure 1: Probability density surfaces for lattice proteins (n = 18, **HP** alphabet, m=5, square lattice). (a): structure distance (relative moves) vs. h, (b): structure distance (contacts) vs. h, (c): same as (a) but cubic lattice, (d): energy distance vs. h.

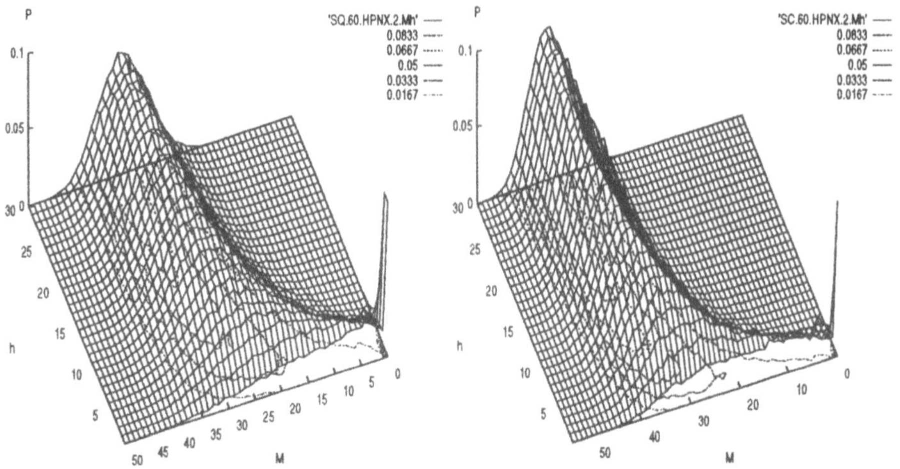

Figure 2: Probability density surfaces for lattice proteins (n = 60, HPNX alphabet, m=2): structure distance (relative moves M) vs. h on a square lattice (a) and a cubic lattice (b). (Data are cutoff at $h = 30$.)

3 Computations

Assessing the performance of the gCGA we have shown that increasing m yields better results[24,30]. At fairly small look-ahead values an average success rate of 10% and a performance within 80% of the optimal energy for can be obtained. In general, increasing m lowers energy and increases compactness and the number of contacts. The contacts, except **HH** remain rather unchanged, indicating that compactness results from a tighter core. A small number of **PP**-contacts implies that they are surface exposed without being explicitly penalized. The major reason for improved efficiency is that, the more the chain "looks ahead", the deeper a trap along the folding pathway can be overcome[24].
We compute large ensembles of random structures for short chains (n = 18) on a square and a simple cubic lattice. We generated 500 reference strings and 5 mutations for all hamming distances. Convergence of this uniform sampling procedure is fast. We checked the influence of the alphabet, the look ahead parameter m and the lattice. We calculated the conditional probability p that two structures (energies) have a distance m or c (or e respectively) given that their underlying sequences have Hamming distance h. Some instructive examples are reported in figs. 1 to 3, more comprehensive results will be reported elsewhere. The overall shape looks, similar to RNA landscapes[10,11], like half a horseshoe. Peaks at $h = 1$ and $M = 0$ refer to the number of neutral point mutations i.e. strictly identical structures. The probability to find a closely related structure

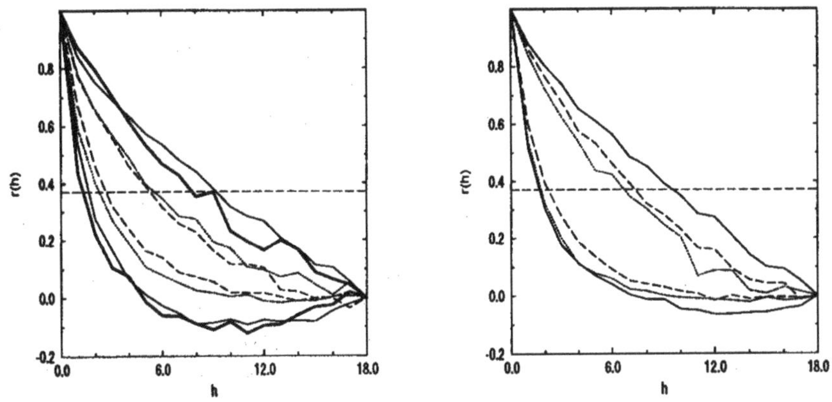

Figure 3: Lattice protein landscapes for the square lattice (a) and the cubic lattice (b). Autocorrelation functions $r(h)$ for energies (upper, nearly straight lines) and structure (relative moves, lower graphs) distances are shown for search depth $m = 5$ (thin lines) and 11 (thick lines), for the HP (full line), the HP' (dotted line) and the HPNX (dashed lines) alphabet.

is rapidly shifted to a random distribution with increasing h. Above a certain "critical" value h_{cr} the probability density becomes independent from h and the structure ensemble is essentially randomized. This defines something like a quantitative measure for a neighborhood size and corresponds roughly to the characteristic lengths (see below). This suggests that the majority of local optima as obtained by the gCGA can be found in a close neighborhood of any random structure. The structure density surfaces for D_{R_h} (Fig. 1a) and $\hat{D}_C$ (Fig. 1b) have a similar shape although the structure measures are based on completely different definitions. Hence the overall shape of the density surfaces do not depend on the usage of a certain structure notion. The density surface for the cubic lattice (Fig. 1d) shows faster randomization which is intuitively clear since shape space is much larger. Still there is a significant number of neutral mutations. To illustrate the versatility of our approach we also report the density surfaces for length $n = 60$ and the **HPNX** alphabet on the square and the cubic lattice (Fig. 2). There the number of neutral mutations is significantly larger which supports an assumption by Lipman and Wilbur [33] about the increasing probability of neutral mutations with larger chains. Also the shift of the average structure distance to higher values becomes more pronounced for the cubic lattice.

The energy density surfaces (Fig. 1c) look different: energies are stronger correlated and again there is a significant number of neutral mutations. At small

h, however, the distribution is rather bell shaped and rapidly broadens. Since most structures are relatively compact, in the case of the **HP** alphabet most structures have 8,9 or at most 10 contacts and the most frequent energy distance is 1. This is of course not the case for different alphabets and longer chains (data not shown).
We then computed autocorrelation functions following Equn. 3. It can be clearly seen that correlations are influenced only slightly by the search depth. Results of structure statistics depend strongly on the particular alphabet and correlations are approximately HPNX > HP' > HP. Energies are less sensitive to mutations than structures which is a result of the high degeneracy of lattice models, that is the correspondence of more than one structure to the MFE state [3]. Larger alphabets, however, have energy landscapes that are more rugged. This reflects the larger number of possible states in energy space and a smaller degeneracy. It is certainly interesting to note that most of these results are similar to findings from RNA secondary structures [11,13].

4 Discussion

We presented and implemented an approach to characterize fitness landscapes of lattice proteins. Clearly enough our results on folding single instances are not unexpected from the "lattice protein point of view". We think, however, that our results are significant in the sense they constitute an important new method for understanding certain features of relevance for the evolution of biopolymers:

- Combining the **HP** model with the concept of relative moves and applying a fast approximation algorithm, makes it feasible to investigate ensembles large enough for a statistical characterization of fitness landscapes. It was also shown that the performance tradeoffs of the algorithm allow it to handle larger chains and thereby address biologically meaningful problems.

- Structure Landscapes of **HP**-type lattice proteins are very rugged. This suggests that there are many local optima and evolutionary strategies may easily get stuck. Yet energies are higher correlated i.e. less sensitive towards point mutations than structures. This is definitely a consequence of using random sequences that usually fold to multiple ground states [3]. Since uniquely folding sequences are rare it is reasonable to assume that evolution from one "unique folder" to another is even more difficult and requires more mutations. Larger alphabets reduce this degeneracy and energy and structure correlations correspond to a similar fitness criterion.

- The ruggedness depends strongly on the size of sequence space and shape space. Larger alphabets smoothen both, the folding landscape and the fitness landscapes. This is another analogy to the fitness landscapes of RNA secondary structures and meets some earlier claims [24] that real proteins need a larger sequence space not only for chemical diversity but also for smooth evolution.

- The probability density surfaces also imply that a significant amount of neutrality complies with the possibility of a fast exploration of shape space [o]. The number of neutral mutations for larger Hamming distances, however, is small. This seems to be a clear contradiction to observations in real proteins that are very robust with respect to point mutations. On one hand this can be attributed to the crudeness of the **HP** model since each mutation actually corresponds to more mutations in a larger alphabet. On the other hand it may result from using an approximation algorithm that typically finds local optima.
  The issue of neutral evolution also deserves a closer look since earlier work in the **HP** - models by Lipman and Wilbur [33] postulated the existence of extended neutral sets in sequence space and that their frequency increases with sequence length.

- In spite of significant changes on single structure properties, ensemble properties are hardly influenced by the search depth. This is particularly interesting in the light of most recent results on RNA secondary structures [13] where ensemble properties are robust with respect to the chosen algorithm and will be the subject of more detailed studies.

Since we used several simplifications, we view our results as a very crude model of realistic processes of the "real world" analogy. Major caveats to our studies are certainly the restriction to very simple models and the usage of an approximation algorithm without performance guarantee. Future work will focus on a comparison to other algorithms, alphabets and fitness criteria to refine the methods presented in this work.

Acknowledgments

We thank Prof. P. Schuster for excellent facilities, W. Hart, K. Dill (at PMMB IV), W. Fontana, M. Vingron for useful discussions, P. Stadler and I. Hofacker for computational help and Sean ODonohue for proofreading. We are indebted to 2 (of 3) referees who helped with constructive criticism to refine the work by commenting its contents and not the language.

---

[o]This was termed *shape space covering* [14,11].

References

1. H.S. Chan and K.A. Dill. *Physics today*, **2**:24, 1993.
2. K.F. Lau and K.A. Dill. *Macromolecules*, **22**:3986, 1989.
3. K.A. Dill, *et al. Protein Science*, **4**:561, 1995.
4. K.A. Dill, *Biochemistry*, **29**:7133, 1990.
5. C. Levinthal. *J. Chim. Phys.*, **65**:44, 1968.
6. D. Shortle. *Protein Science*, **7**:991, 1996.
7. M. Kimura. *The Neutral Theory of Molecular Evolution*. Cambridge University Press, Cambridge, 1983.
8. J. Maynard-Smith. *Nature*, **225**:563, 1970.
9. P. Schuster. *J. Biotech.*, **41**:239, 1995.
10. W. Fontana, *et al. Phys. Rev. E*, **47**:2083, 1993.
11. W. Fontana, *et al. Biopolymers*, **33**:1389, 1993.
12. M. Huynen, *et al. Proc. Natl. Acad. Sci. USA*, **93**:397, 1996.
13. M. Tacker, *et al. Eur. Biophys. J.*, subm, 1996.
14. P. Schuster, *et al. Proc. R. Soc. Lond. B*, **255**:279, 1994.
15. K. Yue, *et al. Proc.Natl.Acad.Sci.USA*, **92**:325, 1995.
16. E.I. Shakhnovich and A. Gutin. *J. Chem. Phys.*, **93**:5967, 1990.
17. E. I. Shakhnovich and A.M. Gutin. *Proc. Natl. Acad. Sci., USA*, **90**:7195, 1993.
18. M. Karplus and A. Sali. *Curr. Opn. Struct. Biol.*, **5**:58, 1995.
19. C. Chothia. *1992*, **357**:543, Nature.
20. G. M. Crippen and V. N. Mairov. In *Proc. Pacific Symposion on Biocomputing 96.* L. Hunter, T. Klein *eds.*:160, World Scientific, 1996.
21. S. Govindarajan and R. A. Goldstein. *Proc. Natl. Acad. Sci. USA*, **93**:3341, 1996.
22. A. Renner, *et al. preprint*, 1996.
23. N. Madras and A. D. Sokal. *J. Stat. Phys.*, **50**:109, 1987.
24. E. Bornberg-Bauer. PhD thesis, University of Vienna, 1995.
25. R. Unger and J. Moult. *Bull. Math. Biol.*, **55**:1183, 1993.
26. R. Unger and J. Moult. *J. Mol. Biol.*, **231**:75, 1993.
27. P. Stolorz. *Proc. 27th Hawaii Intl. Conf. on System Sciences*, 1994.
28. J. E. Solomon and D. Liney. *Biopolymers*, **36**:579, 1995.
29. W. E. Hart and S. C. Istrail. *J. Comp. Biol.*, **3**:53, 1996.
30. E. Bornberg-Bauer. In *Proceedings of German Conference on Bioinformatics*. Leipzig, 1996.
31. A.J. Guttmann and J. Wang. *J. Phys. A: Math*, **24**:3107, 1991.
32. A.J. Guttmann. *J. Phys A: Math*, **22**:2807, 1989.
33. D. J. Lipman and W. J. Wilbur. *Proc. R. Soc. Lond. B*, **245**:7, 1991.

ACCURATE MEAN-FORCE PAIRWISE-RESIDUE POTENTIALS FOR DISCRIMINATION OF PROTEIN FOLDS

Boris A. Reva[1,2], Alexei V. Finkelstein[3], Michel F. Sanner[1] and Arthur J. Olson[1]
[1]Department of Molecular Biology, The Scripps Research Institute, 10666 North Torrey Pines Road, Ca 92037, USA;
[2]on leave from Institute of Mathematical Problems of Biology Russian Academy of Sciences, 142292, Pushchino, Moscow Region, Russian Federation;
[3]Institute of Protein Research, Russian Academy of Sciences, 142292, Pushchino, Moscow Region, Russian Federation

We present two new sets of energy functions for protein structure recognition. The first set of potentials is based on the positions of alpha- and the second on positions of beta-carbon atoms of amino acid residues. The potentials are derived using a theory of Boltzmann-like statistics of protein structure by Finkelstein *et al*[1]. The energy terms incorporate both long-range interactions between residues remote along a chain and short-range interactions between near neighbors. Distance-dependence is approximated by a piecewise constant function defined on intervals of equal size. The size of this interval is optimized. A database of 222 non-homologous proteins was used both for the derivation of the potentials, and for the "threading" test originally suggested by Hendlich *et al*[2]. For threading, we used 102 non-homologous protein chains of 60 to 200 residues. The energy of each of the native structures was compared with the energy of 45 to 20 thousand alternative structures generated by threading. Of these 102 native structures 94 have the lowest energy with alpha-carbon-based potentials, and even more, 100 of these 102 structures, have the lowest energy with the beta-carbon-based potentials.

1 INTRODUCTION

The possibility of predicting protein structure from amino acid sequence is limited by errors in the energy parameters[3] and the combinatorial complexity of the problem. Prediction is a feasible task only with energy functions that allow fast and efficient sorting over many conformations. To this end, a residue-residue approximation is usually used which attributes all atomic interactions to single points placed one per residue.

Physically, such potentials should come as the result of averaging over all interactions at the atomic level between amino acid residues, and between residues and solvent molecules. However, direct calculations of such mean-force potentials are not currently possible both because of methodological difficulties and the lack of reliable atomic energy functions. Therefore, there is significant interest in finding alternative ways to derive simplified energy functions.

There have been several attempts to derive energy functions from structural data on proteins. Initially such potentials were used to predict secondary structure[4-6]; now with the rapidly increasing protein database, there are many attempts to derive potentials for estimating the energy of the tertiary structure (see for review Refs. 9-14).

Most of the approaches exploit Boltzmann's principle: that frequently observed states correspond to low energy states[7-15]. However, the physical origin of Boltzmann-like statistics in proteins, which form unique 3D structures rather than ergodic ensembles of separate residues, was analyzed only recently[1].

In this study we apply the results of that analysis to derive energy functions from known protein structures. Our approach is similar to the one originally used by Sippl[8]. We derive pairwise, distance-dependent, "mean-force" potentials, treating separately long-range and short-range interactions. However, our method of choosing the reference state for long-range interactions and our treatment of short-range interactions differ from the approach used by Sippl.

2 METHODS

Our task is to estimate the energy of interaction, $\varepsilon_{\alpha\beta}(r)$, for a pair of residues α and β (α, β = Gly, Ala,...), where the inter-residue distance r is defined from positions of the C_α (or C_β) atoms. Our estimates of $\varepsilon_{\alpha\beta}(r)$ follow from the theory of Boltzmann-like statistics of protein structures[1]. This theory shows that the requirement for overall thermodynamic stability of unique protein folds results in the observed Boltzmann-like statistics of their elements.

Let us consider a large database of protein structures, and define $N^s_{\alpha\beta}$ as the number of all $\alpha\beta$–pairs occupying positions $i, i+s$ along a chain (i is any position); and $N^{1s}_{\alpha\beta}(r)$ as the number of these pairs at a distance r.

According to Ref.1, the expected value of $N^{1s}_{\alpha\beta}(r)$ is:

$$N^{1s}_{\alpha\beta}(r) = AN^s_{\alpha\beta}M^s(r)\exp\left[-\Delta E^s_{\alpha\beta}(r)/RT_c\right] \tag{1}$$

Here A is a distance- and residue-independent normalization constant; $M^s(r)$ is the probability of finding $i, i+s$ residues at a distance r in the total set of globular folds, (i.e. $M^s(r)$ is proportional to the number of folds where residues $i, i+s$ are at a distance r), T_c is the characteristic temperature of freezing of native folds ($\sim 300K$), R is the gas constant, and $\Delta E^s_{\alpha\beta}(r)$ is the effective interaction energy:

$$\Delta E^s_{\alpha\beta}(r) = \varepsilon^s_{\alpha\beta}(r) + E^s_{\alpha\beta}(r)\,, \tag{2}$$

where $\varepsilon^s_{\alpha\beta}(r)$ is the energy of direct interaction between residues α and β at a distance r, and $E^s_{\alpha\beta}(r)$ is the mean (averaged over all the possible environments of the pair $\alpha\beta$ in stable protein structures) energy of indirect interaction of α and β, i.e. the interaction mediated by all the surrounding residues.

Thus,

$$\frac{N^{1s}_{\alpha\beta}(r_1)}{N^{1s}_{\alpha\beta}(r_2)} = \frac{M^s(r_1)}{M^s(r_2)}\cdot\exp\left(-\frac{\left[\varepsilon^s_{\alpha\beta}(r_1)-\varepsilon^s_{\alpha\beta}(r_2)\right]+\left[E^s_{\alpha\beta}(r_1)-E^s_{\alpha\beta}(r_2)\right]}{RT_c}\right), \tag{3}$$

which corresponds to Eq.10 of Ref.1 where the term Δ_E therein would now include $\varepsilon^{s}_{\alpha\beta}(r_1) - \varepsilon^{s}_{\alpha\beta}(r_2)$, while $E^{s}_{\alpha\beta}(r_1) - E^{s}_{\alpha\beta}(r_2)$, which depends on the possible amino acid environment of the αβ pair, would contribute to both Δ_E and $\Delta_\sigma/2RT_c$ terms.

The direct residue-to-residue interaction energy can be estimated as

$$\varepsilon^{s}_{\alpha\beta}(r) = -RT_c \ln\left[\frac{N^{1s}_{\alpha\beta}(r)}{N^{s}_{\alpha\beta} \cdot M^{s}(r)}\right] + RT_c \cdot \ln A - E^{s}_{\alpha\beta}(r) \quad (4)$$

2.1 *Long-range interactions*

When residues are remote in the chain ($s > s_0 \gg 1$), so that they can be at a distance where they do not interact, the precise value of s is not important. Moreover, the order of residues in a pair (αβ or βα) is also not important. Then the value of $\varepsilon_{\alpha\beta}(r) = \varepsilon_{\beta\alpha}(r)$ for the long-range interactions can be estimated as

$$\varepsilon_{\alpha\beta}(r) = -RT_c \ln\left[\frac{N^{1}_{\alpha\beta}(r)}{N_{\alpha\beta} \cdot M(r)} \Big/ \frac{N^{0}_{\alpha\beta}(\geq R_c)}{N_{\alpha\beta} \cdot M^{0}(\geq R_c)}\right] - [E_{\alpha\beta}(r) - E_{\alpha\beta}(\geq R_c)] \quad (5)$$

Here $N^{1}_{\alpha\beta}(r)$ are the number of cases where the remote (separated by more than s_0 chain residues) αβ and βα pairs occur at a distance r (or rather in an interval $r \pm \Delta/2$; the value of the resolution interval Δ will be optimized below); R_c is the minimal distance where direct interactions between any pair of residues is absent, i.e. $\varepsilon_{\alpha\beta}(r \geq R_c) = 0$; $N^{0}_{\alpha\beta}(\geq R_c)$ are the number of cases when $r_{\alpha\beta} \geq R_c$ or (more precisely, $r_{\alpha\beta} \geq R_c + \Delta/2$, for a given resolution Δ); $N_{\alpha\beta}$ is the total number of the remote αβ and βα pairs; $M(r)$ and $M^{0}(\geq R_c)$ are the probabilities of finding the remote residue pairs at the distances r (or rather from $r - \Delta/2$ to $r + \Delta/2$) and $r \geq R_c$, respectively, in the total set of globular folds. The term $E_{\alpha\beta}(\geq R_c)$ is the average energy of the indirect interactions at $r \geq R_c$; because of the averaging over the distances $r \geq R_c$, this term is small and can be neglected. The term $E_{\alpha\beta}(r)$ can be neglected at small distances $r < R_c$ where a direct interaction of two residues is strong.

Thus,

$$\varepsilon_{\alpha\beta}(r) = -RT_c \ln\left[\frac{N^{1}_{\alpha\beta}(r)}{N^{*1}{}_{\alpha\beta}(r)}\right] \quad (6)$$

where

$$N^{*1}{}_{\alpha\beta}(r) = N^{0}_{\alpha\beta}(\geq R_c)\frac{M(r)}{M^{0}(\geq R_c)} = N^{0}_{\alpha\beta}(\geq R_c)\frac{\sum_{\alpha\beta} N^{1}_{\alpha\beta}(r)}{\sum_{\alpha\beta} N^{0}_{\alpha\beta}(\geq R_c)}; \quad (7)$$

here the ratio of probabilities $M(r)/M^0(\geq R_c)$ is approximated by the ratio of the total number of all remote residue pairs found at a distance r, to the total number of all residue pairs at all the distances $r \geq R_c$; (sums are taken over all the $20 \cdot (20+1)/2 = 210$ kinds of residue pairs).

In formula (5), $N^1_{\alpha\beta}(r)$ represents the pairwise distribution, which depends on the energy of interaction between residues α and β; $N^{*1}_{\alpha\beta}(r)$ represents the pairwise distribution extrapolated to the distances of inter-residue interactions from the non-interaction region. Thus, equation (5) is a potential of mean-force as it is defined in statistical physics[16].

2.2 Short-range interactions depending on distance between residues

In this study, short-range interactions are defined as the ones between residues occupying positions "i,i+2", "i,i+3", "i,i+4" along a chain, that corresponds to $s_0 = 4$ (see Fig.1a).

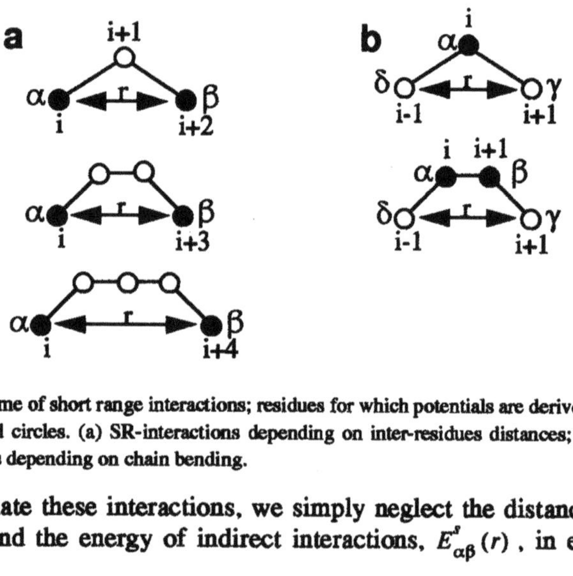

Fig. 1: A scheme of short range interactions; residues for which potentials are derived are shown by filled circles. (a) SR-interactions depending on inter-residues distances; (b) SR-interactions depending on chain bending.

To estimate these interactions, we simply neglect the distance-independent term, $\ln A$, and the energy of indirect interactions, $E^s_{\alpha\beta}(r)$, in equation (3) to obtain:

$$\varepsilon^s_{\alpha\beta}(r) = -RT_c \ln\left[\frac{N^{1s}_{\alpha\beta}(r)}{N^{*1s}_{\alpha\beta}(r)}\right] \tag{8}$$

where

$$N^{*1s}_{\alpha\beta}(r) = N^s_{\alpha\beta} \cdot M^s(r) = \sum_r N^{1s}_{\alpha\beta}(r) \frac{\sum_\alpha \sum_\beta N^{1s}_{\alpha\beta}(r)}{\sum_\alpha \sum_\beta \sum_r N^{1s}_{\alpha\beta}(r)} \quad ,s=2,3,4 \tag{9}$$

The value $N^{1s}_{\alpha\beta}(r)$ is calculated as a number of αβ pairs having positions $i, i+s$ in a chain and the distance between $r-\Delta/2$ to $r+\Delta/2$ in space in the total set of globular folds.

The definition of potentials given in (6) and (8) are different in two ways: the reference state for short-range interactions is chosen as the average energy of an interacting pair rather than a state where interaction is absent (the latter is not possible for neighbor residues); also for short-range interactions we distinguish between pairs αβ and βα.

2.3 Short-range interactions depending on chain bending

The distance between two residues in positions $i, i+s$ also depends on residues which occupy intervening positions (see Fig1b): these residues determine the local chain stiffness.

To take into account these interactions we introduce two "bending-energy" terms:

$$u^1_\alpha(r) = -RT_c \ln\left[\frac{\tilde{N}^1_\alpha(r)}{\tilde{N}^{*1}_\alpha(r)}\right] \text{ and } u^2_{\alpha\beta}(r) = -RT_c \ln\left[\frac{\tilde{N}^1_{\alpha\beta}(r)}{\tilde{N}^{*1}_{\alpha\beta}(r)}\right] \tag{10}$$

where

$$\tilde{N}^1_\alpha(r) = \sum_\delta\sum_\gamma \tilde{N}^{1s=2}_{\delta\alpha\gamma}(r) \tag{11}$$

$$\tilde{N}^{*1}_\alpha(r) = \tilde{N}^{s=2}_\alpha \cdot M^{s=2}(r) = \sum_\delta\sum_\gamma\sum_r \tilde{N}^{1s=2}_{\delta\alpha\gamma}(r)\frac{\sum_\delta\sum_\gamma N^{1s=2}_{\delta\gamma}(r)}{\sum_\delta\sum_\gamma\sum_r N^{1s=2}_{\delta\gamma}(r)} \tag{12}$$

and

$$\tilde{N}^1_{\alpha\beta}(r) = \sum_\delta\sum_\gamma \tilde{N}^{1s=3}_{\delta\alpha\beta\gamma}(r) \tag{13}$$

$$\tilde{N}^{*1}_{\alpha\beta}(r) = \tilde{N}^{s=3}_{\alpha\beta} \cdot M^{s=3}(r) = \sum_\delta\sum_\gamma\sum_r \tilde{N}^{1s=3}_{\delta\alpha\beta\gamma}(r)\frac{\sum_\delta\sum_\gamma N^{1s=3}_{\delta\gamma}(r)}{\sum_\delta\sum_\gamma\sum_r N^{1s=3}_{\delta\gamma}(r)} \tag{14}$$

In formulae (12)-(13) $\tilde{N}^{1s=2}_{\delta\alpha\gamma}(r)$ and $\tilde{N}^{1s=3}_{\delta\alpha\beta\gamma}(r)$ are the numbers of cases for which a residue α or, correspondingly, a residue pair αβ intervenes in a δγ-pair at distances r-Δ/2 to r+Δ/2, see Fig.1b; (index s shows a separation between δ and γ); $\tilde{N}^{s=2}_\alpha$ and $\tilde{N}^{s=3}_{\alpha\beta}$ are the total numbers of cases for which a residue α or, correspondingly, a residue pair αβ occurs in intervening positions. Thus, the same δαγ fragment contributes to both $u^1_\alpha(r)$ and $\varepsilon^{s=2}_{\delta\gamma}(r)$ potentials. However, the correlation between these potentials is negligible since the number of different amino acid types, 20, is great.

All the potentials (the chain-bending potentials, the short-range distant-dependent potentials, and the long-range potentials) have the form of a piecewise constant function of the distance. The optimal size of the resolution intervals Δ of these functions is established below.

3 RESULTS AND DISCUSSIONS

In order to study the accuracy of our potentials we repeated the test done by Sippl and coworkers[2]. In this test 101 proteins of different sizes and structural classes were used to derive potentials and to evaluate their accuracy using the "threading" method. Among the 101 proteins, 65 of length less than 200 residues were chosen; for each of these proteins, potentials were derived using the remaining 100 original proteins. Then, for any selected protein of length L, all the segments of length L from the 100 protein set were used as alternative structures. Energies of these structures were estimated with the corresponding potentials.

We repeated this test with our energy functions (Eqs.6,8,10) using the same set of proteins. Potentials were derived for both C_β and for C_α atoms (for the threading test with C_β potentials, absent C_β atom positions in Gly-residues were replaced by positions of corresponding C_α atoms).

The cut-off distance $R_c = 14\mathring{A}$ was chosen. Below $14\mathring{A}$ one can expect a direct interaction of long side chains. Above this distance, any direct interaction is absent. The maximal distance between the residues participating in short-range interactions (4 residues along a chain) is in concordance with the interaction cut-off $R_c = 14\mathring{A}$.

Positions of the native conformations in the energy-sorted list for 65 proteins obtained with different potentials are given in Table 1:

Table 1: Position of the native conformation in the energy-sorted list for 65 proteins obtained with different potentials.

PDB code	$C_\beta 2^a$	$C_\beta 2^b$	$C_\alpha 2^b$	$C_\beta 1^b$	$C_\alpha 1^b$
1ins.A	423	207	1994	96	23
1mlt.A	54	363	303	1	494
1gcn	2267	1992	547	2481	188
1ins.B	173	263	881	845	341
1ppt	39	96	571	43	643
1rhv.4	30	7	109	19	6
1bds	1	1	1	1	1
1crn	14	1	1	1	1
5rxn	2414	1	278	1	44
1fdx	28	1	5	1	2
1ovo.A	1	1	1	1	3
4pti	1	1	2	1	1
2mt2	1	1	66	1	26
2ebx 1cse.I	1	1	1	1	1
1sn3	10	1	1	1	1
1ctf	1	1	1	1	1
1hoe	25	1	151	1	20
2abx.A	71	2	1	2	2
3icb	3	1	1	1	1
2pka.A	1	1	1	1	1
351c	2	1	2	1	1
1cc5	12	1	1	1	1
2b5c	1	1	1	1	1
1hip	6	1	1	1	1
2gn5	35	15	113	322	66

PDB code	$C_\beta 2^a$	$C_\beta 2^b$	$C_\alpha 2^b$	$C_\beta 1^b$	$C_\alpha 1^b$
3fxc	1	1	1	1	1
1hvp.A	3	1	4	1	1
1pcy 1wrp.R	1	1	1	1	1
4cyt.R	1	1	1	1	2
2ssi	1	1	1	1	1
2cdv	18	1	9	1	1
1rei.A 1acx 1cpv 2c2c 1hmq.A	1	1	1	1	1
2pab.A 1paz	1	1	1	1	1
155c	2	1	2	1	2
1pp2.R 1bp2 1rn3	1	1	1	1	1
2ccy.A	5	1	1	1	1
2aza.A 1lz1 3fxn 2hhb.A 2pka.B	1	1	1	1	1
2hhb.B 2lhb 2sod.O 1mbd 1lh4	1	1	1	1	1
4dfr.A 2lzm 2sga 3wga.A 4dfr.A	1	1	1	1	1
2alp 1gcr	1	1	1	1	1
1hmg.B	14	1	1	1	1
2stv 3adk 4sbv.A	1	1	1	1	1
Avr:[c]	3.0	1.7	2.7	1.6	2.1

a. C_β atom based potentials derived in[2] at the resolution interval of 2Å.

b. C_β atom and C_α atom based potentials derived according to Eqs. (6), (8) and (10) at the resolutions of 2Å and 1Å, respectively.

c. Average position is defined as the mean geometrical: $\langle P \rangle = \exp\left(\sum_{i=0}^{65} \frac{\ln(P_i)}{65}\right)$ where P_i is the position of a protein i.

One can see from the Table 1 that for short non-globular chains (hormones 1ppt, 1gcn; the individual insulin chains 1ins.A and 1ins.B; the membrane attacking peptide 1mlt and a small component of the rhinovirus protein coat 2rhv.4), whose conformations are probably stabilized by interactions within molecular complexes, neither of the approaches give satisfactory ranking; for larger proteins the new potentials show significantly better accuracy than those used by Sippl and coworkers in the previous work[2].

In Table 2 we compare contributions of different energy terms into protein structure recognition. For long-range (LR) energy terms we also considered the alternative definition of the reference state used in the Refs. 2 and 8.

The results in Table 2 show that long-range energies derived with the reference state of eq.(7) are significantly more accurate than the ones derived with the reference state of the Ref. 2. One can also see that the main contribution in protein structure recognition is achieved with only four energy terms (long-range, [eq.6], and three short-range ones, [eq.(8), s=2,3,4]). This could be another reason for improvement of the native structure ranking in comparison to the Ref.2, where fifteen energy terms were used, since the more energy functions derived from the limited database, the bigger the statistical error.

One can also see that the accuracy of potentials derived from a particular set of proteins depends on the size of the resolution Δ, and that C_β based potentials are always more accurate, than C_α based ones.

Table 2: Average positions of the native conformation in the energy sorted list of 65 proteins obtained with different combinations of C_β based potentials.

C_β based potentials	Resolution in (Å)	
	2.0	1.0
used in the work[2]	3.0	-
derived by Eqs. (6),(8),(10)	1.7	1.6
LR[§] derived with the reference state of the work[2]	5.4	4.1
LR derived by Eqs.(6), (7)	2.6	2.8
SR distance-dependent only derived by Eq.(8)	8.8	7.5
SR bending energy only derived by Eq.(10)	44.5	28.4
SR derived by Eqs.(8) and (10)	5.8	4.4
LR and SR distance-dependent of Eqs.(6) and (8)	1.7	1.6
LR and SR bending energy of Eqs.(6) and (10)	2.0	2.1

[§]The reference state of the work[2] is calculated as: $N^{*1}{}_{\alpha\beta}(r) = N^0_{\alpha\beta}(\le R_c)\dfrac{M(r)}{M^0(\le R_c)}$, compare to the definition of Eq.(7).

The accuracy of the statistics-derived potentials must also depend on the size of the database. The database used in the Ref.2 was relatively small, so it was of-interest to see the results obtained by using a larger one. For this purpose we used a list of low-homology (less than 25%) proteins provided by Hobohm and Sander[17].

Table 3: List of PDB codes of 222 non-homologous proteins used in the threading tests.

1311	1531	1abr.B	1add	1amg	1amp	1aor.A	1aoz.A	1arb	1ars
1ash	1atp.E	1aya.A	1bam	1bet	1bnh	1bp2	1buc.A	1cau.A	1cau.B
1ccr	1cew.I	1cfb	1chm.A	1cks.B	1clc	1cmb.A	1cpc.A	1cpc.B	1crl
1cse.I	1csh	1ctn	1ctt	1cus	1cyg	1cyo	1dhr	1dlc	1dpb
1dsb.A	1dyn.A	1eca	1ede	1eft	1fnc	1fru.A	1fxi.A	1gky	1gmf.A
1gof	1gpb	1gpr	1grj	1hdc.A	1hdg.O	1hjr.A	1hlb	1hle.A	1hmt
1hsl.A	1htm.D	1htp	1huc.B	1hur.A	1hvd	1iae	1inp	1irk	1isc.A
1ivd	1knb	1lba	1ldm	1lga.A	1lis	1lki	1lpb.B	1lpe	1lts.A
1lts.D	1mat	1min.B	1mld.A	1mls	1mmo.B	1mmo.D	1mmo.G	1mnc	1mol.A
1mpp	1mrj	1msc	1mup	1nar	1nba.A	1nch.A	1ndh	1nfp	1nhk.1
1omp	1osa	1oyc	1pbe	1pbp	1pbx.A	1pfk.A	1pgs	1phg	1pii
1plq	1poc	1pox.A	1ppi	1ppn	1ptx	1pya.B	1qor.A	1rcb	1rcf
1rib.A	1rsy	1rtm.1	1rtp.1	1rva.A	1sac.A	1sbp	1scs	1scu.A	1scu.B
1ses.A	1snc	1sxc.A	1tca	1tgx.A	1thv	1tie	1tph.1	1trk.A	1tss.A
1ttb.A	1wht.B	1wsy.B	1xyl.A	1ypt.B	1ytb.A	1zaa.C	256b.A	2acg	2acq
2alp	2aza.A	2bbk.H	2blt.A	2cba	2ccy.A	2cdv	2chs.A	2cpl	2ctc
2dkb	2dnj.A	2dri	2ebn	2end	2er7.E	2fal	2fd2	2gbp	2gst.A
2hbg	2hhm.A	2hpd.A	2hpe.A	2kau.B	2kau.C	2liv	2mad.1	2mnr	2mta.C
2nac.A	2pf1	2pgd	2pia	2pol.A	2por	2prk	2rn2	2rsl.B	2sas
2scp.A	2sil	2tgi	2tmd.A	3aah.A	3cd4	3chy	3est	3gap.B	3gly
3grs	3pga.1	3sdh.A	3sic.I	3tgl	4blm.A	4enl	4fgf	4fxn	4gcr
4mt2	6taa	7icd	7pcy	7rsa	8abp	8acn	8atc.A	8atc.B	8cat.A
8tln.E	9rnt								

From this list of 472 proteins we chose those with resolution better than 2.5Å and with no structural defects (chain gaps, significant distortions of bond lengths, missing residues), resulting in a database of 222 non-homologous proteins (see Table 3).

For threading we chose those having from 60 to 200 residues, resulting in 102 sequences. For each of these sequences we extracted potentials from the remaining 221 proteins and then used structural backbones of these proteins as alternative conformations for threading.

The results of these threading tests are presented in Tables 4 and 5. A comparison of Tables 4and 1 shows that accuracy of the potentials improves with the database size. Besides, Table 4 shows that the most accurate potentials are derived at an optimal resolution interval, Δ, used for approximating energy functions: a bigger interval will resolve fewer details of the potential, a smaller one will yield poorer statistics, and therefore larger errors.

The average ranking as well as average relative deviation of the native structure energy from the mean energy of alternative structures ("Z"-score, see the definition in legend to Table 4) are optimal when Δ=1.0-0.5Å for both C_α and C_β atom based potentials.

Table 4: Average characteristics of the threading test obtained for C_α and C_β atoms based potentials at different resolutions Δ.

Resolution (in Å)	Positions			Z-score			Positions			Z-score		
	T	LR	SR	T	LR	SR	T	LR	SR	T	LR	SR
	C_α atom based potentials						C_β atom based potentials					
3.0	1.5	2.5	24.1	5.2	4.5	2.9	1.13	1.5	2.6	6.7	5.5	4.3
2.0	1.3	2.4	4.7	5.5	4.5	3.6	1.08	1.5	1.9	6.9	5.5	4.8
1.0	1.16	2.4	2.4	5.7	4.6	4.1	1.06	1.5	1.3	7.2	5.6	5.3
0.5	1.18	2.4	2.1	5.9	4.6	4.4	1.09	1.4	1.4	7.4	5.6	5.5
0.25	1.18	2.4	2.8	5.8	4.5	4.3	1.08	1.4	1.8	7.3	5.5	5.3

T, LR, SR stand for average position of the native structure for the total, the long range and the short-range energies; the average position of 102 native structures is found by the formula given in Table 1; the Z-score is defined as $(E_{avr} - E_{nat})/\sigma$, where E_{avr} is the average energy, E_{nat} is the native structure energy and σ is the standard deviation of energies of alternative structures from E_{avr}.

For both types of potentials, long-range interactions give approximately two thirds of the total energy of the native structure. They provide equal accuracy in all the range of Δ from 3 to 0.25Å. Short-range interactions give virtually the same contribution in recognition of the native structure, but only at the resolution Δ of 1Å. When Δ is bigger than 1Å, the details of the short-range potentials are poorly resolved; when Δ is smaller than 1Å, statistical errors increase and become a limiting factor for precision of the complete energy function.

The C_β atom-based potentials are more accurate than the C_α ones because they better approximate the relative positions of centers of residues.

Table 5 gives the details of the threading experiment for 102 proteins with C_α and C_β based potentials, derived at the resolution interval of 1.0A.

Table 5: Characteristics of the native conformation position in the energy sorted list for 102 proteins obtained for C_α and C_β based potentials derived at 1.0Å resolution.

PDB code	Thread-ings	C_α poten-tial		C_β poten-tial		PDB code	Thread-ings	C_α poten-tial		C_β poten-tial		PDB code	Thread-ings	C_α poten-tial		C_β poten-tial	
		P[a]	Z[b]	P[a]	Z[b]			P[a]	Z[b]	P[a]	Z[b]			P[a]	Z[b]	P[a]	Z[b]
1tgx	45359	1	3.8	11	3.5	2mad	31907	1	5.8	1	6.6	1mls	26760	1	5.9	1	8.8
4mt2	45137	13	3.8	1	6.0	4fgf	31907	1	4.6	1	6.1	2rn2	26605	1	5.7	1	6.6
1cse	44696	1	4.3	1	6.1	7rsa	31907	1	6.0	1	6.6	1hlb	26298	1	5.4	1	7.7
1ptx	44476	2	5.0	1	6.7	2acg	31718	1	9.2	1	12.0	1mup	26298	1	4.9	1	6.7
1cks	41423	1	4.3	1	4.8	1ttb	31347	1	6.0	1	6.5	1gpr	26145	1	6.5	1	8.5
1zaa	39903	714	2.0	29	2.9	2ccy	31347	1	4.5	1	6.2	1hjr	26145	1	6.8	1	9.2
1cyo	39254	1	4.9	1	5.5	3chy	31162	1	6.0	1	8.7	1mnc	26145	1	6.3	1	8.5
1mol	37963	2	3.3	1	5.1	1msc	30979	1	4.3	1	4.7	1311	25550	1	6.5	1	8.2
1fxi	37534	1	5.2	1	6.3	1rcb	30979	1	5.4	1	7.2	1cpc	25550	1	6.3	1	9.0
1nch	37107	1	3.9	1	6.4	2aza	30979	1	6.1	1	7.8	1mmo	25550	1	4.1	1	5.9
7pcy	37107	1	6.5	1	8.5	1hmt	30618	1	5.4	1	6.0	2cpl	25257	1	6.9	1	8.1
2hpe	36894	1	5.9	1	7.8	1htp	30618	1	4.7	1	5.8	1tie	24968	1	7.0	1	7.2
1aya	36473	1	6.1	1	7.1	1lis	30618	1	6.0	1	7.6	1rcf	24538	1	7.1	1	8.8
2kau	36473	1	4.5	1	6.2	1poc	30087	1	5.3	1	6.8	1cpc	24111	1	6.9	1	9.7
1lts	36055	1	5.7	1	6.3	1rsy	29911	1	4.2	1	5.9	1lki	24111	1	7.6	1	9.7
1cmb	35847	19	3.0	1	3.7	1snc	29911	1	4.2	1	5.3	2scp	23829	1	5.8	1	8.1
9rnt	35847	1	4.5	1	6.8	1eca	29736	1	5.9	1	9.0	4gcr	23829	1	8.7	1	9.3
256b	35435	1	3.9	1	5.3	2end	29563	1	5.9	1	7.1	3cd4	23275	1	5.1	1	6.0
2fd2	35435	1	6.7	1	7.8	4fxn	29391	1	7.9	1	9.2	1hur	23000	1	7.2	1	8.9
1bet	35230	1	5.6	1	5.9	1pbx	28710	1	6.1	1	9.3	1ytb	23000	1	7.6	1	8.9
2cdv	35230	1	3.6	1	4.2	1nhk	28540	1	6.2	1	7.8	1cau	22863	1	4.9	1	6.9
3sic	35230	1	6.4	1	9.4	1lpe	28371	1	4.5	1	6.7	1cau	22460	1	4.8	1	6.4
1cew	35027	2	4.8	1	5.6	3sdh	28203	1	5.6	1	8.1	1531	22326	1	4.9	1	7.1
1rtp	34827	1	4.3	1	6.8	1lba	28036	1	7.0	1	8.5	1lts	22326	1	6.7	1	7.9
1ccr	34430	2	3.7	1	5.3	2fal	28036	1	6.7	1	9.2	2sas	22326	1	6.1	1	8.1
2tgi	34232	1	5.3	1	6.6	8atc	28036	1	6.6	1	8.3	1gky	22193	1	8.2	1	8.5
1dyn	34035	1	3.5	1	5.3	1ash	27870	1	5.7	1	7.3	1knb	22193	1	6.5	1	8.0
2chs	33839	1	5.2	1	6.4	2hbg	27870	1	6.9	1	10.8	1dsb	21935	1	6.5	1	8.4
2hmz	33840	1	4.2	1	5.9	2mta	27870	1	6.4	1	7.8	1isc	21426	1	8.2	1	10.7
1gmf	32868	1	5.4	1	6.9	1osa	27707	1	6.1	1	7.4	1tss	21173	1	4.6	1	5.6
2rsl	32674	1	6.1	1	7.8	1rtm	27547	1	6.1	1	7.3	1cus	20797	1	8.9	1	10.5
2pf1	32481	2	3.7	1	5.5	1grj	27230	1	5.3	1	6.7	2alp	20672	1	7.2	1	9.6
1bp2	32098	1	5.4	1	5.8	1sxc	27230	1	7.1	1	9.0	1bam	20425	1	7.5	1	7.9
1htm	32098	1	3.4	1	4.1	1wht	26916	1	5.0	1	4.9	1iae	20425	1	7.3	1	8.6

a. Position of the native conformation's energy in the energy sorted list.

b. Z-score defined as $(E_{avr} - E_{nat})/\sigma$, where E_{avr} is the average energy, E_{nat} is the native structure's energy and σ is the standard deviations of energies of alternative structures.

The potentials successfully recognize the native structure: only 8 proteins for C_α atom based potentials and only 2 for C_β ones are not in the lowest energy for their native structures. It is important to note the large "Z-scores": the bigger the relative deviation of the native energy from the mean energy, the higher probability that the native structure will have the lowest energy among any other competing conformations. We have also checked if the results of threading are biased by the fact that potentials are extracted from the same protein set which is subsequently used as a source of templates for threading: the set of set of 222 proteins was divided in half. The first 111 proteins (set A) was used to extract the potentials; the second set of 111 proteins (set B) was used for threading experiments with these potentials. The obtained ranking of native structures is essentially the same as reported in Table 5.

4 CONCLUSION

In this work we have developed a consistent approach to derive phenomenological energy functions using the theory of Boltzman-like statistics of protein structure.

We have tested the approach to derive pairwise, distance-dependent potentials using the positions of C_α or C_β atoms. The energy function includes both long-range interactions between residues which are remote along a chain, and short-range ones between near chain neighbors. The distance dependence of the energy functions is approximated by a piecewise constant function defined on intervals of equal size. The size of this interval is optimized to preserve as much detail as possible without introducing excessive error due to limited statistics.

Results of these tests demonstrate that our new approach to derive potentials performs better than the previous one used by Sippl and co-workes[8,2]. Our's is more accurate in treatment of some important details of both short- and long-range potentials and therefore performs better. It is noteworthy that a similar improvement of performance has been obtained by Sippl[15] at the cost of adding of a "surface" term in the energy function and atomic description of residues, i.e. for the cost of inclusion of many additional statistical information.

The ability of our potentials to recognize protein structure was also checked on 102 non-homologous proteins 60 to 200 residues in length. Each of the sequences had to choose among a corresponding set of alternative structures obtained by threading the sequence through the backbones of 222 proteins. Most of the 102 protein sequences (94 for C_α-atom based potentials and 100 for C_β-ones) recognized their native structures.

Our studies also show that long-range and short-range interactions are equally important in protein structure recognition. As the statistics of short-range interactions are poorer than those of long-range ones, short-range interactions become the "bottle-neck" for improving the accuracy of statistical potential functions.

In our tests the best ranking of native structures was achieved for potentials approximated at a resolution of 1Å, which is obviously far from a detailed representation of the actual energy functions. We can further improve the potentials by enlarging the database.

In estimating the role of simplified pairwise potentials for the protein folding problem, one should not expect to explain all of the details of protein structure. However, these potentials can be useful for efficient discrimination of a small number of the favorable conformations from a vast number of unfavorable ones.

ACKNOWLEDGMENTS

This work was supported by NIH Grant PO1GM38794 (to AJO). The research of AVF was supported in part by an International Research Scholar's Award No. 75195-544702 from the Howard Hughes Medical Institute and by NIH Fogarty Research Collaboration Grant No. TW00546. Authors are thankful to Drs. B.Duncan and G.Morris for careful reading and improvement of the manuscript.

REFERENCES

1. Finkelstein, A., Badretdinov, A., Gutin, A. *Proteins* **23**, 142, (1995)
2. Hendlich, M., Lackner, P., Weitckus, S., Floeckner, H., Froschauer, R., Gottsbacher, K., Casari, G., Sippl.,M. *J.Mol.Biol.* **216**, 167, (1990)
3. Finkelstein, A., Badretdinov, A., Gutin, A. *Proteins* **23**, 151, (1995)
4. Ptitsyn O.B., Finkelstein A.V. *Biofizika* (USSR) **15**, 757, (1970)
5. Chou, P.Y. and Fasman, G.D. *Biochemistry* **13**, 211, (1974)
6. Sternberg, M.J. *Anti-Cancer Drug Design* **1(3)**, 169, (1986)
7. Pohl, F.M. *Nature New Biology* **234**, 277, (1971)
8. Sippl, M. *J.Mol.Biol.* **213**, 859, (1990)
9. Sippl, M.J. *Current Opinion in Structural Biology* **5**, 229, (1995)
10. Jernigan, R., Bahar, I. *Current Opinion in Structural Biology* **6**, 195, (1996)
11. Rooman, J., Wodak, S. *Protein Engineering* **8**, 849, (1995)
12. Godzik, A., Kolinski, A., Skolnick, J. *Protein Science* **4**, 2107 (1995)
13. Miyazawa, S., Jernigan, R. *J.Mol.Biol.* , **256**, 623 (1996)
14. Thomas, P.D., Dill, K.A. *J.Mol.Biol.* **257**, 457, (1996)
15. Sippl, M.J. *J.Comput.-Aided Mol.Design* **7**, 473 (1993)
16. Mayer, J.E., Geppert Mayer, M., *Statistical Mechanics*. Wiley & Sons, 1977
17. Hobohm, U., Scharf, M., Schneider, R., Sander, C. *Protein Science* **1** , 409, (1992)

REAL TIME SURFACE RECONSTRUCTION FOR MOVING MOLECULAR FRAGMENTS

M.F. SANNER and A.J. OLSON
The Scripps Research Institute, 10666 North Torrey Pines Road, La Jolla, CA 92037, USA

Recently we introduced the Reduced Surface as an efficient tool to built molecular surfaces. We describe here how this geometric construct can be used to efficiently reconstruct the solvent excluded surface of a protein for which the coordinates of a subset of atoms are changing. We show that, the complexity of that operation is not dependant upon the size of the molecule and is in O[$t\log(t)$] where t is the maximum of the number of probes and atoms involved in the reconstruction of the surface. The algorithms described here have been implemented and tested on several proteins. The triangulation of the solvent excluded surface of proteins in which a side chain was changing conformation could be updated at rates ranging from 7 to 22 frames per second. We also applied this method to compute the surface area fluctuation of the FIV protease undergoing a constrained molecular dynamics simulation (16 mobile residues). Rate of 6 frames per second were obtained in this case.

1 Introduction

Molecular surfaces are widely used in molecular modeling[1] to describe hydration effects[2-7] and to visualize and study molecular properties and interactions[8-12]. Several algorithm to compute such surfaces have been presented[13-18]. A method to interactively deform a molecular surface using control points was proposed by Klein *et al.*[19]. Recently, we described a program called MSMS[20] to compute a triangulation of the solvent excluded surface with a complexity in time in O[$n\log(n)$] for a molecule made of n atoms. This algorithm is based on the use of the *reduced surface*[20,21] which provides a compact way to store the geometric information needed to generate several molecular surfaces: van der Waals (VdW), solvent accessible[22] (SAS) and solvent excluded[23] (SES) surface. The performance of this algorithm allowed us to envision using it in some interactive applications such as "molecular sculpting" where the surface provides interactive feed-back on the impact of conformational changes on shape. The method presented here also drastically reduces the CPU time required to compute molecular surfaces in the case of singularities badly handled by MSMS.

After briefly defining the reduced surface and its main properties, we present algorithms to update in real time the SES of a molecule when a subset of atoms is moving. Updating of the surface implies identifying and removing faces, edges and vertices in the reduced and solvent excluded surface and reconstructing these surfaces. The complexity of the presented algorithm is discussed and the timings of several examples of molecular sculpting are reported. We also used these algorithms to update the surface of the FIV protease undergoing constrained molecular dynamics. We report rates for updating the triangulated representation of its solvent excluded surface as well as the time needed to analytically compute the surface area at every step.

1.1 Reduced Surface Definition

Like the SES and the SAS, the reduced surface is defined using a spherical probe of radius *rp* representing the volume of a solvent molecule. When the probe is simultaneously in contact with three or more atoms it is in a *fixed position* because it cannot roll further without losing contact with at least one of the atoms. The polygon obtained by connecting with line segments the centers of the atoms on which the probe is lying in a fixed position is a *face of the reduced surface* (RS-face). The atom centers are *vertices of the reduced surface* (RS-vertices) and the line segments are *edges of the reduced surface* (RS-edges).

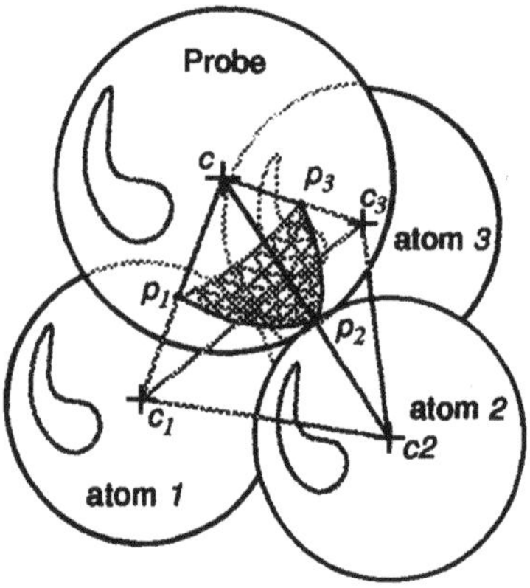

Figure 1: Probe in a fixed position defining an RS-face (c_1,c_2,c_3), an SES spherical reentrant face (p_1,p_2,p_3) and an SAS vertex *c*.

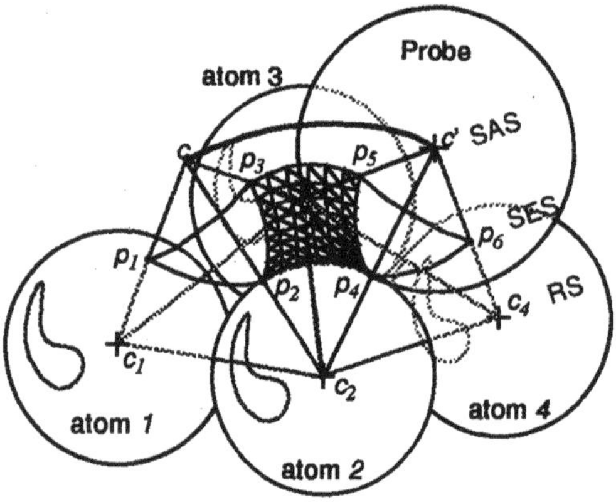

Figure 2: Probe rolling over two atoms defining an RS-edge (c_2,c_3), an SES toroidal face (p_2,p_4,p_5,p_3) and an SAS edge (c,c').

Figure1 shows a probe in a fixed position and the RS-face it defines. In some cases, the probe may roll completely around a pair of atoms without colliding with a third atom, the RS-edge joining the centers of these two atoms will be called a *free RS-edge* because it doesn't belong to any RS-face. Similarly, when the probe can roll on an atom without touching any other atom its center will be called a *free RS-vertex*. The polygons associated with all fixed positions of the probe and the free RS-edges and RS-vertices define the reduced surface. This surface can be made of several components each of them made of several closed surfaces connected by RS-vertices and/or free RS-edges.

1.2 *Reduced Surface Properties*

Under the assumption that the probe is never in contact with more than three atoms at a time, the faces of the reduced surface are triangles. There is an *outer component* that encloses all components that are not reduced to a single free RS-element. Geometrical properties of the reduced surface have been described previously[20]. In particular, one can show that for a protein made of n atoms the number of RS-faces and RS-edges grow as a linear functions of n and we gave an algorithm to compute the outer component of this surface in $O[n\log(n)]$ operations.

It should be noted that the reduced surface provides all the geometric information necessary to build the SAS and the SES. Figure 1 shows how an RS-face (c_1,c_2,c_3) corresponds to a spherical reentrant SES-face (p_1,p_2,p_3) and an SAS vertex c. Similarly, figure 2 shows the relationship between the RS-edge (c_2,c_3), the SES spherical reentrant face (p_2,p_4,p_5,p_3) and the SAS edge (c,c'). In the same way every RS-vertex corresponds to a contact face of the SES and an SAS face. It is also important to realize that the RS-vertices are located at atom centers providing a direct hint about which parts of the reduced surface need to be updated when some atoms move.

2 Updating the surfaces after a subset of atoms has moved

Let us assume that we have computed, for a molecule made of n atoms and a given probe size, the reduced surface, the analytical model of the SES and its triangulation and that these surfaces are available in the data structures described in our previous work[20].

The following algorithms will update these surfaces for a subset of m atoms which have been assigned new positions and/or radii. In the following we will refer to these atoms as the "*moving atoms*". To update the surfaces means to delete the obsolete parts of the reduced and analytical SES, reconstruct these surfaces and triangulate the newly created SES-faces.

2.1 *Updating the Reduced Surface*

An RS-face needs to be updated in the two following cases: one of its vertices is the center of a moving atom or secondly a moving atom has an intersection with the probe corresponding to the face. In the latter case, this RS-face will not belong to the updated reduced surface and has to be deleted. In the first case, this RS-face may or may not be part of the updated reduced surface. To find out, one needs to check the new probe position for intersections with all other atoms. In terms of complexity, this is as expensive as deleting and reconstructing the face. Therefore all these faces are systematically deleted. RS-edges shared by deleted RS-faces are deleted, as well as RS-vertices for which all faces they belong to, have been deleted. Free edges of the reduced surface with at least one vertex located at the center of a moving atom are deleted as well.

As mentioned in section 1.2 every face, edge and vertex of the reduced surface corresponds to a face in the analytical description of the solvent excluded surface. The SES-faces corresponding to the deleted elements of the reduced surface are tagged for deletion.

To reconstruct the reduced surface, we apply the same algorithm as the one used to construct the initial reduced surface[20]. This algorithm starts from an initial face defining a fixed probe position and "rolls" the probe over an RS-edge to the next fixed position defining the neighbor face (see Fig. 2). This operation was referred to as the "*treatment of an edge*". This recursive algorithm is executed as long as there are edges to be treated. In our case, after the out-dated parts of the reduced surface have been deleted, we are left with a number of RS-edges which belong to only one face (Fig. 3). Any such face-edge pair can be used to start this algorithm. Every RS-vertex which belongs to a reconstructed RS-face or RS-edge is then checked for free RS-edges using the algorithm described previously[20].

This procedure will re-build a closed RS-component and new free RS-edges if there are any. In the case where a subset of one or more atoms moves far enough from the rest of the molecule to form its own component, this component wouldn't be found. For this to happen, this subset of atoms has to move further than a probe diameter away from any RS-vertex belonging to a re-built RS-face or RS-edge. Another assumption made for this algorithm to work is that there is at least one face of the reduced surface that is not deleted. If this is not the case the problem is equivalent to recomputing the whole surface.

2.2 Reduced Surface Update Complexity

For every RS-vertex we know its associated RS-faces. Therefore, the RS-elements having at least one vertex located at the center of a moving atom can be selected in order m operations for m moving atoms.

To find the RS-faces for which a moving atom collides with the associated probe, one has to test the probes in a fixed position against every moving atom. In fact, only probes close enough to the moving atoms have to be considered. Let us call k the number of probes in fixed positions close to any moving atom during the entire course of motion. These probes can be selected once at the beginning and at every update we can build a BSDtree[20] for these probes and the ones created during the previous update. This tree can be built in O[$k$log(k)] operations and enables the testing of any moving atoms for intersections with fixed probes in O[log(k)] operations.

The algorithm to re-build the reduced surface also uses a BSDtree to select close atoms while treating an edge. This tree has to be re-built for every update to include the new positions of the moving atoms. Let us call l the number of atoms involved in the reconstruction of the reduced surface at any step. These atoms can be selected before hand and the tree can be build in O[$l$log(l)]. Once this tree is built, an edge of the reduced surface can be treated in O[log(l)] operations.

Both, the number k of probes and the number l of atoms involved in the update depend on the number m of moving atoms as well as on the compactness of the set of moving atoms. Their upper bound is the number of atoms n, but for applications like molecular sculpting, both are independent of n and the complexity of updating the reduced surface is in O[$t$log(t)] where $t = \max(l,k)$.

2.3 *Updating The Analytical Description Of The Solvent Excluded Surface*

The SES-faces to be deleted have been tagged during the update procedure of the reduced surface. These faces are now deleted along with all SES-edges shared by two deleted SES-faces and SES-vertices shared only by deleted SES-faces (Fig. 3). SES-edges shared by a spherical reentrant face and a deleted toroidal face are deleted as well. This is done in order to be able to re-construct the SES using the same procedure as the one used to build it initially.

The procedure to build the SES starts by creating a spherical reentrant face corresponding to an initial face of the reduced surface. For every edge of this initial RS-face, the spherical reentrant triangle corresponding to the neighbor RS-face is created along with the toroidal reentrant face connecting these two spherical reentrant faces (Fig. 2). This recursive algorithm stops when all the edges and faces of the reduced surface have been treated at which point all the reentrant faces of the analytical SES have been created.

To re-build the SES we start this algorithm on any reconstructed RS-face. Once, all reentrant faces are created the contact faces are found by building cycles of convex edges belonging to toroidal reentrant faces. This analytical surface description is then submitted to the same singularity handling algorithm as the one used for the initial SES. This algorithm will correct the self intersecting parts of the SES by checking singular edges that appeared during the SES reconstruction.

The complexity to update the analytical description of the solvent excluded surface is a linear function of the number of vertices, edges, and faces deleted in

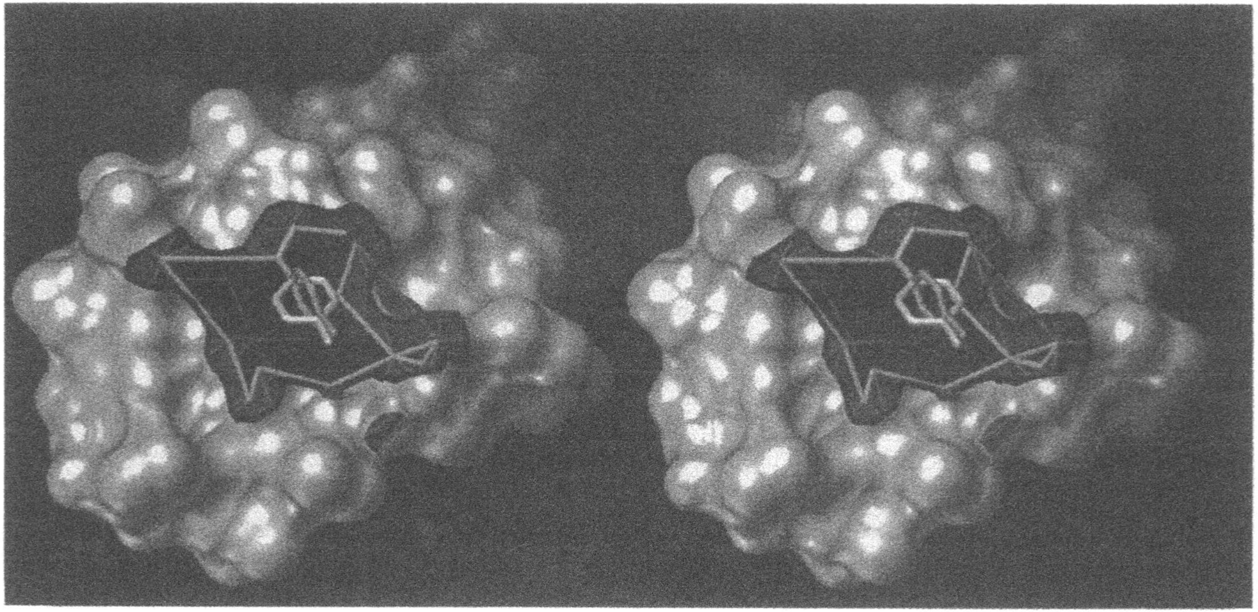

Figure 3: Unchanged solvent excluded and reduced surface for a side chain rotation. The CHI 2 angle of tyrosine 29 in Crambin (1crn) was incremented by 90 degrees. The obsolete parts of the reduced and solvent excluded surface were deleted. The contours of the remaining parts of these surfaces are shown in bold. This is a cross-eyed stereo-diagram

the reduced surface. This number is $O[m]$ for m moving atoms.

2.4 Updating The Triangulation Of The Solvent Excluded Surface

In MSMS the triangulation of an SES-component was stored in dynamically allocated arrays, one for the vertices and one for the faces. To enable an efficient update of the triangulation we have modified this data structure. Now, the triangulation is stored with the analytical surface description. Every SES-vertex is its own triangulation vertex. Every SES-edge holds an array of triangulation vertices used for its discrete representation and finally, every SES-face stores an array of internal triangulation vertices (not on the edge or at the vertices) and an array of triplets of vertices pointers describing the triangular faces.

When an SES-face is deleted, its triangulation is deleted too. Updating the triangulation of the SES simply requires the triangulation of the newly created faces using the same, template based, procedure as the one used for the initial triangulation.

3 Results

To evaluate the performance of the algorithms described here, we timed two types of surface reconstruction experiments. First we modified the conformation of a single side chain in proteins of different sizes, next we progressively increased the number of moving atoms for the same protein. All times reported in that section are given in seconds and have been obtained on a Dec Alpha 250 running at 233 Mhz.

3.1 Protein Side Chain rotation

We have chosen a set of seven proteins with evenly distributed sizes ranging from 327 to 3263 atoms. For each of these proteins, shown in table 1, we selected a solvent accessible side chain allowing a 360 degree rotation about its CHI1 or CHI2 angle while remaining at the surface of the protein. Steric repulsion was not taken into account and some moving atoms can get very close to some fixed atoms during the rotation. We incremented the value of the rotatable torsion angle in steps of 5 degrees and updated the SES triangulated at a density of 1.0 vertex/Å^2.

We report in table 1 the average CPU time per update and the average number of RS-faces deleted per update. The update rate ranges from 22/sec. for CRAMBIN to 7/sec. for LIVER ALCOHOL DEHYDROGENASE and CYTOCHROME P450. These values show that our implementation still is molecule size dependant. This dependency was expectable because our implementation relies to a large extent on the use of existing procedures written for MSMS and our data structure doesn't yet allow storage of lists of reconstructed faces, edges and vertices, sometimes forcing procedures to check all elements of a surface to find out which ones need attention. Nevertheless, the rates achieved still enable real time manipulation of the side chains in fairly large proteins. The times indicated here include reading the new coordinates of the moving atoms from a different file at every step. As expected, the number of RS-faces deleted at each step correlates well with the number of moving atoms.

Table 1: Timing for 71 surface updates after modifying a single side chain conformation in proteins of different sizes.

Protein	Number of atoms	Rotatable side chain	Modified torsion angle	Average update time (sec.)	Average removed RSF face	Moving atoms
1crn	327	TYR-29	CHI 2	0.045	27.75	6
1fd2	848	ARG-106	CHI 1	0.058	23.07	6
2lzm	1309	LYS-34	CHI 1	0.068	14.72	4
3pgm	1854	TRP-75	CHI 1	0.125	32.20	9
7abp	2338	GLU-42	CHI 1	0.104	15.86	4
5adh	2787	GLN-299	CHI 1	0.145	16.56	7
3cpp	3263	GLN-343	CHI 1	0.145	14.73	4

3.2 Constrained Dynamic Trajectory

The trajectory of the FIV protease mutant D30N,D30'N undergoing a constrained molecular dynamics (MD) simulation was used to evaluate the update rate dependency upon the number of moving atoms. During this 55 picosecond MD simulation, made to monitor side conformations in the active side, most of the protein was held fixed. Only 16 residues corresponding to 100 atoms of the protease were allowed to move. The simulation was done with Biosym's program Discover under the following conditions: a temperature of 350 degree Kelvin and a time step of 10^{-15} second. It started with 5000 steps equilibration

Table 2: List of the moving residues in the FIV protease MD simulation.

1	ILE 1037	5	LEU 2029	9	LEU 1029	13	ILE 2037
2	VAL 1059	6	ASN 2030	10	ASN 1030	14	VAL 2059
3	GLY 1060	7	THR 2031	11	THR 1031	15	GLY 2060
4	GLY 1061	8	GLY 2032	12	GLY 1032	16	GLY 2061

followed by 50,000 steps of simulation. Every hundredth step the conformation was saved. We took every tenth conformation (a conformation every picosecond) out of the 500 ones saved during the simulation. For these 50 conformations we measured the time to update the surface according to the number of atoms whose positions were taken from the simulation. We made 13 runs progressively increasing the number of residues with moving atoms. The column "Residues" in table 3 reports the range of residues (as reported in table 2) taken as mobile in every run. We report the CPU time to reconstruct the SES triangulated at a density of 1.0 vertex/$Å^2$ and the number of RS-faces deleted over 50 updates.

Table 3: Timing for 50 updates of the SES of FIV for an increasing number of moving atoms.

Run	1	2	3	4	5	6	7	8	9	10	11	12	13
Residues	1	1-2	1-4	1-5	1-6	1-7	1-8	1-9	1-10	1-11	1-13	1-14	1-16
Nb. atoms	8	15	23	31	39	46	50	58	66	73	85	92	100
RS-Faces	384	1796	2798	2798	3248	3333	3973	3973	4077	4115	5045	6121	6809
Time (sec.)	3.8	6.5	8.8	8.3	9.0	9.3	10.3	10.4	10.4	10.6	12.1	13.7	14.6

In this experiment the dependency upon the size of the protein is a constant and the increase in time corresponds to the increase of the number of RS-elements and SES-elements that have to be updated. Figure (4.A) shows that the time to reconstruct the surfaces grows as a linear function of the number of RS-faces deleted. Since all side chains do not contribute equally to the surface the dependency upon the number of moving atoms (figure 4.B) is not as straight.

When all 16 residues are allowed to move approximately 8% of the reduced and solvent excluded surfaces is reconstructed and triangulated at each update with a rate of 3 updates per second. This number should improve as the data structures will allow to make the reconstruction molecule size independent.

3.3 Analytical surface area calculation

The 50 conformations extracted from the MD simulation presented in 3.2 were used to evaluate the time needed to analytically compute the area of the SES. All 16 residues (100 atoms) were considered mobile. For every conformation we updated the reduced surface and the analytical representation of the SES and recomputed the surface area. The average time per update was 0.17 second which is equivalent to almost 6 frames per second.

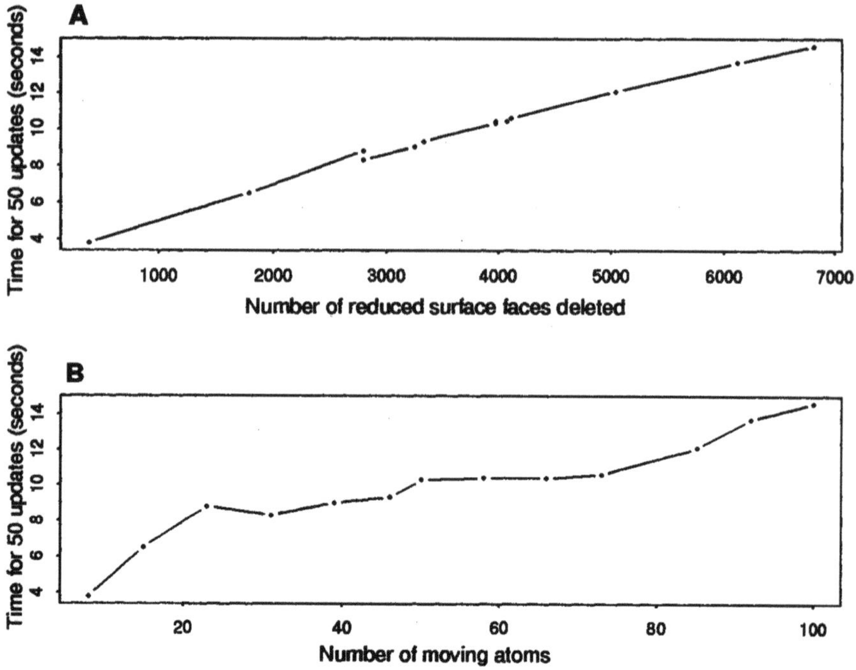

Figure 4: Time for 50 updates of the triangulated SES of the FIV protease during the MD simulation as a function of the number of moving atoms (A) and deleted RS-faces(B).

4 Discussion and conclusion

We have presented an algorithm to reconstruct the reduced and solvent excluded surface of a molecule when a subset of atoms is moving. The performance of this algorithm enables real-time *sculpting* of molecular surface. A user can select a side chain of a protein, modify its conformation and see the surface move along with atoms as the torsion angles are modified. This enables the use of molecular surfaces as a visual cue showing the influence of such conformational changes on the molecule's shape. The only condition for the described algorithms to work is that for every update, at least one RS-face of the previous surface remains unchanged. The complexity of an update operation is in $O[t\log(t)]$ where t is the maximum of the number of probes and the number of atoms involved in the update operation. This number t is a function of the number of moving atoms and of the amplitude of the motion.

Although our implementation still shows a dependency upon the size of the molecule, this can be overcome. This dependency occurs mainly because we implemented these algorithms as an extension to the existing program MSMS[20]. Many procedures used to build the initial surfaces are used by the surface updating algorithm. These procedures often run over all faces, edges and vertices of the surfaces creating a size dependency which is reflected by lower update rates for larger molecules. However, the results show that even with this limitation one can achieve real time surface update on fairly large molecules. In many applications the set of moving atoms is compact and the amplitude of their motion is limited. Knowledge of these conditions helps reducing the complexity of the problem. A known restriction is that, if atoms move far enough from the rest of the molecule to form their own component, they will be omitted and the algorithm will simply close the main component of the reduced surface. Typically, this will not happen when only covalent torsions are modified. In other applications where covalency is not maintained, this component can be identified in $O[m\log(t)]$ operations for m moving atoms. The complexity is partly due to the use of BSDtrees which require, in the current implementation, to be reconstructed at every update.

The times and update rates presented here were obtained for a triangulation vertex density of 1.0 vertex / Å^2. Higher density will multiply the required CPU time by a constant but it is straightforward to implement a scheme where the surface would be updated with a low triangulation density during the motion and with a higher density as the motion stops.

Analytical surface area can be computed without having to triangulate the solvent excluded surface. The speed achieved in this case would enable inclusion of such a term in a minimization process. Method for rapid calculation of buried surface areas are currently under development.

This type of application requires a very robust program because of the large number of molecular surfaces computed. MSMS was tested against a large set of proteins and proved to be robust. Still, in some cases it restarts the calculation after modifying the radii of some atoms. This happens mainly because of numerical instability in handling singularities. The algorithms presented here are useful in such cases because MSMS no longer has to recompute the whole surface, but simply updates it after modifying some atomic radii.

Acknowledgments

The authors thank Garrett Morris for providing the HIV protease trajectory coordinates and Jean Claude Spehner for his contributions to the definition and study of the reduced surface. This work was supported by NIH grants number P01GM38794 and P41 RR08065-02. This is publication number xxxx-MB from The Scripps Research Institute.

References

1. M.L. Connolly, T.J. O'Donnell, S. Warde. *Network Science*. April issue (1996). http://edisto.awod.com/netsci/Issues/Apr96/toc.html.
2. J. Vila, R.L. Williams, M. Vásquez and H.A. Scheraga, *Proteins: Structures, Functions and Genetics,* **10(3)**, 199 (1991).
3. K.A. Palmer and H.A. Scheraga, *J. Comp. Chem.* **12**, 505 (1991).
4. W.C. Still, A. Tempczyk, R.C. Hawley and T. Hendrickson, *J. Am. Chem. Soc.* **112**, 6127 (1990).
5. C. Zheng, C.F. Wong and J.A. McCammon, *Biopolymers*, **29(14)**, 1877 (1990).
6. I. Tuñòn, E. Silla and J.L. Pascual-Ahuir, *Protein Engineering,* **5(8)**, 715 (1992).
7. R.M. Jackson, M.J.E. Sternberg, *Nature*, 366 (1993).
8. C.L. Fisher, J.A. Tainer, M.E. Pique and E.D. Getzoff. *J. Mol. Graphics*, **8**, 125 (1990).
9. C.D. Zachmann, S.M. Kast, J. Brickman. *J. Mol. Graphics.* **13**, 89 (1995)
10. F.E. Blaney, C. Edge and R.W. Phippen. *J. Mol. Graphics.* **13**,165 (1995)
11. B.S. Duncan and A.J. Olson, *Proceedings of the 13th Molecular Graphics Society Meeting* (1994).
12. R.N. Norel, S.L. Lin, H.J. Wolfson and R. Nussinov. *J. Mol. Biol.*, **252**, 263 (1995).
13. R.J. Zauhar and R.S. Morgan, *J. of Comp. Chem.*, **11(5)** 603 (1990).
14. E. Silla and F. Villar, O. Nilsson, J.L. Pascual-Ahuir and O. Tapia, *J. Mol. Graphics*, **8**, 168 (1990)..
15. G. Perrot,B. Cheng,K.D. Gibson,J. Villa, K.A. Palmer, A. Nayeem, B. Maigret and H.A. Scheraga, *J. Comp. Chem.*, **13(1)**, 1 (1992).
16. M.L. Connolly, *J. Mol. Graphics*, **11**, 139 (1993).
17. A. Varshney, W.V. Wright and F.P. Brooks Jr., *IEEE Computer Graphics and Applications*. **15(5)**, 19 (1994).
18. F. Eisenhaber, P. Lijnzaad, P. Argos, C. Sanders and M. Scharf, *J. Comp. Chem.*, **16(3)**, 273 (1995).
19. T.E. Klein, C.C. Huang, E.F. Pettersen, G.S. Couch, T.E. Ferrin and R. Langridge, *J. Mol. Graphics*, **8**, 16 (1990).
20. M.F. Sanner, A.J. Olson and J.C. Spehner. *Biopolymers*, **38**, 305 (1996).
21. Sanner M.F. *Ph.D. dissertation thesis: Modeling and applications of molecular surfaces*. Université de Haute-Alsace, France (1992).
22. B. Lee and F.M. Richards, *J. Mol. Biol.*, **55**, 379 (1971).
23. F.M. Richards, *Ann. Rev. Biophys. Bioeng*, **6**, 151 (1977).

Finding Association Rules on Heterogeneous Genome Data

K. Satou, G. Shibayama, T. Ono[†] Y. Yamamura[†]
E. Furuichi[‡] S. Kuhara[†] and T. Takagi

Human Genome Center, Institute of Medical Science, The University of Tokyo, 4-6-1 Shiroganedai, Minato-ku, Tokyo 108, Japan.

†*Graduate School of Genetic Resources Technology, Kyushu University, 6-10-1 Hakozaki, Higashi-ku, Fukuoka 812, Japan.*

‡*Fukuoka Women's Junior College, 4-16-1 Gojo, Dazaifu, Fukuoka 818-01, Japan.*

A novel approach for discovery of knowledge from genome data, which has been recently watched with interest in the research area of database, is applied to finding unified rules spreading over sequence, structure, and function of protein. As the result of experiments using data extracted from PDB, SWISS-PROT, and PROSITE, some association rules stating sequential/structural/functional aspects of two kinds of endopeptidases were found.

1 Introduction

Intelligent management of huge amounts and heterogeneous genome data is one of the important research areas in bioinformatics. Advanced technology in AI and database are highly needed to achieve the goal, that is, providing molecular biologists with a powerful and comfortable genome analysis environment. In this research area, we studied the application of deductive database technologies to the analysis of protein structural data, and developed a database system named PACADE.[13,22] One of the results of the study was that a structural similarity search mechanism was devised and implemented on PACADE.[21] Through the similarity search function, a user can retrieve protein substructures similar to a substructure specified by the user from a viewpoint of distance, angle, and length of secondary structures.[20]

As a step to go further beyond database search which inevitably requires a user to describe query and a set of rules, we planned to study an approach which is reversal in the sense that a system generates rules from data. This direction of research meets an emerging research area in computer science, which is called *Data mining (Knowledge Discovery) from Databases* and aiming at the extraction of knowledge from a large amount of data in databases. As to genome data, *Inductive Logic Programming (ILP)* is actively applied from this area. According to results reported by Muggleton et al., ILP seems promising, especially in some kind of prediction problems.[14] However, in case the target concept to be learned is not well-defined, another type of machine learning should be used because we can not give positive and/or negative examples.

An attractive problem of data mining called "Discovery of *association rules*" was first posed in 1993 by Agrawal et al.[1] The simplicity of its basic framework, robustness against a large amount of data, and intuitive readability on the semantics of the resulting association rules imply its potential applicability to many real-world problems. Therefore, it has been actively studied in both of the theory and application sides. Nevertheless, there are still few application studies on extraction of association rules from genome data in spite of its suitability for this research area. In this study, we tried to discover association rules concerned with the amino acid sequence, structure, and function of protein from heterogeneous genome database. As a result of these experiments using public genome database concerned with protein, some association rules stating sequential/structural/functional aspects were found.

2 Associating Large and Various Genome Information

As is commonly known, three kinds of information about protein, that is, sequence, structure, and function, are said to be closely related. However, though discovery of unified rules through this information has been actively studied for a long time, it has been solved only partly up to now because it is a large and complicated problem. Prediction of protein structure can be regarded as verification of such rules as a working hypothesis. Since establishing prediction methodology with high precision means not only knowing the principles of protein folding but also designing new proteins with a desired function, there have been many studies on protein structure prediction with various approaches. For example, molecular dynamics, 3D-1D,[6] threading, AI approaches including neural net,[18] decision tree over regular pattern,[24] etc. However, in spite of these attempts, even precision of secondary structure prediction is still not at a satisfactory level. In addition to rules associating sequence with structure, it is more important to find rules related to the function of protein. As to prediction of function from sequence, motif finding using homology search, multiple alignment, and machine learning techniques is one of the major approaches.[11] However, since the definition of protein function is obscure, there is still room for trying a new approach.

When an attempt to use such a prediction comes up against a brick wall, there may be important but unnoticed viewpoints spreading over various levels of information. Therefore, a knowledge discovery system which can point out unnoticed association buried under large and various genome data is needed to make a breakthrough. Moreover, it also needed to pigeonhole and grasp large and complicated problems like correlation among sequence, structure, and the function of protein. These are the motivations of this study in which a data mining approach, recently watched with interest, is applied to finding association rules concerned with sequence, structure, and function of protein from heterogeneous genome database.

3 Association Rules

3.1 Terminology

The basic framework for discovery of association rules was first shown in the context of customer transaction database gathered by retail sellers.[1] Suppose that the data about a set of items are stored in a database as follows:

trans_id	`bread`	`butter`	`rice`	`milk`	`soy sauce`
1	1	1	0	1	0
2	0	1	0	0	1
3	1	0	0	0	1
4	1	1	0	1	1
5	1	1	1	0	0

In this database, binary data for five items mean whether they were bought or not, in a transaction trans_id. From such a database, sets of items called *large itemsets*, whose elements tend to be frequently bought together, are retrieved in the first step. There is a user-defined threshold value called *minimum support* on the frequency of retrieved large itemsets. For example, {**`bread, butter, milk`**} is retrieved under the condition **`minimum support = 1`** because its support is 2. Then in the second step, large itemsets are processed into association rules which have head and body in both sides of the implication. In this step, another threshold value called *minimum confidence* is used to delete inaccurate rules. This value is computed by dividing the support of the head (= frequency of head item) by the support of the body itemset. For example, an association rule **`bread, butter`** $\Rightarrow$ **`milk`** survives under the condition **`minimum confidence = 60%`** because it is 66.6% confident.

3.2 Related Works

The research topics of association rules can be roughly classified into the following 4 types:

[Performance improvement] From the beginning, it has been pointed out that the naive algorithm for finding large itemsets is inefficient.[1] Houtsma et al. mapped the problem of finding large itemsets into operation of relational database through SQL queries and named the algorithm SETM.[10] Agrawal et al. proposed an excellent pruning method named Apriori algorithm for eliminating useless candidate itemsets which must not be large itemsets. On the other hand, Agrawal et al. and Shintani et al. separately proposed parallel algorithms and reported results on a shared-nothing parallel computer.[2,25]

[Postprocessing of association rules] There exist apparently redundant or insignificant association rules from some viewpoints, i.e. statistic or user-defined. Corresponding to the terminology for "data mining", elimination of such rules can be called "refinement", which has been actively studied.[12,7,26] Visualization of resulting rules is another type of postprocessing having the same objective.[12,7]

[Application] Since the basic framework is not dependent on the initial application problem, it has a wide applicability in nature. An example is analysis of telecommunication network alarm databases.[8] Another example is an application to the retrieval of closely-related pages from WWW data resources,[16] where the weighted association rule is used for associating keywords. Concerning genome data, we tried to discover association rules from signals in mammalian promoter sequences.[23]

[Semantic extension of association rules] The semantics of the association rule `bread, butter` $\Rightarrow$ `milk` is limited to a propositional one. To make association rules richer, efforts to extend its semantics are needed. Srikant et al. tackled the problem of handling (interval of) numerical value, and proposed a sophisticated framework for finding quantitative association rules including numerical values.[26]

3.3 Comparison with ILP

Obviously, discovery of association rules is not a conflicting one with ILP, rather a complementing one because the latter is classified as learning from examples, and the former needs no examples. An ILP system like GOLEM [14] and FOIL [17] generates a logic program with first-order syntax and semantics, which is not achieved in association rules.

On the other hand, the framework for finding association rules has some good points:

- The cost of computation is lower comparing with ILP. This means a robustness against a large amount of data.
- The value of association rules can be estimated in intuitive measures.

3.4 Heterogeneous Data

In the example shown in subsection 3.1, there were no explicit classifications among the items and they were homogeneous in a sense. However, the simplicity of the basic framework of discovering association rules allows heterogeneous sets of items to occur in the attributes. Figure 1 illustrates our aim in this study:

protein name	sequence feature1	sequence feature2	structure feature1	function1	function2
name1	1	0	1	0	1
name2	0	0	1	1	0
name3	1	0	0	1	0
name4	1	0	1	1	1
name5	1	1	1	0	0

⇓ Data Mining

`sequence feature1, structure feature1` ⇒ `function2`
`(support=2, confidence=66.6%)`

Figure 1: Sketch of Data Mining on Heterogeneous Genome Data.

4 Methods and Materials

4.1 Data for Mining

Before performing the data mining illustrated in figure 1, proteins have to be characterized from sequential, structural, and functional viewpoints. In this study, we chose the following four data sources, which are related to each other by using PDB [5] entry names as keys:

[Sequential feature] PROSITE[4] is a dictionary of protein sites and patterns. If a PROSITE pattern matches to a SWISS-PROT[3] entry, there is a description of the pattern in the entry.

[Similar substructures as a structural feature] Using PDB as data source, PACADE can perform some kinds of structural similarity searches over the data of secondary structures. The similarity searches are roughly classified based on the following two points:

Rule set
If a user is interested in a specific structure, e.g. a supersecondary struc-

ture like Greek key, jelly roll, and meander, he can use a rule set for the structure. If he does not want to stick to any specific structure, he can use a rule set for any structure that consists of continuous secondary structures including α-helices, β-strands, and/or random coils.

In such a rule set, there are some parameters defining structural similarity, which are related to distance, angle, and length of α-helix and β-strand. By tuning these parameters, a user can specify his preference about error ranges of similarity. In this study, we set $\pm$ 60 degrees for angle, $\pm$ 6 angstrom for distance, and $\pm$ 15,40,50 residues for length of β-strands, α-helices, and random coils, respectively.

Direct or indirect similarity
PACADE can compute indirect similarity relationships as well as direct ones.[19] In the former case, starting from a specific substructure in a specific protein, the system iteratively performs a direct similarity search until no indirectly similar structures are found.

In this study, first we computed all the directly similar substructures that consisted of continuous three α-helices or β-strands allowing random coils between two of them (we call such a substructure *3-stranded*). An example of the answers which PACADE returned is below.

```
structure(2,6,"1lya") is similar to structure(19,23,"1aaj")
structure(2,6,"1npc") is similar to structure(19,23,"1aaj")
structure(2,6,"2cdv") is similar to structure(16,20,"9wga")
                              ⋮
```

The first and the second argument of the predicate **structure** represent the sequential numbers of starting and ending secondary structures in the protein represented by the third argument. Then, the 3-stranded substructures in the answers are mapped to integers.

```
1772 is similar to 1622
1779 is similar to 1622
1818 is similar to 1306
          ⋮
```

After that, 3-stranded substructures are classified into closures of indirectly similar ones. Sequential numbers are also assigned to the closures.

closure	sequential number of it
{1622, 1772, 1779, ...}	21
{1306, 1818, ...}	23
⋮	⋮

Finally, from these data, we generated the following data, each of which states "some of substructures in a closure *num* occur somewhere in a protein *pdbcode*".

```
1aaj  21
1lya  21
1npc  21
2cdv  23
9wga  23
 ⋮     ⋮
```

To keep the database consistent, we eliminated the entries such as the entries of DNA/RNA, the entries which have no SEQRES records, and the entries whose ATOM records have no data of residues. As a result of this filtering, 187 PDB entries as source data were selected and used to generate the above data for mining. Moreover, Kabsh and Sander's method was used to make up for the mistakes and inconsistencies in secondary structure data in PDB. We think these filtering and refining for PDB data are enough to keep the quality of the structural data for mining.

The reason why we did not take already published protein structure sets (SCOP,[15] FSSP[9]) is as follows:

- These structure sets only states structural similarity from a viewpoint of the whole protein or the whole chain of amino acid. Therefore, if these structure sets are used instead of search results of PACADE, the data mining system can not discover any associations concerned about characteristic substructures buried under the whole structure of protein.

[EC number as function] Enzymes are classified, based on their functions, in four levels of hierarchy, which are represented as EC numbers. SWISS-PROT entries for enzymes have descriptions of their EC numbers. To characterize proteins, we used part of the EC number in two ways, that is, the number of the 1st-2nd level and the number of the 1st-2nd-3rd level.

[SWISS-PROT keyword as function] Keywords in a SWISS-PROT entry include functional, structural, or other categorical characterization.

Part of the above four kinds of data could not be related to each other because of key mismatch. For instance, a protein `1aec` in PDB had no corresponding entry in SWISS-PROT. Starting from the 187 PDB entries, 181 out of the 187 had corresponding SWISS-PROT entries; 137 had matching PROSITE motifs; and 114 were enzymes with EC numbers. Of course, the 181 proteins had some keywords in corresponding SWISS-PROT entries. The following table illustrates these data assembled for mining.

pdb code	{1187,...,699}	SPPR=UBIQUITIN_CONJUGAT	EC3= 6.3.2	EC2= 4.2	SPKW= SIGNAL	...
1aaj	0	0	1	0	1	...
1aak	1	1	0	0	0	...
1abe	1	0	0	0	0	...
...	...	...	...	...	...	...

In this table, **SPPR** means PROSITE motif, and **SPKW** means keyword. These were extracted from SWISS-PROT entries. {1187,...,699} is an abbreviation of a set of 39 indirectly similar substructures including two substructures, 1187 and 699.

4.2 System

In this study, we adopted SETM algorithm and implemented it as Perl scripts and Sybase RDBMS on Sun 690MP. Only two threshold values, that is, minimum support (=5) and minimum confidence (=65%) were used. Since we did not use maximum support, some inconvenience about generation of a large amount of useless association rules was conjectured. For example, **SPKW=3D-STRUCTURE** marks too high support (=181) because this keyword means that there is a corresponding entry in PDB. Instead of using maximum support, we post-processed the resulting association rules to delete the rules which include items of too high supports.

Besides items of high supports, there was one more conjectured inconvenience. Since the items EC2 and EC3 are apparently related to each other, useless rules such as EC3=1.2.3 => EC2=1.2 will be generated. Such rules were also deleted in the postprocessing phase.

5 Experimental Results

As the result of the mining, 182388 association rules were generated. After the postprocessing phase, it was decreased to 586 when the maximum support was set to 50. In the case of a maximum support 30, it was furthermore decreased to 381. The following 2 long rules are examples out of the 381 rules.

> {1161,...,865}, SPKW=SERINE PROTEASE, SPKW=ZYMOGEN,
> SPPR=TRYPSIN_HIS, SPPR=TRYPSIN_SER => EC3=3.4.21 (100%, 6 sp.)
>
> {4356,...,808}, SPKW=ZYMOGEN, SPKW=ASPARTYL PROTEASE,
> SPPR=ASP_PROTEASE => EC3=3.4.23 (100%, 6 sp.)

In this section, we analyze and discuss focusing on the 381 rules.

5.1 Classification based on EC Numbers

234 out of the 381 rules included a description of EC number. The following two tables show the breakdown.

EC number	the number of rules
EC2=1.1	2
EC2=2.1	1
EC2=2.7	1
EC2=3.1	5
EC2=3.2	2

EC number	the number of rules
EC3=1.1.1	4
EC3=3.2.1	2
EC3=3.4.21	171
EC3=3.4.23	46

We can say that most of such rules are concerned with only two kinds of EC numbers, that is, EC3=3.4.21 and EC3=3.4.23. Other rules were not interesting since only the EC numbers and a few SPKW occurred in them like the following example rules.

```
SPKW=GLYCOSIDASE => EC2=3.2 (83%, 10 sp.)
SPKW=NUCLEASE,SPKW=ENDONUCLEASE => EC2=3.1 (85%, 6 sp.)
```

5.2 Serine Endopeptidases and Aspartic Endopeptidases

Rules related to EC3=3.4.21 and EC3=3.4.23 represent associations in serine endopeptidases and aspartic endopeptidases, respectively. These 171+46 rules consisted of items in the following tables.

items related to serine endopeptidases	sp.
{1161,...,865}	26
{1299,...,4355}	6
SPPR=TRYPSIN_HIS	9
SPPR=TRYPSIN_SER	9
EC3=3.4.21	13
SPKW=SERINE PROTEASE	13
SPKW=ZYMOGEN	21

items related to aspartic endopeptidases	sp.
{4356,...,808}	7
SPPR=ASP_PROTEASE	7
EC3=3.4.23	7
SPKW=ASPARTYL PROTEASE	7
SPKW=ZYMOGEN	21

Only the item SPKW=ZYMOGEN occurred in both of the two kinds of rules. The occurrence of other items in the rules agree with known biological knowledge.

[1ppf]
Human Leukocyte Elastase (HLE) (Neutrophil Elastase (HNE)) (EC 3.4.21.37)

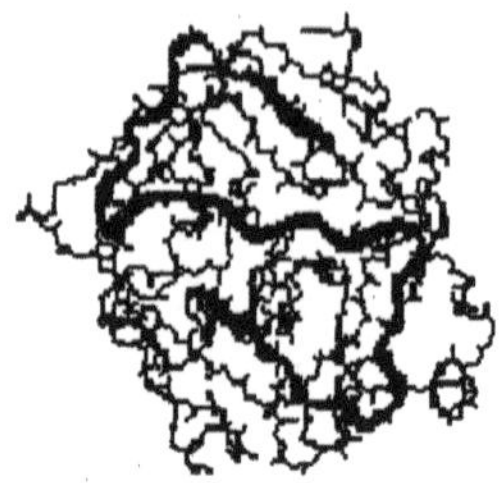

[2cga]
Chymotrypsinogen *A
(EC 3.4.21.1)

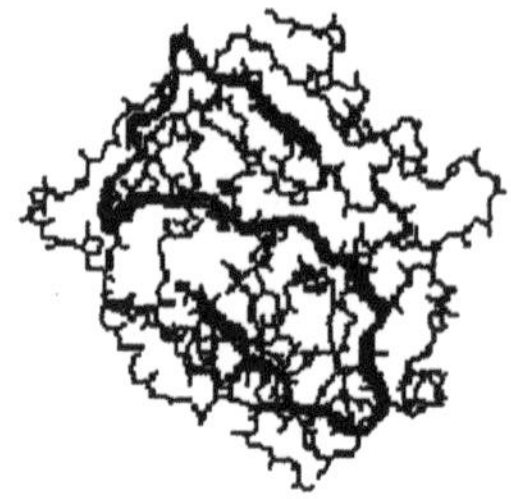

[2pka]
Kallikrein A
(EC 3.4.21.8)

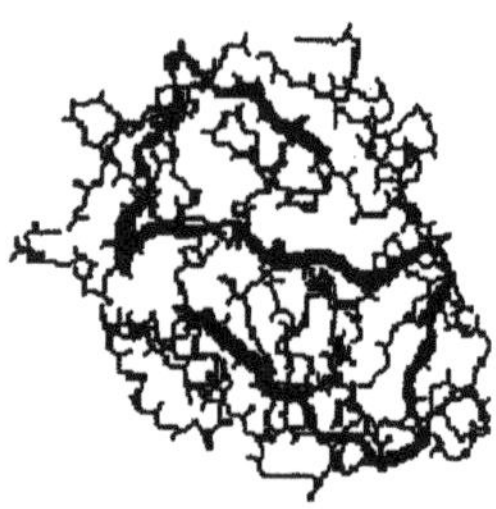

[3est]
Native Elastase
(EC 3.4.21.11)

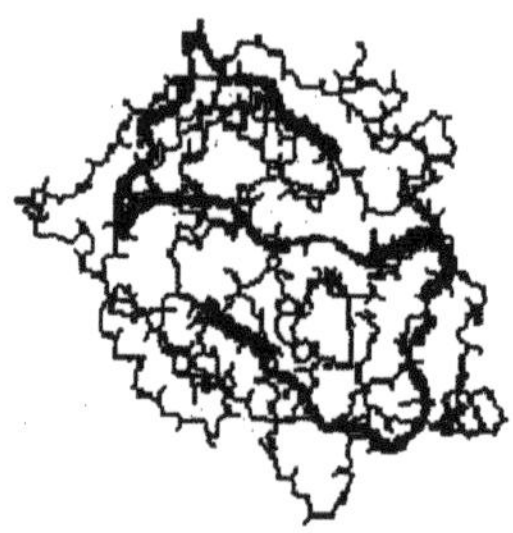

[3rp2]
Mast Cell Protease II Precursor (EC 3.4.21.-)

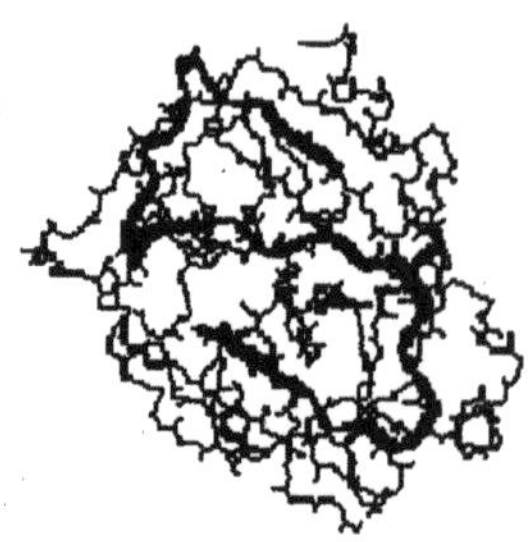

[4ptp]
Beta Trypsin
(EC 3.4.21.4)

Figure 2: Graphical display of six serine endopeptidases.

Figure 2 shows the six serine endopeptidases which have similar substructures included in {**1299,...,4355**}, where the substructures are emphasized as dark and wide ribbons. Even if the substructure seems to be unrelated to the active site of these enzymes, it illustrates that the data mining method can be used to find substructures common to proteins which have the same function.

5.3 Discussion

There may be two reasons why almost all rules were concerned with serine and aspartic endopeptidases.

- Since these two enzyme families are among the most frequently found ones in the 187 proteins used here, this result may be biased.

- It is known that, according to experimental results on structural classification of proteins, these two enzyme families have distinctive structures compared with other proteins.

However, as to structure-structure association, there should be more association rules unrelated to serine and aspartic endopeptidases. We think that this result is caused by the loose definition of structural similarity mentioned in 4.1. Loose definition makes the resolution of classification low, which forces some of clusters to merge together. Since such a set of substructures with too high support are eliminated in the postprocessing phase, it does not occur in the resulting 381 rules focused in this section.

6 Concluding Remarks

In this study, we tried to find hidden association rules buried under large and various genome data. The experimental results were encouraging, but some problems came to the surface. For instance, background knowledge about propositionalization of source data should be used to eliminate uninteresting rules like `EC3=1.2.3 => EC2=1.2`. Moreover, visualization must also be needed to grasp a huge amount of association rules when we extend this experiment to more and various genome data.

Acknowledgments

This work was supported in part by a Grant-in-Aid for Scientific Research on Priority Areas, "Genome Science," from the Ministry of Education, Science, Sports and Culture in Japan.

References

1. R. Agrawal, T. Imielinski, and A.N. Swami: *ACM SIGMOD*, pp.207-216 (1993).
2. R. Agrawal and J.C. Shafer: *IBM Research Report RJ 10004* (1996).
3. A. Bairoch and R. Apweiler: *NAR*, Vol.24, pp.21-25 (1996).
4. A. Bairoch, P. Bucher, and K. Hofmann: *NAR*, Vol.24, pp.189-196 (1995).
5. F.C. Bernstein, T.F. Koetzle, G.J.B. Williams, E.F. Meyer, M.D. Brice, J.R. Rodgers, O. Kennard, T. Shimanouchi, and M. Tasumi: *JMB*, 112, pp.535-542 (1977).
6. J.U. Bowie, R. Luthy, and D. Eisenberg: *Science* ,253, pp.164-169 (1991).

7. T. Fukuda and S. Morishita: *Technical Report of IEICE*, DE95-6 (1995-05), pp.41-48 (1995).
8. K. Hätönen, M. Klemettinen, H. Mannila, P. Ronkainen, and H. Toivonen: *ICDE'96* (1996).
9. L. Holm, C. Ouzounis, C. Sander, G. Tuparev, and G. Vriend: *Protein Science*, 1, pp.1691-1698 (1992).
10. M. Houtsma and A. Swami: *ICDE'95*, pp.25-33 (1995).
11. T. Ishikawa, S. Mitaku, T. Terano, T. Hirosawa, M. Suwa, and B. Seah: *Proc. of Genome Informatics Workshop 1995*, pp.39-48 (1995).
12. M. Klemettinen, H. Mannila, P. Ronkainen, H. Toivonen, and A.I. Verkamo: *3rd International Conference on Information and Knowledge Management*, pp.401-407 (1994).
13. S. Kuhara, K. Satou, E. Furuichi, T. Takagi, H. Takehara, and Y. Sakaki: *Proc. of the 24th HICSS*, Vol.I, pp.653-659 (1991).
14. S. Muggleton, R.D. King, and M.J.E. Sternberg: *Proc. of the 25th HICSS*, Vol.1, pp.685-696 (1992).
15. A. G. Murzin, S. E. Brenner, T. Hubbard, C. Chothia: *JMB*, 247, pp.536-540 (1995.)
16. H. Nishimura, K. Ito, H. Kawano, and T. Hasegawa: *Seventh Data Engineering Workshop (DEWS'96)*, pp.79-84 (1996).
17. J.R. Quinlan: *Machine Learning*, Vol.5, No.3, pp.239-266 (1990).
18. B. Rost and C. Sander: *Proteins*, 19, pp.55-77 (1994).
19. K. Satou, E. Furuichi, S. Hashimoto, Y. Tsukamoto, S. Kuhara, T. Takagi, and K. Ushijima: *Journal of Japanese Society for Artificial Intelligence*, Vol.11, No.3, pp.440-450 (1996).
20. K. Satou, E. Furuichi, T. Takagi, and S. Kuhara: *Proc. of the 27th HICSS*, Vol.V, pp.160-169 (1994).
21. K. Satou, E. Furuichi, T. Takagi, S. Kuhara, and K. Ushijima: A. Makinouchi ed., *Proc. of International Symposium on Next Generation Database Systems and Their Applications (NDA'93)*, pp.130-137 (1993).
22. K. Satou, E. Furuichi, K. Takiguchi, T. Takagi, and S. Kuhara: *CABIOS*, Vol.9, No.3, Oxford Univ. Press, pp.259-265 (1993).
23. G. Shibayama, K. Satou, and T. Takagi: *Proc. of Genome Informatics Workshop 1995*, pp.108-109 (1995).
24. S. Shimozono, A. Shinohara, T. Shinohara, S. Miyano, S. Kuhara, and S. Arikawa: *Proc. of the 26th HICSS*, pp.763-772 (1993).
25. T. Shintani and M. Kitsuregawa: *Proc. of Joint Symposium on Parallel Processing 1996(JSPP'96)*, pp.97-104 (1996).
26. R. Srikant and R. Agrawal: *SIGMOD'96* (1996).

Enumerating Suboptimal Alignments of Multiple Biological Sequences Efficiently

Tetsuo SHIBUYA, Hiroshi IMAI
Department of Information Science, Faculty of Science, University of Tokyo
7-3-1 Hongo, Bunkyo-ku, Tokyo 113, Japan

The multiple sequence alignment problem is very applicable and important in various fields in molecular biology. Because the optimal alignment that maximizes the score is not always biologically most significant, providing many suboptimal alignments as alternatives for the optimal one is very useful. As for the alignment of two sequences, this suboptimal problem is well-studied[6,9,12], but for the alignment of multiple sequences, it has been considered impossible to investigate such suboptimal alignments because of the enormous size of the problem. The optimal multiple alignment can be obtained with A* algorithm[4,5], and an efficient algorithm for the k shortest paths problem on general graphs is discovered recently[1]. We extend these algorithms for computation of set of all aligned groups of residues in optimal and suboptimal alignments, and for enumeration of suboptimal alignments. The suboptimal alignments are numerous. Thus we discuss what kind of suboptimal alignment is unnecessary to enumerate, and propose an efficient technique to enumerate only necessary alignments. The practicality of these algorithms are demonstrated through experiments. Moreover, the property of suboptimal alignments of multiple sequences are also examined through experiments.

1 Introduction

The multiple alignment is a problem to obtain the alignment of multiple sequences with the highest score based on some given scoring criterion between characters. This problem appears in various fields of molecular biology such as the prediction of three dimensional structures of proteins and the inference of phylogenetic tree.

The method using dynamic programming (DP) is well-known for the alignment problems. This method needs $O(n^d)$ time and space for d sequences of length at most n. This method can be applied when n is not so large and d is 2 or 3, but for larger problems, it is impractical. The A* algorithm is a well-known algorithm for the general optimization and search problems. This algorithm can reduce the search space dramatically if a powerful estimator is used. Thus the A* algorithm with upper bounding operation is proposed recently for computing the optimal alignment of multiple sequences[4,5].

A suboptimal alignment is an alignment whose score is close to the optimal one. The optimal alignment based on the scoring criterion is not always the biologically most significant alignment, and such candidates as suboptimal alignments for the best alignment are often required. In fact, in case of aligning two sequences, the suboptimal alignments problem are well-studied[6,9,12] and used for many applications such as predicting protein structure and so on[7,8,11].

```
REAFSQAIWRATFAQVPESRSLFKR==
ADFLV-ALF-EKFPDSANFFADFKGKS
KNG-S-LLFGLLFKTYPDTKKHFKHFD
LAAVF-TAYPDIQARFPQFAGK-DVAS
GSGVE-ILY-FFLNKFPGNFPMFKKLG
```

(a) The optimal alignment

```
REA | FSQ | AIWRATFAQVPESRSLFKR==
ADF | LV- | ALF-EKFPDSANFFADFKGKS
KNG | -S- | LLFGLLFKTYPDTKKHFKHFD
LAA | -VF | TAYPDIQARFPQFAGK-DVAS
GSG | -VE | ILY-FFLNKFPGNFPMFKKLG
```

(b) A suboptimal alignment

```
REAFSQAIWRATFAQVPESRS | LF | KR==
ADFLV-ALF-EKFPDSANFFA | DF | KGKS
KNG-S-LLFGLLFKTYPDTKK | HF | KHFD
LAAVF-TAYPDIQARFPQFAG | -K | DVAS
GSGVE-ILY-FFLNKFPGNFP | MF | KKLG
```

(c) Another suboptimal alignment

```
REA | FSQ | AIWRATFAQVPESRS | LF | KR==
ADF | LV- | ALF-EKFPDSANFFA | DF | KGKS
KNG | -S- | LLFGLLFKTYPDTKK | HF | KHFD
LAA | -VF | TAYPDIQARFPQFAG | -K | DVAS
GSG | -VE | ILY-FFLNKFPGNFP | MF | KKLG
```

(d) Unnecessary alignment to check

Figure 1: Examples of suboptimal alignments of multiple protein sequences

In multiple alignment problem, with these methods for only two sequences, we can see suboptimal alignments of each pair of sequences[12], but these are not the accurate suboptimal alignments of all the sequences.

Enumeration of the suboptimal alignments had not been considered as very practical even in the case of aligning two sequences[6,12]. But such enumeration becomes easier because a new efficient algorithm for the k shortest paths problem is proposed by Eppstein[1,10]. This algorithm enumerates the k shortest paths in $O(k+n+m)$ time and space after having constructed the shortest path tree from the source or the destination for any graph with non-negative m edges and n vertices.

In this paper, we first discuss the method to obtain E_Δ, which represents all aligned groups of residues in optimal and suboptimal alignments which are at most Δ worse than the optimal, by extending the A* algorithm, and based on this extended A* algorithm and the Eppstein algorithm, we go on to discuss the methods for the enumeration problem. Figure 1 shows some examples of suboptimal multiple alignments of protein fragments. (a) is the optimal alignment, and (b), (c) and (d) are suboptimal alignments. The regions bounded by boxes are the regions which are different from the optimal alignment. (b) and (c) have only one such region. On the other hand, (d) has two, both of which appear also in (b) or (c). Thus, if we check suboptimal alignments one by one, examining (d) may be of no use: we can reconstruct (d) from (b) and (c). Thus we propose a new enumeration algorithm which does not enumerate such unnecessary alignment as (d) based on the algorithms above. We further show the efficiency and practicality of these algorithms and the property of these suboptimal alignments through experiments on groups of protein sequences. In the experiments, we will show that both the number of the alignments and the enumeration time are drastically reduced by ignoring such unnecessary alignments.

2 Computation of a Subgraph Related to Suboptimal Alignments

E_Δ is a set of vertices which are used by the s-t path whose length is at most Δ longer than the shortest path. In this section, we first introduce A* algorithm[4,5], and then extends it to compute E_Δ efficiently.

2.1 A Algorithm for Multiple Sequence Alignment*

The multiple alignment problem can be easily transformed to the shortest path problem on some grid-like directed acyclic graph with no negative edges. Let S_k be the kth sequence of d sequences to be aligned, and $n_k = O(n)$ be the length of S_k. Then suppose a directed acyclic graph $G = (V, E)$ such that $V = \{(x_1, \ldots, x_d) | x_i = 0, 1, \ldots, n_i\}$ and $E = \{(v, v+e) | v \in V, e \in [0,1]^d, e \neq \mathbf{0}\}$. In this graph, a path from $s = (0, \ldots, 0)$ to $t = (n_1, \ldots, n_d)$ corresponds to an alignment of the sequences.

In the alignment problem of two sequences, the length of an edge is defined from the score table between characters, and the length of a path from s to t equals the score of the corresponding alignment. In multiple alignment problem, the sum of all the scores for alignments of pairwise sequences is generally used as the score. Thus the score of the alignment equals the length of the corresponding path, defining length of each edge as the sum of the lengths of the corresponding edges in the graphs of pairwise alignments. This longest path problem can be easily transformed to the shortest path problem[4,5].

The A* algorithm will not search the whole graph in finding the shortest path if a good estimate for the shortest path length from each vertex to t can be used. Ikeda and Imai[4] show the following estimator is very useful in case $d > 2$. Let G_{ij} be the corresponding graph to the alignment of S_i and S_j, v_{ij} be the corresponding vertex in G_{ij} to v in G, and $L^*(u, v)$ be the shortest path length from u to v. Then $h(v) = \sum_{1 \leq i < j \leq d} L^*(u_{ij}, v_{ij})$ can be used as a powerful estimator for the multiple alignment problem. This estimator is easily be shown to be dual feasible, *i.e.* $l(u, v) + h(v) \geq h(u)$. Hence the A* algorithm can be applied as following.

1. For each of i and j $(1 \leq i < j \leq d)$, apply DP to graph G_{ij} from t_{ij} to calculate $L^*(v_{ij}, t_{ij})$ for each v_{ij} in V_{ij}.
2. Modify the length of edge (u, v) in G as follows, using $h(v)$ above, and compute the shortest path with Dijkstra method.

$$l'(u, v) = l(u, v) + h(v) - h(u) \tag{1}$$

Note that the time and space used for the DP is negligible, if d is large. A vertex in the graph for alignment has $2^d - 1$ edges going out from it, and the A* algorithm examines all the descendant vertices and keeps in a heap the information about all of them. If an upper bound $L^+(s, t)$ for the s-t shortest path, which corresponds to the lower bound of the score of the alignment, is given, the necessary space for the heap can be reduced[4,5] and the computing time is also reduced: we can ignore w such that $L^*(s,v) + l(v,w) > L^+(s,t)$, when we examine the descendant vertices of v. This is called the enhanced A* algorithm.

2.2 Upper Bounding Technique for Computing E_Δ

E_Δ is a set of vertices which are used by the s-t paths whose lengths are at most Δ longer than the shortest path, and it corresponds to all aligned groups of residues in optimal and suboptimal alignments in original problem. This problem is well-studied[5,6,9,12], and computing this set E_Δ with A* algorithm is not so complicated. For any path p from s to t, the modified path length by the expression (1) is only $h(t) - h(s)$ longer than the original length. This value is not relevant to p, thus E_Δ on the modified graph is same as the original one. Hence, first we modify the edge lengths, and then we can obtain E_Δ with the Dijkstra method as follows[5].

1. Search from s by the Dijkstra method until the shortest path from s to t is discovered.
2. Search successively until a vertex v, to which the shortest path from s is more than Δ longer than the s-t shortest path, is discovered.
3. Modify the length of each edge (u,v) to $\delta(u,v)$ as follows:
$$\delta(u,v) = l(u,v) + L^*(s,u) - L^*(s,v) \tag{2}$$
Then apply the Dijkstra method from t until a vertex from which the shortest path to t is longer than Δ is discovered in this modified graph. E_Δ is the set of vertices searched in this step.

A vertex in the graph for the multiple alignment has $2^d - 1$ edges going out from it, and the Dijkstra algorithm examines all the descendant vertices and keeps the information about all of them. If an upper bound $L^+(s,t)$ for the s-t shortest path is given, we can also reduce the necessary space for heap as in the case of computing the optimal solution with enhanced A* algorithm: we can ignore w such that $L^*(s,v) + l(v,w) > L^+(s,t) + \Delta$, when we examine the descendant vertices of v.

In general, such kind of an upper bound is difficult to obtain. However, we can use the actual shortest path length obtained in step 1 for the upper bound in step 2: we can ignore w such that $L^*(s,v) + l(v,w) > L^*(s,t) + \Delta$.

3 Enumeration of Suboptimal Alignments

In this section, we first introduce Eppstein algorithm[1] briefly, and then extend it for the alignment problem. Moreover, we propose a new enumeration method to avoid unnecessary alignments in enumeration.

3.1 Eppstein Algorithm

Eppstein[1] proposed an algorithm which finds implicitly the k shortest paths for the graph G with non-negative m edges and n vertices regardless of cycles, in $O(m + n + k)$ time after the shortest path tree is constructed. Eppstein[1] also proposed an easier algorithm of $O(m + n \log n + k)$ time.

In the algorithm, we use $\delta(u, v)$ for the edge (u, v) as in equation (2). This $\delta(u, v)$ denotes how much longer the path will be using the edge (u, v) than the optimal path by way of v, and therefore this value is always non-negative.

If an edge (u, v) is on the shortest path tree, $\delta(u, v)$ is zero, otherwise, it is called a sidetrack and $\delta(u, v)$ may not be zero. If we go along an s-t path p other than the shortest path, there must be sidetracks on the path, and we define $sidetrack(p)$ as the nearest sidetrack from s within them.

Let $(tail(p), head(p))$ be $sidetrack(p)$. Then we can suppose a heap, in which the parent of a path p is a path which is same as p from $head(p)$ to t, but go along the shortest path from s to $head(p)$ instead of using $sidetrack(p)$. We define this parent of p as $parent(p)$ and we call p a child of $parent(p)$. The root of the heap is the shortest path, and all the paths from s to t appear in the heap once. In this heap, p is $\delta(sidetrack(p))$ longer than $parent(p)$.

The basic concept of the Eppstein algorithm is to modify this path heap to 4-heap. From this heap, we can obtain the k shortest paths in $O(k)$ time[2], or $O(k \log k)$ time in sorted form. The following is the outline of this algorithm:

1. Construct the shortest path tree from s to all the other vertices.
2. For each vertex v, construct $H_G(v)$, that is, a 3-heap of sidetracks (u', u), such that u is on the shortest path from s to v, ordered by $\delta(u', u)$. Let the length from the root of $H_G(v)$ to a node n be $\delta(u, v)$, where n represents sidetrack (u, v).
3. For each v in G, make an edge from each node in $H_G(v)$ which represents a sidetrack (u', u) to the root of $H_G(u')$, and define the length of this new edge as the value of the root.
4. Make a new node for each v in G, and make an edge from this node to the root of $H_G(v)$. Let the length of this edge be δ of the root. Let this new graph be $P(G)$.

Then we can find a heap $H_v(G)$ in $P(G)$ for any v, considering the root as the node made in step 4 for v, and the value of a node as the length from the root to the node. There is a one-to-one correspondence between the nodes in $H_v(G)$ and the paths from v to t in G, and the k smallest nodes in this virtual heap $H_v(G)$ correspond to the k shortest path. Moreover, we can easily restore the path from the node of the heap, which can be done in $O(n')$ time where n' is the size of the output alignment. For more details, see the paper[1].

Note that the shortest path tree in step 1 is constructed generally by the Dijkstra method, but for problems such as the alignment problem, we can also use DP. Eppstein showed the step 2 can be done in $O(n+m)$ time, but this is a complicated algorithm and takes much time in practice, and we use a far more easier algorithm that can be done in $O(n \log n + m)$ time, which is also proposed by Eppstein[1]: we make $H_G(v)$ one by one from s to the other vertices along the shortest path tree, sharing as many nodes as possible.

3.2 Extending Eppstein Algorithm to Reduce Memory Space

In this subsection, we discuss our approach for enumeration of all the suboptimal alignments whose scores are at most Δ lower than the optimal one. The original Eppstein algorithm requires searching all over the graph, and requires much memory. But it is evident that we only have to apply the Eppstein algorithm in the subset E_Δ after computing E_Δ as in the previous section, and then search the Eppstein's heap structure with the depth first method.

However, if we use the easier $O(n \log n + m)$ algorithm in step 2 of Eppstein algorithm, we do not have to compute E_Δ additionally. First, we must take the step 1 and 2 in the subsection 2.2, using upper bounding technique. These procedures cannot be skipped. After these procedures, we implement the Eppstein algorithm as follows:

1. Construct the Eppstein's heap structure only on the shortest path.
2. Search for suboptimal solutions which are at most Δ worse than the optimal (root) from the root of $H_s(G)$ with depth first search method. If we encounter $H_G(v)$ which has not been constructed yet, we construct the heap structures of vertices on the shortest path from s to v for which we have not constructed heaps yet.

With this method, when we finish enumerating all the suboptimal alignments, the set of vertices for which we constructed the Eppstein heap is also E_Δ. Thus we do not have to compute E_Δ additionally. Notice that this technique can be used in general graphs other than the graphs for alignments.

3.3 Avoiding Unnecessary Alignments

As we will show in the next section, the suboptimal alignments of multiple sequences are numerous. In examining the suboptimal alignments one by one, we should select alignments worth taking time to see. For this requirement, we introduce a notion of alignment class D_i as follows:

Definition 1 *D_i is a class of alignments which have i regions, which are sets of consecutive columns in the alignment, different from the alignment in D_0. There is only one alignment in D_0, and the alignment in D_0 is one of the optimal alignments which is arbitrary chosen.*

In Figure 1, the optimal alignment (a) is in D_0 (and none of the others are in this class), suboptimal alignments (b) and (c) are in D_1, and suboptimal

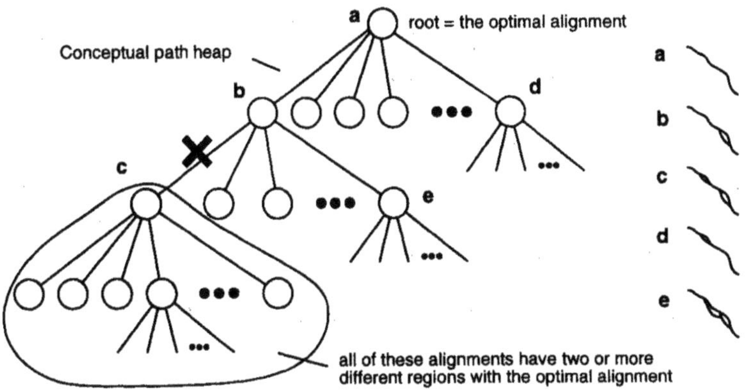

Figure 2: An example of a conceptual path heap. We can easily construct a heap which does not contain unnecessary alignments such as **c** and its all descendants.

alignment (d) is in D_2. We can easily construct alignments in D_i ($i \geq 2$) and their scores from alignments in D_0 and D_1. Thus alignments in D_i ($i \geq 2$) are unnecessary to enumerate in many cases.

The technique to avoid such alignments in D_i ($i \geq 2$) in enumeration of suboptimal alignments is rather simple: when we search the Eppstein's heap structure, if *head*(p) of s-t path p is on the s-t shortest path and *parent*(p) is not the shortest path, ignore p and its children (defined in subsection 3.1). Note that it is possible to construct a heap structure for enumerating only alignments in class D_1. Accordingly we can efficiently enumerate only the alignments in class D_1. Moreover, notice that we can extend this algorithm for enumerating alignments in class D_i ($i < d$) for any d.

3.4 Extracting Knowledge from Eppstein Heap

As mentioned by Eppstein[1], the Eppstein heap has a good feature: some of numerical values for each suboptimal solutions can be obtained in $O(1)$ time with some simple pre-process of $O(|E_\Delta|)$ time. In the case of multiple alignment problem, these can be obtained in such an efficient way for example: the number of aligned groups in which all residues are same, the number of indels, the score computed with another score table different from the table used in computing the optimal solution, the length of the alignment, and so on.

4 Experimental Results

In this section, we examine the efficiency of our approach and investigate the properties of suboptimal alignments through experiments. In the experiment, we used the PAM-250 matrix, and linear gap penalty bx where x is the gap length and b is the minimum value in the PAM-250 matrix, -8. All the experiments are done on Sun Ultra 1 with 128 megabyte memory.

4.1 *Case with High Similarity*

We first did experiments on a group of 8 sequences with high similarity in Table 1. According to it, the average scores per amino pair of these pairwise alignments are about 2.5 to 4. Add to this, the optimal score of multiple alignment of all these 8 sequences is 33129 and its length is 456, thus the average score per amino pair of this alignment is $\frac{33129}{456 \cdot \binom{8}{2}} \approx 2.59$ (Table 2). These are higher than in the experiment in the next subsection.

Table 1: Sequences of EF-TU and EF-1α to be aligned and their scores of pairwise sequence alignments. We use the top d sequences in this table in the experiments.

Sequences			Pairwise Scores						
Species	Protein	Length	Met	Tha	Thc	Sul	Ent	Pla	Sty
Halobacterium marismortui (Hal)	EF-TU	421	1329	1314	1221	1109	1099	1000	971
Methanococcus vannielii (Met)	EF-TU	428		1336	1247	1150	1176	1087	1045
Thermoplasma acidophilum (Tha)	EF-1α	424			1311	1261	1233	1063	1072
Thermococcus celer (Thc)	EF-1α	428				1132	1130	1049	991
Sulfolobus acidocaldarius (Sul)	EF-1α	435					1192	1131	1099
Entamoeba histolytica (Ent)	EF-1α	430						1584	1551
Plasmodium falciparum (Pla)	EF-1α	443							1636
Stylonychia lemnae (Sty)	EF-1α	446							

As for computing alignments of less than 8 sequences, we could apply the simple A* algorithm. However, for alignment of the 8 sequences, we used the upper bounding technique (enhanced A*) because 128 megabyte memory is not enough for computing with the simple A* algorithm: we used in the experiment the optimal solution as the upper bound to see the best efficiency of this enhanced algorithm. In any case, we used the upper bounding technique after the optimal solution is obtained.

According to Table 2, the DP takes a lot of time compared with the A* algorithm when d is small, but it is negligible when d is large. This table also shows that, the additional searching time required for computing suboptimal solutions is not so much as long as Δ is not much larger than in these experiments: it requires at most twice the time in total as in the case of computing only the optimal alignment in these experiments if $\Delta \leq 40$.

Figure 3, Table 3 and Table 4 show the results of enumerating the suboptimal alignments. Figure 3(a) shows that there are enormous number of suboptimal alignments, and the number increases exponentially as Δ increases. However, in Figure 3(b), we can see the number of suboptimal solutions is dramatically reduced by ignoring alignments in class D_i ($i \geq 2$). The number of the alignments enumerated in this way is only 0.0003% ($d = 4$) to 0.4% ($d = 8$) of all the alignments in case $\Delta = 30$ (see Table 4): it seems difficult to

Table 2: Searching time (sec) by the A* algorithm in the experiment on the d sequences of EF-TU and EF-1α. In case $d = 8$, the enhanced A* utilizing the optimal score is used. Note that only DP is used in case $d = 2$.

	$d=2$	$d=3$	$d=4$	$d=5$	$d=6$	$d=7$	$d=8$
best score	1329	3970	7709	12314	18101	24912	33129
Pre-process DP	0.32	1.00	4.30	7.23	11.1	16.0	20.5
Search (optimal)	-	0.18	0.52	3.35	19.6	426	5427
Search ($\Delta = 10$)	-	0.18	0.60	3.63	20.9	439	5686
Search ($\Delta = 20$)	-	0.22	0.73	4.17	23.1	462	6735
Search ($\Delta = 30$)	-	0.27	0.93	5.00	26.9	498	8027
Search ($\Delta = 40$)	-	0.33	1.23	6.22	31.5	552	9623

Table 3: Size of E_Δ and Eppstein's heap structure in the experiments on d sequences of EF-TU and EF-1α. The heap size in the table does not include the number of nodes made in step 4 of Eppstein algorithm, which is same as $|E_\Delta|$.

Δ		$d=2$	$d=3$	$d=4$	$d=5$	$d=6$	$d=7$	$d=8$
10	$\lvert E_{10}\rvert$	503	485	513	553	534	579	540
	heap size	437	277	411	503	454	674	404
20	$\lvert E_{20}\rvert$	1101	595	609	689	691	799	784
	heap size	7184	1010	1266	1701	1750	2604	2672
30	$\lvert E_{30}\rvert$	1447	946	817	901	864	1246	1316
	heap size	12983	4949	3417	3997	3594	7552	8539
40	$\lvert E_{40}\rvert$	2011	2528	1170	1249	1156	1973	2254
	heap size	17934	25861	8648	10036	7785	18407	23973

check significance of all the suboptimal alignments at most 10 worse than the optimal, but in our method, we can do it. Accordingly, the enumeration time is also reduced drastically(see Table 4).

Observing Figure 3(a), the number of the suboptimal alignments seems to be similar and irrelevant to d. It is an interesting fact, but this comparison is unfair. The number must be compared between the cases which have same value of $\frac{\Delta}{\binom{d}{2}}$: we must consider Δ per amino pair. For example, it is all right to compare the case $\Delta = 28$ $(d = 8)$ and the case $\Delta = 10$ $(d = 5)$. In this case, the number of suboptimal alignments in the former case is $\frac{7168718}{16112} \approx 444.9$ times as that of the latter case.

Table 4: Enumerating time (sec) when $\Delta = 30$ in the experiment on the d sequences EF-TU and EF-1α. (a) is the case enumerating all the suboptimal alignments, and (b) is the case enumerating alignments in class D_0 (optimal) and D_1. The time of constructing the Eppstein's heap structure is included in the time below.

		$d=2$	$d=3$	$d=4$	$d=5$	$d=6$	$d=7$	$d=8$
(a)	#alignments	38047513	8804702	327522816	85923864	20689104	49633652	13857237
	time (sec)	152.87	54.98	1830.18	510.63	124.55	292.50	109.00
(b)	#alignments	6968	1695	1117	2176	1659	41791	60589
	time (sec)	0.23	0.13	0.32	0.95	2.10	9.83	29.62

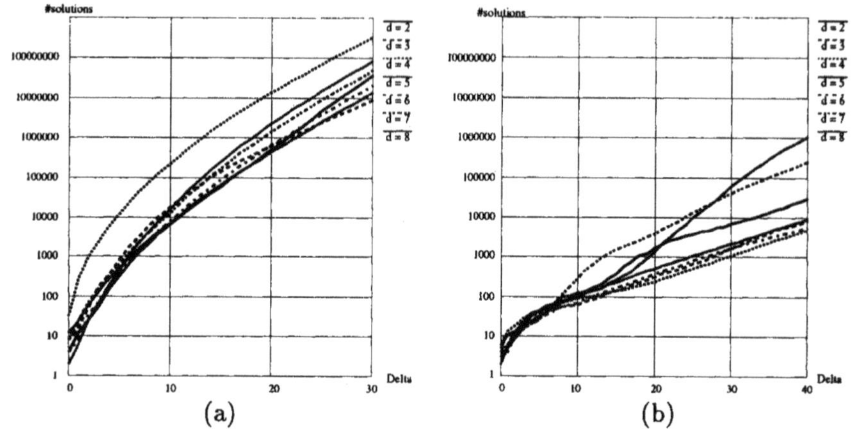

Figure 3: Number of the suboptimal alignments of d sequences of EF-TU and EF-1α whose scores are at most Δ worse than the optimal. (a) is the case enumerating all the alignments. $(0 \le \Delta \le 30)$ (b) is the case enumerating alignments in classes D_0 and D_1. $(0 \le \Delta \le 40)$

According to Table 3, $|E_\Delta|$ and the size of Eppstein heap for this size of Δ is not so large. Thus, the enumeration time in Table 4(b) is small, though it includes times for constructing the heap. In Figure 3(b), the number of suboptimal alignments in class D_1 increases much when $d = 2, 7, 8$ compared with other cases. The reason of this is seen in Table 3. The $|E_\Delta|$ in cases $d = 2, 7, 8$ is larger than the others: there may be many alignments which have a large region different from the optimal. On the other hand, in Figure 3(a), the number of the alignments in case $d = 4$ is large compared with others, but much of these must be combinations of small number of 'necessary' alignments.

4.2 Case with Low Similarity

We next did experiments on 5 globin sequences as in Table 5. According to Table 5, the average scores per amino acid pair of pairwise alignments of them are about 0.2 to 1.3. The score of the optimal multiple alignment of these 5 sequences is 543 and its length is 165, thus the average score per amid acid pair of this alignment is $\frac{543}{165 \cdot \binom{5}{2}} \approx 0.33$, which is lower than the previous case.

Figure 4 and Table 6 show the result of the experiments. According to Table 6(a), the searching time by simple A* algorithm is far longer than in the previous experiments for same d, though the length is short. It is because the estimator of the A* algorithm is not so powerful in case with low similarity.

According to Figure 4, the number of alignments in this experiment is also drastically reduced as in the experiments in the previous subsection by ignoring alignments in class D_i $(i \ge 2)$: the number of alignments in D_1 is only

Table 5: Globin sequences to be aligned and their scores of pairwise sequence alignments.

globin		Length	Apl	Bus	Ct7	Ct3
Lumbricus terrestris - AIII	(Lum)	157	29	15	35	41
Aplysia limacina	(Apl)	146		126	177	140
Busycon canaliculatum	(Bus)	147			111	64
Chironomus thummi thummi - VIIA	(Ct7)	145				191
Chironomus thummi thummi - IIIa	(Ct3)	151				

Table 6: (a) Searching time (sec) by simple A* algorithm, (b) the best score and the size of E_Δ in the experiment on the d globin sequences.

(a)

	$d=2$	$d=3$	$d=4$	$d=5$
Pre-Process DP	0.05	0.27	0.52	0.83
Search (optimal)	-	0.73	7.40	837
Search ($\Delta = 10$)	-	0.85	8.13	865
Search ($\Delta = 20$)	-	0.93	9.43	909
Search ($\Delta = 30$)	-	1.22	11.22	964
Search ($\Delta = 40$)	-	1.63	14.13	1080

(b)

	$d=2$	$d=3$	$d=4$	$d=5$
best score	29	103	354	543
$\|E_{10}\|$	357	508	380	554
$\|E_{20}\|$	776	1184	866	1159
$\|E_{30}\|$	1149	2403	1575	2448
$\|E_{40}\|$	1544	3839	2669	4569

0.004% of that of all the suboptimal alignments in case $d = 5$ and $\Delta = 20$.

As mentioned by Zuker[12], the alignments with low score are not always insignificant. In general, if the lengths of sequences to be aligned are short, the size of E_Δ will be small. However, the size of E_Δ is larger than in the previous experiments for same d and Δ. Hence we can conclude that sequences we use in this experiment is not so significant as in the previous experiment. In this way, we can use the size of E_Δ as a factor of the significance of the alignment.

5 Concluding Remarks

We investigated suboptimal multiple sequence alignments problem. Based on A* algorithm and Eppstein algorithm, we showed that the suboptimal multiple alignments can be enumerated in practical time. We also proposed a new efficient enumeration method. This method enumerates only the alignments which has only one region different from the optimal solution. The suboptimal alignments enumerated in this way are far fewer than by normal enumeration.

Our technique used with some approximate methods is also useful in many cases. Our algorithm can also be applied to many other optimization problems in molecular biology, such as tree-based alignment problem, gene finding problem, and so on. These remain as future works.

Acknowledgement

This work was supported in part by the Grant-in-Aid for Scientific Research on Priority Areas, "Genome Science", from the Ministry of Education, Science,

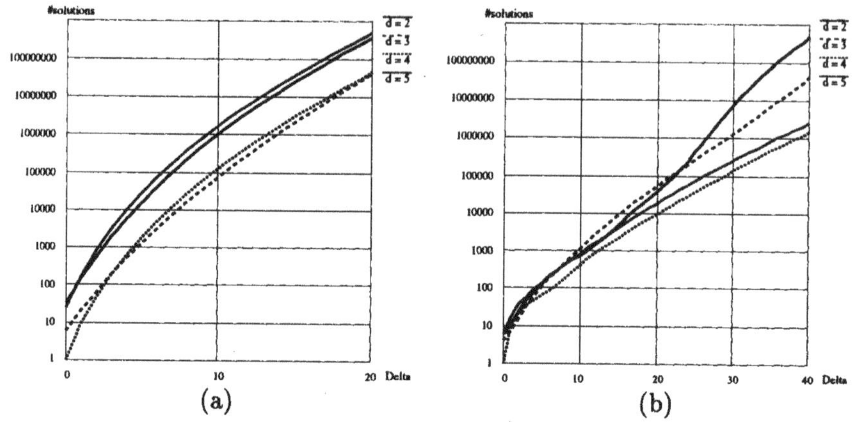

Figure 4: Number of the suboptimal alignments of d globin sequences whose scores are at most Δ worse than the optimal alignment. (a) is the case enumerating all the alignments. $(0 \leq \Delta \leq 20)$ (b) is the case enumerating alignments in classes D_0 and D_1. $(0 \leq \Delta \leq 40)$

Sports and Culture of Japan.

References

1. D. Eppstein, *Proc. IEEE Foundation of Computer Science*, 35: pp.154-165, 1994.
2. G. N. Frederickson, *Information and Computation,* 104: pp.197-214, 1993.
3. J. Gracy, et al., *Protein Eng.* 6: pp.821-829, 1993.
4. T. Ikeda, and H. Imai, *Proc. Genome Informatics Workshop V*, pp.90-99, 1994.
5. T. Ikeda, *Master's Thesis,* Dept. of Info. Sci., Univ. of Tokyo, 1995.
6. D. Naor and D. Brutlag, *Proc. 4th Symp. Combinatorial Pattern Matching,* pp.179-196. Springer-Verlag LNCS 684, 1993.
7. M. A. Saqi and M. J. Sternberg, *J. Mol. Biol.* 219: pp.727-732, 1991.
8. M. A. Saqi, et al., *Protein Eng.* 5: pp.305-311, 1992.
9. G. Shibayama, and H. Imai, *Proc. Genome Informatics Workshop IV,* pp.120-129, 1993.
10. T. Shibuya, et al., *Proc. 2nd Intelligent Transportation Systems,* pp.2031-2036, 1995.
11. M. S. Waterman and M. Eggert, *J. Mol. Biol.* 197: pp.723-728, 1987.
12. M. Zuker, *J. Mol. Biol.* 221: pp.403-420, 1991.

REDOX PROPERTIES OF CYTOCHROME C: NOVEL LINEAR RESPONSE AND HYBRID CONTINUUM–MICROSCOPIC METHODOLOGIES

Thomas Simonson
Institut de Génétique et Biologie Moléculaire et Cellulaire (C.N.R.S.), 1 rue Laurent Fries (C.U. de Strasbourg), 67404 Illkirch France.

Redox properties of yeast cytochrome c are estimated using molecular dynamics combined with a simple linear response approximation, as well as a hybrid continuum–molecular dynamics (COMD) approach. In both approaches, the free energy associated with an electrostatic perturbation (a redox electron) is separated into its relaxation and static (non-relaxation) components. The static component is calculated from the molecular dynamics simulation. The relaxation component is then calculated with a linear response approximation, either from the molecular dynamics, or from a separate continuum calculation. This latter hybrid approach exploits the relative robustness of continuum models for dealing with large perturbations, while avoiding some of their limitations. It is quite general, and could be applied for example to pK$_a$ calculations.

1 Introduction

Electrostatic and dielectric properties of proteins are central to their stability and activity [1]. This is especially obvious in the case of redox and electron transfer proteins, which harvest and orchestrate the flow of much of the energy in the biosphere. A very challenging area is the study of charge screening in these complex, inhomogeneous systems. Various experimental techniques have been used, such as measurements of redox potential shifts [2], pK$_a$ shifts [3], or changes in stability [4], upon mutating charged and polar groups. These techniques provide only indirect information on the protein properties themselves, since they contain a large contribution from solvent relaxation. Dielectric dispersion by dry protein powders [5], and measurements of gas phase basicities of protein ions [6], probe the protein properties directly, but in non-aqueous environments. The presence of a spectroscopic probe can provide a sensitive window into local details of a protein medium. Thus Stark effect measurements have been used to study both the equilibrium electric field [7], and local polarizability [8] at specific protein sites. Time-dependent Stokes shifts of a die complexed with apomyoglobin [9] provide a direct measurement of time-dependent dielectric relaxation. Finally, computer simulations provide a powerful approach, which becomes increasingly attractive as force fields, electrostatic treatments, and computer resources steadily improve [10, 11].

Cytochrome c has served for many years as a model electron transfer protein, and a large body of experimental and simulation data has been accumulated. We have carried out molecular dynamics simulations of yeast cytochrome c in solution in its oxidized and reduced forms, and we have reported recently detailed analyses of its macroscopic and microscopic dielectric properties [12–14]. We report here further calculations of redox properties, using two novel continuum and molecular dynamics methods. The first is a simple linear response approximation, proposed recently by Simonson *et al.* and Levy *et al.* [15–17]. It is used in conjunction with molecular dynamics simulations to calculate the reorganization free energy associated with heme oxidation and reduction, and compared to more rigorous free energy perturbation calculations. This approximation has already been applied to several problems [12–20]. However applications to proteins have been limited, and it is therefore useful to explore its limits further here.

The second method is a new, hybrid, continuum–molecular dynamics (COMD) method for the calculation of electrostatic properties. In this method, the perturbation free energy associated with, say, heme oxidation is decomposed into two components: a relaxation free energy, and a static free energy [21]. The static free energy is calculated from a molecular dynamics simulation, while the relaxation free energy is obtained from a continuum model. The COMD method is quite general, and can be applied to many electrostatic calculations, including pK_a calculations. As a preliminary test, the method is applied here to the calculation of the redox potential of cytochrome c. Additional applications are underway.

2 Methods

2.1 Linear response approximation

When a set of perturbing charges q_i (such as a redox electron) is introduced into the vicinity of a protein, the perturbation free energy has the well-known expression [22]

$$\Delta G = -kT \ln\langle \exp(-U/kT)\rangle_0, \tag{1}$$

where U is the perturbation energy, and the brackets indicate an ensemble average over the unperturbed ensemble. If the perturbation consists of a single redox electron, for example, ΔG is the redox potential. Expanding the above expression in powers of U/kT gives

$$\begin{aligned} \Delta G &= \langle U\rangle_0 - \frac{1}{2kT}(\langle U^2\rangle_0 - \langle U\rangle_0^2) + O([U/kT]^3) \\ &= G_1 + G_2 + G_{nl} \end{aligned} \tag{2}$$

The first term G_1 represents the static component of the perturbation free energy, while the remaining terms G_2 and G_{nl} represent the relaxation free energy [13,21]. If the perturbation consists of a redox electron, the relaxation free energy is identical to the reorganization free energy of electron transfer theory [23]. The linear response approximation truncates the free energy expansion after the second order term G_2, giving a quadratic free energy with respect to the perturbing charges. The remaining G_{nl} is the 'non-linear' component. This truncation is equivalent [17] to assuming a gaussian probability distribution of the perturbing potential (over the unperturbed ensemble). The relaxation free energy can also be written

$$\Delta G - G_1 = G_{rlx} = -kT \ln\langle \exp(-\delta U/kT)\rangle_0, \tag{3}$$

where δU is the deviation of U from its mean. The ensemble averaging is normally done using a microscopic simulation technique—molecular dynamics in the present work.

2.2 COMD: a hybrid continuum–molecular dynamics model

The decomposition of the perturbation free energy into static and relaxation components (above) can be made in continuum models as well as molecular dynamics. It is easy to show (*e.g.* [13,15]) that the relaxation free energy is identical to the self-energy of the perturbing charges. Thus for a redox electron, for example, the relaxation free energy for reduction is the free energy to insert the perturbing electron, with all the protein permanent charges removed. Proton self-energies are routinely calculated as a part of pK_a calculations.

We propose here a novel, hybrid, method, termed COMD, in which the relaxation component of the perturbation free energy is calculated from a continuum model, while the static component ($\langle U\rangle_0$) is calculated from a molecular dynamics simulation. This additional complexity aims to exploit optimal features of each method. Thus, the molecular dynamics model should provide a reasonably accurate estimate of the static component of the free energy, obtained by simply averaging the perturbation over the simulation. While this procedure is known to have significant statistical uncertainty, it is nevertheless free from the more serious approximations of continuum models; the neglect of specific ordering of discrete water moleules for example. On the other hand, the continuum model provides a simple and robust approach to relaxation free energies, which has been tested specifically for this purpose in some detail [13]. Microscopic free energy calculations, either using the linear approximation or the full exponential form (1), are limited with respect to the size of the perturbation that can be tackled (see below, as well as *e.g.* [18,12]), precisely because of lack of convergence of the relaxation free energy. The continuum model, while approximate, is known to be more robust in this respect. It is also completely independent, in this context, of any choice of permanent charge distribution, since the self-energy is calculated without any protein permanent charges; and it is fairly robust with respect to the choice of atomic radii. It does require an assumption for the protein dielectric. Here, the COMD method exploits an important feature of proteins: the optimal dielectric constant to describe relaxation properties is normally different from the low value (1–2) used to describe equilibrium properties [24–26]. This is physically fairly obvious, but has been neglected in most applications of continuum models. By explicitly separating out the relaxation part of the free energy, the COMD method relies clearly on the Fröhlich-Kirkwood dielectric constant, which is unambiguously defined as a linear response coefficient. The Fröhlich-Kirkwood dielectric constants of eight proteins have been calculated recently from molecular dynamics simulations [27, 12, 26]. It was found that while the overall values are surprisingly large (ranging from 11 to 35), values in the protein interior are much lower, ranging from 2 to 4, consistent with earlier empirical estimates [24] as well as powder experiments [5]. For cytochrome c, in particular, the polarizability in the heme vicinity is low [12, 13].

At first glance, the self-energy calculation with the continuum model would appear to require an assumption for the radius of the perturbing charges. This could introduce strong artefacts into the calculation. However in practice, one transfers the perturbing charges from a reference compound, such as a heme in solution, to the compound of interest—the protein-bound heme. In that case there is a systematic cancellation of the radius-dependent part of the free energy.

2.3 Simulations

Two molecular dynamics simulations were performed, of yeast ferro- and ferricytochrome c (abbreviated 1YCC and 2YCC respectively), solvated by 1400 TIP3P waters [28], at 293 K, starting from the crystal structures [29], lasting one nanosecond each. Electrostatic interactions were truncated beyond 12 Å (1 Å = 0.1 nm). The Charmm/Param19 empirical force-field was used [30]. A soft spherical boundary potential of radius 24 Å was used to confine the system. Simulations were done with the program X-PLOR [31].

Continuum calculations were performed with the program Delphi [32] using the protein crystal structure.

In the redox calculations, the redox electron is assumed to be distributed equally on the four nitrogen atoms that bind the heme iron.

3 Results

3.1 Heme oxido-reduction: linear response free energy calculations

Free energies to oxidize reduced cytochrome c (1YCC), and to reduce oxidized cytochrome c (2YCC), are reported in Table 1. The free energies are decomposed into the first-order term G_1, the second-order term G_2, and higher-order terms G_{nl} (eq. 2). By averaging over these 'forward' and 'backward' free energy estimates, we obtain another estimate of the 1YCC oxidation free energy. This estimation is equivalent to performing the oxidation in two steps, *i.e.* through a half-oxidation of 1YCC and a half-reduction of 2YCC. This two-step protocol is closer to a full-fledged free energy calculation, and should be more accurate.

We first observe the performance of the linear response approximation. The quality of the linear response approximation is measured by the magnitude of the non-linear terms, which are significant for the full reduction of 1YCC, but negligible for the half-oxidation and half-reduction. Thus the linear response approximation to the relaxation free energy is accurate, in this case, for a perturbation as large as a half-electronic charge; it is inaccurate for perturbation by a full electronic charge

Second, we can analyze further the accuracy of the relaxation free energy by assuming that the probability distribution of the equilibrium electrostatic potential is gaussian on the heme. This was shown to be the case at all the C_α positions in cytochrome c, over the thermally accessible range of conformations [13]. It has also been observed in the active site of histidyl tRNA synthetase (T. Simonson, unpublished). The analysis goes as follows. Calculation of G_{rlx} (eq. 3) involves integrating the product of $\exp(-\delta U/kT)$ by the probability distribution $p(\delta U)$, which we are assuming to be gaussian. This product is another gaussian, $w(\delta U)$, displaced with respect to $p(\delta U)$ by $-\sigma^2/kT$, where σ is the standard deviation of U. In order to calculate the integral accurately, the peaks of p and w must overlap sufficiently. In other words, our simulation must sample the regions that contribute most to the integral. This will be the case if the shift σ^2/kT is not much larger than the width σ of p. Thus the condition to reliably integrate is

$$\sigma \sim kT. \tag{4}$$

If on the contrary the fluctuations of δU are much larger than kT, we cannot be sure of the accuracy of a single step calculation of the relaxation free energy; the unperturbed ensemble does not sufficiently sample the tails of the probability distribution $p(\delta U)$. This does not necessarily mean that linear response is inaccurate. Its accuracy appears in several cases to hold up beyond the region where $\sigma \sim kT$ [18]. Thus we find empirically that we can calculate G_{rlx} in a single step with linear response, even in cases when the simulation data would not by itself give us confidence to do so. Indeed, this empirical robustness is precisely what makes linear response useful.

For the present data, $\sigma = 1$ kcal/mol for the 1YCC simulation (considering the perturbation to 2YCC, *i.e.* $\delta q = 1$). Thus the integration of the exponential in (1) should be moderately accurate, and we can compare the total relaxation free energy to the linear response approximation with some confidence. Therefore the deviation from linear response seen in this case is probably significant, even though the statistical error in G_1 is of the same magnitude.

Our third observation is that the average perturbation energies, or G_1, appear to be quite noisy, as has been seen in other studies. Thus our 'forward' and 'backward' free energy estimates (lines 1 and 2 in Table 1) agree closely for their relaxation components, but disagree completely for the static components. The 'two-step' estimate (line 5) is effectively the average of the previous two. The real uncertainty in G_1 is therefore at least ±5 kcal/mol, despite the small apparent statistical error.

Our estimate of the oxidation free energy of 1YCC is thus 9±5 kcal/mol. Our estimate of the relaxation, or reorganization free energy is much more precise: G_{rlx} = -0.80±0.02 kcal/mol. This low reorganization free energy reflects the low polarizability of the protein matrix around the heme, and the absence of nearby solvent. Indeed, recall that this relaxation free energy includes the contribution of explicit solvent. Bulk solvent is not present however in our simulations, since we simulated the protein in 24 Å water droplets, surrounded by vacuum. A simple Born estimate of the bulk solvent contribution to the relaxation free energy is -7 kcal/mol, giving a total of G_{rlx} = -7.8 kcal/mol, including now the effect of bulk solvent.

In classical electron transfer theory, this reorganization free energy is directly related to the activation free energy G^* for transfering an electron from ferro-cytochrome c to ferri-cytochrome c: $-2G_{rlx} = 4G^*$. Thus $G^* = -G_{rlx}/2$ = 3.9 kcal/mol. In contrast, the free energy to introduce a negative charge into a heme-sized cavity in bulk water would be on the order of -80 kcal/mol, giving an activation free energy of 40 kcal/mol. Thus the low polarizability of the protein matrix around the heme has a dramatic effect on the electron transfer kinetics; we expect that qualitatively similar results would hold for electron transfer between cytochrome c and its physiological partners cytochrome c oxidase and reductase. Similar results were obtained by Warshel and coworkers with a Protein Dipole Langevin Dipole model [33].

Table 1: Heme oxido-reduction: linear response results

	δq^e	G_1	G_2	G_{nl}	ΔG
1YCC[a] → 2YCC[b]	-1	4.7 (4)	-0.8 (2)	-0.15	3.8 (4)
2YCC → 1YCC	1	-13.6 (4)	-0.8 (2)	0.14	-14.3 (4)
1YCC → 1/2YCC[c]	-0.5	2.4 (2)	-0.2 (1)	-0.02	2.1 (2)
2YCC → 1/2YCC	+0.5	-6.8 (2)	-0.2 (1)	-0.01	-7.0 (2)
1YCC → 1/2YCC → 2YCC	-1				9.1[d] (3)

Results are in kcal/mol. Uncertainties on the last digits in parentheses. [a]Ferri-cytochrome c. [b]Ferro-cytochrome c. [c]Half-oxidized, half-reduced intermediate state. [d]Obtained by adding together the two previous half steps. [e]Magnitude of perturbing charge.

3.2 COMD hybrid methodology

We now adopt the hybrid COMD viewpoint to attack the same problem: calculation of the free energy to transfer an electron from ferro-cytochrome c to ferri-cytochrome c. We therefore retain the molecular dynamics estimate of the static component of the free energy, but use a continuum model to calculate the relaxation component. We just saw how well the linear response approximation and the molecular dynamics approach appears to work for this calculation, so that a continuum model would not actually present any practical advantage here. We perform the calculation merely as an illustration of the hybrid methodology; other applications will be presented in the future.

We consider separately the radius-dependent contribution to the self-energy, and the remaining contribution, as discussed above (Methods). The radius-dependent contribution is in fact the Born free energy to embed the perturbing charge in a homogeneous, infinite medium having the dielectric constant of the protein (see [13] for details). In ordinary applications, as pointed out above, the radius-dependent contribution would systematically cancel when a reference compound is considered. In the present application, there is no reference compound, and we will actually explicitly calculate the radius-dependent part, keeping in mind its artificial character. For the protein dielectric constant ϵ_p we assume various values between one and two, based on theoretical calculations of the dielectric constant in the heme region [12].

With $\epsilon_p = 1$ we obtain G_{rlx} = -16.9 kcal/mol. The radius-dependent part of the self-energy is obviously zero (ϵ_p=1), so only the surrounding solvent contributes to the relaxation free energy. This result can be compared with the molecular-dynamics-plus-Born-correction result of -7.8 kcal/mol, which contains however a contribution from the protein medium itself.

With $\epsilon_p = 2$, the self-energy is -8.3 kcal/mol, not including the radius-dependent term. If we incude the radius-dependent term, the total self-energy is much too large. To reproduce the molecular dynamics result, we require ϵ_p smaller than 2. Assuming $\epsilon_p = 1.2$, we obtain agreement with a radius of 4 Å. This low protein dielectric is not unreasonable, when comparing to molecular dynamics results, which do not contain explicit electronic polarizability. A cavity radius of 4 Å is close to values used in continuum treatments of charged perturbations (photoexcitation) on an indole ring [34].

4 CONCLUSION

We have presented an application of a simple linear response method, proposed earlier [15–17], to calculate electrostatic perturbation free energies in proteins. The linear response approximation appears to be accurate for a perturbing charge inserted on the heme group of cytochrome c. The low polarizability seen here for the heme environment is of obvious functional relevance.

We have also proposed a novel hybrid continuum–molecular dynamics approach for electrostatic free energies. While the application considered was somewhat artificial, the method is quite general, and should be useful for pK_a calculations in particular. It has two advantages in principle: first, it should be able to exploit the robustness of continuum models for handling rather large perturbations, while still allowing the inclusion of important discrete water molecules through the static free energy term, where they are likely to contribute most. Second, it incorporates automatically the distinction between the static and relaxation free energies: it has been pointed out in the past and recently [24, 13, 25] that these two components should probably not be calculated with a single dielectric model, but should each have a specific treatment, as in the present approach.

Acknowledgments

Simulations were done on the C90 computer of the IDRIS supercomputer center of the Centre National de la Recherche Scientifique.

References

1. M. Perutz. Electrostatic effects in proteins. *Science*, 201:1187–1191, 1978.
2. R. Varadarajan, T.E. Zewert, H.B. Gray, and S.G. Boxer. Effects of buried ionizable amino acids on the reduction potential of recombinant hemoglobin. *Science*, 243:69–72, 1989.

3. A.J. Russell and A.R. Fersht. Rational modification of enzyme catalysis by engineering surface charge. *Nature*, 328:496–500, 1987.
4. H. Nicholson, W.J. Becktel, and B.W. Matthews. Enhanced protein thermostability from designed mutations that interact with α helix dipoles. *Nature*, 336:651–656, 1988.
5. S. Bone and R. Pethig. Dielectric studies of protein hydration and hydration-induced flexibility. *J. Mol. Biol.*, 181:323–326, 1985.
6. P.D. Schnier, D.S. Gross, and E.R. Williams. Electrostatic forces and dielectric polarizability of multiply protonated gas-phase cytochrome c ions probed by ion/molecule chemistry. *J. Am. Chem. Soc.*, 117:6747–6757, 1995.
7. D.J. Lockhardt and P.S. Kim. Internal Stark effect measurement of the electric field at the amino terminus of an α helix. *Science*, 257:947–951, 1992.
8. M.A. Steffen, K. Lao, and S.G. Boxer. Dielectric asymmetry in the photosynthetic reaction center. *Science*, 264:810–816, 1994.
9. D.W. Pierce and S.G. Boxer. Dielectric relaxation in a protein matrix. *J. Phys. Chem.*, 96:5560–5566, 1992.
10. C.L. Brooks III, M. Karplus, and M. Pettitt. Proteins: a theoretical perspective of dynamics, structure and thermodynamics. *Adv. Chem. Phys.*, 71:1–259, 1987.
11. A. Warshel. *Computer modelling of chemical reactions in enzymes and solutions*. John Wiley, New York, 1991.
12. Thomas Simonson and David Perahia. Internal and interfacial dielectric properties of cytochrome c from molecular dynamics simulations in aqueous solution. *Proc. Natl. Acad. Sci. USA*, 92:1082–1086, 1995.
13. Thomas Simonson and David Perahia. Microscopic dielectric properties of cytochrome c from molecular dynamics simulations in aqueous solution. *J. Am. Chem. Soc.*, 117:7987–8000, 1995.
14. Thomas Simonson and David Perahia. Dielectric properties of proteins from simulations: tools and techniques. *Comp. Phys. Comm.*, 91:291–303, 1995.
15. T. Simonson, D. Perahia, and G. Bricogne. Intramolecular dielectric screening in proteins. *J. Mol. Biol.*, 218:859–886, 1991.
16. T. Simonson, D. Perahia, and A. T. Brünger. Microscopic theory of the dielectric properties of proteins. *Biophys. J.*, 59:670–90, 1991.
17. R. Levy, M. Belhadj, and D. Kitchen. Gaussian fluctuation formula for electrostatic free energy changes. *J. Chem. Phys.*, 95:3627–3633, 1991.
18. P. Smith and W.F. van Gunsteren. Predictions of free energy differences from a single simulation of the initial state. *J. Chem. Phys.*, 100:577–584,

1994.
19. G.S. Del Buono, F.E. Figueirido, and R. Levy. Intrinsic pKa's of ionizable residues in proteins: an explicit solvent calculation for lysozyme. *Proteins*, 20:85–97, 1994.
20. J. Aqvist, C. Medina, and J.E. Samuelsson. A new method for predicting binding affinity in computer-aided drug design. *Prot. Eng.*, 7:385–391, 1994.
21. L. Landau and E. Lifschitz. *Statistical Mechanics*. Pergamon Press, New York, 1980.
22. R. H. Fowler and E. A. Guggenheim. *Statistical Thermodynamics*. Cambridge University Press, 1939.
23. R. Marcus. *Ann. Rev. Phys. Chem.*, 15:155, 1964.
24. M. Gilson, A. Rashin, R. Fine, and B. Honig. On the calculation of electrostatic interactions in proteins. *Journal of Molecular Biology*, 184:503–551, 1985.
25. L. Krishtalik, A.M. Kuznetsov, and E.L. Mertz. Electrostatics of proteins: a description in terms of two dielectric constants simultaneously. *Biophys. J.*, 70:A225, 1996.
26. Thomas Simonson. Accurate calculation of the dielectric constant of water from simulations of a microscopic droplet in vacuum. *Chem. Phys. Lett.*, 250:450, 1996.
27. P. Smith, R. Brunne, A. Mark, and W.F. van Gunsteren. The dielectric constant of trypsin inhibitor and lysozyme calculated from molecular dynamics simulations. *J. Phys. Chem.*, 97:2009–2014, 1993.
28. W. Jorgensen, J. Chandrasekar, J. Madura, R. Impey, and M. Klein. Comparison of simple potential functions for simulating liquid water. *J. Chem. Phys.*, 79:926–935, 1983.
29. A. M. Berghuis and G. D. Brayer. Oxidation state-dependent conformation changes in cytochrome c. *J. Molec. Biol.*, 223:959–976, 1992.
30. B. Brooks, R. Bruccoleri, B. Olafson, D. States, S. Swaminathan, and M. Karplus. Charmm: a program for macromolecular energy, minimization, and molecular dynamics calculations. *J. Comp. Chem.*, 4:187–217, 1983.
31. A. T. Brünger. X-PLOR *version 3.1, A System for X-ray crystallography and NMR*. Yale University Press, New Haven, 1992.
32. K. Sharp. *DelPhi, Version 3.0*. Columbia University, 1988.
33. A.K. Churg and A. Warshel. Control of the redox potential of cytochrome c and microscopic dielectric properties in proteins. *Biochemistry*, 25:1675–1681, 1986.

34. P.L. Muino and P.R. Callis. Hybrid simulations of solvation effects on electronic spectra: indoles in water. *J. Chem. Phys.*, 100:4093–4109, 1994.

PROTEIN SUPERFAMILY MEMBERS AS TARGETS FOR COMPUTER MODELING: THE CARBOHYDRATE RECOGNITION DOMAIN OF A MACROPHAGE LECTIN

RONALD E. STENKAMP[1,3], ALEJANDRO ARUFFO[1,2] & JÜRGEN BAJORATH[1,2]

[1]Department of Biological Structure, University of Washington, Seattle, WA 98195

[2]Bristol-Myers Squibb Pharmaceutical Research Institute

3005 First Avenue, Seattle, WA 98121

[3]Corresponding author, phone , fax, electronic mail:

phone: (206)-685-1721

fax: (206)-543-1524

e-mail: stenkamp@u.washington.edu

Abstract

Members of protein superfamilies display similar folds, but share only limited sequence identity, often 25% or less. Thus, it is not straightforward to apply standard homology modeling methods to construct reliable three-dimensional models of such proteins. A three-dimensional model of the carbohydrate recognition domain of the rat macrophage lectin, a member of the calcium-dependent (C-type) lectin superfamily, has been generated to illustrate how information provided by comparison of X-ray structures and sequence-structure alignments can aid in comparative modeling when primary sequence similarities are low.

Introduction

Members of emerging protein superfamilies are generally thought to adopt a similar global fold, despite sharing only low sequence similarity. As targets for comparative protein modeling [1], members of protein superfamilies, for which at least some structural information is available, appear attractive as it is usually possible to generate approximate three-dimensional models for many of these molecules. However, the low level of sequence similarity shared by these proteins makes it difficult to generate topologically meaningful alignments relative to potential structural template(s) [1], and hence the accuracy of such models is often limited and insufficient for more detailed applications.

The well studied immunoglobulin superfamily (IgSF) [2] can be considered a paradigm for the similarities and relationships of sequences and structures in protein superfamilies. Structural studies on a variety of proteins or protein domains belonging to the IgSF, whose sequence similarity is often limited to two conserved cysteines and a few hydrophobic (core) residues, have revealed many variations of the basic immunoglobulin fold [3]. Despite the knowledge of these structures and many IgSF sequences, it remains difficult to identify, by sequence comparison, closely related templates for model building of IgSF molecules with unknown structure.

The situation is even more problematic for protein superfamilies for which, in contrast to the IgSF, only one structure has been determined and where, in consequence, information from structure comparison (ie, the identification of structurally conserved and variable regions in different proteins) is not available to complement multiple sequence alignments. Until recently, this has been the case for the calcium-dependent (C-type) lectin superfamily [4]. C-type lectin domains, which typically share less than 30% sequence identity, specifically bind mono- or oligosaccharides in a calcium-dependent fashion and function as carbohydrate recognition modules in many mammalian proteins [5]. The C-type lectin domain of the mannose binding protein from rat (MBP) was the first structure of a C-type lectin domain determined [6] and revealed a novel and rather unusual protein fold, consisting of about 50% loops and other extended regions of unusual secondary structure [6]. This structure has served as template for model building of other C-type lectins [7].

More recently, the structure of the C-type lectin domain of E-selectin, a cell adhesion molecule, has been determined [8] as well as structures of the closely related human homolog of rat MBP [9,10]. Structure comparison of MBP and E-selectin [8,11] has, in conjunction with multiple sequence comparison [12], improved the ability to construct meaningful models of other members of the C-type lectin superfamily [11,13]. We illustrate this here by building a model of the C-terminal extracellular carbohydrate recognition domain of the rat macrophage lectin (ML) [14], a type II transmembrane glycoprotein receptor with specificity for galactose and N-acetylgalactosamine [14,15].

Methods

X-ray structures of E-selectin at 2.0 Å resolution [8] and of MBP at 1.7 Å resolution [16] were compared by backbone superposition as described [11]. Structurally conserved regions were identified by sequential least squares superposition of backbone segments of increasing length followed by root mean square deviation (rmsd) comparison. Backbone segments which superimposed with an rmsd of less than 1 Å were determined, and a structure based sequence alignment was generated. This structure-oriented alignment was complemented by multiple sequence comparison of ML, selectins [12] and other C-type lectins (not shown) to better understand the structural relevance of C-type lectin consensus residues. Backbone regions which are structurally conserved in MBP and E-selectin provided the framework for the ML model. The backbone conformations of structurally variable regions in MBP and E-selectin and regions including insertions and deletions relative to ML were approximated by conformational search [17]. Side chain replacements were modeled in conformations as similar as possible to the original conformation or, for structurally unconstrained positions, using a rotamer search procedure [18]. The initially assembled model was refined by some energy minimization, and the stereochemistry of the refined model and its sequence-structure compatibility [19] were assessed.

Results and Discussion

The sequences of the carbohydrate recognition domains of ML, MBP, and E-selectin are less than 30% identical. Comparison of the MBP and E-selectin X-ray structures reveals significant differences in some regions, although both proteins adopt the same global fold. However, structural conservation in MBP and E-selectin includes two regions of extended unusual secondary structure. The information obtained from structure comparison has been incorporated in a topological alignment of MBP and E-selectin which reflects the spatial equivalence of residues (Figure 1). The comparison allows a better definition of conserved C-type lectin core regions and of variable structural elements (Figure 2) than has been possible on the basis of only the MBP structure. This was illustrated by comparison of E-selectin model and X-ray structures [13]. The knowledge of similarities and differences in these two structures with limited sequence similarity provides the basis for more accurate sequence alignments to model other members of this protein superfamily.

The sequence of the macrophage lectin was aligned against this template by matching core residues, structurally constrained positions and consensus residues in structurally conserved regions. Using these criteria, regions including insertions and deletions could be assigned with some confidence. Structurally conserved regions in MBP and E-selectin were thought to be also conserved in ML and included in the model. Other backbone segments were considered variable, and their conformations were approximated by conformational search calculations. Following side chain modeling, the model was energy refined and its stereochemistry was assessed.

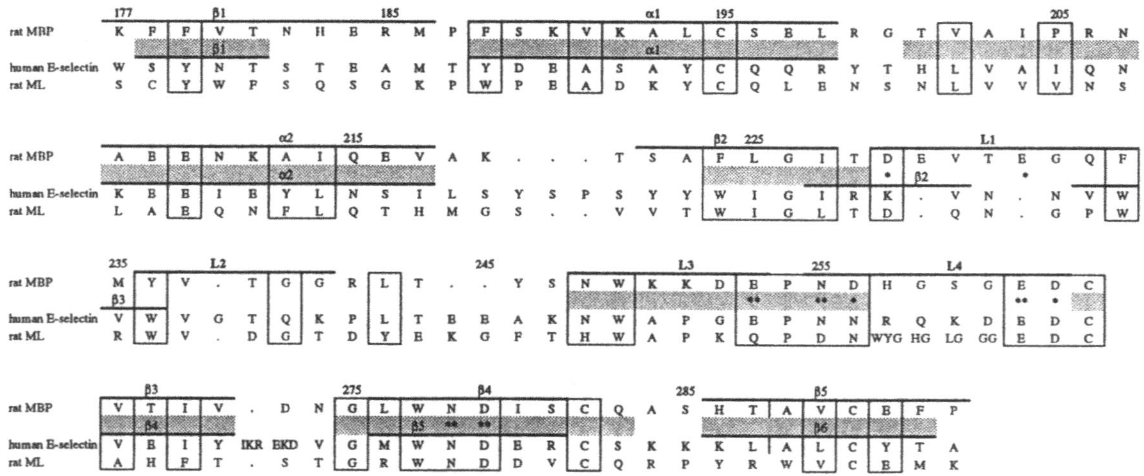

Figure 1. Topological alignment of the C-type lectin domains of human E-selectin and rat MBP, based on structural comparison. The sequence of rat ML was aligned against this template. The major secondary structure elements in MBP and E-selectin are labeled. L1-L4 are extended regions of non-classical secondary structure in MBP. Residues which participate in the formation of two calcium binding sites in MBP are labeled with one and two asterisks, respectively. Residues thought to be determinants the C-type lectin fold are boxed. Horizontal shading shows the structurally conserved regions in MBP and E-selectin. Residue numbers are given for ML.

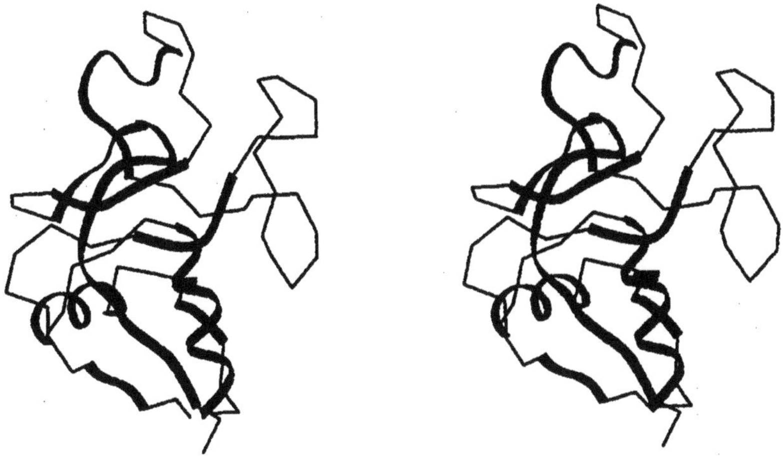

Figure 2. Stereo view of structurally conserved regions in MBP and E-selectin (thick lines) according to Figure 1 mapped on a trace of the MBP C-type lectin fold.

How sound were the assumptions on which the modeling of ML was based? Ultimately, the question can not be answered prior to experimental structure determination. However, the inverse folding approach [20] has provided a variety of methods for threading and the assessment of sequence-structure compatibility which are particularly relevant for model building attempts in the presence of low sequence homology. Here the energy profile method of Sippl [19] has been applied to analyze the sequence-structure compatibility of the ML model (Figure 3). The obtained profile is, in terms of the overall negative value of the average residue interaction energies, indicative of an overall correctly folded model with no substantial errors in the core regions. The analysis is not expected to identify a number of errors such as incorrectly modeled loop conformations, but provides a critical assessment of the reliability of the initial structure-oriented sequence alignment and of the finalized model beyond a determination of its stereochemistry.

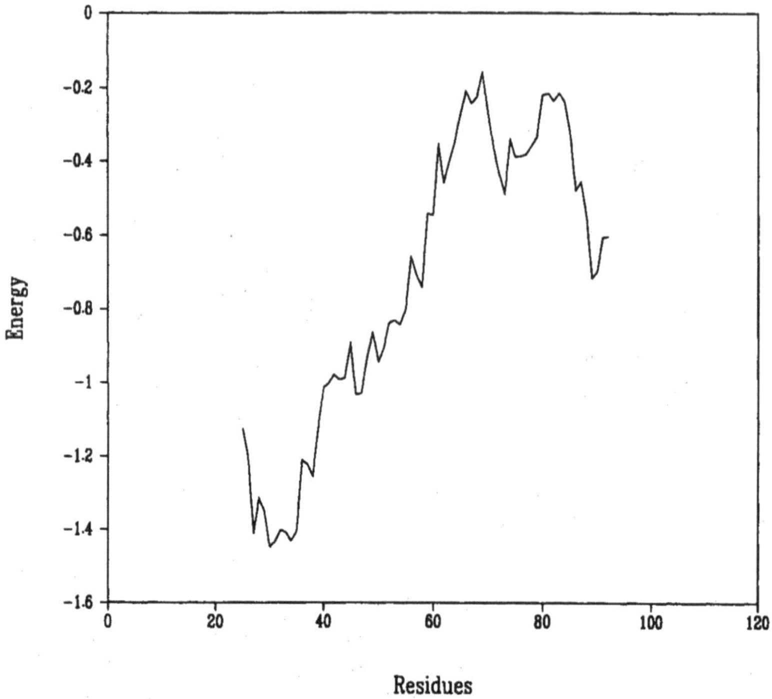

Figure 3. Energy profile of the ML model. Pairwise average residue interaction energy is given in units of E/kT (E, interaction energy in kcal/mol; k, Boltzmann constant; T, temperature in K) and calculated at each residue position using a fifty residue window for energy averaging.

Figure 4 shows the ML model in comparison to the MBP and E-selectin structures. A functional calcium binding site in MBP which is directly involved in carbohydrate binding [16] is predicted to be conserved in ML suggesting that details of the protein-carbohydrate interactions are similar. In contrast, residues surrounding this calcium binding sites and their spatial arrangements differ in all three structures. These ML residues can be selected based on the model and their contribution to specificity can be assessed experimentally. Another unique feature of ML compared to MBP and E-selectin is a five residue insertion in a calcium binding loop.

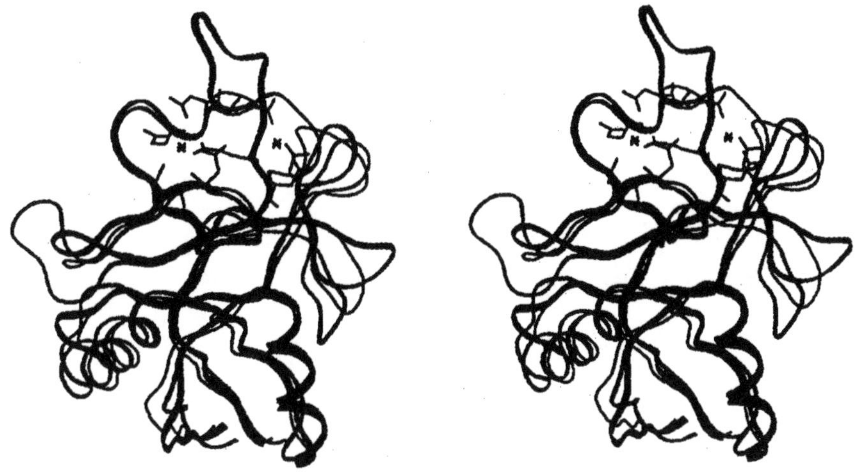

Figure 4. Superposition of C-type lectin domains. The backbones of the MBP and E-selectin structures and the ML model are traced in thin, medium, and thick line, respectively. The orientation is similar to figure 2. ML residues of calcium binding sites fully conserved in MBP, E-selectin, and ML (left) or partially conserved in MBP and ML (right) are shown.

Conclusions

Although members of protein superfamilies are, in principle, promising targets for comparative molecular modeling, the generation of detailed models is often difficult due to low sequence similarities and limited availability of structural data. The generation of reliable models is more straightforward once results from multiple sequence and structure comparison are combined in a meaningful way, as exemplified by studies on C-type lectins such as ML.

References

1. J. Bajorath *et al, Protein Sci.* **2**, 317 (1993).
2. A.F. Williams *et al, Immunol.* **6**, 381 (1988).
3. P. Bork *et al, J. Mol. Biol.* **242**, 309 (1994).
4. K. Drickamer, *J. Biol. Chem.* **263**, 9557 (1988).
5. K. Drickamer, *Curr. Opin. Struct. Biol.* **3**, 393 (1993).
6. W.I. Weis *et al, Science* **254**, 1608 (1991).
7. J. Bajorath and A. Aruffo, *J. Biol. Chem.* **269**, 32457 (1994).
8. B.J. Graves *et al, Nature* **367**, 532 (1994).
9. S. Sheriff *et al, Nature Struct. Biol.* **1**, 789 (1994).
10. W.I. Weis and K. Drickamer, *Structure* **2**, 1227 (1994).
11. J. Bajorath and A. Aruffo, *Protein Sci.* **5**, 240 (1996).
12. J. Bajorath and A. Aruffo, *Biochem. Biophys. Res. Comm.* **216**, 1018 (1995).
13. J. Bajorath et *al, Bioconjug. Chem.* **6**, 3 (1995).
14. M. Li *et al, J. Biol. Chem.* **265**, 11295 (1990).
15. S.T. Iobst and K. Drickamer, *J. Biol. Chem.* **271**, 6686 (1996).
16. W.I. Weis *et al, Nature* **360**, 127 (1992).
17. R.E. Bruccoleri and J. Novotny, *Immunomethods.* **1**, 96 (1992).
18. J. Bajorath and R.M. Fine, *Immunomethods.* **1**, 137 (1992).
19. M.J. Sippl, *Proteins* **17**, 355 (1993).
20. S.J. Wodak and M.J. Rooman, *Curr. Opin. Struct. Biol.* **3**, 247 (1993).

DEFINITE-CLAUSE GRAMMARS FOR THE ANALYSIS OF *CIS*-REGULATORY REGIONS IN *E. COLI*

D. THIEFFRY[1], D.A. ROSENBLUETH[2], A.M. HUERTA[1], H. SALGADO[1], and J. COLLADO-VIDES[1*]

[1]*Centro de Investigación sobre Fijación de Nitrógeno. Universidad Nacional Autónoma de México. Cuernavaca A.P. 565-A, Morelos 62100, México*

[2]*Instituto de Investigaciones en Matemáticas Aplicadas y en Sistemas. Universidad Nacional Autónoma de México, Ciudad Universitaria, México D.F., 04510, México*

* *Corresponding author*

Based on an extensive collection of σ70 associated regulatory mechanisms, a grammatical model has been constructed that define the functional positions and combinations of sites within DNA regulatory regions. The syntactic rules and the dictionary implemented in a Prolog program were coupled to consensus matrices used as "sensors" to integrate a syntactic recognizer. A systematic comparison between the syntactic recognizer and the standard weight matrix methodology is presented using 12 regulatory proteins and the whole collection of about 130 σ70 DNA regulatory regions. On the average an increased sensitivity of 5 to 10 fold is obtained with this novel approach.

1. Introduction

As DNA sequence data are accumulating at a fast pace, matching them with their functional characterization is becoming more urgent. Besides the established experimental methods, one thus looks more and more for theoretical methods able to automatically generate a preliminary, trustable, characterization of new sequences (see, for example, EBI's GeneQuiz [3] and GeneCrunch [20]). In this respect, the characterization of transcriptional regulatory sites is of particular importance. However, even though the DNA binding sites of many regulatory proteins have already been thoroughly experimentally determined, it is still difficult to accurately predict the occurrence of similar sites in new sequences.

In the seventies, the characterization of *cis*-regulatory sites involved the definition of consensus sequences. But, in most cases, these consensus sequences performed poorly in discriminating true sites from the genomic background. These consensus sequences were soon significantly improved by taking into account the frequency of each base in each site position ("consensus matrix"), sometimes including the possibility of gaps and/or position correlation [1, 10, 11, 13-15, 17, 21-23, 27, 30]. However, in spite of being mathematically well grounded, these methods are still often clumsy in discriminating true from false sites. A common drawback of all these programs results from a compromise between high specificity (i.e., recognition of only true sites) and high sensitivity (i.e., recognition of all true sites).

Seaching for improvements of these methods, several authors are developing sophisticated scoring schemes or filters. With the same goal in mind, we prefer to keep the consensus definition rather simple, but to take advantage of additional biological information that restricts the significant sites to certain positions and combinations of them. The biological principles of the σ70 *E.coli* promoter collection have been formalized in the form of a grammar that uses transformational rules and terminal symbols corresponding to the complete protein binding sites within a regulatory DNA region [4-8].

In this paper, we attempt to show how the combination of syntactic rules and consensus matrices allows a drastic selection of the sites matched by a given consensus matrix. Since the sites identified by the parser must occur at positions and/or in combinations which are known to be functional in other sequences, they are more likely to be functional than other matching sites. We summarize the results obtained for a set of 12 σ70 associated regulatory protein, chosen among those having the highest number of characterized sites and the best established consensus matrices according to their random expected frequencies.

2. Methods

DNA sequences for the regulatory domains of σ70 promoters were obtained from GenBank. The precise location of the initiation of transcription was assigned after comparison of (i) the GenBank file, with (ii) the position indicated in the literature, and with (iii) the position indicated in a review paper [16].

Scripts were written in Perl [28] to generate the following set of sequences:

1) A set of 128 extended and oriented σ70 associated promoter sequences, covering from around -200 to +40, with respect to the annotated transcription starting site (+1) of each promoter. Each sequence corresponds to a line in Figure 1 of [12] where the position and regulatory function for each site has been experimentally determined.

2) A collection of functional binding sites for 39 transcriptional regulatory proteins, mostly coming from our σ70 promoter collection. Sequences for binding sites that regulate one or more parallel promoters are included only once, whereas sequences for sites that regulate two divergent promoters are included twice, one sequence being the inverted complement of the other.

The matching of weight matrices and DNA sequences discussed below was always done with the set of 128 oriented promoter sequences. The input for generating the weight matrices of the different regulatory proteins was a collection of files, each with the set of all extended functional sites for a given protein. These extended sites were extracted from the set of functional sites mentioned above, using the central positions obtained from the literature. Their size was that reported in the literature plus six bp on each side (see Table I in Collado-Vides 1993b).

A multiple-alignment program that selects the alignment matrix optimizing information content, "wconsensus", was used to generate a set of best matrices. Wconsensus determines ungapped multiple alignments of unknown prior width [14, 15]. The alignment matrix selected for each protein was the one with the lowest expected frequency that includes all the sites. Once the matrix and the aligned sequences for each protein were obtained, we re-computed the new central positions for each sequence in relation to the +1 of the respective promoters, and used them as reference in the following computations. Another program, developed in the group of G. Stormo, "patser", is then used to score DNA sequences with the matrices obtained [25]. In all runs of wconsensus and patser, we used equal base frequencies and the default parameters.

The grammatical model used has already been published elsewhere [4-8]. Briefly, the principles incorporated into the grammatical model are: i) the existence of a proximal obligatory site for any promoter, ii) binding sites in a given promoter can be grouped into sets that work coordinately in a mechanism of regulation, and iii) each regulator can bind to a characteristic set of functional positions. In addition, we include a summary of the corresponding rules in appendix 1a and an example of a parse tree for a "promoter sentence" in appendix 1b. For a more detailed description of the methodology, see the references.

This model has been implemented using the programming language Prolog. As Prolog was designed as a language for programming natural-language applications [24], it is therefore specially suited for describing grammars like ours, that involve non context-free dependency relationships. A short description of our implementation is given in appendix 2.

3. Results

We developed a series of Perl scripts that perform the following tasks automatically:

1) To run "wconsensus", and extract: (i) the best alignment (i.e., with the lower expected frequency), and (ii) the corresponding consensus matrix for each of the 39 sets of cis-regulatory binding sites.

2) To generate a table summarizing the main characteristics for each protein of the alignments obtained: (i) the number of sequences used, (ii) the alignment/matrix width, and (iii) the corresponding sample size adjusted information content [14].

3) To run patser to calculate the lowest matching scores among each set of original sites; these scores are then included in a table, later used to fix the

Table 1. Comparison of weight matrices vs. grammatical recognition.

Protein (W:alignment width, IC: information content (bits), T: threshold)	Scores intervals: Functional sites/Grammar+Patser/Patser							
	5-10	**10-15**	**15-20**	**20-25**	**25-30**	**30-35**	**Totals**	**Ratios**
AraC (W:12, IC:8.38, T:10.55)	-	6/8/161*	3/3/4	0/0/0	0/0/0	0/0/0	9/12/165	1/1.33/18.33
ArgR (W:24, IC:15.71, T:18.82)	-	1/49/646*	0/9/116	5/6/12	6/6/6	0/0/0	12/70/780	1/5.83/65
CRP (W:24, IC:12.21, T:6.94)	4/34/209*	12/31/102	17/18/26	4/5/5	0/0/0	0/0/0	37/88/342	1/2.38/9.24
FNR (W:19, IC:13.48, T:19.59)	-	-	1/1/2*	4/5/10	3/3/3	0/0/0	8/9/15	1/1.13/1.88
GlpR (W:23, IC12.27, T:16.49)	-	-	2/4/48*	8/8/11	0/0/0	1/1/1	11/13/60	1/1.18/5.45
LexA (W:21, IC:18.27, T:17.01)	-	-	1/1/5*	1/1/2	8/8/8	1/1/1	11/11/16	1/1/1.46
MalT (W:11, IC:6.10, T:10.66)	-	8/9/43*	0/0/0	0/0/0	0/0/0	0/0/0	8/9/43	1/1.13/5.38
MetJ (W:10, IC:8.27, T:5.80)	3/49/596*	10/12/47	0/0/0	0/0/0	0/0/0	0/0/0	13/61/643	1/4.69/49.46
PhoB (W:18, IC:13.30, T:8.85)	1/17/260*	1/30/452	2/2/20	7/8/10	0/0/0	0/0/0	11/49/742	1/4.45/67.45
PuR (W:17, IC:19.09, T:19.01)	-	-	1/1/1*	3/3/6	5/5/6	0/0/0	9/9/13	1/1/1.44
PutA (W:12, IC:8.03, T:11.53)	-	6/11/86*	2/3/5	0/0/0	0/0/0	0/0/0	8/14/91	1/1.75/11.38
TyrR (W:19, IC:13.38, T:9.35)	1/9/53*	0/23/161	7/12/21	7/8/8	0/0/0	0/0/0	15/52/243	1/3.47/16.2

Three classes of sequences within the different threshold intervals are indicated: the functional sites used to construct the weight matrices, those found with the syntactic recognizer coupled to weight matrices as sensors, and those found with *Patser* alone (for information about the scoring scheme, see Stormo, 1990). For instance, for AraC in the interval of 10 to 15 bits there are 6 functional sites, 8 sites found by the grammar with patser, and 161 sites found with patser alone. *In this interval we only counted scores greater or equal to the corresponding threshold.

thresholds (i.e., the lower site scores) when searching for matching sites in putative regulatory sequences.

4) To run patser with pre-defined scoring intervals for each consensus matrix, counting the number of matching sites, and saving these figures in a table.

5) To repeat again step 4 for each matrix, but this time looking for matching sites at positions and in combinations pre-defined by the syntactic rules.

Here, we present the results obtained for 12 proteins, selected among 39 because they correspond to both a significant number of sites and a reasonably good consensus matrix. We used these 12 matrices to compare the performances of their sole use vs. their combination with syntactic rules (points 4 and 5). Note that, for each protein, only a small subset of the 128 promoter sequences were used to generate the corresponding dictionary, whereas the test sequence set always consists of the whole collection of 128 oriented promoter sequences.

The results are summarized in Table 1. It can be seen that the sets of protein sites are quite heterogeneous. Indeed, the information content corresponding to the best alignments/matrices of the 12 sets of sites covers a wide range of scores, from 5.80 to 19.59 bits. For each of the 12 selected proteins we give the number of sites found per score interval, first using the grammatical recognizer combined with patser, and then using patser only. The number of original sites falling in each scoring interval have also been included for comparison.

In some cases, including FNR, LexA and PurR, the consensus matrix alone is already a good discriminant of the corresponding regulatory sites. Not surprisingly, these three proteins are related to consensus matrices with high information content. However, the ArgR and PhoB consensus matrices are also characterized by a high information content but are much less selective. This is because these two proteins involve weak sites that lower the threshold.

In the last column of each sub-table, one can compare the selectivity of both methods through the corresponding (matching sites/true sites). In most cases, it can be observed that the combination of syntactic rules with consensus matrices is about 5 to 10 times more selective. This is already a significative amelioration which could still be improved by sharpening either the matrices and/or the syntactic rules.

Looking at the scoring classes in more detail, it can be seen that most of the time both methods give the same number of matching sites for the highest scores, usually very close to the number of functional sites. This might imply that selective pressure forbids such strong sites at wrong positions.

Thus, the syntactic rules further select the consensus matching sites, especially in the case of low score classes. In other words, the grammatical rules are particularly useful to eliminate weak presumptive sites.

4. Conclusions and perspectives

Cis-regulatory syntactic rules summarize functional information which is not included in the widely used consensus matrices. The combination of both types of information in a simple algorithm proves to be quite powerful, especially in the case of poorly conserved sites, increasing selectivity by a factor of 5 to 10. With the simple matrices and rules used here, significative numbers of false positive sites are still found in some cases, including those of ArgR, CRP, MetJ, PhoB, and TyrR. A deeper analysis of each of these cases might help us derive more selective algorithms (a preliminary analysis of ArgR, LexA and TyrR cases can be found in [19]). However, the remaining "false positive" sites are to be evaluated carefully. Certainly, these sites are more likely to be functional, as they occur in known functional positions relative to the transcription start site, as well as in known functional combinations (occurrence of a proximal obligatory site, etc.).

The main goal of implementing the syntactic recognition of regulatory regions is to apply it to reveal potential regulatory signals in new unannotated DNA sequences. We have initiated a systematic analysis of a collection of about 300 new putative promoter sequences. In these cases, the transcription start site ("+1") is already characterized and the syntactic recognizer can be directly used. In other cases, specific programs have to be used to first localize putative +1 sites. In collaboration with G. Hertz (University of Colorado, Boulder, USA), we are working on a combination of the syntactic parser together with a specific σ70 promoter recognizer. This strategy may help to strengthen the predictive power of standard recognition methods of promoters thanks to the additional biological information that is incorporated into the syntactic recognizer.

However, definitive answers could only come from experiments. In this respect, it would be interesting to compare our results with, for instance, observations on gene regulation derived from 2-D gel global protein analyses performed in *E.coli* [26] and studies on global patterns of gene expression [2, 29].

In parallel, we are working on the extension of our syntactic parser to the whole collection of σ70 associated proteins. To deal with the proteins that only have a few characterized sites, a version of the syntactic parser that can use sequences of specific sites instead of consensus matrices has to be developed. In the process, we should also be able to compare the use of consensus matrices vs. the use of original aligned sequences for the whole collection.

It is important to emphasize that the grammatical methodology is not limited to use consensus matrices to detect binding sites for individual proteins. Any other algorithm could equally be used as a "sensor" to detect signals located at particular positions and in specified combinations. See for instance the application of this methodology in gene recognition [9]. For instance, a method based on secondary structure to identify protein-binding sites could in principle be equally used in a syntactic recognition system.

The selectivity when using the syntactic recognizer raises on the average 5 to 10 times when compared with the standard methodology. Although these are preliminary results, they are encouraging and provide a motivation to work on collecting, organizing, and analyzing larger sets of regulatory collections of sequences. These could include other types of promoters in bacteria, and more generally, eukaryotic regulatory domains.

Acknowledgments

This work was supported by a grant from DGAPA-UNAM to J.C.-V. and D.A.R., and by a grant from Conacyt to J.C.-V. We acknowledge Gerald Hertz for the use of his programs, for fruitful discussions, and for sharing regulatory sequences that helped us to correct inconsistencies in the location of the initiation of transcription. Collaboration with G. Hertz was initiated at the 1995 Aspen Workshop on Patterns in Biological Sequences. We acknowledge Ernesto Leyva for writing the program to re-compute positions of sites.

Appendix 1a: Context-free skeleton of the σ70 grammar

This appendix shows the context-free skeleton of our grammar. For a justification of this skeleton see (Collado-Vides, 1992).

$$
\begin{array}{lll}
Pr''' & \rightarrow & D\text{-}Op\ \ Pr'' \\
Pr'' & \rightarrow & Pr' \mid I'\ \ Pr' \mid IC'\ \ Pr' \mid HI'\ \ Pr' \\
Pr' & \rightarrow & Pr \mid Pr\ \ Op' \\
I' & \rightarrow & D\text{-}I\ \ I(R) \\
D\text{-}I & \rightarrow & Is \\
Op' & \rightarrow & Op(R)\ \ D\text{-}Op \\
D\text{-}Op & \rightarrow & Ops \\
IC' & \rightarrow & D\text{-}IC\ \ IC(R) \\
D\text{-}IC & \rightarrow & ICs \\
HI' & \rightarrow & D\text{-}HI\ \ HI(R) \\
D\text{-}HI & \rightarrow & Is\ \ Ops \\
Is & \rightarrow & \varepsilon \mid I\ \ Is \\
Ops & \rightarrow & \varepsilon \mid Op\ \ Ops \\
Ics & \rightarrow & \varepsilon \mid IC\ \ ICs
\end{array}
$$

where the standard notation is used, that is, X → Y is read "rewrite X as Y"; the "|" is used in optional rules where the left symbol can be rewritten in different alternative ways; ε stands for the empty string. The start symbol is *Pr'''*. The nonterminals are: *Pr'''*, *Pr''*, *Pr'*, *I'*, *D-I*, *Op'*, *D-Op*, *I-C'*, *D-IC*, *HI'*, and *D-HI*. The terminals are: *Pr*, *I(R)*, *Op(R)*, *IC(R)*, *HI(R)*, *I*, *Op*, and *IC*. The dictionary entries are: *Pr*, *I(R)*, *Op(R)*, *IC(R)*, and *HI(R)*. Except for *Pr*, all of these entries have contextual information.

Regulatory sites in a given promoter are grouped into "phrases". There are three basic types of phrases, positive phrases (I', or IC'), negative phrases Op' and heterologous phrases HI'. The simplest phrases contain one or several sites for the same regulator, whereas IC' contain sites for different activators, and HI' contain both activator and repressor sites. The fact that any σ70 promoter must have a proximal site is reflected in the condition that any phrase involves a referential "(R)" proximal site. Any phrase X contains also a category for duplicated or multiple optional sites which are generated from the D-X symbols (i.e., D-I for duplicated activator sites). Since a derivation can involve combinations of phrases and different functional positions for each protein, the grammar generates a large number of regulatable arrays.

Appendix 1b: An example of a parse tree

The parse tree corresponding to the phrase [[Op,d,i,-93],[I,d,j,-44],[I,c,j,CRP,-62.5],[Pr,lac],[Op,c,i,LacI,+9],[Op,d,i,+402]] is presented in the Figure 1.

Figure 1. Example of a parse tree.

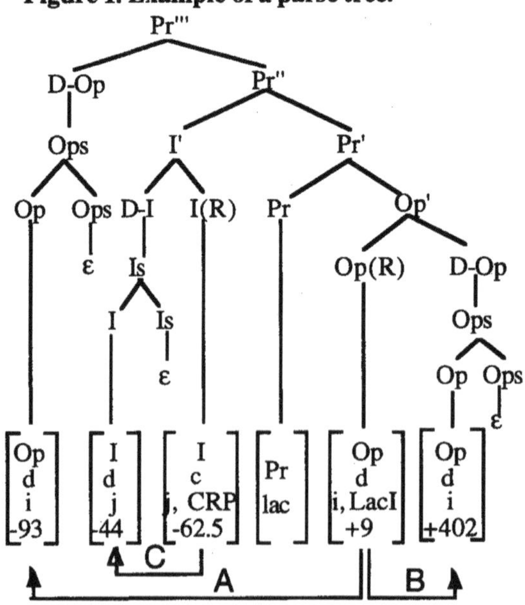

Appendix 2: Prolog implementation of the σ 70 grammatical model

Difference lists. As a first approximation for representing the productions of the σ70 grammar, we can employ "difference lists," as is commonly done in Prolog when using "definite-clause grammars" (DCG) [18]. The first production, for example:

$$Pr''' \rightarrow D\text{-}Op \;\; Pr''$$

is written in DCG syntax as:

```
'Pr3' --> 'D-Op', 'Pr2'.
```

where we have replaced the original primes by digits, and we have enclosed the predicate symbols in quotes, to conform to standard Prolog syntax for predicate symbols. This DCG clause abbreviates the following Prolog clause:

```
'Pr3'(X,Z) :- 'D-Op'(X,Y), 'Pr2'(Y,Z).
```

The intended meaning of each predicate p(X,Y) is that there is a string starting at X and ending at Y which belongs to the formal language p. String concatenation is achieved by using the same variable Y as the ending of the string in 'D-Op' and the beginning of the string in 'Pr2'.

Contextual information. A problem with the above representation is that it lacks contextual information. (Such information is depicted in Figure 1 as arrows connecting the leaves of the parse tree.) The DCG formalism, allows us to incorporate contextual information with additional argument places. These argument places can be viewed as transferring information between nodes which are siblings in the parse/proof tree. Note, however, that we wish to transfer information between *leaves* of the parse tree. Hence, given two leaves that must communicate with each other, we added argument places to all their ancestors which are not common to both leaves.

For example, the information transfer represented with the arrow labeled A, is implemented with an argument place added to the subgoals in the first production:

```
'Pr3' --> 'D-Op'(A), 'Pr2'(A).
```

Right-to-left construction. Another elaboration results from the order in which we want to construct certain portions of the parse tree. Prolog builds parse/proof trees using a left-to-right discipline. If we followed such a regime, we would have to build some parts of the tree which depend on information contained in the dictionary *before* accessing the dictionary. For instance, the number (and contents) of the 'Op' leaves to the left of the 'I' leaves depends on the information represented by the arrow labeled A. Such information is contained in the dictionary under an 'Op(R)' entry. Therefore, to build trees in an efficient way, we must override Prolog's default left-to-right order. It is possible to do so by making explicit the hidden arguments of the DCG shorthand, and writing the subgoals from right to left, so that by selecting the leftmost subgoal, Prolog first constructs the rightmost sibling.

```
'Pr3'(X,Z) :- 'Pr2'(A,Y,Z), 'D-Op'(A,X,Y).
```

Dictionary. Consider now the representation of the dictionary entries. The tree in Figure 1 can be generated with the following dictionary:

```
'Op(R)'([p(i,-93)],[p(i,+402)],[[i,'LacI',+9]|X],X).
'I(R)'([p(i,-44)],[[i,'CRP',-62.5]|X],X).
```

where the terms with the p function symbol are used to group an *index*, say i, with a site position, say -93.

The first argument place of the 'Op(R)' predicate is a list of the optional sites to the *left* of the obligatory site (arrow A in Figure 1) of that dictionary entry. The second argument place of this predicate is a list with the optional sites to the right of its associated obligatory site (arrow B in appendix 1b). Finally, the third argument place of such a predicate contains the information about the obligatory site.

Similarly, the first argument place of the 'I(R)' predicate is a list of the optional sites, all of which are to the left of the associated obligatory site. The second argument place of this predicate represents the obligatory 'I(R)' site.

For example, the term p(i,-93) generates the leftmost 'Op' leaf, which is an optional site associated with the obligatory site 'LacI'.

Indexes. Note that to be able to determine which obligatory site is associated with a given optional site, we must rename the indexes of the different dictionary entries. In this case, we map the i index for the 'I(R)' entry to a new j index, as appears in appendix 1b. Such a renaming is performed with additional argument places.

Subsets of optional sites. The last step in our implementation includes the computation of *subsets* of optional sites. Each list of optional sites in a dictionary entry represents a set of which *any* subset is taken as a valid set of optional sites. This change is achieved by incorporating a predicate subset(Sub,Xs) which is intended to hold when Sub is a subset of Xs.

References

1. O.G. Berg and P.H von Hippel, "Selection of DNA binding site by regulatory proteins. Statistical-mechanical theory and application to operators and promoters" *J. Mol. Biol.* **193**, 723 (1987)
2. S.E. Chuang, D.L. Daniels and F.R. Blattner, "Global regulation of gene expression in *Escherichia coli*" *J. Bacteriol.* **175**, 2026 (1993)
3. G. Casari, M. Andrade, P. Bork, J. Boyle, A. Daruvar, C. Ouzounis, R. Schneider, J. Tamames, A. Valencia, and C. Sander, "Challenging times for bioinformatics" *Nature* **376**, 647 (1995)
4. J. Collado-Vides, "The search of a grammatical model of gene regulation is formally justified by showing the inadequacy of context-free grammars" *CABIOS* **7**, 321 (1991)
5. J. Collado-Vides, "A grammatical model of the regulation of gene expression" *Proc. Natl. Acad. Sci.USA* **89**, 9405 (1992)
6. J. Collado-Vides, "A Linguistic Representation of the Range of Transcription Initiation of σ70 Promoters: I. An Ordered Array of Complex Symbols with Distinctive Features" *Biosystems* **29**, 87 (1993)
7. J. Collado-Vides, "A Linguistic Representation of the Range of Transcription Initiation of σ70 Promoters: II. Distinctive Features of Promoters and Their Regulatory Binding Sites" *Biosystems* **29**, 105 (1993)
8. J. Collado-Vides in *Integrative Approaches to Molecular Biology*, "Integrative representations of the regulation of gene expression" Eds. J. Collado-Vides, B. Magasanik and T.F. Smith (MIT Press, Cambridge Mass, 1996)
9. S. Dong and D.B. Searls, "Gene structure prediction by linguistic methods" *Genomics* **23**, 540 (1994)
10. K. Frech, G. Herrmann and T. Werner, "Computer-assisted prediction, classification, and delimitation of protein binding sites in nucleic acids" *Nucleic Acids Res.* **21**, 1655 (1993)
11. J.A. Goodrich, M.L. Schwartz and W.R. McClure, "Searching for and predicting the activity of sites for DNA binding proteins: compilation and analysis of the binding sites for *Escherichia coli* integration host factor (IHF)" *Nucleic Acids Res.* **18**, 4993 (1990)
12. J.D. Gralla and J. Collado-Vides in *Cellular and Molecular Biology: Escherichia coli and Salmonella*, "Organization and Function of Transcription Regulatory Elements" Eds. F.C. Neidhardt, R. Curtiss III, J. Ingraham, E.C.C. Lin, K.B. Low, B. Magasanik, W. Reznikoff, M. Schaechter, H.E Umbarger and M. Riley (2nd ed., Washington, D.C. American Society for Microbiology, 1996)
13. D.K. Hawley and W.R. McClure, "Compilation and analysis of *Escherichia coli* promoter DNA sequences" *Nucleic Acids Res.* **11**, 2237 (1983)
14. G.H. Hertz, G.W. Hartzell-III and G.D. Stormo, "Identification of consensus patterns in unaligned DNA sequences known to be functionally related" *CABIOS* **6**, 81 (1990)

15. G.H. Hertz and G.D. Stormo in *Bioinformatics and Genome Research*, "Identification of consensus patterns in unaligned DNA and protein sequences: a large-deviation statistical byasis for penalizing gaps" Ed. H.A. Lim and C.R. Cantor (World Scientific Publ., Singapore, 1995).
16. Lisser S. and Margalit H. (1993). "Compilation of *E.coli* mRNA promoter sequences". *Nucleic Acids Res.* **21**: 1507-1516.
17. M.C. O'Neill, "Consensus methods for finding and ranking DNA binding sites. Application to *Escherichia coli* promoters" *J. Mol. Biol.* **207**, 301 (1989)
18. F.C.N. Pereira and , D.H.D. Warren, "Definite clause grammars for language analysis - A survey of the formalism and a comparison with augmented transition networks." *Artificial Intelligence* **13**, 231 (1980)
19. D. Rosenblueth, D. Thieffry, A. M. Huerta, H. Salgado and J. Collado-Vides, "Syntactic recognition of regulatory regions in Escherichia coli" *CABIOS* **12** (in press).
20. M. Scharf, R. Schneider, G. Casari, P. Bork, A. Valencia, C. Ouzounis and C. Sander in *Intelligent Systems for Molecular Biology 1994 (ISMB94)*, "GeneQuiz: a workbench for sequence analysis" (AAAI Press, Stanford, CA, 1994).
21. T.D. Schneider, G.D. Stormo, L. Gold and A. Ehrenfeucht, "Information content of binding sites on nucleotide sequences" *J. Mol. Biol.* **188**, 415 (1986)
22. R. Staden, "Computer methods to locate signals in nucleic acid sequences" *Nucleic Acids Res.* **12**, 505 (1984)
23. R. Staden, "Methods for calculating the probabilities of finding patterns in sequences" *CABIOS* **5**, 89 (1989)
24. L. Sterling, and E. Shapiro, *The Art of Prolog* (2nd edition. MIT Press, Cambridge, MA, 1994)
25. G. Stormo, "Consensus patterns in DNA" *Meth. Enzym.* **183**, 211 (1990)
26. R.A VanBogelen, K.Z. Abshire, A. Pertsemlidis, R.L. Clark and F.C. Neidhardt in *Cellular and Molecular Biology: Escherichia coli and Salmonella*, "Gene-protein database of *Escherichia coli* K-12, Edition 6" Eds. F.C. Neidhardt, R. Curtiss III, J. Ingraham, E.C.C. Lin, K.B. Low, B. Magasanik, W. Reznikoff, M. Schaechter, H.E Umbarger and M. Riley (2nd ed., Washington, D.C. American Society for Microbiology, 1996)
27. P.H. von Hippel and O.G. Berg, "On the specificity of DNA-protein interactions" *Proc. Natl. Acad. Sci.USA* **83**, 1608 (1985)
28. L. Wall and R.L. Schwartz, *Programming Perl* (O'Reilly and Associates, Inc., Sebastopol, Ca, 1991).
29. M.X. Wang and G.M. Church, "A whole-genome approach to *in vivo* DNA-protein interactions in *E.coli*" *Nature* **360**, 606 (1992)
30. F. Wolfertstetter, K. Frech, G. Herrmann, and T. Werner, "Identification of functional elements in unaligned nucleic acid sequences by a novel tuple search algorithm" *CABIOS* **12**, 71 (1995).

ENUMERATION OF FLUX ROUTES THROUGH COMPLEX BIOCHEMICAL REACTIONS

JONATHAN WAGG & PETER SELLERS
The Rockefeller University, 1230 York Avenue, N.Y., N.Y., 10021, U.S.A

In the present work, a general algorithm for enumeration of the flux routes via which a chemical species "flows" through a complex biochemical reaction is outlined and presented by way of a biological example, a kinetic model for potassium ion permeation through a voltage-gated ion channel. The algorithm is readily amenable to computer based implementation and when used in conjunction with an existing algorithm provides a convenient means for simulation of the equilibrium and steady-state isotope exchange kinetics of complex biochemical reactions.

1. Introduction

Protein-catalyzed reactions are complex, because they proceed from a set of reactants to a set of products via a mechanism comprising multiple elementary reactions; the binding/dissociation of reactant(s) and product(s) to/from intermediate states of the catalyst and interposed conformational transitions of this protein. Intermediate states of the catalyst appear in the chemical equations for the elementary steps and partial reactions of the overall reaction but not in the chemical equation for the overall reaction.

Isotopes may be used as labeled (tagged) atoms to characterize the steady-state kinetics of partial components of a complex biochemical reaction[1], e.g., the rates of ATP-ADP exchange in an ATPase cycle or the transmembrane fluxes of a chemical species in a transporter cycle. In particular, if a partial reaction is associated with a chemical group exchange between a specific reactant/product pair, then by labeling an atom of that group in the respective reactant (product), one may measure the rate at which that group subsequently appears in product (reactant). These measurable rates are the isotope exchange rates of the complex reaction[2,3,4,5]. A flux route for a chemical species, X, is a sequence of steps through part of a complex reaction, via which X is exchanged from a reactant (product) to a product (reactant).

The principal object of this paper is to provide a programmable procedure to enumerate flux routes through complex biochemical reactions. Such a procedure is a prerequisite in an otherwise well-determined mathematical procedure for modeling the equilibrium and steady-state isotope exchange kinetics of such reactions[6].

2. Glossary of Terms

Elementary Reaction (Process): An elementary process is one for which the mechanism of reaction is given directly by its stoichiometric equation. It consists of two transitions of chemical state (state transitions), one in each of the forward and reverse directions (see below).

State transition: A state transition is a single change from one chemical state to another via an elementary process. Individual chemical states will be designated with lower case subscripts, x_i, x_j,.....

Transition Rates: The rates of transition across an elementary step between the states x_i (the set of reactants) and x_j (the set of products) will be designated $r_{i,j}$ and $r_{j,i}$. These rates are generally assumed to be given by $k_{i,j}.[x_i]$ and $k_{j,i}.[x_j]$, respectively, where $k_{i,j}$ and $k_{j,i}$ denote the rate coefficients governing the rates of the respective transitions and $[x_i]$ and $[x_j]$ denote the chemical activities of x_i and x_j, respectively.

Conditional Probabilities: For chemical states from which multiple state transitions occur it is possible to assign probabilities for the occurrence of each transition conditional upon there having occured a single state transition. To assign such a conditional probability to the state transition x_i to x_j one proceeds as follows: (i) identify the full set of mutually exclusive state transitions that x_i may undergo. This set should be all inclusive for the overall reaction or system of reactions of interest; (ii) write the appropriate rate equation for each transition; (iii) determine the ratio of the rate of the transition x_i to x_j to the sum of the rates of all transitions (including x_i to x_j) in which x_i is involved. This ratio is the required conditional probability and will be designated $C_{i,j}$.

Complex Reaction: A reaction comprised of more than one elementary process.

3. Basic Approach

The algorithm that will be used to make an exhaustive list of all flux routes is similar to that previously used to solve a different problem, finding all possible mechanisms for a given overall reaction[7], which is simpler than the present problem, because it can be solved with no information other than the overall reaction and a list of elementary reactions. The problems are different because a flux route represents a mechanism for a partial component of an overall reaction and as such includes intermediate states on both sides of its chemical equation and, in general, does not include all reactants and products of the reaction. Nonetheless, since both problems are combinatorial, they are amenable to solution using comparable (but different) approaches.

To determine a flux route for a chemical group/species, X, we need, not only the chemical equation that describes each elementary reaction, but, if that species appears more than once on either side of a chemical equation, we need to know for each X on the left which X on the right represents the identical particle. Therefore, instead of a list of elementary reaction equations, the procedure for listing flux routes will start with an expanded list, in which elementary steps have been replaced by more than one reaction whenever there are alternate ways in which the particle X^* can be positioned on the two sides of its chemical equation. The particle is starred to distinguish it from other particles of X. For instance, in place of the reaction: XX + JX ↔ JXXX; one might write the following three reactions: X*X + JX ↔ JXX*X, XX* + JX ↔ JXXX* and XX + JX* ↔ JX*XX. For a given system of reactions there may be a number of ways to replace a given reaction step, each associated with a specific set of structural assumptions. For example, with different structural assumptions the above replacement reactions above could have been: X*X + JX ↔ JX*XX, XX* + JX ↔ JXX*X and XX + JX* ↔ JXXX*. An unequivocal expansion will only be possible in those cases were relevant detailed structural information about the reaction system is available. When this information is not available one must necessarily assume a given structure since this replacement procedure is requisite to sucessfully enumerating a set of flux routes.

The expanded list is then used to set up an input matrix whose rows characterize specific reactions from this list and whose columns represent the intermediate states (left) and reactants and products (terminal species) of the overall reaction (right). This matrix is then processed according to a defined set of operations to yield another matrix whose rows charaterize the flux routes through the system of reactions and whose columns correspond to the elementary reactions that were characterized in the rows of the input matrix. These procedures will now be presented by way of a biological example, a 5 step two-site single-file pore model for a potassium ion channel.

4. A Sample System with 5 Elementary Reaction Steps

Fig. 1 presents a two-site single-file pore model for potassium ion (K) permeation through a voltage-gated ion channel[8]. Numbers in square brackets denote different occupancy states of the channel and encircled numbers denote transitions between these states. For all states, O denotes an unoccupied channel binding site and K denotes occupancy of a site by a potassium ion. The site on the left is assumed to be accessible from only the extracellular compartment whilst that on the right is assumed accessible from only the intracellular compartment. Accordingly, steps 4 and 5 represent interaction of K ions with the extracellular accessible site and steps 1 and 2 denote interaction with the other site. Ion translocation across the membrane is mediated by step 3 and involves the "hopping" of a K ion from one site to the other. The efflux of K ions (movement from the intracellular compartment to the extracellular compartment) through this system of reactions and across the membrane involves the binding of K from the intracellular compartment (via step 1 or 2), a hopping of this ion from one site to the other (via step 3) and a subsequent dissociation of this ion into the extracellular compartment (via step 4 or 5). The corresponding influx of K ions (movement from the extracellular compartment to the intracellular compartment) involves a converse set of reaction steps; the binding of K from the extracellular compartment (via step 4 or 5), a hopping of this ion from one site to the other (via step 3) and a subsequent dissociation of this ion into the intracellular compartment (via step 1 or 2).

One may assign rate coefficients to the steps of this mechanism and for a given set of steady-state conditions, solve for the steady-state distribution of channel between the different intermediate states. These may then be used to calculate the

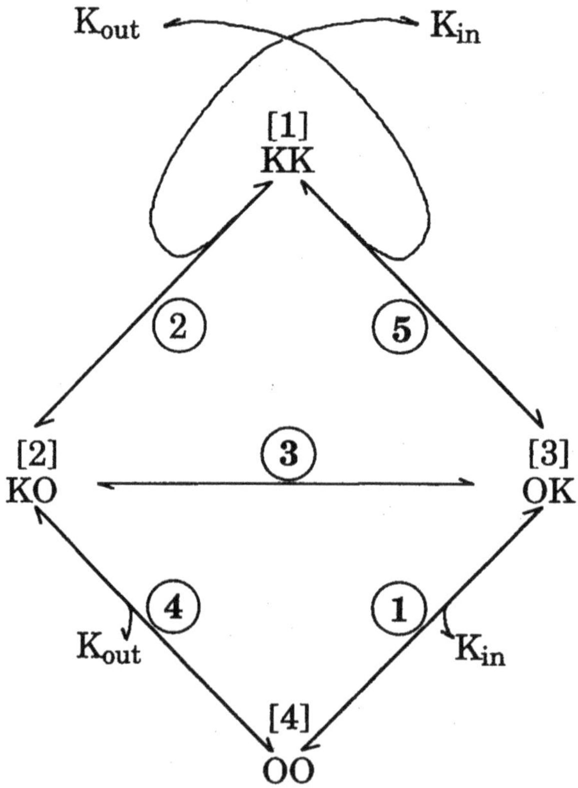

Figure 1. A two-site single-file pore model for potassium ion (K) permeation through a voltage-gated ion channel[8]. See text for details.

net steady-state flux of potassium ions through the mechanism. For example, the predicted net efflux of K (movement out of the cell) via the mechanism is then given by the net rate of reaction across step 3, $r_{3,2} - r_{2,3}$, or by the sum of the net rates at which K leaves the mechanism to enter the extracellular compartment via steps 4 and 5, i.e., $(r_{2,4} - r_{4,2}) + (r_{1,3} - r_{3,1})$. This net efflux is equal to the difference between the unidirectional efflux and influx of K. However, in general, these latter fluxes may not be equated to the sum of the unidirectional rates of potassium release into the extracellular compartment, i.e., $r_{1,3} + r_{2,4}$. This is because some of the K exiting the mechanism via these steps represent ions that entered from the extracellular compartment. As a consequence, a more extensive series of calculations are necessary in order to solve for the efflux and influx of K. These involve: (i) enumeration of all flux routes for K through the mechanism and (ii) subsequent application of a well-determined mathematical procedure[6].

4.1. Enumeration of Flux Routes

The model presented in Fig. 1 comprises a set of 5 elementary steps. These are listed below (list (1)) in the order they are numbered in Fig. 1, OO + K_{in}↔OK, KO + K_{in}↔KK, OK↔KO, KO↔K_{out} + OO, KK↔K_{out} + OK. As indicated already, this list of elementary reactions is inadequate for our purposes, but the following list (list (2)) contains the additional information needed to make the problem solvable: 1. K*O + K_{in}↔K*K, 2. KO + K^*_{in}↔KK*, 3. K*K↔K^*_{out} + OK, 4. KK*↔K_{out} + OK*, 5. OK*↔K*O, 6. K*O↔K^*_{out} + OO, 7. OO + K^*_{in} ↔OK*.

Before considering the mathematical solution of the flux route problem, let us look at this example intuitively. Each of the above 7 equations provides a forward step → or a backward step ← that can be used in putting together a flux route from K^*_{in} to K^*_{out}. Since we are only interested in following the progress of K*, we may temporarily ignore the species without K* and write a modified list (list (3)) as follows: 1. K*O↔K*K, 2. K^*_{in}↔KK*, 3. K*K↔K^*_{out}, 4. KK*↔OK*, 5. OK* ↔K*O, 6. K*O↔K^*_{out}, 7. K^*_{in}↔OK*. A flux route from K^*_{in} to K^*_{out}, for the purposes of the enumeration procedure, can be defined as a sequence of chemical species without repetitions, where every successive pair is taken from the above list, using whatever arrow goes in the direction of the sequence. (In this example only → arrows are used.) By inspection it can be seen that the flux routes are as follows:

K^*_{in} → OK* → K*O → K^*_{out}
K^*_{in} → KK* → OK* → K*O → K^*_{out}
K^*_{in} → OK* → K*O → K*K → K^*_{out}
K^*_{in} → KK* → OK* → K*O → K*K → K^*_{out}

To arrive systematically at a complete list such as this, we can look at the problem as one in linear algebra and solve it with the algorithm described in the next section.

4.2. A Vector Decomposition Algorithm

The problem of listing flux routes is essentially that of finding all non-intersecting paths between two points in a network of line segments that represent first-order elementary chemical reactions. In that sense it is simpler than the problem of listing all mechanisms in a chemical network, where we cannot assume that the elementary reactions are first-order or treat them as such. Nevertheless, we shall use an algorithm[7] that is applicable to both problems. It is a procedure for decomposing a vector in every possible way into a linear combination of linearly independent components, where the components must be selected from a given list. Now, supposing we have such an algorithm at our disposal, let us see how it would be applied to the flux route problem.

Returning to the example, consider the 6-dimensional vector space generated by the 6 species in the system that contains K*, i.e., K^*_{in}, K^*_{out}, KK*, K*K, OK*, K*O. Seven vectors in this space characterize the elementary reactions connecting pairs of these species: R_1 = - K*O + K*K; R_2 = - K^*_{in} + KK*; R_3 = - K*K + K^*_{out} ; R_4 = - KK* + OK*; R_5 = - OK* + K*O; R_6 = - K*O + K^*_{out} ; R_7 = - K^*_{in} + OK*. The reverse reaction in each case would be characterized by a change of signs. Not all the vectors in this list are linearly independent, but the vector decomposition algorithm will decompose the vector, R = - K^*_{in} + K^*_{out}, in every possible way into a linear combination of linearly independent vectors selected from the list R_1, R_2, R_3, ..., R_7. Choosing linearly independent ones will insure that each flux route is non-self-intersecting. The algorithm, as we shall see, will produce four decompositions of the vector R, namely: R = $R_5 + R_6 + R_7$; R = $R_2 + R_4 + R_5 + R_6$; R = $R_1 + R_3 + R_5 + R_7$; R = $R_1 + R_2 + R_3 + R_4 + R_5$. These correspond to the flux routes that were previously arrived at by inspection.

The present example is simple enough that the algorithm can be gone through step-by-step. First of all, the vectors R_1 through R_7 are written as rows in a matrix with the coefficients of the species in R (that is, K^*_{in} and K^*_{out}) being placed at the right end of the row. This gives the following matrix (matrix (1)):

	KK*	OK*	K*O	K*K	K^*_{in}	K^*_{out}
R_1	0	0	-1	1	0	0
R_2	1	0	0	0	-1	0
R_3	0	0	0	-1	0	1
R_4	-1	1	0	0	0	0
R_5	0	-1	1	0	0	0
R_6	0	0	-1	0	0	1
R_7	0	1	0	0	-1	0

Next, use row operations to put the matrix in row echelon form. This can be done in various ways, but will always lead to zeros in the last two rows and in the preceding row a combination of the original rows corresponding to one of the desired flux routes. The row operations written to the left of the following row-echelon matrix (matrix (2)) show one way in which the desired form can be achieved.

	KK*	OK*	K*O	K*K	K^*_{in}	K^*_{out}
R_4	-1	1	0	0	0	0
R_5	0	-1	1	0	0	0
R_1	0	0	-1	1	0	0
R_3	0	0	0	-1	0	1
$R_1 + R_3 + R_5 + R_7$	0	0	0	0	-1	1
$R_1 + R_3 - R_6$	0	0	0	0	0	0
$R_2 + R_4 - R_7$	0	0	0	0	0	0

This shows that $R_1 + R_3 + R_5 + R_7$ is a flux route, and that all other flux routes are obtainable from it by adding linear combinations of the two cyclic routes $R_1 + R_3 - R_6$ and $R_2 + R_4 - R_7$. In other words, for every pair (x,y) of coefficients the expression: $R_1 + R_3 + R_5 + R_7 + x(R_1 + R_3 - R_6) + y(R_2 + R_4 - R_7)$; equals $(-K^*_{in} + K^*_{out})$. The expression can be rewritten as: $(1 + x)(R_1 + R_3) + y(R_2 + R_4) + R_5 - xR_6 + (1 - y)R_7$. This will be a flux route, that is, it will be non-self intersecting, if x and y are chosen to minimize the number of elementary reactions in it. This is done by setting as many as possible of the coefficients (1 + x), y, x, (1 - y) equal to zero. This means setting them equal to zero two at-a-time and solving for x and y. There are 6 ways this can be done, but two of them do not yield any solutions, namely, the pairs $1 + x = 0$, $x = 0$ and $y = 0$, $1 - y = 0$. In the remaining cases we get (x,y) equal to (-1, 0), (-1, 1), (0, 0), (0, 1). Putting these values of x and y in the general expression above, we get a complete list of flux routes: $R_5 + R_6 + R_7$, $R_2 + R_4 + R_5 + R_6$, $R_1 + R_3 + R_5 + R_7$, $R_1 + R_2 + R_3 + R_4 + R_5$.

This procedure is readily programmable, and the amount of computer time it takes is proportional to the number of ways of setting a certain number of coefficients equal to zero in the general expression for flux routes. If the row-echelon matrix has r rows of zeros and n rows altogether, then the computing time is proportional to the binomal coefficient n(n-1)...(n-r+1)/r!. The only aspect of programming that needs special mention is that care must be taken to avoid repeated solutions.

4.3. Calculating Steady-state Unidirectional K Fluxes

The enumeration of flux routes for a specified chemical species through a system of reactions provides a basis for subsequent calculation of the steady-state unidirectional fluxes of this species through quantitatively explicit formulations of the system and/or for the derivation of analytical expressions for these fluxes. Below we provide a brief outline of the procedures previously developed for calculation of these fluxes[6] as applied to the sample system of 5 reactions.

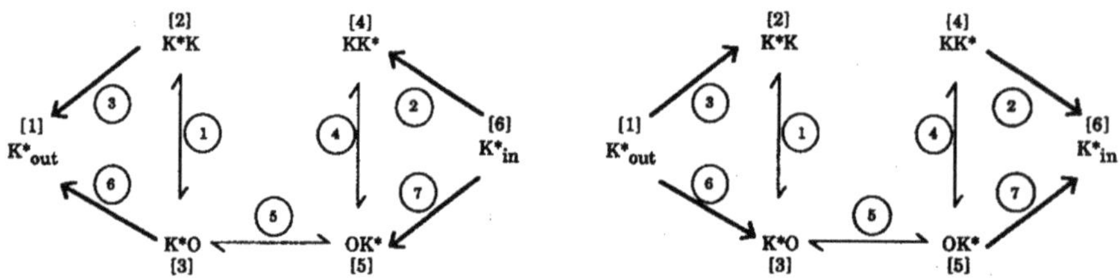

$$
A = \begin{array}{c} \\ [1] \\ [2] \\ [3] \\ [4] \\ [5] \\ [6] \end{array}
\begin{array}{c} \begin{array}{cccccc} [1] & [2] & [3] & [4] & [5] & [6] \end{array} \\
\begin{bmatrix}
0 & 0 & 0 & 0 & 0 & 0 \\
C_{2,1} & 0 & C_{2,3} & 0 & 0 & 0 \\
C_{3,1} & C_{3,2} & 0 & 0 & C_{3,5} & 0 \\
0 & 0 & 0 & 0 & C_{4,5} & 0 \\
0 & 0 & C_{5,3} & C_{5,4} & 0 & 0 \\
0 & 0 & 0 & r_{6,4} & r_{6,5} & 0
\end{bmatrix} \end{array}
$$

$$K_{efflux} = (I - A)^{-1}(6,1)$$

$$
B = \begin{array}{c} \\ [1] \\ [2] \\ [3] \\ [4] \\ [5] \\ [6] \end{array}
\begin{array}{c} \begin{array}{cccccc} [1] & [2] & [3] & [4] & [5] & [6] \end{array} \\
\begin{bmatrix}
0 & r_{1,2} & r_{1,3} & 0 & 0 & 0 \\
0 & 0 & C_{2,3} & 0 & 0 & 0 \\
0 & C_{3,2} & 0 & 0 & C_{3,5} & 0 \\
0 & 0 & 0 & 0 & C_{4,5} & C_{4,6} \\
0 & 0 & C_{5,3} & C_{5,4} & 0 & C_{5,6} \\
0 & 0 & 0 & 0 & 0 & 0
\end{bmatrix} \end{array}
$$

$$K_{influx} = (I - B)^{-1}(1,6)$$

Figure 2. Top: Set of reaction routes derived from enumerated flux routes and used to calculate K influx and efflux via mechanism of Fig. 1. Efflux routes shown on left and influx routes shown on right. Bottom: Matrices, A (left) and B (right), derived from the above influx and efflux routes.

(i) From the enumerated flux routes establish a set of reaction routes [see[6]] for K efflux and another set for K influx. This is achieved by: (a) identifing the set of reaction steps comprising the full set of enumerated flux routes, in this case the steps comprising list (3); (b) replacing all bidirectional steps directly involving K with single transitions (referred to as entry and exit transitions). For efflux routes, the replacement transitions should be in the direction of K^*_{in} binding and K^*_{out} dissociation (see Fig. 2, top left) whilst for influx routes, they should be in the converse direction, i.e., the replacement transitions should be in the direction of K^*_{out} binding and K^*_{in} dissociation (see Fig. 2, top right).

(ii) Assign rate coefficients to the steps of the original expanded list (list (2)) and solve for the steady-state probabilities of intermediate species and the unidirectional rates of reaction across all steps of the list. Subsequently, assign conditional probabilities, Ci,j, to all transitions as outlined above (see section 2).

(iii) For each set of reaction routes obtained in (i) above (the efflux and influx routes, respectively), arrange the corresponding set of conditional probabilities (calculated as outlined above) into a corresponding square matrix in which the elements in the ith row and jth column equal the conditional probability for the transition from the ith to the jth state. Replace the probability for the occurrence of entry transitions (transitions for which K enters the system of reactions) with the rates of these transitions. In this way one obtains a matrix, A, derived from the set of efflux routes (see Fig. 2, bottom left) and another matrix, B, derived from the set of influx routes (see Fig.2, bottom right). Subtract each matrix from its respective identity matrix and invert the resulting matrices. It can be shown that the elements $(I\text{-}A)^{-1}_{(6,1)}$ and $(I\text{-}B)^{-1}_{(6,1)}$ give the steady-state unidirectional efflux and influx of K, respectively.

5. A Sample System with 12 Elementary Reactions

The previous example involved a membrane bound protein catalyst which had two sites that could be occupied by K. Fig. 3 presents a three site, single-file model for K permeation through a voltage-dependent ion channel, i.e., a membrane bound catalyst, OOO, with 3 sites[9]. It represents a simple extension of the mechanism presented in Fig. 1. and comprises a set of 12 elementary steps. These are listed below (list (4)) in the order they are numbered in Fig. 3,

$OOO + K_{in} \leftrightarrow OOK$	$OOK \leftrightarrow OKO$	$KOO \leftrightarrow K_{out} + OOO$
$OKO + K_{in} \leftrightarrow OKK$	$OKO \leftrightarrow KOO$	$KOK \leftrightarrow K_{out} + OOK$
$KOO + K_{in} \leftrightarrow KOK$	$OKK \leftrightarrow KOK$	$KKO \leftrightarrow K_{out} + OKO$
$KKO + K_{in} \leftrightarrow KKK$	$KOK \leftrightarrow KKO$	$KKK \leftrightarrow K_{out} + OKK$

In addition to this information we need the following, which shows how a particle designated by K* can be positioned on each side of each of the above equations. This results in the following expanded list (list (5)) of 22 reactions:

$OOO + K^*_{in} \leftrightarrow OOK^*$	$OOK^* \leftrightarrow OK^*O$	$K^*OO \leftrightarrow K^*_{out} + OOO$
$OK^*O + K_{in} \leftrightarrow OK^*K$	$OK^*O \leftrightarrow K^*OO$	$K^*OK \leftrightarrow K^*_{out} + OOK$
$OKO + K^*_{in} \leftrightarrow OKK^*$	$OK^*K \leftrightarrow K^*OK$	$KOK^* \leftrightarrow K_{out} + OOK^*$
$K^*OO + K_{in} \leftrightarrow K^*OK$	$OKK^* \leftrightarrow KOK^*$	$K^*KO \leftrightarrow K^*_{out} + OKO$
$KOO + K^*_{in} \leftrightarrow KOK^*$	$K^*OK \leftrightarrow K^*KO$	$KK^*O \leftrightarrow K_{out} + OK^*O$
$K^*KO + K_{in} \leftrightarrow K^*KK$	$KOK^* \leftrightarrow KK^*O$	$K^*KK \leftrightarrow K^*_{out} + OKK$
$KK^*O + K_{in} \leftrightarrow KK^*K$		$KK^*K \leftrightarrow K_{out} + OK^*K$
$KKO + K^*_{in} \leftrightarrow KKK^*$		$KKK^* \leftrightarrow K_{out} + OKK^*$

If the procedure described earlier is applied to this set of 22 reactions, then 112 flux routes will be found. It is not feasible to go through the algorithm by hand in

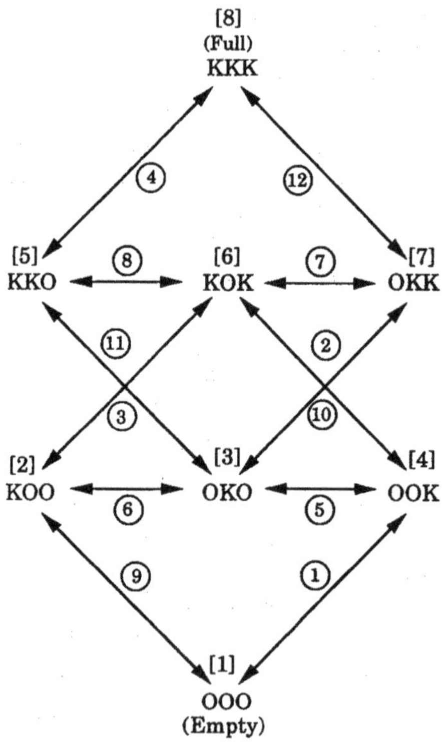

Figure 3. A three-site single-file pore model for potassium ion (K) permeation through a voltage-gated ion channel[8]. For details see text.

this case, but it is easy to get an overview of the possible routes by observing that they correspond to all non-intersecting paths from K^*_{in} to K^*_{out} in the following diagram.

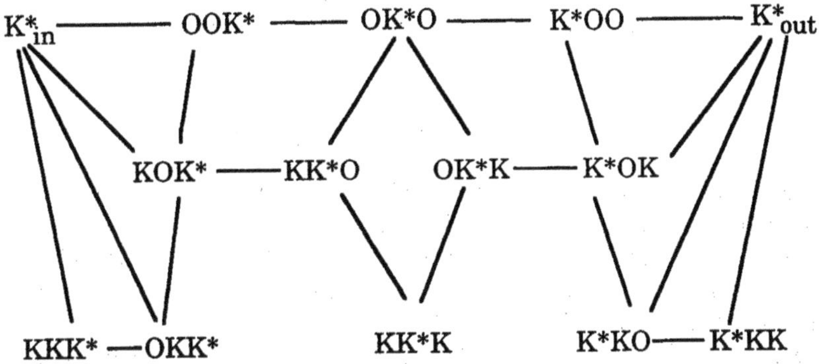

Each line segment in the diagram corresponds to one of the 22 reactions involving K*, simplified by ignoring chemical species that do not involve K*. List (5) and the enumerated flux routes provide the basis for the calculation of the unidirectional fluxes of K through this mechanism.

SUMMARY

From a computational viewpoint the procedure that has been described starts with a matrix whose rows characterize elementary reactions and whose columns represent chemical species with the intermediates on the left and the terminal species on the right. When this matrix has been processed in the manner described above, we end up, essentially, with another matrix whose rows characterize chemical mechanisms or flux routes and whose columns correspond to the elementary reactions that were characterized in the rows of the input matrix. The information contained in the latter matrix, the full set of flux routes for a chemical species through a system of reactions, may be used in conjunction with the expanded list of reactions from which the input matrix was derived and a method developed by Wagg[6] to calculate the steady-state unidriectional fluxes of this species through quantitatively explicit formulations of the system and/or for the derivation of analytical expressions for these fluxes.

The algorithm presented in this paper and related methods are readily amenable to computer based implementation and are currently being incorporated into an existing software package (SCoP; distributed by Simulation Resources of Berrien Springs, MI, USA) to facilitate modeling the equilibrium and/or steady-state isotope exchange kinetics of complex biochemical reactions.

ACKNOWLEDGMENTS

The authors want to thank David C. Gadsby for his support and encouragement and Mari Kuwabara for assistance in the preparation of figures. The work presented in this paper was supported by HHMI and NIH HL-36783

REFERENCES

1. Wagg, J. & Chapman, J.B. "Steady-state Rate Analysis: Application to Biological Transport. J. theor. Biol. 174:45-59 (1995)
2. Temkin, M.I. "The Kinetics of Transfer of Labeled Atoms by Reaction" In: "The use of tracers to study heterogeneous catalysis" Annals of the New York Academy of Science. 213:79-89 (1973)
3. Segel, I.H. "Isotope Exchange" Chapter 10 In: "Enzyme Kinetics Behavior and Analysis of Rapid Equilibrium and Steady-State Enzyme Systems" John Wiley & Sons. New York (1975)
4. Britton, H.G. "The Concept and Use of Flux Measurements in Enzyme Studies: A theoretical analysis" Arch. Biochem. Biophys. 117:167-183 (1966)
5. Cleland, W.W. "Enzyme Kinetics" Ann. Rev. Biochem. 36:77-112 (1967)
6. Wagg, J. "A Method for Defining Steady-state Unidirectional Fluxes Through Branched Chemical, Osmotic and Chemiosmotic Reactions" J. theor. Biol. 128:375-385 (1987)
7. Happel, J. & Sellers, P.H. "Analysis of the Possible Mechanisms for a Catalytic Reaction System" Advances in Catalysis. 32:273-323 (1983)
8. Hille, B. & Schwarz, W. "Potassium Channels as Multi-Ion Single-File Pores" J. Gen. Physiol. 72:409-442 (1978)
9. Hille, B. Ionic Selectivity, Saturation, and Block in Sodium Channels. A Four-Barrier Model. J. Gen. Physiol. 66:535-560 (1975)

USING THE RADIAL DISTRIBUTIONS OF PHYSICAL FEATURES TO COMPARE AMINO ACID ENVIRONMENTS AND ALIGN AMINO ACID SEQUENCES

LIPING WEI, RUSS B. ALTMAN†, JEFFREY T. CHANG
Section on Medical Informatics
Stanford University, MSOB X215
Stanford, CA 94305-5479
{wei, altman, jchang}@smi.stanford.edu
415-725-3394
†Corresponding author.

We have performed a comprehensive analysis of the microenvironments surrounding the twenty amino acids. Our analysis includes comparison of amino acid environments with random control environments as well as with each of the other amino acid environments. We describe the amino acid environments with a set of 21 features summarizing atomic, chemical group, residue, and secondary structural features. The environments are divided into radial shells of 1 Å thickness to represent the distance of the features from the amino acid C_β atoms. We make the results of our analysis available graphically over the world wide web. To illustrate the validity and utility of our analysis, we used the amino acid comparative profiles to construct a substitution matrix, the WAC matrix, based on a simple summary of the computed environmental differences. We compared our matrix to BLOSUM62 and PAM250 in BLAST searches with query sequences selected from 39 protein families found in the PROSITE database. Although BLOSUM62 was the most sensitive matrix overall, our matrix was more sensitive for some families, and exhibited overall performance similar to PAM250. Our results suggest that the radial distribution of biochemical and biophysical features is useful for comparing amino acid environments, and that similarity matrices based on the geometric distribution of features around amino acids may produce improved search sensitivity.

Introduction

The twenty amino acids provide a useful basis set of chemical functionality for constructing protein macromolecules. Small microenvironments within proteins derive their important structural and functional characteristics from the physical interactions between the amino acids. In large part, the tolerance of protein macromolecules to mutation depends on the critical features of the lost amino acid, and the ability of the new amino acid to replace these features. Miyata et al. have shown that in proteins that have preserved their structure throughout the process of evolution, the frequency of amino acid substitution is correlated with the physico-chemical similarities between the exchanged amino acids (Miyata *et al.*, 1979). A mutation in which an amino acid is replaced by one with similar physico-chemical properties is more likely to be accepted than one in which the new environment disrupts the protein's 3D conformation. Thus, similarity matrices derived from empirical substitution frequencies often serve to confirm the physical similarity of two amino acids by showing a high frequency of substitution in protein sequences.

The tolerance of a microenvironment for one amino acid or another, however, is not directly a function of the properties of the lost amino acid (it is, after all, lost!), but is rather a direct function of the properties of the environment surrounding the lost amino acid. If a new amino acid is compatible with the environment, then it will be accepted as a replacement, and the resulting energy of interaction will be acceptable. If the new amino acid is incompatible with the environment, then the unfavorable interaction energies may significantly destabilize the protein or render it inactive. Thus, it is useful to examine the environments of amino acids in order to understand the likelihood that various substitutions will be acceptable. This can be done for single amino acid environments using molecular dynamics, in order to assess the suitability of a mutation (Grantham, 1974; Jones, 1975). It is also useful, however, to characterize the environments for multiple superimposed instances of each amino acid in order to uncover regularities and patterns that may only be discernible from averaged ensembles.

We have previously developed a general purpose system, FEATURE, for representing and characterizing protein microenvironments using a broad set of properties (Bagley & Altman, 1995). The FEATURE system takes a set of aligned sites that share some structural or functional significance, and a set of control sites without such significance (nonsites). The system creates shells of 1 Å thickness out to 10 Å and compares the distribution of values for a variety of properties (shown in Figure 1) in the shells of the sites with those of the nonsites. Significant properties within each shell are determined using the Wilcoxon Rank Sum test (Ott, 1992). The FEATURE system thus provides information about the distance of various features from a central point in the site. It is therefore somewhat different from other feature-based systems in which the relative geometry of features is not represented (Grantham, 1974; Jones, 1975). We have shown that FEATURE can also divide an environment into small three-dimensional cubes in its analysis, although at a cost of decreased statistical significance of the findings (Bagley et al, 1995). In this paper, we use the radial system to study the microenvironments surrounding ~100 instances of each of the twenty amino acids. We describe the properties of each amino acid against a background of random amino acids. We also describe all amino acids' specific properties compared to each other, thus illustrating the physico-chemical and structural differences between the environments of pairs of amino acids.

In order to illustrate one possible application of our analysis, we have used a straightforward interpretation of our amino acid comparison data to generate a new similarity matrix, WAC, for sequence comparison. We compared the performance of WAC to that of BLOSUM62 (Henikoff & Henikoff, 1992) and PAM250 (Dayhoff *et al.*, 1978), using the BLAST search program (Altschul *et al.*, 1990). Given a query sequence and a matrix, BLAST uses the matrix to extract protein sequences, from a database, that contain high local alignment scores with the query. We also compared WAC with Rao's matrix, which is based on physico-chemical properties of the amino acids themselves, instead of the environments around them (Rao, 1986).

Methods

Analysis of Amino Acid environments

In these experiments, we compared the average environments of each amino acid against a random set of background amino acids, as well as against the environments of the other amino acids. The original system runs in Common Lisp, but was ported to Microsoft Visual C++ v4.0 running on a Pentium Pro/200 in order to accommodate the larger data sets required for these experiments. The amino acid data were taken from a set of 20 proteins from the PDB (1ACX, 1AVR, 1F3G, 1FKF, 1GAL, 1IPD, 1PAF, 1PDA, 1PYP, 1REC, 1RHD, 1SNC, 1TEN, 2ACT, 2BP2, 2BPA, 2HIP, 3GLY, 4TMS, 9INS; Bernstein *et al.*, 1977) with resolution finer than 3Å, with no significant structural similarities (Holm & Sander, 1994), and with no homologous sequence or function. The average sequence length of the proteins in this set was 268.

Property based on:	Property Name
Atom	Atom Name
	Hydrophobicity
	Charge
	Positive Charge
	Negative Charge
	Charge with HIS
Chemical group	Hydroxyl
	Amide
	Amine
	Carbonyl
	Ring-system
	Peptide
Residue	Residue type
	Hydrophobicity Classification 1
	Hydrophobicity Classification 2
Secondary structure	Secondary Structure Classification 1
	Secondary Structure Classification 2
Other Properties	Van Der Waal volume
	B-factor
	Mobility

Figure 1 List of microenvironment properties used by FEATURE.

For each amino acid, 5 random instances were chosen from each protein. For proteins with less than 5 instances of an amino acid, all instances were used, thus slightly less than 100 sites were sampled. Each amino acid site was centered on the Cß atom to maximize the observable effects of the side chain while still maintaining a comparable site across all 20 amino acids. The Cß atom position of Glycine was estimated based on the average position of the superimposed Cß atoms from all other amino acids. The ~100 sites of each amino acid were compared to the ~100 sites of each of the other amino acids, as well as 100 nonsites chosen randomly from the other amino acids.

From each comparison, data for 21 properties describing the biochemical and biophysical milieu were collected radially, in 10 concentric 1Å shells. Each observed feature was assigned to a volume shell depending on its distance from the site center. For example, a negative charge observed at 5.7Å would be assigned to shell 6, describing the features at 5-6Å. Since the property values do not necessarily have a normal distribution, a non-parametric test, the Wilcoxon Rank Sum test, was used to determine the statistical significance of the differences between the observed values of sites and nonsites for a property at a given radius (Ott, 1992). Properties and associated radii are reported for which the statistical significance exceeds certain threshold ($p=0.005$ in our experiments). The results are available on the WWW at *http://smi.stanford.edu/projects/helix/pubs/wacpsb/* On this page, a matrix of amino acids is presented, and selection of a cell within the matrix produces a graphical comparison of the amino acids.

Generating A Similarity Matrix

The Wilcoxon test yields a t-value that describes the difference between sites and nonsites for a property at a volume. The overall difference between two amino acids can be calculated by taking the sum of the squared t-values for each property and volume. This yields a single number that represents comparatively the differences between the features found in the amino acid pair. Some properties are slight variations of others, and to avoid double-counting, were not used in the analysis. Thus, for example, we have two different classifications of secondary structure (that divide secondary structural space slightly differently) and we only used one of them. Similarly, we used only a single hydrophobicity classification.

The summed differences in the amino acid pairs were used to create a 24 by 24 similarity matrix, the WAC matrix. The matrix was scaled with respect to BLOSUM62 using a linear least-squares regression. The values for the B amino acid were calculated by taking the frequency-weighted average of the D and R values. The Z and X values were calculated similarly, using the E, Q values and all values, respectively. The * entries were filled with the lowest values found in the entire matrix. The frequencies of the amino acids were obtained from the SWISS-PROT Release 33.0 Release Notes.

Evaluation of the WAC Matrix

The performance of the WAC matrix was evaluated based on its sensitivity in detecting related protein sequences in the same family. 39 families were randomly picked from the PROSITE v13.1 database. Out of each family, the most distant protein sequence was chosen as the query. A BLAST search using the WAC, BLOSUM62, and PAM250 matrices was run for each query (Altschul et al., 1990). Rao's matrix, as published in (Rao, 1986), was also tested on several queries. The BLOSUM62 and PAM250 matrices were obtained from the same GCG v8.1 software package as BLAST (GCG, April 1991). The default values of E(xpect)=10 and W(ordlength)=3 were used. The Expect parameter instructs BLAST to discard sequences whose score is lower than a score that would be expected to occur 10 times by chance. The L(istsize) was increased from L=250 to L=500 so that the list of sequences found by the BLAST search was not truncated.

Results

The amino acid comparison tables are made available on the WWW. Figure 2 shows three comparison grids between two closely related amino acids, GLU and ASP, between two more distantly related amino acids, ASP and PHE, and between GLU and PHE.

The amino acid microenvironment data was used to construct the WAC amino acid similarity matrix. Since very few significant differences were found when comparing an amino acid's environment to itself (resampled), the similarity values along the diagonal are the highest in the matrix. The mean of all values is -0.945 with a standard deviation of 1.90. WAC has a correlation of 0.8136 with BLOSUM62. Figure 3 shows the position-by-position difference between WAC and BLOSUM62. WAC has a correlation of 0.7683 with Rao's matrix.

Figure 4 compares the results of the BLAST search using WAC, BLOSUM62, and PAM250. In 11 out of the 39 groups, all 3 matrices correctly identified every sequence. WAC correctly identified more sequences than BLOSUM62 in 3 groups, less in 16 groups. When compared to PAM250, WAC correctly identified more sequences in 11 groups, and less in 12. However, in the groups whose average sequence length is greater than 450 (12 groups), WAC found either the same number or more sequences than BLOSUM62. Conversely, WAC did not perform as well on shorter sequences. Rao's matrix did not perform as well as the other matrices (data not shown).

Discussion

The amino acid comparison grids show features consistent with the known differences between amino acids. In particular, the radial information is useful in distinguishing some closely related amino acids. For example, the primary difference between the environments of ASP and GLU is due to the greater length

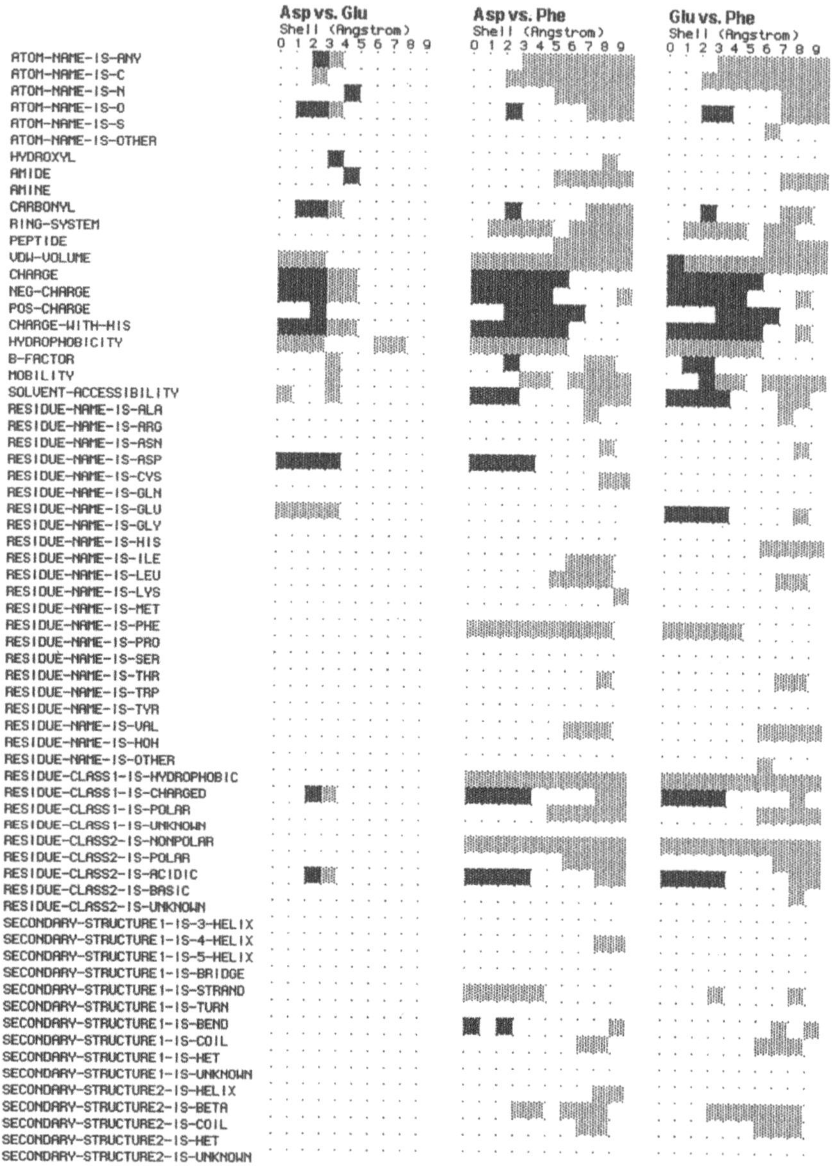

Figure 2 Sample analyses. Properties, listed along the left-hand column, were analyzed at 1Å volumes up to 10Å from the C_β carbon. The volumes for which the properties were significantly more prevalent for the first sites are marked in light grey, and dark grey for the second. Most properties are self-explanatory, and represent the presence of a particular atom, chemical group, residue type or type of secondary structure. "Asp vs. Glu" shows much fewer significantly different properties than "Asp vs. Phe" and "Glu vs. Phe," indicating that ASP and GLU are more closely related to each other than they are to PHE.

of GLU. Thus, although they share numerous features, GLU tends to have more features out to the 5-6 Å shell, while the ASP features extend to only 4-5 Å shell. Similarly, a comparison of VAL and LYS shows that the long chain of LYS occupies different volume than VAL, and so the distribution of surrounding atoms is quite different. If we want to determine the most defining features of amino acids comparison, we could apply a stricter threshold of statistical significance than the current p=0.005.

For some amino acids, there is considerable rotational freedom in the sidechain that leads to a variety of possible positions distal to C_β. Our work has averaged over all these conformations in order to produce an "average" surrounding environment. Clearly, for particular proteins such an average would not be appropriate, and it would be preferable to model a particular subset of possible conformations. In this analysis, we have combined all orientations in order to have a general comparison of features over a wide range of proteins and microenvironments. It is remarkable that most of the key physical features are reflected in the differences in the surrounding distributions.

We focused on comparing WAC with BLOSUM62 because BLOSUM62 has been shown to have good performance (Henikoff & Henikoff, 1993; Vogt *et al.*, 1995), and it is the current default of BLAST search. In the WAC-BLOSUM62 difference matrix (Figure 3), all the diagonal entries are less than or equal to zero, while most of the off-diagonal numbers are greater than zero. This suggests that WAC is more tolerant to mutations than BLOSUM62. In database searches, WAC performed on par with PAM250 and slightly below BLOSUM62, even though WAC was not derived from amino acid substitution frequency patterns (Figure 4). The diagonal elements of our WAC matrix are all the same, because there are few significant differences between two sets of randomly chosen environments both centered around the same amino acid. We could use the comparison of individual amino acids against a random background in order to gain an estimate of the uniqueness of each amino acid environment. Such a refinement might improve the performance of our matrix with respect to BLOSUM62, which shows a clear variation in substitution likelihood along the diagonal.

The WAC matrix is derived from a simple statistical difference between the biochemical, biophysical, and structural environments of amino acids. The comparative microenvironment descriptions for each amino acid are based on statistical analyses of superimposed amino acids randomly chosen from a set of nonhomologous proteins, and are presented on the web page. The use of nonhomologous proteins ensures that we get a general measure of similarity of the environments surrounding amino acids. However, we can also produce context-dependent similarity matrices by using a selected set of proteins or selected regions within proteins (Koshi & Goldstein, 1995). The broad set of properties considered give a fairly comprehensive look at the critical features of amino acids. Some of the properties are purposefully redundant because we believe that there are many alternative viewpoints from which to study a microenvironment. These redundant properties were not used in creating the summary score for the WAC matrix construction. The detailed data sets are available upon request from the authors.

The use of the PROSITE groups and BLAST to perform a comparison of the matrices is discussed in (Henikoff & Henikoff, 1993). Despite the idiosyncrasies of PROSITE, such as its very stringent requirements for family membership, it represents the most reliable collection of related sequences that form a good gold-standard for large scale similarity searches. The BLOSUM62 matrix is derived from an analysis of the substitution frequencies in the conserved blocks within the BLOCKS/PROSITE databank. Because BLAST focuses on high scoring ungapped alignments, it may be that BLOSUM62 is especially well suited for performing well in BLAST searches. Nonetheless, the wide use of BLAST and the good average performance of BLOSUM62 make this type of evaluation very attractive, and a good benchmark.

In our study, WAC generally performs well for groups that have larger average sequence lengths. One possible reason is that smaller proteins have fewer structural constrains. Miyata et al. (Miyata et al., 1979) observed that in those low-constraint regions, amino acid substitution depends less on the extent of physico-chemical properties of substituted amino acids. Thus similarity matrices based on physico-chemical properties would be expected to perform poorly. We do not yet have enough data to make any statistically significant conclusions about the range of protein sizes that are best suited for use of our matrix.

The approach we used to calculate the WAC matrix is fundamentally different from that of other similarity matrices. The difference between WAC and matrices calculated from observed and expected frequencies, such as BLOSUM62 (Henikoff & Henikoff, 1992) and PAM250 (Dayhoff et al., 1978) is obvious—WAC is computed entirely from differences in the observed average environment surrounding amino acids without respect to any multiple alignment. WAC is also different from matrices that are derived from physico-chemical parameters, such as Rao's matrix (Rao, 1986) and Miyata's matrix (Miyata et al., 1979). WAC does not simply compare the physico-chemical properties of the amino acids themselves. Instead, the numbers in WAC come from statistical difference between physico-chemical and structural features of the micro-environments of amino acids, and have a built-in representation of the radial distribution of these features. This may explain the overall better performance of WAC over Rao's

The representation and characterization system we use is general purpose. In this paper, we applied the system to study the environments of amino acids, and then used the representation to make a similarity matrix. In other work, we have used the system to study the properties of calcium binding sites, disulfide-bonding state of Cysteines, and serine proteases (Bagley & Altman, 1995; Bagley & Altman, 1996). We have also developed a scoring scheme, based on the representation system, to recognize the occurrence of protein sites in new, unannotated structures (Wei & Altman, 1996), and have achieved high accuracy in

	C	S	T	P	A	G	N	D	E	Q	H	R	K	M	I	L	V	F	Y	W	
	-5	1	1	2	0	3	3	1	2	3	3	2	1	2	1	1	1	2	2	2	C
		0	0	1	-1	0	0	-1	-2	0	0	0	0	1	1	1	1	0	1	2	S
C	4		-1	1	0	2	1	0	0	2	1	1	1	1	1	1	0	0	1	1	T
S	0	4		-3	1	2	2	0	0	1	2	2	1	3	3	3	2	4	2	4	P
T	0	1	4		0	-1	2	0	-2	1	2	0	0	2	1	1	1	2	2	3	A
P	-1	0	0	4		-2	0	-1	0	2	1	1	1	3	2	3	1	1	1	0	G
A	0	0	0	0	4		-2	-1	0	1	-1	0	0	2	2	2	2	2	2	3	N
G	0	0	0	0	-1	4		-2	-2	-1	0	1	0	2	-1	1	0	-1	0	1	D
N	0	1	1	0	0	0	4		-1	-2	-1	-1	-2	1	-1	0	-2	-1	-2	1	E
D	-2	-1	-1	-1	-2	-2	0	4		-1	0	-1	-1	1	3	2	1	3	2	2	Q
E	-2	-2	-1	-1	-3	-2	0	0	4		-4	0	1	2	2	2	2	1	-2	2	H
Q	0	0	1	0	0	0	1	-1	0	4		-1	0	1	1	1	1	1	1	3	R
H	0	-1	-1	0	0	-1	0	-1	-1	0	4		-1	1	1	0	-1	1	0	1	K
R	-1	-1	0	0	-1	-1	0	-1	-1	0	0	4		-1	1	0	0	2	1	3	M
K	-2	0	0	0	-1	-1	0	-1	-1	0	0	2	4		0	-1	-1	0	1	3	I
M	1	0	0	1	1	0	0	-1	-1	1	0	0	0	4		0	0	1	1	3	L
I	0	-1	0	0	0	-2	-1	-4	-4	0	-1	-2	-2	2	4		0	1	1	3	V
L	0	-1	0	0	0	-1	-1	-3	-3	0	-1	-1	-2	2	1	4		-2	0	-1	F
V	0	-1	0	0	1	-2	-1	-3	-4	-1	-1	-2	-3	1	2	1	4		-3	-1	Y
F	0	-2	-2	0	0	-2	-1	-4	-4	0	0	-2	-2	2	0	1	0	4		-7	W
Y	0	-1	-1	-1	0	-2	0	-3	-4	1	0	-1	-2	0	0	0	0	1	4		
W	0	-1	-1	0	0	-2	-1	-3	-2	0	0	0	-2	2	0	1	0	2	1	4	
	C	S	T	P	A	G	N	D	E	Q	H	R	K	M	I	L	V	F	Y	W	

Figure 3 WAC similarity matrix (Lower) and difference matrix (Upper) obtained by subtracting the BLOSUM62 matrix from the WAC matrix position by position.

recognizing calcium binding sites, disulfide-bonding Cysteines, and ATP binding sites.

The use of microenvironmental information is not limited simply to the comparison of average amino acid environments, but could be applied to specific environments within specific structural families. Bowie and Eisenberg have shown that environmental attributes can be used for a dynamic programming-based scheme for fold recognition (Bowie *et al.*, 1991). Our environmental attributes, including radial information, may also be suitable for this task. In addition, our environmental attributes could be used to create scoring functions for evaluating the detailed fit of a sequence to a structural fold in the manner of current threading techniques (Bryant & Lawrence, 1993; Jones *et al.*, 1992; Sippl & Weitckus, 1992).

Conclusions

We have performed a comprehensive analysis of the environments surrounding amino acids. Our analysis differs from previous analyses in that we maintain

Group	Description	Avg Length	Query	Sensitivity WAC	BLOSUM62	PAM250
PS00216	Sugar Transport Protein	516	Q06221	89	77	80
PS50003	PH Domain	901	P35401	11	6	1
PS00221	MIP Family	295	P42067	100	97	81
PS01080	Apoptosis regulator	220	Q07440	71	71	71
PS01047	Heavy Metal Associated Domain	657	P46839	57	57	61
PS00850	Glycine Radical	475	P13316	75	75	75
PS00687	Aldehyde Dehydrogenase	527	P30841	100	100	100
PS00667	NADH Dehydrogenase	318	Q00242	100	100	100
PS00499	C2 domain	631	P27715	90	90	56
PS00437	Catalase 1	515	P11934	100	100	100
PS00316	Thaumatin	214	P13867	100	100	100
PS00249	PDGF	212	P01128	100	100	100
PS00242	Integrin Alpha	1086	P34446	100	100	100
PS00239	Receptor Tyrosine Kinase	1051	P42159	100	100	100
PS00162	Eukaryotic CO2 Anhydrase	280	P28651	100	100	100
PS00120	Lipase Serine Active Site	435	P25234	7	7	7
PS00113	Adenylate Kinase	210	P43412	100	100	100
PS00110	Pyruvate Kinase	523	P22200	100	100	100
PS00049	Ribosomal Protein L14	125	P46767	100	100	90
PS00039	DEAD ATP helicase	514	P38719	100	100	100
PS00021	Kringle Domain	718	P00748	100	100	100
PS00013	Prokaryotic Lipoprotein attachment	286	P29722	2	2	1
PS01033	Globin	147	Q03331	1	2	5
PS00190	Cytochrome c	111	Q02469	0	1	0
PS00259	Gastrin	84	P09040	14	17	6
PS00267	Tachykinin	43	P22691	7	11	9
PS00201	Flavodoxin	157	P41050	83	87	74
PS00192	Cytochrome b	309	P15585	82	86	81
PS00233	Insect Cuticle	141	P26967	41	47	47
PS00237	G-Protein Receptor	402	P16849	34	44	32
PS00287	Cysteine protease inhibitor	226	P35479	33	45	41
PS00636	DNAJ	412	P36540	3	24	5
PS00018	EF-hand Calcium Binding	236	P39047	55	77	5
PS00418	Potex Carlavirus Coat	251	P22172	77	100	96
PS01124	Thermonuclease	272	P26950	47	73	65
PS00262	Insulin	101	P15131	60	94	92
PS00272	Snake Toxin	65	P28375	35	82	86
PS00197	Ferredoxin	214	P07771	36	85	85
PS00027	Homeobox	337	P31367	30	87	88

Figure 4 BLAST Search Data. A BLAST search was performed for each matrix using a query chosen from each PROSITE group. The sensitivity of a matrix is the percentage of the group members detected.

some information about the geometry and relative distances between features in a radial shell around Cβ of the amino acids. We have shown that our analysis produces detailed maps of the environmental differences between each amino acid and the other amino acids. We have further illustrated one practical use of our analysis, in the creation of a similarity matrix, the WAC matrix, based on a simple statistical summary of the differences between two sets of average amino acid environments. The performance of the WAC matrix is remarkable given the simplicity of its derivation, and suggests that refinement may lead to improved performance.

Acknowledgments

RBA is a Culpeper Medical Scholar, and this work was supported by the Culpeper Foundation and by NIH grants LM-05652 and LM-06244. The computing environment was provided by the CAMIS resource under NIH LM-05305. JTC is supported by the Howard Hughes Summer Fellowship from the Department of Biological Sciences. The BLAST searches were performed using the computing resources of CMGM. We thank Lee Kozar for his help with running BLAST search.

References

Altschul, S. F., Gish, W., Miller, W., Myers, E. W. & Lipman, D. J. (1990). Basic local alignment search tool. *Journal of Molecular Biology* **215**(3), 403-410.

Bagley, S. C. & Altman, R. B. (1995). Characterizing the microenvironment surrounding protein sites. *Protein Sciences* **4**, 622-635.

Bagley, S. C. & Altman, R. B. (1996). Conserved Features in the active site of nonhomologous serine proteases. *Folding & Design*, in press.

Bowie, J. U., Lüthy, R. & Eisenberg, D. (1991). A method to identify protein sequences that fold into a known three-dimensional structure. *Science* **253**, 164-170.

Bryant, S. H. & Lawrence, C. E. (1993). An empirical energy function for threading protein sequence through the folding motif. *Proteins: Structure, Function, and Genetics* **16**, 92-112.

Dayhoff, M. O., Schwartz, R. M. & Orcutt, B. C. (1978). A model of evolutionary change in proteins. *Atlas of Protein Sequence and Structure* **5, suppl. 3**, 345-352.

GCG. (April 1991). Program Manual for the GCG Package 7 edit., 575 Science Drive, Madison, WI, USA 53711.

Grantham, R. (1974). Amino acid difference formula to help explain protein evolution. *Science* **185**(154), 862-4.

Henikoff, S. & Henikoff, J. G. (1992). Amino acid substitution matrices from protein blocks. *Proceedings of the National Academy of Sciences of the United States of America* **89**, 10915-10919.

Henikoff, S. & Henikoff, J. G. (1993). Performance evaluation of amino acid substitution matrices. *Proteins: Structure, Function, and Genetics* **17**, 49-61.

Holm, L. & Sander, C. (1994). The FSSP database of structurally aligned protein fold families. *Nucleic Acids Research* **22**, 3600-3609.

Jones, D. D. (1975). Amino acid properties and side-chain orientation in proteins: a cross correlation appraoch. *Journal of Theoretical Biology* **50**(1), 167-83.

Jones, D. T., Taylor, W. R. & Thornton, J. M. (1992). A new approach to protein fold recognition. *Nature* **358**(6381), 86-9.

Koshi, J. M. & Goldstein, R. A. (1995). Context-dependent optimal substitution matrices. *Protein Eng* **8**(7), 641-5.

Miyata, T., Miyazawa, S. & Yasunaga, T. (1979). Two types of amino acid substitutions in protein evolution. *Journal of Molecular Evolution* **12**, 219-236.

Ott, L. R. (1992). *An introduction to statistical methods and data analysis*. fourth edit, Wadsworth Publishing Company, Belmont, CA 94002.

Rao, M. J. K. (1986). New scoring matrix for amino acid residue exchanges based on residue characteristic physical parameters. *International Journal of Peptide and Protein Research* **29**, 276-281.

Sippl, M. J. & Weitckus, S. (1992). Detection of native-like models for amino acid sequences of unknown three-dimensional structure in a data base of known protein conformations. *Proteins: Structure, Function, and Genetics* **13**, 258-271.

Vogt, G., Etzold, T. & Argos, P. (1995). An assessment of amino acid exchange matrices in aligning protein sequences: the twilight zone revisited. *Journal of Molecular Biology* **249**, 816-831.

Wei, L. & Altman, R. B. (1996). A general method for recognizing protein sites, in preparation.

TRANSFAC DATABASE AS A BRIDGE BETWEEN SEQUENCE DATA LIBRARIES AND BIOLOGICAL FUNCTION

E. WINGENDER, H. KARAS, R. KNÜPPEL
Gesellschaft für Biotechnologische Forschung mbH,
Mascheroder Weg 1, D-38124 Braunschweig

The TRANSFAC database contains information about regulatory DNA sequences and the proteins (transcription factors) binding to and acting through them. It may thus serve as a dictionary for the biological meaning of these sequence elements. Moreover, the TRANSFAC data can be used to describe these elements, to define consensi and matrices for elements of certain function, and thus to provide means of identifying regulatory signals in newly unravelled genomic sequences.

1 Introduction

Great efforts are presently undertaken to sequence whole genomes. To assign a biological function to these sequences, most investigators and particularly those which think of applying genomic data for medical or biotechnological purposes start looking for identification of splice sites / open reading frames and try to assess the biological function of the putative gene product. However, the genome of a complex organism represents a highly dynamic network of positively and negatively cross-regulating elements. These components are *cis*-acting DNA elements of approximately 5-25 base pairs in length, clustered in the promoter and enhancer regions of a gene, and *trans*-acting factors that regulate transcription of the gene (transcription factors). Up to now, hundreds of transcription factors have been identified, many of them have been cloned and disclosed as members of certain classes and families[1] (Wingender, submitted). The sequence of a regulatory signal within the genome and the availability and properties of a transcription factor that can interact with this element define the biological function of that DNA element. Thus, to be able to decipher the language of the genomic operating instructions, we have to have a dictionary of the genomic "words" and their meaning. In this paper, we describe the approach of the TRANSFAC database[2, 3] to achieve this goal, and we briefly describe the sequence analysis programs which can be used in connection with the database.

2 Structure of the TRANSFAC database

The dictionary of a natural language is just a list of two columns, the "words" in their basic form and their meaning(s). However, when starting to analyze the genomic language, we just have a number of inflected forms of the words, i. e. variants of a consensus sequence, all of them having a similar but slightly different meaning. This meaning is given by the transcription factor(s) that binds to this element either with high or low affinity, in a way that is exclusive or amenable to competition with other factors. Since we don't know yet the way and meaning of inflection in most cases, we have to list all these elements along with the binding factor(s), and then we have to have an additional list which describes the biological properties of the transcription factors.

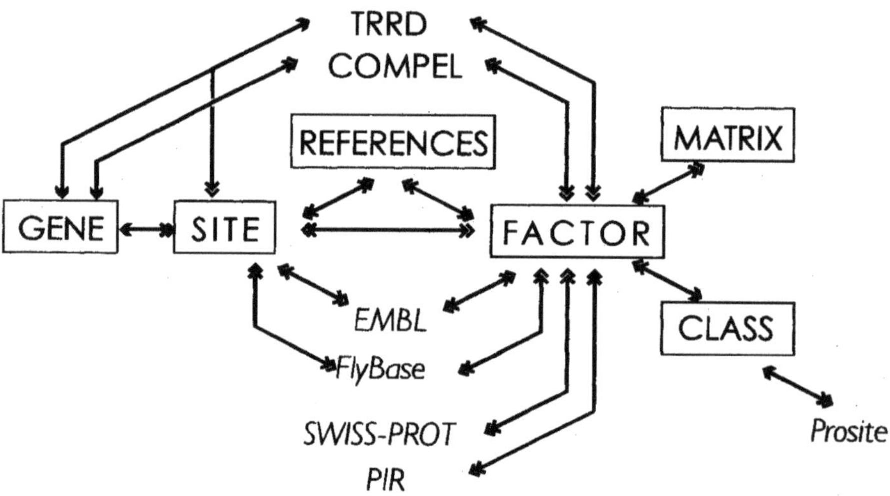

Fig. 1: Structure of the TRANSFAC database as it appears under the World Wide Web. Double arrowheads on either side indicate n:n relations, single arrowheads on one and a double arrowhead on the other side represent 1:n relations. Genuine TRANSFAC tables are boxed, closely connected databases (TRRD, COMPEL) are given in normal lettering, external databases linked to TRANSFAC tables are shown in Italics.

Thus, the main axis of the relational TRANSFAC database is the n:n relation between the SITE and the FACTOR table. SITE gives information about the location of individual regulatory sequence elements within their genes, experimental evidence, and the sequence itself which is position-sensitively linked to a corresponding entry of the EMBL data bank. Also given are the cellular context in which the function of a certain site has been investigated, and the references to the original publication. While most of these data are connected through n:n relations in the internal relational model, they have been included in the individual SITE entries in the exported ASCII flat file and in the WWW version (Fig. 1).

If the interaction of a certain site with a defined transcription factor has been experimentally proven, the corresponding FACTOR entry is linked. It contains data about the physico-chemical, structural and functional properties of the factor, including its occurrence or proven absence in certain cells / tissues. If the corresponding data are available, the FACTOR entry is also linked to the EMBL data library, to SWISS-PROT and PIR, for *Drosophila* items to FlyBase as well. Nevertheless, we started to insert also the protein sequences themselves which for many splice variants are not easily accessible from the large databases and thus required some editing. They will be available with one of the next releases.

Separate tables which are linked to the FACTOR table are CLASS, which will be described below, and MATRIX. The MATRIX table contains nucleotide distribution matrices (weight matrices) deduced from aligned binding sites. These sites may be authentic genomic binding sites or synthetic sequences which have been selected from pools of random oligonucleotides.

"On top" of the SITE table, a new GENE table has been generated. It contains just the full denomination of the gene, its acronym(s), and the gene classification as proposed by P. Bucher and the Eukaryotic Promoter Database (EPD). The main purpose of the GENE table, however, is to provide a link to the Transcription Regulatory Region Database (TRRD).[4] Therefore, this table is identical in both databases. GENE as well as FACTOR are also linked to the COMPEL database on composite elements.[5]

The TRANSFAC database release 3.0 comprises the following number of entries:

SITE	4299 entries	
Genomic sites		3760 entries (880 genes)
Artificial sites		316 entries
Consensus sequences		223 entries
FACTOR	1763 entries	
CELL	816 entries	
CLASS	27 entries	
MATRIX	246 entries	

As more and more genes have been cloned and more recombinant transcription factors are available, a rapidly growing number of publications describing binding sites appears, many of them in journals which previously had quite distinct scopes (e. g., virological, immunological, endrocrinological journals). This makes updating a database like TRANSFAC extremely laborious. Therefore, the main focus of updating its contents for release 3.0, and also the forthcoming release 3.1, is on the FACTOR table which has now numerous new and updated old entries on bZIP, bHLH, Myb- and Ets-like, paired, homeo, POU, and HMG factors as well as several other, minor classes.

3 Transcription factor classification

Many transcription factors have been discovered to belong to a large class such as bZIP (basic domain-leucine zipper) or homeo domain. These assignments are part of the FACTOR table, an 1:n relation links FACTOR entries to those of the CLASS table, where the particular class features are explained. As external links, CLASS contains cross-references to the PROSITE database. We recently made an attempt to incorporate these class definitions into a more comprehensive transcription factor classification scheme (Wingender, submitted). For this, we grouped the 24 classes to the following four superclasses according to the overall topology fo their DNA-binding domains:

1 Basic domains
2 Zinc-coordinating DNA-binding domains
3 Helix-turn-helix
4 β-Scaffold factors with minor groove contacts

The most prominent classes within superclass 1 are the bZIP, bHLH and bHLH-ZIP transcription factors. Additionally, some smaller classes such as those of the NF-1-like factors have been tentatively assigned to this group. The zinc-coordinating domains first of all comprise the classes of Cys_4 zinc fingers of nuclear receptor and GATA-type and of Cys_2His_2-type, but also the Cys_6 zinc cluster proteins of GAL4 type. Superclass 3 comprises the big class of homeo domain proteins, but also the Paired box, Winged Helix, heat shock factors, tryptophan clusters (with the families of Myb-, IRF- and Ets-like factors) and TEA domain proteins. The most problematic superclass may be the fourth one, since any combination of classes grouped here exhibits several common properties, but none of these features is shared by all of them. The classes within superclass 4 are the Rel-homologous factors, p53, MADS box factors, TATA-binding proteins and HMG domain factors. Nearly all classes are subdivided into families and, where appropriate, into subfamilies. However, there are some classes / families whose structure has not yet been resolved. Therefore, the whole classification scheme should be considered as a dynamic system.

4 Sequence scanning tools

We have established a pattern search module (PatSearch) that enables to check a novel sequence for the occurrence of sequence elements as they are contained in the TRANSFAC SITE table. In contrast to other sequence-scanning programs,[6, 7] it takes advantage of the special notation of sequences in the database, where the nucleotides are given in capital or small letters depending on the importance attributed to them by the authors. It is also able to use consensus IUPAC strings for searching.
To assess the statistical significance of a match of a given pattern of length l, we calculate a weight W using

$$W = \sum_{i=1}^{l} \log_4(1/p_i) \qquad (1)$$

Here, p_i is the probability that the i-th position of the search pattern (either a sequence element or a IUPAC consensus string in 15 letter code) matches. Neglecting the possibility of unequal frequency of nucleotides in the sequence to be analyzed, we obtain p_i = 0.25 for a match in any unambigously defined pattern position, 0.5 for a mtach in double degenerate positions (IUPAC codes S, W, R, Y, K, M), 0.75 for triple degeneracy (codes B, D, H, V) and 1 for undefined positions (code N). Thus, a maximal weight W_{max} is assigned to each search pattern assuming matching with another sequence in each position. This value can be used for pre-selection of patterns to avoid unnecessary output due to frequently matching very short and/or highly degenerate patterns.

The program uses a simple algorithm for the search; the nucleotides of the sequence and of the patterns are represented in a four-bit code allowing fast search for matching by a bitwise-AND operation. The program is controlled by three parameters that are chosen by the user. The first parameter is the fraction of allowed mismatches in the core region of the pattern (given in capital letters in the database). The default value is set to zero excluding any mismatch. The second parameter is the percentage of allowed mismatches in the flanking region. The last parameter defines an output threshold in terms of the W/W_{max} ratio, which ranges between zero (no match) and 1 (perfect match).

The matrices of the TRANSFAC MATRIX table can be used for constructing consensus sequences in terms of IUPAC strings, or for sequence analysis with appropriate routines such as MatInspector.[8] The latter is available as a service through the World Wide Web, WWW (http://transfac.gbf-braunschweig.de or http://www.gsf.de/BIODV). It uses a library which has been cleared by those matrices which are not restrictive enough for useful analysis.

These "soft" matrices have been found for factors with a highly relaxed binding site specificity, e. g. C/EBP. To further define their binding sites, we considered structural features of the DNA of potential importance. For this kind of analysis, we align experimentally proven binding site for a certain factor and create average structural profiles for eight different structure parameters (width and depth of major and minor groove, total bending angle of the DNA axis, twist angle, rise and inclination). These parameters were taken from a library of all hexanucleotides, containing the structural description for the central dinucleotide step.[9] From this library, the profile of any DNA sequence can be generated very rapidly and used for comparison with the stored characteristic profile of the site of interest by applying a simple root mean square (rms) routine. However, this tools is still in an experimental stage in that those parameters have to be identified which are really indicative for each factor. Thus, we found that a widening of the minor groove width is an useful auxiliary criterion for the identification of TATA-boxes,[9] and that the major groove width profile shows some characteristics for bZIP class factors (unpublished results).

When running either scanning routine under the World Wide Web, the output contains active hyperlinks to the FACTOR entries whose connected patterns matched. In future, this output will be supplemented by regulatory pathways the matching factor may be part of, be it a signal transduction pathway or part of a regulatory genetic network. These tools are presently under development.

5 Biological applications

Using pattern search tools with the sequence elements and IUPAC consensus strings compiled in the TRANSFAC database, we identified a potential CRE element in the promoter of the human parathyroid hormone (PTH) gene. Deviating from the canonical TGACGTCA by an A in the fifth position, it exhibited a low responsibility towards cAMP.[10] Elements with the core sequence TGACATCA were found also in several other genes and were demonstrated to interact with AP-1 and/or CREB/ATF-like factors. However, no cross-competition could be seen for protein binding using an AP-1 consensus sequence,[10] whereas purified recombinant CREB clearly binds to this sequence (Wingender & Bischoff, unpublished results).

Using the TRANSFAC matrix library together with the MatInspector program, several elements and even clusters of potential T-cell relevant transcription factor binding sites could be identified in the gene encoding rat RT6. The T-cell relevant sites have been mainly found associated with one of two transcription start sites, TSS-2, which is the major one in adult spleen cells.[11]

6 Discussion

Using experimental data about regulatory signals in eukaryotic genomes as they are deposited in the databases TRANSFAC,[2, 3] TRRD[4] and COMPEL,[5] we shall be able to identify the context sensitivity of their meaning. As in natural language, a certain word / sequence element may adopt a different meaning when placed in a different context. The next step thus should be to extend the dictionary to this type of context-sensitive kind of semantics. However, the experimental basis is still poor, compared with the number of genes and regulatory regions present in the genome. We thus have to undertake attempts that take potential binding sites into consideration as well, as they are predicted by the most reliable tools presently available. We described above tools that may be suitable to identify inflected words (PatSearch) as well as word stems (MatInspector, ProfileSearch) on the basis of statistical and structural considerations. Additional programs will significantly improve the definition of "word stems" / consensus descriptions, such as those established by ConsIndex and used by ConsInspector.[12] Finally, more elaborate approaches for linguistic analyses and formalizing the grammar of the genome can be expected to bring a major breakthrough in the future.

Acknowledgements

This work was supported by the German Ministry of Education, Science, Research and Technology (Project no. 01 IB 306 A) and by the European Commission (BIO4-CT95-0226).

References

1. E. Wingender, "Gene Regulation in Eukaryotes" (VCH Weinheim, 1993)
2. E. Wingender, "Compilation of transcription regulating proteins" Nucleic Acids Res. 16, 1879 (1988)
3. E. Wingender, P. Dietze, H. Karas and R. Knüppel, "TRANSFAC: A database on transcription factors and their DNA binding sites" Nucleic Acids Res. 24, 238 (1996)
4. O. V. Kel, A. G. Romachenko, A. E. Kel, A. N. Naumochkin and N. A. Kolchanov, "Data representation in the TRRD - a database of transcription regulatory regions of the eukaryotic genomes" Proceedings of the 28th Annual Hawaii International Conference on System Sciences; IEE Computer Society Press, Los Alamitos, CA 5, 42 (1995)
5. O. V. Kel, A. G. Romaschenko, A. E. Kel, E. Wingender and N. A. Kolchanov, "A compilation of composite regulatory elements affecting gene transcription in vertebrates" Nucleic Acids Res. 23, 4097 (1995)
6. D. S. Prestridge, "SIGNAL SCAN: A computer program that scans DNA sequences for eukaryotic transcriptional elements" Comp. Appl. Biosci. 7, 203 (1991)
7. D. S. Prestridge, "SIGNAL SCAN 4.0: additional database and sequence formats", Comp. Appl. Biosci. 12, 157 (1996)
8. K. Quandt, K. Frech, H. Karas, E. Wingender and T. Werner, "MatInd and MatInspector - New fast and sensitive tools for detection of consensus matches in nucleotide sequence data" Nucleic Acids Res. 23, 4878 (1995)
9. H. Karas, R. Knüppel, W. Schulz, H. Sklenar and E. Wingender, "Combining structural analysis of DNA with search routines for detection of transcription regulatory elements", Comp. Appl. Biosci., in press
10. E. Rupp, H. Mayer and E. Wingender, "The promoter of the human parathyroid hormone gene contains a functional cyclic AMP-response element" Nucleic Acids Res 18, 5677 (1990)
11. F. Haag, G. Kuhlenbäumer, F. Koch-Nolte, E. Wingender and H.-G. Thiele, "Structure of the gene encoding the rat T cell ecto-ADP-ribosyltransferase RT6", J.

Immunol., in press (1996)

12. K. Frech, G. Herrmann and T. Werner, "Computer-assisted prediction, classification, and delimitation of protein binding sites in nucleic acids" Nucleic Acids Res. 21, 1655 (1993)

A NEW APPROACH TO PROTEIN FOLD RECOGNITION BASED ON DELAUNAY TESSELLATION OF PROTEIN STRUCTURE

W. ZHENG, S.J. CHO, I.I. VAISMAN, and A. TROPSHA*

The Laboratory for Molecular Modeling, Division of Medicinal Chemistry and Natural Products, School of Pharmacy, University of North Carolina, Chapel Hill, North Carolina 27599-7360

We propose new algorithms for sequence-structure compatibility (fold recognition) searches in multi-dimensional sequence-structure space. Individual amino acid residues in protein structures are represented by their C^{α} atoms; thus each protein is described as a collection of points in three-dimensional space. Delaunay tessellation of a protein generates an aggregate of space-filling, irregular tetrahedra, or Delaunay simplices. Statistical analysis of quadruplet residue compositions of all Delaunay simplices in a representative dataset of protein structures leads to a novel four body contact residue potential expressed as log likelihood factor q. The q factors are calculated for native 20 letter amino acid alphabet and several reduced alphabets. Two sequence-structure compatibility functions are computed as (i) the sum of q factors for all Delaunay simplices in a given protein, or (ii) 3D-1D Delaunay tessellation profiles where the individual residue profile value is calculated as the sum of q factors for all simplices that share this vertex residue. Both threading functions have been implemented in structure-recognizes-sequence and sequence-recognizes-structure protocols for protein fold recognition. We find that both profile and total score based threading functions can distinguish both the native fold from incorrect folds for a sequence, and the native sequence from non-native sequences for a fold.

1 Introduction

The inverse protein folding approach to protein folding problem has become increasingly popular in recent years. It relies heavily on the available structural information about x-ray or NMR characterized proteins that can be obtained from the Brookhaven Protein Data Bank.[1] The analysis of this information has shown convincingly that the variety of protein conformations, or folds is, in fact, limited.[2,3,4] Thus, the practically intractable conformational search problem, associated with protein folding, is reduced to the search for sequence-structure compatibility, or protein fold recognition.

The search for compatibility in the sequence-structure space[5] can be done using two protocols. The sequence-recognizes-structure protocol implies searching for the most compatible protein structure for a sequence. Alternatively, structure-recognizes-sequence protocol involves searching for the most compatible protein sequence for a structure.[6] Since both protocols require the evaluation and ranking

---

* Please send reprint requests to this author

of the results of threading, the compatibility between sequence and structure needs to be evaluated quantitatively with a fitness function.

Most threading functions proposed so far (e.g.,[7,8,9]) require a definition of a contact between residues (reviewed recently[10,11]). Many existing definitions of contact residues are often based on an arbitrary distance criteria.[12,13,14] Because such definition is not objective, the resulting threading potentials may depend on the chosen criteria of a contact.

Recently, we applied statistical geometry approach[15,16] to the analysis of protein structure.[17,18] Individual residues in protein structures are represented by their C^{α} atoms. Delaunay tessellation of a protein generates an aggregate of space filling, irregular tetrahedra or Delaunay simplices. Each Delaunay simplex defines objectively four unique nearest neighbor residues (vertices of the simplex). Thus, for the first time, this approach affords unambiguous identification of all contact residues in sets of four natural nearest neighbors in a folded protein structure. Our recent statistical analysis of the quadruplet composition of all Delaunay simplices in a representative protein dataset led to the first four-body residue contact potential.[17]

In this paper, we describe several new four body contact potentials based on Delaunay tessellation of representative dataset of x-ray characterized proteins. We also report two new threading functions computed from these potentials. The first function describes the total sequence-structure compatibility score, and the second function is analogous to the 3D-1D structure profile, originally proposed by Bowie *et al.*[3] We show that in all tested cases both threading functions can distinguish between native and non-native folds for a protein sequence and correctly select native sequence for a protein fold.

2 Computational details.

2.1 Representative dataset of protein structures.

We used Sander's 25% dataset[19] which included 365 protein chains with greater than 2Å resolution and no more than 25% sequence identity between any two protein sequences. The following 43 protein chains were excluded from the analysis due to a number of factors such as the presence of unnatural (modified) amino acids, structural gaps (i.e., absence of coordinates for at least one residue), or description of an entry as theoretical model: 1bbtl; 1bbt4; 1bgeb; 1bpb; 1brd; 1cpt; 1ddt; 1efm; 1glcg; 1glt; 1gox; 1gp1a; 1gsgp; 1huw; 1lla; 1mfbh; 1mina; 1pda; 1pdga; 1ppba; 1pspa; 1pte; 1ptsa; 1rec; 1smra; 1sto; 1tabi; 1tfd; 1tie; 1tpla; 1wsya; 2crd; 2dnja; 2hmza; 2ila; 2plv1; 2reb; 3cox; 3hhrc; 3hvtb; 4htci; 4ts1a; and 5fbpb.

2.2 *Statistical geometry of proteins.*

The Brookhaven PDB files in the dataset were initially preprocessed to extract the coordinates of C^{α} atoms from individual chains listed in Sander's database.[19] Delaunay tessellation of proteins in the dataset was performed with the **qhull** program.[20] The programs to perform the statistical analysis of the residue composition of Delaunay simplices were written in C programming language.

2.3 *Four body contact potentials.*

The nature of Delaunay tessellation suggests that the residue contact potential should be calculated as four-body potential. This potential was calculated in the form of log likelihood factor q as follows:

$$q_{ijkl} = \log \frac{f_{ijkl}}{p_{ijkl}} \tag{1}$$

where i, j, k, l are any four amino acid residues, f_{ijkl} is the observed normalized frequency of occurrence of a given quadruplet, and p_{ijkl} is the expected frequency of occurrence of a given quadruplet. The q_{ijkl} shows the likelihood of finding four particular residues in one simplex. Further details of these calculations were described elsewhere.[17]

2.4 *Threading functions.*

Based on Delaunay tessellation of protein structures, we have developed two independent threading functions . The **total score** function is the sum of q factors for all quadruplets of amino acids observed in a protein after tessellation, i.e.:

$$S = \sum_{i=1}^{n_q} q_i \tag{2}$$

where q_i is the statistical potential for i-th quadruplet and n_q is the total number of quadruplets in a protein. The protocol employed for the no gap *structure-recognizes-sequence* threading was as follows. (1) Tessellate a template structure. (2) Generate 2,500 random sequences of the same length as the native sequence by randomly assigning an amino acid to each position in a sequence according to its observed frequency of occurrence in the training dataset. This procedure ensures that the ensemble of generated sequences has the same observed average frequency of occurrence for each amino acid as in the training dataset. (3) Thread each random sequence through the template and determine new amino acid compositions of Delaunay simplices. (4) Calculate the total score for each random sequence. (5) Calculate Z_{seq} score for the native sequence from the following equation:

$$Z_{seq} = \frac{S_n - \overline{S}_{seq}}{SD_{seq}} \tag{3}$$

where S_n is the total score for native protein, and $\overline{S}_{seq}$ and SD_{seq} are the average and standard deviation of the total scores for all random sequences, respectively.

The following protocol was employed for no gap *sequence-recognizes-structure* threading. (1) For each native (query) sequence, select a subset of protein structures with a sequence length not less than that of the query sequence. (2) Extract all substructures with continuous sequence of the same length as the query sequence from each protein structure of the subset. This creates a library of alternative conformations for the query sequence. (3) Tessellate each substructure. (4) Thread query sequence through each tessellated substructure and calculate a total threading score. (5) Calculate the Z_{str} score from the following equation:

$$Z_{str} = \frac{S_n - \overline{S}_{str}}{SD_{str}} \tag{4}$$

where S_n is the total score for native sequence/structure, and $\overline{S}_{str}$ and SD_{str} are the average and standard deviation of the total scores after threading the native sequence through all structures, respectively.

We have also introduced the **3D-1D Delaunay tessellation profile** threading function. The profile score for each residue is calculated as the sum of q factors (cf. Eq. 1) of all quadruplet compositions in which this residue participates. Plotting this value for each residue as a function of the residue number generates a 3D-1D structure profile. Following Bowie *et al.*,[3] we have generated profiles by applying a sliding window average over 21 residues.

3 Results.

3.1 Four body contact potentials and threading functions based on 20 letter amino acid alphabet.

Delaunay tessellation of all 322 protein chains (66,852 amino acid residues) in the dataset generated 387,880 simplices. Obviously, the current relatively small size of the Protein Data Bank is insufficient to derive meaningful statistical potential for all theoretically possible $20^4 = 160{,}000$ quadruplets. Thus, as in our earlier work,[17] we have postulated that the composition of Delaunay simplices is order independent, i.e., all different order-dependent combinations of four residues have been considered as the same composition. Thus, the maximum theoretical number of such combinations of 8,855.[17] In our dataset, 8,818 compositions have occurred at least once, with the average frequency of 44 occurrences per composition. The q factors were calculated from Eq. 1. For those 37 combinations that never occurred in the dataset, we assumed that their likelihood of occurrence was low; thus, their q factors were assigned the value of -1.5 which is slightly lower than the lowest q factor calculated for any observed composition. The four body statistical potential based on the 20 letter amino acid code is referred to as ***20L***.

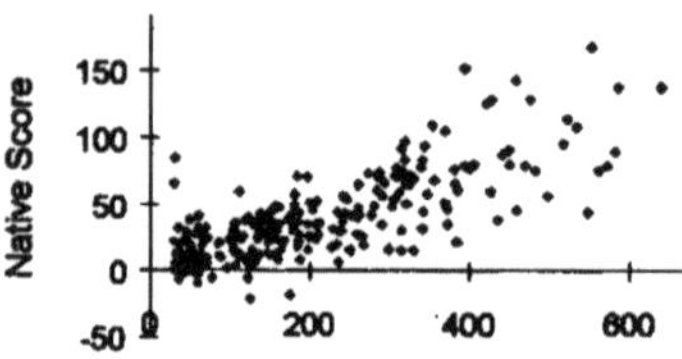

Figure 1. Total threading scores for all proteins in the dataset (cf. Eq. 4).

Based on the values of q factors for 8,855 quadruplet compositions, we have calculated total threading scores (cf. Eq. 2) for all proteins in the dataset. The results are plotted in Figure 1. As a general trend, these scores were higher for proteins with longer sequences. Using the algorithm described above, we have also calculated Z_{str} scores for 55 native protein sequences of different length (Figure 2). The Z_{str} scores were positive for all tested protein sequences which indicates that each native sequence was able to distinctly recognize its native structure. The fact that scores were also higher for proteins with longer sequences indicates that the recognition of native structure by these long sequences was manifested stronger.

Concurrently, we have calculated Z_{seq} scores for all proteins in the dataset (Figure 3). These calculations are significantly faster than calculations of Z_{str} scores since they do not require a tessellation step for every calculation (see Computational Details). Again, the values of Z_{seq} scores were generally higher for bigger proteins. However, for several small proteins, Z_{seq} scores were negative which means that for small proteins, a certain fraction of random sequences had total threading scores higher than that of the native sequence. This observation is discussed below.

Figure 2. Z_{str} scores for 55 proteins of different length (cf. Eq. 6).

Figure 3. Z_{seq} scores for all proteins in the database (cf. Eq. 5).

3.2 Four body contact potentials based on three letter amino acid alphabet.

In order to improve the statistics, we have derived four body contact potentials using two reduced alphabets of amino acids. The first set of such potentials was based on a three letter classification of amino acids recently implemented by Srinivasan and Rose in their LINUS algorithm for protein structure prediction.[21] According to this classification, based on the average buriedness of amino acids in x-ray characterized proteins, amino acids are considered as hydrophobic (Cys, Ile, Leu, Met, Phe, Trp, Val), amphiphilic (Ala, His, Thr, Tyr), or polar (Pro, Gly, Ser, Asp, Asn, Glu, Gln, Arg, Lys). The q factors for this alphabet were calculated from Eq. 1. All 15 theoretically possible combinations were actually observed, with the average frequency of 25,859 occurrences for each composition. This potential is referred to as ***3L***.

3.3 Four body contact potentials based on six letter amino acid alphabets.

The second set of four body potentials was obtained using the following six letter classification proposed by Goldstein et al.[22] on the basis of mutation frequencies of amino acid residues in Dayhoff 250 PAM Matrix[23]: c - Cys alone; s - Ser, Thr, Pro, Ala, Gly; n - Asn, Asp, Glu, Gln; h - His, Arg, Lys; v - Met, Ile, Leu, Val; and f - Phe, Tyr, Trp. The q factor values for this alphabet which we will refer to as ***6L*** potential were calculated from Eq. 1. All 126 theoretically possible combinations were observed with almost 3,100 occurrences for each composition on average.

Finally, we have combined the ***6L*** alphabet with our earlier classification of Delaunay simplices into five different types (***5T***) based on the patterns of separation of vertex residues in a primary sequence[17] to generate ***6L5T*** potential. These five classes include: class 4, where all four residues of the simplex are consecutive in the protein sequence; class 3, where three residues are consecutive, and the fourth is distant in the sequence; class 2, where two pairs of consecutive residues are distant in sequence; class 1, where two residues are consecutive, and two other residues are distant from the first two and from each other; and class 0, where all four residues are distant from each other. The two residues were defined as distant if they were separated by one or more residues in a protein sequence.

In order to generate this ***6L5T*** potential, Eq. 1 was modified to calculate the log likelihood of each quadruplet composition of six letters for each of the five classes as follows:

$$q^t_{ijkl} = \log\frac{f^t_{ijkl}}{p_{ijkl}} \tag{1a}$$

where i, j, k, l are any four letters of the ***6L*** alphabet, t is one of the five types, f^t_{ijkl} is the observed frequency of occurrence of the quadruplet composition of the given type calculated as the observed number of the particular i, j, k, l combination of the given type divided by the total observed number of all compositions of the given type, and p_{ijkl} is the expected frequency of occurrence.[17] The maximum number of different possible combinations for each of the five types using ***6L*** alphabet was obviously also 126. We have observed 126, 126, 125, 125, and 119 combinations for classes 0, 1, 2 (one combination is missing), 3 (one combination is missing), and 4 (seven combinations are missing), respectively. As in the case of the ***20L*** potential, for those combinations that were never observed in the database we have assigned the low q factor values of -0.5 for classes 2 and 3 and -1.0 for class 4 (the lowest observed values of the q factor were -0.308, -0.306, and -0.839 for classes 2, 3, and 4, respectively).

3.4 The ability of threading functions to distinguish native and misfolded proteins.

In order to test and compare the effectiveness of threading functions based on different amino acid alphabets, we have threaded several native sequences through both native and deliberately misfolded protein structures. As was initially described by Novotny et al.,[24] the deliberately misfolded structure can be obtained by assigning the native sequence to a different folded protein structure of the same sequence length. Several such pairs of structurally unrelated proteins of the same length were extracted from the Brookhaven database by Holm and Sander,[25] and we have used their dataset in this work.

For each pair of proteins with the same sequence length, we considered the results of four threadings: two threadings of the native sequences through their native structures, and two cross-threadings of the native sequences through the alternative templates. The results of these threadings using total score based threading functions for different amino acid alphabets are presented in Table 1. For each group of proteins with the same sequence length we first report the total and Z_{seq} scores for native sequences followed by the results of cross-threading. For all

Table 1. The effectiveness of threading functions to discriminate between native and misfolded structures.

Seq.[a]	Struct.[a]	Seq. Length	Total Score[b]				Z_{seq} Score[c]			
			20L	*3L*	*6L*	*6L5T*	*20L*	*3L*	*6L*	*6L5T*
1ppt	1ppt	36	0.97	-2.01	0.17	1.90	0.86	0.37	0.96	1.82
1cbh	1cbh	36	20.35	-0.58	10.15	13.89	4.12	1.15	2.81	3.59
1ppt	1cbh	36	-3.46	-2.77	-3.59	-2.03	-0.92	0.17	-0.75	0.01
1cbh	1ppt	36	-9.92	-5.13	-8.07	-8.03	-2.14	-1.36	-1.30	-0.91
1fdx	1fdx	54	35.09	9.52	34.38	39.99	4.69	3.25	4.43	5.67
5rxn	5rxn	54	17.65	1.01	17.23	18.77	5.21	2.70	5.32	5.88
1fdx	5rxn	54	-13.76	-6.87	-8.42	-7.26	-0.90	-1.06	-0.85	-0.47
5rxn	1fdx	54	-7.30	-4.57	-3.34	-7.75	1.12	0.38	1.21	0.58
3b5c	3b5c	85	6.76	4.21	10.39	12.17	2.80	3.01	3.37	4.25
1hip	1hip	85	3.51	4.29	8.33	13.77	3.63	2.99	3.89	5.01
3b5c	1hip	85	-0.39	1.15	5.34	-1.67	1.49	2.45	2.11	1.14
1hip	3b5c	85	-32.77	-11.51	-14.83	-17.07	-1.98	-1.44	-0.58	-0.48
2ssi	2ssi	107	7.37	17.83	19.51	27.75	3.41	5.85	5.20	6.79
2cdv	2cdv	107	41.23	11.22	14.40	16.01	5.99	3.65	3.80	4.38
2ssi	2cdv	107	-25.53	-9.49	-18.19	-19.37	-1.01	-0.76	-1.10	-0.77
2cdv	2ssi	107	-21.24	-10.32	-19.70	-22.40	-0.33	-0.51	-0.44	-0.34
2paz	2paz	123	37.39	24.05	21.37	29.44	7.10	7.20	5.07	6.99
1bp2	1bp2	123	18.09	-1.19	9.27	7.37	2.39	1.84	1.67	2.09
2paz	1bp2	123	-15.70	-6.81	-6.20	-4.14	0.33	0.38	0.61	1.62
1bp2	2paz	123	-14.29	-15.92	-11.58	-15.56	-0.17	-1.09	-0.16	-0.06
3rn3	3rn3	124	18.51	4.57	11.35	21.43	4.91	3.21	3.73	5.32
1p2p	1p2p	124	18.31	1.69	17.57	17.97	2.38	2.15	2.12	2.75
3rn3	1p2p	124	-36.74	-13.95	-23.58	-29.16	-0.75	-0.80	-0.42	-0.53
1p2p	3rn3	124	1.77	-17.25	3.42	-5.75	1.02	-1.03	0.83	0.56
2i1b	2i1b	153	22.10	19.45	20.26	34.51	5.19	6.79	4.69	7.18
1lh1	1lh1	153	32.44	22.29	12.12	18.79	4.93	3.82	2.81	4.79
2i1b	1lh1	153	-39.00	-29.48	-24.79	-33.58	-1.39	-2.05	-1.45	-1.93
1lh1	2i1b	153	-21.47	-9.44	-5.87	-5.17	-0.84	-0.42	0.24	1.15
2cyp	2cyp	293	59.33	18.70	40.65	52.98	8.38	5.90	6.31	8.38
1rhd	1rhd	293	57.27	53.04	38.90	58.86	8.49	9.70	6.83	9.72
2cyp	1rhd	293	-36.62	-26.92	-15.10	-31.33	0.36	0.33	0.31	-0.14
1rhd	2cyp	293	-65.47	-36.42	-44.35	-53.53	-1.21	-0.89	-1.70	-1.12

[a]PDB abbreviation.
[b]Calculated from Eq. 2 using 20L, 3L, 6L, and 6L5T statistical potentials.
[c]Calculated from Eq. 3 using 20L, 3L, 6L, and 6L5T statistical potentials.

four alphabets the total scores for native sequence/structure threadings were always higher than for cross threadings. Similarly, the Z_{seq} scores for native sequence/structure threadings were always positive and higher than for threading native sequences through misfolded structural templates. However, the distinction between native and misfolded structures was clearly more pronounced for ***20L*** and ***6L5T*** alphabets. Although, as we have discussed above, Z_{seq} scores were low and sometimes even negative for small proteins (cf. Figure 3) the fact that these scores were lower for misfolded proteins indicates that a native sequence assigned to a misfolded template behave more like a random sequence for this template. It is worth noting that not all of the proteins analyzed in Table 1 were included in the training dataset used to derive four body potentials.

We have also compared 3D-1D Delaunay profiles for all pairs of native and misfolded structures. The results for two pairs of different lengths are shown on Figures 4a and 4b for ***20L*** and ***6L5T*** potentials, respectively. For both potentials and in all tested cases, the profiles for deliberately misfolded structures run distinctly lower than for native structures. The separation of profiles for folded and misfolded structures was usually greater for profiles derived with ***6L5T*** potential.

4 Discussion

Based on Delaunay tessellation of protein structures, we have introduced two new threading functions for protein fold recognition. We have shown that with any of these functions, one could correctly detect native folds for all tested sequences as well as find native sequences for the vast majority of folds. The results suggest that this new approach to fold recognition could be successfully used for inverse protein structure prediction.

The inverse folding prediction of protein structure can be achieved by two alternative protocols: threading of a query sequence through a library of known folds in order to find the most compatible fold, or threading all sequences through a structural template in order to find the most compatible sequences. These two approaches are fully complementary and systematic application of both protocols in principle leads to complete exploration of the sequence/structure space. However, one might expect that the results of testing both protocols on the currently available sequence-structure subspace (i.e., protein structures deposited in the Brookhaven

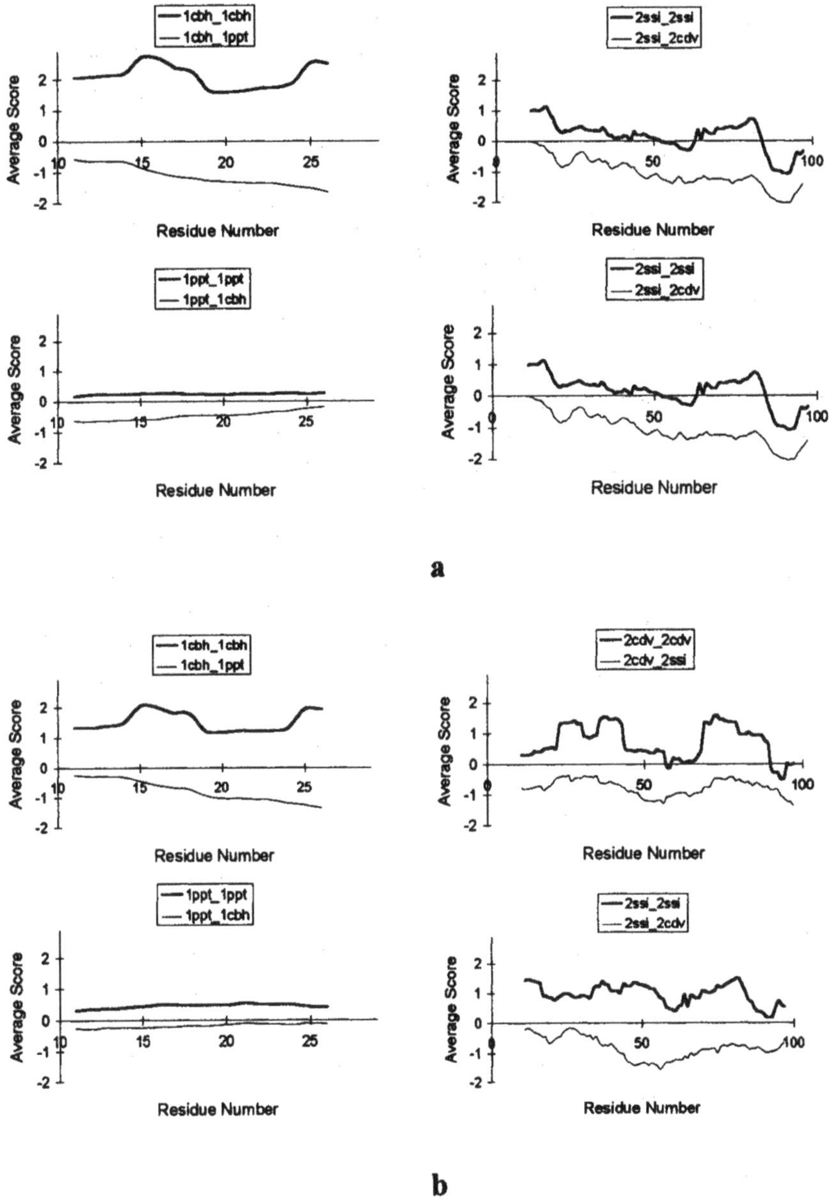

Figure 4. Comparison of 3D-1D Delaunay tessellation profiles for native and deliberately misfolded structures. The profiles are calculated with *20L* (a) and *6L5T* (b) potentials. The first three letter abbreviation in each legend corresponds to the PDB code for the sequence and the next three letter abbreviation corresponds to the PDB code for the structure.

database) could be qualitatively different in terms of distribution of Z scores. It is generally agreed that each native sequence may assume only one unique fold which will be the most energetically favorable conformation of the native sequence. Consequently, with any adequate threading function one should never find an alternative conformation with the threading energy lower than that for the native fold. So, the Z_{str} scores for sequence recognizes-structure protocols should always be positive. Indeed, in the case of our total score based threading function we have observed only positive Z_{str} scores in all tested cases (Figure 2 and Table 1).

On the other hand, the fact that different sequences may assume similar folds suggests that there may be several non native sequences that will be better suited for a native fold. In fact, this assumption constitutes the theoretical basis of the experimental protein engineering. Therefore, random exploration of the sequence space for a particular fold may in principle generate several sequences with total threading scores higher than that of the native sequence. As a result, Z_{seq} scores in some cases may be quite low and even negative. In fact, we have observed this phenomenon for several native protein structures, especially small ones (Figure 3). It appears quite attractive to test experimentally whether these sequences can fold into the structure for which they score higher than the native sequence.

3D-1D Delaunay profiles represent an alternative way to distinguish the native from non-native folds. In all tested cases, the profiles for misfolded structures were significantly lower than for native structures for all different four-body potentials and the best results were achieved with *6L5T* potential. We believe that the latter potential affords the best balance between the number of experimental observations of quadruplet compositions and the adequacy of the reduced representation of natural amino acid alphabet.

All threading protocols and functions considered in this work have been developed for the non-gapped sequence-structure alignment. Currently, these protocols can be applied to find the best structure among alternative conformations generated for instance as a result of homology model building or in the process of x-ray or NMR structure determination. The development of new threading protocols that will allow threading with gaps is in the focus of our ongoing work in the area of inverse protein folding.

5 Acknowledgments

This work was supported in part by PHS grant MH 40537, Center grants HD03310 and MH33127, and the School of Pharmacy Faculty Seed Grant Program. W.Z. acknowledges the graduate assistantship from EPA/UNC Toxicology Research

Program, Training Agreement #T901915, with the Curriculum in Toxicology, UNC-CH.

References

1. F.C. Bernstein et al, *J. Mol. Biol.* **112**, 535 (1977).
2. J. Richardson, *Adv. Protein Chem.* **34**, 167 (1981).
3. J.U. Bowie *et al*, *Science* **253**, 164 (1991)
4. C. Chothia, *Nature* **357**, *543* (1992).
5. H.W. Hellinga and F.M. Richards, *Proc. Natl. Acad. Sci.* **91**, *5803* (1994).
6. S.J. Wodak and M.J. Rooman, *Curr. Opin. Struct. Biol.* **3**, *247* (1993).
7. S. Miyazawa and R. L.Jernigan, *Macromolecules* **18**, *534* (1985).
8. G.M. Crippen and V.N. Maiorov, In *The Protein Folding Problem and Tertiary Structure Prediction* (Birkhäuser, Boston; 1994, pp 231-277).
9. S.H. Bryant and C.E. Lawrence, *Proteins* **16**, *92* (1993).
10. A. Godzik *et al*, *Prot. Sci.* **4**, *2107* (1995).
11. A. Godzik, *Struct. Curr. Biol.* **4**, *363* (1996).
12. D.P. Yee *et al*, *J. Mol. Biol.* **241**, *557* (1994).
13. M.J. Behe *et al*, *Proc. Natl. Acad. Sci. USA*. **88**, *4195* (1991).
14. M.J. Sippl *et al*, In *The Protein Folding Problem and Tertiary Structure Prediction* (Birkhäuser, Boston, 1994, pp 353-407).
15. J.D. Bernal, *Nature* **183**, *141* (1959).
16. A.Okabe *et al.*, Spatial Tessellations: Concepts and Applications of Voronoi Diagrams. (Chichester, Wiley; 1992).
17. A. Tropsha *et al.*, In *Pacific Symposium on Biocomputing '96*; Eds. L. Hunter and T.E. Klein (World Scientific, Singapore, 1995, pp 614-623).
18. R.K. Singh *et al.*, *J. Comput. Biol.* **3**, *213* (1996).
19. U. Hobohm and C. Sander, *Protein Sci.* **3**, *522* (1994).
20. C.B. Barber *et al.*, The Quickhull Algorithm for Convex Hull. Tech. Rep. GCG53, Geometry Center, University of Minnesota, Minneapolis, MN 55454.
21. R. Srinivasan and G.D. Rose, *Proteins* **22**, *81* (1995).
22. R.A. Goldstein et al, *Proc. Natl. Acad. Sci. USA* **89**, *9029* (1992).
23. D.G. George et al, In *Macromolecular Sequencing and Synthesis*; Ed. D. H. Schlesinger (Liss, New York, 1988, pp 127-149).
24. J. Novotny *et al*, *J. Mol. Biol.* **177**, *787* (1984).
25. L. Holm and C. Sander, *J. Mol. Biol.* **225**, 93 (1992).

www.ingramcontent.com/pod-product-compliance
Lightning Source LLC
LaVergne TN
LVHW051924120926
847902LV00009B/71